MW00773620

John LaFarge

and the Limits

of Catholic

Interracialism

1911–1963

John LaFarge

and the Limits

of Catholic

Interracialism

1911–1963

David W. Southern

Louisiana State University Press

Baton Rouge and London

05 04 03 02 01 00 99 98 97 96   5 4 3 2 1

Designer: Rebecca Lloyd Lemna

Typeface: Garamond

Typesetter: Impressions, a Division of Edwards Bros., Inc

Printer and binder: Thomson-Shore, Inc.

Library of Congress Cataloging-in-Publication Data

Southern, David W.
    John LaFarge and the limits of Catholic interracialism, 1911–1963
    / David W. Southern.
          p.   cm.
    Includes bibliographical references and index.
    ISBN 0-8071-1971-1 (cl : alk. paper)
    1. La Farge, John, 1880–1963. 2. Jesuits—United States—
    Biography. 3. Civil rights workers—United States—Biography.
    4. Afro-American Catholics—History—20th century. 5. Church and
    social problems—Catholic Church.   I. Title.
    BX4705.L237S68   1996
    261.8'348'0092—dc20
    [B]   95-44178
                                                               CIP

Map and excerpts from *The Manner Is Ordinary* copyright 1954, renewed 1982 by John
LaFarge, reproduced by permission of Harcourt Brace & Company.

For Marcy, who knows why

Contents

Illustrations

Abbreviations Used in Notes

Am   *America*

CICNYP   Catholic Interracial Council of New York Papers. Catholic University of America, Washington, D.C.

CICCP   Catholic Interracial Council of Chicago Papers. Chicago Historical Society, Chicago.

IR   *Interracial Review*

JLFP 1 / JLFP 2   John LaFarge Papers, Accessions one and two. Special Collections, Georgetown University Library, Washington, D.C.

MIO   John LaFarge, *The Manner Is Ordinary.* New York, 1954.

Preface

In the last thirty years of his life the Jesuit priest John La-Farge, who lived from 1880 to 1963, was widely recognized as the most influential Catholic spokesman on black-white relations in the United States. He founded the Catholic Interracial Council of New York in 1934, which for the next quarter century was the "most important [Catholic] church organization engaged in the promotion of racial justice."[1] A prolific writer and gifted publicist, LaFarge was instrumental in coaxing the Catholic church toward a more liberal position on race in the pre–*Brown* v. *Board of Education* era. In the early 1930s, well in advance of his church, he denounced racism as a sin and a heresy, and in 1937 he elaborated his ideas about the relationship between Catholic doctrine and race relations in a seminal book entitled *Interracial Justice*. The book made such an impression on Pope Pius XI that he secretly employed LaFarge to write an encyclical on racism and anti-Semitism.

Born into the social register in Newport, Rhode Island, John LaFarge was the son of a famous painter and art critic of the same name. His parents, older siblings, and family friends regarded young LaFarge as something of a prodigy. He exhibited an early aptitude for the piano

1. Jay P. Dolan, *The American Catholic Experience: A History from Colonial Times to the Present* (Garden City, N.Y., 1985), 369.

and foreign languages, and he displayed a strong intellectual and spiritual bent. At age eleven he decided he would one day become a priest.[2]

After graduating from Harvard University in 1901, he prepared for the priesthood in Innsbruck, Austria. Although he was ordained in 1905, he decided he was not suited to be a diocesan priest and instead entered the Society of Jesus. Steeping himself in academics and contemplation over the next five years, LaFarge seemed destined for a doctorate and a quiet niche in Catholic academia. But his ever-fragile health began to fail in 1910 as he grappled with scholastic philosophy at Woodstock College in Maryland. For therapy, his superiors sent him to the Jesuit missions in southern Maryland in 1911. The Maryland experience, which lasted fifteen years, marked a turning point in his life. Coming into contact with a large black proletariat for the first time, much of which was Catholic, LaFarge quickly recognized the gap between the universalist Catholic creed and racist Catholic practices. He responded by plunging into racial work, striving to provide separate but equal access to worship and education for black Catholics. His work in southern Maryland culminated in 1924 with the founding of the Cardinal Gibbons Institute, the "Catholic Tuskegee."

In 1926 the editor-in-chief of the influential Jesuit weekly *America* summoned LaFarge to New York City. For the rest of his life he served on the editorial staff of the magazine, acting as editor-in-chief from 1944 through 1948. In New York the cosmopolitan priest threw himself into a flurry of diverse social activism, holding offices in numerous Catholic organizations. However, the Jesuit's greatest achievements came from his leadership of the Catholic Interracial Council. Through its official journal, the *Interracial Review,* the New York council served as a national clearinghouse of racial information for Catholics and provided an organizational model for other cities to follow.

Driven by a deep spiritual faith and a strong belief in the unifying mission of Catholicism, LaFarge patiently bored from within the American church for almost half a century, trying to change what was essentially a racist institution. As a publicist, he significantly improved the image of the church with respect to black leadership. After a decade as leader of the interracial movement, LaFarge had defused a great deal of the suspicion about the Catholic church that prevailed among black

2. The story of the LaFarge family can be found in the autobiography of John LaFarge, *MIO.*

civil rights leaders, and he established close relationships with blacks such as Roy Wilkins, Lester Granger, and A. Philip Randolph.

Pioneers in the "Negro apostolate" suffered many slings and arrows at the hands of fellow Catholics, but by the time of LaFarge's death (just hours after President John F. Kennedy's assassination), civil rights was becoming a fashionable cause. Late in life, the Jesuit received numerous civil rights awards from Catholic, Protestant, and Jewish organizations and commendations from popes and American presidents as well. In 1963, at the age of eighty-three, LaFarge capped off his fifty-year fight for interracial justice by participating in the famous March on Washington.

In spite of all the recognition he received during his career, LaFarge has now been largely forgotten. In explaining to my academic friends who LaFarge was, I am reminded of a cartoon that once appeared in the *New Yorker*. The cartoon featured a boy gazing at a large picture of Charles Lindbergh on the museum wall and saying to his father: "If everyone thought what he did was so marvelous, how come he never got famous?"[3]

The Lindbergh name, of course, continues to attract attention, but even to the generally well-read, LaFarge is virtually unknown. In hundreds of noted books about the civil rights movement, LaFarge goes unmentioned. It was only after several years of study in race relations that I encountered the Jesuit while researching a book about the influence of *An American Dilemma*, Gunnar Myrdal's classic study of the race problem.[4] LaFarge, I discovered, had written two reviews of the Swede's book. More research revealed that LaFarge had written two books on race relations prior to the publication of Myrdal's book, neither of which was mentioned in *An American Dilemma*. Further investigation revealed that LaFarge and other Catholic interracialists roundly resented the fact that non-Catholic scholars such as Myrdal constantly ignored their work. All of this piqued my interest in LaFarge and his movement. Moreover, my initial research left me wondering why no one had written a scholarly book about the man who for so

3. Quoted in Andrew M. Greely, "The Vanishing Hero," in *Between Two Cities: God and Man in America*, ed. Thurston N. Davis, S.J., Donald R. Campion, S.J., and L. C. McHugh, S.J. (Chicago, 1962), 312.

4. See David W. Southern, *Gunnar Myrdal and Black-White Relations: The Use and Abuse of "An American Dilemma," 1944–1969* (Baton Rouge, 1987), 11, 98.

many years was deemed the most prominent Catholic voice for interracial justice.

Other scholars have lamented the lack of such a work. Recently
the black Benedictine historian Cyprian Davis wrote, "Today there is
needed another assessment on LaFarge's teaching on race in the perspective of the last forty years."[5] As Father Davis' comments imply,
other assessments of LaFarge have been made. Most of these, however,
have not been critical studies based on archival research, and none has
presented the complete story of LaFarge's racial apostolate. Quiet and
polite, conciliatory and charming, Father LaFarge, or "Uncle John" as
he was known to his younger colleagues at Campion House, was an
icon to Catholic interracialists. After the journalist's death, several Jesuits who worked on his voluminous papers began biographies of
LaFarge, but none reached fruition.[6] The Jesuit priest Edward S. Stanton completed a eulogistic doctoral dissertation on LaFarge in 1972,
but he died more than a decade later with his projected full-scale biography of LaFarge still unfinished. Stanton did manage to write several
essays on LaFarge that added to the substantial list of panegyrics by
Catholic writers. In one of these essays, published in an anthology aptly
called *Saints Are Now,* Stanton exalted, "And because God possessed
his soul so completely, Uncle John became, for many who knew him
well, the only authentic saint they had ever met."[7]

More useful to me have been two scholarly and critical dissertations
done at the Catholic University of America. In 1975 Marilyn Wenzke
Nickels covered in detail LaFarge's involvement in the controversial

5. Cyprian Davis, O.S.B., *The History of Black Catholics in the United States* (New
York, 1990), 315.

6. According to the article "Jesuit Says Pius XI Asked for Draft," *National Catholic
Reporter,* December 22, 1972, p. 4, the Jesuits Walter Abbott, Harry Sievers, and Thomas
Breslin began or contemplated biographies of LaFarge.

7. Edward S. Stanton, S.J., "John LaFarge," in *Saints Are Now: Eight Portraits of
Modern Sanctity,* ed. John J. Delaney (New York, 1983), 93. See also Stanton's "John
LaFarge's Understanding of the Unifying Mission of the Church, Especially in the Area
of Race Relations" (Ph.D. dissertation, St. Paul University, Ottawa, 1972), and "The
Manner Was Ordinary," *Am,* 129 (November 24, 1973), 397–99. The publisher Robert
Giroux told Stanton that LaFarge was "too well-mannered and courtly" to appeal to the
modern reader (Robert Giroux to Edward Stanton, January 19, 1982, in box 1, folder 4,
Edward S. Stanton Papers, Boston College). In addition, see the hagiography of Glenn
D. Kittler, "The Manner Was Extraordinary," in *The Wings of Eagles* (Garden City, N.Y.,
1966), 149–86; and Jacques Maritain, "Father LaFarge," *IR,* 33 (February, 1960), 31.

and fateful Turner affair of 1932 and 1933, and the Reverend Martin A. Zielinski completed a history of the Catholic Interracial Council of New York in 1989. Three recent books that touch on the subject of the Catholic church and blacks have also been helpful. Peter McDonough includes a perceptive chapter on LaFarge in his monumental study of American Jesuits, *Men Astutely Trained,* and Stephen Ochs's wide-ranging book on the Josephites and the fight for black priests, *Desegregating the Altar,* contains much that was valuable for this undertaking. This assessment also applies to *The History of Black Catholics in the United States* by Cyprian Davis.[8] All historians who write about Catholic social action are inevitably indebted to path-breaking scholars such as Robert D. Cross, Aaron Abell, David J. O'Brien, William M. Halsey, and Joseph M. McShane.[9]

Despite the great strides of Catholic scholarship since Vatican II, Catholic history still lies on the margins of American history. I agree with Leslie Tentler that greater efforts are required to integrate Catholic history into the whole of the nation's history.[10] I hope this volume in some way contributes to that end.

8. Marilyn Wenzke Nickels, "The Federated Colored Catholics: A Study of Three Variant Perspectives on Racial Justice as Represented by John LaFarge, William Markoe, and Thomas Turner" (Ph.D. dissertation, Catholic University of America, 1975), published almost verbatim as *Black Catholic Protest and the Federated Colored Catholics, 1917–1933: Three Perspectives on Racial Justice* (New York, 1988); Martin A. Zielinski, " 'Doing the Truth': The Catholic Interracial Council of New York, 1945–1965" (Ph.D. dissertation, Catholic University of America, 1989); Peter McDonough, *Men Astutely Trained: A History of the Jesuits in the American Century* (New York, 1992); Stephen J. Ochs, *Desegregating the Altar: The Josephites and the Struggle for Black Priests, 1871–1960* (Baton Rouge, 1990); and Cyprian Davis, *History of Black Catholics.* Also helpful was Martin A. Zielinski, "The Promotion of Better Race Relations: The Catholic Interracial Council of New York, 1934–1945" (M.A. thesis, Catholic University of America, 1985).

9. Robert D. Cross, *The Emergence of Liberal Catholicism in America* (Cambridge, Mass., 1958); Aaron I. Abell, *American Catholicism and Social Action* (Notre Dame, Ind., 1963); David J. O'Brien, *American Catholics and Social Reform: The New Deal Years* (New York, 1968), and also *Public Catholicism* (New York, 1989); William M. Halsey, *The Survival of American Innocence: Catholicism in the Era of Disillusionment, 1920–1940* (Notre Dame, Ind., 1980); and Joseph M. McShane, *"Sufficiently Radical": Catholicism, Progressivism, and the Bishops' Program of 1919* (Washington, D.C., 1986).

10. Leslie Woodcock Tentler, "On the Margins: The State of American Catholic History," *American Quarterly,* 45 (March, 1993), 122.

This task of integration is a daunting one, but no more difficult than trying to decipher the mystery of the Catholic church itself. To echo what V. O. Key once said about the American South, of books about the Catholic church there is no end. As one of my colleagues put it, "Almost every generalization about what Catholics and Catholicism are like turns out to be contradicted by hundreds of examples." People who were born into the church and have studied it intensively have warned about the "cobwebby irrationality of the world's oldest bureaucracy." Then, too, my task was further complicated by dealing with the Janus-like, much-praised and much-maligned Society of Jesus, a powerful "mutation within Catholicism."[11]

And there looms the puzzle of LaFarge himself, "an almost exquisitely complicated bundle of contradictions," as one student of the Jesuit judged.[12] Moreover, LaFarge seldom revealed himself, not even in private correspondence. Not surprisingly, the devout man mirrored many of the paradoxes of the Society of Jesus, a religious order that strained to reconcile tradition and change, medievalism and modernity, the mystical and the practical.[13] Reviewing LaFarge's autobiography in 1954, Jacques Barzun marveled at the "flexible duality" in the priest, who, without blinking an eye, switched from the mystical and obscure to the practical and mundane. It is unusual to find an American leader of LaFarge's stature described by his colleagues as "unostentatiously ordinary" and utterly "without flair," a retiring man of monumental patience who put a high priority on making "a minimum of heat."[14] So fiercely loyal was LaFarge to the institutional church that his efforts to reform it seemed almost out of character.

Ironically, many of the same qualities that explain the Jesuit's successes as a reformer also account for his shortcomings. For example,

---

11. Patrick Allitt to the author, August 22, 1991; Gary McEoin, *Memoirs and Memories* (Mystic, Conn., 1986), 153. See also Scott R. Safranski, *Managing God's Organization: The Catholic Church in Society* (Ann Arbor, Mich., 1985), which destroys many stereotypes about the church.

12. Peter McDonough to the author, February 3, 1992.

13. McDonough, *Men Astutely Trained,* ix, xii, xvi; Rene Fulöp-Miller, *The Power and Secret of the Jesuits,* trans. F. S. Flint and D. F. Tait (New York, 1930), 404; J. C. H. Aveling, *The Jesuits* (New York, 1981), 350–55, 370–72.

14. Jacques Barzun, "Not to Count the Cost," *New York Times Book Review,* February 14, 1954, p. 1; interview of Robert C. Hartnett, S.J., by Edward S. Stanton, December 1, 1980, and Robert A. Graham, S.J., to Edward Stanton, October 13, 1981, both in box 1, folder 1, Stanton Papers, Boston College.

LaFarge's optimism and his heroic patience underlay many of his achievements, but these characteristics also bound him to a philosophy of genteel gradualism and robbed him of a sense of urgency about the race problem. He naïvely believed that it was possible to effect a slow, orderly racial revolution, without the risk of disorder or violence. His aristocratic background and his Eurocentric bias, which often aided him in the racial apostolate and in higher-echelon Catholic politics, saddled him with a lingering paternalism and an ambivalence about black culture. These last two traits, combined with his staunch clericalism, gave him a mindset that helps explain his complicity in the assault on the Federated Colored Catholics in the early 1930s and his shabby treatment of the black couple who ran the Cardinal Gibbons Institute, Victor and Constance Daniel.

Because of the Catholic church's poor historical record on the issues of slavery and race, Catholic apologists have had a tendency to canonize racial liberals who were "ahead of the church." LaFarge is a case in point. While the Jesuit was in front of his church in race relations, he was an exceedingly cautious reformer who was slow to condemn segregation and reluctant to support nonviolent direct action by blacks. Moreover, a staunch theological and ecclesiastical conservative, he functioned comfortably in the pre–Vatican II church. Although this book records LaFarge's important achievements (done in the face of daunting institutional obstacles), its aim is not to lionize LaFarge simply because he strode slightly ahead of a Jim Crow church. This work in fact illustrates that many activists inside the Catholic church, to say nothing of those outside it, were more advanced on the race issue than was LaFarge. Catholic priests such as Thomas J. Harte, John Cooper, William M. Markoe, George H. Dunne, Claude Heithaus, Paul Furfey, and Joseph Fichter and laypersons such as Dorothy Day, John O'Connor, Dennis Clark, and Mathew Ahmann astutely criticized LaFarge and pointed out the limitations of Catholic interracialism.

Judgments aside, it is hoped that this book adds to the historical literature by illuminating the many ironies, paradoxes, ambiguities, and dilemmas surrounding the long fight against racial injustice that LaFarge and his associates waged. One of my basic aims has simply been to provide a detailed record of LaFarge's racial work, since none now exists. I want to stress, however, that this is not a book about black Catholics. Nor is this a book about Catholic theology or spirituality, though I necessarily consider all of these topics. This study rather centers on LaFarge and his reading of the race problem for nearly half a century. A comprehensive look at black Catholics per se was beyond the scope of this already substantial project. The sources on black Catholics are scattered and elusive. Although Cyprian Davis has given us a fine survey of black Catholic history, much monographic work, including the topic of black Catholic influence on the various Catholic interracial councils and the civil rights movement in general, remains to be done.

Acknowledgments

In preparing this book, I have incurred many debts. I would therefore like to thank some of the people and organizations that have assisted me with this project. I owe much to the National Endowment for the Humanities, the American Council of Learned Societies, the American Philosophical Society, and the Cushwa Center for the Study of American Catholicism, all of which provided research grants that enabled me to visit and examine the pertinent and far-flung archival depositories. Thanks also go to Westminster College and Dean Richard E. Mattingly for a sabbatical during the 1991–1992 academic year, which allowed me time off from teaching duties to write this book.

Additionally, I want to thank Peter McDonough, Stephen J. Ochs, Patrick Allitt, Daniel J. Kane, Louise Daniel Hutchinson, the Reverend Peter E. Hogan, S.S.J., and the Reverend Emmett Curran, S.J., for reading portions of the book in manuscript form. I also want to express my deepest appreciation for the efforts of Christine N. Cowan, whose heroic copy editing has greatly improved this book. All offered helpful criticism and saved me from embarrassing errors. They are, of course, in no way responsible for the errors of interpretation or errors of fact that remain.

I also owe thanks to a large number of librarians and archivists. At the risk of leaving out many of those who provided vital assistance to me, I would like to single out the following persons for their cheerful and efficient service: Nicholas B. Scheetz, manuscript librarian at Georgetown University; Archie Motley, curator of archives and manuscripts at the Chicago Historical Society; Esme Bhan, research associate at the Moorland-Spingarn Research Center at Howard University; the Reverend Peter E. Hogan, director of the Josephite Archives in Baltimore; Nancy Merz, associate archivist at the Jesuit Missouri Province Archives in St. Louis; Anne Crowley, S.N.P., archivist at the Catholic University of America; the Reverend Paul A. Fitzgerald, S.J., head archivist at Boston College; and Phil Runkel, archivist at Marquette University. In addition, I want to thank Lorna Mitchell, Liz Hauer, and Barbara Ault, all staffers of Reeves Library at Westminster College, who have been immensely helpful to me over the long course of this project. The following activists and scholars granted me interviews of great value in the development of this book: the Reverend Monsignor George G. Higgins, the Reverend William B. Faherty, S.J., the Reverend Martin A. Zielinski, Jacqueline E. Wilson, Dennis Clark, Mathew Ahmann, and Guichard Parris. Finally, the highest tribute goes to my wife, Marcy, whose infinite patience and understanding, to say nothing of her expert and tireless proofreading, helped sustain me in this effort.

John LaFarge

and the Limits

of Catholic

Interracialism

1911–1963

1

A LaFarge and a Jesuit, Too

John LaFarge seemed destined to make a mark on his times. One hardly would have guessed, however, that he would do it as a Roman Catholic priest. LaFarge was born into the social register in Newport, Rhode Island, on February 13, 1880, "brought into daylight," as he put it, by a black midwife at the family home on 10 Sunnyside Place. He was the ninth and last child of the elder John LaFarge, an eminent artist of his time, and Margaret Mason Perry, a woman with impressive bloodlines. This couple perpetuated a distinguished French-American family whose members had a passion for travel, adventure, and intellectual and artistic pursuits.[1]

The LaFarge name reached the United States in the person of Jean Frédéric de la Farge, the grandfather of the Catholic priest. Born in 1786, this young lieutenant participated in the ill-fated Napoleonic expedition of 1803 to reclaim Santo Domingo from Toussaint L'Ouverture and his black revolutionaries. After three years of captivity as a "white slave," he escaped and made his way to Philadelphia and then to New York. He married Louisa Binsse de Saint-Victor, whose father, Louis François Binsse, was a prominent figure in the French emigré colony in New York City. Eventually Jean Frédéric made a fortune in shipping. He owned extensive property in upstate New York near Lake

---

1. *MIO,* 34–35. Many of the details about LaFarge in this chapter are taken from this autobiography. For short eulogies of LaFarge, see Glenn D. Kittler, "The Manner Was Extraordinary," in his *Wings of Eagles,* 149–86, and Stanton, "John LaFarge," 71–93.

Ontario and the St. Lawrence River, where he established the town of LaFargeville. Later, at his wife's urging, the couple escaped the frigid winters of northern New York by settling permanently in Manhattan.[2] Eventually, the American branches of the two French families dropped the particles from their names and became simply LaFarges and Binsses. This French connection of genes proved an American windfall, producing an array of prominent Americans in the nineteenth and twentieth centuries.

Jean Frédéric and Louisa's son John was born in New York City in 1835. The elder John LaFarge attended St. John's College (later Fordham University) and Mount St. Mary's College at Emmitsburg, Maryland. He contemplated a career in law, but after graduation he embarked upon a leisurely two-year tour of Europe in 1856, a perquisite for those with parents of ample means and a taste for the finer things of life. Prominent literary kin on his mother's side, such as Maximilien Binsse de Saint-Victor and his son Paul, hosted the young American in Paris. There he indulged his early interest in drawing by studying under Thomas Couture, an innovative teacher and technician in painting. He also observed the great masterpieces of art across the continent and had contact with the Pre-Raphaelites in London.[3]

Back home in 1859, the elder John LaFarge began to study with the Romantic painter William Morris Hunt at his studio in Newport, Rhode Island. LaFarge developed into a fine colorist and draftsman who was situated strategically somewhere between the Romantics and the Realists.[4] Like Paul Gauguin, he ventured into the South Seas to escape the rush of modern life, but he could not abandon himself to the primitivism that made his European counterpart famous. Critics have suggested that he was perhaps too traditional and intellectual to blaze new paths in modern painting.[5]

Still, LaFarge carved out a formidable niche in American art by becoming one of the best muralists and decorators of the nineteenth

2. *MIO*, 8–10; Royal Cortissoz, "John LaFarge [1835–1910]," *Dictionary of American Biography*, X, 530.

3. *MIO*, 10, 17; Oliver W. Larkin, *Art and Life in America* (rev. ed.; New York, 1960), 199; Cortissoz, "John LaFarge," 531.

4. Royal Cortissoz, *John LaFarge: A Memoir and a Study* (1911; rpr. New York, 1971), 208–209, 262; Milton Brown *et al.*, *American Art* (Englewood Cliffs, N.J., 1979), 288; Larkin, *Art and Life*, 212, 275, 297.

5. Matthew Baigell, *Dictionary of American Art* (New York, 1979), 201.

century. He rediscovered and revived the lost art of stained glass windows in America. After he was hired by Henry H. Richardson to decorate the Trinity Church in Boston in 1876, his services were much in demand by thriving architectural firms such as McKim, Mead, and White. A noted art critic and biographer of LaFarge called *The Ascension,* a mural done for the Ascension Church in New York City, "the greatest painting of a religious subject produced anywhere in LaFarge's time." As a decorator he was a master of mass and nuance, and hundreds of his "opaline" windows graced public and private buildings in America. Two generations of LaFarges stood in his mammoth shadow and inevitably measured themselves against his considerable legacy.[6]

LaFarge's talents extended beyond painting and decorating. He also had a literary gift and a knack for brilliant conversation, talents he employed as an art critic, travel writer, and lecturer. The Library of Congress cites eleven books by the artist. A 1979 textbook on American art described LaFarge as "the most cultured and sophisticated artist working in the United States in the late nineteenth century." Above all, he was a highly cerebral man. In his autobiography Henry Adams wrote that LaFarge "alone owned a mind complex enough to contrast against the commonplaces of American uniformity." The renowned Bostonian added that LaFarge's stimulating conversation was invested with "infinite shades and refractions of lights, and with color toned down to the finest gradation." Van Wyck Brooks marveled at his "subtle mind, brooding and profound." His "French type of mind" fascinated Adams, who accompanied the painter on his voyages to Japan and the South Seas. According to the pessimistic Yankee, who was struggling mightily to comprehend the rapid change of the late nineteenth century, LaFarge had "ownership" of the meaning of the twelfth century. LaFarge encouraged Adams to travel to France to meditate on medieval cathedrals, a journey that led to his classic *Mont-Saint-Michel* and *Chartres.*[7]

6. Quotation in Cortissoz, "John LaFarge," 532–33; Larkin, *Art and Life,* 285–87, 296; interview of Wer LaFarge (great-grandson of the artist) by Edward Stanton, in box 1, folder 2, Stanton Papers.

7. Brown *et al., American Art,* 288; Henry Adams, *The Education of Henry Adams: An Autobiography* (Boston, 1918), 369–71; Van Wyck Brooks, *New England: Indian Summer* (New York, 1940), 76; *MIO,* 10; Keith R. Burch, "Charles Eliot Norton, Henry Adams, and the Catholic Church as a Symbol of Order and Authority," *Catholic Historical Review,* 75 (July, 1989), 423–38.

The fusion of LaFarge and Binsse blood was further enriched when in 1860 the muralist married Margaret Perry of Newport, Rhode Island. The naval hero Oliver Hazard Perry was Margaret's grandfather, and his brother Commodore Matthew Calbraith Perry was her great-uncle. On her mother's side of the family, she descended from Benjamin Franklin through the Sergeant family of Philadelphia, a noted family in its own right. Miss Perry and LaFarge had mutual friends in William and Henry James. Like LaFarge, the James brothers, destined for fame in the literary and intellectual world, also studied painting under William Morris Hunt, though, it seems, with meager results. It was the brothers who introduced LaFarge to Miss Perry, an attractive woman who at the time had several eager suitors. Perry was an Episcopalian, but she dutifully converted to Catholicism soon after her marriage to LaFarge. In this process she was assisted by Isaac Hecker, another New England convert who founded the Paulists.[8]

As the 1870s drew to a close and Margaret approached forty, she agonized over the prospect of having another child. Her eldest had been born in 1862, and eight other children had followed. One of these was stillborn, and another, Raymond, died in infancy. Adding to Margaret's distress was the fact that her domineering and absentee husband had thrust all the household responsibilities on her. The troubled matron therefore looked to her confessor for help, but he only advised her to trust the Lord and let nature take its course. Thus, on a wintry February day in 1880, the second John LaFarge was born. His was not a promising beginning. Apparently, no one expected the pale, feeble baby to live through the day. The absentee father was not even informed about the birth of his last child until his son was out of danger.[9]

John LaFarge spent his youth in the captivating locale of Newport among charming and witty family members and their many esteemed friends. Henry Adams was "Uncle Henry" to the LaFarge children. Both Henry and William James were lifelong friends of the family. John's eldest brother Grant counted Theodore Roosevelt among his closest friends. Some other family friends singled out in LaFarge's autobiography were the novelist Edith Wharton and Frédéric-Auguste Bartholdi, the designer of the Statue of Liberty. Two of John's older brothers, Grant and Bancel, followed in their father's steps and made

8. *MIO*, 17–25.
9. *Ibid.*, 34–35.

names for themselves as architects and designers. Another brother, Oliver, became a successful executive with General Motors. Two of LaFarge's nephews, Christopher Grant and Oliver Hazard Perry, the sons of Grant LaFarge, went to Harvard and achieved recognition in the art and literary worlds: Christopher as a novelist, journalist, and architect; Oliver as a Pulitzer-Prize-winning novelist and benefactor of Native Americans. In keeping with the times, the LaFarge women primarily assumed supporting roles, but most of them managed to marry well.[10]

Despite the many advantages of his privileged birth, LaFarge did not have a particularly happy childhood. Although his autobiography is sketchy on some of the crucial events of his career, he nonetheless made it explicit in his memoirs that as a youth he deeply resented his father's prolonged absences and general inattention toward him. When the elder LaFarge was not on a trip to Japan, the South Seas, or Europe, he often stayed in his New York studio rather than at the family home in Newport. Even on those rare occasions at home, he was so absorbed in his work that the son found him largely unapproachable. Thus, the young boy scarcely knew his aging father. He approached this shadowy paternal figure with "fear" and "fascination." When the artist returned home from the South Seas in 1891, the younger LaFarge recalled that he "was glad to know that [he] really had a father in fact," for his recollection of him up to then "had been quite indefinite."[11]

Inevitably, the son became very attached to his long-suffering mother, and he resented his father's neglect of her. In her loneliness his mother fell back on her adopted religion and became a deeply pious and orthodox Catholic, unlike her free-spirited and footloose spouse. Like his mother, young John developed a strong sense of sin, causing him to think rather darkly about his worldly and somewhat anticlerical father, who looked at life with "dry, humorous cynicism." In his autobiography he pointedly accused the elder LaFarge of withdrawing his love from his wife and implied philandering by the patriarch. How much the youth knew of his father's private life is uncertain, but in later

10. *Ibid.*, 14, 17, 42, 58–59, 174, 177; "Christopher Grant LaFarge," "John Louis Bancel LaFarge," and "Oliver Hazard Perry LaFarge," all in *New Catholic Encyclopedia*, VIII, 313–16; *MIO*, 9, 56; Francis S. Childs to Edward Stanton, October 17, 1981, in box 1, folder 8, Stanton Papers.

11. *MIO*, 3–4.

life the straitlaced priest must have winced at reading his father's reminiscences of the South Seas. These exotic vignettes included descriptions of "the splendid nakedness of the savages," the incessant flirting of half-clad young girls, and the constant drinking of the narcoticlike *kava.*[12]

In any case, the son made a great effort to satisfy his mother's plea that he love his father, warts and all. Later in life the priest celebrated his father's accomplishments as another instance of triumphant American Catholicism, though he judged his father's art to be more uniquely "Catholic" than it really was. At the same time, he bemoaned the fact that most of his father's work adorned Protestant churches and public places rather than the institutions of his Roman faith.[13]

It is clear that LaFarge was simultaneously attracted and repelled by his father. Although it probably would not add much to the hard truth of history, a psychoanalyst could speculate at length on such father-son, mother-son relations. In any event, young John shared many personality traits with his father (and other members of his family). As one friendly observer of the LaFarge family wrote, they were a "cerebral rather than an emotional lot." The LaFarges, he continued, all seemed to have a certain "dryness" and aloofness that made them "saturnine in temperament and sardonic in conversation." Like his father, John was fastidious, aloof, and often ill. Above all, the youngster was bookish and introspective. The most satisfying times in his childhood were the countless hours he spent reading on the back porch of the Redwood Library in Newport. Here he devoured novels, poetry, biography, and history. At the age of ten he edited a monthly magazine for the neighborhood called *Sunlight.* His extraordinary gift for languages emerged early. In addition to the French that he absorbed from relatives and early study, he learned Danish from a neighbor. Eager to use his acquired skills, one day he excitedly rowed a skiff out into the Newport harbor to converse with Danish sailors. Before he was out of high school, he had also learned Icelandic and Gaelic. He subsequently became fluent in more than a dozen major languages.[14]

12. *Ibid.,* 7, 29–33, 49–53, 131; John LaFarge, *Reminiscences of the South Seas* (Garden City, N.Y., 1912), 68, 87–88, 114, 274.

13. *MIO,* 30–33. See also his articles, "A Catholic Painter on the Masters," *Am,* 10 (January 31, 1914), 392–94; "The Mind of John LaFarge," *Catholic World,* 140 (March, 1935), 701–10; and "LaFarge and the Truth," *Am,* 52 (March 30, 1935), 586–88.

14. Chaucey Stillman to Edward Stanton, May 11, 1982, in box 1, folder 7, Stanton

One talent LaFarge did not inherit was the ability to draw. Try as he would, he never even learned to write legibly, and he was painfully bereft of mechanical ability. As if to compensate him elsewhere, though, he had a keen ear for music. He became an accomplished pianist, studying intensely under private teachers at home and later at Harvard. His sister Frances remembered the "everlasting tinkle" of Johann Sebastian Bach and Wolfgang Amadeus Mozart in the house. Wherever he went, whether it was the seminary in Innsbruck, Austria, or pastoral duty in rural Maryland, he managed to have a piano. Surprisingly, his multitalented father had no interest in music and startled his progeny when one day he thundered that the most appealing music to him was the kind that made "the least sound."[15]

As a kind of prodigy, LaFarge found it difficult to attract young friends with similar interests. Insofar as he made personal contacts outside his immediate family, they tended to be learned adults. One of his mentors was Dr. Herman J. Heuser, who lived near LaFarge's sister and her husband and was a professor of scripture at St. Charles Borromeo Seminary in Overbrook just outside Philadelphia and the founder in 1889 of the *American Ecclesiastical Review.* Heuser patiently fed the inquiring mind of the fifteen-year-old, but one day he cautioned LaFarge: "Look out, young fellow. You are merely cultivating your intellect and neglecting your heart." The professor continued, "What you need is less brains and more heart."[16] This was the first of many such warnings he would receive.

But LaFarge remained aloof and eccentric as a youth. He showed no interest or talent in sports. All his life he suffered from poor digestion and was plagued by a "rebellious interior." Stomach trouble forced him out of high school in his sophomore year, and he and his mother temporarily moved to New York City to live with his father and continue his education under a private tutor. In New York he had surgery for appendicitis and experienced a slow recovery. Because of his delicate

---

15. *MIO,* 7, 45–47, 84.

16. *Ibid.,* 56; Joseph G. Hubbert, C. M., " 'Less Brains and More Heart': Father Herman J. Heuser, Founder of the American Ecclesiastical Review," *U.S. Catholic Historian,* 13 (Winter, 1995), 95–122.

health and his talents, his mother and his older siblings were inclined to pamper the "baby" of the family.[17]

If frail physically, LaFarge was spiritually robust. He claimed that he had decided to become a priest at the age of eleven. At this tender age, he recalled, the clerical vocation became "an all-dominating purpose in my life." Perhaps he was so vocationally fulfilled in later life that he exaggerated how early and how definite his career choice had been. He admits in his memoirs to some uncertainty in that even at Harvard his "mind was not fully made up to the priesthood." Nevertheless, it is clear that LaFarge was as precocious spiritually as he was intellectually. Moreover, his devout mother encouraged this side of him. He read many of her religious books, and not only did he read a pocket-sized Bible three times, but he slept with it under his pillow. Then, too, he diligently perused a Latin missal and Cardinal Henry Edward Manning's book *The Eternal Priesthood*, both given to him by priests. LaFarge remembered that at the age of seven he was deeply moved when his "mother had consecrated [him] to the Blessed Virgin." His first communion at the age of ten equally awed him. The mysteries surrounding Jesus Christ, the Blessed Virgin, and the Eucharist began to envelop his thoughts. The prepubescent lad was thrilled, as he recalled, by "the grandeur and sweep of Catholic dogma."[18] A genuine calling was in the making.

Still, the youngster was puzzled by his attraction to the priesthood. He had never been an altar boy or particularly close to any of the local priests. Nor had he attended parochial schools (the public schools had had better teachers). Furthermore, no one in his family had ever aspired to the priesthood. His kin regarded his interest as a passing phase of adolescence. Moreover, he himself doubted whether he was suited for the priesthood. He considered himself "self-centered," "reserved," "fastidious," and fragile, whereas a priest, he thought, should be someone who was unselfish, outgoing, adaptable, and hearty. Besides that, the family already projected the young man as some kind of professor, probably in languages. Only later did LaFarge realize that he might be both a scholar and a priest.[19]

When time came to choose a college, LaFarge considered Georgetown, Columbia, and Harvard Universities. He decided against Cath-

17. *MIO*, 54–56, 69–70.
18. *Ibid.*, 49–54, 61.
19. *Ibid.*, 37, 49, 52.

olic Georgetown because it had a reputation for poor food, a chief concern for someone who constantly suffered from bad digestion. Family members divided on the other two institutions. The persuasiveness of Theodore Roosevelt, then police commissioner of New York City and one who knew LaFarge's tastes, tipped the balance in favor of the prestigious institution at Cambridge. In 1897 John became the first member of the LaFarge family to enter Harvard, along with another freshman named Robert Frost. Since President Charles Eliot's elective system was in place, the would-be priest loaded his course of study with biblical languages: Latin, Greek, Hebrew, Syriac, and Aramaic. Although he had an opportunity to study with some of the best minds in the country, he was generally disappointed with his classes. With the exception of a few courses such as French medieval history under Professor Charles Cross, he found his classes uninspiring. As he put it, "the tradition of the German university hung heavily over Harvard." He hoped to penetrate the spirit of Aeschylus or Aristophanes, but instead he spent endless hours analyzing the structure of the Greek stage. Rather than immersing himself in the philosophy of Aristotle's *Nicomachean Ethics,* he spent all his time grappling with the Greek language's moods and tenses.[20]

LaFarge's sour memories of Harvard did not hinge solely on pedestrian instruction. He was lonely, especially in his freshman year. His relationship with his academic adviser was "perfunctory." He knew none of the students, and he did not make friends easily. He did not drink, smoke, or, apparently, seek sexual encounters. He paid no attention when, shortly after he arrived on campus, Harvard drubbed Yale in football, 30–0. Despite some attempts to improve his health with exercise, he found himself with a "constant feeling of utter physical weakness." The "food was bad, and the evenings dreary," he recollected. The quality of his nourishment, of course, plagued his rebellious stomach. Living in Harvard Yard was next to primitive, and it seemed worse because it contrasted sharply with certain luxurious conditions outside the yard where the wealthiest students tended to reside.[21]

He also "resented" St. Paul's, the Catholic church located on the grounds of the university. He believed this Catholic edifice gave Prot-

20. *Ibid.,* 49, 58–64.
21. *Ibid.,* 59–60, 69; Edward S. Stanton, unpublished draft of John LaFarge biography, n.d. [1982(?)], in Stanton Papers.

estants a poor image of Catholicism. The plain wooden Romanist structure contrasted sadly with the magnificent Episcopalian Trinity Church
on Copley Square, which was adorned with some of his father's finest
murals and stained glass. St. Paul's congregation came primarily from
the working class, and its pastor and his assistants, LaFarge charged,
were inept and meanly anti-Harvard.[22]

What bothered LaFarge most about Harvard, however, was what
he regarded as the "utter lack of interest in the spiritual welfare of
students." He believed that the faith of many Catholics deteriorated or
was entirely lost at Harvard because of the institution's hostility or
indifference to religion. Many Catholics simply hid their faith, but
LaFarge joined a small group that revived the defunct Harvard Catholic
Club. Although instances of outright anti-Catholicism were rare, he
perceived a sense of hostility toward all religions among most of the
faculty. Singling out the renowned George Santayana as particularly
hostile to supernatural belief, he accused the witty and popular professor of weakening the faith of many students. At first he attended the
crowded Wednesday evening seminars of the noted philosopher and
poet, but when Santayana snidely questioned LaFarge about his belief
in Catholic dogma, he stalked out of the room, never to return. On
Santayana's death in 1952, LaFarge penned a bitterly harsh commentary
on the Spanish-American philosopher, condemning his anticlericalism
and his intellectual "confusion."[23]

After LaFarge left Cambridge, he continued to express his concern
about the spiritual health of Catholic students on non-Catholic campuses. In 1904, while still a seminarian, LaFarge tried to enlist William
O'Connell, the soon-to-be archbishop of Boston, in a campaign for
better spiritual care of such Catholic students. In addition, he followed
up with a lengthy report on conditions of Catholic students at Harvard
that figured prominently in the launching of the Newman Movement.
In the 1920s, however, LaFarge totally abandoned the movement and
argued that Catholic attendance at non-Catholic schools should be discouraged altogether. In the 1940s LaFarge reversed himself again and
supported Newman centers. The historian John Whitney Evans puzzled over these flip-flops and finally concluded that they occurred be-

22. *MIO*, 65.
23. *Ibid.*, 62–64, 68–69; John LaFarge, "Feature 'X,' " *Am*, 88 (October 11, 1952),
42–43.

cause of LaFarge's "innate capacity to transcend the times by growing with them." A more plausible answer is that the ever-obedient priest was simply following the changing Jesuit party line and that of its mouthpiece, *America.* Certainly, "visionary intellect," the term Evans uses in depicting LaFarge, does not accurately describe the staunchly orthodox and triumphalist Catholic of the early twentieth century.[24]

On his becoming an associate editor of *America* in 1926, LaFarge's first series of articles consisted of four essays on education that might have been called "Godlessness and man at Harvard." In these articles he was responding to the brewing intra-Catholic controversy about the Newman Movement and the charges inside and outside the church that Catholic schools were producing few people of intellectual distinction. Speaking as one who had attended both a prestigious secular university in America and an esteemed Catholic institution in Europe, the seminary at Innsbruck, Austria, LaFarge argued that Harvard had "bungled and muffed" the job of liberal education because of narrow specialization, cold rationalism, and the lack of a genuine core curriculum. Even worse, Harvard left out the very soul of culture in its curriculum. The purpose of culture, LaFarge asserted, was to lead one's thoughts "onward and upward to a unified ideal of conduct" based on the "Divine Humanity of Jesus Christ." The proper study of humankind, according to the Jesuit, was not man but God. Secular humanism left a vacuum that only Christian humanism could fill. LaFarge fairly trumpeted his conclusion: "Jesuit schools are today what Harvard University is still striving to become, a school for liberal education."[25]

Thus, the Harvards and Yales were "too dangerous, too proximate an occasion of [spiritual] lapse" for Catholics, and they should be avoided if at all possible. He insisted that his Harvard experience taught him that a "Catholic atmosphere" could not be created on a neopagan campus. Even in a friendlier and more democratic setting than Harvard, he maintained, a "Catholic Foundation" on campus would create hostility in non-Catholics owing to the separation of Catholic students in

24. *MIO,* 65–66; John Whitney Evans, "John LaFarge, *America,* and the Newman Movement," *Catholic Historical Review,* 64 (October, 1978), 614, 617–21.

25. Quotations in John LaFarge, "Harvard Culture and Jesuit Humanism," *Am,* 34 (January 9, 1926), 300, 302, and "Harvard Culture and Jesuit Humanism, II," *Am,* 34 (January 16, 1926), 326–27. On articles critical of Catholic education, see George Shuster, "Have We Any Scholars?," *Am,* 33 (August 15, 1925), 418–19, and Charles Lischka, "The Death of Doctors," *Am,* 33 (September 19, 1925), 435–36.

Newman centers. LaFarge suggested that the only useful thing to be done for Catholics at non-Catholic institutions was to provide a nearby parish church with a devoted and caring staff.[26]

Fighting the partisan education wars probably colored LaFarge's memories of Harvard in a negative way. Actually, his autobiography shows that he enjoyed many happy times at Cambridge. He remained active in alumni affairs, attended class reunions regularly through old age, gave several lectures at the school, and proudly accepted an honorary degree from his alma mater. It is true, however, that his best times at Harvard occurred in the company of mature adults, most of them his relatives or priests. He often visited his uncle Thomas Perry, a tutor in modern languages at Harvard. At his uncle's home he regularly played piano in a trio with two of Perry's daughters. He frequently sought the company of Agnes Irvin, a cousin who was dean of Radcliffe College and who served an excellent soup that agreed with his finicky stomach. There were also visits with William James, professor of philosophy at Harvard and an old friend of the family, and with Aunt Lilla Perry of the Cabot family. Further, LaFarge joined several organizations, such as the Hasty Pudding Club, the Shakespeare Club, and the Musical Club. He also was chosen to be on the editorial board of the *Harvard Monthly*.[27]

Nevertheless, this quiet, intense young man clearly did not mesh smoothly with the surroundings at Harvard or the larger world beyond. John Ropes, a professor of history whom LaFarge admired greatly, was the first person at Harvard to pull the priggish young man aside and advise him "to learn to know the common crowd." LaFarge took the advice seriously but regretted that while at Harvard he "somehow never got around to it."[28]

From the beginning of his college experience, LaFarge thought in terms of preparing himself for the seminary, though his notion of what that entailed was vague. He was determined to keep himself on a strict regimen, which included weekly confession. Spurning the priests at

26. John LaFarge, "Harvard and the Foundation," *Am*, 34 (February 6, 1926), 402–404, and "In Place of Foundation," *Am*, 34 (February 13, 1926), 424–25. See the even more anti-Newman views of the editor-in-chief of *America*, Wilfred Parsons, in "Chaplaincy, Newman Club or Catholic College?," *Am*, 35 (September 4, 1926), 488–89.

27. *MIO*, 62, 69–74.

28. *Ibid.*, 70.

nearby St. Paul's, he chose as his confessor Father Thomas I. Gasson, the Jesuit rector of Boston College. He also confided in the Reverend E. Winchester Donald, the sagacious and broad-minded rector at the LaFarge-decorated Trinity Church. As he began to consider where he would study for the priesthood, Father Gasson recommended theological studies at the University of Innsbruck in Austria. The idea of study abroad appealed to LaFarge, but his father and his brother Grant still opposed his vocational choice. Family support was crucial, especially for the funding of study abroad. Again, Theodore Roosevelt intervened and argued that the devout young man had a vocation and should be allowed to pursue it. Roosevelt's persuasiveness won the point, and in July of 1901, LaFarge set sail for Europe.[29]

As a free-lance seminarian at Innsbruck, LaFarge could live where he wished. Rather than lodging at the Canisianum, the Jesuit-controlled living area for theology students, LaFarge took an apartment in town in order to learn more about the students attending the large, state-run university. Soon, however, he grew exceedingly lonely. By the new year he had moved into the spartan confines of the Canisianum, where he adapted remarkably well to the primitive conditions of unheated rooms and outdoor facilities. These, along with the plain, well-cooked food, somehow seemed to improve his fragile health.[30]

LaFarge also enjoyed his classes at Innsbruck. The Jesuit professors were always available to students in or out of class. He found the teaching more profound and stimulating than at Cambridge. Professors, he recalled, encouraged students to ask questions. His only regret was that he did not get a solid grounding in scholastic philosophy, the type of inquiry favored by Pope Leo XIII. Although the mandatory early morning meditation at the Canisianum was rarely enforced, LaFarge conscientiously acquired a lifelong habit of early prayer and Mass.[31]

While in Europe the young American took on several signal biases that sank deeply into his being. In the anticlerical nationalism of Italian students, many under Austrian rule, LaFarge got a "foretaste of Hitler and Mussolini," and he acquired a strong bias against antipapist liberalism in France. He also acquired a strong aversion to the socialistic

29. *Ibid.*, 59–60, 66–67, 76, 81.
30. *Ibid.*, 83–84, 91–93.
31. *Ibid.*, 99–100.

ideas that were gaining credence in Europe. Finally, he berated the "miserable results" achieved by the mingling of church and state functions at the state university in Innsbruck and elsewhere in Europe.[32]

Although a foreign student, LaFarge was never long without the company of American relatives. Since he had no classes during the summers and on holidays, he was free to do as he pleased. Fortunately, his family had the means and the interest in Europe to enable him to exploit these vacation periods. In the summer of 1902 his mother and his sister Frances toured parts of Austria and Germany with him. During the Easter vacation of 1903, he had a general audience with the frail and failing Pope Leo XIII, and he saw the future pope Benedict XV in Rome. In the summer of 1903 his mother and his sister Margaret joined LaFarge in Paris. From there they toured the French provinces and visited numerous relatives. In England they had a leisurely two-week visit with Henry James, who had not only been influenced by the seminarian's father but had once been romantically attracted to his mother. On his vacation in the summer of 1904, the aspiring priest returned to the States, where he found his father alone at Newport, his mother having gone to visit relatives on the West Coast. His father was in an unusually approachable mood, so they spent much time together. The patriarch now seemed fully reconciled to his son's vocation and was thrilled to find that his youngest had become "quite charming and human."[33]

That same summer LaFarge pleaded with Bishop William O'Connell to work for better spiritual care of Catholic students at Harvard. He also observed activities in the various local parishes around Newport. At this point LaFarge decided that he was not suited to be a diocesan priest. He hungered for a more challenging version of obedience and poverty than was usually required of a secular priest; he sought self-abnegation that would draw him closer to an understanding of the sacrificial love of Jesus Christ. In the course of an eight-day retreat in his final year at Innsbruck, LaFarge decided to join a religious order. His Jesuit retreat master convinced him that his destiny lay with the Society of Jesus.[34]

32. *Ibid.,* 86–87, 104, 108.
33. *Ibid.,* 103–17.
34. *Ibid.,* 117–18.

His choice of religious orders entailed a strange irony. As LaFarge set sail for Europe in 1901, his mother's final words had been, "Don't let them make you a Jesuit." The son's reply had been, "Mother, dear, nothing can ever make me a Jesuit." This exchange later "mystified" LaFarge, for he claimed that in 1901 he had never entertained the idea of becoming a Jesuit.[35] Highly defensive about the Society of Jesus in later life, he never tried in his autobiography to explain the source of his mother's anxiety. But her suspicions about the Jesuits were hardly atypical, even for a devout Catholic. Commemorating the 450th anniversary of the order founded by Ignatius Loyola in 1540, one analyst said of the Jesuits: "They have been the most respected and admired and mistrusted and feared and beloved and detested of all Catholic religious orders."[36] The dictionary typically cites the following as one definition of *Jesuit* (usually in the lower case): "one given to intrigue or equivocation: a crafty person: casuist"; and it defines *jesuitry* as "principles or practices ascribed to the Jesuits (as the practice of mental reservation, casuistry, and equivocation)—usually used disparagingly." Legions of famous writers from John Donne to Aldous Huxley have turned venomous pens on the Jesuits. Voltaire's satiric and picaresque *Candide* is perhaps the most effective anti-Jesuit book ever written.[37]

As the medieval synthesis began to crumble, the Jesuits became unremitting critics of the modern world. They nevertheless strove to effect a compromise between medievalism and modernity, and they helped consummate the marriage between the Renaissance and the enlightened absolutism of early modern Europe. As the shock forces of the Counter Reformation, Jesuits marshaled science and humanistic knowledge to combat Protestantism and secularism. Confident that they had discovered an exquisite synthesis of knowledge and virtue, these "astutely trained men" came to dominate Catholic education. Their enemies, however, charged that the crafty sons of Ignatius originated nothing of value but only manipulated the findings of others toward sinister parochial ends. In the words of Blaise Pascal, the sev-

35. *Ibid.*, 76–77.

36. E. F. Porter, "The Strike Force of God," St. Louis *Post-Dispatch*, September 15, 1991, Sec. G, pp. 1, 6. In his book *The Jesuits in Modern Times* (New York, 1928), LaFarge simply ignored all criticism of the order.

37. *Webster's Third New International Dictionary* (Springfield, Mass., 1986); Aveling, *The Jesuits*, 2, 44–48, 189.

enteenth-century French philosopher and mathematician, "The Jesuits have tried to combine God and the world, and have only earned the contempt of God and the world."[38] In his 1973 memoirs Michael Harrington, a former Catholic who was subjected to Jesuit schooling, marveled, like Leon Trotsky, at the closed and comprehensive system of thought dispensed by the "priestly Machiavellians"—a system he compared to Marxism in its absolutism.[39]

Born in the age of discovery and pledged to papal missions, Jesuits provided the advance agents of Western colonialism, heroically attempting to penetrate alien cultures and devoutly seeking mortification and converts. A former officer in the Spanish army, Ignatius of Loyola fashioned the Society of Jesus along military lines. The Spaniard expected total devotion and loyalty to the church. He once said, "What appears white to my eyes, I take for black if the hierarchic Church so decides."[40]

Although idealistically and zealously given to God and church, the Jesuit order produced many prudent and pragmatic men who gained cultural and political influence throughout the world. Their priests became confessors and counselors to popes as well as to powerful monarchs and nobles. Their political intrigue and influence caused both Catholics and non-Catholics to implicate the religious order in the murders of kings, queens, and popes.[41]

Not surprisingly, the largest and most powerful religious order excited envy, suspicion, and distrust, especially from older religious orders such as the Dominicans and Franciscans. The very name of the Society of Jesus indicated hubristic tendencies in the order: were not all priests companions of Jesus? By the mid-eighteenth century several European countries had banned the Society of Jesus. In 1773 Pope Clement XIV suppressed the order and put its general in the papal

38. Pascal, quoted in Aveling, *The Jesuits,* 252; Fülöp-Miller, *Power and Secret,* 404–405, 487; McDonough, *Men Astutely Trained,* xv–xvi, 136–67, 460–63, *passim.*

39. Michael Harrington, *Fragments of the Century* (New York, 1973), 8–9, 14.

40. Friedrich Gontard, *The Chair of Peter: A History of the Papacy,* trans. A. J. Peeler and E. F. Peeler (New York, 1964), 420–21, 504–505, and quotation by Ignatius is on 421. See also Thomas Bokenkotter, *A Concise History of the Catholic Church* (Garden City, N.Y., 1977), 255–56, and John P. Marshall, "Diocesan and Religious Clergy: The History of a Relationship," in *The Catholic Priest in the United States: Historical Investigations,* ed. John Tracy Ellis (Collegeville, Minn., 1971), 386–88.

41. Aveling, *The Jesuits,* 190, 225–27.

fortress of Castel Sant'Angelo, where he died a few years later. In the papal bull that suppressed the Jesuits, Clement charged that the society had enslaved the papacy and had gained inordinate privileges and monopolies. The papal ban was lifted in 1814, but the order was suppressed in several countries in the late nineteenth century, including Spain, France, Germany, and Italy. Gesu, Jesuit headquarters in Rome, was vacant from 1870 to 1893, but the order recovered and regained prominence, if not complete trust, in the Catholic world of the twentieth century.⁴²

In any case, his mother's fear that LaFarge would become a Jesuit probably stemmed more from personal observations than from Catholic history. After all, while he was at Harvard, LaFarge's confessor was a Jesuit who directed him to a Jesuit-run school of theology in Innsbruck. At the same time, an Episcopalian minister in Boston predicted that LaFarge would become a Jesuit. As a boy he had read and was impressed by the Jesuit theologians Jacques Philippe Lallemant and Jean Pierre De Caussade. Early in his study in Europe, a fellow student, noticing the tone of LaFarge's comments and questions in class, said of the American: "You will be a Jesuit. I always know them." It seems natural that a boy groomed by the family to be a professor would be attracted to an order that dominated Catholic education. And the vows of poverty, chastity, and obedience required by the order seemed more like opportunities than obstacles to the austerely pious youth. In the first of the nine books that he wrote, LaFarge celebrated the Jesuit tradition and explained how the faithful execution of his vows enabled him to do God's work efficiently. The Jesuit precept that "the manner is ordinary" seemed tailored for LaFarge, and this dictum became the title of his autobiography.⁴³

All priests, of course, took the vow of chastity, but to LaFarge chastity was not just a lofty ideal: it was an achievement. Before embarking for Europe in 1901, his much-traveled father took the innocent youth aside and in very candid language warned him about "a certain type of woman" who might get him into "trouble." The startled son

42. *Ibid.*, 200–204, 272, 279–82, 285, 300, 316; John W. O'Malley, S.J., *The First Jesuits* (Cambridge, Mass., 1993), 27, 28, 367–68; Geoffrey Cubitt, *The Jesuit Myth: Conspiracy Theory and Politics in Nineteenth-Century France* (New York, 1993), 41, 43, 53, 193–96, 261, 281, 197–215.

43. *MIO*, 27, 66, 76, 124, 133; LaFarge, *Jesuits in Modern Times*.

assured his father that there would be no difficulties with women.[44] By including this frank and uncharacteristic passage about sex in his memoirs, the only such self-reference in his voluminous writings, LaFarge apparently wanted to stress his self-control in carnal matters. Or perhaps he wanted to say something about his adventurous father, for whom he had mixed feelings.

In addition to the vows of poverty, obedience, and chastity, the Jesuit order vowed allegiance to the pope. In order to serve the pope with the greatest efficiency, Jesuits molded themselves to be tough, militant, and mobile spiritual soldiers of Rome, unencumbered by restrictive habit, hierarchical ambitions, or onerous rules of ritual piety.[45] Loyalty to the pope came easily for LaFarge. In his lifetime he personally met five pontiffs and never once uttered a recorded private or public word of harsh criticism against any pope. On an Easter trip in 1905, he, with a group of Innsbruck seminarians, had the special privilege of a private mass with Pope Pius X, the pontiff who in 1907 would find virtually every form of modern thought to be sinful in his encyclical *Pascendi Dominici Gregis.* Pius X gave a silent blessing to each seminarian in the Innsbruck group. According to LaFarge, when it was his turn the pope focused on him with a hauntingly steady gaze of his "gray-blue eyes." Greatly moved by this encounter, LaFarge felt that the pope's "grave glance penetrated into his very soul."[46]

LaFarge was ordained on July 26, 1905, in the university church at Innsbruck. There his mother, sister Margaret, cousin Henry Bancel Binsse, and several European relatives witnessed his first mass. He had received special permission from the general of the Jesuits and his bishop in Providence to receive holy orders before becoming a Jesuit. He was in effect a free-lance ecclesiastic who was free to pursue any number of courses, such as working toward a doctorate. He nevertheless decided in the fall of 1905 to enter St. Andrew-on-Hudson in Poughkeepsie, New York, for his novice training. As he approached the station in New York City for the last train to Poughkeepsie on November 13, he realized he was in danger of missing it. The gate had

44. *MIO,* 77.
45. Porter, "Strike Force of God," Sec. G, p. 1.
46. *MIO,* 121–22. On Pope Pius X, see James Hennesey, S.J., *American Catholics: A History of the Roman Catholic Community in the United States* (New York, 1981), 196–203, and McShane, "*Sufficiently Radical,*" 3.

already closed, and the conductor was shouting, "All aboard." In a rather anxious state LaFarge exclaimed: "For heaven's sake open the gate and let me through! I am *leaving the world* on this train and *must* make it." He did.[47]

Normally, a person underwent fifteen years of rigorous training to become a Jesuit. First came the novitiate, two years of prayer and spiritual testing. Then came the juniorate, two years of reading mostly Latin and Greek texts. At the beginning of the juniorate, the aspiring priests were allowed to put "S.J." after their names and to take their first vows. Then came three years of philosophy, after which a three-year regency followed. The latter usually entailed teaching in Jesuit high schools and colleges. Finally, the seminarian studied theology for four years. Ordination took place after three years of theological study. The tertianship, a year of prayer, contemplation, and spiritual assessment, was scheduled early in the priest's career. With the exception of the regency, Jesuit training took place in isolated rural settings where fewer temptations against "Angelic Chastity" would be likely. The rule of *tactus* meant no physical contact between seminarians, a precaution against homosexuality. The system was rigid, repetitive, collective, and closed. Everything the young scholastic read, wrote, or heard (radio by the 1920s and ultimately television) was controlled by superiors. Even if the exacting process began in adolescence, the average age of those who stayed the course would be over thirty.[48]

In his autobiography LaFarge said little about his classical and humanities studies at St. Andrew. He instead focused on the spiritual formation and the obedience training that the scholastics underwent. Although Jesuits were exempt from many penitential practices common to other orders, stress was laid on the complete surrender of one's will and judgment to superiors. The novice was forced to experience brutal humility. He had to ask permission to do almost everything outside the prescribed routine, no matter how trivial; and much was prescribed. It was a rule-driven society that aimed at blind obedience and conformism. A rule even taught Jesuits how to act in the throes of death. Long ago the spiritual regimen had been meticulously set down by St. Ignatius in the *Spiritual Exercises.* The English priest J. C. H. Aveling

47. *MIO*, 123–27, 130.
48. McDonough, *Men Astutely Trained*, 136–67; George Reimer, *The New Jesuits* (Boston, 1971), 8, 12.

branded this mystical collection of instructions jotted down by Ignatius over years of strenuous meditation as "antique, strange, and almost savage."[49] The exercises were designed to help a subject experience heaven and hell, rapture and pain. They held out the prospect of imitating Christ in his sufferings. Protestants saw them as the work of the devil or as "secret magic arts." Some modern analysts have seen the *Exercises* as a psychological masterpiece because of its power to control the human mind. Jesuits regularly engaged in thirty-day retreats given over to prayer, meditation, and mortification. The idea was to "interiorize" humility and obedience and focus on the redemptive love of Christ.[50]

LaFarge produced reams of notes on his spiritual gymnastics. Never would there be a more interiorized Jesuit. Nor was there a more loyal one. Throughout his life he strongly resented any criticism of his religious order. In the 1930s, for example, the black Catholic interracialist Guichard Parris happily informed LaFarge that he planned to do his doctoral dissertation on a French bishop named Henri Baptiste Gregoire (1750–1831). Gregoire, who served in the Estates General and several legislative assemblies during the French Revolution, was a great defender of Jews and a tenacious foe of slavery. Because he took an oath to uphold the civil constitution and favored limiting the power of the pope and bishops, however, he was at odds with the Vatican and its supporters. Not surprisingly, LaFarge abruptly cut off Parris' discussion of Gregoire.[51] In fact, the priest's intense loyalty to Jesuit authority explains, in part, why the secret encyclical on racism that LaFarge wrote for Pope Pius XI in 1938 was aborted (see Chapter 8).

After leaving St. Andrew in 1907, LaFarge taught humanities at the Jesuit colleges of Canisius in Buffalo and Loyola in Baltimore. He was

49. Kittler, "The Manner Was Extraordinary," in *Wings of Eagles,* 160; Aveling, *The Jesuits,* 45; Fulöp-Miller, *Power and Secret,* 19–23. The Jesuit O'Malley, in *First Jesuits,* 25, 47–48, 128–33, 163, 342, basically defends, albeit subtly, the sixteenth-century order against all critics, always seeing the first Jesuits as sensible and practical moderates. He also sees the *Spiritual Exercises* as a key element in making the Jesuit order distinctive and admits that Ignatius, in seeking the "direct experience of God," undermined his health by intense and prolonged prayer, fasting, and self-flagellation. See also Cubitt, *Jesuit Myth,* 279, 281.

50. Fulöp-Miller, *Power and Secret,* 5–8, 10, 15.

51. Interview of Guichard Parris by the author, New York, July 22, 1985; "Henri Baptiste Gregoire," *New Catholic Encyclopedia,* VI, 755. See also John W. Donohue, "Recovering Black History," *Am,* 157 (July 25, 1987), 35–37.

relieved to escape dissension-ridden Canisius after a semester, for it was in the throes of ethnic and jurisdictional disputes. His semester at Loyola was more pleasant, but evidence suggests that he was less than a successful teacher owing to his reserved manner. In the summer of 1908 LaFarge entered Woodstock College in Maryland, where he took courses in theology and philosophy. Finally exposed to Thomistic philosophy, his intellectual satisfaction ran high.[52]

That LaFarge would express in his 1954 autobiography his deep reverence for Thomism and his admiration for Pope Pius X attests to his theological conservatism and his loyalty to the institutional church. When LaFarge was at Woodstock, the crackdown on modernism and liberal thought in the church was in full force. For many years Catholic historians have referred to this period as a "witch-hunt," the beginning of an inquisition in the church by the pope and the antimodernists that they judge as intellectually catastrophic. In the decade after 1907, they maintain, a "climate of fear" gripped the church as the hierarchy and the clergy unleashed vigilantes in every diocese to seek out critics of encrusted dogma. Suspicious books were removed from the shelves of seminary libraries, and seminarians came under even stricter surveillance. Catholic journals were so censored and exaggeratedly orthodox that they became painful to read.[53]

All told, LaFarge devoted fewer than two pages in his memoirs to the modernist controversy and said not a word about the damage done by the pope's purge. LaFarge revealed not a trace of sympathy for censured or excommunicated modernists, and he never once mentioned Pope Leo XIII's 1899 condemnation of "Americanism," an act that seriously set back the very social Catholicism that LaFarge would later champion. Nor was there a line of sympathy for the probing Catholic thinkers of the *New York Review* nor for Father John A. Zahn, arguably the foremost Catholic scientist of the period, nor for the brilliant English Jesuit George Tyrrell—all excommunicated or silenced by the church about the time LaFarge entered Woodstock College. LaFarge conceded in his memoirs that Pope Pius X lacked some "finer degrees of sympathy," but he argued that the modernists endangered the faith

---

52. *MIO*, 140–42; Stanton, "John LaFarge," 77.

53. *MIO*, 128–29, 142; Dolan, *American Catholic Experience*, 319; Bokenkotter, *Concise History*, 331–34; Hennesey, *American Catholics*, 196–203; Aveling, *The Jesuits*, 334.

and that the "drastic action of Pius X in his encyclical *Pascendi*" (the twentieth-century *Syllabus of Errors*) was necessary to save the church. Then, quickly brushing aside the questions raised by the modernists, LaFarge moved on to recount his mystical sojourn at Lourdes when he was a seminarian. He claimed that the following sentence concerning the miraculous cures of Lourdes, which was featured in the popular *Song of Bernadette*, was his (though the film gave him no credit): "For those who believe in God no explanation is needed; for those who do not believe in God no explanation is possible."[54] In short, the Jesuit expressed no regret about the intellectual suppression and sterility thrust upon the church in the early twentieth century.

In spite of LaFarge's enthusiasm for scholastic study, life at Woodstock did not remain serene for long. During his second year at the college, he got bogged down in the translation of a long, difficult theological article for the *Catholic Encyclopedia*. The task caused enormous stress on the young scholar. Debilitating him further was the three-week, mid-summer pilgrimage of Woodstock students to southern Maryland. This trip would have been a lark for a normal young person, but the fierce heat weakened LaFarge. On top of that, his father had come down with a lingering illness before the pilgrimage and died later that fall. When he returned from his father's funeral, he was on the verge of a mental and physical breakdown. Sadly, his hope for a doctorate and a career in Catholic academia slipped away. The rector informed the young priest that he was at the fork in the road: "You have the choice, Father LaFarge, of being a live jackass or a dead lion."[55]

For rest and recuperation, his superiors assigned LaFarge to a rural church in southern Maryland. Then, after another easy and brief assignment at a church in Philadelphia, his therapy took a curious turn. His superiors made him assistant chaplain of the Catholic mission on notorious Blackwell Island in New York harbor. For eight months he labored on "Welfare Island" among thousands of convicts, indigents, and tubercular cases. He worked nonstop offering Mass, preaching, and counseling. He administered the last rites more than three thousand times. All his life LaFarge had been intensely engaged in learning, but Blackwell Island gave him a new kind of education. It was, he wrote, "a school of life and death."[56]

---

54. *MIO*, 128–29.
55. *Ibid.*, 142–47.
56. *Ibid.*, 148–52.

Amid the horror in New York harbor, the Newport aristocrat had finally taken up that prescribed "run with the common crowd." For the first time in his life, his heart began to grow in pace with his intellect. An entirely new world of opportunity for empathetic growth opened up to LaFarge in 1911 when his superiors sent him off to the Jesuit missions in southern Maryland.

2

Southern Maryland, 1911–1926

On September 13, 1911, Father John LaFarge boarded a steamer in Washington, D.C., that was bound for Leonardtown, Maryland. Located about eighty miles south of the nation's capital, Leonardtown was the center for several of the twenty-two Jesuit missions in Charles and St. Mary's Counties. Flanked by the Potomac River on one side and the Chesapeake Bay on the other, these were the two southernmost counties on the peninsula that stretched southward from Washington, D.C. The region was isolated, having no major roads or railway system. South of Leonardtown lay St. Mary's City, the first capital of Maryland and the cradle of Anglo-Saxon Catholicism in America. Here the *Ark* and the *Dove* landed in 1634 with three Jesuits on board for the spiritual guidance of the colonists and the conversion of the natives. Here Lord Baltimore hoped to establish a haven for Catholics in the bitterly anti-Catholic English colonies. The Catholic domination of Maryland was short-lived, though, and soon Catholics constituted a religious minority subject to penal laws that handicapped them politically, educationally, and socially.[1]

Although the Catholic outpost eventually fell under Protestant dominance, St. Mary's County still had a significant Catholic presence when LaFarge arrived. This original center of American Catholicism, however, was now but a backwater slice of agrarian America with a distinctive Old South flavor; and it was still missionary territory for

1. *MIO*, 155–57.

the Jesuits. With the exception of his tertianship, the mandatory religious retreat for Jesuits, at St. Andrew-on-Hudson in 1917 and 1918, LaFarge spent the next fifteen years of his life in this insular society. In these years the Progressive Era peaked and faded, World War I came and went, and the Jazz Age roared to a crescendo. Assigned to a setting of drowsy rusticity, LaFarge was far removed from the major national events, including the profound changes occurring in the urban parishes of the North. These years, nonetheless, were decisive ones for him. Here he devoted his life to the Negro apostolate.

When LaFarge arrived in Leonardtown, he was a man of thirty-one years whose character and habits were well formed. He was tall and royally thin and had a patrician bearing with fine features to match. Acquaintances and close relatives agreed on his common characteristics. He was soft-spoken, humble, intellectual, and dedicated. One relative described him as simultaneously "simple" and "incredibly complex." Another saw him as somewhat withdrawn and "impenetrable." Spurning the spotlight, he was content, as one acquaintance put it, to be a "back row flutist in a large orchestra." One observer recalled that he was a "wonderfully polite" and diplomatic person who could say unpopular things without angering others. To be sure, he was a man of monumental prudence, seemingly born without a reckless bone in his body. To Edward S. Stanton, his Jesuit biographer, he was a "truly holy man," a creature of "sweet reasonableness."[2]

Everyone who knew him commented on his subtle sense of humor, his forgetfulness, and his deficient motor skills. His humor was the type dispensed with a twinkle in the eye, the kind that drew a chuckle rather than a belly laugh. When a man told LaFarge that his young daughter liked priests but disliked sisters, he replied, "That kind grow up to be mother superiors." Another time, when some friends sent him a clock for Christmas, LaFarge thanked them profusely. His description of his old clock explained why: "My present timepiece is O.K. on the general progress of time, but is hopelessly vague on details of hours and minutes. Moreover, Campion House, being on D.C., is inhospitable to electric clocks."[3]

2. Interview of Wer LaFarge, n.d., and interview of Margaret Lloyd, n.d., both in box 1, folder 2, Stanton Papers; David S. Toolan, S.J., to Edward Stanton, October 6, 1981, in box 1, folder 3, Stanton Papers; interview of Dennis Clark by the author, Philadelphia, June 15, 1988; Stanton, "John LaFarge," 71, 87.

3. Edgar W. Wilcox to Edward Stanton, September 7, 1981, in box 1, folder 2,

His absent-mindedness started early and became legendary over the years. One day he rode a horse about a mile to say mass and lecture at the Xaverian school for boys near Leonardtown. After he finished his lecture, he returned on foot to the rectory. As he began to drift off to sleep that night, he suddenly realized that he had left his horse tied to a tree in front of the school. This necessitated a late-night hike to retrieve his hungry mount. Later in the 1920s, when automobiles came to the county, LaFarge parked cars and forgot where he put them. Later still, as a globe-trotting speaker, he sometimes forgot the site of his lectures and headed off in the wrong direction. Several times he had to call back from the train station or the airport to his Jesuit quarters to find out where he was supposed to be going.[4]

The Jesuit's lack of physical coordination manifested itself in many commonplace instances, from opening a can of food to getting out of a buggy, but most dramatically in driving an automobile. He seemed never to have learned the function of the clutch on his Model T Ford. Mud, gravel, and dust flew in all directions when he advanced his vehicle. More than once, a team of sturdy horses had to extricate LaFarge from a ditch. Local mechanics could tell his car just by its damaged clutch.[5]

But there was no clumsiness in the manner in which LaFarge carried out his pastoral mission in southern Maryland. He buried himself in his work and got a new sense of himself. Moreover, these fifteen years determined that his life work would be devoted primarily to bettering the position of African Americans within the Catholic church and the nation.[6] The long experience in the South among poverty-ridden, ill-educated, and oppressed blacks brought about an amazing transformation of the young and highly cultured aristocrat from Rhode

Stanton Papers; John LaFarge to G. Patterson, George K. Hunton, and others, December 26, 1954, in letter box 29, CICNYP.

4. *MIO,* 178; recollections of Robert C. Hartnett, S.J., about John LaFarge, December 1, 1980, in box 1, folder 10, and James McGinley to Edward Stanton, n.d., in box 1, folder 5, both in Stanton Papers.

5. *MIO,* 170, 219; interview of Beth McCoy, n.d., in box 1, folder 2, and interview of [?] Emerick, n.d., both in Stanton Papers.

6. Interview of John LaFarge by Mort Young, New York *Journal-American Sun,* March 4, 1962; National Council of Catholic Men, *Christian Action* [pamphlet] (Washington, D.C., 1956), 1, in box 43, folder 22, JLFP 1.

Island. Before coming to Maryland he had, in his own words, seen only "fragments of human life," but in St. Mary's County he saw an "entire social process" unfold. Because of his arduous duties and the isolation, LaFarge had little time or opportunity for intellectual pursuits, but he was richly compensated by the human contact and the sense that he was sorely needed in the missions. At Leonardtown LaFarge inherited from an elderly Jesuit an equally ancient horse named Morgan. The veteran horse knew the mission territory so well that he automatically stopped at the Catholic residences in need of priestly service. On top of that, if Morgan saw a buggy approaching from the opposite direction, he pulled over to the side of the road, expecting a neighborly conversation to ensue. This kind of human interaction was beneficial to the aloof priest. At last he was able to heed the advice that Dr. Heuser had offered him many years before when he was an intense adolescent, namely, to let his heart find its "due place." Equally important, when LaFarge later became the most prominent Catholic spokesman on black-white relations, his lengthy experience in southern Maryland gave him added authority on the race question.[7]

During his tenure in Maryland LaFarge was assigned to three different sites in St. Mary's County. From 1911 to 1915 he was attached to the Jesuit Mission in Leonardtown, along with five other Jesuits. The Jesuits served the churches and outlying missions some twenty to thirty miles inland. These missions could only be reached by horse and buggy over treacherous roads that could more accurately be called paths or by boat across imposing creeks and rivers. Missionary priests spent days on the road in searing heat and numbing cold, celebrating Mass, preaching sermons, conducting baptisms and marriages, directing catechetical centers, and visiting the sick and infirm. The churches were depressingly plain and sometimes incomplete, offending LaFarge's keen aesthetic sensibility. It was at a church in a state of crude incompleteness that a black snake fell on LaFarge's head in the midst of a sermon. Despite such trials, traveling priests enjoyed the deservedly renowned southern hospitality. The faithful of southern Maryland showed great reverence for their priests (as long as they did not try to alter racial mores), and the rural laity awaited itinerant clergymen with eager anticipation. Many of the isolated families had a priest's room in their

7. *MIO*, 159, 169–70, 205.

house. When a priest entered the front yard, it was said, a chicken died in the backyard. The natives referred to the provisioning of the clergy as "eating the priest."[8]

In 1915 LaFarge was transferred a few miles southward to St. Inigoes Manor near St. Mary's City. One of his duties was to minister at St. James Church to some newly arrived Slavs, few of whom could speak English. Here his talent for language served him well. Since he had some knowledge of Polish (and he was already reading Fyodor Dostoyevsky's *Crime and Punishment* in Russian to pass the lonely hours), his superiors trusted him to acquire the necessary fluency in the Slavonic language. Quickly he gained enough mastery of the foreign tongue to preach simple sermons and hear the confessions of the members of the Slav colony.[9]

After his tertianship in 1917 and 1918, his superiors assigned him to St. Michael's at Ridge, about six miles south of his previous post at St. Inigoes. There he labored until 1926, when he was called to New York City to begin a new career in journalism. In all of these Maryland assignments, LaFarge became increasingly preoccupied with the physical, spiritual, and moral welfare of the large number of black Catholics in the county. At the time of the Civil War, blacks, four-fifths of whom were slaves, outnumbered whites 8,415 to 6,798 in St. Mary's County. When LaFarge arrived in the county, blacks made up about 40 percent of the population, with possibly a third or a fourth of them being Catholic.[10] Even though less than a fifth of Maryland's overall population was black, de jure segregation came to Maryland in the early twentieth century. In 1904 the legislature passed a Jim Crow law that applied to many public places, but in a close vote legislators failed to disfranchise blacks. In 1911 the state passed a law to segregate housing, but it was

8. *Ibid.*, 163–64.

9. *Ibid.*, 179–80, 205.

10. Bayly E. Marks, "Skilled Blacks in Antebellum St. Mary's County, Maryland," *Journal of Southern History,* 53 (November, 1987), 539; Stanton, "John LaFarge," 79. There are no reliable figures on how many Catholics, black or white, resided in St. Mary's County in the early twentieth century, but see John T. Gillard, S.S.J., *The Catholic Church and the American Negro* (Baltimore, 1929), 48, 50. According to Gillard's 1928 survey, the Baltimore archdiocese had the third highest number of black Catholics in the United States, second only to New Orleans and the Lafayette diocese in Louisiana. Even so, Gillard's count shows that only about 22,000 black Catholics lived in all of Maryland and the District of Columbia in 1928.

struck down by the Supreme Court in 1917. In the 1920s the Ku Klux Klan, perhaps more anti-Catholic than antiblack, had a resurgence in Maryland.[11]

While white Catholics in southern Maryland constituted a religious minority of struggling small farmers and fishermen (LaFarge compared them to the Irish minority in the North), black Catholics had even worse problems. As Catholics they were a minority within a despised minority, and as blacks they faced daily the stress and humiliation of white racism. As LaFarge recalled, if a pastor treated a black person as a human being, he would be charged with "moving the Negro 'out of his place.' "[12] Although most blacks worshipped in the same churches as whites in southern Maryland, they were confined to galleries apart from whites or they attended services at times different from when the majority worshipped. As a Catholic character said in a Harry Sylvester novel about the Maryland missions: "Sure, we make niggers set in the back of the churches, and the Protestants don't let them in at all." Unvarnished Jim Crow Catholicism had come to St. Mary's County in 1905. There, blacks withdrew from St. Michael's in Ridge when the white organist refused to play on an instrument that had been played by black hands. This incident led to the establishment of the all-black St. Peter Claver Church. As a rising tide of racism and segregation spread across the land in the so-called Progressive Era, the trend in the Catholic church was toward "racial parishes." In the South the first two decades of the century constituted a time of widespread disfranchisement and horrific lynching and torching. From 1906 to 1915, 620 African Americans died by rope and fagot. As blacks began to flee to the North, race riots became a regular occurrence in the large, Catholic-filled, urban centers above the Potomac.[13]

The pictures taken of southern Marylanders by the Farm Security Administration during the Great Depression are no less haunting than

11. Robert J. Brugger, *Maryland: A Middle Temperament, 1634–1980* (Baltimore, 1988), 420–22, 426, 611. On the rise of segregation, see C. Vann Woodward, *The Strange Career of Jim Crow* (3rd rev. ed.; New York, 1974).

12. *MIO*, 162–63, 191–92.

13. *Ibid.*, 190; Harry Sylvester, *Dearly Beloved* (New York, 1942), 70. On rising racism and segregation, see Dolores Egger Labbe, *Jim Crow Comes to Church: The Establishment of Segregated Parishes in South Louisiana* (2nd ed.; Lafayette, La., 1971); I. A. Newby, *Jim Crow's Defense: Anti-Negro Thought in America, 1900–1930* (Baton Rouge, 1965); and David W. Southern, *The Malignant Heritage: Yankee Progressives and the Negro Question, 1901–1914* (Chicago, 1968).

those by Walker Evans in *Let Us Now Praise Famous Men,* by Evans and James Agee. A recent documentary collection on St. Mary's County titled *But Now When I Look Back* reveals through government photographs and black eyewitnesses the primitive conditions and the poverty that many African Americans had to endure.[14]

Things were not always so bad as they were in the 1930s in southern Maryland. Ninety percent of the area's economy was tied to farming and fishing. It was not the risky one-crop agriculture, which was at the mercy of fluctuating world markets, but a more diversified, subsistence type of farming, and it largely enabled the region to escape the post–World War I agricultural depression that hit many commercial farming areas. Southern Marylanders raised corn, wheat, oats, tobacco, and vegetables, and they had plenty of hogs, chickens, oysters, crabs, and fresh fish. They supplemented their diets with squirrel, rabbit, raccoon, and waterfowl. Apples, cherries, and various berries grew in abundance. Families grew tired of gastronomical fare that outsiders would have considered delicacies: oysters and crabcakes, for example. If food was ample, money was often scarce. Many supplemented their income by trapping muskrat, mink, raccoon, and skunk. Others made money from bootleg liquor, especially after the onset of Prohibition. While life was hard and unglamorous for most, there were many pleasures for the common folk. Blacks enjoyed an endless array of festivals, fairs, church socials, and outdoor sporting events. Many remembered the charm of the countryside between the Chesapeake and the Potomac. Elvare Gaskin, a black woman who lived in the village of Scotland, recalled her youth on the peninsula: "It's beautiful walking at night, with the moon and the stars. The environment engulfed us—honeysuckles, magnolias . . . everything had a clean smell. . . . And in the first of the spring all fruit trees would be blooming. . . . You could smell the apples and the peaches and the grapes. . . . And when the sweet potato vines came full bloom, I'd just dive down there, make believe I was swimming." [15] When blacks of St. Mary's County looked back, they also remembered stable families and a tight-knit community. Often they found ways to transcend the oppressive social system that stacked the cards against them.

14. James Agee and Walker Evans, *Let Us Now Praise Famous Men* (Boston, 1941); Andrea Hammer, *But Now When I Look Back: Remembering St. Mary's County Through Farm Security Administration Photographs* (Westminster, Md., 1988).

15. Hammer, *But Now When I Look Back,* 1, 21, 23, 47, 57, 61–63, 67–68, 83.

LaFarge marveled at how blacks clung to the Catholic faith under such adverse circumstances. Many walked several miles in all kinds of inclement weather to worship in a Catholic church. Still, in the years after emancipation many had left the faith to join Protestant churches that became the center of black community life. In his Jesuit fashion, LaFarge set out to assess the problem of black Catholics in an analytical way. He began to explore the sociology and history of the area. He lamented that there was "an absence of historical sense" in both races in the county. (LaFarge, his interest aroused, eventually wrote several articles on the history of Catholic Maryland.) The past was a touchy subject with blacks. If lacking in formal study of the past, blacks in St. Mary's County certainly had enduring memories. LaFarge found that when it came to the church, black Catholics spoke about the past with "great bitterness." They especially remembered that the Jesuits at Inigoes Manor had held slaves, not unlike four other Jesuit manors in Maryland and several Catholic orders around the South and border areas. After church officials discovered that some 300 slaves under Jesuit care were being neglected physically and spiritually (and thus providing a source of scandal for the church), the Jesuit general in Rome gave the priestly masters in Maryland permission to sell the slaves under certain conditions. In 1838 the Jesuits sold 272 black slaves, but this action brought only more scandal. Against Rome's orders, families were broken up in the sale, and, furthermore, most of the slaves fell into the hands of Protestant masters in the Deep South (for more on this, see Chapter 3). Despite LaFarge's tendency to sugarcoat Catholic history, in his memoirs he described this antebellum episode as a "blunder" and an act of "real cruelty."[16]

In terms of race relations, Maryland's Catholic past was tragic. LaFarge judged that in earlier times "simpler means" could have accomplished a vast amount of good between the races. He saw that now the traditional economic interdependence between the races was fading, causing the races to drift further apart. The church, LaFarge lamented, had failed to seize its golden opportunity to work for racial fairness. He observed that most of the Jesuits in the missions safely confined

16. *MIO*, 157–58, 161, 184–89, 219. See Robert Emmett Curran, S.J., "Splendid Poverty: Jesuit Slaveholding in Maryland, 1808–1838," in *Catholics in the Old South: Essays on Church and Culture,* ed. Randall M. Miller and Jon L. Wakelyn (Macon, Ga., 1983), 125–46.

their activity to spiritual matters and dared not rock the social boat. He
sensed that a racial storm was brewing in the land. What could reasonably be done by conscientious Catholics to promote racial justice?
LaFarge asked himself this question over and over on his long, solitary
buggy rides. What was the Christian / Catholic answer to the riddle of
race?[17]

The pace of life in the Maryland hinterland gave him time to ponder
deeply how Catholic theology applied to the social and human relationships of his time. It provided the occasion for deep meditation
about the "Jesuit ideal" and led to the publication of his first book, *The
Jesuits in Modern Times,* in 1928. Although the book dealt almost exclusively with the spiritual side of the church mission, LaFarge pointed
out that St. Ignatius' first endeavor for the church, a home for wayward
girls, had a "distinct *social* end in mind." Once in Maryland, he recalled
with more appreciation the debates about Catholic social doctrine that
had so animated his Italian and German colleagues at Innsbruck. Back
then he had often been roundly offended because many of the European students embraced the radical ideologies of socialism or fascism.
LaFarge, however, now scrutinized the entire social and religious picture in southern Maryland and slowly began to sift and integrate the
factors that he deemed pertinent to change. In keeping with his irenic
personality, LaFarge did not opt for heroic or confrontational poses to
effect the racial transformation that he considered essential to meet the
ideals of Catholic charity and justice. Given the hostility toward blacks
in the county and the apathy of the Catholic hierarchy, he ruled out
being a "bull in an ecclesiastical china-shop." LaFarge could well have
been Sylvester's model for the priest Laurence Kane in *Dearly Beloved,*
his novel about the Maryland missions. Kane was saintly and racially
liberal, but he was also diplomatic, cautious, and ever aware that many
parishioners suspected him of being one of the "nigger-loving" Jesuits.[18]
If cautious, LaFarge, like Kane, never wavered once he adopted a strategy. He determinedly and optimistically set to work, relying on supernatural faith and heroic patience to carry the day (or the decades). In a
word, his answer for racial progress was education.

There is no evidence that LaFarge followed the debate raging in
the early twentieth century between the militant protest leader W. E. B.

17. *MIO,* 157, 168–69, 192, 207.
18. John LaFarge, *Jesuits in Modern Times,* 1, 73–74; *MIO,* 168–69, 192, 203–204;
Sylvester, *Dearly Beloved,* 83–84, 95, 120.

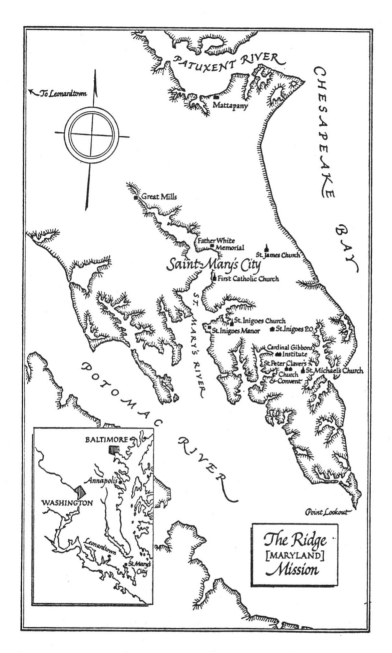

The Ridge Mission: The Jesuit Missions in St. Mary's County, Maryland. Map copyright 1954 and renewed 1982 by John LaFarge, reproduced by permission of Harcourt Brace & Company.

John LaFarge, Artist and
Father of the Reverend
John LaFarge (no date).
Photograph courtesy of
John LaFarge, S.J., Papers,
Georgetown University
Library, Washington,
D.C.

The Home of the Rever-
end John LaFarge, 10 Sun-
nyside Place, Newport,
Rhode Island, 1988. Pho-
tograph courtesy of Paul
Harrison.

Reverend John LaFarge, S.J., and Children at St. James School, St. Mary's County, Maryland, *ca. 1923*. Photograph courtesy of John LaFarge, S.J., Papers, Georgetown University Library, Washington, D.C.

Father LaFarge (far right), Schoolchildren, and an Unidentified Jesuit at St. Peter Claver Church, Ridge, Maryland, 1928. Photograph courtesy of John LaFarge, S.J., Papers, Georgetown University Library, Washington, D.C.

Du Bois (1868–1963) and the accommodationist Booker T. Washington (1856–1915). During his years in Maryland, he made no mention of the National Association for the Advancement of Colored People (NAACP), which was founded just two years before he came to Leonardtown. Nor did LaFarge raise serious questions about segregation while in Maryland. He clearly favored Booker T. Washington's gradualist strategy of education and self-help, a plan that emphasized duties and downplayed rights, integration, and any form of militant protest. He agreed with the Tuskegee educator that blacks as an underdeveloped people needed a practical or vocational education, but he also argued that they needed religious faith. "The gift of faith," he declared, "must be perfected through study and the hearing of the Word." Unlike Washington (who was a Protestant and a stern moralist), LaFarge maintained that only Catholic education instilled the morality vital to preserve families and to ward off the social decay that he saw as threatening the black community. Moreover, he insisted that only Catholicism could effectively combat modern menaces such as socialism, communism, secularism, and, yes, Protestantism.[19]

Unfortunately, education was extremely poor or nonexistent for blacks in southern Maryland. The segregated public schools for both races were execrable, a "mere farce," in LaFarge's words. The school term for blacks lasted four months, with no required attendance. The school buildings were one-room shacks with no indoor plumbing. Many of the black teachers had no more than a fifth-grade education. In 1920 Maryland spent $36.03 on each white pupil and $13.20 on each black student. Although Catholics operated two academies in the area for the more affluent classes, LaFarge noted that local Catholics had no parish schools.[20] This failing he vowed to remedy.

In his tenure in Maryland, LaFarge helped establish at least four parish schools, two for each race. Two were started at St. James near St. Mary's City before the war, and two were begun at Ridge in 1918, one for whites at St. Michael's and one for blacks at St. Peter Claver's. He vividly recollected what an immense strain these school put on him

19. *MIO*, 193, 204. On the Du Bois-Washington controversy, see August Meier, *Negro Thought in America, 1880–1915: Racial Ideologies in the Age of Booker T. Washington* (Ann Arbor, Mich., 1963).

20. *MIO*, 177–78; George H. Callcott, *Maryland and America, 1940 to 1980* (Baltimore, 1985), 145.

from 1918 to 1922. He felt "abandoned" and "helpless." Sometimes his only refuge was the piano he had brought down from Newport and the record player that allowed him to hear his beloved classical music. His "refractory digestion" was as bad as ever, and he had to endure a constant struggle to staff the schools he established. Given the primitive or incomplete quarters for teachers in St. Mary's County and the demand for parochial schools all over the nation, it was difficult to recruit nuns to come to southern Maryland and even more difficult to entice them to stay. Funding the schools was another pressing problem, something that was largely beyond the resources of the poor parishes. LaFarge experienced "deep revulsion" at raising funds for the schools. This task entailed making many trips to New York, where he had to appeal to the pocketbooks of his affluent friends and relatives, rather than, as he wished, ministering to their souls. He conceded that if he had foreseen the trouble involved in the school projects, he probably would never have started them. His efforts, however, brought certain rewards. His contact with people and his lectures to New Yorkers forced him to analyze and articulate the race problem in Maryland. The schools also served hundreds of youngsters who got their first chance at a Catholic education.[21] Furthermore, the art of raising money would prove to be indispensable for his long and successful career in the racial apostolate.

In his final years in Maryland, LaFarge looked beyond the parish school. He was instrumental in the founding of the Cardinal Gibbons Institute in 1924, a secondary school for blacks that he later hailed as the first national educational project for African Americans established by Catholics and the seedbed for the Catholic interracial movement. The institute was designed as a school of practical education based on the Tuskegee model of vocational training and the Danish folk school, which stressed community education. LaFarge also hoped that the institute would speak to the worsening conditions of black farmers and would preserve the rural family as well as help both races find common ground on which to work out their differences. He hoped to retard the

---

21. *MIO*, 196, 198–99, 202–204; Edwin Warfield Beitzel, *The Jesuit Missions in St. Mary's County, Maryland* (2nd ed.; Abell, Md., 1976), 277. Stanton credited the priest with starting eight schools in "John LaFarge," 80. In *The Premier See: A History of the Archdiocese of Baltimore, 1789–1989* (Baltimore, 1989), 306, Thomas W. Spalding cites St. Mary's County for exceptional growth in Catholic schools, without mentioning LaFarge.

southern migration to the city, where blacks were thrown in with white ethnic immigrants, primarily Catholics. He believed a situation was being created that promised violent racial explosions like those at the end of World War I.[22]

Originally, plans had been made by the Xaverian Brothers to build a reform school for black youths in St. Mary's County. Cardinal James Gibbons had given $8,000 to purchase land for the school, and over a hundred acres was bought along the Potomac River near St. Peter Claver's, the black church at Ridge. The Xaverians backed out, however, and in 1916 Fathers LaFarge, Brent Matthews, and Abraham Emerick, all from the Jesuit mission at St. Inigoes, began to lobby hard for an educational institution for blacks instead of a reform school. But the plan, except for the purchase of land, lay fallow until after the war. With the death of Cardinal Gibbons in 1921, LaFarge made a renewed effort to get the project started again. He consulted several people at the newly created National Catholic Welfare Conference (NCWC), including Father R. A. McGowan, assistant director of the Social Action Department, and Arthur C. Monahan, an expert on southern education in the Education Division. Father Monahan suggested that they start a coeducational school staffed by blacks and open to students of all religions. LaFarge also raised the matter with Dr. Thomas Wyatt Turner, a professor of biology at Howard University. The son of a Maryland sharecropper, Turner founded the Committee of Fifteen during World War I, a group of black Catholics formed to fight racial discrimination in the church.[23]

In early 1921, plans for the establishment of a black school were approved by Michael J. Curley, the new archbishop of Baltimore. The archbishop appointed an interracial lay board for the school, selecting

22. *MIO*, 207, 210–15; John LaFarge, "A Catholic Folk School," *Am*, 37 (June 18, 1927), 233–34; John LaFarge, "The Baltimore Rural Life Conference," *Am*, 33 (November 21, 1925), 129–31; John LaFarge, "The Meaning of Cardinal Gibbons Institute," *Chronicle*, 2 (November 29, 1929), 7. LaFarge's claim that the institute at Ridge was the first Catholic national educational project might be disputed since Xavier University was founded earlier in New Orleans by Mother Drexel. However, Xavier was not fully operational until after the school in Maryland had opened.

23. *MIO*, 209–11; "Items From My Diary, 1915–1916," pp. 3–4, in box 23, folder 2, JLFP 1; Nickels, *Black Catholic Protest*, 32, 227. See also Marilyn Wenzke Nickels, "Thomas Wyatt Turner and the Federated Colored Catholics," *U.S. Catholic Historian*, 7 (Spring–Summer, 1988), 215–32.

himself as chairman and retired admiral William S. Benson as vice-chairman. The impressive board of trustees, which included Senator David I. Walsh of Massachusetts and Turner, hired the black educators Victor Hugo Daniel as principal and his wife, Constance E. H. Daniel, as assistant principal. The Daniels held membership in an elite group that one historian has branded the "aristocrats of color." Although most of the American black elite lived comfortably, they did not constitute an aristocracy of wealth. Theirs was an aristocracy of culture, talent, and education. Many of the black upper class descended from free antebellum blacks, and most of them had blood lines running toward both the white and black races, as did the Daniels. To say that this elite was "Negro" would have been, in most cases, biologically inaccurate. To say that they were "black" would have been, more often than not, a chromatic absurdity. Although the black elite was proud of its cultural roots and championed cultural diversity, most of its members believed in integration and were acutely sensitive to racial discrimination and the insult of Jim Crow.[24]

Victor Hugo Daniel (1884–1967) was born in the Danish West Indies (since 1917 the U.S. Virgin Islands), one of five children who descended from a family of colonial government officials and shipbuilders at Charlotte Amalie, St. Thomas. One of his ancestors was an early nineteenth-century immigrant from Genoa by the name of Joseph Nathaniel D'Anielli, later anglicized to Daniel. Rather than work in the family shipyard, Victor's father, Joseph Nicholas, became a civil servant and ultimately the secretary to the French Consulate in Haiti. After an apprenticeship as a boilermaker, Victor escaped secondary training in Denmark by emigrating to the United States in 1908. He enrolled at Tuskegee Institute and graduated with the class of 1911. While there, he became a close associate of Dr. George Washington Carver, the famous black agricultural scientist. After earning his degree, Victor taught at Tuskegee and nearby secondary schools, St. Joseph High School in Montgomery, Alabama, among others. During World War I, in lieu of military service, he did agricultural defense work in Kansas. After the war he joined the faculty at the Bordentown Manual and Industrial School for Negroes in New Jersey. "Very European" in bearing, Daniel was a light-skinned African American who was highly intelligent, well-

24. Willard B. Gatewood, *Aristocrats of Color: The Black Elite, 1880–1920* (Bloomington, Ind., 1990), 7, 13, 44–45, 149–53, 180, 300.

read, and dignified in appearance. He loved opera, and he loved to tell folktales from his native islands. Although warm and compassionate with members of his large family, he tended to be a rather reserved and private man. Victorian in culture, he prized punctuality, discipline, and hard work. He never swore, and he was a staunch Catholic.[25]

Constance Eleanor Hazel Daniel (1894–1963) was born in St. Paul, Minnesota, the fourth child of William Augustus Hazel and Rosa Elizabeth Grosvenor Hazard. Her father's family descended from a free black family in North Carolina who had moved to Cambridge, Massachusetts, to escape the growing Negrophobia that threatened free blacks in the 1850s. William Hazel (1854–1929) was educated in the public schools of Cambridge and received college training at Cooper Union in New York. He became a pioneer black draftsman, architect, and stained-glass artisan who worked for the prestigious Boston firm of S. J. F. Thayer. In 1887 Hazel relocated to the St. Paul-Minneapolis area, where he was the western representative of the New York architectural firm of Louis Tiffany as well as the manager of the Brown & Haywood Stained Glass Company. While in Minnesota, the architect filed three discrimination suits against public businesses that refused to serve him, winning one of them. After fifteen years in Minnesota, he moved his family back to Massachusetts to join the Hazel clan in Cambridge. In 1909 William Hazel took a position on the faculty of Tuskegee, where he taught architectural engineering until 1919. Then he was hired by Howard University to establish a school of architecture. Everywhere William Hazel went, he engaged in civil rights activity.[26]

Daniel also descended from free blacks on her mother's side of the family. Her maternal grandmother, Martha Armstead Hazard, was born a slave in Virginia, the illegitimate daughter of a white plantation owner. A visiting white man from Connecticut, the family story goes, fell in love with the mulatto beauty, purchased her freedom, took her off to New England, and married her. Thus, the mother of Constance Daniel,

25. Most of the information on Victor and Constance Daniel has been supplied by their daughter, Louise Daniel Hutchinson of Washington, D.C. Now retired, Hutchinson was formerly Director of Research and senior staff historian for the Smithsonian Institution's Anacostia Museum. She is also the family historian.

26. Louise Daniel Hutchinson, "Building on a Heritage," *American Visions,* 4 (August, 1989), 11; Louise Daniel Hutchinson to the author, June 6, 1992; Louise Daniel, "A Study of My Family," 4–5, a paper for Sociology 180 under Dr. E. Franklin Frazier at Howard University, *ca.* 1949–1950, copy in the author's possession.

Rosa Elizabeth Hazard, was born in Rhode Island in 1852. She graduated from Providence High School and attended Rhode Island Normal School and the New England Conservatory of Music. Miss Hazard was the first black teacher employed by General Samuel Armstrong at Hampton Institute in Virginia.[27]

Constance Daniel enjoyed a secure childhood among a large tribe of kinfolk in Cambridge, and she received a superior education. After attending some of the best secondary schools in the area, she studied at Spelman Seminary (later a college) in Atlanta. She enrolled at Tuskegee when her father came there to teach in 1909. After graduating in 1912, she married Victor Daniel in 1916. She taught in secondary schools in Alabama and in Kansas before she accompanied her husband to Bordentown, New Jersey. Constance was a highly literate and cultured woman: a lover of words, she enjoyed crossword puzzles and anagrams and had a passion for literature; music was a second great and abiding interest. She also adored her father and took up his causes. She rejected any hint of black inferiority, often repeating the following to her children: "You will be something in spite of, not nothing because of!" Stoic, iron-willed, and passionate in her principles, she had an educational mission and was bent on speeding the betterment of African Americans. Not least, she was a mother and a stern disciplinarian who early exposed her children to the rigor and reward of learning. The Daniels arrived at Cardinal Gibbons Institute in 1924 with four children, and during their decade at Ridge their progeny doubled.[28]

The Cardinal Gibbons Institute opened with great fanfare in the fall of 1924. Father McGowan of the NCWC preached the sermon, and Father Charles Uncles, a Josephite from Baltimore and one of five African American priests at the time, celebrated mass. The first class at the institute consisted of twenty-eight boys and girls. The enrollment in the second year increased to fifty-two. Besides serving as a general secondary and vocational school for blacks, the institution acted as an agricultural extension unit for the surrounding area. It held annual agricultural fairs, one of which was attended by Carver, and it organized a Negro Health Week and a Children's Day and held summer camps for black youths.[29]

27. Hutchinson to the author, June 6, 1992; Daniel, "Study of My Family," 1, 3.
28. Hutchinson to the author, June 6, July 23, 1992.
29. *MIO*, 212; "Report of the Principal of Cardinal Gibbons Institute for Year 1925–1926," in letter box 24, CICNYP.

Within two months after the opening of Cardinal Gibbons Institute, Dr. Turner founded the Federated Colored Catholics (FCC), a national federation that was an outgrowth of the Committee of Fifteen Turner had started in World War I. The stated purpose of the FCC was to bring black Catholics closer together, to advance Catholic education for African Americans, and "to seek to raise the general Church status of the negro and to stimulate colored Catholics to a larger participation in racial and civic affairs." Turner was the driving force of the FCC and its perennial choice for president. Since Turner had been involved in the planning of the institute, the FCC adopted the school at Ridge as a special project.[30] Because of the FCC's financial support of the institute, LaFarge, officially the chaplain of Cardinal Gibbons Institute, became involved in federation activity in order to encourage its continued support of the school.

But the Cardinal Gibbons Institute closed its doors in 1933, a victim of the Great Depression and of white Catholic apathy. LaFarge, who continued to exert considerable influence over the institute after he moved to New York in 1926, never gave the slightest hint to the public that the school was in trouble. As late as 1932, LaFarge wrote a report about the glowing health of the institute in the Catholic magazine *Commonweal* and touted it as the embodiment of the "Catholic idea" of education. He praised the black principal and his wife lavishly.[31]

Actually, the black school suffered from inadequate white Catholic support and funding from the beginning. Only a gift of $35,000 from the Knights of Columbus in 1923 allowed Gibbons Hall, the main campus building, to be built in time for the opening of the school the following year. After that, the Catholic church did little financially to sustain the school. Archbishop Curley, the nominal head of the institute's board, was a social and racial conservative just up from Florida to replace Cardinal Gibbons. A blunt, outspoken Irishman who was a great builder and a champion of the working class, Curley nevertheless was exceedingly cautious on the race question. He essentially saw the

30. News Clipping, December 29, 1924, in Thomas W. Turner Papers, Moorland-Spingarn Research Center, Howard University, Washington, D.C.; Nickels, "Thomas Wyatt Turner," 225–26; "Proposed Negro School in Southern Maryland," in box 24, carton 4, CICNYP.

31. John LaFarge, "The Cardinal Gibbons Institute," *Commonweal*, 15 (January 17, 1932), 433–35. See also "N.Y. Catholics Hear Fr. LaFarge Plead for Racial Justice," New York *Age*, December 14, 1929, p. 3.

school at Ridge as a means to convert blacks. His interest in the struggle for racial equality was nominal at best. The institute survived as long as it did because of grants from the General Education Board and the Julius Rosenwald Fund, gifts from some of LaFarge's wealthy friends, and, most of all, the heroic efforts and sacrifices of the Daniels.[32]

Lack of funds meant human discomfort and physical decay at Ridge. During the first year the students virtually had to camp out in Gibbons Hall, the sole building on campus. In the second year a dormitory and a farmhouse for the principal and his family were constructed. Maintenance of buildings and machinery was constantly deferred. Victor Daniel had to perform myriad duties as administrator, teacher, mechanic, carpenter, plumber, agricultural agent, and fund raiser. His work was so taxing that he suffered a physical breakdown after four or five years. From then on, his feisty and talented wife practically ran the school until its closure.[33]

Another serious problem with the school was the rift between the Daniels and the whites on the board of trustees. The Daniels charged that certain members of the board tried to dictate, down to the pettiest detail, how the institute should be run. They especially resented Father Monahan of the NCWC, the executive secretary of the board who meddled incessantly in the school's administration.[34] A difference in educational philosophy between the Daniels and the board caused dissension. Although the black educators had studied at Tuskegee, they both strongly rejected the idea that blacks should be restricted to one kind of education. They saw the need of liberal as well as vocational education, and they both had great respect for Du Bois and the NAACP, especially Mrs. Daniel. Confident in their professional skills and proud of their race, neither educator meekly accepted the arbitrary or petty commands of white outsiders, not even priests.[35]

32. Michael J. Curley, Archbishop of Baltimore, to John LaFarge, December 1, 1922, Ridge Letters, John LaFarge Papers, New York Historical Society, New York. On Curley, see Thomas Spalding, *Premier See*, 322, 334, 345–46.

33. Victor Daniel, "Report of the Principal," in box 24, folder 4, CICNYP; Constance Daniel to John LaFarge, n.d., in box 23, folder 4, JLFP 1; "The Cardinal Gibbons Institute: A Brief History," *Colored Harvest*, 15 (September–October, 1927), Maryland Ridge Papers, Josephite Archives, Baltimore.

34. The Daniels-Monahan feud will be covered in Chap. 6.

35. Victor H. Daniel, "What Type of Education?," *Chronicle*, 2 (November, 1929), 3–6; Louise Daniel Hutchinson to the author, July 10, 1992.

Additionally, Constance, unlike her husband, was only a nominal Catholic. She left the Unitarian church because of racial snubs doled out by some of its ministers and because her future husband was Catholic. After converting to her spouse's religion at Tuskegee, however, she discovered that racism was rampant in the Catholic church as well. Constance shared her concern with the chaplain of the institute, John LaFarge. No doubt, the two must have discussed many of the things they had in common beyond their concern about racism in the church. Indeed, their lives intersected in a number of strange ways that must have sparked some lively conversation between them. For instance, Constance's mother was born, as was LaFarge, in Newport, Rhode Island. Her father William Hazel worked as an architect with the artist John LaFarge on the Trinity Church in Boston. Growing up, Constance played in the Cambridge streets with the children of Harvard faculty about the time LaFarge was completing his degree nearby. Both the priest and the educator were accomplished pianists. And if the genealogy of the Daniel-Hazel family is correct, they may have been related by blood, for one of the "black" Hazards (James) was supposedly the illegitimate son of Oliver Hazard Perry, one of LaFarge's illustrious ancestors.[36]

In any case, in early 1925 Constance Daniel poured out her feelings to LaFarge about the racist behavior she had encountered from Catholic priests and bishops. She told him in a long letter that she had not gone to confession for years because she had lost all respect for white priests, LaFarge excepted. In concluding her letter, Daniel declared: "If race and creed clash, creed will have to go. I am a Negro first."[37]

The letter thoroughly disturbed LaFarge. He responded with an eight-page letter, chastising Daniel for her lack of faith in the church and for her resorting to racial chauvinism. He said he was "shocked" by her revelations about racism in the church, but he told her to be patient. Justice, he counseled, was inevitable because "the Catholic Church from her intrinsic holiness *infallibly renders justice in the end.*" He maintained that already a majority of Catholics in the world, in-

36. Hutchinson, "Building on a Heritage," 11; Constance Daniel to Dr. Robert A. Daniel, June 24, 1959, courtesy of Louise Daniel Hutchinson; Daniel, "Study of My Family," 1, 3.

37. Constance Daniel to John LaFarge, January 30, 1925, in box 20, folder 1, JLFP 1.

cluding the pope, rejected racism and that this majority would be heard "in due time." The Jesuit urged prudence, patience, and faith in the meantime, larding his letter generously with cautionary adjectives he deemed appropriate for the guidance of such a spirited woman. Among the words used were "non-aggressive," "dispassionate," "gradual," "moderate," and "conciliatory."[38]

Daniel responded with a fiery letter of eleven pages. She informed LaFarge in so many words that he had not solved any of her problems or convinced her of anything with his cautionary advice. She, too, believed in ultimate justice, she said, but blacks could not afford to wait for the white Catholic hierarchy to hand it to them. The distinction that LaFarge made between the sinless church and prejudiced Catholics—a distinction that was a lifelong theme of his—did not impress her. She duly scolded LaFarge for preaching that the Catholic church alone had the answer to the race problem. She said there was no evidence for his claim, and she reminded him that non-Catholics were doing much more for blacks than were Catholics. She also argued that Protestant and secular blacks "had been trained to mental exercise" and were far in advance of timid black Catholics. In short, Daniel called for black protest against all racial discrimination, especially that perpetuated by the church itself. Inevitably, she invoked the name of Du Bois. She conceded that the editor of the NAACP's *Crisis* magazine had a "scathing tongue," but she argued that his facts were "a thousand times more scathing."[39] From 1925 until the Cardinal Gibbons Institute closed, Constance Daniel constantly fenced with LaFarge and white board members, just as she did in the letter.

Subsequently, the closing of the Cardinal Gibbons Institute in 1933 was ugly and acrimonious. Shortly before the closing of the school, LaFarge teamed up with another Jesuit, Father William Markoe of St. Louis, to remove Turner from the presidency of the FCC. In that heated and divisive episode of 1932 and 1933 (see Chapter 5), the Daniels sided with Turner, which made the two educators even more suspect in LaFarge's eyes. Suffice it to say here that LaFarge covered up the prob-

38. John LaFarge to Constance Daniel, February 3, 1925, in box 20, folder 1, JLFP 1.
39. Constance Daniel to John LaFarge, February 6, 1925, in box 20, folder 1, JLFP 1. Daniel fits the portrait of the "New Negro" of the 1920s as described by Alain Locke, ed., *The New Negro: An Interpretation* (New York, 1925), and Nathan Irving Huggins, *Harlem Renaissance* (New York, 1971).

lems and controversy surrounding the Cardinal Gibbons Institute, demonstrating a pattern of behavior he would exhibit again and again in regard to race-related matters. He later exaggerated the influence of the school, writing in his memoirs that it "worked as a powerful instrument with which to awaken the dormant consciences of the Catholic public." Two pages earlier, however, the priest confessed that there was a paralyzing "general public indifference" about the Catholic Tuskegee.[40]

In any event, the Jesuit used his tie with the institute to work his way into a position of influence within the FCC. His interaction with the Daniels, particularly Constance, however, revealed how little LaFarge appreciated the protest side of the black movement in the 1920s and 1930s. His counsel to her demonstrated how poorly he responded to an intellectual and militant black Catholic, to say nothing of those outside Catholicism. He had a considerable distance to travel before he became a genuine racial liberal.

Although LaFarge often expressed the view that the Cardinal Gibbons Institute provided a sterling example of interracialism in action, the facts were somewhat different. In truth, while the institute's students, teachers, and local administrators were black, the school was under the thumb of the Catholic hierarchy and white priests such as LaFarge and Monahan. The institute, therefore, did not differ significantly from the segregated public schools of the South. Nevertheless, LaFarge was correct in saying that his experience with the Cardinal Gibbons Institute constituted an important step in his long journey toward a deeper understanding of the racial dilemma in America.

It must be remembered that LaFarge formulated his basic strategy for assisting black Catholics and improving race relations in a location with a Deep South flavor and in an era when racism was raw and escalating throughout the nation. His was a conservative, gradualistic plan—a plan that he held to for several years with only slight modification and embellishment. The strategy put education of both blacks and whites at the center. It acquiesced in legal segregation and assumed that local blacks did not mind sitting in the gallery of the church or having a white priest as their pastor. Because of the gratitude of his black parishioners, LaFarge persuaded himself that he could fully serve the pastoral needs of the Jim Crow church known as St. Peter Claver.

40. *MIO*, 213, 215.

In southern Maryland he also took on an agrarian bias and preached that blacks were better off on the farm. Insisting that only parochial schools could provide the proper education for Catholics, he argued against bills that would have provided federal aid to public education. He seemed opposed to almost all forms of federal intrusion, most notably that forced on the country by "the contemptible spirit of these fanatics," the Protestant-led prohibitionists.[41]

While in Maryland LaFarge began to indulge in a false optimism about racism and the South that thereafter would shape his outlook. Despite the stigmatization and systematic oppression of blacks in southern Maryland, he insisted that "bitter and prejudiced people are a minority." Like southern liberals in the first half of the twentieth century, he put his hope in the "Silent South." He believed that a majority of southern whites were well disposed toward blacks but feared to show their true feelings because of an aggressive minority of race baiters. Someday, he and southern liberals projected, this liberal majority would come forth, and the South would rid itself of racial wrongs. In the meantime, any intervention of the federal government into racial matters, LaFarge and white southerners argued, would invite disaster.[42]

As I stated earlier, begging money for schools in Maryland was a traumatic experience for LaFarge. However distasteful this activity was, though, it forced him, in his words, to "come out of [his] shell" and to put his efforts in a broader perspective in order to appeal to the Catholic Club of New York and similar groups.[43] His reflections also led to his first articles on blacks, which were published by the influential Jesuit weekly *America*. These pieces showed a sincere concern for the plight of African Americans, but they also revealed a paternalistic, some would even say patronizing, attitude toward blacks that afflicted many white Catholics working in the racial apostolate in the early twentieth century.[44]

41. John LaFarge, "Following the Prussian Model," n.d., in box 10, folder 4, JLFP 1, argues against the Smith-Towner bill of 1919; the quotation on prohibitionists is in John LaFarge, "Calumnies Against France," *Am*, 21 (August 2, 1919), 426.

42. *MIO*, 193. On the concept of the "Silent South" and southern liberals, see Morton Sosna, *In Search of the Silent South: Southern Liberals and the Race Issue* (New York, 1977).

43. *MIO*. 199.

44. On the paternalism of Catholics in general and the Josephites in particular, see Ochs, *Desegregating the Altar, passim;* on the paternalism of the editors of *Commonweal,*

LaFarge's first article on race relations appeared on December 17, 1921. In "Full Measure for the Negro," he grieved that blacks had not secured "the most valuable elements in our white men's civilization." He declared further: "The principles, skill, discoveries and erudition of the white man can undoubtedly be communicated to those of another race. . . . The Negro is entitled to the best, the very best that the white man can give him." The Jesuit argued that a tendency toward radicalism, emotionalism, and materialism took a greater toll on the morality and the civic mindedness of the "susceptible Negro" than on those of whites. In addition, he commented on how the "Creator appears to have given him [the black man] a special power of voicing in music and folk-song the home love of all Americans, white as well as colored." In his next article on blacks a week later, he continued in this vein. "He [the Negro] is our ward," LaFarge wrote, "entrusted to us by God's Providence." Whites must take the African American by the hand and advance him to where he is "no longer in the imitative, gregarious stage, but a human being capable of thinking rightly for his own good." As the historian Jay P. Dolan has observed, when Catholic leaders talked about blacks, they thought in terms applied to the American Indians. The remedy for both the black and red "wards" was schooling that would effect a profound transformation of their cultures and align them with that of whites.[45]

In a 1925 article in *America* that reeked of paternalism, LaFarge expressed doubt as to whether a simple black farmer from his parish could understand the controversy over "Evolution" and religion, even though the parishioner had read the views of a learned black churchman on the issue in a black newspaper. Since this black minister apparently believed that Darwinism and religion could be reconciled, LaFarge wondered if the farmer could profit from a clear-cut discussion of the topic in the *Catholic Mind,* a magazine that he had left for the parishioner's use. In tune with Pope Pius X's condemnation of all modernism in 1907, LaFarge scoffed at the confusion on the issue of evo-

see Paul E. Czuchlewski, "Liberal Catholicism and American Racism, 1924–1960," *Records of the American Catholic Historical Society of Philadelphia,* 85 (March–June, 1974), 144–62.

45. John LaFarge, "Full Measure for the Negro," *Am,* 26 (December 17, 1921), 197–98; John LaFarge, "The Immediate Negro Problem," *Am,* 26 (December 24, 1921), 221–22; Dolan, *American Catholic Experience,* 43, 359–60.

lution by non-Catholics. And he doubted whether this African American reader of the black press could really understand the *Catholic Mind,* which was not written exclusively "for *his* race" as the Jesuit assumed was the case with the black newspaper.[46]

As the above quotations indicate, the denominational jingoism of LaFarge matched his paternalism. Most of his sectarian promotion occurred when he discussed the topic of education. In his first exposure to a national audience through *America,* LaFarge quoted a report of the Southern University Race Commission as follows: "The solution of all human problems rests upon rightly directed education." This education, he admonished, could not be the "half-measure of the secular semi-educator." It had to be education based on "sound Catholic principles." With unswerving confidence, LaFarge insisted that "the colored man's destinies are safest and surest when in the hands of Catholic leaders and Catholic educators." He proclaimed that "the Catholic Church alone holds the keys to the best elements in the white man's civilization" and asserted that "the Church alone can reach his [the Negro's] mind and heart." Only the Catholic church "has the key to true progress," he wrote. It "can give the Negro principles, methods, habits, by which he can learn to solve his own problems . . . by building up his intellectual power and moral character."[47]

Although LaFarge conceded that Protestants spent far more money and effort on blacks than did Catholics and confessed that blacks were the "weakest link in the Catholic Church," he argued that the race problem was a unique opportunity for his denomination, a view he never relinquished. To guide blacks and whites toward racial peace and justice would be, he declared, "a jewel in the crown of our Church in this country and a safeguard of our Republic."[48]

LaFarge remembered his Maryland years as the seedbed of the interracial movement, but in his early articles in *America* he did not rule out all-black organizations as a means of improving race relations and advancing the black cause. In his first article on race relations, written while the black nationalist Marcus Garvey was in his heyday, LaFarge

46. John LaFarge, "The Doctor and the Cantaloupes," *Am,* 33 (June 23, 1925), 443–44.

47. LaFarge, "Immediate Negro Problem," 221; LaFarge, "Full Measure for the Negro," 198.

48. LaFarge, "Full Measure for the Negro," 198; LaFarge, "Immediate Negro Problem," 221.

called for a "solid union of all American colored Catholics." In the early 1920s LaFarge showed great respect for Turner. He lauded the black leader's definition of the so-called Negro problem as a problem not of the black community's making. Quoting Turner, LaFarge wrote, "The real problem is not that of the Negro's capacity but of the white men's attitude [toward blacks]." Early on, Turner and LaFarge adopted the view that the race problem was a "white man's problem," a concept more popularly advanced by the Swedish economist Gunnar Myrdal in his classic book on race, *An American Dilemma*, published in 1944.[49]

LaFarge also acknowledged that the absence of black Catholic leaders militated against the retention and conversion of blacks for the Catholic church. "The Negro alone, with rare exceptions," he claimed, "can fully understand the Negro, can obtain from him full confidence." He realized that the best weapon to recruit and retain blacks would be black priests. LaFarge also discerned black suspicions about the white-dominated church and its lack of interest in black vocations. But the possibility of raising a black clergy in the 1920s seemed so remote to LaFarge that he simply noted discussion was beginning to increase on this neglected subject. Given the dim prospects for black priests, LaFarge put his hope in a black laity trained as teachers, catechists, industrial supervisors, labor leaders, and health officials.[50]

The Jesuit scholar Stanton portrayed LaFarge as a great "pastoral theologian." That is, he stressed the priest's success in making practical application of Catholic theology to social and human relationships. At this point in his career, though, LaFarge did little more than assert that the Catholic church was uniquely equipped to rescue the black minority from all its bondage. Other than general references to Christian charity and justice, he gave no reason the Catholic church was especially obligated or favored in the work of racial redemption over, say, Protestants, Jews, or secular groups. Indeed, he frequently acknowledged that non-Catholics had surpassed Catholics in the racial field. In his early writing he did not delve into Catholic history or theology to show why he believed Catholicism had the inside track to solving the

---

49. LaFarge, "Full Measure for the Negro," 198; LaFarge, "Immediate Negro Problem," 222; Gunnar Myrdal, *An American Dilemma: The Negro Problem and Modern Democracy* (New York, 1944), 669.

50. LaFarge, "Immediate Negro Problem," 222–23. For the failure of the church to raise a black clergy, see Ochs, *Desegregating the Altar.*

great American social dilemma. Nor did he refer to papal encyclicals such as Pope Leo XIII's *Rerum Novarum,* an 1891 prolabor manifesto, or to the doctrine of the Mystical Body of Christ, which later became mainstays in his argument that Catholicism has special application to the race problem. Interestingly, he never mentioned the historic Bishops' Program of Social Reconstruction. This seminal document came out of World War I and was largely conceived and drafted by Father John A. Ryan, the preeminent American pastoral theologian of the era.[51]

In the 1920s the American Catholic church had not yet translated its verbal flirtation with a social gospel into concrete programs. It would be many years before the racial dimensions of social Catholicism would begin to be known to a significant number of American Catholics. While in Maryland LaFarge thus had little in the way of institutional doctrine to guide his practical efforts to better the spiritual and material lot of black Catholics. Ironically, LaFarge became more of a pastoral theologian after he left rural Maryland for the cement canyons of New York City.

To put LaFarge's doctrinal and racial views in better perspective and to understand more fully the forces and ideas with which he had to contend in the establishment of his racial apostolate in New York in the late 1920s, it is necessary to interrupt this chronological-biographical narrative now and review the state of Catholic social doctrine prior to the watershed years of the 1930s. For proper context it is also mandatory to explore more precisely how Catholic social teaching related to African Americans.

51. Stanton, "John LaFarge's Understanding," 242; Dolan, *American Catholic Experience,* 342–44.

3

Catholic Social Teaching and African Americans

"Nineteenth-century Catholicism preached an individual gospel, not a social gospel." Unlike European Catholics or American Protestants, Catholics in the United States did not develop an integrated social philosophy, let alone a nationally organized program of social action. On many of the burning social and political questions of the nineteenth and early twentieth centuries, the American church remained mute. The Catholic church's response to industrialization and its many ramifications, Joseph M. McShane argues, was "confused, ineffective, and devoid of passion and intellectual depth."[1] Even after Father Ryan and the NCWC laid the theoretical and organizational groundwork for social Catholicism in the early twentieth century, the American church refused to face the race question in a true spirit of catholicity and, in fact, acquiesced in racist tendencies that were deeply ingrained in American culture.

Primarily a devotional institution, the American Catholic church revealed itself in four characteristic traits: "authority, sin, ritual, and the miraculous." The one "true church" was, above all, a hierarchical institution whose orthodoxy insisted that the institutional church was divine and unchanging.[2] This ahistorical view of the church guided the

---

1. Dolan, *American Catholic Experience,* 231; McShane, *"Sufficiently Radical,"* 5.
2. Dolan, *American Catholic Experience,* 221, 303–304.

Catholic hierarchy, which was headed by a pope who claimed direct succession from the apostle St. Peter. Pope Pius IX, who reigned from 1846 to 1878, led a church that was under siege spiritually, intellectually, politically, and even militarily. The last pope to have a minister of war, Pius IX reacted strongly to the escalating attacks on Catholic absolutism that came from all directions, whether from the republican guns of Giuseppe Garibaldi's assault on the Papal States or from the imperial troops of Napoleon III who imprisoned the pope in the Vatican or from the Machiavellian politics of Otto von Bismarck who orchestrated the *Kulturkampf.* Pius IX lashed out at the secular world in his *Syllabus of Errors* in 1864. The document condemned virtually the entire Enlightenment, including the American principles of freedom of speech and freedom of religion. The pope vowed that the church would make no compromise with "progress, liberalism, and modern civilization."[3]

Pius IX strengthened the doctrine of papal infallibility in matters of faith and morals. And since the church in the United States was officially missionary territory until 1908, it technically came under the direct control of Rome and tended to be emphatically "papalist." After 1870, the famous dictum "Rome has spoken; the case is closed" accurately mirrored the American church's authoritarian cast.[4]

The doctrine of papal infallibility also bolstered the status of bishops and the clergy as authority filtered downward. The bishop became a diocesan pope who had the trappings of royalty. A well-known joke in Catholic circles was that after a bishop was ordained he would never eat a bad meal or hear the whole truth. The priest, the local mediator of the divine order, dispensed the all-important sacraments to the ritually starved laity. For this the laity looked upon the priest with profound reverence. Below him, however, real authority vanished. As a Catholic journalist put it: "Only those within the hierarchy had rights. All outside approached as supplicants." Given the authoritarian nature of the nineteenth-century church, American Catholics tended to be docile and submissive before church officials.[5]

3. Pius X, quoted in David O'Brien, *Public Catholicism,* 102. See also Bokenkotter, *Concise History,* 11.

4. John Cogley, *Catholic America* (New York, 1973), 68–73; "Rome has spoken" quotation in Dolan, *American Catholic Experience,* 222.

5. Cogley, *Catholic America,* 218; Dolan, *American Catholic Experience,* 222–25; McEoin, *Memoirs and Memories,* 158; Dolan, *American Catholic Experience,* 224–25.

Like many Protestant denominations of this era, the Catholic church was also preoccupied with the idea of sin, its prayer books stressing confession and the horrors of hell. The celibate priesthood seemed to place an inordinate emphasis on sins associated with sex. In 1942 the Catholic novelist Sylvester, echoing the times, had one of the characters exclaim, "A Catholic is someone who thinks that the only two mortal sins are sex and murder, in that order." [6] Priests often busied themselves with the minutiae of sexual misconduct, as did some of the great church fathers. Aquinas, for example, warned that masturbation was worse than incest.[7]

Preoccupation with sin led Catholics to a militantly negative view of the outside world and fostered a strong anti-Protestantism. Catholics learned from their prayer books that Protestants were a "perishing and debauched multitude of heretics and infidels." The harsh attitude toward Protestants retarded interfaith efforts for social action until the 1960s.[8]

Catholic emphasis on sin was related to ritual and a belief in the miraculous. The worshiper approached the divine through solemn and splendid ritual that involved Mary, the saints, relics, incense, candles, holy water, and rosary beads. The Eucharist was "the epitome of liturgical theater." The belief that the bread and the wine became the body and blood of Christ required a sense of the miraculous. Shrines such as Lourdes in France drew tens of thousands who sought miracle cures for their bodily afflictions.[9] Taken together, the culture of authority, sin, ritual, and the miraculous tended to create an insular and conservative Catholic society that was pietistic, docile, anti-intellectual, and fatalistic. These traits militated against the emergence of a social or public Catholicism geared to the problems of the modern era.

Another factor hindering the development of social doctrine lay in the makeup of the Catholic minority, which overwhelmingly consisted

---

6. Dolan, *American Catholic Experience*, 225–29; Sylvester, *Dearly Beloved*, 188.

7. Some feminists relate the obsession with sexuality to the subordination of women, for instance, Uta Ranke-Heinemann, *Eunuchs for the Kingdom of Heaven: Women, Sexuality, and the Catholic Church*, trans. Peter Heinegg (New York, 1990), 233, 311. See also Karen Kennelly, ed., *American Catholic Women: A Historical Exploration* (New York, 1989).

8. Dolan, *American Catholic Experience*, 228.

9. *Ibid.*, 229, 233–35.

of immigrant, working-class people. In 1789 approximately 25,000 Catholics lived in the United States, with about 15,000 in Maryland. By the time of the Civil War, however, there were over 3,000,000 Catholics. After 1880, large numbers of Catholics poured in from eastern and southern Europe. Poles and Italians contributed the largest numbers of Catholics after the Irish and Germans. By 1930 almost twenty million Catholics resided in America, or about one-sixth of the total population. As ethnic colonies proliferated in northern cities, the Catholic community sounded like a Tower of Babel. In 1907 Boston had forty-two foreign language parishes. In 1922, 40 percent of American bishops were foreign born, and 60 percent of them were Irish. Many of the hierarchy and clergy had received their education abroad; many of the bishops, in Rome. Most of the immigrants were ill-educated peasants. As late as 1940, 66 percent of the Catholic population was lower class.[10]

The influx of this poor, non-Protestant mass of people provoked fear and resentment among the Anglo-Saxon majority, and regular nativist outbursts took place, the worst in the 1850s, the 1890s, and the 1920s.[11] The antiforeign feeling helped to engender a siege mentality among Catholics. The internal nationalistic and ethnic divisions in the church focused the hierarchy's attention on unity and order rather than on social justice. Marginal and persecuted Catholics found refuge in ritual and the infallibility of the pope and the church. The immigrant church concerned itself with bricks and mortar, interest-group politics, and personal piety, and it shied away from reform movements.[12] Indeed, Protestant-dominated reform movements, including the Social Gospel, were often infected with raw anti-Catholicism and racism.[13]

10. Forrest G. Wood, *The Arrogance of Faith: Christianity and Race in America from the Colonial Era to the Twentieth Century* (Boston, 1991), 354–55; George M. Marsden, *Religion and American Culture* (New York, 1990), 132; Dolan, *American Catholic Experience*, 127–36, 357, 362; Elizabeth McKeown, *War and Welfare: American Catholics and World War I* (New York, 1988), 42.

11. On nativism and the ordeal of the immigrants, see John Higham, *Strangers in the Land: Patterns of American Nativism, 1860–1925* (New York, 1955), and Kenneth T. Jackson, *The Ku Klux Klan in the City, 1915–1930* (New York, 1967).

12. McShane, *"Sufficiently Radical,"* 15, 17–18; David J. O'Brien, "The Church and American Culture During Our Nation's Lifetime," in *The Catholic Church and American Culture: Reciprocity and Challenge,* ed. Cassian Yuhaus, C.P. (Mahwah, N.J., 1990), 15–18.

13. On the antiforeignism and racism of reformers, see Richard Hofstadter, *The*

Not surprisingly, few Catholics tried to imitate the Social Gospel of the late nineteenth century. Led by the Protestant ministers Washington Gladden and Walter Rauschenbusch, the Social Gospel denounced unregulated capitalism, social Darwinism, and the "gospel of wealth" as un-Christian. They blamed widespread poverty not on the immorality of the workers but on the economic system. They stressed Christian cooperation instead of ruinous competition, and they preached that high morality could not be expected among poor industrial workers mired in wretched social conditions. Some supported the class politics of the Populists, and some even embraced "Christian socialism," but mostly they advocated a moderate reform package that was similar to what became known as progressivism. The Social Gospel culminated in the formation of the Federal Council of Churches of Christ in 1908.[14]

Little influenced by Protestant liberalism, the social thought and action of Catholics was rather a pragmatic response to the immediate social conditions of the time. Faced with widespread poverty common to the unskilled industrial worker, Catholics began to organize charitable organizations. St. Vincent de Paul, the most important of these Catholic organizations in the nineteenth century, was founded in 1845. The church also began to build hospitals and orphanages. By 1880, 119 Catholic hospitals and 267 orphanages had been built. Between 1887 and 1906, Catholics completed 225 more hospitals. Since most Catholic activists saw poverty as a natural condition, they dispensed charity to individuals with little thought of indicting the economic system.[15]

In the late nineteenth century, however, some Catholics looked to the labor movement as a remedy for poverty and a vehicle for social reform. Many Catholic workers joined the Knights of Labor, which was founded in 1869. Terence V. Powderly, an Irish-born Catholic, headed the Knights at the peak of its power in the 1880s, when the federation had nearly a million members. The organization welcomed

---

Age of Reform: From Bryan to FDR (New York, 1955), 60–93, 176–82; Idus A. Newby, *Jim Crow's Defense: Anti-Negro Thought in America, 1900–1930* (Baton Rouge, 1965); and Southern, *Malignant Heritage,* 43–54, 67–85.

14. See especially Washington Gladden, *Applied Christianity: Moral Aspects of Social Questions* (New York, 1886); Walter Rauschenbusch, *Christianity and the Social Order* (New York, 1907); and Charles H. Hopkins, *The Rise of the Social Gospel Movement in American Protestantism, 1865–1915* (New Haven, 1940).

15. Dolan, *American Catholic Experience,* 323–25, 328.

men and women of all creeds and colors into one, large industrial union. Possibly two-thirds of its members were Catholic. This broadly reformist, even utopian, union got crucial support from a powerful American prelate, Archbishop Gibbons of Baltimore. Because of conservative opposition in the American hierarchy to the Knights of Labor, the pope was on the verge of condemning the federation. In 1887, however, Gibbons persuaded Pope Leo XIII not to condemn the Knights. He also prevailed upon the Vatican not to put Henry George's liberal *Progress and Poverty*, published in 1879, on the Index of forbidden books. The pope's approval of the controversial Knights, the support of labor by Cardinal Gibbons and other liberal members of the hierarchy, and the rise of a sizable number of firebrand "labor priests" such as Edward McGlynn, Peter C. Yorke, and Peter E. Dietz marked an important advance for the church in the direction of social Catholicism.[16]

Many analysts, however, date the beginning of modern Catholic social doctrine with Pope Leo XIII's historic encyclical of 1891, *Rerum Novarum (On the Condition of Labor)*. Although aimed primarily at the church's archenemy socialism and filled with rhetoric that was frequently condescending and paternalistic toward the working class, *Rerum Novarum* was the first comprehensive attempt by the Vatican to address the "social question" in the new industrial age. It was also prolabor and critical of unregulated capitalism.[17] Searching for a "middle way" between savage capitalism and heretical socialism, the pope maintained that the marketplace could not be divorced from religious precepts of morality and justice. The church, Rome asserted, could not be silent on grave questions involving individual dignity and the health of the family. Commenting on *Rerum Novarum*, Bishop John Spalding

16. *Ibid.*, 329–33, 338–39, 341–42; Henry J. Browne, *The Catholic Church and the Knights of Labor* (Washington, D.C., 1949), 190, *passim;* Anthony Sean Pastor-Zelaya, "The Development of Roman Catholic Social Liberalism in the United States, 1887–1935" (Ph.D. dissertation, University of California, Santa Barbara, 1988), 14, 28–37.

17. Peter Hibblethwaite, "The Popes and Politics: Shifting Patterns in 'Catholic Social Doctrine,'" *Daedalus,* 111 (Winter, 1982), 86–87; Bokenkotter, *Concise History,* 311, 314–16, 320; Mary E. Hobgood, *Catholic Social Teaching and Economic Theory: Paradigms in Conflict* (Philadelphia, 1991), 107. An English translation of *Rerum Novarum* can be found in *Catholic Social Thought: The Documentary Heritage,* ed. David J. O'Brien and Thomas A. Shannon (Maryknoll, N.Y., 1992), 14–39.

of Peoria said that "the mission of the Church is not only to save souls, but also to save society."[18]

The potential of Leo XIII's encyclical was not realized in America because the American hierarchy was deeply divided on a host of issues: parochial schools, national and ethnic parishes, and the rate of the Americanization of the church, for example. Liberal bishops such as Gibbons, John Ireland, Denis O'Connell, and John K. Keane, building on the ideas of the earlier Americanizers Isaac Hecker and Orestes Brownson, tried to adapt the church to an American context. "A free church in a free society" was their slogan. They quarreled bitterly with conservative bishops, who put Catholicism above Americanism; and both sides appealed to Rome for support of their views. In one of the most confusing episodes in modern Catholic history, Pope Leo XIII condemned "Americanism" in an 1899 letter, *Testem Benevolentiae*. The Americanist controversy, very complex in itself, spilled over into European squabbles and involved "modernism," an even more radical challenge to Catholic dogma. Some scholars suggest that what the pope censured in 1899 was not really Americanism but European modernism.[19]

Whether or not Americanism was a "phantom heresy," its embrace of historicism constituted a sure sign of modernism to conservatives.[20] Bishop Spalding seemed to confirm conservative suspicion when, in response to the pope's censure of Americanism, he defiantly proclaimed, "The Church lives in history and must speak to its age."[21] In

18. Spalding, quoted in Abell, *American Catholicism and Social Action*, 77.

19. David O'Brien, *Public Catholicism*, 61, 96, 208; Ochs, *Desegregating the Altar*, 74; Michael Gannon, "Before and After Modernism: The Intellectual Isolation of the American Priest," in *Catholic Priest*, ed. John Ellis, 293–383. See generally Thomas T. McAvoy, *The Americanist Heresy in Roman Catholicism, 1895–1900* (Notre Dame, Ind., 1963).

20. Scott R. Appleby, *"Church and the Age Unite!": The Modernist Impulse in American Catholicism* (Notre Dame, Ind., 1992), 185, 206, is one of several scholars who have recently argued for the relatedness of Americanism and modernism. But see also Margaret M. Reher, "Americanism and Modernism—Continuity or Discontinuity?," *U.S. Catholic Historian*, 1 (Summer, 1981), 87–103, and William L. Portier, "Modernism in the United States: The Case of John R. Slattery," in *Varieties of Modernism*, ed. Ronald Burke, Gary Lease, and George Gilmore (Mobile, Ala., 1986), 77–97.

21. Spalding, quoted in David O'Brien, *Public Catholicism*, 123. For the view that Spalding was in conflict with *Testem Benevolentiae*, see David P. Kellen, "Americanism

addition, most Americanists openly embraced religious liberty and the separation of church and state. In 1895, four years before the letter condemning Americanism, Leo XIII had informed Americanists that these liberal concepts did not meet the test of Catholic orthodoxy.[22] Moreover, the cooperation of Americanists with Protestants exposed liberals to charges of "religious indifference," that is, of holding one religion to be as good as another. Nor did the liberals' advocacy of American exceptionalism set well with the pope and his European advisers. Like Lincoln in another context, Archbishop Ireland preached that American Catholicism was the last best hope of Catholicism on earth. Liberals such as Ireland boldly promoted Catholicism as the basis of America's "manifest destiny." Triumphalist liberals could cooperate with Protestants because they feared them so little. In Ireland's words, Protestantism as a religious system was in the "process of dissolution" and was "without value as a doctrine or moral power."[23]

If Leo XIII presented an obstacle to liberal Catholics, the next pope was anathema to them. In 1907 Pope Pius X lowered the ecclesiastical boom on a cluster of ideas known as modernism. His 1907 encyclical *Pascendi Dominici Gregis* condemned such ideas as historicism, modern biblical criticism, and Darwinism. After *Pascendi*, the Vatican established vigilante committees in each diocese that sought to exterminate every trace of modernist thought. Modernist thinkers such as Alfred Loisy in France and George Tyrrell in England were excommunicated, and several American liberals were silenced. The *New York Review*, perhaps the finest Catholic theological journal in America, was closed down in 1908.[24]

Revisited: John Spalding and *Testem Benevolentiae*," in *The Inculturation of American Catholicism, 1820–1900*, ed. William L. Portier (New York, 1988), 404–54.

22. Winthrop S. Hudson, *Understanding Roman Catholicism: A Guide to Papal Teachings for Protestants* (Philadelphia, 1959), 105; Margaret Mary Reher, *Catholic Intellectual Life in America: A Historical Study of Persons and Movements* (New York, 1989), 73; Arnold Sparr, *To Promote, Defend, and Redeem: The Catholic Literary Revival and the Cultural Transformation of American Catholicism, 1920–1960* (Westport, Conn., 1990), 5.

23. Dolan, *American Catholic Experience*, 309, 314, 316; Ireland, quoted in Marvin R. O'Connell, *John Ireland and the American Catholic Church* (St. Paul, Minn., 1988), 280.

24. Bokenkotter, *Concise History*, 335; Dolan, *American Catholic Experience*, 318–20; Appleby, "*Church and the Age Unite!*," 117–66, 169, 206, 230–35.

Ironically, in the early twentieth century Catholicism took the path of Protestant fundamentalism, the most anti-Catholic force in America, in proscribing modernistic thought so completely. Thinking was out; devotional piety and loyalty to Rome were in. Original thought and original research became original sin. As one observer put it, "For a time American Catholicism acted as if it had inherited a mandate to . . . enforce the moral code of nineteenth-century cultural Protestantism."[25]

Intellectual dry rot, therefore, afflicted much of American Catholicism before World War I. As late as the mid-1950s, Father John Tracy Ellis lamented the scarcity of Catholic intellectuals. According to William M. Halsey, Catholicism entered the twentieth century with a mindset of "blustering negativism." During the fabled period of reform known as the Progressive Era, Catholics largely stood on the sidelines.[26]

John Ryan, however, was splendidly in tune with the reform impulse of the Progressive Era. Born in 1869 to Irish immigrants in the small farming village of Vermillion, Minnesota, Ryan grew up among prairie Populists and talk of economic justice. He became a priest in 1898 and attended Catholic University for graduate study in moral theology. His 1906 doctoral dissertation, "A Living Wage," argued that economic policies should be shaped by moral principles and that wages should be sufficient to sustain a worker and his family in health and dignity. A man of action, Ryan allied himself with non-Catholic progressives and helped enact a minimum-wage law for Minnesota. In 1909 he set forth a broad reform program that included legislation for a minimum-wage law, an eight-hour workday, prohibition of child labor, and the right to strike. He even suggested ownership of public utilities and progressive taxes. With the publication of *Distributive Justice* in

25. Marsden, *Religion and American Culture,* 177–93; Reher, *Catholic Intellectual Life,* 98; Bokenkotter, *Concise History,* 333–35; Martin E. Marty, *An Invitation to American Catholic History* (Chicago, 1986), 145; Gannon, "Before and After Modernism," in *Catholic Priest,* ed. John Ellis, 350; Edward Duff, S.J., "The Church and American Public Life," in *Contemporary Catholicism in the United States,* ed. Philip Gleason (Notre Dame, Ind., 1969), 123.

26. Cross, *Emergence of Liberal Catholicism,* 111; John Tracy Ellis, *American Catholics and the Intellectual Life* (Chicago, 1956), *passim;* Gerald P. Fogarty, *The Vatican and the American Hierarchy from 1870 to 1965* (Stuttgart, 1982), 190–93; Halsey, *Survival of American Innocence,* 9; Hennesey, *American Catholics,* 207, 210, 212–13; McShane, "*Sufficiently Radical,*" 15, 17–18.

1916, Ryan had formulated the most comprehensive social justice program ever offered by an American Catholic.[27]

Although Ryan was a populist / progressive, he was no modernist. Staunchly orthodox in everything theological and institutional, he, like Leo XIII in *Rerum Novarum,* used Thomistic thought to attack amoral market capitalism. Although some Catholic conservatives thought Ryan's ideas too socialistic, he did succeed in opening a modest and safer door to Catholic Americanism in the early twentieth century.[28]

Many liberal Catholics such as Ryan recognized World War I as a perfect opportunity to prove their patriotism and to assimilate more fully into the American mainstream culture. Attempting to unify the Catholic response to the war, the bishops established the National Catholic War Council in 1917. Through the council, they sought to showcase Catholic enthusiasm for the war (only four cases of conscientious objection by Catholics were recorded). In 1919 the National Catholic War Council became the National Catholic Welfare Council, and later in 1922 the permanent organization replaced the word *Council* with *Conference.* In 1919 the NCWC incorporated most of Ryan's social agenda into a document known as the Bishops' Program of Social Reconstruction. These developments stunned non-Catholic liberals. Upton Sinclair called the new stance of the church a "miracle." The war thus increased Catholic unity, visibility, and pride, and it ended the American hierarchy's "masterly inactivity" on the social and political front.[29]

Would the grand social agenda of the bishops be implemented, or was it just window dressing? From the beginning, weaknesses in the bishops' program became evident. First of all, the program was only

27. Dolan, *American Catholic Experience,* 342–43; John A. Ryan, *A Living Wage: Its Ethical and Economic Aspects* (New York, 1906); John A. Ryan, "A Program of Social Reform by Legislation," *Catholic World,* 89 (July, 1909), 433, and (August, 1909), 608–44; Francis L. Broderick, *Right Reverend New Dealer: John A. Ryan* (New York, 1963), 85.

28. Reher, *Catholic Intellectual Life,* 113, 119; McShane, "*Sufficiently Radical,*" 50–51; Hobgood, *Catholic Social Teaching,* 227.

29. Dolan, *American Catholic Experience,* 342–44; Pastor-Zelaya, "The Development of Roman Catholic Social Liberalism," 96–97; Marty, *Invitation to American Catholic History,* 160–61; Halsey, *Survival of American Innocence,* 9; McShane, "*Sufficiently Radical,*" 55–56, 81, 83, 87–88, 123; Peter Guilday, ed., *The National Pastorals of the American Hierarchy, 1792–1919* (Washington, D.C., 1923), 295–98, 303–304, 317–40; Dolan, *American Catholic Experience,* 345.

"semicanonical" and therefore not binding on all Catholics. Second, Pope Pius XI feared that the organization might threaten papal power. Third, the 1920s was not a time that favored liberal reform. Most bishops soon lost interest in the program and fell in with the conservative spirit of the time. Moreover, the heightened visibility of ethnicity and Catholicism stemming from the war unleashed a new wave of nativism. Despite all the rhetoric about the compatibility of Americanism and Catholicism, a "strenuous and exhausting" dualism remained in the Catholic mind as the church remained primarily an immigrant institution hampered by a siege mentality. Priests continued to be more interested in Marian devotions and novenas than in social justice.[30]

To be sure, the war increased the power and prestige of the hierarchy. Powerful prelates such as George Mundelein, the archbishop of Chicago, ushered in a fabulous decade of building that resulted in an explosion of Catholic schools, churches, hospitals, and community centers. More representative of the church than any social program was the 1926 International Eucharist Congress held in Chicago. For five days the church, under Archbishop Mundelein's imperial guidance, put on a rich display of pageantry. Over 100,000 spectators watched as legions of Catholic organizations and some fifty brightly dressed and bejeweled cardinals marched along Michigan Avenue. It was a stunning example of triumphalist Catholicism. The "awakening giant," America's largest religious denomination, now looked to shape the nation's future. Catholics felt they alone had staved off modernism and rejected the nihilism of the postwar period, perpetuating what Halsey has called the "survival of American innocence."[31]

During the war unprecedented cooperation between Catholics, Protestants, and Jews had occurred. In the 1920s, however, the gap between Catholics and other faiths may have widened. More and more, Catholic leaders blamed the ills of the world on Protestantism and secularism (and often had trouble making distinctions between the two).

30. McShane, *"Sufficiently Radical,"* 25, 88, 278–79, 444–49; Hennesey, *American Catholics*, 230–31; David J. O'Brien, "The American Priest and Social Action," in *Catholic Priest*, ed. John Ellis, 443; David O'Brien, *Public Catholicism*, 126, 220.

31. Cogley, *Catholic America*, 79–82; Dolan, *American Catholic Experience*, 350, 355; Edward R. Kantowicz, *Corporation Sole: Cardinal Mundelein and Chicago Catholicism* (Notre Dame, Ind., 1983), 215, 241, *passim*; Martin E. Marty, *The Noise of Conflict, 1919–1941* (Chicago, 1991), 146–48, Vol. II of Marty, *Modern American Religion*; Halsey, *Survival of American Innocence*, 3.

Ignoring the mainline Protestant "goodwill movement" toward other faiths, Catholic spokesmen suggested that the most bigoted fundamentalists spoke for Protestantism. Michael Harrington, a follower of Dorothy Day in the 1940s, remembered the "sullen ethnocentrism" of his Protestant-hating classmates in college. In the 1920s Pope Pius XI brusquely turned down invitations to participate in international congresses that sought greater unity among Christians. He forbade Catholics attending any of the congresses, and in a 1928 encyclical the pope said that Christian unity could only be achieved if Protestants rejoined the "one true Church of Christ." The pope additionally forbade Catholics engaging in any interfaith discussions of theological issues. Since these issues tended to spill over into moral and social questions, this prohibition meant that Catholics contributed only negatively to ecumenical efforts in the social field. For example, in the 1920s and 1930s Catholics remained aloof from the newly formed National Conference of Christians and Jews.[32]

Even the most liberal Catholics made statements in the 1920s that aroused fear and consternation among non-Catholics. In a 1922 book titled *The State and the Church,* Ryan agreed with Rome that true religion (read Catholicism) should have a favored place in the government. George N. Shuster, an editor of the liberal magazine *Commonweal,* wrote in 1928, "Had it not been for the grotesque stupidity of Protestants, we would long since have built up in this country a system of denominational schools subsidized and to some extent supervised by the state."[33] The most broad-minded Catholics seemed not to understand why non-Catholic Americans reacted so strongly to their expressed contempt for public schools, then the pride of the nation. It would be many years before Catholics cooperated comfortably with Protestants and Jews on an agenda of social and political reform.

32. David O'Brien, *Public Catholicism,* 194; Benny Kraut, "A Wary Collaboration: Jews, Catholics, and the Protestant Goodwill Movement," in *Between the Times: The Travail of the Protestant Establishment in America, 1900–1960,* ed. William R. Hutchison (New York, 1989), 212, 214; Michael Harrington, *Fragments of the Century* (New York, 1973), 5; Pope Pius XI, quoted in Lerond Curry, *Protestant-Catholic Relations in America* (Lexington, Ky., 1972), 92; McShane, "*Sufficiently Radical,*" 2, 5; Dolan, *American Catholic Experience,* 228; Cross, *Emergence of Liberal Catholicism,* 221.

33. Reher, *Catholic Intellectual Life,* 119; George N. Shuster, *The Catholic Spirit in America* (1928; rpr. New York, 1978), 175; Martin J. Bredeck, *Imperfect Apostles: The Commonweal and the American Catholic Laity, 1924–1976* (New York, 1988), 165.

Although Ryan and the NCWC opened the door for social Catholicism to advance in the 1920s, not many took advantage of it. In fact, the Great Depression did more than any number of Catholic social treatises or encyclicals could ever do to galvanize Catholics for social action.[34]

The theological fathers of Catholicism acted as if the transcendent church had no past but only "an eternal present." The secular idea of history meant little to those who believed the church was divine and unchanging. Subjecting dogma to history was one of the modernist sins condemned by Pope Pius X. So the church really had no dialectic in the early twentieth century, only static and immutable categories of meaning. According to the Catholic historian Eric Cochrane, the ahistorical assumptions of Catholic theology not only affected Catholic historians but became the curse of Catholic intellectuality. Furthermore, in the words of William J. McGill, Catholic historians often acted as "uncritical purveyors of in-group mythology."[35]

Before the Catholic *glasnost* of the 1960s, even the best Catholic historians fell short of standards set by the modern historical profession.[36] The founding fathers of American Catholic history—historians such as John Gilmary Shea (1824–1892), Peter K. Guilday (1884–1947), and John Tracy Ellis (1905–1993)—assumed the infallibility of church dogma and favored the hierarchy over the laity. Guilday, the founder of the *Catholic Historical Review* in 1915, once proclaimed, "Religion

34. David O'Brien, *Public Catholicism*, 157; Dolan, *American Catholic Experience*, 408.

35. Garry Wills, "Memories of a Catholic Boyhood," *Esquire*, 75 (February, 1971), 117; McEoin, *Memoirs and Memories*, 170–71; Gannon, "Before and After Modernism," in *Catholic Priest*, ed. John Ellis, 352; James Hennesey, S.J., "Church History and the Theologians," *U.S. Catholic Historian*, 6 (Winter, 1987), 2, 4, 12; Eric Cockrane, "What Is Catholic Historiography?," *Catholic Historical Review*, 61 (April, 1975), 188; William J. McGill, "Something of Worth from Boeotia: The Presidential Addresses of the American Catholic Historical Association, 1920–1968," *Catholic Historical Review*, 56 (April, 1970), 41.

36. Czuchlewski, "Liberal Catholicism and American Racism," 144–46; Randall M. Miller, Introduction to *Catholics in the Old South*, ed. Miller and Wakelyn, 4; David J. O'Brien, "American Catholic Historiography: A Post-Conciliar Evaluation," *Church History*, 37 (March, 1968), 80–94; Moses Rischin, "The New American Catholic History," *Church History*, 41 (June, 1972), 225–29.

is the all-important thing in the world, and every religion, save the Catholic religion, lacks something essential." Even the younger Ellis could not break entirely free of apologetic and celebratory history.[37]

Nor was the bulk of Catholic history before the 1960s written by the outstanding historians mentioned above. Rather, polemicists, untrained in historical method and with very large and dull denominational axes to grind, wrote most of it. Their histories were largely about the hierarchy, for the hierarchy, and by the hierarchy (and clergy). They corrected allegedly false histories concocted by Protestants and blamed Protestants and secularism for Catholic shortcomings. They not only denied any conflict between Catholicism and American principles, but they practically claimed that Catholics had invented religious freedom and republicanism. Protestants, they argued, were no friends to liberty. According to the liberal archbishop John Ireland, "Protestantism did nothing for liberty," except perhaps to foster "political anarchy."[38]

Liberty aside, few subjects brought more distortion and cover-ups from Catholic writers than did slavery and racism. Priests in the black apostolate frequently acted as modern spin doctors. While they looked to better race relations in the future, they definitely improved those in the past by exaggerating the racial tolerance of Catholics. In his voluminous writings, LaFarge often asserted that slavery and racism derived from Protestant culture and were foisted on Catholics. He argued that though Spaniards displayed repulsive cruelty toward natives, they still were kinder and gentler slaveholders than Protestants because of their religion. LaFarge often coached Catholics on how to answer Protestants if they criticized Catholic shortcomings with respect to race relations. "American Catholics may reply, with historical truth, that the drastic North American racial pattern is none of their own creation," LaFarge instructed. "It was laid by persons of other faiths," he continued, "and is out of harmony with the principles and traditions of the Catholic Church."[39]

37. Much of this paragraph, including quotations, comes from J. Douglas Thomas, "A Century of American Catholic History," *U.S. Catholic Historian*, 6 (Winter, 1987), 25–49. Shea, Guilday, and Ellis also stressed the compatibility of Catholicism and Americanism, but see David O'Brien, *Public Catholicism*, 126, 220, and Gannon, "Before and After Modernism," in *Catholic Priest*, ed. John Ellis, 297, on duality in Catholicism.
38. Ireland, quoted in Marty, *Invitation to American Catholic History*, 132–33.
39. See, for example, the following works by John LaFarge: "The Survival of the Catholic Faith in Maryland," *Catholic Historical Review*, 21 (April, 1935), 14–15; *No*

Several other Catholic spokesmen echoed the charge that American racism was the product of "rank Calvinism," and they assured Catholics that their church had "nothing in its racial record of which to be ashamed." Even John Dorsey, one of five black priests in America in the 1920s, admitted that he told black Catholics that racism did not exist in the church. The Reverend John Cooper, an anthropologist at Catholic University, was exceptional in rejecting such apologetics. In 1934 he wrote, "There have been few blacker blots on Christian history than our comparative failure to prevent, combat, and uproot Negro slavery." [40]

Both secular historians and post–Vatican II Catholic scholars have now thoroughly documented the church's complicity in the enslavement of black Africans. From medieval times Christian Rome considered all non-Christians fair game for bondage, regardless of complexion. In 1452 Pope Nicholas V gave the king of Portugal power "to despoil and sell into slavery all Moslems, heathen and other foes of Christ." Although several popes subsequently condemned the slave trade, the Catholic church never treated slavery itself as a sin; nor did abolition enter into Catholic dogma as the antislavery movement swept across the liberal West in the nineteenth century. In truth, the church recognized "just servitude" and found slavery compatible with natural law, requiring only that Catholics treat slaves humanely and give them religious instruction and the appropriate sacraments. The 1852 Plenary Council of American bishops confronted the slavery issue with resounding silence. According to the historian Randall Miller, "The Church won social and political acceptance in the South by sanctifying the secular order of slavery and states' rights." Although Roger Taney, the Catholic chief justice of the United States, declared in the 1857 *Dred Scott* decision that blacks "had no rights which the white man was

---

Postponement: U.S. Moral Leadership and the Problem of Racial Minorities (New York, 1950), 132, 142–46; *The Catholic Viewpoint on Race Relations* (Garden City, N.Y., 1956), 53; "Doing the Truth," *IR,* 7 (March, 1934), 33; and "The Humility of St. Martin de Porres," *IR,* 35 (September, 1962), 204–207.

40. William L. Portier, "John R. Slattery's Vision for the Evangelization of American Blacks," *U.S. Catholic Historian,* 5 (Winter, 1986), 38; John T. Gillard, S.S.J., "The Negro Looks to Rome," *Commonweal,* 21 (December 14, 1934), 195; John T. Gillard, S.S.J., *Colored Catholics in the United States* (Baltimore, 1941), 56; Ochs, *Desegregating the Altar,* 241; John M. Cooper, "Christ and the Other Sheep," *Ecclesiastical Review,* 90 (May, 1934), 455.

bound to respect," LaFarge had great respect for the Maryland jurist, once describing him as "saintly" and "truly noble-hearted."[41]

Although many Catholics have argued that slavery in Catholic countries was more benign than in Protestant nations, the evidence indicates that Catholics in the United States treated their slaves no better than did non-Catholics.[42] In addition, Carl N. Degler argues in his comparative study of Catholic Brazil and the generally Protestant United States that "Brazilian slavery was physically harsher than North American." Furthermore, the slaves of Catholic masters in North America often had no access to clergy and received no religious instruction. Despite significant differences in law and culture, it seems that slavery was equally oppressive in Catholic and non-Catholic countries.[43]

What distinguished the Catholic practice of slavery most dramatically from the Protestant was that the Catholic church itself owned slaves. The Protestant clergy in the South could rightly plead that they

41. Nicholas V, quoted in Louis Ruchames, "The Sources of Racial Thought in Colonial America," *Journal of Negro History,* 52 (October, 1967), 253; Wood, *Arrogance of Faith,* 357; Madeleine Hooke Rice, *American Catholic Opinion in the Slavery Controversy* (1944; rpr. Gloucester, Mass., 1964), 152; Randall M. Miller, "Slaves and Southern Catholicism," in *Masters and Slaves in the House of the Lord: Race and Religion in the American South, 1740–1870,* ed. John B. Boles (Lexington, Ky., 1988), 130; bishops, quoted in Guilday, ed., *National Pastorals,* 154, 192; Wood, *Arrogance of Faith,* 358–60; Randall M. Miller, "A Church in Cultural Captivity: Some Speculations on Catholic Identity in the Old South," in *Catholics in the Old South,* ed. Miller and Wakelyn, 14; Taney, quoted in Richard H. Sewell, *A House Divided: Sectionalism and Civil War, 1848–1865* (Baltimore, 1988), 58; John LaFarge, "American Catholics and the Negro, 1962," *Social Order,* 12 (April, 1962), 154.

42. Wood, *Arrogance of Faith,* 356–57; Rice, *American Catholic Opinion,* 41–43; Maria Genoino Caravaglios, *The American Catholic Church and the Negro Problem in the XVIII–XIX Centuries* (Rome, 1974), 74; Randall M. Miller, "The Failed Mission: The Catholic Church and Black Catholics in the Old South," in *Catholics in the Old South,* ed. Miller and Wakelyn, 160.

43. Carl N. Degler, *Neither Black nor White: Slavery and Race Relations in Brazil and the United States* (New York, 1971), 69. Two earlier works that argued slavery was more humane in Latin America are: Frank Tannenbaum, *Slave and Citizen: The Negro in the Americas* (New York, 1947), and Stanley Elkins, *Slavery: A Problem in American Institutional and Intellectual Life* (Chicago, 1959). For arguments to the contrary, see, in addition to Degler, Winthrop D. Jordan, *White over Black: American Attitudes Toward the Negro, 1550–1812* (Chapel Hill, N.C., 1968), 198–99, 604–606; David Brion Davis, *The Problem of Slavery in Western Culture* (Ithaca, N.Y., 1966), 223–61; and Marvin Harris, *Patterns of Race in the Americas* (New York, 1964), 65–78.

had no power over their parishioners. But the Vatican and the hierarchy claimed ultimate power and therefore had ultimate responsibility in the matter of slavery. John Carroll of Maryland, the first archbishop in America, had many slaves. Moreover, several religious orders and dioceses owned slaves.[44] It was an embarrassment to LaFarge that his religious order had been one of the largest slaveholders in Maryland. LaFarge and other apologists coped with this difficulty by stressing the kindness of Jesuit slaveholders and by suggesting that the priests eventually sold the slaves for religious reasons.[45]

The true story is somewhat different. The Maryland Jesuits, who controlled five large estates of about twelve thousand acres and owned some 300 slaves, sold 272 blacks in 1838. The main reason for the sale was not religious principle but the poor management and debt of the Jesuit estates. Reports by Catholic investigators revealed that the Jesuits neglected their slaves both physically and spiritually. In 1821 a Jesuit observer said that the slave quarters were "almost unfit for human beings to live in." The sale of the slaves, however, created more scandal, for the Jesuits sold the slaves to Protestant planters in Louisiana, and the sale caused the breakup of slave families, thereby going against orders from Rome to keep families together. Thomas Mulledy, the Maryland provincial, was called to Rome and chastised by the Jesuit general for his handling of the sale. He remained in Rome for three years of rehabilitation before he returned to the states. The Jesuits, however, found good use for the $115,000 gained from the sale of the slaves. Some of the money was used for church pensions and retirement of the Georgetown College debt, but the bulk of it, $90,000, was invested in Jesuit training.[46]

In any case, the Catholic hierarchy continued to treat the slavery question as a nonmoral issue. The noted Catholic historians Guilday and Ellis hailed the church's neutrality on the moral issue of slavery a

44. Wood, *Arrogance of Faith*, 355, 357; Cyprian Davis, *History of Black Catholics*, 38–39, 72, 82, 116.

45. See, for example, Edward D. Reynolds, S.J., *Jesuits for the Negro* (New York, 1949), 36–43.

46. R. Emmett Curran, S.J., "Splendid Poverty: Jesuit Slaveholding in Maryland, 1805–1838," in *Catholics in the Old South*, ed. Miller and Wakelyn, 125–46. See also Miller, "Slaves and Southern Catholicism," *ibid.*, 129; Cyprian Davis, *History of Black Catholics*, 36–37; Wood, *Arrogance of Faith*, 356; and Thomas Spalding, *Premier See*, 6, 113.

wise choice because it allowed Catholicism to escape the divisive fate of the Protestant churches. The threat of schism in American Catholicism, however, was slight. Southern bishops and clergy readily parroted the proslavery arguments of the Old South, and their northern counterparts tended to view slavery as a "necessary evil." Clearly, northern Catholics were more concerned about the positive evils of anti-Catholic abolitionists in the Know-Nothing and Republican parties. Many abolitionists equated slavery and "priestcraft" as similar kinds of human bondage, except that one was physical, one psychological. William Lloyd Garrison, the leading abolitionist editor, described Irish Catholics as a "mighty obstacle in the way of negro emancipation." The assertive John Hughes, the immigrant archbishop of New York from 1850 to 1864, gave some credence to these abolitionist charges. Not only did Hughes call Protestants "infidels" and "heretics," but he spoke against the emancipation of the "big Black beast." In 1863 the *Metropolitan Record,* New York's archdiocesan newspaper, asked why white men were dying for blacks, a race of people who could not "escape the primal curse put upon them." No doubt, such talk helped incite many New York Catholics against blacks. In 1863 in the so-called draft riots, Irishmen rose up and killed scores of innocent African Americans.[47]

Given the overwhelming domination of Protestants in the South and the dearth of Catholic abolitionists, it is little wonder that there were probably no more than 100,000 to 200,000 black Catholics in the United States at the end of the Civil War. About three-fourths of these Catholics were located in Maryland and Louisiana. Catholic slavemasters fared poorly in holding or converting blacks. Unlike in the Protestant churches, there were no black preachers in the Catholic church. Slaves tended to identify with black preachers and emotional, song-filled Protestant worship. Many nominal black Catholics deserted the

47. Peter Guilday, *A History of the Councils of Baltimore* (New York, 1932), 169–70; John Tracy Ellis, ed., *Documents of American Catholic History* (2nd ed.; Milwaukee, Wisc., 1962), 378–83; Ochs, *Desegregating the Altar,* 18; Rice, *American Catholic Opinion,* 120–21; Garrison, quoted in Tyler Anbinder, *Nativism and Slavery: The Northern Know Nothings and the Politics of the 1850s* (New York, 1992), 45; Hughes, quoted in Ochs, *Desegregating the Altar,* 32, and Anbinder, *Nativism and Slavery,* 112; *Metropolitan Record,* quoted in John C. Murphy, *An Analysis of the Attitudes of American Catholics Toward the Immigrant and the Negro, 1825–1925* (Washington, D.C., 1940), 49–51, 53; Wood, *Arrogance of Faith,* 363.

church and, as one servant put it, joined the "American religion" of Protestantism. Whites in the North treated the tiny minority of black Catholics, if they were aware of their existence, with cold suspicion or indifference, and black Protestants looked on them as a curiosity. The Irish scorned blacks because the latter were Republican and Protestant and competed with the Irish for menial jobs; blacks were hostile to the Irish because they were Democrats opposed to emancipation. Until the second half of the twentieth century, most blacks thought of the Catholic church as a "white man's church."[48]

Martin J. Spalding, the archbishop of Baltimore, wanted to change the church's image and convert blacks. In late 1865 Spalding wrote to Archbishop John McCloskey of New York that the status of blacks was ripe for discussion by the American hierarchy at the upcoming Second Plenary Council. In a memorable statement Spalding penned the following: "It is a golden opportunity for reaping a harvest of souls, which neglected may not return."[49] Born to a slaveholding family in Kentucky, Spalding was the former bishop of Louisville and a supporter of the Confederacy. During the Civil War he told the Roman Congregation of the Propaganda that liberated blacks "ordinarily became miserable vagabonds, drunkards, and thieves." In spite of these views, Archbishop Spalding was sincerely interested in winning black souls. The archbishop, who was named the apostolic delegate for the Second Plenary Council, put before the American hierarchy a plan backed by the Roman Curia that called for the evangelization of African Americans. The plan included a special bishop or apostolic delegate to oversee all mission activity among blacks. Besides increased missionary work for blacks, Spalding wanted the bishops to discuss more "Negro sisterhoods," a special collection for black missions, and separate parishes for blacks.[50]

The post–Civil War council faced grave problems in administering a chaotic and rapidly growing church. Despite these problems, toward

48. Ochs, *Desegregating the Altar,* 20–22; Miller, "Slaves and Southern Catholicism," in *Masters and Slaves,* ed. Boles, 131–44; Cyprian Davis, *History of Black Catholics,* 58–59; Wood, *Arrogance of Faith,* 363; Dolan, *American Catholic Experience,* 360.

49. Spalding, quoted in Cyprian Davis, *History of Black Catholics,* 117–18.

50. Ochs, *Desegregating the Altar,* 38–39. Two struggling black sisterhoods were established in 1829 and 1842 (pp. 23–26), the Oblate Sisters and the Sisters of the Holy Family, respectively. These poor relatives of the church often taught in black schools and worked in black orphanages.

the end of the council the bishops devoted an extraordinary session to the race issue. In this stormy session, the bishops vehemently rejected most of Spalding's recommended changes. Archbishop Peter Kenrick of St. Louis threatened to resign if a special bishop was appointed to oversee racial missions. Bishop John Quinlan of Mobile, Alabama, said he could do nothing for "heretical Negroes." Archbishop McCloskey of New York objected to a special collection that would go mostly to southern dioceses. In the end the bishops reached a consensus on only three ideas in regard to African Americans: that "sudden liberation" had been a mistake for blacks because they had "peculiar dispositions and habits" and were in considerable need of "moral restraint"; that greater pastoral care for blacks was needed; and that each bishop should be in complete command of his diocese. The bishops pleaded for European missionaries "through the bowels of mercy" to devote their lives to African Americans.[51]

The harvest of souls that Archbishop Spalding hoped for did not materialize. The growth of black Catholics in America from 1865 to 1940 was exceedingly slow. Thousands of blacks abandoned the Catholic church after the Civil War. One study indicated that 65,000 blacks left the church in just one section of Louisiana immediately following the war. In 1940 only about 300,000 black Catholics resided in America. When Father John E. Burke reported on blacks to the apostolic delegate in 1913, he opined that since the Civil War the church had lost more blacks than it had gained. From 1865 to the mid-1920s, the percentage of black Catholics in the overall black population dropped from 4 to 2 percent.[52]

Former slaves flocked to the African Methodist Episcopal and the African Methodist Episcopal Zion churches, congregations formed in the North in the early nineteenth century. After 1865, southern blacks

51. Cyprian Davis, *History of Black Catholics*, 119, 120, 122; "Transcript of Second Plenary Council," typescript of Josephite News Letter, November–January 1966–67, in Josephite Archives, Baltimore; Caravaglios, *American Catholic Church*, 209; Guilday, ed., *National Pastorals*, 221.

52. Albert J. Raboteau, "Black Catholics: A Capsule History," *Catholic Digest* (June, 1983), 37; Miller, "Failed Mission," in *Catholics in the Old South*, ed. Miller and Wakelyn, 168; Cyprian Davis, "The Holy See and American Black Catholics: A Forgotten Chapter in the History of the American Church," *U.S. Catholic Historian*, 7 (Spring–Summer, 1988), 175; John E. Burke, "Our Negro Mission Field," *Am*, 30 (March 15, 1924), 534.

founded new churches, largely Baptist and Methodist. By 1890 only slightly more than a tenth of blacks remained in white-dominated Protestant churches, also mainly Baptist and Methodist. These churches, however, engaged in large-scale missionary activity in the South after the Civil War. The American Missionary Association (AMA), largely financed by the Congregational church, spent $7 million on blacks before 1890. It opened several schools of higher education for blacks, including Atlanta and Fisk Universities, Hampton Institute, and Talladega and Tougaloo Colleges. By the mid-1880s the AMA supported fifty-seven schools and eight colleges. One-half of all blacks in college in 1940 were in mainline Protestant institutions. Occasionally, frustrated priests in the black apostolate pointed out the Protestant achievements in black education and welfare in order to stir Catholics to greater efforts. In 1924, for instance, the Jesuit magazine *America* noted that the Methodists alone had nineteen high schools, professional schools, and colleges for blacks.[53]

All told, Catholic efforts on behalf of African Americans before World War I were minimal and their achievements puny. The historian James Hennesey summed it up in this manner: "Neither the official church nor individual Catholics were outspoken in their zeal for racial justice." Exceptional individuals such as John Boyle O'Reilly, editor of the Boston *Pilot,* and Archbishop Ireland stepped forth and spoke out against racism in the church in this period. For the most part, though, the hierarchy and clergy primarily addressed the concerns of the immigrant church in the urban centers of the North and paid scant attention to blacks, 90 percent of whom lived in the heavily rural areas of the South.[54]

The only religious congregation exclusively devoted to the evangelization of African Americans was the Josephites, or the Mill Hill Fathers of England, founded in 1866 by the Reverend Herbert Vaughan (later a cardinal). Five Josephites, Vaughan and four priests, arrived in Baltimore in 1871 in answer to the appeal of the Second Plenary Council for black missions. The Josephite congregation barely survived its

53. Ochs, *Desegregating the Altar,* 34–35; David W. Wills, "An Enduring Distance: Black Americans and the Establishment," 170, and Dorothy C. Bass, "Ministry on the Margin: Protestants and Education," 56, both in *Between the Times,* ed. William Hutchinson; "The Great Task of Negro Education," *Am,* 30 (March 1, 1924), 486.

54. Hennesey, *American Catholics,* 193.

first decade in America. Three of four Josephites died in the first year. Lack of manpower, internal divisions, hierarchical apathy (even hostility), and widespread racism plagued the group. Only the brilliant, dynamic leadership of the Irishman John R. Slattery rescued the Josephites.[55]

Born in 1851 in New York to affluent parents, Slattery attended public schools and the City College of New York before he entered St. Charles College, a preparatory Sulpician seminary. An eye problem forced him to withdraw from the seminary, and upon recovery he enrolled at Columbia University to study law. But after hearing Father Vaughan preach about the black missions in 1872, Slattery was off to Mill Hill, a suburb of London, to prepare for entry into the Josephites. In 1878 Vaughan appointed Slattery the American provincial. A brilliant administrator, Slattery kept the undermanned, underfinanced order from dissolution. In 1893 the American Josephites separated from their English cousins, and Slattery became the first superior general of the American congregation during one of the worst decades in American race relations. The 1890s witnessed the segregation, disfranchisement, and wholesale lynching of blacks: 169 blacks died at the hands of vigilantes in 1892.[56]

The successes of the Josephites under Slattery did not come easily. In 1893 there were but five Josephites, the same as in 1871. They suffered constant insults (they were often called "nigger priests") and neglect from the hierarchy. The Third Plenary Council, which met in Baltimore in 1884 under the guidance of Archbishop Gibbons, failed to act decisively on the race issue. One action it did take, however, aided the Josephites. The council approved an annual collection for blacks and Indians and set up a Negro and Indian Commission composed of two bishops. The first five years of the special collection brought in $361,000 or about one cent per Catholic per year.[57]

Early in his ministry Slattery concluded that no harvest of black souls was possible until the church had a black clergy. The Second and Third Plenary Councils flatly turned down plans for a black priesthood. Bishops did not want blacks in their seminaries and would not

55. J. G. Snead-Cox, *The Life of Cardinal Vaughan* (2 vols.; St. Louis, 1910), I, 168–78; Ochs, *Desegregating the Altar,* 3, 37, 43–51.

56. Ochs, *Desegregating the Altar,* 84–85; Southern, *Malignant Heritage,* 11.

57. Ochs, *Desegregating the Altar,* 36, 62–63.

place them in their dioceses if they received holy orders. Many saw the black priest as a threat to white supremacy. To elevate a black man to the priesthood of Christ with all the respect and prestige attached thereto, it was thought, could lead to social equality and race mixing. The lack of black priests not only worked against the conversion of blacks; it also bred paternalism among the white clergy, who supposedly spoke for blacks, and tended to instill docility in the black laity. There were no Catholic Nat Turners or Frederick Douglasses in the nineteenth century.[58]

Slattery set to work with his usual dynamism and established an integrated Josephite feeder college and seminary in Baltimore. The first black Josephite, Charles Randolph Uncles, was ordained in 1891. Only four black American priests had preceded Uncles. Three of them were the Healy brothers: James, Alexander, and Patrick. These extremely light-skinned mulattoes were born slaves on a Georgia plantation, products of an Irishman and his black common-law wife. The Healy brothers did not identify with African Americans and were seldom perceived as black. The first dark-skinned African American to receive holy orders was Augustine Tolton, who was born a slave in Missouri in 1854. Tolton was ordained in 1886 and held pastorates in Illinois in Quincy and Chicago. Like the preparations for the Healy brothers, his seminary training and ordination took place abroad.[59]

The ordination of Father Uncles was a fine start for Slattery, but the quest for a black priesthood was in part undermined by his own paternalism. Although, strictly speaking, Slattery did not believe in the intellectual inferiority of blacks, he believed that slavery and cultural conditioning had caused blacks to have less "moral restraint" than whites. His ambivalence about blacks could be seen in the derisive terms he used for the minority—terms such as "Sambo" and "Deriah." Far from practicing affirmative action, Slattery applied a tougher standard to black seminarians than to white. Because he doubted the ability of young black men to remain chaste, he would not let them enter the seminary until age thirty, five years later than for whites. Moreover, black seminarians would have their study interrupted for field work, during which more observation of their moral conduct could be un-

58. *Ibid.*, 3–4, 10–11; Miller, "Failed Mission," in *Catholics in the Old South,* ed. Miller and Wakelyn, 149–50.

59. Ochs, *Desegregating the Altar*, 10, 64, 78–79.

dertaken by white overseers. An admirer of Booker T. Washington, Slattery deemphasized black rights, urged "patient forebearance" by blacks, and told them to "leave politics alone."[60]

Still, there was explosive opposition to Slattery's struggle for a black clergy. In addition, the three black priests that Slattery started on their way to ordination had stormy and, ultimately, tragic careers. Finally, the condemnation of Americanism by Pope Leo XIII in 1899 drove Slattery, an ardent Americanist, to despair. In 1904 he left the church and became a full-fledged modernist. In 1906 he wrote in the *Independent* magazine, "If anything in this world is certain, it is that the stand of the Catholic Church toward the negro is sheer dishonesty."[61]

Slattery's apostasy almost caused the dissolution of the Josephites. Between 1907, when the last of Slattery's protégés was ordained, and World War II, the Josephites did not raise one black to the priesthood. When Father Uncles died in 1933, there were only two black priests in the entire United States. By 1945 the figure had risen to only twenty-one. By contrast, the tiny Episcopal church, the denomination most similar to the Catholic church in structure and doctrine, was able to raise eighty-six blacks to the priesthood between 1866 and 1900.[62]

From the Civil War through World War II, the trend was toward segregation in the Catholic church. Missionary efforts by religious orders such as the Josephites actually hastened the trend. More and more, Jim Crow parishes replaced Jim Crow pews in white-dominated churches. Increasing hostility between the races after the Civil War led many blacks to request separate churches. Racial parishes coincided with the establishment of ethnic parishes that accommodated various nationalities such as Germans, Italians, and Poles. Sometimes Catholics used the terms "race" and "nationality" interchangeably. The Second Plenary Council of 1866 allowed racial parishes as an expedient, but they became increasingly the rule after the 1890s. Unlike the black Protestant churches, however, black Catholics almost never had a black pastor.[63]

60. *Ibid.*, 70, 80, 88, 93, 113–14, 118, 133, 152–62, 169–70, *passim;* Cyprian Davis, *History of Black Catholics*, 145–62.

61. Ochs, *Desegregating the Altar*, 74–75, 89, 121–33.

62. *Ibid.*, 37, 78–79, 135, 144–62, 164–75, 194–97, 318–19, 398, 456–57.

63. Cyprian Davis, *History of Black Catholics*, 159; Labbe, *Jim Crow Comes to*

The fate of most black Catholics was in the hands of racist or accommodating southern bishops and paternalistic religious orders. Cardinal Gibbons, the preeminent prelate from the 1880s until his death in 1921, was a paternalist who viewed blacks as members of a lower order of being. In a eulogy for the black Josephite priest John Plantevigne, he challenged blacks to prove themselves "worthy of love and respect." Gibbons, in alliance with other prominent bishops, thwarted several attempts by the Vatican to raise the status of blacks in the church.[64]

Certain individuals, to be sure, tried to reverse the un-Catholic behavior of the church in the area of race relations. Speaking at St. Augustine's in Washington, D.C., Bishop Ireland proclaimed, "No church is a fit temple of God where a man because of his color is excluded or made to occupy a corner." Ireland's influence helped Stephen Theobald, an African American, receive seminary training, ordination, and a pastorate in St. Paul, Minnesota. Katharine Drexel, who was beatified in 1988, devoted her life to the betterment of blacks and Indians after an 1891 audience with the pope. The daughter of a textile mogul, Drexel inherited a fortune and spent a large part of it funding the congregation she founded, the Sisters of the Blessed Sacrament for Indians and Colored People. Her younger sister, Louise Drexel (later Mrs. Edward Morrell), also became a generous benefactor of African American projects. Mother Katharine Drexel opened Xavier University in New Orleans in 1931, the first Catholic school of higher education for blacks.[65]

But blacks could not depend on the kindness of a few isolated white Catholics to purge the church of racial discrimination. Nor could black

---

Church, 1–16, 18–19, 34–37, 69, 82–84; Dolan, *American Catholic Experience,* 365–66; Jamie T. Phelps, O.P., "John R. Slattery's Missionary Strategies," *U.S Catholic Historian,* 7 (Spring–Summer, 1988), 204–205; John McGreevy, " 'Race' and Twentieth Century American Catholic Culture," *Cushwa Working Papers,* University of Notre Dame, Series 24, No. 4 (Spring, 1993), 14–17.

64. Gibbons, quoted in Ochs, *Desegregating the Altar,* 174, 266; William A. Osborne, "The Race Problem in the Catholic Church in the United States: Between the Time of the Second Plenary Council (1866) and the Founding of the Catholic Interracial Council of New York (1934)" (Ph.D. dissertation, Columbia University, 1953), 175–80.

65. Ireland, quoted in John Paul Muffler, "This Far by Faith: A History of St. Augustine's, the Mother Church for Black Catholics in the Nation's Capital" (Ph.D. dissertation, Columbia University, 1989), 153; Ochs, *Desegregating the Altar,* 163, 276; LaFarge, *Catholic Viewpoint,* 57; Cyprian Davis, *History of Black Catholics,* 135–36, 254.

Catholics depend on a black clergy that was virtually nonexistent; it therefore devolved upon the black laity to fill the leadership gap. In the nineteenth century Daniel Rudd stood out as a trailblazer in black lay leadership. Born in 1854 to Catholic slaves in Bardstown, Kentucky, Rudd moved to Springfield, Ohio, after the Civil War. In 1886 he began a weekly newspaper called the *Ohio State Tribune*, retitled the *American Catholic Tribune* a year later. Rudd was a devout Catholic and church loyalist who endeavored to tie the destiny of American blacks to "Holy Mother Church." He felt compelled to "refute the slander" that the Catholic church was "inimical to the negro race." Hailing Catholicism as a "true friend" of African Americans, he declared, "The Catholic Church alone can break the color line." [66]

Despite his intense loyalty to the church, Rudd was not uncritical. He took issue with racist acts by white Catholics and spoke out against lynching and the spread of segregation. Rudd also promoted "race pride" and black politicians. He was as proud of his color as he was of his church. A frequent lecturer throughout the Midwest, South, and the East, Rudd spread his message widely. In 1888 he first publicized the idea of holding a national black congress to unite black Catholics to "take up the cause of race." With the approval of Archbishop William Henry Elder of Cincinnati, Cardinal Gibbons, Father Slattery, and even Pope Leo XIII, Rudd and his allies scheduled a black congress for January 1 through 4, 1889, in Washington, D.C. Although national black congresses originated in the 1830s, Protestant ministers dominated the antebellum conventions. Lacking a black clergy, Catholics lagged behind black Protestants in political activity. Nevertheless, the five Catholic African American Congresses that met from 1889 through 1894 constituted a remarkable first step toward establishing an authentic black voice in American Catholicism. [67]

The first black Catholic congress was enthusiastic and joyful. About a hundred delegates met in one of the oldest and proudest black parishes in the land, St. Augustine's, and heard addresses by Cardinal Gibbons, Archbishop Elder, and Father Slattery, the last speaking on "The Negro in the Priesthood." Also speaking to the congress was the

66. Cyprian Davis, *History of Black Catholics*, 164–66.
67. *Ibid.*, 163, 166–73; David Spalding, C.F.X., "The Negro Catholic Congresses, 1889–1894," *Catholic Historical Review*, 55 (October, 1969), 353; Thomas Spalding, *Premier See*, 287.

first recognized black priest in America, Augustine Tolton. The tremendous enthusiasm for Tolton belied the myth that blacks preferred white priests. In a statement drawn up at the end of the congress, the delegates described the event as a "humble experiment" that they hoped would be "an entering wedge" in breaking the wall of color prejudice. The delegates called for more schools, hospitals, orphanages, jobs, and better housing but did not criticize the church directly. Blacks emerged from the congress in an optimistic mood, and they topped off the affair by meeting with President Grover Cleveland in the White House.[68]

In the next four congresses, held at Cincinnati, Philadelphia, Chicago, and Baltimore, a slow but perceptible radicalization of the delegates occurred. Even so, the Catholic conclave still sounded obsequious at times, such as when it declared that the existence of two black priests in the United States illustrated the "divine truth of Catholic religion." According to black historian Cyprian Davis, there also emerged at the congresses something approaching a "black theological consciousness." Significantly, the congresses unveiled a number of well-educated and talented black Catholic leaders and gave them a forum in which to express their ideas. In the fourth black congress, which was held in conjunction with the second general American Catholic lay congress, Charles N. Butler, an employee of the Treasury Department, spoke out boldly for "civil equality." In fact, as the congresses continued, condemnations of Catholic racism escalated. The delegates established a Committee of Grievances in 1891, and in 1894 it sent letters of protest to American bishops and routed a protest message to the pope through the first apostolic delegate. By the final congress Slattery was so alarmed at the increasingly militant protest that he implored the delegates to trust "time and silence" and to shun haste and anger.[69]

Perhaps the most interesting revelation emanating from the five black Catholic congresses and the two general lay congresses between 1889 and 1894 is that even the most liberal among the hierarchy and clergy feared lay activity, whether black or white. Cardinal Gibbons, Archbishop Ireland, and Father Slattery all reacted negatively to the progressive boldness of the lay congresses. It is not clear if the Vatican put an end to these congresses, but it is unmistakable that the American

68. Cyprian Davis, *History of Black Catholics,* 163, 173–74; Ochs, *Desegregating the Altar,* 77.
69. Cyprian Davis, *History of Black Catholics,* 175–94.

hierarchy wanted no more of them. Worn down by the opposition, Rudd ceased to publish the *American Catholic Tribune* in 1899 and settled down in obscurity in Arkansas.[70] The condemnation of Americanism by Leo XIII in the same year, combined with Pius X's attempt to exorcise modernism from Catholicism less than a decade later, amounted to a left hook and a right cross on the jaw of progressive thinking in the church.

Although historians have labeled the first two decades of the twentieth century the Progressive Era, it marked the nadir for African Americans. The progressive presidents Theodore Roosevelt and Woodrow Wilson acted on the premise that blacks were innately inferior to whites, and most progressives joined the racist and imperialistic stampede of the early twentieth century. In Europe the credo of the "white man's burden" resonated loudly, and the intellectual groundwork for Nazism was being laid. The world at the turn of the century and after was truly obsessed with color and race.[71]

The condition of blacks at the turn of the century stimulated Thomas Wyatt Turner, a devout Catholic, to fight racism with all the more determination. Born into a poor Catholic family in southern Maryland in 1877, Turner attended the black public schools for eight years. He then entered an Episcopalian secondary school for blacks in St. Mary's County, the center of the Jesuit missions but an area without parish schools for blacks or whites. After finishing preparatory school, Turner was offered a scholarship by Lincoln University in Pennsylvania, with the stipulation that he become an Episcopalian. Refusing the offer, he walked penniless to Howard University in Washington, D.C. He entered Howard in 1897 and graduated in 1901, the same years that the slightly younger LaFarge attended Harvard. Turner enrolled for graduate study at Catholic University, which had not yet adopted a policy of excluding blacks, but he was short on money, so he had to drop his plans for graduate school in favor of teaching high school science in Baltimore. In 1913 Turner returned to Washington, D.C., and took a job as professor of biology at Howard. While there, he

---

70. *Ibid.,* 193, 214; Hennesey, *American Catholics,* 190–92; David O'Brien, *Public Catholicism,* 114–15.

71. Southern, *Malignant Heritage,* 82–85. For a classic statement on the race problem as the problem of the age, see W. E. B. Du Bois, *The Souls of Black Folk* (1903; rpr. New York, 1961).

continued his studies in biology and completed his doctorate at Cornell University in 1921. In 1924 he moved from Howard to Hampton Institute in Virginia, where he would teach until retirement.[72]

Growing up in southern Maryland, Turner acquired a strong aversion to racial discrimination. As a child he had learned the ideal of color blindness from a nearby Quaker family. Often moving in a non-Catholic black world made him bolder than most cloistered Catholics, black or white. In 1895 he reverently attended the funeral of Frederick Douglass, the militant black integrationist. In 1912 he successfully sued the Chesapeake and Atlantic Railroad for putting him, a first-class ticket holder, in a Jim Crow smoking car. While a high school teacher, he became the secretary of the original branch of the Baltimore NAACP. Returning to Washington, D.C., as President Wilson took office, he opened a membership drive for the NAACP in the capital city. At this time he strongly believed that the hierarchy and the clergy would purge racism from the Catholic church. When Wilson and his southern advisers began to segregate federal bureaucracies in Washington, D.C., in 1913, Turner dashed off a letter to Cardinal Gibbons, asking him to send a letter of protest to the president. Gibbons politely refused his request, prompting the black educator to take up his pen again and write two protest articles for the *Missionary* in 1915 and 1916. In them Turner expressed his dissatisfaction with the church's refusal to provide a Catholic education for blacks, especially beyond the elementary level. He experienced this firsthand when a student of his was turned away at Catholic University because of his race.[73]

During World War I Turner was particularly offended by the overt racism that permeated the nation's military mobilization. He learned that not only were American troops segregated by color but there was no agency designated to assist black Catholic servicemen. The Young Men's Christian Association (YMCA) and the Young Women's Christian Association (YWCA) served Protestants, and the Knights of Columbus catered only to white Catholics. Nor did the newly formed National Catholic War Council have any black representation on it. These facts galvanized a group of five blacks to schedule meetings at

72. Nickels, "Thomas Wyatt Turner," 216–17. See also Nickels, *Black Catholic Protest,* 19–22.

73. Unpublished autobiography of Thomas Wyatt Turner, 13, 50, 52, 68, and "Legal Actions," both in Turner Papers; Nickels, *Black Catholic Protest,* 22–27.

Turner's home to discuss the situation. By 1917 the group had grown, and it began to call itself the "Committee of Fifteen." The committee set forth a broad agenda, the essential elements being to bring a closer union among all black Catholics, to eradicate all obstacles that kept blacks from enjoying the "full temporal graces" of the church, to secure for blacks equal opportunity for educational, economic, and spiritual programs, and to raise the status of black Catholics. The committee further requested admission to the Knights of Columbus and the National Catholic War Council.[74]

By 1919 Turner's group had broadened its name to the Committee for the Advancement of Colored Catholics. Taking advantage of the new annual meetings of the American hierarchy, the committee sent the bishops a long letter protesting racism in the church in general and specifying areas in which it desired change. The members also sought, unsuccessfully, an audience with the apostolic delegate in hopes that he would relay their concerns to the Vatican. High on the committee's priorities were black education, the raising of a black clergy, acceptance of blacks at Catholic University, more money for black welfare, and representation of blacks on all church boards affecting the opportunities of African Americans. The ad hoc committee also pointed out how much more non-Catholics were doing for blacks and stressed the idea that only blacks could adequately assess their own needs.[75]

In its communication with the bishops, the committee singled out the Josephites for excluding blacks from their seminary. Turner wrote a strong letter to the rector of the seminary, the Reverend E. R. Dyer, who flatly admitted the exclusion of blacks and blamed southern bishops for the policy. Dyer exclaimed, "It is a condition not a theory which confronts us." Dyer's response to Turner documented the astonishing racism at every level of the church. Turner replied that it was unreasonable to expect blacks to respect bishops or clergy who denied Catholic teachings of universal brotherhood. Turner also questioned whether the bishops had the luxury of accommodating unreasoning bigots in the church. Dyer, stung by Turner's criticism of bishops, shifted his argument in a follow-up letter and blamed prejudiced white seminarians for black exclusion. Turner followed up with a passionate

74. Nickels, *Black Catholic Protest,* 31–32.
75. Nickels, "Thomas Wyatt Turner," 221–22.

condemnation of the "sin of race prejudice," a position that white liberals such as LaFarge would not take for another fifteen years.[76]

The indictment of the Josephites by black Catholics led to a long and acrimonious debate between the two groups that stretched into the 1930s, a feud that eventually involved LaFarge. Louis B. Pastorelli, the superior general of the Josephites from 1918 to 1942, made sure that no black Josephites were ordained. At the same time, he engaged in "stonewalling, half-truths, and carefully planned counterattacks" in order to deny it; and Cardinal Gibbons supported Pastorelli's antiblack actions.[77]

Despite such setbacks, Turner pressed onward. He heeded the advice of the black priest John Dorsey to "Agitate, Agitate!" As a southern black, Turner could feel the subtlest racism in his bones, and the overt cases occurred frequently enough to stoke his indignation. Traveling to a science convention in Kansas City, Missouri, right after World War I, Turner stopped in St. Louis for Sunday mass. An usher rudely directed him to a pew in the back of the church.[78]

Such events convinced Turner that a permanent organization was needed to combat racism in the church. In late December of 1924 Turner and his allies turned their ad hoc committee into the FCC, which held its first annual convention a year later and elected Turner as its president. Essentially, the FCC continued to promote the agenda the wartime committee had originated. After 1925 the black organization directed mountains of correspondence to the hierarchy and the clergy, complaining of racist snubs and calling for more Catholic education for blacks and for more black priests. Father LaFarge initially supported the FCC, and the FCC supported LaFarge's most important project in Maryland, the Cardinal Gibbons Institute.[79]

How much impact did the black congresses of the late nineteenth century and the agitation of Turner and his wartime committee have on American Catholicism? Undoubtedly, the greatest impact was on black Catholics. The lively and hopeful congresses from 1889 to 1894

76. *Ibid.*, 225; Nickels, *Black Catholic Protest*, 28–29; Phelps, "Slattery's Missionary Strategies," 205; Ochs, *Desegregating the Altar*, 229–30.

77. Ochs, *Desegregating the Altar*, 214–15, 237–38.

78. Dorsey, quoted *ibid.*, 241; Nickels, "Thomas Wyatt Turner," 227.

79. Nickels, *Black Catholic Protest*, 42–61, 235–36, 239–42.

and the large annual conferences of the FCC from 1925 to 1932 demonstrated the widespread black discontent in the church and the will
to fight discrimination. The conferences also unveiled capable black
leaders who were dedicated, disciplined, full of race pride, and eminently Catholic in their spirituality. Furthermore, the black protest
movement attracted white support from important priests such as
LaFarge, William Markoe, James Gillis, and McGowan of the Social
Action Department of the NCWC.[80]

In the main, however, the hierarchy, most of the clergy, and the
white laity remained solid in their support of the racial status quo.
Although the American bishops surprised many in formulating a plan
of social reconstruction in 1919, they refused to address the explosive
racial situation at the end of World War I. The bishops' conference of
1919 indulged in glittering generalities about the church making "no
distinction of race or nation," but it added nothing practical to the
plenary councils of 1866 and 1884.[81] Between 1920 and 1933 the American bishops raised the race issue but once. They did little but rue the
fact that "when we give thousands, they [Protestants and Jews] give
tens of thousands and millions" to race projects, and "where we have
hundreds in the field, they have thousands."[82]

The black Catholic protest, nevertheless, made some impact on the
Vatican. The race riots of 1919 disturbed Pope Benedict XV, and
through his secretary of state he urged the American bishops to put the
racial outbreaks on their agenda for discussion. Davis' recent research
in the Vatican Archives turned up a bulging file labeled "Condizione
dei Negri," indicating the concern over this issue in Rome. Until 1908,
the American church was technically under the direct control of the
Congregation of the Propaganda; after 1908, the Sacred Consistorial
Congregation kept a close eye on the United States. These two Roman
congregations, often working through the apostolic delegate to the
United States, watched the American church's racial conduct with
growing interest. In 1904 Cardinal Girolama Maria Gotti of the Prop-

80. Cyprian Davis best analyzes black advances in *History of Black Catholics*, 193–
208, 221, 238–60, *passim*. On William Markoe, see William Barnaby Faherty, S.J., *Rebels
or Reformers? Dissenting Priests in American Life* (Chicago, 1988), 69–77, and Nickels,
Black Catholic Protest, 136–209, 289–93, 298–300.

81. McShane, *"Sufficiently Radical,"* 160; Guilday, ed., *National Pastorals*, 287,
309–10.

82. Bishops, quoted in Osborne, "The Race Problem in the Catholic Church," 72.

aganda sent a letter to Apostolic Delegate Diomede Falconio, reporting that he had good evidence that the American church's treatment of blacks was "humiliating and entirely different from that of whites." The only practical result of the pressure from Rome, though, was the establishment in 1907 of the Catholic Board for Mission Work among the Colored People. Although headed by the liberal and dedicated John Burke, pastor of a black church in New York City, the board was restricted to publicity, fundraising, and distribution of money.[83]

In 1912 the Consistorial Congregation and the Propaganda again stepped up pressure on the American church through the apostolic delegate to expand its efforts in the black apostolate, particularly stressing the necessity of an increase in the ordination of blacks. Archbishop Giovanni Bonzano, the apostolic delegate, prevailed upon Father Burke to make another report on the racial activities of the church. Burke's 1913 report documented the continuing failures of the church to convert and treat blacks according to Catholic doctrine. One new suggestion in the report was a recommendation for a separate college and seminary for the education of black priests. In 1920 the Society of the Divine Word, headquartered in Holland, accepted the Vatican challenge to raise a black clergy. The religious order opened a segregated seminary in Greenville, Mississippi, which moved intrastate to Bay St. Louis in 1923. In the 1930s the Bay St. Louis seminary would produce the first significant numbers of black priests in America. The Jim Crow seminary was popular with the segregation-minded hierarchy, but it was controversial among blacks. In the 1920s the black priests Dorsey and Theobald publicly criticized the plan. Since the hierarchy would not integrate feeder colleges and seminaries, however, the practical choice seemed to be either no black priests or a segregated seminary. Without commenting on the issue of segregated seminaries, Popes Benedict XV and Pius XI issued encyclicals, in 1919 (*Maximus Illud*) and 1926 (*Rerum Ecclesiae*), respectively, that promoted native clergies. In 1926 Pius XI consecrated six Chinese bishops to make his point.[84]

83. Cyprian Davis, "The Holy See and American Black Catholics," 170–79; Ochs, *Desegregating the Altar,* 138–43, 264. Giotti probably received much of his information from an influential Belgian Josephite named Joseph Anciaux, who in 1903 sent to Rome a forty-six-page exposé of the American church entitled "To the Holy See Concerning the Wretched Conditions of Negro Catholics in America."

84. Cyprian Davis, "The Holy See and American Black Catholics," 173–79; Ochs, *Desegregating the Altar,* 246–57, 271, 281, 283.

The strong and largely successful resistance of the American hier-archy to the Vatican on the race issue belied the idea that the Roman bureaucracy was an efficient monolith. If America's race problem pre-sented a "moral dilemma" to the nation, the Vatican had yet to create one in the minds of American Catholics. If anything, blacks saw a hard-ening of antiblack attitudes in the "white man's church." Mary Church Terrell, one of the original founders of the NAACP and the National Urban League, wrote in 1918 that Catholicism had become "tainted with a cruel, unreasonable un-Christlike race prejudice." Terrell un-doubtedly noticed that no Catholics were among the founding mem-bers of these two pioneer civil rights organizations. Du Bois, the fore-most black leader of the time, rudely and often alluded to the racial hypocrisy of American Catholicism. In 1925 he wrote in the *Crisis:* "The Catholic Church in America stands for color separation and dis-crimination to a degree equalled by no other church in America, and that is saying a great deal." [85]

A challenging situation therefore faced Father LaFarge in 1926 as he took his racial apostolate from southern Maryland to New York City. There he would encounter the mounting problems that stemmed from the Great Migration of blacks to northern cities. There he would view close up the Harlem Renaissance and the unfolding saga of the "New Negro." And, most important, there he would soon confront the fateful choice of whether to support Thomas Turner and the FCC in the escalating black protest movement or venture forth on a different course.

85. Terrell, quoted in Gatewood, *Aristocrats of Color,* 295; Nancy J. Weiss, *The National Urban League* (New York, 1974), 52; W. E. B. Du Bois, "The Catholic Church and Negroes," *Crisis,* 30 (July, 1925), 121.

4

"The Pilgrim," New York, and the Jazz Age

Father LaFarge was at his mother's bedside in Newport when she died on May 2, 1925. On that very day he received a call from Laurence J. Kelly, the Jesuit provincial of Maryland-New York. LaFarge had once been an assistant to Kelly when the latter was the pastor at St. Aloysius in Leonardtown, Maryland. The Jesuit provincial asked the mourning priest to stop by the New York headquarters of the Jesuit weekly *America* on his way back to Maryland. He was to see Wilfrid Parsons, the new editor-in-chief of the magazine. Parsons and LaFarge had both entered St. Andrew-on-Hudson in 1905 for their Jesuit training. Parsons wanted LaFarge to join the staff of the magazine at once, but the latter requested time to put his Maryland affairs in order.[1]

LaFarge was particularly concerned about the Cardinal Gibbons Institute, an institutional infant of one year and still in need of close parental attention. In the following year LaFarge tried to shore up the institute and the other black projects he had started in southern Maryland. He then embarked for New York City, where he reported to Campion House on West 108th Street, the stately, newly acquired Jesuit house and editorial offices of *America*. On August 7, 1926, the maga-

---

1. *MIO*, 225–26; John LaFarge, "Father Wilfrid Parsons," [1958], copy in *America* Collection, Georgetown University, Washington, D.C.

zine first carried LaFarge's name on its masthead as an associate editor. There his name would remain, later in his capacities as executive editor and editor-in-chief, until his death on November 24, 1963. Becoming a journalist, like his assignment to southern Maryland, marked a turning point in his life. "Life began for Fr. LaFarge, not at forty," a eulogist wrote in 1963, "but at forty-six." Although LaFarge is known today primarily as an activist in the area of race relations, for almost forty years his name was more broadly associated with *America* and progressive Catholic journalism.[2]

America began publication in 1909, the year Theodore Roosevelt left the presidency. A board consisting of all the Jesuit provincials in North America laid down the guidelines for the new periodical. Its purpose, according to the board, was to inform the public about the progress of the Catholic church and to discuss current events from a Catholic perspective. Its directives called for the magazine to nip in the bud any errors, "whether doctrinal or historical, concerning the Catholic faith, Christian morals, ecclesiastical discipline, the Apostolic See, and the Catholic Church." The provincials prescribed a journal that was nonpolitical and given to "strict avoidance of proselytism." The provincials warned that any criticism of Catholics had to be done with respect, so as not to give "legitimate offense." More important, if there were any criticism of the hierarchy or other prominent Catholics, the provincials themselves, and possibly the father general, should be consulted. The provincials advised that non-Catholic writers should be used sparingly. "Much less," they insisted, "should women be among the regular contributors to the magazine," and if that unhappy prospect occurred, "the article should not appear over the female writer's name."[3]

The first editorial of the magazine in 1909 was silent about the journalistic strictures imposed on it from above, but it was no less sanguine than the provincials about the exalted calling of the magazine. The editors claimed that it intended to survey all the relevant questions of the day and to present "an authoritative statement of the position of the Church in the thought and activity of modern life." From the be-

2. *MIO*, 226; "John LaFarge, S.J. (1880–1963)," *Am*, 109 (December 7, 1963), 725. For works that emphasize LaFarge's racial activism, see Nickels, *Black Catholic Protest;* Ochs, *Desegregating the Altar;* Stanton, "John LaFarge's Understanding"; and Zielinski, " 'Doing the Truth.' "

3. "Directives of Very Reverend Xavier Wernz Concerning Publication of a New Periodical in North America, 1909," in box 1, folder 2, JLFP 1.

ginning the magazine tended to be progressive by Catholic standards, but by the standards of the Progressive Era, it was often starkly conservative. The first issue of the periodical, however, vowed to "stimulate effort and originate movement for the betterment of the masses." At the same time, the magazine vehemently attacked all types of socialism, and it rejected Darwinism with equal vigor.[4] In a 1927 response to a Protestant minister's charge that Catholicism was reactionary and had no appeal to the intellect, the editors concluded that only the Catholic Church, "with its theory of development," had "any provision for orderly progress." *America* gave strong verbal support to the Bishops' Program of Social Reconstruction after World War I. The magazine, however, preached a kind of nineteenth-century stewardship, and it abhorred federal power, fearing a Protestant-dominated government might be used against the Catholic church. The magazine therefore was very reluctant to support any kind of federal regulation, as LaFarge would discover with respect to the crime of lynching. In commenting on a deadly train wreck in 1919, the editors argued that a capitalist should provide his employees with a living wage and safe working conditions or "resign." Paul L. Blakely, who in the 1920s and 1930s shaped *America*'s editorial page more than anyone, including the editor-in-chief, was a southerner with an implacable states' rights orientation. He filled editorials and his numerous articles with jeremiads against federal intrusion, particularly in the field of education. Because of staffers like Blakely, the journal also showed heightened concern about women working outside the home. The editors warned in 1919 that such work was a dangerous distraction from woman's true calling of marriage and procreation.[5]

Like most Catholic spokesmen of the time, the controlling provincials and the editors were neither liberal nor conservative but both. *America* never approached a consistent liberal stance until Blakely died and LaFarge became the chief editor in the early 1940s. Still, when LaFarge joined the staff of *America*, it was already the most quoted Catholic journal in the country and was considered by many influential

4. "Editorial Comment," *Am*, 1 (April 17, 1909), 5; "Catholicism and Socialism," *ibid.*, 8–9; "Darwinism and Popular Science," *ibid.*, 44.

5. "Is the Catholic Religion Progressive?," *Am*, 38 (November 5, 1927), 77; "May a Corporation Lawfully Kill?," *Am*, 21 (April 26, 1919), 74–75; Paul L. Blakely, "The Same Old Bull," *Am*, 21 (June 7, 1919), 222–24; "A New Menace to the Family," *Am*, 21 (May 31, 1919), 204–205.

Catholics and non-Catholics alike to be the official voice of American Catholicism.[6] Although the day-to-day yoke of the governing board was not especially heavy, the trustees clearly controlled the editors. Proving too liberal and independent for the provincials, Parsons was unceremoniously removed from his editorial post in 1936 in a way that seemed distasteful to his friend LaFarge. When Parsons died in 1958, LaFarge asked his Jesuit provincial about the reasons for Parsons' earlier dismissal. The New York provincial Thomas E. Henneberry told him confidentially that Parsons commissioned too many articles by "non-Catholics and Jews."[7]

One can be sure that the ever-obedient LaFarge took the journalistic directives from above quite seriously. His journalistic behavior would indicate that he not only heeded the 1909 directives of the provincials but those of Pope Leo XIII as well. In an 1895 letter to the American church (*Longingua Oceani*), Leo XIII advised Catholic journalists to seek a united front and to avoid questioning "the decisions and acts of bishops," since publicists "exert no small influence upon the opinions and morals of the multitude."[8]

Once in place at *America,* LaFarge wrote prolifically, and the breadth of his commentary is truly impressive. Owing to his rich background and his broad interests, LaFarge cast a wide intellectual net in his writing. On December 4, 1926, he began a weekly column called "With Script and Staff," which he always signed "The Pilgrim," a title of self-reference used by Ignatius of Loyola in his autobiographical writings. He assured his readers that the Pilgrim was "not a wanderer" and that "the road, wherever it leads, is the Homeward Road," where the faithful meet in the "fullness of Christ." Often LaFarge discussed several topics in each column. In his first column, for example, he took up three separate topics in addition to his introductory paragraph on the Pilgrim. One of them concerned a convention of "Freethinkers" in Rome. Here LaFarge quoted a fascist deputy who had harangued free-

6. Cogley, *Catholic America,* 175, 178; "Analysis of *America,*" n.d. [1940?], in box 7, folder 48, JLFP 2.

7. Thomas E. H. Henneberry to John LaFarge, December 24, 1958, box 21, folder 1, JLFP 1. A future editor-in-chief of *America,* Robert C. Hartnett, S.J., reported later that one of the reasons for Parsons' removal was that he criticized the movie index of the archdiocese of Chicago and offended the powerful Cardinal Mundelein (Interview of Hartnett by Stanton, December 1, 1980, in Stanton Papers).

8. Quoted in John Ellis, ed., *Documents of American Catholic History,* 506.

thinking conventioneers, telling them that "the only possible form of ethics is that which Jesus Christ laid down in the Gospel . . . in the Catechism, in interpretation, tradition, and in Catholic teaching." The following year LaFarge used his column for a strong defense of Pope Pius XI's collaboration with Benito Mussolini. Not only did the Italian dictator make the trains run on time; he also mended fences with the Vatican in the Lateran Treaty and Concordat of 1929.[9]

LaFarge's column was a potpourri of history, literature, art, current events, and Catholic apologetics. In his first six months as associate editor, he wrote on such items as agriculture, birth control, China, communism, Harry Houdini, the Ku Klux Klan, divorce, mental illness, education, the "breakup of Protestantism," motion pictures, and Uganda. Because of his family background and his linguistic abilities, LaFarge also had responsibility in the weekly chronicle for news items on France, the Soviet Union, and Eastern Europe.[10] In volume thirty-six of *America*, which included material from October 16, 1926, to April 9, 1927, he also wrote ten signed articles and several book reviews. Even though volume thirty-six contained the Jesuit's series of four articles on race relations, neither in this nor in any subsequent volume did his racial writings make up more than a fraction of his journalistic output. LaFarge's interests were indeed catholic in their breadth.

Once in New York City, LaFarge greatly accelerated his nonracial activities. He became increasingly active in the National Catholic Rural Life Conference and served on the board of directors from 1928 to 1946, the executive board in the 1930s, and in the vice-presidency in the early 1940s. In his autobiography LaFarge devoted an entire chapter to "The 'Green Revolution.'" He expressed great admiration for the Jesuit John Rawe, the inspiration for the rural life movement, and for the priest who became its chief administrator for three decades, Luigi Ligutti. Rawe was a Nebraskan with anti-city biases, a sort of Catholic version of William Jennings Bryan who propounded the agrarian myth, Peter McDonough believes, with a "zany sweetness." LaFarge made

9. John LaFarge, "With Script and Staff," *Am*, 36 (December 4, 1926), 185, and 37 (May 7, 1927), 90. On Catholics and fascism, see Wilson D. Miscamble, C.S.C., "The Limits of American Catholic Antifascism: The Case of John A. Ryan," *Catholic Historical Review*, 76 (December, 1990), 531; McDonough, *Men Astutely Trained*, 78; and John P. Diggins, *Mussolini and Fascism: The View from America* (Princeton, 1972), 183, *passim*. More on this topic will come in Chap. 8.

10. *MIO*, 227.

the connection between the rural life movement and the race problem most explicit in his advertisements of the Cardinal Gibbons Institute. He frequently alluded to the hardships of black farmers in his copious writings and speeches on rural life. He denied, however, that he favored a utopian back-to-the-land movement, even though he sought joint ventures with the anti-industrial, southern agrarians of *I'll Take My Stand*. Furthermore, when he spoke in rural areas, his speech was often indistinguishable from the romantic effusions of Rawe. LaFarge, like Rawe, preached a message that equated the land with a desired moral order that was withering in the urban landscape of America. To Catholic thinkers who were greatly alarmed at rising communist and fascist movements and were disgruntled with amoral, marketplace capitalism, the agrarian ideal proved alluring just as it was becoming more and more illusory. With 80 percent of American Catholics living in the city, the rural life movement constituted yet another weak and little-known Catholic subculture struggling to gain recognition. LaFarge conceded that his rural life seeds fell on "stony soil," but his Maryland experience and the Cardinal Gibbons Institute made the rural life movement almost mandatory for the Jesuit. Besides, it was an impeccable Catholic Action program that LaFarge found irresistible. In addition to seeking to increase and improve Catholic life on the land, the National Catholic Rural Life Conference stated that one of its major goals was "to convert the non-Catholics living on the land."[11]

LaFarge also became deeply involved with the liturgical movement after settling in New York and devoted a significant amount of writing to this cause. He was a member of the National Liturgical Conference and the Liturgical Arts Society, serving as chaplain in the latter organization for many years. Although elitist in membership, the liturgical movement had a progressive angle as well as an aesthetic one in that it strove for greater participation of the laity in the mass. To put it mildly, LaFarge became quite excited at the prospect of getting congregations to experience the thrill of Gregorian chants.[12]

11. *Ibid.*, 227–40. See also LaFarge, "Two Catholic Conventions: The Rural Life Program," *Am*, 42 (November 9, 1929), 104–105, "A Peach County Stabilizer," *Am*, 43 (July 5, 1930), 306–307, and "Religion and the Land," *Catholic Mind*, 38 (August 8, 1940), 281–90; McDonough, *Men Astutely Trained*, 89–95, 518; and Twelve Southerners [John Crowe Ransom *et al.*], *I'll Take My Stand: The South and the Agrarian Tradition* (New York, 1930).

12. *MIO*, 172–73, 285–93, 389–91; John LaFarge, "Doing the Truth," *Chronicle*, 3

At least two other nonracial activities of LaFarge deserve mention. He was a founding member of the Catholic Association for International Peace (CAIP) in 1927. This activity exemplified his abiding concern with the unifying mission of Catholicism. Neither for war nor for pacifism, CAIP took the typically Catholic middle-of-the-road or third-way approach that questioned both unrestricted national sovereignty and one-worldism. Finally, LaFarge was one of the leading figures in the St. Ansgar League, which was established in 1926. Its most distinguished member was Sigred Undset, the Danish novelist. The league took on the formidable task of the Catholic reconquest of Scandinavia (and Iceland).[13] Predictably, LaFarge's activism prompted some of his fellow clergymen to dub him a champion of "lost causes."

Whether racial justice was a lost cause or not, the American Catholic church found the rising racial violence during and after World War I difficult to ignore. Nor could it any longer seriously argue that the race problem was strictly a southern phenomenon to be dealt with by Catholic missions below the Potomac. In an editorial of July 19, 1919, "Catholics and the Negro Question," *America* opined that the North shared blame for racial inequity and was perhaps more hypocritical than the South on the issue of race relations. Although the magazine lauded the "heroic" priests and nuns who worked for the spiritual welfare of blacks, it charged that the general apathy of Catholics on the subject was "scandalous." In addition, the magazine warned that the color-blind Reds were making appealing overtures to the oppressed minority, and it warned that the Bolsheviks might entrap the black masses unless Catholics evangelized them. In spite of the alarm sounded by *America*'s editors, they seemed to count on an infinite patience among blacks. Just one week before the bloody race riot in Chicago, *America* praised the stoicism and meekness of blacks under provocation. The vices of blacks, the editors declared, sprang from their poor environment, but their virtues were self-made. And those virtues, they proclaimed, were best manifested in the African American who was "patient, humble, affectionate, a lover of his home and his children, loyal to his friends and with a heart too child-like long to cherish resentment."[14]

(June, 1930), 462–63; David O'Brien, "The American Priest and Social Action," in *Catholic Priest*, ed. John Ellis, 446–47.

13. *MIO*, 249–51, 387–88; Patricia McNeal, *Harder than War: Catholic Peacemaking in Twentieth-Century America* (New Brunswick, N.J., 1992), 10–12.

14. "Catholics and the Negro Question," *Am*, 21 (July 19, 1919), 380. For earlier,

When a shrill and burgeoning Ku Klux Klan appeared in the North after the war, defaming Catholics as much as blacks, it inevitably drew *America's* attention to the race problem. The Jesuit weekly opened its pages to a significant number of articles about African Americans in the 1920s. In fact, *America* was ahead of the times in capitalizing the word *Negro*, even in advance of LaFarge and William Markoe, the Jesuit crusader for racial integration in St. Louis.[15] Before LaFarge had written his first articles on race in late 1921, the young Father Markoe had become *America's* primary spokesman on race. In the early 1920s he contributed over twenty articles on the race problem to the weekly. After LaFarge arrived at Campion House in 1926, however, he became the magazine's recognized "Negro expert."

LaFarge's four-part series on black-white relations in 1926 basically repeated the themes he had articulated earlier in Maryland, namely: education is all-important for solving the race problem; the Negro is the ward of the white man; blacks are more susceptible than whites to materialism and radical movements; blacks are better off on the farm; black vocations are needed to convert the race; only Catholicism has a clue to the solution of the race question, though Protestants have more racial achievements; and, finally, all must have the patience of a Job in the face of the racial dilemma. The series, however, also sounded some new themes and contained some changes in emphasis that reflected LaFarge's new environment in New York. He geared the first article, titled "The Catholic's Voice in Negro Guidance," to the urban North. LaFarge informed the reader that the black population in New York City had increased from 60,666 in 1900 to 251,340 in 1926. The black population in the city actually soared by 115 percent in the 1920s, ballooning to 327,106 at the end of the decade. Without mentioning the changing neighborhoods or the rapid increase of racial parishes (about a quarter were now in the North), LaFarge described the urban racial scene as "dynamic" and "explosive." Raising a new theme on which he would become increasingly alarmist, the Jesuit admonished his readers that the communists were urging the Negro to "cast loose all that ties

---

typical references to the race question, see "Notes and Comment," *Am*, 14 (October 23, 1915), 47–48, and (March 11, 1916), 527.

15. Wilfrid Parsons, "The World's Work and Kukluxism," *Am*, 30 (March 8, 1924), 493–95. LaFarge tended not to capitalize *Negro* in drafts of his early writing, and Markoe's first letter to *America* put *Negro* in the lower case (21 [August 9, 1919], 451).

him to God and man and country." Moreover, he pointed out that the race problem was tied up with other crucial problems such as education, labor, health, and housing. Another reason he cited as necessitating action was simply that the Negro, "an ordinary human being like the rest of us," deserved elementary justice.[16]

LaFarge added that academic study of the race problem, though vital, was not enough. What was needed, he claimed, was more personal interaction between individual whites and blacks. This new theme was thrust upon him by the cold impersonality of the large northern city, and it pointed ahead to his founding of the Catholic Interracial Council. LaFarge concluded the article by saying that the racial situation had been transformed by intersecting developments and that Catholics had no choice but to face the race problem. If it were approached correctly, he suggested, the race question could be made into a Catholic issue with a Catholic solution. He argued strongly that, given the grave nature of the race problem, silence on the issue by Catholics would be "imprudent" and "unjust." The second article, undistinguished in comparison with the first, called for greater support of black Catholic missions and the need for black vocations.[17]

LaFarge's third article had much more substance and fewer religious overtones, challenging Catholics to render full justice to the African American, including "life, liberty, and pursuit of happiness." LaFarge discussed the many obstacles that prevented black conversion to Catholicism, the most significant factor being that northern blacks now bitterly resented all segregation and discrimination practiced by the church. He revealed that of fifteen hundred blacks who received college degrees in 1925, only five were awarded by Catholic institutions. He therefore issued a plea for more action by white Catholics in black missions and cited the National Urban League (but did not mention the NAACP) as a good example to emulate. With Constance Daniel's words still fresh in his memory ("I am a Negro first"), LaFarge warned that neglect of blacks invited an "unhealthy spirit of racial solidarity" based on "an entirely materialistic basis." Yet he applauded

16. John LaFarge, "The Catholic's Voice in Negro Guidance," *Am*, 36 (October 23, 1926), 32–33. On New York blacks, see also Gilbert Osofsky, *Harlem: The Making of a Ghetto, 1890–1930* (New York, 1968).

17. LaFarge, "The Catholic's Voice," 32–33, and "The Blue Horizon," *Am*, 36 (October 30, 1926), 56–57.

blacks for understanding the necessity for patience in dire times. Then he added cryptically that in racial matters the church might even have to go beyond patience and require "some degree of silence in certain instances."[18]

The final article of the series focused on the "handicaps" of the race, particularly the lack of "Christian character training." He alluded to the insights of Booker T. Washington, his favorite non-Catholic, in regard to racial correctness. The challenge, he indicated, was to tie the wisdom of the Tuskegee master to the locomotive of unrivaled Catholic ideals. He also suggested that the spiritual efforts on behalf of blacks by Katharine Drexel and the Josephites were insufficient to convert blacks. Economic measures and social justice, he argued, were also necessary. In his conclusion LaFarge proclaimed that black Catholics represented a challenge to "Catholic manhood" and to the "genuineness of . . . Catholicity."[19]

No one agreed with that conclusion more than Thomas Turner, the black president of the FCC. Turner responded to the LaFarge series with a letter to the editor, published in *America* in February of 1927. Turner first congratulated the priest on his articles, saying that they explained the ineffectiveness of missionary efforts aimed at blacks. The next paragraph, however, launched an attack on white priests in the racial field. Turner charged that they all had an attitude problem and needed to "develop their [black] charges so that they can be looked upon as no longer subject to pure tutelage."[20] Turner clearly believed that clerical paternalism was not one of those "certain instances" that the church should camouflage with silence. Although beholden to LaFarge, who was then very supportive of the FCC and about to host its third annual convention in New York City, Turner had already begun to chafe under clerical paternalism. LaFarge, now in close proximity to the militant New Negro of Harlem, displayed a growing anxiety over signs of racial chauvinism.

Interestingly, LaFarge expressed no opinion on the Dyer Anti-Lynching Bill that was introduced in 1922. *America* editorialized

18. John LaFarge, "The Crux of the Mission Problem," *Am,* 36 (November 6, 1926), 80–81.

19. John LaFarge, "Hardcover," *Am,* 36 (November 13, 1926), 109–11. See, too, his "Doing the Truth," *Chronicle,* 4 (August, 1931), 512–13.

20. Thomas Turner, "The Negro in the Church," *Am,* 36 (February 5, 1927), 414.

against such federal legislation throughout the 1920s—a stand that elicited strong objection from the NAACP. The editors responded to the black organization with their all-purpose answer: "It is our opinion that for local disorders local remedies are best." This answer convinced neither blacks nor most white liberals since no lyncher had ever been prosecuted in the South. Inasmuch as LaFarge would soon enthusiastically endorse the antilynching bill, it appears that he was, for the time being, practicing "true and perfect obedience" to superiors and not a little prudence as well.[21]

One of the common themes running through LaFarge's racial writings in this period was optimism. If Catholics failed to support black missions, if members of the church consistently acted in a racist manner, and if Protestants continually bested Catholics in the racial field, LaFarge still remained upbeat. His religious faith did not allow pessimism. "The Catholic Church," he said, "never admits any problem in human relations is insoluble." Besides, pessimism was the disease of modernist intellectuals.[22] Moreover, LaFarge's lack of interest in the theological concept of original sin steered him in an optimistic direction. Latter-day Jansenists and Calvinists might use the concept to illuminate the dark corners of human conduct, and more pessimistic interpreters of the Bible might stress self-idolatry to explain the terrible tenacity of race prejudice, but LaFarge declared repeatedly that racial justice was inevitable.

LaFarge's analyses of race and racism account in part for his naïve optimism. Race, he asserted, was a mere accident of geography and history. "The real strength of the truly Catholic position," he wrote in 1929, "is in the ignoring of race." He constantly stressed that racism resulted from ignorance, and he argued that racism had to be learned.[23] Given the amount of racism in evidence, LaFarge might have asked why so many people, against their better nature, learned bigotry so easily and so well. Was not a great deal of the white ignorance about

21. "Lynching and Its Prevention," letter to editor from Herbert J. Seligmann, Director of Publicity, NAACP, *Am,* 44 (October 11, 1930), 24. See also the editorials "Lynching on the Wane," *Am,* 37 (January 14, 1928), 335, "Lynching Ebbs and Flows," *Am,* 43 (September 20, 1930), 560, and "Investigating Lynching," *Am,* 44 (October 18, 1930), 30; LaFarge, *Jesuits in Modern Times,* 40.

22. John LaFarge, "Catholic Negroes Take Stock," *Am,* 48 (February 4, 1933), 430.

23. Quoted in Nickels, *Black Catholic Protest,* 250; John LaFarge, "Doing the Truth," *Chronicle,* 5 (May, 1932), 90–91, and "Catholic Negroes Take Stock," 430.

race willful? Moreover, why could not the grace-endowed hierarchy divest itself of this debilitating ignorance? Divorced from any discussion of history, class, economics, or social psychology (and without condemnation of racism as a sin that required personal confession and institutional rectification), the view that ignorance was the sole cause of racism constituted a rather shallow approach to a deep and enduring problem.[24] In his novel about the Jesuit missions in southern Maryland during the 1930s, Sylvester commented on how Catholics escaped accountability for their racist sins owing to their "invincible ignorance." His liberal white protagonist observed that ignorance had become "a theological term, a very providential one, the same sort of term that saves the followers of Father Coughlin in the eyes of the Church."[25]

Another salient characteristic of the priest's writing was its emphasis on the spiritual and the supernatural. Even when LaFarge argued about race relations in terms of materialistic expediency, he always attempted to frame the debate on higher, nonmaterialistic grounds. He maintained, for instance, that it was in the best economic interest of whites to elevate blacks. The proper motivation for black uplift, however, was Christian love and justice. Likewise, he held that the superior argument for the formation of a black clergy was not based on its utility for the conversion of African Americans. Rather, he pointed out, the failure to elevate blacks to the priesthood denied one of the holy sacraments to an entire race. Eschewing appeals to the American creed, he clearly believed that social justice arguments sounded more plausible and more Catholic when they downplayed economics, sociology, and race and when they were pitched at the highest metaphysical level. In addition, LaFarge, like most Jesuits, tried to work some compromise between the deductive Thomism favored by Rome and modern

24. For analyses of racism that differ from LaFarge's, see, for example, Pierre Van den Berghe, *Race and Racism: A Comparative Approach* (New York, 1967), and *The Ethnic Phenomenon* (New York, 1987); Joel Kovel, *White Racism: A Psychohistory* (New York, 1970); Harmannus Hoetink, *Slavery and Race Relations in the Americas: Comparative Notes on Their Nature and Nexus* (New York, 1973); and Howard Schuman, Charlotte Steeh, and Lawrence Bobo, *Racial Attitudes in America: Trends and Interpretations* (Cambridge, Mass., 1985). These sources are discussed in Southern, *Gunnar Myrdal and Black-White Relations*, 275–86, 296–306.

25. Sylvester, *Dearly Beloved*, 257.

thought. These inclinations gave his prose an uneven and often abstract and detached quality that had limited appeal to the average reader.[26]

Like many Catholic spokesmen, LaFarge constantly sounded the triumphalist horn of Catholicism throughout the 1920s. After World War I the Catholic resurgence, a mingling of confidence and insecurity, created a Catholic counterculture that originated scores of what Halsey has called little "communities of purpose," including such organizations as the Catholic Library Association in 1921, the Catholic Philosophical Association in 1926, and the Catholic Book Club in 1928. This Catholic propensity, unfortunately, had a negative side. It often entailed presumptuous exclusivism and denominational chauvinism in which Catholics wrapped themselves in a cocoon of not-so-splendid isolation. LaFarge exemplified this tendency. In 1931 he proclaimed, "Catholic teaching is the only certain guarantee of human rights in the world today." Two years later he gloated, "The Church is the one authentic, entirely consistent messenger of social justice in the world today." Because the church "alone knows the *true goal* of life, she alone," he asserted, "can solve the race problem." He was not unlike Mary McGill, the editor of *Catholic Girl,* who confided to Wilfrid Parsons: "We are so SURE. That characteristic would hurt me, if I didn't believe. I think I would hate people who are so sure and set apart, if I were not so favored with our *Supreme Gift.*" Such confidence, as one historian of Catholic liberalism has observed, could work against reform in the church by inviting self-satisfied complacency.[27]

Furthermore, on the other side of LaFarge's Catholic boosterism lay anti-Protestantism, which, to be sure, was more than matched by the anti-Catholicism that infected Protestants during this period. Although LaFarge sometimes cited Protestant achievement in the racial field as a prod to Catholics, in the end he always belittled the heirs of Martin Luther. His Jesuit biographer had to concede that LaFarge's views on Protestants contained "streaks of intolerance."[28] Like Pope

26. Nickels, *Black Catholic Protest,* 250, 260. See Aveling, *The Jesuits,* 325, on the attempted compromise between Thomism and modern thought.

27. Halsey, *Survival of American Innocence,* 1–2, 18, 56–57; Sparr, *To Promote, Defend, and Redeem,* 49–50; John LaFarge, "Doing the Truth," *Chronicle,* 4 (June, 1931), 463, and "Saturday Evening Session," *Chronicle,* 4 (October 4, 1931), 626; Mary McGill, quoted in Halsey, *Survival of American Innocence,* 51; Czuchlewski, "Liberal Catholicism and American Racism," 147.

28. Stanton, "John LaFarge's Understanding," 92.

Pius XI, he ridiculed the Protestant quest for unity in the international congresses held in the 1920s. The answer for Protestants, LaFarge advised, was for the lost sheep to return to the "one true Church of Christ." Protestantism, he held, was flawed by "private choice" and inherent disunity. The Catholic church was not seeking unity, LaFarge boasted, because she already had it.[29] In a revealing article, LaFarge described the decline of Catholicism in an unnamed town in the Northeast as an unmitigated disaster. The result in this case was that the "klan, the Mason, and the Odd Fellows" had become "all-powerful," and mixed marriages were undermining what Catholicism was left. The outcome, LaFarge lamented, was a "lapse into paganism" with the Protestant sects consuming "what Christianity is left." Nor did LaFarge always show a Christian tolerance in intra-Catholic squabbles. John Whitney Evans, a Catholic priest who hailed LaFarge as a visionary intellect, charged that the priest was uninformed, unfair, and dogmatic in his opposition to Father John O'Brien and the Newman Movement in the 1920s.[30]

Some contemporary analysts, however, have suggested that the term "Catholic intellectual," at least as applied to the early twentieth century, was oxymoronic. As it always has been, the brightest and best of persecuted minority groups dissipate an inordinate amount of intellectual energy promoting and defending their kind rather than blazing new trails of thought. Free and disinterested pursuit of knowledge and ideas, the essence of intellectualism, was not commonplace among a Catholic clergy so bombarded with neat bundles of received wisdom and so subjected to restrictive rules in their educational training. The English cardinal John Henry Newman, one of the luminaries of nineteenth-century Catholicism, felt that Jesuits were particularly unbalanced intellectually. Newman once said of a Jesuit friend, "Now his simple duty is to be obedient—alas, how difficult in the case of sensitive minds, with intellectual and logical perceptions." Certain men of "hard mind" were capable of doing it, Newman believed, "but there are those whom it crushes."[31]

29. John LaFarge, "With Script and Staff," *Am,* 37 (September 3, 1927), 498, and "The Cloud at Lausanne," *Am,* 37 (September 17, 1927), 509–10. See also Wilfrid Parsons, "The Unity of the Church at Lausanne," *Am,* 37 (September 17, 1927), 543.

30. John LaFarge, "Winterburg Unvisited," *Am,* 38 (February 18, 1928), 464; Evans, "LaFarge, *America,* and the Newman Movement," 633–34.

31. Sparr, *To Promote, Defend, and Redeem,* 15; David J. O'Brien, "Dialogue: How

Certainly the Catholic priesthood was at an intellectual disadvantage compared to the liberal Protestant tradition that produced the Social Gospel and Reinhold Niebuhr. In Pavlovian fashion, the Catholic clergy reacted to rather than read the signs of the time. Nurtured in a culture that disdained Protestantism and ecumenism, LaFarge was equally jaundiced about secularism and liberalism. In 1927 he proclaimed, "American secular colleges are the platforms and the loudspeakers of the infidel group." He deprecated the secular geniuses of the time as agents of a repellent atheism. In his writings he branded as dangerous men such renowned thinkers as Clarence Darrow, Bertrand Russell, Julian Huxley, and even Albert Einstein. He perceived that atheism lurked in the latter's time-space theories. In a word, LaFarge denigrated the contributions of a great number of the most celebrated minds of the era.[32]

Although LaFarge never defined liberalism precisely, he seemed to lump it indiscriminately with secularism and atheism. In fact, his assault on "Liberalism" (always capitalized) seemed more appropriate to the anticlerical liberalism of Europe and Latin America than to the more tolerant variety found in the United States. In an article called "How Liberal Is a Liberal?," LaFarge suggested that any ideology with a materialistic basis could not be truly liberal. He associated secular liberalism with industrial slavery, divorce, birth control, trial marriage, and state education. Liberalism, he charged, produced not liberty but the license to do evil.[33]

Without a doubt, however, LaFarge believed that the greatest evil of the twentieth century was communism. He branded it the greatest calamity since the Reformation. To LaFarge, this all-consuming dread seemed to be, more or less, a lurid extension of Protestantism, secularism, and liberalism, stretched out to the most distant point on the spectrum of modern evil. At the height of the Cold War, LaFarge referred

---

Has American Catholic Intellectual Life Changed over the Past Thirty Years?," *U.S. Catholic Historian*, 4 (Spring, 1985), 183–85; Edward Wakin and Joseph F. Scheuer, *The De-Romanization of the American Catholic Church* (New York, 1966), 261; Newman, quoted in Aveling, *The Jesuits*, 323.

32. John LaFarge, "With Script and Staff," *Am*, 41 (May 25, 1929), 162, and (September 7, 1929), 522–23; John LaFarge, "Poisoning Negro Youth," *Am*, 44 (January 24, 1931), 376–77.

33. John LaFarge, "How Liberal Is a Liberal?" *Am*, 38 (January 28, 1928), 387–89. See also his "Spain's New Liberty," *Am*, 45 (July, 1931), 318.

to communism as the "new Calvinism." He traced his anticommunism back to his student days in Austria, before the Russian Revolution. In his memoirs he applauded the honesty of liberals who had shown the courage to recant their naïve fellow-traveling, but he remained bitter over their "stupidity" toward people like himself who were right too early, who, he wrote, "suffered a painfully clear vision of organized political atheism . . . at the close of the First World War."[34] He, like many Catholic thinkers in this period, devoted a great deal of his journalistic output to eviscerating atheistic Bolshevism.

It was only when the soft-spoken LaFarge discussed communism that a real urgency, even a touch of theatrics, seeped into his gray prose. Detailing the communist atrocities against clergymen in China in 1928, he described the death of one priest at the hands of Chinese communists: "It took three hours for them to saw off his head with a rusty knife . . . but [he] remained steadfast to the end." (Ironically enough, despite his stand against racism, LaFarge never once described the lynching of a black person.) From the 1920s on, he used the threat of communism to heighten racial concern. He suggested that blacks, like Jews, had an affinity for the communist line. In a 1931 letter to a priest who was writing about black education, LaFarge advised the author that he needed "a little more strategy." As was often the case, the strategy he suggested was to show that black students in non-Catholic schools were unduly susceptible to communist appeals.[35] LaFarge at times seemed to subsume the race problem under the Red menace. Between 1930 and 1933 he wrote seventeen signed articles, four columns, and any number of editorials on the subject of communism. In 1933 he pleaded with president-elect Franklin D. Roosevelt not to extend recognition to the Soviet Union, saying that Christians should not clasp the hand that had pledged to destroy them.[36]

34. *MIO*, 243, 298, and "Our People Have Courage, an Extraordinary Spirit," *U.S. News & World Report*, February 22, 1960, p. 79; Stanton, "John LaFarge's Understanding," 102.

35. John LaFarge, "With Script and Staff," *Am*, 39 (June 9, 1928), 211; John LaFarge to Richard McKeon, S.J., August 9, 1931, in box 1, folder 2, Stanton Papers.

36. Stanton, "John LaFarge's Understanding," 101–102; John LaFarge, "Does the Russian Government Love the Negro?," *Chronicle*, 4 (April, 1931), 410–11, and "Shall We Recognize Russia?," *Am*, 48 (February 18, 1933), 472–73. See also LaFarge's articles "What Catholic Education May Forget," *Am*, 45 (August 22, 1931), 471–72; "Will the Negro Turn Communist?," *Am*, 47 (May 14, 1932), 133–35; and "The Appeal of Bolshevism," *Am*, 48 (December 3, 1932), 201–203.

LaFarge kept well-informed about blacks and was an inveterate clipper of articles on the subject. Most of his information necessarily came from non-Catholic sources. In 1928 he singled out Carter Woodson's *Journal of Negro History* for praise. Asking if black history had "any especial interest for [white] Catholics," LaFarge explained that it could illuminate many of the problems related to black Catholic missions. He expressed no interest in black history or black culture per se, but he asked Catholic writers to flood the *Journal of Negro History* with articles that revealed the beneficence of the Catholic church toward blacks.[37]

One Catholic source that LaFarge drew on was the Reverend Francis J. Gilligan. Ordained in 1924, Gilligan became a close friend of LaFarge and a valuable member of the black apostolate. The publication of his 1928 book, *The Morality of the Color Line,* was a significant event in the history of Catholic black-white relations. Originally a doctoral dissertation done under the progressive reformer Ryan at Catholic University, Gilligan's work was perhaps the first extended treatment of the race problem by an American Catholic in this century. Viewing the problem as a moral question, Gilligan concluded that racism was a grave sin. Despite this bold charge, Gilligan's treatise was replete with equivocation. Like Booker T. Washington, he stressed black duties over rights and order over protest, and he made several concessions to segregation. Although he drew on the cultural anthropology of Franz Boas, he nevertheless suggested a natural aversion between the races and handled the questions of social equality and interracial marriage in an awkward and paternalistic manner. Yet, overall, the book represented an advance in thinking about race relations in the American Catholic church.[38]

Although Gilligan's book served as a source for Catholic racial activism, no Catholic document rivaled *Quadragesimo Anno* for its

37. Clippings on blacks in "Fine Arts—Negroes," in box 3, folder 17, JLFP 1; John LaFarge, "The Unknown Field of Negro History," *Am*, 39 (July 21, 1928), 349–50.

38. Francis J. Gilligan, *The Morality of the Color Line: An Examination of the Right and Wrong of the Discrimination Against the Negro in the United States* (Washington, D.C., 1928), esp. x, 54–55, 194–98, 208–11, 213–14. In a letter to the author, dated August 11, 1989, Father Gilligan was rather apologetic about his earlier views on segregation and miscegenation. See LaFarge's praise of Gilligan's work, John LaFarge to John H. Ziegler, October 29, 1953, in box 8, folder 2, JLFP 1. For examples of Gilligan's later writings, see "Jim Crow and the White Worker," *Am*, 44 (April 4, 1931), 623–24, and a series of essays on blacks in the *Chronicle* from November, 1930, through September, 1931.

impact on social Catholicism. Pope Pius XI's 1931 encyclical was a veritable pep talk for LaFarge and all those in the social apostolate. An update of *Rerum Novarum* on its fortieth anniversary, *Quadragesimo* became the key document of Catholic liberalism and served simultaneously as the Catholic path to the New Deal and the antidote to socialism. The papal directive, while strongly sanctioning private property, assailed laissez-faire capitalism and called for a living wage and distributive justice. Disdaining a world that had "almost fallen back into paganism," the pope proffered a "third way," one that found capitalism flawed but salvageable and socialism unredeemable.[39] Franklin D. Roosevelt described *Quadragesimo Anno* as "one of the greatest documents of modern times."[40]

Quadragesimo uniquely incorporated elements of both liberalism and socialism but encased them discreetly in a Catholic philosophy and theology that inclined toward conservative hierarchy and order. The pope devoted little space to hardcore communism, claiming its evil was all too clear. But he cautioned Catholics against a moderate and rising socialism, whose programs, he admitted, "often strikingly approach the just demands of Christian social reformers." The pope, however, allowed "no connivance with error." Even mild socialists, he argued, had not abandoned their belief in class warfare and the abolition of property. Thus, his conclusion was decisive. "No one," he said, "can be at the same time a sincere Catholic and a true socialist." Unfortunately, Catholic social teaching contained conflicting ideological elements that tended to war against one another. Furthermore, Vatican solutions were often quaintly anachronistic (guilds and corporatism, for example) and utopian, because they assumed social harmony as natural. In addition, the encyclical was drafted in obscure, pontifical Latin, making it difficult to translate into meaningful contemporary terms.[41]

39. Lawrence B. DeSaulniers, *The Response in American Catholic Periodicals to the Crises of the Great Depression, 1930–1935* (New York, 1984), 8, 11–15; Garry Wills, *Bare Ruined Choirs: Doubt, Prophecy, and Radical Religion* (Garden City, N.Y., 1972), 50; John LaFarge, "The New Labor Encyclical," *Am*, 45 (June 6, 1931), 204. *Quadragesimo* is in *Catholic Social Thought*, ed. O'Brien and Shannon, 42–79, and pope quotation on p. 75.

40. Franklin Roosevelt, quoted in George Q. Flynn, *American Catholics and the Roosevelt Presidency, 1932–1936* (Lexington, Ky., 1968), 17.

41. Pope, quoted in *Catholic Social Thought*, ed. O'Brien and Shannon, 67–69; David Hollenbach, S.J., *Claims in Conflict: Retrieving and Renewing the Catholic Hu-*

Even Catholics who paid some attention to encyclicals often seemed unsure of what to make of them. Garry Wills has shown that seldom were encyclicals meant to lay out infallible moral guidelines, as LaFarge sometimes seemed to imply. Normally, popes used encyclicals to exhort and instruct, but they seldom revised dogma or proscribed specific behavior. In addition, the principle of "subsidiarity" left a large loophole for conservative Catholics. Much like the Jeffersonian states' rights philosophy, the Catholic concept of subsidiarity held that problems should be solved at the lowest level of social organization: first family, then church, local government, state, and nation. This was a formula made for opposing collective action at the national level. In any event, most American Catholics apparently paid no attention to encyclicals. When New York governor Al Smith was quizzed about them, he reportedly answered, "Will somebody tell me what in the hell an encyclical is?"[42]

The 1931 encyclical, like its illustrious forerunner of 1891, never referred directly to blacks or the American race problem. Nevertheless, American priests in the racial apostolate relied heavily on such encyclicals. This was particularly true for LaFarge, since he seldom alluded to the Bible or to secular sources such as the Declaration of Independence as a basis for racial activism. LaFarge therefore became a meticulous exegete of papal statements, teasing out of them every possible inference for the race problem. He had planned an elaborate celebration of *Rerum Novarum*'s fortieth anniversary in Harlem well before the release of *Quadragesimo*. LaFarge thus viewed the new encyclical as a "golden opportunity to present the true attitude of the Catholic Church on the matter of social justice to the Negro population." He also believed that the Harlem rally would combat the "wretched Communist propaganda" that he felt was now pervasive there. The Harlem gath-

---

man *Rights Tradition* (New York, 1979), 162, 207; Hobgood, *Catholic Social Teaching,* 98, 101–102, 107, 109, 117–18, 122–23, 215, 227; John A. Coleman, S.J., "Neither Liberal nor Socialist: The Originality of Catholic Social Teaching," in *One Hundred Years of Catholic Social Thought: Celebration and Challenge,* ed. John A. Coleman (Maryknoll, N.Y., 1991), 25, 33, 35, 39–40.

42. Garry Wills, *Politics and Catholic Freedom* (Chicago, 1964), Introduction, 23, 37, 53, 55, 61–62, 79, 138–53, 194–207, 210, 224, *passim.* On subsidiarity, see Patrick Allitt, *Catholic Intellectuals and Conservative Politics in America, 1950–1985* (Ithaca, N.Y., 1993), 91, 94–95, 114. Smith is quoted in Hennesey, *American Catholics,* 252. See also the editorial "The Force of Papal Encyclicals," *Am,* 37 (April 30, 1927), 55.

ering on May 17, 1931, featured several noted black speakers from the fields of labor, education, and race relations, including Mary McLeod Bethune.[43]

LaFarge persistently presented Pius XI's encyclical as proof that the church possessed the key to the race question. He offered it as evidence to the Catholic Laymen's Union, an all-black group that he started in 1928. Into this cohort, the future nucleus of LaFarge's Catholic Interracial Council, he invited about twenty carefully picked black businessmen and professionals from New York City. As spiritual director of the Laymen's Union, he sought to mold these hand-picked blacks into "good Catholics" and participants in Catholic Action as defined by the pope: namely, lay action for the advancement of Catholicism under the direction of the hierarchy. Emphasizing the spiritual, LaFarge conducted three-day retreats and an annual communion mass breakfast for the group. He instructed the members in Catholic doctrine, meditation, and humility. Additionally, he tutored the men in public speaking and manners, hoping to groom them for interaction with educated white Catholics as the first step toward interracial understanding. The group also held public forums every month to discuss social issues. These discussions covered the waterfront of Catholic Action, including birth control and divorce. LaFarge's quiet, humble manner captured the group's confidence. Having done that, he gradually introduced the members of the organization to the church's view of the race question, assuring everyone of Catholicism's deep and abiding concern for blacks. This was the LaFarge technique: start with noncontroversial spiritual activity among black elites and slowly ease into more problematical social questions.[44]

The men of the Laymen's Union never embarrassed LaFarge with radical demands or intemperate language. They tended to be a conserv-

---

43. LaFarge, "The New Labor Encyclical," 203–204, and "Doing the Truth," *Chronicle*, 4 (July, 1931), 489–90; Ryan, quoted in Miscamble, "Limits of American Catholic Antifascism," 523–38; John LaFarge to Msgr. Stephen J. Donahue, March 5, 1931, in box 1, folder 39, JLFP 2; editorial "The Negro and the Encyclical," *Am*, 45 (May 30, 1931), 174–75.

44. George K. Hunton, *All of Which I Saw, Part of Which I Was: The Autobiography of George K. Hunton* (Garden City, N.Y., 1967), 56, 61–64; Osborne, "The Race Problem," 166–67; interview of Robert C. Hartnett, S.J., by Edward Stanton, March 18, 1981, in Stanton Papers; John LaFarge, "Memorandum of Laymen's Union Retreat," in box 32, folder 1, JLFP 1.

ative lot. A group picture that accompanied a LaFarge article about the organization in the *Interracial Review* in 1934 showed nineteen of them, resplendent in formal evening dress, with their spiritual director near the center. Myles A. Paige, a leading member of the group who had learned LaFarge's social philosophy well, declared in a formal address that a good Catholic could never vote for a socialistic candidate. Edward E. Best, a physician who championed "patience under oppression," condemned all race-consciousness as the mother of hatred and strife.[45] With the exception of Guichard Parris, who emigrated from Guadeloupe in 1917, none of these black men took leadership roles in the broader civil rights movement. As a teacher and a scholar, Parris himself was an exception within the business-oriented group. He was the harshest critic of the Catholic church, too. Parris graduated Phi Beta Kappa from Amherst and pursued graduate study in French literature at Columbia University. In the 1940s he became a member of the publicity department of the National Urban League. Revealingly, Parris' 1990 obituary in the New York *Times* made no reference to his leadership in Catholic interracialism.[46]

On the whole, most of the men in the Laymen's Union were not representative of the increasingly militant black intelligentsia that was led by Du Bois, James Weldon Johnson, and A. Philip Randolph. The posture of the men in the Laymen's Union more closely resembled that of the segregated black seminarians at Bay St. Louis, Mississippi, who in their long years of training received stern lessons in order and humility from white overseers. One black seminarian, Orion F. Wells, wrote in 1929 that in "God's Church 'a thousand years are as a day.' . . . The progress of the Holy Mother Church [*sic*] is slow and almost imperceptible in the solution of the Race Problem." If the church progressed slowly, the Laymen's Union progressed not at all. Holding scant attraction for young black Catholics, the union's membership aged and decreased to fifteen in the 1940s.[47]

---

45. For a picture of the group in tuxedoes, see John LaFarge, "The Laymen's Union," *IR*, 7 (April, 1934), 42; copy of address by Myles A. Page, n.d., in box 1, folder 41, JLFP 2; Edward E. Best, "Race-Consciousness in the Negro," *IR*, 9 (August, 1936), 118–19.

46. Interview of Guichard Parris by the author, New York, July 22, 1985; John W. Donahue, "Recovering Black History," *Am*, 156 (July 18–25, 1987), 35–36; obituary of Guichard Parris, New York *Times*, November 16, 1990.

47. Orion F. Wells, "The Attitude of the Catholic Church Toward the Colored

Because of his relationship with the FCC in the 1920s, LaFarge naturally took his loyal black followers from New York into Thomas Turner's organization. The FCC had supported LaFarge's Cardinal Gibbons Institute, and in return it received free advice and services from an increasingly influential Jesuit who duly promoted the new black organization in *America*. As soon as he landed in New York, however, the Jesuit quietly began a sustained effort to alter the structure and purpose of the FCC, vowing to make the black agency into a genuine Catholic Action group. His involvement in the FCC would significantly determine, for good or for ill, the direction of Catholic policy in race relations for a generation to come.

Man," *St. Elizabeth's Chronicle,* 2 (March, 1929), 14; list of members, in box 32, folder 1, JLFP 1; Thomas J. Harte, C.Ss.R., *Catholic Organizations Promoting Negro-White Relations in the United States* (Washington, D.C., 1947), 161; Stanton, "John LaFarge's Understanding," 83.

5

Interracialism Versus Black Protest
LaFarge and the FCC, 1927–1933

In the months prior to the fourth convention of the FCC, which was held in New York City in 1927, LaFarge advised Thomas Turner repeatedly that the black federation suffered from inadequate programs and faulty structure. He told Turner that he was studying Catholic organizations carefully in order to find out what worked best. After LaFarge came to New York, he increasingly placed more stress on interracial contact as the answer to the race problem. Although no organizational changes materialized at the 1927 New York meeting, LaFarge's promotional report on the convention in *America* suggested that he had begun to shape the organization to his own way of thinking. "As a practical means of obtaining a *right understanding with the rest of the Catholic body*" (my emphasis), LaFarge noted in his report, "the formation of a Catholic interracial committee was recommended, similar to the secular or non-Catholic committees which have already proved their usefulness in so many parts of the United States."[1] Here one can detect the emerging interracial philosophy of the eventual founder of the Catholic Interracial Council of New York

1. Nickels, *Black Catholic Protest*, 242; John LaFarge, "The Federation of Colored Catholics," *Am*, 36 (January 1, 1927), 284; John LaFarge to Thomas Turner, July 27, 1927, in Turner Papers; John LaFarge, "After Two Centuries," *Am*, 37 (October 1, 1927), 584.

(CICNY), a strategy that LaFarge more and more insisted was the "right," indeed the only, understanding of the race problem in the context of American Catholicism.

As racial tensions rose in early twentieth-century America, interracial organizations gained increasing favor with racial progressives. Examples included the NAACP in 1909, the National Urban League in 1911, the southern-based Commission on Interracial Cooperation in 1919, and, most important to LaFarge, the Commission on Race Relations in 1922. Although LaFarge learned much about interracialism from non-Catholics, he was loath to give them credit. Prior to World War II his Catholic exclusivism worked against generous attribution. If one read only LaFarge's writings in this period, one might conclude that Catholics invented the concept of interracialism. For example, George E. Haynes (1880–1960), who was almost perfectly contemporaneous with LaFarge, widely disseminated ideas that were practically identical to those of LaFarge, but his ideas predated LaFarge's by several years. In 1922, Haynes, who earned a Ph.D. at Columbia University and was a founding member of the Urban League, became the executive director of the Commission on Race Relations for the Federal Council of Churches, the first black to hold an executive position in that agency. In the same year Haynes published a book called *The Trend of the Races,* which sold 600,000 copies within months. He argued in his book that interracial contact between educated men and women under pleasant circumstances provided the right formula to improve race relations. Only interracial cooperation between the best of both races, he maintained, would stave off festering black radicalism. In 1923, Haynes originated Race Relations Sunday, during which white and black congregations exchanged parishioners and ministers. LaFarge never duly acknowledged Haynes's pioneering work, giving but a bare reference to the black Protestant in his seminal 1937 book, *Interracial Justice.*[2]

2. John Hope Franklin and Alfred A. Moss, Jr., *From Slavery to Freedom: A History of Negro Americans* (6th ed.; New York, 1988), 287–90, 319–20; William M. Tuttle, Jr., *Race Riot: Chicago in the Red Summer of 1919* (New York, 1984), 251–58; George Edmund Haynes, *The Trend of the Races* (New York, 1922), 158–59, 173–75; Samuel Kelton Roberts, "Crucible for a Vision: George Edmund Haynes and the Commission on Race Relations, 1922–1947" (Ph.D. dissertation, Columbia University, 1974), 86, 100, 102–103; David W. Wills, "An Enduring Distance: Black Americans and the Establishment," in *Between the Times,* ed. William Hutchinson, 172–75, 178–79; John LaFarge,

LaFarge, however, participated in several secular interracial seminars in this period. It seems that LaFarge wanted to create a Catholic presence at these seminars to refute charges that the Catholic church was a white man's religion. Moreover, he apparently believed that Catholic attendance could foreclose the temptation for Protestant, Jewish, and secular liberals to use interracial seminars as an anti-Catholic forum. LaFarge therefore represented *America* at the National Interracial Conference in Washington, D.C., in December, 1928. He also attended a meeting sponsored by the American Interracial Seminar in which he had contact with Franz Boas, E. Franklin Frazier, Robert E. Park, and Charles S. Johnson.[3]

Meanwhile, LaFarge was pressuring Turner to pursue a more definite interracial strategy at the FCC. The 1928 FCC convention in Cincinnati employed the NCWC to hold a seminar on industrial problems in which black and white workers discussed problems of the workplace, a feature that became a regular part of subsequent conventions.[4] This innovation most likely came from LaFarge's growing influence in the black organization. Bringing in NCWC organizers meant that more and more whites would play important roles in FCC activities.

At the 1929 FCC convention in Baltimore, LaFarge was but one of several white clerics who participated in the program. His detailed report on the convention in *America* gave a clue as to the direction in which LaFarge wanted to guide the FCC. In his report he quoted a brief passage from Turner's presidential address: "Ours is not a grievance organization. Ours is simply to encourage the highest ideals and to enable our people to cooperate with the best influences of Church and State." This part of Turner's address, it turns out, was actually a peace offering to the hostile Josephites, but LaFarge seized upon it as descriptive of the FCC. Further on, however, LaFarge quoted a lengthy and strongly worded resolution by the FCC that condemned racial discrimination in Catholic schools. After quoting the passage, though, LaFarge put his gloss on it, commenting, "This resolution was pro-

---

Interracial Justice: A Study of the Catholic Doctrine of Race Relations (1937; rpr. New York, 1978), 169.

3. Roberts, "Crucible for a Vision," 113–14; John LaFarge, "Opportunity for the Negro," *Am*, 40 (February 2, 1929), 406–407; Hubert C. Henry to John LaFarge, January 5, 1930, in box 49, folder 6, JLFP 1.

4. See the historical report on the FCC in the *Chronicle*, 4 (September, 1931), 546–47.

pounded in no ways [*sic*] in the spirit of criticism, but simply as a statement of undeniable fact."[5] If LaFarge did not put words in Turner's mouth, he clearly attempted to soften their sting. He downplayed the fact that the FCC was a black protest organization that made demands on the hierarchy to end racial discrimination in the church. While LaFarge condemned racial prejudice and discrimination, he contradictorily refused to acknowledge the salience of race and racism.

Because of his connection with the Cardinal Gibbons Institute, LaFarge was aware that his interracial philosophy exposed him to charges of inconsistency. He also realized that some of the northern members of the FCC were not too enthusiastic about a Jim Crow, Tuskegee-style school in southern Maryland. In an article in October, 1929, LaFarge therefore defended the institute as an agency that provided agricultural extension service for the white community and one that was guided by an integrated board of trustees. He was so concerned about the image of the institute that he asked Turner to write a letter to *Commonweal* to refute the impression that the black school was a "back-to-the-farm movement" and to counter the idea that it was "racial" rather than interracial. LaFarge stressed the view that the school was genuinely representative of the broadest and best Catholic Action.[6] It was, in truth, a black school controlled by whites and by none more than by LaFarge.

By the end of the 1930 convention in Detroit, LaFarge had engineered the passage of a new set of directives that slanted the FCC in the direction of an interracial, Catholic Action, hierarchy-controlled organization. Although Turner acquiesced at the time, some of the more militant blacks in the FCC grew alarmed at the pattern of events. But before we examine the pivotal Detroit convention, a closer look at the previous convention in Baltimore is in order, for there a festering feud between black Catholics and the Josephites reached critical mass.

At the 1929 convention of the FCC, the Baltimore-based Josephite congregation prepared for battle. Its superior general Louis Pastorelli had heard that the FCC planned to use the convention to force his

5. John LaFarge, "Colored Catholics Discuss Their Situation," *Am*, 41 (September 14, 1929), 544–46, and "The Baltimore Convention," *Chronicle*, 2 (October, 1929), 3–7; "Fifth Annual Convention, Federated Colored Catholics of America," in box 3, folder 16, JLFP 1.

6. John LaFarge, "The Meaning of Cardinal Gibbons Institute," *Chronicle*, 2 (November, 1929), 7–8; John LaFarge to Thomas Turner, April 7, 1931, in Turner Papers.

hand on the issue of black priests. Having long forsaken John Slattery's quest for a black clergy, Pastorelli attempted to cover up the true facts of the matter. Turner realized that the order's hostility posed a threat to the success of the FCC, so he sought to smooth over their differences. The Josephites, after all, ran most of the black missions in the Deep South and had influence over the all-black Knights of Peter Claver, a fraternal organization analogous to the all-white Knights of Columbus. The congregation, however, advised southern blacks to stay away from the FCC. It reviled those "Yankee Negroes," the ingrates who, the Josephites charged, slandered the only Catholic congregation dedicated expressly to the care of black Catholics.[7]

Sensing an FCC trap in Baltimore, Pastorelli was prepared. Although the superior general stayed away from the convention, he sent the Reverend Thomas Duffy as his mouthpiece. Duffy delivered a long, defensive policy speech to open the convention. After declaring that his congregation believed "absolutely and unqualifiedly in colored priests," he then attempted to justify the fact that there was only one elderly black priest among the Josephites. He also sniped at critics of the order, intimating that they were devious persons who resorted to "trickery" and "chicanery" to defame the religious congregation. Finally, Duffy fired a shot at the clerical allies of the FCC, calling them "armchair missionaries" with no experience in the monolithically racist, white South, where Josephites did their heroic work.[8]

Although LaFarge had labored in the rocky vineyards of southern Maryland for fifteen years, the Josephites clearly perceived him as one of the primary armchair missionaries who aided and abetted their detractors. After all, no priest had worked longer or more intimately with the FCC than had LaFarge. However, another Jesuit, William Markoe, was attending his first FCC convention in Baltimore, and he would soon attract more hostility from the Josephites than LaFarge could ever have imagined. A remarkable man given to grand schemes, Markoe differed dramatically in personality from LaFarge: he was loud, bold, convivial, profane, and charismatic. Unlike LaFarge, he liked to shock people and keep provincials and bishops on edge.[9] Interestingly, he was

---

7. Ochs, *Desegregating the Altar,* 230–31, 279.

8. *Ibid.,* 226–45; "Address Delivered by Rev. Thomas J. Duffy at the Convention of the Federated Colored Catholics, September 1, 1929," typescript in John T. Gillard Papers, Josephite Archives, Baltimore.

9. Interview of Claude H. Heithaus, S.J., by Marilyn W. Nickels, June 5, 1973,

born, like LaFarge, into a distinguished and comfortable French-American family in St. Paul, Minnesota, in 1892. Markoe (originally Marcous) descended from French Huguenots who migrated to the Virgin Islands in the seventeenth century and became wealthy plantation owners. In 1770 Abram Markoe left the islands, settled in a grand mansion on Chestnut Street in Philadelphia, and became a captain of some note in the American Revolution. Since a Markoe woman married the grandson of Benjamin Franklin, Father Markoe and LaFarge were distant cousins. One of the grandsons of Captain Markoe took the family name to the frontier land of Minnesota, where he became a substantial landowner, prominent citizen, pioneer balloonist, and a convert to Catholicism. One of the pioneer's sons, James C. Markoe, married Mary Prince and became a successful physician in St. Paul. The couple had six children, four sons and two daughters (both daughters became nuns). One of his sons, William, entered St. Louis University in the fall of 1912.[10]

Although blacks were few in Minnesota, young Markoe nevertheless had African Americans on his mind. First, Markoe had the example of the integrationist archbishop John Ireland in his home state. Second, he had guilt feelings because of his slaveholding ancestors. Last, Markoe seemed to crave contact with what he fancied to be an exotic black world. Throughout his life he searched the big cities of America for black Markoes, some of whom he believed were related to him by blood. Young Markoe moved comfortably in black culture. Declaring it was superior to white culture, he spent many convivial hours in bars with famous black athletes and entertainers. He boasted that most of his friends were black, and he lamented that he had no "black blood" in his veins. When he was exiled by superiors to a remote Indian res-

---

transcript in Josephite Archives, Baltimore; interview of William Barnaby Faherty, S.J., by the author, September 2, 1986. See William M. Markoe, "An Interracial Role: Memoirs of Rev. William M. Markoe, S.J., 1900–1966" (Typescript, 1967), copy in the Jesuit Missouri Province Archives, St. Louis. See also Cyprian Davis, *History of Black Catholics*, 221–22.

10. Jeffrey H. Smith, *From Corps to CORE: The Life of John P. Markoe, Soldier, Priest, and Pioneer Activist* (St. Louis, 1977), 25–29, 38; "Stripes in Flag Creation of MU Priest's Ancestor," Milwaukee *Sentinel*, July 4, 1968, clipping in William M. Markoe Papers, Marquette University Library, Milwaukee, Wisc.; Markoe, "Interracial Role," 1–2, 141, 201.

ervation in 1941, far from any blacks, he described himself as "a fish out of water."[11] If LaFarge preached interracialism, Markoe lived it.

When Markoe arrived in St. Louis in 1912 and was first introduced to racial segregation, he thought that he had landed in a black southern city.[12] During his novitiate, his superiors assigned Markoe the task of feeding poor blacks from the area, some of them descendants of Jesuit slaves. Within months Markoe began to think in terms of spiritual provisions and black evangelization. During his next five years in St. Louis, he and other like-minded scholastics visited countless black homes, set up catechetical centers, started schools, and erected two churches for blacks. To his great joy, Markoe's older brother John, a 1914 graduate of West Point, joined him as a seminarian in 1917. Even more handsome, magnetic, and daring than William, the former college football star and captain of an all-black cavalry unit had one terrible weakness: he was an alcoholic. This condition ended his military career. In 1917 the Markoe brothers and their fellow seminarians Austin A. Bork and Horace Frommelt signed a pledge "to give and dedicate our whole lives and all our energies, as far as we are able and it is not contrary to a pure spirit of perfect indifference and obedience, for the salvation of the Negroes in the United States."[13]

Before LaFarge had published his first article on blacks in *America*, Markoe had contributed five articles on black-white relations to the magazine and had aroused no little controversy with his views.[14] In

11. Markoe, "Interracial Role," 160, 399, 412–13, 587, 592; William Markoe, "Miscegenation and Jesuit Thinking," *I.S.O. Bulletin* (January, 1947), 3.

12. Markoe, "Interracial Role," 1. On St. Louis Catholics and race, see Donald J. Kemper, "Catholic Integration in St. Louis, 1935–1947," *Missouri Historical Review*, 73 (October, 1978), 2; Lawrence O. Christensen, "Race Relations in St. Louis, 1865–1966," *Missouri Historical Review*, 78 (January, 1984), 123–36; William Barnaby Faherty, S.J., *Dream by the River: Two Centuries of St. Louis Catholicism, 1766–1980* (rev. ed.; St. Louis, 1981), 26–27; and Kenneth P. Feit, typescript on St. Louis Jesuits [no title], 1969, in Jesuit Provincial Archives, St. Louis.

13. Markoe, "Interracial Role," 7–12, 38–40, 342–43; Reynolds, *Jesuits for the Negro*, 94–99; Smith, *From Corps to CORE*, 10–12, 35–54, 56–59, 86, *passim;* "Shrine of Our Lady, Saint Stanislaus Seminary, Feast of the Assumption, 1917," in box 3, Markoe Papers.

14. See, for example, the following by William Markoe: letter to the editor, *Am*, 21 (August 9, 1919), 451; "Viewing the Negro Supernaturally," *Am*, 23 (June 19, 1920), 200–201; "The New Race Problem," *Am*, 23 (October 9, 1920), 582–84; "A Solution of the

substance Markoe's essays did not differ greatly from those of LaFarge in the 1920s and the 1930s. The main difference between them lay in style and emphasis. Markoe's prose possessed a rude energy lacking in the work of the irenic LaFarge. If LaFarge shunned confrontation, Markoe found it satisfying that his articles caused "wide comment, discussion, controversy, and considerable irritation." His prose crackled with the use of theatrics, exaggeration, heavy sarcasm, and exclamation points. In his second article Markoe assured whites that the black man was a moral and rational being who would not "some dark night draw his razor and cut our throats." Naming names and citing figures, Markoe denounced Catholic racism more directly than did LaFarge. As early as 1921, he declared that race prejudice was a grave sin; he shamed whites for slavery and the rape of black women that produced millions of mulattoes. "I defy any man," he challenged, "to prove that the white American is the moral superior of the black." [15]

Markoe also attacked segregation with greater vehemence and specificity than LaFarge. He assailed segregation as expensive, impractical, injurious to black conversion, and repugnant to God. Schools were just as much religious institutions as churches, he argued, and should never be segregated, except in the South where law required it. Bolder still, Markoe responded with directness to complaints that integration led to social equality and miscegenation, a habit that LaFarge considered wildly imprudent. Markoe averred that the mingling of the races in "semi-family life" at school would not corrupt white children. In any case, he insisted, racial intermingling in churches and schools would have to be risked for the sake of Christian justice. Moreover, he reminded his readers, marriage was a holy sacrament that could not be denied on grounds of race. When Markoe sent a particularly shrill article on miscegenation to *America* in 1926, the editors rejected it. LaFarge undoubtedly influenced the decision. Published two years later

New Race Problem," *Am*, 24 (November 27, 1920), 125–26; "Social Equality and Catholic Schools," *Am*, 24 (January 29, 1921), 350–52; "Catholics, the Negro, a Native Clergy," *Am*, 25 (September 24, 1921), 535–37; "Negro Morality and a Colored Clergy," *Am*, 26 (November 12, 1921), 79–81; "Negro Higher Education," *Am*, 26 (April 1, 1922), 558–60; "The Importance of Negro Patriotism," *Am*, 28 (January 27, 1923), 344–45; "The Importance of Negro Leadership," *Am*, 29 (October 13, 1923), 605–606; "Claver Clubs in Operation," *Am*, 30 (April 5, 1924), 590–92.

15. Markoe, "Interracial Role," 17–18, "New Race Problem," 583, "Negro Morality and a Colored Clergy," 80, and "Catholics, the Negro, a Native Clergy," 535.

in Markoe's parish journal, the article held that white disgust over miscegenation lay at the heart of the race problem. Although Markoe denied that blacks generally desired marriage with whites, he maintained
that a "natural sex impulse tending to amalgamation" afflicted the "great
unwashed masses." [16] It is difficult to fathom his true aims in this rambling piece, other than to shock the faculty at St. Louis University to
whom it was originally delivered.

Wanting to shock no one, LaFarge saw the issue of social equality
and intermarriage as no-win issues for Catholicism and tried to avoid
them as much as possible. With his growing emphasis on interracialism,
however, he could not evade the issue entirely. In 1930 he devoted a
short paragraph in "What Do Colored Catholics Want?" to arguing
that blacks, above all, did not want social equality "in the obnoxious
sense attached to this word." Two years later he again explained what
social equality did and did not mean. LaFarge admitted that he did not
know whether blacks craved social fellowship with whites, but he conceded that interracial events necessitated some social amenities. But
"friendly intercourse of serious workers," he added, "did not necessarily create a situation" that led "naturally to intimacies and prolonged
relationships that may be good or bad for many or any reasons." [17]
LaFarge's veiled references to social equality and miscegenation were
cast in language that revealed how uncomfortable he was with the topics
and how much he feared them in the hands of someone as uninhibited
as Markoe. LaFarge knew that miscegenation was a club that racists
wielded against all who worked for racial reform—a fact that in no way
deterred Markoe.

Clashing styles and temperaments, then, tended to drive the two
Jesuits apart. As an editor of *America*, LaFarge took it upon himself to
police for proper prudence all publications about blacks. Markoe
groused that he lost his "national forum" after LaFarge arrived in New
York, for Markoe never had another article on race relations published

16. Markoe, "Solution of the New Race Problem," 126, and "Social Equality and
Catholic Schools," 351–52; William Markoe, "The Mission Crusade and Negro Education," *Am*, 27 (June 3, 1922), 154–56; Markoe, "Social Equality and Catholic Schools,"
350–52; William Markoe, "The Soul of the Colored Man," *Am*, 24 (March 5, 1921), 474–
75, letter to the editor, *Am*, 24 (January 15, 1921), 308, and "The Negro's Viewpoint,"
St. Elizabeth's Chronicle, 1 (April, 1928), 3–4, 16, 32.

17. John LaFarge, "What Do the Colored Catholics Want?," *Am*, 43 (September
20, 1930), 566–67, and "Doing the Truth," *Chronicle*, 5 (April, 1932), 72–73.

in the Jesuit weekly after LaFarge joined the staff. The intramural competition between the two was evident at an early date. Markoe first
became aware of LaFarge when he received a letter from him complaining that the St. Louis Jesuit had not given recognition to LaFarge's
writings or to his pet project, the Cardinal Gibbons Institute.[18]

While in his final years of theological studies in St. Louis, Markoe
engaged in a frenzied schedule of activities among blacks. In addition
to his local activism, his articles for *America,* and his studies (on the
last he seemed to concentrate little), he began to spend more time as a
volunteer at St. Elizabeth's, the racial parish that had served the entire
city of St. Louis since 1873. Shortly after Markoe's ordination in 1926,
the provincial put him in charge of St. Elizabeth's. In his memoirs he
recalled the excitement of the moment by commenting, "The entire
Negro population of St. Louis was my flock."[19]

Under Markoe St. Elizabeth's became a hub of social activity. The
parish sponsored picnics, carnivals, moonlight cruises on the Mississippi, a drum and bugle corps, a parish band, boy scouts, girl scouts,
the Catholic Knights of America, various sodalities, and a host of other
activities. The highlight of parish activities, however, came with the
musical comedies put on by Markoe and his fellow Jesuit Daniel A.
Lord. The author of some fifty plays and thirty-odd books, Lord, like
Markoe, believed in Catholic Action that was "loud, gay, [and] bois-
terous."[20] These plays enjoyed an inspired reception. The black entertainers performed before integrated audiences, and Markoe introduced
the plays with lectures on the evils of racism in St. Louis. He believed
that the plays made the first "small dents" in the local caste system and
established a better climate for interracial cooperation.[21]

Markoe was a man who sought and achieved many racial "firsts."
He claimed a record number of black conversions in the late 1920s and
early 1930s. He drew up plans for a new black church that included a
large auditorium, a gymnasium, and a swimming pool, but the De-

18. Markoe, "Interracial Role," 18–19, 87.
19. *Ibid.,* 41–52, 90.
20. Hennesey, *American Catholics,* 250; Daniel A. Lord, S.J., *Played By Ear* (Chicago, 1956), viii; Daniel A. Lord, "Lessons from a Musical Comedy," *Chronicle,* 3 (July,
1930), 153, 155; Markoe, "Interracial Role," 175–77, 122–25, 212–13, 349, 366–67. See
also Joseph T. McGloin, *Backstage Missionary: Father Dan Lord, S.J.* (New York, 1958).
21. Markoe, "Interracial Role," 137–38, 349.

pression and hierarchical opposition ultimately stymied his plans.[22] In June of 1932 Markoe aired the first *Interracial Hour* over WEW, the St. Louis University radio station. He also experimented with Claver Clubs, each one "a little inter-racial commission." In 1931 he created a new organization called the White Friends of Colored Catholics, which he completely integrated into the "social, cultural, recreational, and financial" life of his black parish.[23]

The irony of a dedicated integrationist pastoring a Jim Crow church was not lost on Markoe. He claimed that he accepted the assignment only as a springboard to a national Catholic movement—a movement that would doom segregation. To further that goal, in March of 1928 he began a parish journal entitled *St. Elizabeth's Chronicle.* No ordinary parish sheet, the monthly journal stated in its first issue that its goal was to reveal the church's "eternal principles" of "Justice and Charity" and to prove to blacks that Catholicism alone had the power to transform a racist society. Markoe sent copies of the journal to black parishes all over the country and solicited news items from them. By November of 1928 the periodical asked for suggestions for a new title that would bespeak its rising "national prominence."[24] Markoe had found the outlet that he had lost at *America.*

His stock on the rise with blacks, Markoe arrived in Baltimore in 1929 to find the Josephites up in arms against Turner and the FCC.[25] The Josephites also believed that LaFarge and Markoe were conspiring with the FCC to embarrass them on the issues of black vocations and segregation. Years later Markoe commented that if the Josephites had only known that he was there to "infiltrate" the FCC, they might have

22. *Ibid.*, 211–12. Reynolds, *Jesuits for the Negro*, 119–20, believes that Markoe exaggerated his number of conversions and slighted that of others. See drawing of church plant in *St. Elizabeth's Chronicle*, 2 (January, 1929), 11, and "Historical Sketch of St. Elizabeth's Parish," *Chronicle*, 4 (September, 1931), 564, and Markoe, "Interracial Role," 341–42.

23. "The Chronicle on the Air," *Chronicle*, 5 (August, 1932), 137; Markoe, "Claver Clubs in Operation," 592; William Markoe, "How Help the Negro?" *Am*, 32 (January 3, 1925), 271–72; Markoe, "Interracial Role," 61, 179.

24. Markoe, "Interracial Role," 91, 109; William Markoe, "The St. Elizabeth's Chronicle," *St. Elizabeth's Chronicle*, 1 (March, 1928), 7; editorial "Wanted—A New Name for the 'Chronicle,'" *St. Elizabeth's Chronicle*, 1 (November, 1928), 10.

25. For Markoe's impact on blacks in St. Louis, see William Barnaby Faherty, S.J., *The Religious Roots of Black Catholics in St. Louis* (St. Louis, 1977), 76, 111–13, 127–28.

welcomed him with open arms. Markoe in fact had sized up the FCC
as a Jim Crow organization and expressed dismay that neither LaFarge
nor Turner took "umbrage at it." Despite his misgivings about the federation, he offered to let it use his parish journal as its official organ.
Having no mouthpiece of its own, the FCC readily accepted his offer.
Markoe then dropped the name of the parish from the title of the journal, and it became *The Chronicle*. Although it was advertised as the
official organ of the FCC, Markoe controlled the journal and was the
sole arbiter of its contents. In his autobiography he cited Baltimore as
a turning point for him and the FCC. "Now we had really infiltrated,"
Markoe crowed.[26]

Markoe, no doubt, exaggerated, after the fact, how suddenly he
made his decision to subvert the FCC. He rather kept his plans hidden
in the months following the Baltimore convention and managed to gain
the trust of Turner and other influential FCC members. In 1930 he
promoted the FCC in editorials such as "Just Watch Us Grow." In July
of 1930, though, Markoe dropped a clue about his real feelings toward
the federation in an article entitled "Our Jim Crow Federation." Commenting on the executive meeting of the FCC the previous June, he
disclosed that there was mounting criticism that the FCC was a Jim
Crow organization, but he coyly defended the agency by explaining
that the title of the organization was really a misnomer. The overriding
goal of the FCC, he wrote, was "a closer union between [*sic*] all Catholics." He reminded readers how many whites were involved in the
FCC, including the editor of its official journal, and how dedicated the
organization was to Catholic Action, which he defined as "lay cooperation with the hierarchy of our country for the advancement of the
Kingdom of Christ."[27] At this point no one in the FCC suspected that
this blackest of white men had any plans to sabotage Turner's protest
movement.

On May 31, 1930, Markoe set out on a long tour to promote the
Chronicle and, more circumspectly, to make the federation more "interracial in character." He traveled to New York, Philadelphia, Pittsburgh, Washington, D.C., Baltimore, Buffalo, Cincinnati, Columbus,
Detroit, and Chicago. Everywhere Markoe went, he remembered,

26. Markoe, "Interracial Role," 129–31.

27. "Just Watch Us Grow," *Chronicle*, 3 (June, 1930), 132; William Markoe, "Our
Jim Crow Federation," *ibid.* (July, 1930), 149–50.

he was "feted as a champion of Catholicism among Negroes, and of the rights of Negroes within the Church, especially by Catholic Negroes."[28]

In New York LaFarge received Markoe warmly, for despite their differences, they had made common cause in regard to the FCC. Markoe described them accurately as "a strange pair, not too compatible." He saw LaFarge as an older, more conservative priest who, while sincere in his efforts to help the minority, was "not quite black enough himself." He judged that LaFarge was an "ultra prudent," "safety first man." Markoe, however, was "rash and reckless" and tended to see prudence as a sin, at least when used as "an alibi for neglect." He hailed LaFarge as a "scholar," but he branded himself a "champion dropout" who detested the academy, especially the Ivy League variety. One might add that Markoe was a first-rate organizer, whereas LaFarge was a reserved man of ideas who preferred to leave many of the organizational details to trusted subordinates. Although an activist, LaFarge found his inspiration through prayer, meditation, and intellectual thought. The contemplative life nearly drove Markoe crazy; he dreaded mandatory retreats in secluded places, absent any black flock for him to shepherd. During his tertianship in 1928 and 1929, he virtually came unhinged in the first month and nearly suffered a breakdown.[29]

Although Markoe was ambitious, in the East he deferred to LaFarge's "seniority," and his "decided superiority." He even offered the New York journalist a monthly column in the *Chronicle*. LaFarge agreed and began his column, "Doing the Truth," the following year. Meanwhile, the time was ripe for Jesuit collaboration. Turner had come down with a serious illness and had to cancel a European trip. It was doubtful he would even be able to attend the fall convention in Detroit. Even when well, the officers of the FCC were occupied with making a living. The situation gave LaFarge and Markoe a golden opportunity to plan the coming convention.[30]

At this juncture a controversial book appeared that further exacerbated the bad feelings between the Josephites and the FCC. John Gillard, a young, able, and rapidly rising Josephite, had just finished his doctoral dissertation and was preparing it for publication at the time

28. Markoe, "Interracial Role," 138–39.
29. *Ibid.*, 2, 4, 43, 119–20, 139–41, 143.
30. *Ibid.*, 139, 141; Nickels, *Black Catholic Protest*, 177–78.

of the Baltimore convention. Early in 1930 it appeared as *The Catholic Church and the American Negro*. As scholarly and prolific as LaFarge and as brash and opinionated as Markoe, Gillard was Pastorelli's secretary and acted as his mouthpiece through the Josephites' official magazine, *Colored Harvest*. Evidence suggests that Pastorelli was already grooming the young priest to be the next superior general of the order.[31]

Most of Gillard's book had a scholarly flavor, filling a statistical and historical void concerning African American Catholics, but the last part covered contemporary issues and was given to undocumented speculation. Here Gillard trotted out the most demeaning racial stereotypes, stressing the low level of intellectuality and the high level of sexuality of blacks. Although Gillard claimed to favor a black clergy, he was transparently negative about the prospects of raising black priests. He concluded that Pope Pius XI's 1926 *Rerum Ecclessiae* on the necessity of native clergies did not apply to the United States. The Baltimore priest reproached black leaders for having a "chip-on-the-shoulder" attitude that resulted in capricious appeals to the hierarchy over imagined racial slights. It is highly revealing that in recounting the Josephite saga, Gillard never mentioned John Slattery, the American father of the Baltimore congregation.[32]

Although Gillard's book received glowing assessments in most Catholic periodicals, LaFarge and various blacks attacked it with acerbic pens. When Gillard sent a copy of his book to LaFarge, he said with a tone of satisfaction that it would surely "irritate" some people. LaFarge replied coldly: "I doubt if much is achieved by irritation. . . . In the long run, I think, more is accomplished by pacific methods."[33] He nonetheless irritated most of the Josephite congregation with his review of Gillard's book. After some brief complimentary remarks on the first five parts of the book, LaFarge trained his guns on Gillard's "personal conjectures," which he characterized as given to the "half-truth" and the "sweeping statement." He upbraided Gillard for his stereotypical remarks about blacks and claimed that they served to create

31. Ochs, *Desegregating the Altar*, 299, 301. Information on Gillard and his book is located in boxes 3 and 4, Gillard Papers, and in "The Josephite Harvest Centennial" (Winter, 1987–88), copy in possession of the author.

32. Gillard, *Catholic Church and the American Negro*, 82, 86–87, 90–92, 225–27, 236–37, 239, 255–56, *passim*.

33. John LaFarge to John Gillard, May 11, 1930, in Gillard Papers. Clippings of several favorable reviews can also be found in "Scrapbook—Clippings," in Gillard Papers.

an atmosphere of "distrust" and "pessimism." LaFarge listed and discussed many of Gillard's offending remarks and provided the page numbers where they appeared. He especially criticized Gillard's "speculations" about the "hereditary tendencies" and "hyper-sexuality" of blacks. He also lambasted a passage from the book that had managed to infuriate black reviewers: "The prospective missioner to the Negro must have a natural adaptability to the child-like mentality of this infantine race." LaFarge further arraigned Gillard for ambivalence on the desirability of black priests and contended that the Josephite had twisted the pope's encyclical on native clergies. Finally, he took belligerent exception to the book's advertisement as the "official" view of the Catholic church.[34]

Turner reviewed Gillard's book two months later in the *Chronicle* at greater length and with more venom. While repeating many of the criticisms made by LaFarge, he wrote in more detail about past Josephite transgressions. Where LaFarge had seen ambivalence on the question of black priests, Turner charged Gillard with outright "propaganda against a race clergy." On several points Turner went beyond LaFarge's critique, disclosing a crucial difference of perspective from that of the priest. For example, he criticized Gillard for ignoring black thinking and black leadership in the church. Turner argued that Gillard treated the African American like a "zoological specimen." Ironically, in light of later events, Turner complained that the book attempted to "rationalize the idea of 'separatism' in national and church life."[35]

Other black reviewers treated Gillard's book similarly. Not surprisingly, Constance Daniel skewered Gillard in a review that was published in *Opportunity,* the official journal of the Urban League. She characterized the book as the "tactless blunderings of a young and overzealous priest" who had no idea that educated blacks existed. The Baltimore *Afro-American* also thrashed Gillard soundly for his stereotypical treatment of blacks. Finally, Carter Woodson unleashed a withering barrage on the book in his own *Journal of Negro History.* After flailing Christianity in general for its racial hypocrisy, Woodson then zeroed in on the Josephites for "failing ingloriously to face courageously such

34. John LaFarge, "Father Gillard's Study of the Catholic Negro," *Chronicle,* 3 (July, 1930), 151–52.
35. Thomas Turner, "Father Gillard's Book," *Chronicle,* 3 (September, 1930), 205–207.

questions as the need for a Negro clergy, race distinctions, and segregation." In concluding, Woodson compared the Josephites unfavorably with LaFarge and Markoe. He noted that the two Jesuits had won the esteem of blacks around them, but he claimed that the Josephites were "hated by the very Negroes among whom they toiled for generations."[36]

Gillard responded to LaFarge in a lengthy letter, complaining that the review of his book was "devastating" and "unfair." He charged that LaFarge's review had focused on just one part of the book and contained only six lines of praise as opposed to eighty-six of blame. Gillard vigorously defended his characterizations of blacks, claiming they were based on the "collective experiences" of countless missionaries. The Josephite argued, moreover, that the "child-like mentality" of blacks was corroborated by psychological tests given to them in World War I.[37]

LaFarge replied to Gillard in an even longer letter (four typed pages in length). He indicated that Gillard should have thought about the possible consequences before wandering blindly into the controversial area of racial characteristics. He asserted that he in no way could allow the book's erroneous message to be seen as the official word of the Catholic church, for that would be highly injurious to the church's quest for black converts. LaFarge repeated many of the same charges he had leveled in his review, especially stressing that the book wrongly posited the "singularity" of blacks by dwelling on black-white differences. He warned Gillard that whites were just waiting to "seize upon" expressions such as "child-like mentality." He further underscored his belief that such characterizations had no scientific validity. Although LaFarge stood his ground, the peace-loving Jesuit concluded his frank letter in a conciliatory vein, commenting that the "cause is too big for any one man or even [one] school of men's thoughts."[38]

36. Constance Daniel, review of *The Catholic Church and the American Negro*, by John T. Gillard, in *Opportunity* (August, 1930), 247–48, copy in Gillard Papers; "Unfair Generalizations," Baltimore *Afro-American*, July 5, 1930; Carter G. Woodson, review of *The Catholic Church and the American Negro*, by John T. Gillard, in *Journal of Negro History*, 15 (July, 1930), 106–107. See Woodson's negative comments on interracialism in Lorenzo J. Greene, *Working with Carter G. Woodson, the Father of Black History: A Diary, 1928–1930*, ed. Arvarh E. Strickland (Baton Rouge, 1989), 221.

37. John Gillard to John LaFarge, June 30, 1930, in box 5, folder 55, JLFP 2.
38. John LaFarge to John Gillard, July 1, 1930, in box 5, folder 55, JLFP 2.

Gillard seemed partially mollified by LaFarge's letter. He replied that the "exchange of ideas" was beneficial and that "an electrical storm often clears the atmosphere." Gillard, however, charged that LaFarge had given ammunition to "intellectual" blacks who would "take down the pants" of the Josephites. Later in the summer LaFarge met with Gillard in Washington, D.C., to try to iron out some of their differences, but the differences remained. On September 30 he sent a letter to Gillard that brought up a touchy issue in the Josephite camp. La-Farge criticized the Josephites for having an *"undue* fear" of southern bishops in regard to the ordination of black priests. LaFarge speculated that the bishops needed the Josephites more than the Josephites needed them, and therefore the order should be more forthright on the necessity of black priests. "I believe," he wrote, "that it is no longer prudence, but a grave imprudence, to be too timid in stating boldly and clearly the essential rights of the Negro as a human being, both in the natural order, and the economy of the Church." LaFarge lectured Gillard that the number of educated blacks was rapidly increasing and the strength of the black press was growing. Lay blacks could not be put off when they demanded "essential human rights," LaFarge warned. Significantly, however, LaFarge added that "the brakes must be applied when things tend against faith or morals." If lay blacks tended toward "un-Catholicity," he told Gillard, their task was "slowly, steadily . . . [to] guide them into the true Catholic manner of expression: to move from the racial to the human viewpoint."[39]

Despite the search for common ground, relations between the Jesuits and the Josephites went from bad to worse. Edward G. Brunner, a veteran Josephite located in New Orleans, collaborated closely with Gillard to fight what they now considered a Jesuit-FCC plot to slander the Josephites. Brunner offered to serve as a proxy warrior for Gillard, advising him to steer clear of public debate with Turner and his henchmen. Since Markoe had made his parish journal the official voice of the FCC, the Josephites considered him a marked man. They believed that Markoe not only had opened up his *Chronicle* to "ignorant and ill-willed" people but had also invaded their territory in the South to stir up unlettered blacks against them. Their resentment knew no bounds

39. John Gillard to John LaFarge, July 3, 1930, and John LaFarge to John Gillard, September 30, 1930, both in box 5, folder 55, JLFP 2.

after Markoe gave a spirited address before a convention of the Knights of Peter Claver in Oklahoma. The speech was subsequently published in the organization's official organ, *The Claverite,* and Markoe later bragged that he had "aroused them [the delegates] to a high pitch of militance." Brunner told Gillard that Markoe was a "zealous ass" and a "demagogue" afflicted with a grotesque "Superiority Complex." [40]

Determined to strike back, Brunner first sent anonymous letters to Markoe and his provincial, but eventually he confronted the Jesuit priest directly in a letter on August 28, 1930. His letter assailed Markoe as an imprudent and ignorant man who had opened the *Chronicle* to "slanderous innuendo" against the Josephites. As for Turner and his crowd, Brunner said they were "race men" first and Catholic incidentally. [41] In two hefty letters to Brunner, Markoe not only defended himself in his sledgehammer prose but also stood up for Turner and his allies. Markoe assured Brunner that the black leaders of the FCC were all good Catholics. He explained to him that the FCC, with Jesuit help, was becoming well organized and thoroughly Catholic. [42]

Meanwhile, Gillard trained his guns on Turner, trying first to remove him from the presidency of the FCC and finally attempting to turn the hierarchy against the federation. Gillard's correspondence shows he believed he had LaFarge's assurance that Turner would be removed sometime after the Baltimore convention in 1929. When this did not occur, Gillard sulked in his tent. Trying to keep some unity in the racial apostolate, LaFarge went to Baltimore to try to persuade Gillard to participate in the 1931 convention in St. Louis. At first Gillard made his appearance in St. Louis contingent upon LaFarge's promise that Turner would be ousted at the convention. LaFarge replied later that he had thought it over and decided it would be "rash of [him] to make such a definite assurance." LaFarge explained to Gillard that he feared forcing the issue of Turner's presidency might only strengthen

40. Edward G. Brunner to John Gillard, September 11, 22, 1930, and October 5, December 9, 1931, all in Gillard Papers; Markoe, "Interracial Role," 152.

41. Brunner to Gillard, September 11, 1930, and Edward Brunner to William Markoe, August 28, 1930, both in Gillard Papers. Brunner seemed to become increasingly reactionary. As rector of Epiphany College in the early 1940s, he stoutly resisted the superior general's efforts to promote black vocations (see Ochs, *Desegregating the Altar,* 377–82, 388).

42. William Markoe to Edward Brunner, September 20, 24, 1930, both in Gillard Papers.

the black leader and his loyal backers. The last part of LaFarge's letter consisted of vague hints about converting the leadership of the FCC to a proper course of action—hints so vague that they were probably lost on Gillard, who did not fully appreciate how far LaFarge and Markoe had already succeeded in altering the FCC. Although he thought LaFarge was guilty of cowardly vacillation in regard to Turner, Gillard agreed to attend the St. Louis convention anyway. To fend off further attacks by blacks and Jesuits, however, he preached, in his words, a "good dogmatic sermon" and gave a sober historical lecture at St. Louis. He celebrated noncontroversial Catholic Action and preached that saving souls was superior to social reform and that eternal salvation took precedence over sociology.[43]

Obviously, nothing LaFarge did in the way of sanitizing the FCC satisfied Gillard, who greatly exaggerated the hostility the Jesuit and Turner felt toward the Josephites. Judging the Josephite missions in the Deep South as vital, LaFarge tried everything he could to appease the Josephites, short of sacrificing all his principles. Even Turner tried to smooth the troubled waters. In response to Woodson's negative review of Gillard's book, Turner wrote a letter to the editor of the *Chronicle* arguing that Woodson had been wrong in saying all blacks hated the Josephites. He praised the work of the congregation and predicted that the FCC and the Josephites would experience "a more productive cooperation than we have had in the past." Later Turner wrote to Pastorelli and informed him that he had expressly forbidden any negative discussion of the Josephites at the Baltimore convention. After the St. Louis convention, however, even LaFarge concluded that the Josephites seemed intent on continuing the dispute.[44]

Convinced that the FCC had not been curtailed by LaFarge, Gillard portrayed the federation in the *Colored Harvest* as un-Catholic and anticlerical. In the spring of 1932 he informed Archbishop Curley that the FCC was "coercing the Hierarchy into certain lines of action"

43. John LaFarge to John Gillard, June 16, 1931, and John LaFarge to John Gillard, n.d. [June, 1931 (?)], both in box 5, folder 55, JLFP 2; John Gillard to L. J. Welbers, S.S.J., May 5, 1932, in Gillard Papers; "The Seventh Annual Convention Program," *Chronicle,* 4 (September, 1931), 551–54.

44. John LaFarge to Michael J. O'Neil, S.S.J., n.d., in box 1, folder 42, JLFP 2; Thomas Turner, letter to the editor of the *Chronicle,* Thomas Turner to Louis B. Pastorelli, superior general of the Josephites, July 8, 1931, and John LaFarge to Thomas Turner, October 16, 1931, all in Turner Papers.

and making judgments on issues that were purely religious. Gillard exclaimed to the archbishop, "I always thought the Catholic Church was directed from the Head down, not from the feet up." A few days earlier Gillard had laid his case against the FCC before Emmett Walsh, the archbishop of Charleston, South Carolina, and the chairman of the administrative board of the NCWC. Gillard tried to persuade Walsh that the FCC consisted primarily of northern blacks who were no more representative of black Catholics than were the Knights of Peter Claver. He maintained that the sole purpose of the organization was "agitation" and that, owing to its loose organization, the federation was beyond hierarchical control.[45]

Gillard vented his spleen more completely in a letter to a fellow Josephite in San Antonio, Texas, the Reverend L. J. Welbers. Gillard told Welbers he had once thought that LaFarge was sincere but no more. Oddly enough, he now believed LaFarge was being duped by Turner. As for Markoe, Gillard called him an irresponsible man with a "messianic complex." And Turner, he asserted, was a devious man who "hate[d] the Josephites" and served as the "self-appointed 'pope' of the colored Catholics in the United States." Additional charges against the three leaders of the federation saturated the steamy letter. In conclusion, Gillard vowed to do everything possible to "disband" the FCC. The following month Gillard asked Markoe not to reprint any of Gillard's articles in the *Chronicle*.[46]

Gillard, of course, had it all wrong about who was being duped. The Detroit convention of 1930 represented a turning point in the history of the FCC. In the executive meeting of the FCC in January of 1930, LaFarge took charge (Markoe and Turner were absent) and put together the agenda for the forthcoming convention. The "directive regulations" passed later in Detroit were published in March in the *Chronicle* under the title "Catholic Action as the Objective of the Federation: Some Suggestions for the Second Day of Detroit." Describing Catholic Action as *"apostolic,"* LaFarge applied his definition to a variety of areas such as education, the retreat movement, young people's

45. Ochs, *Desegregating the Altar,* 311; John Gillard to Archbishop Michael J. Curley, April 13, 1932, and John Gillard to Archbishop Emmett Walsh, April 5, 1932, both in Gillard Papers.

46. Gillard to Welbers, May 5, 1932, and John Gillard to William Markoe, June 29, 1932, both in Gillard Papers.

welfare, rural life, the liturgical movement, foreign and home missions, and the "Interracial Movement." His main point was that the FCC should be organized so it could carry out many of these activities that reached above and beyond mere racial protest and aimed at the greater glory of Catholicism. By August of 1930 the *Chronicle* advertised itself as a "National Monthly Inter-racial Magazine," and LaFarge came away from Detroit confident that the transformation of the FCC had begun. In the *Chronicle* he rejoiced that the "great programs of Catholic Action [had been] adopted as our own." He prayed that the convention themes would "lead to deeds worthy of our high ideals!" (LaFarge's use of an exclamation point, unlike Markoe's, was extremely rare.) The Jesuit did not mention that the Detroit rules mandated strict ecclesiastical approval and guidance of all FCC chapters. Throughout this period LaFarge campaigned constantly to ban individual, at-large membership in the FCC, for he, like Gillard, feared that un-Catholic individuals might slip into the federation. The best he could do, however, was to limit voting to chapters rather than to individuals.[47]

Two years later, when the Turner affair came to a climax, several of the founding members of the FCC claimed they had warned Turner that the Detroit regulations threatened lay leadership. For example, G. A. Henderson, one of the vice-presidents of the FCC, recalled in 1932: "I foresaw this trouble, in Detroit, and spoke to Doctor Turner . . . saying that the Detroit Rules gave an entering wedge for the clergy to get control of the Federation."[48]

But Turner, who was contesting several issues before the American hierarchy in 1931, wanted to retain support of the clergy. He thus paid lip service to Catholic Action and reminded the FCC chapters that the Detroit rules required ecclesiastical approval by local church officials. Turner, however, sounded a note of caution, saying he was "not at all blind to certain difficulties" that could arise under the Detroit regulations. He nevertheless argued that the improvement of black Catholics was "contingent upon harmonious relationships existing between . . .

47. "Catholic Action as the Objective of the Federation," *Chronicle,* 3 (May, 1930), 51–52, 66; John LaFarge to William Markoe, January 25, 1930, in box 8, folder 24, JLFP 1; reference to the title in *Chronicle,* 3 (August, 1930), 197; John LaFarge, "Two Echoes of the Convention," *Chronicle,* 3 (November, 1930), 271–72; John LaFarge, "Principles Underlying the Federated Colored Catholics," in box 3, folder 16, JLFP 1.

48. G. A. Henderson to H. M. Smith, secretary of the FCC, November 18, 1932, in Turner Papers.

organizers and clergy, and chapters and clergy." Only in June of 1932 did Turner mention the growing alarm of some blacks that "Detroit was entirely new and endangered their hopes for Lay control and Lay participation in Catholic matters." Even at that point, however, Turner still reached out for clerical support.[49]

Meanwhile, the 1931 FCC convention in St. Louis gave Markoe his day in the sun. The convention, which met for three days in early September, proved the largest and most successful to that time. Markoe described the events lovingly in his autobiography. On Sunday morning a magnificent procession of over five hundred clergy and laity representing some seventy thousand black Catholics marched from St. Elizabeth's to the St. Louis University church of St. Francis Xavier. To Markoe's surprise, his old nemesis, John Glennon, the archbishop of St. Louis, showed up to welcome the delegates and guests. Glennon, who harbored decidedly antiblack views, had earlier refused Markoe's invitations to speak and had denied him the use of the archdiocese's St. Louis Cathedral for the ceremonies. At St. Francis Xavier's the Reverend Stephen Theobald, one of three black priests in the United States, celebrated a solemn high mass. Endorsements poured in from the pope, from the apostolic delegate, and from more than a score of cardinals and bishops.[50]

What stuck in Markoe's mind about the convention is revealing. He noted that the telegram from Cardinal Eugenio Pacelli, the secretary of state at the Vatican and the future Pius XII, omitted the word *colored* from the federation's title. He exulted as St. Elizabeth's choir entertained the delegates with the "blues." He relished the evening address by Father Theobald, a native of British Guiana who had studied law at Cambridge University before becoming a protégé of Archbishop Ireland in St. Paul. The black priest scolded the university for excluding blacks and did so in the school's auditorium in front of the school's

---

49. Thomas Turner, "Address Made at Detroit Convention," *Chronicle*, 3 (December, 1930), 289; Thomas Turner, "Official Letter of the Federated Colored Catholics," *Chronicle*, 4 (September, 1931), 541; Thomas Turner, "Our Detroit Regulations," *Chronicle*, 5 (June, 1932), 110–11; Thomas Turner to Gustave Aldrich, March 18, 1931, in Turner Papers.

50. Markoe, "Interracial Role," 187–201; "The Seventh Annual Convention Program," *Chronicle*, 4 (September, 1931), 551–54; John LaFarge, "The Bridge at St. Louis," *Am*, 45 (September 26, 1931), 585–87.

president. Markoe admired Theobald's courage. Interestingly, in 1924 Theobald had written Turner that he would be "beheaded" if he "dared associate with a lay movement" like the FCC. Most of all, Markoe enjoyed the interracial dance held at the university, an event that Markoe calculated would set off alarm bells in the minds of the Jesuit bureaucracy and Archbishop Glennon. "Maybe," Markoe said of the dance, "we were too Catholic!" [51]

The crucial fact about the convention remains that LaFarge and Markoe prodded the FCC further along in the direction of Catholic Action and interracialism and further away from the emphasis on black protest and race leadership. Markoe filled the *Chronicle* with calls for more interracial activity in the months prior to the meeting. The huge flyers that advertised the convention carried below the title of the organization the following subheading: "America's Most Important Interracial Congress." [52] LaFarge, too, pressured Turner, harping incessantly on the "Detroit Rules" and "procedures." He encouraged ever more nonracial activities and ever purer apostolic Catholic Action by the FCC in the quest of a larger Catholicity. [53] On June 19, 1931, LaFarge suggested that the entire structure of the federation be changed, making the presidency largely honorary and giving real control to a permanent secretary and a small board of trustees. He also proposed that two names be offered by the nominating committee for every position in the FCC. More dramatically, a month later LaFarge threatened to resign from the FCC unless the Detroit rules were upheld in a federation dispute in Philadelphia. When William Bruce, backed by William Prater, national field agent of the FCC, disputed Father Vincent Dever's control of federation activity in Philadelphia, LaFarge emphatically demanded that Turner see to it power remained in Dever's hands or he would resign from the organization. At stake, LaFarge

51. Markoe, "Interracial Role," 188, 190, 199–201; Stephen Theobald, "Our Hope and Aspirations," *Chronicle*, 4 (November, 1931), 656–59; Stephen Theobald to Thomas Turner, May 23, 1924, in Turner Papers; Hunton, *All of Which I Saw*, 107–108.

52. William Markoe, "The Annual Convention—1931," *Chronicle*, 4 (June, 1931), 457–58, and "Plans For the National Convention," *ibid.* (July, 1931), 488; "The Need for Greater Inter-Racial Activity," *ibid.* (August, 1931), 520–21; copy of flyer in Turner Papers; Markoe, "Interracial Role," 203–304.

53. See, for example, John LaFarge to Thomas Turner, April 1, 7, 1931, both in Turner Papers.

insisted, was *"the whole question of ecclesiastical authority."* Moreover, the Jesuit charged, the black organizers Prater and Bruce were rude, dishonest, and insufficiently Catholic.[54]

It is telling that less than two months later, at the St. Louis convention, Prater was replaced as national field agent by Elmo Anderson. Anderson was president of the LaFarge-created Catholic Laymen's Union and had recently become the executive secretary of the Catholic Board for Mission Work among the Colored People. The board, located in New York, was headed by LaFarge's friend the Reverend Edward D. Kramer. Anderson's appointment suggested several things. He essentially became the national organizer of the FCC, a post similar to the position of executive secretary that LaFarge had recommended to replace the presidency. And Anderson, as an employee of the mission board, would have more time to devote to the FCC than Turner, a busy professor at Hampton. Finally, through Anderson and LaFarge, the FCC might be able to tap some of the funds that the Board of Colored Missions expended on black missions. This funding amounted to about $400,000 in 1930, none of which had gone to the FCC. In his last report as field agent at the 1931 convention, Prater expressed some of the rising frustration that existed in the FCC concerning the increasing white control of the organization. "The Federation is not enslaved," he cried out. "Catholic men and women can come together for any good purpose without the sanctions of any church head."[55]

Despite some signs of rebellion at St. Louis, LaFarge had to be pleased with the convention. He had installed one of his black disciples as national organizer, and he had beaten back attempts from the Philadelphia chapter to amend the Detroit rules. Only LaFarge's suggestion that the nominating committee present two names for every elected position had not passed. Perhaps this program was his way of signaling to Gillard his good faith in trying to ease Turner out of the presidency. In any case, LaFarge put his usual conservative gloss on the FCC convention in the pages of *America*. He depicted the convention as a "bridge" between black and white, poor and affluent. Emphasizing

---

54. John LaFarge to Thomas Turner, June 19, July 13, 1931, both in Turner Papers.

55. Nickels, *Black Catholic Protest*, 84–85, 266; Eugene J. McGuinness to Thomas Turner, November 26, 1930, in Turner Papers; William Prater, "Report of Field Agent of the Federated Catholics of the United States, 1931," *Chronicle*, 4 (November, 1931), 666.

Catholic duties over black rights, he rejoiced that Catholic Action had been proclaimed the "chief aim" of the federation. He saluted the FCC for its broadened perspective and praised the delegates for condemning birth control as immoral as well as "socially and economically unsound." Most important, LaFarge proclaimed that the barrier that had separated blacks and whites had been bridged. The "Federation's membership," he boasted, "is [now] open to all who have the welfare of the Negro at heart." Privately, LaFarge told the Jesuit Richard McKeon that providence had placed the leadership of Catholic Negroes "in our hands."[56]

In St. Louis, Turner exhibited the strain of the "twoness" of being black in America, a thought that Du Bois had expressed so eloquently in his classic *The Souls of Black Folk* (as a minority within a minority, Turner in fact was subjected to a "threeness"). On the one hand, Turner's presidential address in 1931 was more militant than ever. As the Depression deepened, Turner stressed even more the tragic side of black life. He spoke of how petty discriminations had elevated black emotions to "fever heat." He raked white society over the coals for waging war on an oppressed people and thundered that the church had done little to fight racial discrimination or raise a black clergy. The upshot, Turner grieved, was that the "Negro Catholic" was "standing on the brink of spiritual disaster." The resolutions passed by the delegates were equally militant, demanding equality of opportunity in worship, education, and economics. The delegates also condemned lynching and expressed their resentment at being called a "problem" by whites.[57]

On the other hand, Turner acquiesced in the Jesuits' continued efforts to apply the Detroit regulations and emphasize Catholic Action. He in fact apologized for his hypercritical remarks in St. Louis and took pains to praise LaFarge ("the untiring friend" of the FCC), Markoe, and other white priests without whom, Turner announced, "very little progress" could have been made. Turner also did LaFarge's bidding in the Philadelphia controversy by strongly backing Father Dever

56. Nickels, *Black Catholic Protest*, 80–81, 84, 264; John LaFarge, "The Bridge at St. Louis," 586–87; John LaFarge to Richard McKeon, S.J., January 22, 1932, in box 1, folder 2, Stanton Papers.

57. Du Bois, *Souls of Black Folk*, 17; Thomas Turner, "The Social Order and the Catholic Negro," *Chronicle*, 4 (November, 1931), 650–54, and "Platform of the Federated Colored Catholics," *Chronicle*, 4 (September, 1931), 549.

over the black activists Bruce and Prater, lest the Jesuit carry out his threat to leave the FCC.⁵⁸

Outwardly, St. Louis marked the apex of FCC morale and harmony. LaFarge and Markoe felt good because they believed they had molded the FCC into a genuine Catholic organization. In 1931 most blacks inside and outside the FCC hailed the two Jesuits as true friends of the African American. Black federation members especially appreciated them for the national publicity they afforded the group. LaFarge, for example, saw to it that Rome was informed about the FCC through the semiofficial Vatican newspaper *Osservatore Romano.* Turner told Markoe that St. Louis was a "splendid success" because of him. "The result was glorious," he beamed, "not a hitch anywhere; everyone cooperated to the fullest." Black newspapers such as the Chicago *Defender* and the New York *Age* proclaimed the indispensability of the two Jesuit priests to the black cause.⁵⁹

Nevertheless, LaFarge pressed on with his plans to reform the FCC. The executive committee of the federation met in New York in January and again in June of 1932 and agreed to revise the constitution and bring it in line with the Detroit directives. In addition, the committee selected New York City as the site of the next convention. The locations of the conventions in 1931 and 1932 speak volumes about the direction of events. If Detroit was an "entering wedge," New York would blow the door wide open for the metamorphosis of the FCC. During the summer before the convention, LaFarge primed black Catholics with publications and private letters, exhorting them to incorporate into the FCC structure virtually every idea he had recommended to them since coming to New York. In his regular column in the *Chronicle,* he reported, much as Markoe had in "Our Jim Crow Federation," that some delegates had suggested a name change for the organization. He pointed out that the name " 'National Catholic Inter-Racial Fed-

58. Thomas Turner, "A Letter from the President of the Federation," *Chronicle,* 4 (June, 1931), 455; Turner, "Social Order and the Catholic Negro," 654; H. M. Smith to Thomas Turner, August 8, 1931, Thomas Turner to William Bruce, July 16, 29, 1931, and Thomas Turner to C. J. Foster, July 10, 1931, all in Turner Papers.

59. Nickels, *Black Catholic Protest,* 70; Thomas Turner to William Markoe, September 16, 1931, in Turner Papers; "Federated Catholics Ready for Seventh Annual Confab," Chicago *Defender,* August 22, 1931, and article, title unclear, New York *Age,* August 1, 1931, both clippings in box 3, folder 16, JLFP 1.

eration,' whether desirable or not," indicated what had actually occurred in the FCC.[60]

In two lengthy letters to Turner in August, LaFarge expressed what
would eventually emerge as one of the essential differences between
him and the FCC president. LaFarge maintained that the church must
take the long, slow course of educating the white laity on the racial
question. He argued that direct protest to the hierarchy could not be
successful until there was an "improvement in the *general* attitude of
the Catholic public." The Jesuit speculated that shrill protest might
cause another type of interracial organization to be "imposed by authority." He pointedly reminded Turner that the hierarchy had the
"right and duty not merely to advise, but to prescribe the norms according to which [racial activity] shall be conducted in specific
instances."[61]

Markoe was also about the FCC's business. Actually, Markoe, always at odds with his superiors, had been removed as pastor at St.
Elizabeth's immediately before the St. Louis convention, but his con-
siderate replacement did not announce the change until after the convention. Now Markoe let it be known that he could devote all of his
time to the federation. LaFarge therefore brought him to New York to
plan the 1932 convention. Markoe spent two months in a rented office
in New York City and put out two issues of the *Chronicle* there. He
brought along his invaluable secretary, a young black intellectual named
Hazel McDaniel Tableau. The two made many side trips to Harlem and
around the Northeast to "propagandize" the chapters, as Markoe put
it, to the idea of interracialism.[62]

Again, Turner seemed to accommodate himself to the desires of
LaFarge and Markoe. He hoped to keep the FCC unified in order to
accomplish several immediate goals. He, as usual, was occupied in 1932
with presenting appeals for black rights to the pope and to the American hierarchy. He also deeply involved himself in the case of William
Lane, a black seminarian who had finished a large part of his training
but could find no bishop to sponsor him for ordination and placement

60. Nickels, *Black Catholic Protest*, 89, 91–92; John LaFarge, "Doing the Truth,"
Chronicle, 5 (April, 1932), 72–73, and (July, 1932), 130–31.
61. John LaFarge to Thomas Turner, August 6, 24, 1932, both in Turner Papers.
62. Markoe, "Interracial Role," 226–35.

after his original sponsor bailed out. In addition, Turner devoted a great deal of time attempting to end the exclusion of blacks from Catholic University. After much negotiation between Turner and Catholic authorities, James W. Ryan, the rector of the university, finally informed him, "The time is not ripe to admit colored students." LaFarge also grieved for the black seminarian, and he supported Turner's efforts to integrate Catholic University. But he did so quietly, behind the scenes, instructing Turner at one point not to include his name in a letter of protest about Lane to the apostolic delegate.[63]

Turner's deference to LaFarge and Markoe actually indicated the growing strength of the Jesuits in the federation. LaFarge and Markoe had brought into the FCC many new members who had strong loyalties to them. Trying to please the Jesuits, Turner regularly made public statements such as "the chief aim [of the FCC] is not to 'fight discrimination,' as some have claimed."[64] All the while, however, he was receiving complaints from founding members that they were unhappy with the increasing clerical control of the organization. Eugene A. Clark announced that he strongly opposed the proposed constitutional changes because he felt that under them it would be impossible to do anything "without ecclesiastical approval." Turner showed some signs of uneasiness himself when in March he asked Markoe not to publish the proposed constitutional revisions in the *Chronicle*. In a charged letter to a Josephite priest in April, he spoke out against discrimination and bemoaned the paucity of "Race leaders" among Catholics. Turner remarked that secular black groups had achieved much more and in less time than black Catholics. LaFarge seemed to answer Turner in his column in the August *Chronicle*. "The Catholic Church works without haste," the Jesuit wrote. "She is neither feverish nor fretful."[65] Turner,

63. Thomas Turner to Pope Pius XI, August 24, 1932, and Thomas Turner to the American Hierarchy, n.d. [1932], both in Turner Papers; Ryan, quoted in Ochs, *Desegregating the Altar,* 310; Pietro Fumasoni-Biondi, apostolic delegate to the United States, to Thomas Turner, February 23, 1932, and John LaFarge to Thomas Turner, January 19, February 19, 1932, all in Turner Papers.

64. Thomas Turner, "The Spirit of the Federated Colored Catholics," *Chronicle,* 5 (May, 1932), 92. See also his "Our Detroit Regulations," 110–11.

65. Eugene A. Clark to Thomas Turner, August 18, 1932, in Turner Papers; William B. Bruce, "An Open Letter to the Members of the Federated Colored Catholics of the United States," March 15, 1932, in box 3, folder 16, JLFP 1; Thomas Turner to L. J.

however, was increasingly pessimistic and impatient about events in Depression-ridden America. His rhetoric grew more strident and his tone more urgent. The future to him was, more and more, at hand.

Clearly, Turner would have to fight in New York to recapture some of the original purpose of the federation and reclaim his leadership. But LaFarge and Markoe now had many advantages. The extravaganza put on in New York, which exceeded the one in St. Louis in size and pomp, was impressive to black Catholics accustomed to receiving little attention. In the opening ceremonies, a spectacular procession made its way to St. Patrick's Cathedral, where the convention mass was celebrated. Around four thousand blacks attended the service. The FCC now claimed to represent a hundred thousand black Catholics, about half of all those in the United States. Black and Catholic newspapers gave the convention front-page coverage, and the secular press in the area, including the New York *Times,* gave it extensive notice as well. Some fifty priests attended, all white. Father Theobald had died shortly after the St. Louis convention, depriving black Catholics of any leadership from the black clergy. Another conspicuously absent was Father Dever from Philadelphia. On the eve of the convention, he had confided to Turner, "I do not think it wise to let the impression grow that a few of us white members of the Federation are running it."[66] Having no such reservations, Markoe took Dever's place as chairman of the constitutional revision committee.

Because of months of careful preparation, LaFarge and Markoe gained control of the convention. The executive committee changed the name of the FCC to the National Catholic Federation for the Promotion of Better Race Relations, and it approved a constitutional revision that eliminated the words *colored* and *Negro* from the basic charter as much as possible. Although Turner gave in to these changes, he still clearly considered "racial solidarity and racial improvement" the key goals of the federation; and, above all, he reasoned that the feder-

Welbers, April 30, 1932, in Turner Papers; John LaFarge, "Doing the Truth," *Chronicle,* 5 (August, 1932), 151.

66. Hazel McDaniel Tableau, "Federated Colored Catholics Make History in New York City Convention," *Chronicle,* 5 (October, 1932), 195, 198–200; "Catholics Vote to Change Name of Federation," Baltimore *Afro-American,* September 10, 1932; "Pope Pius Cables Convention," New York *Times,* September 4, 1932; Vincent Dever to Thomas Turner, September 1, 1932, in Turner Papers.

ation had to remain "as an instrument of the Negro layman."[67] Turner seemed to be hoping against the odds that any changes would prove to be largely cosmetic.

Although Markoe attended to most of the programmatic details of the convention and thus clashed most directly with Turner, engaging with the president in spirited arguments about the objectives of the organization, it should be remembered that it was LaFarge who brought Markoe to New York two months prior to the convention. Moreover, when the quiet patrician took the floor of the executive meeting and argued so vehemently for changing the federation's name, he astounded Markoe and the New York delegates with his uncharacteristic passion. After the convention LaFarge was quoted as follows: "An organization designed to promote better race relations should itself be interracial in character." Under the heading "Name Change Voted by Negro Catholics," the New York *Times* praised the federation for erasing the color line.[68]

As the convention broke up, LaFarge provided the spark that set off an explosion in the revamped federation. As Markoe was leaving New York, LaFarge suggested that he change the name of the *Chronicle* to the *Interracial Review* in order to reflect the mood of the convention. Informed by Markoe of this change on September 23, Turner erupted. He informed Archbishop Curley, the nominal spiritual director of the federation, and Markoe that the St. Louis journal, because of the illegal name change, would be dropped as the official organ of the organization. Markoe, in turn, alerted Turner that the journal, whatever it was called, belonged strictly to him and his religious order and that he would use it as he saw fit. Markoe also defended Elmo Anderson's postconvention appointment of himself as deputy to the national organizer of the federation, adding that his appointment by one of LaFarge's faithful allies did not need the approval of the president or the executive committee.[69]

67. Thomas Turner to Eugene Clark, September 18, 1932, in Turner Papers.

68. Markoe, "Interracial Role," 230, 235–36, 243; Tableau, "Federated Catholics Make History," 199–200; "Name Change Voted by Negro Catholics," New York *Times*, September 6, 1932.

69. Markoe, "Interracial Role," 244; William Markoe to Thomas Turner, September 23, 1932, in Turner Papers; Thomas Turner to Archbishop Michael J. Curley, October 8, 1932, in Gillard Papers; William Markoe to Thomas Turner, October 10, 1932, in Turner Papers.

The battle lines quickly formed after the *Interracial Review* appeared in October. Those who had been suspicious of the Jesuits all along now bombarded Turner and one another with letters expressing their outrage and anxiety.[70] Turner then issued a press release that denounced Markoe in acid prose. For the next three months charges and countercharges flew wantonly from both camps, and the hierarchy cringed as Catholics washed their dirty linen in public. After Turner's press release, Eugene Clark in Washington, D.C., arranged a meeting at his home between Markoe and Turner in hopes of a reconciliation. Also present at the meeting were several of Turner's allies, including Father Alonzo Olds of St. Augustine's, Turner's old parish in Washington, D.C.[71]

Markoe, however, stormed into the city in an offensive mode. He had once defended Turner against his Josephite detractors, but he now judged that the FCC president had "a little bit of the Black Muslim in him." He believed that the sharecropper's son might have good reason to be suspicious of all whites, but he charged that Turner had become a paranoid and dangerous man. When Markoe arrived at the meeting, he refused to shake Turner's hand until the professor apologized for his attack on him in the press. Turner replied that there was no reason for an apology, and the business end of the meeting terminated abruptly. Later, the raffish priest seemed almost shocked at his own behavior. He conceded in his memoirs that his actions constituted a failure of diplomacy and Christian charity, but he reminded the reader that it happened "before the day of dialog and ecumenism"; in addition, he pleaded that he "did not know how else to act."[72]

After the Washington, D.C., confrontation, Markoe traveled to New York to consult with LaFarge, though what transpired between them was not recorded. We do know that soon after their meeting Markoe persuaded George Conrad of Cincinnati, the first vice-president of the federation, to call an executive meeting in Chicago on December 4 to consider the removal of Turner from the presidency. (A regular meeting was scheduled for early January in Washington, D.C.)

70. See, for example, G. A. Henderson to H. M. Smith, November 18, 1932, and Eugene Clark to William Markoe, October 7, 1932, both in Turner Papers.

71. Thomas Turner, "Letter to the Catholic and Secular Press by the President," October [?], 1932, and Eugene Clark to Thomas Turner, November 6, 1932, both in Turner Papers.

72. Markoe, "Interracial Role," 229–30, 249–51.

Turner characterized Conrad, a conservative black lawyer, as a "lackey." Even Markoe confessed that Conrad was an "Uncle Tom." In the Chicago meeting Markoe induced a fraction of the executive committee (nine of twenty-five members, mostly from the Midwest) to evict Turner from office on charges of "unwarranted assumption of power," "false publicity," and "imprudence." The committee dropped the charge of "treason." Turner and his supporters boycotted the meeting and declared it illegal on the grounds that the president did not call the meeting and that two-thirds of the full committee did not vote for the ouster as required by the constitution.[73]

After the Chicago meeting, the war via the press reignited. Markoe used his journal to inveigh against the "type of Negro leader who would prefer to be a 'kingfish' in a Negro organization rather than a respected human being in an interracial group." The *Afro-American* quoted Markoe as saying that Turner's dismissal was caused by his predilection for "racial discrimination."[74] A highly influential and often sensational newspaper, the *Afro-American* fought Turner's fight on the front page, rallying the eastern bloc of black Catholics, who met on January 8, 1933, to reconstitute the old FCC. Cora Grace Inman wrote a series of articles that battered Catholicism and described LaFarge and Markoe as false friends of blacks who insisted on telling blacks what they ought to want. The editors of the newspaper labeled Markoe's "Kingfish" article "ridiculous" and "silly." An article entitled "LaFarge's Old Parish Voted to Support Dr. Turner" aimed at the priest's soft spot for southern Maryland. At the NAACP, Du Bois roasted Markoe and the church. He described Turner and his allies as men who had discarded the meekness expected of black Catholics. They had instead "stood up and talked like men and not begged like supplicants." Du Bois portrayed the controversy as a clear case of white clergymen trying to suppress the voice of black laymen. Ridiculing Markoe's accusation of

73. Nickels, *Black Catholic Protest*, 194; George Conrad to Thomas Turner, October 29, 1932, and Thomas Turner to Carl J. Murphy, January 20, 1933, both in Turner Papers; Markoe, "Interracial Role," 288; "Catholics Oust Dr. Turner," Baltimore *Afro-American*, December 17, 1932; "Catholic Head to Disregard 'Rump' Ouster," Baltimore *Afro-American*, December 24, 1932.

74. William Markoe, " 'Kingfish' Race Leaders," *IR*, 6 (February, 1933), 29; "Priest Advises ANP When Federation Will Meet," Baltimore *Afro-American*, January 7, 1933. Markoe was also quoted to the same effect in the black Norfolk *Journal and Guide*, [January 11(?)], 1933, clipping in Turner Papers.

Jim Crow, Du Bois tartly summed up what he depicted as an old and specious argument: "Don't segregate yourselves! Let's all get together, whites and blacks, and let the wise whites lead you." [75]

Watching gleefully from the sidelines, Father Gillard exclaimed that he was "delighted to learn that 'thieves are falling out.' " The Josephite intriguer charged that LaFarge and Markoe had been manufacturing black radicals for years, but they had not expected one to turn on them. As soon as Turner became a problem, Gillard observed, the Jesuits acted. "Seldom, if ever," he declared, "do Jesuits play second fiddle." [76]

LaFarge, who detested intra-Catholic controversy, laid low during the climax of the Turner affair. He avoided discussion of the federation split in his regular columns, and only in February and March did he obliquely refer to the FCC upheaval. In a February essay in *America*, LaFarge began by quoting Conrad, the newly installed president, who had solemnly pledged the federation to greater obedience to the hierarchy. The most significant feature of the rambling, puffy article was LaFarge's discussion of his long-range racial strategy, which he summed up as "the *general education of the Catholic laity* to the Negro's actual situation, needs and desires." In the *Interracial Review* he defined "interracial" and argued its superiority over "racial," without mentioning the Turner affair. LaFarge concluded the essay by saying that the Negro expected "the white man not to overreach him [and] to work for his

75. On the Baltimore *Afro-American*, see Maxwell Brooks, *The Negro Press Re-Examined* (Boston, 1959), 77–78, 80–81. Cora Grace Inman (a pen name for an unknown writer whom some believed to be Constance Daniel because of the prose style and because Inman's initials corresponded with the abbreviation for the Cardinal Gibbons Institute), "Pots, Kettles, Soap and Water Needed in Catholic Controversy," Baltimore *Afro-American*, February 18, 1933, and "Newest Racket Is Whites Who Pose as Authorities on the Negro," Baltimore *Afro-American*, January 28, 1933; "Kingfish," Baltimore *Afro-American*, February 18, 1933; "LaFarge's Old Parish Votes to Support Dr. Turner," Baltimore *Afro-American*, February 4, 1933. W. E. B. Du Bois, "The Negro and the Catholic Church," *Crisis*, 42 (March, 1933), 68–69. Some of the following articles in the *Afro-American* give the flavor of the debate: "Catholic Federation Constitution Shows that Dr. Turner Was Ousted by 'Rump' Committee," December 17, 1932; "Dr. Turner Absent as Rump Committee Put Him Out," December 17, 1933; "Catholics Sure to Support Dr. Turner," December 31, 1932; "Conrad's Former Neighbor Will Support Dr. Turner," January 7, 1933; "Dr. Turner Says He Still Heads Catholic Federation," January 21, 1933; and "Dr. Turner Asks Where Father Markoe Was When Federation Met Bishops," February 4, 1933.

76. John Gillard to Archbishop Michael Curley, October 10, 1932, in Gillard Papers.

true welfare, not for any personal scheme of political or social self-aggrandizement," words that must have exasperated Turner and his supporters.[77]

The public histrionics of Markoe and the relative silence of LaFarge during the FCC controversy tempt the historian to focus on Markoe and downplay LaFarge's role in Turner's removal.[78] A conspicuously ambitious man in whom many detected a messianic complex, Markoe gloated in his memoirs that he joined the FCC to "infiltrate" it, as we noted earlier. But LaFarge, it must be remembered, was the senior partner of the Jesuit team. It is no surprise that he "laid low" during the controversy, for that was his normal mode of operation during prickly disputes. He abhorred controversy, fearing that it would threaten Catholic solidarity and that non-Catholics would capitalize on it. He obviously tried to distance himself from the rampaging Markoe and to avoid culpability for the acrimonious split in the federation. Arthur Schomburg, the famous Puerto Rican collector of African Americana, said that LaFarge was "as silent as he [was] clever."[79] With Markoe eagerly playing the hatchet man, LaFarge had an opportunity to distance himself from the coup d'etat. It was he, however, who brought Markoe to New York in 1930 and 1932 to organize and enhance clerical control of the FCC. After his disastrous confrontation with Turner in Washington, D.C., Markoe traveled to New York to consult with LaFarge prior to the rump session in Chicago. At the time of Turner's ouster, LaFarge sent a telegram to Markoe, but unfortunately it and any telephone calls between the two have been lost to history. Fortunately, the Turner Papers contain LaFarge's crucial correspondence with the black leader, for it is unaccountably absent from the LaFarge Papers. LaFarge also avoided meaningful discussion of Turner and the federation split in his autobiography and other books on the race question. Markoe, of course, acted decisively and openly in the Turner episode and seemed eager to expose himself in his memoirs. The younger Jesuit maintained, though, that he always bowed to the "seniority" and "superiority" of the New York Jesuit, who during the climax of the Turner affair was always just off stage.[80]

77. John LaFarge, "Catholic Negroes Take Stock," *Am,* 48 (February 4, 1933), 429–31, and "What Is Interracial?," *IR,* 6 (March, 1933), 54–55.
78. See, for example, Nickels, *Black Catholic Protest,* 310.
79. Arthur Schomburg to Thomas Turner, n.d., in Turner Papers.
80. Markoe, "Interracial Role," 141; William Markoe to John LaFarge, December

The dissidents on the East Coast, the New York delegates excepted, certainly held both Jesuits guilty in the breakup of the FCC. Both publicly and privately, Turner depicted LaFarge as a coconspirator. In the pages of the *Afro-American,* he spoke of the "insidious forces" that had undermined black Catholic unity. He told Du Bois that the priests had tried to convert the FCC into a "Jesuit subsidiary." Turner also described LaFarge as a paternalist who used the concept of interracialism to impose clerical control on the federation; and clerical control, he claimed, amounted to an "insidious assault . . . on *Negro leadership.*" Both Jesuits, he wrote Prater, "tried to grab the land, put up their flag, and claim the country for their own." He expressed outrage to the black priest Norman DuKette of Detroit on hearing that LaFarge had pressured Father Olds not to attend the Washington, D.C., meeting of the eastern federation in January of 1933. Finally, Turner put out the story that LaFarge's actions against the FCC were motivated in part by his fear that the federation was going to expose the segregation, or the "ugly spots," in the Jesuit missions in southern Maryland. This charge, whatever its truth, cannot be verified.[81]

Much has been made of LaFarge's humble and dignified manner in this study and elsewhere, but it should not obscure his determination to act as the key Catholic spokesman on racial policy in the United States. We have seen already that as soon as LaFarge became the "Negro expert" at *America,* Markoe immediately lost his access to the magazine. In trying to discern why LaFarge seemed to lose interest in the western federation so quickly, Markoe speculated that his own prominence there may have become too great to suit LaFarge, who may have concluded, Markoe mused, that "the Federation was not big enough for

---

27, 1932, in box 3, folder 16, JLFP 1. LaFarge kept legal notes on handling correspondence, including destroying it; see box 10, folder 3, JLFP 2.

81. "Catholic Head to Disregard 'Rump' Ouster," Baltimore *Afro-American,* December 24, 1932; Thomas Turner, "Statement to [Executive] Committee," January 8, 1933; Thomas Turner to W. E. B. Du Bois, March 3, 1933; Thomas Turner to William Prater, n.d.; Thomas Turner to Father Norman Duckett (Ochs spells the name "DuKette" in *Desegregating the Altar,* 277), March 11, 1933; Thomas Turner to Theobald Wade, date unclear; unpublished autobiography of Thomas W. Turner—all in Turner Papers. See also interview of Thomas W. Turner by Marilyn W. Nickels, March 24, 1973, transcript in Josephite Archives, Baltimore; "Federation Head Tells Why Priests Sought to Oust Him," Baltimore *Afro-American,* January 14, 1933; and Thomas Turner, "Our Federated Colored Catholics," *Voice,* 1 (April, 1934), 2–5, copy in Turner Papers.

both of us." Probably closer to the truth, LaFarge worried about Markoe's capacity to incite controversy and defy Catholic authority. Markoe, for instance, began once again to express his provocative views on interracial marriage in 1933. Despite their great differences, however, the two competing priests had a great deal of admiration for each other. Each professed lasting friendship with the other in his autobiography. Markoe treasured an autographed copy of an anniversary issue of the *Interracial Review* that he received many years later from LaFarge. The inscription read: "To the founder of the *Interracial Review*—Fr. Bill Markoe, S.J.; to the St. John Baptist of the Catholic interracial movement of the U.S. in this century." If LaFarge accorded Markoe the role of John the Baptist, he clearly considered himself the savior of interracialism.[82]

One can also find a hint of LaFarge's ambition in his attitude toward Father Gillard. In his scathing review of Gillard's book in 1930, LaFarge justified his uncharacteristically harsh assault on a fellow priest by pleading that he could not allow the defamation of blacks to stand as the "official view" of Catholicism. Nevertheless, one cannot entirely dismiss Gillard's complaint that LaFarge's review was not only "devastating" but "unfair." Gillard cried out that LaFarge's harsh judgment of his book was "calculated to place [him] in a very unfavorable light." He griped that LaFarge had "put in the minds of Negroes a thought calculated to do injury to [him] and [his] work among them." He accused LaFarge of using his tremendous prestige among blacks to consign the book "to the limbo of apocryphal literature." LaFarge in fact admitted that he gave the book a more positive assessment for the white clientele of *America* than he had for the primarily black readers of the *Chronicle*. Whatever LaFarge's intentions, Gillard, like Markoe, virtually lost his national forum at *America* after 1930. With the pages of that periodical largely closed to him, he became a major writer on race relations for *Commonweal*. Any larger ambitions that the fiery Josephite may have had in the racial field were cut short by his sudden death in 1942 at the age of forty-two.[83]

82. Markoe, "Interracial Role," 309–12. Markoe sent greetings on LaFarge's silver anniversary at *America* (William Markoe to John LaFarge, February 25, 1952, in box 14, folder 27, JLFP 2). On miscegenation, see William Markoe, "Sincerity and Intermarriage," *IR*, 6 (June, 1933), 112–14; *MIO*, 339.

83. John Gillard to John LaFarge, June 30, 1930, John LaFarge to John Gillard,

Although the question of which white priest (or which religious society) would be the Moses of black Catholics was not absent from the Turner affair, it was not the essential question in the dispute. Nor was the central question a matter of racial versus interracial or Catholic versus un-Catholic, as LaFarge and Markoe had claimed. It was rather a question of lay versus clerical and white versus black domination. The blandly optimistic gradualism of LaFarge was pitted against the urgency of black protest aimed directly at the hierarchy and clergy. LaFarge was in the movement for the long haul; his genius lay in patient striving. Turner, who had suffered personal racial insults for over half a century, felt, as Martin Luther King, Jr., did in 1963, that the time for freedom in the church was now. He knew that making the FCC a captive of Catholic Action meant, by definition, that the black laity's interests would be subsumed under the hierarchy's interests. He also understood that at some point he had to resist the steady erosion of black lay power in the FCC if he was to maintain credibility as a person who could inspire a cadre of much-needed black Catholic leaders.

When Turner finally rebelled against white paternalism, LaFarge quickly shed his circumspection and opted for decisive action against the black leader. Although he never publicly disclosed his motivation for moving against Turner, he candidly expressed his rationale in a letter to Archbishop Curley of Baltimore at the time of the rump session. LaFarge informed the archbishop that Turner was a man who had an "anti-clerical slant" and who went "over the heads of his own Negroes" and tried "to stir up the clergy by setting them off one against the other." LaFarge warned that Turner knew "the clergy's respective affiliations, inhibitions: and he [knew] how to play on these to his heart's desire." LaFarge assured Curley that Turner represented only a minority of blacks in the federation and that the reforms had changed the agency from a "racial bloc" to a "really Catholic organization." In his recent history of black Catholics, the black priest Cyprian Davis depicted LaFarge as a principled and dedicated leader but also as an "elit-

---

July 1, 1930, John Gillard to John LaFarge, n.d. [1930], John Gillard to John LaFarge, February 24, 1931, all in box 5, folder 55, JLFP 2; John LaFarge to John Gillard, May 11, 1930, in Gillard Papers. On Gillard's writing for *Commonweal,* see Czuchlewski, "Liberal Catholicism and American Racism," 144–62. Some defenders of Gillard characterize LaFarge as not only paternalistic but patronizing toward subordinates, black and white alike (Father Peter Hogan, S.S.J., to the author, June 9, 1992).

ist" who was incapable of allowing a man such as Turner to lead. "What he [LaFarge] could not do," Davis concluded, "was accept the position of trusting the resourcefulness of blacks themselves, of recognizing the leadership and qualities of blacks."[84] Nickels, who delved deeply into the Turner episode, ultimately concluded that LaFarge "betrayed" the black leader and that he "abandoned" black leadership "whenever his own hierarchical structure seemed threatened."[85]

The removal of such a talented and popular leader as Turner seriously retarded for a generation the development of black leadership in the Catholic church. Father McGowan of the NCWC Social Action Department viewed the federation split as a "tragedy." He characterized charges of anticlericalism against Turner as "ridiculous." In addition to McGowan, Fathers Olds and Dever gave Turner support, though none of them criticized LaFarge or Markoe publicly.[86] There is some evidence that Turner's protest efforts were beginning to have some effect on the bishops in the administrative arm of the NCWC by 1932. Bishop Walsh of Charleston, South Carolina, and Archbishop John T. McNicholas of Cincinnati, key members of the administrative committee, were both old-style paternalists, but they were impressed with the FCC leaders' "thoroughly proper attitude" toward Catholic authority. More egalitarian was the Paulist general secretary of the NCWC, John J. Burke, an influential priest and one of the NCWC's founders. In August, 1932, Burke wrote Turner that he admired his work and that he thought the

84. John LaFarge to Archbishop Michael Curley, December 4, 1932, in Turner File, Josephite Archives; Cyprian Davis, *History of Black Catholics,* 222, 228.

85. Nickels, *Black Catholic Protest,* 312. In her dissertation, "The Federated Colored Catholics," 198, 202, 252, 278–79, 312, *passim,* Nickels gave LaFarge every benefit of the doubt, referring to his silences in the Turner controversy as "non-involvement." In the virtually verbatim reprint of her dissertation published in 1988, Nickels was far more censorious of LaFarge, though she presented no new evidence for the harsher judgment. Others who followed Nickels' earlier, softer tone toward LaFarge are Zielinski, " 'Doing the Truth,' " 9–12; Ochs, *Desegregating the Altar,* 312, 347; and to a lesser extent, Cyprian Davis, *History of Black Catholics,* 228–29. Much more critical of LaFarge is an earlier work by a Catholic priest, Harte, *Catholic Organizations Promoting Negro-White Relations,* 6–8.

86. Raymond McGowan to Thomas Turner, December 22, 1932, January 1, 1933, in Turner Papers. On sympathetic priests, see Eugene Clark to Thomas Turner, November 6, 1932, January 23, 1933, in Turner Papers. In the interview of Msgr. George Higgins by the author, Washington, D.C., July 1, 1986, Higgins maintained that his close associate McGowan was sympathetic to Turner and upset with LaFarge and Markoe.

bishops would favor a conference with the FCC president on racial matters. While friendly in tone, the first paragraph of Burke's missive revealed the petty kind of obstacles black Catholics faced in dealing with the clergy and the hierarchy. Burke scolded the black organization for writing a letter "just addressed 'N.C.W.C.' and beginning 'Dear Friend.' " Protocol took on great significance in the minds of Catholic officials. Nevertheless, Burke arranged for Turner to meet the bishops on the NCWC's administrative committee on November 14. Burke's Paulist biographer believed that the NCWC was being forced to act on the FCC's demands that the church abruptly end some of its most overt discrimination, such as the exclusion of blacks at Catholic University. But when the split in the FCC occurred, the bishops had an excuse to back off the issues that Turner had highlighted.[87]

Turner's eastern followers reclaimed the federation and restored its original name in January, 1933. It once again declared that its primary goals consisted of raising the status of blacks in the church and cultivating black leadership. The eastern federation, however, waned during the following years. It no longer had LaFarge or Markoe or the *Chronicle / Interracial Review* or *America* to advocate its views, and the serious illnesses of Turner and his wife caused the Hampton professor to relinquish the presidency in 1934, though he soon returned to office. But the organization did not attract many young, talented black Catholics, and the older leaders were ultimately worn down by grinding opposition. The FCC dissolved itself in 1952 with a testimonial dinner for Turner (then age seventy-five), two years before the Supreme Court issued *Brown* v. *Board of Education of Topeka.* In closing its books, the black federation stated somewhat prematurely that it was "satisfied . . . that universal Catholic principles are [now] real and tangible."[88]

All the malfeasance attributed to Turner by Markoe and LaFarge, not to mention his defamation by the Josephites, was basically unfounded. Turner was an exemplary practitioner of his faith, much like

87. John J. Burke, C.S.P., to Thomas Turner, August 30, 1932, in Turner Papers; John B. Sheerin, C.S.P., *Never Look Back: The Career and Concerns of John J. Burke* (New York, 1975), 11–12, 207–208.

88. "Rump Catholics Are Denounced in Washington," Baltimore *Afro-American,* January 14, 1933; copy of 1933 resolutions of FCC; "A Testimonial to Thomas W. Turner, Presented by the Federated Colored Catholics of the United States, 1952"—all in Turner Papers. On Turner's health, see "News Notes," *Voice,* 1 (January, 1934), 9, copy in Turner Papers.

the pious and triumphalist Rudd, who had called the black Catholic congresses in the late nineteenth century. Horace B. McKenna, a Jesuit admirer of LaFarge who worked in the Maryland missions in the 1930s, vouched for Turner, whose manner was always "dignified" and thoroughly Catholic in his racial endeavors.[89] Nor was Turner a separatist. Indeed, he had fought Jim Crow all of his life. In an eloquent address to the FCC in 1933, Turner justified the black federation by pointing to similar ethnic organizations such as the Ancient Order of Hibernians (Irish), the Polish Roman Catholic Union, the Knights of St. John and the Catholic Central Verein (German), the Catholic Slovak Union, and so on. He wondered why the Jesuits had not indicted these organizations for practicing separatism. Turner strongly believed that a unified black Catholic voice had to be developed so that blacks could better deal with the discriminatory church. There is no reason to doubt the accuracy of Turner's motivations as he later stated them in his unpublished history of black Catholics: "The prime objective of this black group [the FCC] was the eradication of discrimination and it was felt that blacks could not participate in interracial activities 'from the back of the church.' If discrimination could be abolished, Black clergy and lay leadership would develop, integration would follow, and interracial goodwill could be built."[90] If Turner erred, it was in trusting the Jesuits too much and in compromising too radically the original aims of the federation. While Turner was trying to restore the old FCC in 1933, Daniel Rudd died in poignant obscurity in Bardstown, Kentucky, another black prophet unhonored in his time.[91]

LaFarge erred in preaching that his interracial, Catholic Action strategy constituted the only true path to racial progress. He also blundered by insisting that interracialism and black protest were mutually exclusive concepts. His ideological and tactical rigidity in the early 1930s was extreme and contrasted sharply with his later flexibility. In 1943, for instance, LaFarge told Zacheus Maher, the American assistant

89. Interview of Horace B. McKenna, S.J., by Marilyn W. Nickels, March 24, 1973, transcript in Josephite Archives, Baltimore.

90. Thomas Turner, "Our Federated Colored Catholics," 2–3, and "The History and Heritage of Black Catholics" (Typescript, 1975), n.p., both in Turner Papers. In "The Negro and the Immigrant," *IR*, 6 (February, 1933), 30–31, Markoe disingenuously argued that blacks, unlike European ethnic groups, were fully assimilated and had no need for separate organizations.

91. On Rudd's death, see Cyprian Davis, *History of Black Catholics*, 214.

to the Jesuit general, that "wide variations of interpretations" among Catholics on race relations were legitimate.[92]

LaFarge's vision was hampered by a deeply ingrained paternalism. As Markoe put it, the Newport elitist was not quite black enough. The Jesuit patrician never really fathomed the urgency of black activists such as Turner, and he was unable in this period to work with proud and well-educated blacks without injuring their pride and undermining their leadership potential. While LaFarge was correct in preaching that whites needed to be educated about blacks and to have contact with them, he was wrong in teaching that black rights could not be gained until whites learned to love blacks, supernaturally or otherwise. If it is true that society (or the church) cannot force people to love one another, it is also true that a sincere and determined government can compel its citizens to respect certain basic rights of even despised groups. Perhaps LaFarge also underestimated the potential of the American hierarchy to pursue a truly Catholic course on race. Ironically, for all the easy optimism that pervaded LaFarge's thought, his religious fatalism and his staid gradualism made him appear pessimistic to many non-Catholic liberals.

After the schism in the federation, LaFarge's involvement with the western federation, officially the National Catholic Interracial Federation, diminished rapidly. He missed the next three executive meetings after the New York convention, though he attended the Cleveland convention in September of 1933. While Markoe assumed hands-on leadership in the federation for a time, LaFarge tried to quell rumors of Jesuit conspiracies. He alerted Markoe that the two should not be seen together, lest black delegates whisper, "Oh, oh, here they come!" Ironically, Markoe soon lost interest in the federation himself. He expressed dismay with the weak leadership of Conrad, Turner's obsequious replacement, and grew irritated with the new spiritual director of the federation, Archbishop McNicholas, an archpaternalist given to empty rhetoric and thoughtless condescension toward blacks.[93]

Furthermore, just as Markoe (at least in his own mind) seemed to be riding high, his fortune took a turn for the worse. In late 1933 his

92. LaFarge, quoted in McDonough, *Men Astutely Trained*, 199.

93. Markoe, "Interracial Role," 309–11, 322, 361–64; Nickels, *Black Catholic Protest*, 204–209. See Archbishop McNicholas' address to the Cincinnati convention in *IR*, 6 (October, 1933), 174–76.

new provincial, the Reverend Samuel H. Horine, demanded that the *Interracial Review* be submitted to a Jesuit board of censors. Rather than compromise his journal, Markoe turned the review over to La-Farge in New York. In 1934 he regained the pastorate at his beloved St. Elizabeth's, and after that he paid more attention to parish matters. He attended only one more federation convention, which took place in Cincinnati in 1935. The organization simply evaporated in the late 1930s. Markoe, however, remained an icon to the black community in St. Louis, and he remained at odds with his Jesuit superiors and Archbishop Glennon. In 1941 he was exiled to Mankato, Minnesota, where, he wailed, not "a single Negro lived." Later, in 1951, after a few years of racial activity in Denver, he was banished to Marquette University to teach theology. One can only guess that his superiors knew what constituted purgatory for Markoe, given his need for black company and his distaste for the academy. After the early 1930s he never again played a major role in national racial affairs. Markoe died in Milwaukee in 1969.[94]

After the federation brouhaha, however, LaFarge's national star continued to rise until he was widely recognized as the foremost Catholic spokesman on black-white relations. As his involvement in the National Catholic Interracial Federation waned, he threw himself into other activities, old and new. In 1933 and 1934 he spent a considerable amount of his time dealing with the painful closure of the Cardinal Gibbons Institute and the contentious Victor and Constance Daniel. In late 1933 LaFarge helped found the Northeastern Clergy Conference on Negro Welfare. The event that gave him the greatest claim to historical significance, however, came in 1934 when he founded the CICNY. As the debate was raging over the FCC, LaFarge was contemplating a "more effective organization" to carry out the work of the racial apostolate—an organization over which he could exert maximum control.[95] Turning his back on the western federation, he proclaimed the newly acquired *Interracial Review* as the official organ of the New York council. The momentous events in Catholic black-white relations in the next decade would be staged in New York.

94. Nickels, *Black Catholic Protest,* 205–209; Markoe, "Interracial Role," 337–38, 340–41, 345–49, 361–64, 398.
95. Zielinski, "Promotion of Better Race Relations," 50–51.

Dedication of Cardinal Gibbons Institute, 1924. Directly in the middle in front is Constance Daniel; directly behind her are Victor Daniel, the principal, and Father LaFarge. Photograph courtesy of Alice Bennett, Ridge, Maryland.

Ruth Logan and Constance Daniel at Tuskegee, 1916. Photograph courtesy of Louise Daniel Hutchinson, Washington, D.C.

Victor and Louise Daniel, Early 1920s. Photograph courtesy of Louise Daniel Hutchinson, Washington, D.C.

The Daniel Family at Cardinal Gibbons Institute, ca. 1933. First row, left to right: John, Constance, Elizabeth "Betty" Anne, Victor, and Louise; second row, left to right: Constance Dorothea, William J., Victor Christopher, Marguerite Rosa, and Robert Alphonse. Photograph courtesy of Louise Daniel Hutchinson, Washington, D.C.

Thomas Wyatt Turner, Longtime President of the Federation of Colored Catholics (no date). Photograph from Thomas W. Turner Papers, Box 153-23, Folder 9, Moorland-Spingarn Research Center, Howard University.

Reverend William M. Markoe, S.J., and Children in St. Louis (no date). Photograph courtesy of Jesuit Missouri Province Archives, St. Louis, Missouri.

Reverend John T. Gillard, S.S.J., 1941. Photograph courtesy of Josephite Archives, Baltimore.

Reverend Paul M. Gillis, C.S.P. (no date). Photograph courtesy of the Office of Paulist History and Archives, Washington, D.C.

6

The Fall of the
Cardinal Gibbons Institute
and the Rise of the CICNY

As the Turner affair was being played out in 1932 and 1933, the Democratic presidential candidate Franklin D. Roosevelt defeated the Republican incumbent Herbert Hoover and offered his liberal program to a Depression-racked nation. Under the label of the New Deal, the Democratic party forged a new political majority and ushered in the beginnings of the modern welfare state. Laissez-faire capitalism had staggered to an ignominious crawl under Hoover, and most Americans wanted relief and reform. The charismatic Roosevelt's appeal to the "forgotten man" was not wasted on American Catholics. In the 1930s, for example, Roosevelt garnered more of the white, ethnic, Catholic vote in the northern cities than had Al Smith, the Catholic nominee for the Democratic party in 1928.[1]

Even before the New Deal began, social Catholicism got a boost with Pope Pius XI's *Quadragesimo Anno*, the 1931 update of Pope Leo XIII's 1891 *Rerum Novarum*. Social Catholicism, however, was not just

1. See the monumental work of Arthur Schlesinger, Jr., *The Age of Roosevelt* (3 vols.; Boston, 1957–60). The best one-volume work is William E. Leuchtenburg, *Franklin D. Roosevelt and the New Deal* (New York, 1963). See also Paul Conkin, *The New Deal* (New York, 1967). An excellent anthology is *The New Deal: The Critical Issues*, ed. Otis L. Graham, Jr. (Boston, 1971).

a response to papal teachings; it was also a reaction to American events. In the 1930s Catholics found that one way to bridge the troublesome dualism between Catholicism and Americanism was to become reformers in an era of reform. Noted clergymen such as John Ryan, Francis J. Haas, and most especially the radio priest Charles E. Coughlin (before he deserted Roosevelt in 1935) rendered conspicuous support for the New Deal; the powerful Cardinal George Mundelein of Chicago also became an important enthusiast for Roosevelt's economic policies. The Great Depression and the New Deal thus provided a shot in the arm for the social *magisterium*.[2]

This is not to say that Catholics did not have reservations about the policies of Roosevelt and the New Deal. The Catholic hierarchy and many in the clergy feared that political involvement by church leaders would stir up a new round of anti-Catholicism, and some feared a stronger federal government could be used against a minority faith. Utopian agrarians such as the Jesuit John Rawe ultimately rejected more of New Deal farm policies than they accepted. Most of all, Roosevelt's diplomatic policies in regard to the Soviet Union, Spain, and Mexico made support for the New Deal by the Catholic leadership tenuous. The most solid support for Roosevelt and the Democratic party came from Catholic labor activists, whose activities coincided most congenially with the interests of the largely working-class church. Even the influence of John LaFarge brought only spotty support for Roosevelt's New Deal by the magazine *America*. In fact, the influential weekly campaigned vigorously against a third term for the Hyde Park aristocrat.[3]

2. David J. O'Brien, "The American Priest and Social Action," in *Catholic Priest*, ed. John Ellis, 427; William A. Osborne, *The Segregated Covenant: Race Relations and American Catholics* (New York, 1967), 131; Mel Piehl, *Breaking Bread: The Catholic Worker and the Origins of Catholic Radicalism in America* (Philadelphia, 1982), x, 27, 38, 40–41; Dolan, *American Catholic Experience*, 401–17; Kantowicz, *Corporation Sole*, 173–202, 215, 241. See generally David O'Brien, *American Catholics and Social Reform*; Halsey, *Survival of American Innocence*; Abell, *American Catholicism and Social Action*; Flynn, *American Catholics and the Roosevelt Presidency*; Broderick, *Right Reverend New Dealer*; and Thomas E. Blantz, C.S.C., *A Priest in Public Service: Francis J. Haas and the New Deal* (Notre Dame, Ind., 1982).

3. Editorial "Do We Need a Third Term?" *Am*, 63 (May 25, 1940), 183. On agrarian reformers, see Peter McDonough, *Men Astutely Trained*, 89–95, 98–118; on foreign policy, see George Q. Flynn, *Roosevelt and Romanism: Catholics and American Diplomacy, 1937–1945* (Westport, Conn., 1976); on labor, see Dolan, *American Catholic Ex-*

While supporting many of Roosevelt's policies, Catholic social thinkers continued to search for a Catholic synthesis that transcended the materialistic, secular-oriented New Deal. Catholic intellectuals struggled to meld together the ancient and the new, tradition and reform. "Integration" (nonracial in meaning) became a buzz word among Catholics during the decade. Using the theological doctrine of the Mystical Body of Christ, the natural law reasoning of Thomism, and the ongoing vehicle of Catholic Action, Catholic thinkers tried to articulate a total spiritual and social reality with which to shape the nation. However, such Catholic visions, often vague and contradictory, made almost no impact on the largely devotional laity or on national policies.[4]

Moreover, American Catholic social activists in the 1930s tended to neglect racial matters. There were many reasons for this. Many labor activists, the most prominent component of social Catholicism, were indifferent or hostile to racial change, Dorothy Day (1897–1981), a radical journalist and reformer, and her Catholic Worker movement notwithstanding. Unlike labor activism, racial activism threatened large blocks of the white Catholic laity and went against the racial attitudes of most of the hierarchy.[5] Prelates sympathetic to the economic policies of Roosevelt sometimes harbored strong antiblack attitudes. Cardinal Mundelein, for instance, expressed alarm at the new species of "sassy nigger" invading northern cities and demanding social equality. Despite the exuberant social action in the archdiocese of Chicago, many of the schools built by the enterprising archbishop remained closed to blacks.[6]

Another factor in Catholic inaction was that most blacks lived in the South, where Catholicism was weakest, making it irresistibly easy for Catholics to do nothing and blame the southern caste system on white Protestantism. With less than 2 percent of the Catholic popula-

---

perience, 405–406, and Pastor-Zelaya, "The Development of Roman Catholic Social Liberalism," 4.

4. Philip Gleason, "In Search of Unity: American Catholic Thought, 1920–1960," *Catholic Historical Review,* 65 (April, 1979), 204; Halsey, *Survival of American Innocence,* 60; Dolan, *American Catholic Experience,* 351–52, 407; David J. O'Brien, "Catholicism and Americanism," in *Modern American Catholicism, 1900–1965,* ed. Edward R. Kantowicz (New York, 1988), 110–13.

5. Dolan, *American Catholic Experience,* 405; O'Brien, "American Priest and Social Action," in *Catholic Priest,* ed. John Ellis, 449–50. See also Piehl, *Breaking Bread.*

6. Mundelein, quoted in Ochs, *Desegregating the Altar,* 326; James Sanders, *The Education of an Urban Minority: Catholics in Chicago* (New York, 1977), 207–15.

tion and a minuscule number of priests, blacks simply did not command enough power to tap the church's resources for racial change. Even priests in the racial apostolate confined most of their efforts to black conversion rather than black rights.[7] Hence wholesale discrimination against black Catholics continued in Catholic churches, schools, hospitals, and the like.

Nor did the Roosevelt administration really propose a new deal for blacks. It advocated no special programs for blacks, and it did not challenge the southern caste system. If the president had endorsed racial reform, he would have endangered crucial support for the New Deal by southern Democrats. Roosevelt knew the race issue was a political potato that was too hot to handle, and he risked no political capital on it. He even refused to support the Costigan-Wagner antilynching bill that was introduced in 1934. However, racially liberal New Dealers such as Secretary of the Interior Harold Ickes hired many talented and skilled blacks as advisers for government programs. These government officials included Robert C. Weaver of the Federal Housing Authority (later in 1966 Weaver became the first black cabinet member at Housing and Urban Development), William H. Hastie, assistant solicitor in the Department of the Interior, and Eugene Kinckle Jones, executive director of the National Urban League, who worked in the Department of Commerce. Collectively these government officials were sometimes known as the "black cabinet." Blacks also made gains because of organized labor, which was boosted by the Roosevelt administration with protective legislation such as the National Labor Relations Act, better known as the Wagner Act. Moreover, the new Congress of Industrial Organizations (CIO) welcomed workers of all races. Blacks undeniably received vital benefits from New Deal relief programs and from government efforts to create jobs. Nevertheless, in recent years many historians have tended to discount the racial gains made in the 1930s. John Hope Franklin, for instance, concluded that the status of the "black cabinet" was "nebulous and unofficial" and that none of the black advisers had access to the president or could be considered policy makers. According to Nancy Weiss, blacks "voted for Franklin Roosevelt in spite of the New Deal's lack of a substantive record on race." African

7. Even LaFarge stressed conversion; see, for example, his "The Negro Apostolate," *Commonweal,* 22 (July 5, 1935), 257.

Americans supported him because of the economic benefits of his policies and to some degree because of Eleanor Roosevelt.[8]

In actuality, many of the New Deal programs openly discriminated against blacks, and some inflicted either short-term or long-term damage and strengthened segregation. The Agricultural Adjustment Act, for example, reduced cotton acreage and pushed black tenants off the land. The National Recovery Administration paid blacks lower wages than whites. The government segregated the camps of the Civilian Conservation Corps. The Federal Housing Authority and related agencies perpetuated segregated housing by upholding restrictive covenants through their race-determined lending practices. According to a recent scholarly work on the Tennessee Valley Authority (TVA), this model of "grassroots democracy" engaged in "overt patterns of racial discrimination" and planned a future that retained the racial status quo. Blacks did not remain uncritical. In 1934 both the Urban League and the NAACP in their official journals attacked the TVA for its discriminatory practices. Left-leaning blacks such as Ralph Bunche were even more vocal in their criticism.[9]

Therefore, despite impressive economic and political reform, the 1930s essentially constituted another decade in which significant racial reform was deferred. Blacks thus faced not only extreme economic hardship, but they daily experienced the humiliating caste system that was frequently undergirded by terrorism. The year of Roosevelt's inaugural saw the murder of twenty-eight blacks by lynch mobs.[10]

How much racial change could LaFarge hope to effect in the Catholic church in this climate? Could he build a movement to serve as an instrument of racial progress in the wake of the Turner debacle? In 1934, the year LaFarge created the CICNY, Father John W. Cooper, an anthropologist at Catholic University, assailed Catholics in the *Ec-*

---

8. Franklin and Moss, *From Slavery to Freedom*, 348–49; Nancy J. Weiss, *Farewell to the Party of Lincoln: Black Politics in the Age of FDR* (Princeton, 1983), xiv. See also John B. Kirby, *Black Americans in the Roosevelt Era: Liberalism and Race* (Knoxville, Tenn., 1980). For a more positive view, see Harvard Sitkoff, *A New Deal for Blacks: The Emergence of Civil Rights as a National Issue* (New York, 1978).

9. Nancy L. Grant, *TVA and Black Americans: Planning for the Status Quo* (Philadelphia, 1990), quotations on xvii, 158, but see also 47–72, 109–35.

10. Robert L. Zangrando, *The NAACP Crusade Against Lynching, 1909–1950* (Philadelphia, 1980), 7, 127, 133–35, 140.

clesiastical Review for their complacency in regard to blacks. "Instead of seeking justice for him [the Negro]," Cooper thundered, "we have been pussyfooting and following a weak and spineless compromise, of compromise not merely with facts but also principles."[11] To be sure, LaFarge faced formidable obstacles in trying to steer the church and the Jesuits onto a racial path that was truly catholic.

Ironically, LaFarge himself helped make the path more rocky because of the unfortunate and uncharitable way in which the Cardinal Gibbons Institute was closed. On November 23, 1933, George K. Hunton, secretary of the executive committee of the institute, informed the board of trustees that the committee had decided to close the Tuskegee-style school for blacks within a month.[12] Although the Great Depression helped precipitate its demise, the global economic debacle clearly was not the sole reason for the cessation of the Catholic church's first national educational project for African Americans. White Catholic apathy and mismanagement also figured in its closure. Moreover, the brusque closure of the school in southern Maryland cast negative reflections on Catholicism in the eyes of many blacks. The Turner affair had barely abated before black critics were once again subjecting the Catholic church and its leaders to a public flogging because of their part in suspending activities at the school. Because of his close identification with the Cardinal Gibbons Institute, Father LaFarge would not go unscathed.

On November 3, 1933, the principal, Victor Daniel, advised a prominent board member of the institute that he feared it would be necessary to close the school because of insufficient funds. Other blacks, however, hinted that a church conspiracy was afoot to stifle the black leaders at Ridge. On November 11, Cora Grace Inman reported in the influential Baltimore *Afro-American* that school officials had severely pruned the staff at the institute and were callously undermining the work of the Daniels. (Some antagonists of the Daniels, such as Archbishop Curley, believed Cora Grace Inman was a pseudonym for Constance Daniel since Inman's initials were identical to those of the institute, a charge Daniel vehemently denied.) Inman, who had blasted Fathers LaFarge and Markoe in the earlier Turner affair, smelled a plot

11. John W. Cooper, "Christ and the Other Sheep," *Ecclesiastical Review*, 90 (May, 1934), 456.

12. George K. Hunton to Elmo Anderson, November 23, 1933, in box 4, CICNYP.

by the church to punish the Daniels for their support of Turner. On December 9, 1933, the editors of the *Afro-American* probed the closing of the black school in a series of rhetorical questions laced with a sarcastic tone: "Can it be possible that white Catholic leaders are becoming ashamed of themselves? Can it be that they expect to open the doors of Catholic colleges like Loyola and Notre Dame in Baltimore to all Catholics? Can it be that even the national Catholic university in Washington is going to drop its color bar and become thoroughly Christian?" The black editors complained that they could see "no signs of . . . regeneration within the church." They added, "Closing . . . Gibbons Institute seems merely to be another case of taking away from a group even that *which they seemed to have*" (my emphasis).[13]

Several months later Turner loyalists met at the convention of the reconstituted FCC in Philadelphia. There, William Prater made the implications of the Baltimore newspaper more concrete in his complaint: "We regret to see our educationals dumped, so to speak, in the road like worthless criminals. Should we not have . . . a statement from the proper source as to the reason for such unprecedented action against the principal of the Cardinal Gibbons Institute?"[14]

The period of 1933 and 1934 was a sobering and pivotal time for LaFarge, to say nothing of the Daniels. The split in the FCC had led to a dead end as far as sustaining an effective black Catholic federation. In addition, the closing of the institute at Ridge greatly disturbed LaFarge. He held a special place in his heart for southern Maryland and the Gibbons Institute. As the primary founder of the institution, he always advertised the school as the seedbed of the interracial movement in later years. After coming to New York in 1926, he kept close watch on events at the institute, making numerous trips back to the banks of

13. Victor H. Daniel to Walter E. Kennedy, November 3, 1933, in letter box 24, CICNYP; Cora Grace Inman, "In Catholic Circles," Baltimore *Afro-American*, November 11, 1933; "Race Prejudice Keeps Colored Priests Out," Baltimore *Afro-American*, n.d. [late 1933 or early 1934], clipping in the Maryland, Ridge file, Josephite Archives, Baltimore. Clippings of the following articles from the Baltimore *Afro-American* are in the Gillard-Turner Clippings file, Josephite Archives: editorial "Is the Catholic Church Ashamed of Itself?" December 9, 1933; "Gibbons Institute," December 23, 1933; "Would Reopen Gibbons," December 30, 1933; and "Gibbons Institute Head Still at Farmhouse," January [?], 1934.

14. William Prater, quoted in minutes of FCC, September 1–3, 1934, in Turner Papers.

the southern Potomac. While in Maryland, he had developed a deep interest in the history of the area. In the early 1920s he helped found the Pilgrims of St. Mary's, a group set up to investigate and celebrate the important but largely ignored Catholic heritage of Maryland. LaFarge, in fact, largely instigated the events that led to the erection of a monument to Father Andrew White, the noted Jesuit missionary who in 1634 landed with English immigrants at St. Mary's, Maryland's first capital. LaFarge played a prominent role in the planning for the 1934 tercentennial of that landing, the Catholic equivalent of the 1607 settlement at Jamestown, Virginia.[15]

As attached to it as he was, the institution at Ridge nevertheless proved to be a heavy cross for LaFarge to bear. After coming to New York, he continued to exercise a great deal of authority over the affairs of the institute as the most knowledgeable and dedicated member on the board of trustees. He devoted much of his time to the never-ending task of raising funds for the school. Even in the best of times in the late 1920s, the school had no endowment and was heavily dependent on foundation grants and gifts from a few wealthy individuals. In 1926 LaFarge set up a special fundraising committee for the Cardinal Gibbons Institute and persuaded his brother Oliver, a prominent businessman in New York, to be its chairman. In 1929 the New York *Age* reported on a gala Manhattan affair of 170 people at which LaFarge eloquently promoted the southern school and interracial justice. When his brother's health failed, LaFarge had to resume the major responsibility for raising revenue, a job he thoroughly disliked. By the 1930s the burden of the school was beginning to take its toll on LaFarge. In a 1933 letter to his provincial, he mourned the fact that Catholics had scant interest in the institute and that the Society of Jesus had no serious plan for the education of African American Catholics. About the same time, he sent an unusually emotional letter to a fellow Jesuit in which he complained that for seven years his work for the institute had been a hindrance to his journalism and his intellectual interests.[16]

---

15. See "Philly's Cardinal Praised; Archbishop's Jim Crow Reproved," Baltimore *Afro-American*, April 27, 1935, clipping in Catholic Interracial Councils—Newspaper Clippings folder, Josephite Archives; *MIO*, 217–24. For inquiries to LaFarge about Maryland history, see box 23, folders 1 and 5, JLFP 1.

16. "Catholics Hear Fr. LaFarge Plead for Racial Justice," New York *Age*, December 14, 1929; LaFarge, memorandum on the Cardinal Gibbons Institute, September 12,

The funding problem at the Gibbons Institute weighed heavily on LaFarge. A constant shortage of funds at the school meant an absence of certain basic courses, such as foreign languages. Because of this lack, the institute never received accreditation. But many black schools, with exceptions such as Atlanta and Fisk Universities, had trouble with accreditation, yet they continued to operate. Tuskegee was not accredited as a four-year college until 1935.[17]

Funding was only one—albeit a major one—of the many problems that bedeviled the school. Almost immediate friction occurred between the black administrators of the institute and certain white members on the executive committee of the board. As early as 1927 Admiral William S. Benson, the first vice-president of the board (actually the head of the board since Archbishop Michael Curley of Baltimore was the president), was calling for the resignation of Constance Daniel, the assistant principal. Constance actually resigned after the fray reached a white heat in 1927, but her husband immediately rehired her as a teacher, which brought further complaints from committee members. The Daniels then protested that the committee was "dictating the choice of teachers" at the institute.[18]

Given the rough conditions and low pay (the average pay for a teacher was around $500 a year), the principal had difficulty recruiting teachers with the zeal, patience, and competence to match those of the Daniels. Constance, who would soon be acting principal of the school, was just as apt to hire a Protestant teacher as a Catholic, a trait that did not endear her to the executive committee. In 1931 she wrote a scorching letter to Mother Katharine Drexel charging that graduates from Xavier University, the black institution Drexel founded in New Orleans, made poor teachers and bad role models for young blacks. She judged them vastly inferior to teachers from Tuskegee and Hampton.[19]

One source of profound irritation to the Daniels was Arthur C.

1935, in box 23, folder 4, JLFP 1; John LaFarge to Edward C. Phillips, Provincial of Maryland-New York, June 19, 1933, and John LaFarge to Emile Mattern, S.J., July 20, 1933, both in box 12, folder 11, JLFP 1.

17. Louise Daniel Hutchinson, *Anna J. Cooper: A Voice from the South* (Washington, D.C., 1981), 60.

18. A. C. Monahan to LaFarge, July 7, October 11, 1927, and memorandum on board meeting, date unclear [Jan. 20, 1928 (?)], both in letter box 24, CICNYP.

19. Constance Daniel to Mother Katharine Drexel, July 27, 1931, in box 15, folder 12, JLFP 1.

Monahan, the secretary of the executive committee. An educational expert with the NCWC in Washington, D.C., Father Monahan constantly intervened in the administrative affairs of the black school. In 1928 he requested and acquired from the board the power to approve every expenditure of the institute, no matter how trivial, as if the black administrators were a couple of former felons. Even Lawrence P. Williams, the treasurer of the board and another source of irritation to the Daniels, warned LaFarge that it was imprudent for Monahan to act like a plantation overseer and that it was impractical to micromanage the school from afar.[20]

The differences between the black educators on the one hand and Admiral Benson and Father Monahan of the board on the other came to a head in 1928 and 1929. In response to constant charges of mismanagement and insubordination, Victor Daniel struck back with a long memorandum titled "Statement of the Principal of the Cardinal Gibbons Institute on Turning over to the Executive Committee of the Board of Trustees, Detailed Reports of Enrollment, Operation and Management, Requested by Admiral Benson; Chairman of the Board of Trustees." In this document the principal apparently addressed every charge that had been directed at him and his wife after they arrived in southern Maryland. He, for example, vehemently rejected the claim that he or his wife had dismissed teachers without cause or without due process. He called for changes in the by-laws that would allow him more freedom to recruit and dismiss personnel and generally run the school with more efficiency. He directly accused Benson and Monahan of usurping his authority as principal and charged that the "suggestions" coming from the committee sounded much more like "demands." He blasted Benson for instructing the staff on one of his visits on how the plowing should be done. He noted that appropriations for the school year were often late, forcing him and his wife to pay for expenses out of their personal resources. He charged that the board forced them to admit ill-prepared students who had a fifth-grade ed-

20. Lawrence P. Williams to John LaFarge, July 8, 1927, in box 27, folder 2, JLFP 1. On the issue of expenditures, see "Notes on CGI Executive Meeting," March 11, 1929, in box 27, folder 1, JLFP 1; memorandum of board meeting, n.d., in letter box 24, CICNYP; John LaFarge, "Notes on Executive Committee Meeting," February 21, 1928, in box 27, folder 1, JLFP 1; A. C. Monohan to John LaFarge, July, 1927, in letter box 24, CICNYP; Constance Daniel to John LaFarge, July 4, 1927, September 21 and October 15, 1928, all in box 1, folder 11, JLFP 2.

ucation at inferior local schools and then had the audacity to criticize their slow progress at the institute. The suggestion that partitions be installed between the toilets in the institute's dormitories, he protested, revealed "evidence of prudishness and of a prurient mind." Daniel seemed to bristle most at the directive that he should go on the road to raise money for the institute. He angrily informed the committee that he was already performing as principal, teacher, mechanic, agriculturalist, and maintenance man and that further responsibilities were beyond his human capacity.[21]

At this time LaFarge strongly defended the Daniels against their critics. He promised a concerned board member in 1928 that he would study the difficulties at the institute carefully and, if requested, report to the executive board. LaFarge attended the executive committee meeting on March 11, 1929, and clashed repeatedly with Benson, Monahan, and Williams. The Jesuit succeeded in deleting from the minutes of the previous meeting a "censure" of Victor Daniel for missing an executive meeting because of "physical" problems. He also challenged another censure of the principal for a breach of procedure, namely, writing to the head of the board rather than to the secretary. LaFarge irritably pointed out that he had advised Daniel, when in doubt, to write to the highest authority. Under heavy questioning, Father Aloysius Thibbits, the Jesuit then assigned to the mission at Ridge, admitted that Monahan had characterized LaFarge as a "source of danger" to the well-being of the Gibbons Institute. LaFarge came away from the meeting convinced that Benson and Monahan were unduly hostile and petty toward the Daniels and prejudiced against Jesuits.[22] Like the pharaohs of old, these board members expected the Daniels to make bricks without straw.

Evidence suggests that LaFarge's intervention in 1929 probably hastened the resignation of Monahan. In any case, by 1931 a new secretary of the executive committee had been appointed. During the wrangling over the administration at the Cardinal Gibbons Institute, LaFarge issued a stream of optimistic reports about the school. In the January, 1932, issue of *Commonweal*, for example, he praised the in-

21. "Statement of the Principal . . . ," August 28, 1928, in box 21, folder 15, JLFP 2. LaFarge compiled a detailed list of complaints against the Daniels, in box 1, folder 15, JLFP 2.

22. John LaFarge to H. Taliferro, October 27, 1928, in letter box 24, CICNYP; notes on CGI executive committee meeting, March 11, 1929, in box 27, folder 1, JLFP 1. See also "Memo," May, 1929, in letter box 24, CICNYP.

stitute's great strength and promise and lauded the superior leadership of the black educators. Determined to persuade blacks that the Catholic church was making significant racial advances, he covered up the mounting toll that dissension and the Depression had inflicted on the showpiece school.[23]

Meanwhile, Constance Daniel had been a growing irritant to LaFarge since she first jarred him with her "I-am-a-Negro-first" letter in 1925. Thereafter, she constantly bombarded him with long letters that excoriated Catholic racism and, more specifically, the meddling of the executive committee in the daily affairs of the school. She sent him a series of biting, pencil-drawn cartoons that depicted high-handed board members as meddlesome, paternalistic drones. She also chastised LaFarge for censoring her *Notebook*, a school newspaper that was edited by her but printed in New York under LaFarge's guidance. One other event that particularly rankled the Daniels was the refusal of the Catholic University of America to admit their son Victor Christopher because of his race. A bright student, he not only had graduated from the institute but had received a privately tutored liberal education under his parents. Several times between 1927 and 1932 Constance threatened to resign and return to Boston with her seven children.[24]

Despite the carping of the executive committee, the Daniels received high marks for character, dedication, and administrative excellence from many quarters. Victor's background revealed a man of excellent character and determination. While he had been a good student majoring in electrical engineering at Tuskegee, he was also a campus leader who played varsity football and organized Tuskegee's first track team. At the Manual Training and Industrial School in New Jersey, where he was commandant and dean of the boy's department for six years, Daniel sternly but compassionately trained black youths. Horace McKenna, the Jesuit who reopened the institute in 1936 and worked in the mission field of southern Maryland for many years, knew the Dan-

23. John LaFarge, "The Cardinal Gibbons Institute," *Commonweal*, 15 (January 17, 1932), 433–35.

24. See, for example, Constance Daniel to John LaFarge, July 4, 1927, August [?], September 21, and October 15, 1928, all in box 1, folder 11, JLFP 2; and Constance Daniel to John LaFarge, February 8, 1930, in box 23, folder 4, JLFP 1. Cartoons are in box 1, folder 12, JLFP 2. The information on Victor Christopher's education and rejection at Catholic University comes from a letter, Louise Daniel Hutchinson to the author, June 6, 1992.

iels well. He described Victor as an administrator who demonstrated "zeal, sacrifice, moderation, and intelligence" in coping with the extreme challenges at the institute. McKenna described Victor's wife as a combative woman who possessed "great strength of character and great force of ideas." John R. O'Connell, another Jesuit who visited Ridge in 1926, depicted the principal as "one of the most scholarly and refined gentlemen [he had] ever met."[25]

The demands of the job at Ridge, unfortunately, did not allow the principal the option of moderate work or provide him with adequate time for leisure. He therefore worked himself into physical exhaustion and a nervous breakdown by 1930. Even LaFarge attributed Daniel's breakdown to overwork and lack of recreation. With the onset of his illness, which included partial paralysis, his wife became the de facto principal. An independent committee of educational experts hired by the board to assess the institute in 1932 concluded that Constance Daniel's administration was "energetic, efficient, and progressive." In February of 1932 LaFarge commented in a letter to John Hope, president of Atlanta University, that Constance Daniel was "carrying on splendidly" at the institute, filling in, he added, for the "intense and devoted" principal who had largely created the school.[26]

No amount of work and sacrifice by the black educators could save the school from white Catholic apathy and mismanagement from above, to say nothing of the severest depression the country had ever known. By 1931, expenses at the school began to outstrip revenues. A report on fundraising, done by the John Price Corporation for the school in 1931, concluded that Cardinal Gibbons Institute needed $600,000 to repair the physical plant and make it attractive to students. In 1931 and 1932 the executive committee cut the meager pay of teachers by 10 percent, and between 1931 and 1933 it reduced the teaching staff from seven to three. While LaFarge was drafting rosy scenarios

25. V. H. Daniel, "The Boy," *Tuskegee Alumni Bulletin*, 4 (April, 1922), 7; "Victor H. Daniel, Class of '11, Elected to Principalship of the Cardinal Gibbons Institute," *ibid.*, 6 (July, 1924), 8; interview of McKenna by Nickels, November [?], 1974; Horace B. McKenna, "Twin Silver Jubilee," n.d., in box 10, folder 10, JLFP 2; letter to the editor by John R. O'Connell, S.J., *Am*, 35 (August 7, 1926), 408.

26. Constance Daniel to Thomas Turner, August 7, 1930, in Turner Papers; "Report on the Committee on a Study of the Curriculum and Accessory Matters of the Cardinal Gibbons Institute to the Board of Trustees," August 26, 1932, in letter box 15, CICNYP; John LaFarge to John Hope, February 11, 1932, in box 27, folder 1, JLFP 1.

about the institute for public consumption, Victor Daniel began to reveal some hard truths about the school in his annual report to the FCC at its St. Louis convention in 1931. Daniel reported that the lack of funds had necessitated the termination of classes in chemistry and physics and that students and teachers were "living under certain disadvantages." A few days after this report, LaFarge privately appealed to the president of Georgetown for a $50,000 loan to keep the institute afloat. In the spring of 1932, Daniel asked neighboring farmers for contributions in kind for the struggling institution. By the end of the school year 1932–1933, most of the teachers had not been paid for a year.[27]

In September of 1931 LaFarge hired George K. Hunton to replace Monahan as the secretary of the executive committee of the institute. LaFarge hoped that Hunton's appointment would ease the friction between the Daniels and the committee and also raise enough money to keep the school from folding. Born in 1888 to an Irish family in Claremont, New Hampshire, Hunton attended the College of the Holy Cross, received a degree from the Fordham Law School in 1910, and then joined the New York bar. At Fordham, Hunton fell under the sway of the pioneering social activist Terrence J. Shealy, a magnetic Jesuit who founded the School of Social Studies in 1911. Because of Shealy's influence, Hunton was well versed in the social teachings of the church. Going forth with a social conscience, he worked for the Legal Aid Society of Harlem from 1912 to 1915. After military service in World War I, he entered private practice and became a promoter of the League of Nations and anti–Tammany Hall politics. Hunton, like LaFarge, began to perceive himself as having a weakness for unpopular, or even lost, causes. A tall, slender man with a thinly clipped moustache and "piercing dark-brown eyes," Hunton was drawn to LaFarge's dedication and sincerity regarding the black apostolate. He became a tire-

27. "A Fund-Raising Survey Analysis and Plan for the Cardinal Gibbons Institute," prepared by John Price, 1931, p. 93, in box 27, folder 4, JLFP 1; G. David Huston to Board of Trustees of Cardinal Gibbons Institute, August 26, 1932, in box 23, folder 1, minutes of executive meeting, November 6, 1933, in box 27, folder 1, "Eighth Annual Report of the Principal," June 4, 1932, in box 27, folder 1, all in JLFP 1; "Statement of Financial Conditions of Cardinal Gibbons Institute," January 1, 1931, in letter box 24, CICNYP; Victor Daniel, "Seven Years of Cardinal Gibbons Institute," *Chronicle*, 4 (November, 1931), 665; John LaFarge to W. Coleman Nevils, October 12, 1931, in box 1, folder 9, JLFP 2; notice by Victor Daniel on CGI, April 22, 1932, in letter box 15, CICNYP.

less, lifelong worker for the interracial cause. A bachelor all his life, Hunton wedded himself to the work that LaFarge and others had started. In 1934 he became the executive secretary of the CICNY and the editor of the *Interracial Review,* positions he held until his joint retirement with LaFarge in 1962. In 1931 he and LaFarge began a monumental journey together that terminated at the Lincoln Memorial in the famous 1963 March on Washington. Although he and LaFarge differed greatly in personality (Hunton was noisier, blunter, and much more volatile than LaFarge), the two men had almost identical views on the race question. Like Dorothy Day and Peter Maurin, they constituted one of the great social action teams in American Catholic history. Their association of more than three decades was both personal and professional and extremely close. Hunton characterized LaFarge as an "infinitely kind" man of the "profoundest depths." On LaFarge's death, he exclaimed that the priest had been "my father, my brother, my confidant, my friend and encourager."[28] Although Hunton had a strong temper and often clashed personally with colleagues in his own rank and below, he was compliantly subordinate to the Jesuit leader for the duration of his career.

In 1931, however, Hunton had given little thought to the race question in recent years, and he knew next to nothing about the South. He admitted his lack of contact with educated blacks, and he confessed that he then believed that it would take many years before blacks could develop adequate leadership. Nevertheless, because of the financial exigencies of Cardinal Gibbons Institute, the executive committee empowered Hunton to act decisively to save the school. Given Hunton's limited knowledge about southern education and such blacks as the Daniels, he was almost certain to perpetuate the friction between the black couple and the committee—friction that had occurred in the first place because of the former secretary's excessive intervention into the institute's daily affairs. After Hunton had made an extensive tour of the school, LaFarge immediately realized that the New York lawyer and the Daniels were going to have serious differences. In a long letter to Victor, LaFarge expressed confidence that the black educators could

---

28. Gary McEoin, "Hunton: Pioneer Interracialist," *Ave Maria,* November 17, 1957, clipping in box 5, folder 60, JLFP 2; Hunton, *All of Which I Saw,* 24, 29–50, 275. See also Hunton's obituary in the New York *Times,* November 13, 1967. On Father Shealy, see McDonough, *Men Astutely Trained,* 49–50, 98–99.

work with Hunton. He told them that Hunton would probably not use the full extent of his authority but rather would act with "discretion and be receptive" to their input. LaFarge granted Hunton's inexperience and lack of knowledge about the institute, but he explained that the situation was in a "transitory phase." In any case, he said, the committee had "to work with the persons . . . at hand."[29]

Since Hunton had been carefully hired by LaFarge for $4,000 a year, a fairly good salary in the Depression year of 1931, he was hardly a man who was just "at hand." Whatever the case, the Daniels were not mollified by LaFarge's missive. In a four-page letter to LaFarge, Constance Daniel vented her ample spleen. She accused LaFarge of betraying her trust by letting yet another absentee landlord direct the institute. She also scolded the priest for breaking his promise not to bother her sick husband, a reminder to LaFarge that she, not her husband, was the real principal and that correspondence should be addressed to her. With no intent to be humorous, she threw in her version of how remote micromanagement actually worked at Ridge: "Mr. Kennedy writes to Mr. Hunton—a man without qualifications or experience—to write to the Principal, to write to Mr. Hunton, to write to Mr. Kennedy, what a bill for insurance is for. The Principal, for some unknown reason—is ineligible to write a note saying, 'The insurance is not on the car but on the farmhouse.' " Daniel lamented that the institute was no longer a "creditable and honorable Negro institution" but just one more colored school "very definitely controlled by its Board or its appointees." The local administration, she charged, had been reduced to the "status of more or less commendable clerks . . . . to be closely trained by an untrained white employee." She raged, "We seem . . . as a race to be cursed with paternalism." In reference to LaFarge's previous letter, she chided him for professing to abhor "the smoldering fires of racial discontent" while instigating them in the school and the FCC.[30]

The rising racial discontent of which LaFarge spoke in the summer of 1932 would lead to the sundering of the FCC, a controversy in which the Daniels also got caught up. Father William Markoe noted the absence of the two black educators from the FCC convention in New York in 1932 and judged it "significant." After visiting the Maryland

29. John LaFarge to Victor Daniel, n.d. [May or June, 1932], in box 1, folder 13, JLFP 2.

30. Constance Daniel to John LaFarge, June 7, 1932, in box 1, folder 11, JLFP 2.

school during his promotional tour for the FCC in 1930, Markoe noted that the Daniels followed the militant lights of Du Bois. Constance was scheduled to speak at the convention in New York, but she told Turner that her presence there would be like putting "a stick of dynamite on the platform." Two years earlier, in a letter to Turner, she praised LaFarge as a humble and trustworthy man, but she further advised the president of the FCC "to refrain from too close affiliation with any one group of Religious."[31]

Not surprisingly, the Daniels supported Turner in the FCC controversy. Constance reported to Archbishop Curley in Baltimore, who passed her letter on to LaFarge, that LaFarge had tried to force her and her husband's hand on the "federation matter." LaFarge, of course, failed to turn the black liberals around. At the same time, the Daniels realized that they could never again represent the institute before a federation that, in their view, had been purloined by two dissembling Jesuits. Both the Daniels had written extensively for Father Markoe's *Chronicle,* and Victor was listed as an associate editor of the black federation's official journal. With Turner's ouster from the FCC, however, their contributions to the journal ended. In April, 1933, LaFarge's ally Markoe dropped Victor Daniel's name from the masthead of the journal. Turner also resigned from the board of Cardinal Gibbons in June of 1933, and neither of the Daniels attended the Cleveland convention of the reformed (western) federation that fall. Oddly enough, at Cleveland the board of trustees of the institute gave Victor Daniel the "highest commendation for his successful efforts in actually keeping expenditures within the meager allotment of the budget."[32]

LaFarge still seemed upbeat about the institute when he attended the last commencement exercises under the Daniels in May, 1933, even though the number of graduating seniors had dwindled to ten. He brought the rich Catholic sisters Mother Katharine Drexel and Mrs. Louise Morrell along with him. LaFarge was greatly encouraged that the two heiresses were impressed with the institution and counted

31. Markoe, "Interracial Role," 143, 241; "Program of the FCC Convention, 1932," in letter box 15, CICNYP; Constance Daniel to Thomas Turner, August 29, 1932, and August 7, 1930, both in Turner Papers.

32. See Victor Daniel to Thomas Turner, February 25, 1933, in Turner Papers; Elmo Anderson to Victor Daniel, September 25, 1933, in box 1, folder 9, JLFP 2; Constance Daniel to Archbishop Michael J. Curley, April 14, 1934, in box 10, folder 1, JLFP 2; "Report on Cardinal Gibbons Institute," *IR,* 6 (October, 1933), 140.

themselves as "one of the family." He also indicated that the General Education Board had put up a matching grant that might keep the school afloat. But it appears that once LaFarge decided to act against Turner in the fall of 1932, he also turned his back on the Daniels. On the eve of the FCC's New York convention, he informed Constance Daniel that he had grown tired of battling over jurisdictional matters at the institute. Although he repeated his usual advice that the principal should have enough power for effective administration, he now brusquely warned her that the board had complete power over the affairs of the school.[33]

By 1933, then, LaFarge and Hunton had long lost all patience with the Daniels. They therefore were not disposed to extend a great deal of consideration or even common courtesy to the husband and wife team, not to mention their eight children, when they abruptly decided to close the school. On November 16, 1933, Hunton gave notice to Victor Daniel that the institution would be closed on December 30 and that the staff would be paid through the month of December. The letter from the executive secretary was succinct and legalistic. It contained not a whisper of regret or sympathy for the cashiered staff. The executive committee essentially offered to pay the principal through December on the condition that he relinquish the keys to the institute by December 15 and that he vacate his family from the campus farmhouse by January 1, 1934, that is, in the middle of the winter.[34] Although a lawyer, Hunton took no reading as to whether these terms fulfilled contractual obligations with the Daniels.

On November 21, Hunton informed Victor Daniel that he was authorized to pay the principal the sum of $2,210.06 for his services through the month of December. This amount supposedly was salary owed Daniel through December, but no itemization was included. Daniel replied that his contract called for three months notice of termination, which meant that the institute was responsible for his salary through February, 1934. In addition, he informed Hunton, the board had agreed to pay for his food, heat, light, and laundry expenses. Adding his salary for January and February ($187.50 per month) and ex-

33. John LaFarge to Victor H. Daniel, May 26, 1933, copy of letter in possession of the author, courtesy of Louise Daniel Hutchinson; John LaFarge to Constance Daniel, August 28, 1932, in box 1, folder 11, JLFP 2.

34. George Hunton to Victor Daniel, November 16, 1933, in box 27, folder 1, JLFP 1.

penses for heat, light, fuel, and laundry through the same period, the principal claimed the institute owed him $2,931.06. He also indicated that it was impossible for him to move his large family out of the house by the end of the month. On December 7, as the holiest and most empathetic time of the Christian year approached, the executive committee, chaired by LaFarge, voted to ask Daniel for a copy of his contract. The committee also discussed "what steps should be taken to have Mr. Daniel vacate the farm house on December 31st if possible." [35]

The principal promptly sent a copy of his contract to the committee, which essentially verified his contention about a notice of three months and thus his claim for pay through February. The contract also stipulated expenses for heat, light, and laundry, but it did not mention food. Daniel argued, however, that LaFarge and other officials had orally promised this to him when he came to Ridge. On December 14, Hunton informed Daniel that Helena M. Graydon, a white social worker and former employee of the national YWCA, would take possession of the buildings on campus, the farmhouse excepted, on December 15. [36]

The negotiations between Daniel and the executive committee continued for the next several months and involved an increasing number of people, particularly Walter E. Kennedy, first vice-president of the board, who resided in Baltimore, and John H. T. Briscoe, a Leonardtown, Maryland, lawyer retained by Daniel to represent him. Since the parties could not agree on a settlement, Hunton made a partial payment of $800.00 to Daniel on December 28, 1933. On January 20, Hunton offered Daniel $1,020.00 more to settle. Daniel rejected the offer because he claimed it included only salary and not the maintenance that had been promised. Daniel's lawyer then increased the stakes dramatically by sending a bill to the executive committee on February 1 that totaled $8,207.09. It included about $2,500.00 for food and $1,115.78 for "car expense." Hunton called the figure "preposterous" and on February 20 counteroffered Daniel $1,388.06, which essentially covered

35. George Hunton to Victor Daniel, November 21, 1933, Victor Daniel to George Hunton, December 6, 1933, "Minutes of the Executive Meeting of the Cardinal Gibbons Institute," December 7, 1933, all in letter box 24, CICNYP.

36. See "Maintenance Arrangements Between Cardinal Gibbons Institute and Victor Daniel, Principal, and Constance E. H. Daniel, Assistant Principal," A. C. Monahan to Victor Daniel, June 10, 1924, and Victor Daniel to George Hunton, December 14, 1933, all in letter box 24, CICNYP.

salary owed Daniel. However, Hunton stipulated that the payment would be made only if Daniel signed a waiver releasing the institute from all claims. Daniel refused the offer.[37]

Meanwhile, as Victor Daniel took his stand against the executive committee of Cardinal Gibbons Institute, his family was suffering. Even before the closure of the school was announced, Daniel reported to the executive committee on October 27 that the school desperately needed twenty tons of coal in order for the institute to function properly. He explained that the furnace in his house was built for hard coal and that wood, especially the green wood available, provided inadequate heat and smoked up his residence. He added that his wife, who had resigned from the institute in June, had just returned from "a very serious operation" and her health was further aggravated by the smoky conditions. In a letter to Victor Daniel earlier in the spring of that year, LaFarge acknowledged the couple's problems, signing off with the following: "Hoping Mrs. Daniel is feeling stronger and that you will get a little rest from the strain of the last few weeks." Daniel told Hunton on December 14 that the lack of heat in his house had become "a menace to the health" of his family. By then the children were sleeping four in a bed to keep warm, and books and papers were being burned for heat. Although Daniel continued to hold out for a settlement based on his claims, he indicated to Hunton that he would be willing to accept a partial fulfillment of his contract in order to alleviate his family's suffering. On February 6, he wrote to the treasurer of the institute in New York: "I am very much in need of money to provide heat and food for my family. Will you therefore please send my check for January?"[38]

What Daniel did not reveal to the treasurer was more startling: his eight-year-old daughter, Elizabeth "Betty" Anne, had died on January 8 at Children's Hospital in Washington, D.C. The child, who suffered

37. George Hunton to Victor Daniel, December 28, 1933, in letter box 23, CICNYP; Walter E. Kennedy to George Hunton, January 20, 1934, John Briscoe to Walter Kennedy, February 1, 1934, George Hunton to Walter Kennedy, February 7, 1934, Walter Kennedy to John Briscoe, February 9, 1934, all in letter box 24, CICNYP.

38. Victor Daniel to Walter Kennedy, October 27, 1933, Victor Daniel to George Hunton, December 14, 1933, both in letter box 24, CICNYP; LaFarge to Daniel, May 26, 1933; Victor Daniel to John McBride, treasurer of CGI, February 6, 1934, and John Briscoe to Walter Kennedy, February 20, 1934, both in letter box 24, CICNYP; telephone interview of Marguerite Daniel Johnson (daughter of Victor and Constance Daniel) by the author, Washington, D.C., August 3, 1992.

from rheumatic fever, contracted deadly pneumonia that winter. Betty Anne's funeral mass was held at St. Augustine's in Washington, D.C., with Father Alonzo Olds performing the private service. She was buried in nearby Mt. Olivet Cemetery, for Constance Daniel could not bear to return her daughter's body to Ridge. This tragedy was one in a series of blows that struck the family within a period of little more than a year, and together they almost crushed Constance's indomitable spirit. On June 11, 1933, the black educator's ninth child, a boy named Sosthenes, was stillborn. Shortly after that, she had a mastoidectomy performed in Washington, D.C. With no medical insurance, they had to contend with mounting bills, and the episode turned into a horrible period of physical suffering, mental anguish, and chaos for the family. The normally vocal mother fell strangely silent after the death of Betty Anne. It was too painful for Victor as well to speak of her death. Moreover, Constance suffered guilt feelings, wondering if she had sacrificed her children for some impractical educational and racial ideal.[39]

In those days children of all classes and races died from illnesses that today could easily be prevented or treated successfully with modern medicine. But the Daniels believed there was a connection between Betty Anne's death and the callous treatment they received from the institute. Constance finally broke her silence and spoke her mind to Archbishop Curley on April 14, 1934. In a letter to him she described the circumstances surrounding her daughter's death: "When I came home sick from the hospital, I found the house cold, and a little sick girl, who died later, shivering by a furnace filled with green wood. No reply to requests for fuel, indicated by written contract, has ever been made. Through the below zero weather, in the drafty house . . . my children remained without fuel." The distraught mother charged that the church had treated them in a most un-Christian manner and vowed that it would not get away with "suppression of the truth—à la La-Farge." The archbishop passed along her letter (and all his earlier correspondence with her husband) to LaFarge. Having gotten no help from the Baltimore prelate, Constance finally went public with the

39. Louise Daniel Hutchison, daughter of Victor and Constance Daniel and the Daniel family historian, has provided me with valuable information on her parents: Louise Daniel Hutchinson to the author, June 25, July 10, 23, and August 14, 1992; and telephone interviews of Louise Daniel Hutchinson, June 26, 1992, Washington, D.C., and Marguerite Daniel Johnson by the author.

story of the closing of Cardinal Gibbons Institute in the *Afro-American* on June 30; but she kept a curious silence about the death of Betty Anne.[40]

With negotiations at an impasse, Victor Daniel also appealed to Archbishop Curley, who for months had been deluged with bills for institute expenditures. On November 23, 1933, Curley offered to assist with the school's debt if the closure of the institute did "not get too much publicity." On March 12, in the first of two long letters to the archbishop, Daniel reviewed the history of his case in detail. Both he and his wife took deep offense at Curley's remark that the institute had been an "absolute failure." Daniel assured Curley that not only had he and his wife made the institution function effectively for nine years by their Herculean labors, but they had spent thousands of dollars from their own pockets to keep the school running. Daniel described the executive committee's actions toward them as "crude and insulting." He asked Curley as president of the board to repudiate the committee's "sharp and disgraceful conduct" and see that Christian justice was done. He also threatened to seek secular justice by filing a lawsuit.[41]

The archbishop sized up the situation and quickly wrote to La-Farge. He pressured him and the executive committee to act on Daniel's request, not out of any sense of seeking justice, as his letters to LaFarge and Hunton demonstrated, but because he feared that the former principal would bring the "Archbishop of Baltimore and the Society [of Jesus] before the Civil Tribunal." After the Daniels vacated the house at Ridge around the first of April, the executive committee paid Daniel $1,338.06 and declared "it had done its duty in full." John Briscoe accepted the money for Daniel but warned that it would not be considered as full payment. Even though Daniel refused to release the institute from further claims, Hunton advised Archbishop Curley that it would be better to pay Daniel and "deprive him of a grievance—or the role

40. Constance Daniel to Archbishop Michael J. Curley, April 14, 1934, in box 1, folder 10, JLFP 2; "Trustees' Diverse Views Made Her Quit, Mrs. Daniel Says," Baltimore *Afro-American*, June 30, 1934, clipping in letter box 24, CICNYP.

41. Archbishop Michael Curley to George Hunton, November 23, 1933, in letter box 24, CICNYP; Victor Daniel to Archbishop Michael Curley, March 12, 21, 1934, both in box 1, folder 11, JLFP 2. Archbishop Curley gave $2,500 toward the CGI debt on January 15, 1934 (see Edward C. Phillips, Maryland-New York Provincial, to John LaFarge, January 15, 1935, in box 12, folder 11, JLFP 1).

of martyr and curb his tendency to letter writing and having recourse to the press." [42] Fencing continued between the two camps over the next two or three months. [43] Then Walter Kennedy learned in July that Daniel had indeed filed a suit against officials of the Cardinal Gibbons Institute at Leonardtown. As far as this writer knows, the case never came to trial. Nor is there any evidence of an out-of-court settlement, which seems unlikely given the intransigence of the executive committee and the fact that Daniel, who moved with his family to Washington, D.C., was still threatening to sue the institute in 1937. [44]

Meanwhile, in a report on the Gibbons Institute on January 23, 1934, LaFarge tried to persuade Archbishop Curley to reopen the institute under new management. In assessing the reasons for the school's closure, he placed no responsibility on himself or the board, blaming instead finances and "mistakes" by the Daniels. He informed Curley that blacks did not hold the former principal (Victor) in high regard. Ultimately, however, LaFarge concluded that the archbishop would not reopen the school until the hefty debt was liquidated: in 1935 it amounted to $13,000 plus unknown mortgage obligations. The archbishop set up a committee in Leonardtown to help abolish the debt, and LaFarge himself worked hard to this end. [45] It is clear that the archbishop's main concern was to avoid adverse publicity and to stay disentangled from controversies such as those that flared over the FCC

42. Archbishop Michael Curley to John LaFarge, January 22, 1934, in box 1, folder 9, JLFP 2; Archbishop Michael Curley to John LaFarge, March 15, 1934, George Hunton to Archbishop Michael Curley, April 2, 1934, Archbishop Michael Curley to George Hunton, April 3, 1934, George Hunton to John Briscoe, April 4, 1934, John Briscoe to George Hunton, April 7, 1934, George Hunton to John Briscoe, April 12, 1934, all in letter box 24, CICNYP.

43. See, for example, Victor Daniel to George Hunton, April 23, June 1, 1934, and Victor Daniel to Archbishop Michael Curley, April 17, 1934, all in letter box 24, CICNYP.

44. Walter Kennedy to George Hunton, July 30, 1934, in letter box 24, CICNYP; Victor Daniel to Warren Schuyler, February 10, 1937, in box 1, folder 9, JLFP 2.

45. John LaFarge to Archbishop Michael Curley, January 23, 1934, in box 1, folder 9, JLFP 1. On the debt, see John LaFarge to Edward C. Phillips, March 22, November 11, and December 23, 1934, all in box 12, folder 11, JLFP 1; John LaFarge to Archbishop Michael Curley, January 23, 1934, and John LaFarge to James J. Hoey, May 29, 1935, both in box 1, folder 9, JLFP 2; minutes of the executive meeting, January 18, 1934, in letter box 24, CICNYP; Nickels, *Black Catholic Protest*, 230–32.

and the institute.[46] LaFarge informed the provincial of Maryland-New York, Edward C. Phillips, that Curley was a "frank reactionary" who had no interest in the school or "Negro" work in general. He further charged that the archbishop was "irresponsible" and an "impossible hindrance" to racial endeavors.[47]

LaFarge seldom, if ever, spoke so disparagingly of a member of the hierarchy, but perhaps he had an ulterior motive in this case. LaFarge worked unceasingly in 1933 and 1934 to convince his provincial and even the Jesuit general in Rome that the Society of Jesus should take over the Cardinal Gibbons Institute. He pleaded with Phillips that "the school would not be a burden, but an *investment* for the Society." He elaborated at length: "I am convinced that it *would greatly add to our prestige and appeal for the Jesuit missions abroad, if we could point to a real missionary undertaking at home.* The C.G.I. has a national reputation; and a widespread goodwill." LaFarge further pleaded that taking over the school "would finally settle the vexed question of the Society doing something for the colored." He continued, "This 'something' would be to work with *our* Negroes; in our land; in the way we and no other Religious or seculars can do; in a way that would fit into all of our missions."[48]

This was vintage LaFarge. Constantly trying to nudge superiors into a benign course, LaFarge's facile and well-trained mind always presented a long-range, nuanced view of issues, never, of course, neglecting the problem of the Jesuit image.[49] Although he failed to move the Jesuit hierarchy, he displayed, as always, an extraordinary ability to adapt to the situation. Having lost the case for a Jesuit-controlled Gibbons Institute, he responded by building new interracial organizations around the edges of the rigid Jesuit system and waiting patiently for new openings.

46. On Archbishop Curley and the FCC, see Archbishop Michael Curley to Thomas Turner, March 30, 1933, Archbishop Michael Curley to Eugene Clark, March 28, 1933, and Archbishop Michael Curley to George B. Conrad, December 16, 1932, all in Turner Papers. For a kinder, if still critical, view of Curley, see Thomas Spalding, *Premier See*, 334, 336, 378–80, 385.

47. John LaFarge to Edward Phillips, March 22, 1934, in box 12, folder 11, JLFP 1. See also Edward Phillips to John LaFarge, December 11, 1933, John LaFarge to Edward Phillips, January 12, 1935, and John LaFarge to Vladimir Ledochowski, general of the Jesuits, May 20, 1934, all in box 12, folder 11, JLFP 1.

48. John LaFarge to Edward Phillips, March 22, 1934, in box 12, folder 11, JLFP 1.

49. McDonough, *Men Astutely Trained*, 127–30, 132–34, 186–91, 202.

In the meantime, the best that LaFarge could manage for the school was to persuade the provincial to spare one Jesuit to act as a caretaker at Ridge for one year. When the priest, Richard McKeon, was withdrawn in 1935 (much to McKeon's relief), LaFarge assured the provincial that the Jesuit involvement with the institute and the retreat therefrom would not create "much publicity" or "embarrassment." On May 24, 1935, LaFarge ended his official connection with the school when the provincial approved his resignation from the board. In 1936 the institute was reopened as a secondary day school, and it eventually came under diocesan control. Later renamed Cardinal Gibbons High School, it finally closed for good in 1967. In the summer of 1972 the campus was razed, leaving only the cupola of the original building standing. A memorial to the school was erected and dedicated at Ridge on September 1, 1990.[50]

Like the Turner affair, the closing of the Cardinal Gibbons Institute was not one of LaFarge's finest hours. While he laid grand schemes before the Jesuit provincial on how to exploit the school for the greater glory of the Society of Jesus, he showed small concern for the plight of the Daniel family in the ill-heated farmhouse in Maryland. LaFarge, Hunton, and the executive committee even refused to honor the principal's contractual rights with respect to regular salary until threatened with litigation. Although Victor Daniel may have overstated his monetary claims against the institute, it must be remembered that he and his wife went far beyond the normal call of duty to keep the school in operation. Constance served the entire summer of 1924 without pay as she worked feverishly to prepare the institute for opening. She also served several years as acting principal on the pay of an assistant principal ($1,200 a year) and several months in 1932 and 1933 without any pay at all. Victor Daniel's salary actually dropped from $2,500 in 1924 to $2,250 in 1932. The discrepancy between bachelor Hunton's starting salary of $4,000 and that of the Daniels attests to the priorities of the church and society. In any case, it would be difficult to put a monetary value on what the couple gave to the Catholic school and on what they endured in their nine years in southern Maryland.

50. Edward Phillips to John LaFarge, December 11, 1933, John LaFarge to Edward Phillips, January 12, 1935, and Edward Phillips to John LaFarge, May 24, 1935, all in box 12, folder 11, JLFP 1; Beitzel, *Jesuit Missions,* 292; "Cardinal Gibbons Institute Memorial Dedication," September 1, 1990, copy in possession of the author.

Besides, the Daniels made the supreme sacrifice as parents. They lost their first child born at Ridge, and Constance experienced a still-birth that was no doubt directly related to the grueling stress of her job. The officials of the institute, however, steadfastly refused to recognize Victor Daniel's rightful, that is, documented, claims to reimbursement for heat, light, and sundries, not to mention food. The ridiculously short notice the committee gave the Daniels to vacate the house in the middle of winter amounted to callous negligence. The sole response the black administrators received from church officials on the death of their daughter was a terse note of sympathy from Hunton on January 9, 1934. Family members recall that only one Oblate sister, a black teacher at the institute, paid a visit to the family and offered condolences. George Washington Carver, however, wrote a touching letter to "My beloved children, Mr. and Mrs. Daniel." A part of it read: "How my heart does indeed go out to you at this time. My heart does indeed bleed with yours at the loss of your dear little one. It does however make Heaven nearer and dearer to us."[51]

The silence of LaFarge and Hunton in their autobiographies in regard to the tragedy of the Daniel family speaks loudly. The normally outspoken Hunton revealed only that the closing of the Cardinal Gibbons Institute sucked him into "a losing battle." Hunton indirectly suggested his real feelings toward the Daniels when he wrote that the FCC was an "extremely racial" group that tended to "increase race tensions and promote race hatreds." To be certain, the story of the Cardinal Gibbons Institute has not been one that the church has been eager to tell.[52]

The closing of the institute at Ridge indicated that interracial contact among even highly educated people could foster bad as well as good feelings. The entire affair also raises a complex question: did LaFarge turn his back on the Daniels because the couple preferred the leadership of Turner and Du Bois to his? Many black Catholics in the

51. George Hunton to Victor and Constance Daniel, January 9, 1934, in box 4, CICNYP; Louise Daniel Hutchinson to the author, June 25, 1992; George Washington Carver to Victor and Constance Daniel, February 3, 1934, copy in possession of the author, courtesy of Louise Daniel Hutchinson.

52. Hunton, *All of Which I Saw,* 56, 58–59; George Hunton to Rev. William J. Walsh, October 13, 1938, in letter box 16, CICNYP. Those who have written of LaFarge and the Baltimore archdiocese have tended to ignore the details of the closing of CGI. For example, see Thomas Spalding, *Premier See,* 326, 334, 345–46.

Baltimore-Washington, D.C., area certainly grew embittered about the way the black school was shut down and the way the FCC was emasculated. Remnants of Turner's black federation, the *Afro-American*, and members of the Daniel family saw a link between the closing of the institute and the ouster of Turner. They suggested that the economic explanation for closing the school was manufactured to provide a convenient excuse for getting rid of the Daniels, especially Constance. When LaFarge ventured to Howard University in the spring of 1935 to speak about "dynamic love" in the Catholic church, he faced a sullen gathering of black Catholic academics and activists. After LaFarge's address, Leo S. Holton, a dentist from Howard University, questioned the Jesuit sharply about the exclusion of blacks from Catholic schools and churches. LaFarge replied in his typical manner that the offenders who excluded blacks were individual Catholics, not the divine church. A young Catholic student from South Carolina charged that priests in the South were fighting against sharecroppers' unions and other progressive reforms, and he added that the idea of a Catholic priest lecturing about dynamic love seemed laughable to him. Others, including William Prater, an old ally of Turner, arraigned LaFarge for his part in the FCC schism.[53]

A recently arrived resident of the federal city and a new reporter for the Washington, D.C., *Afro-American* scored the most punishing blows in the clerical-lay Donnybrook, namely, Constance Daniel. She observed that the clergy and hierarchy had voiced an orgy of protest against the proscription of Catholic freedom in Mexico but had remained silent about the wholesale denial of African American rights. Daniel asked rhetorically if anyone there had "ever heard of the Catholic church being accused of stirring up the colored man in defense of his rights as an American citizen." She bemoaned the fact that she had yet to hear a bishop step forth to support the Costigan-Wagner anti-lynching bill. Daniel characterized LaFarge as a trimmer. "He seems to be having considerable difficulty," she said, "in balancing water on both

53. "Philly's Cardinal Praised; Archbishop's Jim Crow Reproved." Louise Daniel Hutchinson, who was born at Ridge and until 1987 was a staff historian at the Smithsonian Institution, believes strongly that there was a link between the school's closing and her mother's militancy. In a letter to the author, dated July 23, 1992, she wrote that "the trustee's stated reason for closing C.G.I., is, at best, a shabby and 'safe' excuse for what only can be described as loathsome and uncharitable conduct by the Catholic church."

shoulders." Under this furious barrage, the priest conceded the racial shortcomings of the Catholic church, but he argued that the primary cause of the race problem, white ignorance, could only be cured by slow and methodical education. LaFarge concluded his defense of Catholicism by casting himself as a model of racial correctness, saying, "Of course, everybody knows where I stand." Predictably, this remark, given recent events, failed to impress the crowd. A skeptical Prater could not resist the opening. "Father LaFarge is correct," Prater said in a mordant tone. "We all know where he stands."[54]

Both Prater and the Daniels had their reasons for being bitter toward LaFarge and the church. In the Daniels' case, the eviction from Ridge made life painfully difficult during the Depression years. At first Constance Daniel worked as a reporter at the *Afro-American,* where she was paid a penny a word. In the late 1930s she took a job in public relations at the federal Farm Home Administration, and she later advised the Farm Security Administration about black personnel and the black community. She vigilantly fought racism and sexism the rest of her life. Kept out of the Washington Press Corps because of her color and gender, she helped found the Capitol Press Club. She served as a ghostwriter for the influential black leader Mary McLeod Bethune and was deeply involved in the desegregationist battles (boycotts and sit-ins or sit-downs) of the capital city in the late 1940s and early 1950s. A member of the progressive and controversial Southern Conference for Human Welfare, she was branded a subversive by Senator Joseph McCarthy, which effectively ended her career in government.[55]

After an unsuccessful campaign by the Baltimore *Afro-American* and Thomas Turner to get Victor Daniel appointed as governor or resident commissioner of the Virgin Islands, the black educator was able to find work in the federal government as a consultant on vocational education. He worked in the Department of Education in Washington, D.C., and did surveys for the Baltimore Board of Education. In 1938 he returned to St. Thomas in the Virgin Islands to take a job as the director of vocational programs at Charlotte Amalie High School.

54. "Philly's Cardinal Praised; Archbishop's Jim Crow Reproved."

55. Louise Daniel Hutchinson to the author, June 25, 1992; Constance Daniel to the Coordinating Committee for Enforcement of Washington, D.C., Anti-Discrimination Laws, August 4, 1951, copy in possession of the author, courtesy of Louise Daniel Hutchinson. Thomas Turner recalled much later that Constance Daniel was bitter and somewhat out of control (see interview of Turner by Nickels).

Three years later he resumed employment at the Manual Training and Industrial School at Bordentown, New Jersey, and worked there as dean of boys until his retirement in 1955. Much appreciated there, Daniel was compared by a local reporter to the lovable fictional character Mr. Chips.[56]

While the bitterness of black Catholics in the 1930s is understandable, it is a fact that LaFarge and all the priests in the black apostolate suffered constant ill-will from white Catholics, from the hierarchy on down. LaFarge no doubt included himself when he wrote, "The priest or missionary engaged in work among the colored often feels himself isolated and looked upon askance by those who ought to venerate the nobility of his calling." LaFarge's detractors at Howard University did not much appreciate the Jesuit's prudent efforts on their behalf, but neither were they fully aware of the depths of his private agitation over the exclusion of blacks from Catholic, and especially Jesuit, institutions (except, of course, in places where the law demanded it).[57]

Since most black Catholics preferred separate worship in racial parishes to marginalization in white-dominated, territorial parishes, their major complaint about the church was that it mandated that black parents provide their children with a Catholic education but often made the requirement impossible to fulfill. Beginning with the migration of blacks to the North in World War I, black Catholics were denied entrance into many elementary and secondary parochial schools, or they were forced to attend more distant segregated schools that spent considerably less money per pupil and often had a curriculum more geared to vocational education. When a well-qualified black student named George Moore was denied admission to a Jesuit preparatory school in Cleveland in the early 1930s, the local bishop ordered the Jesuits to admit him or move out of the diocese. But no white student spoke to Moore during his entire first semester, and racial incidents persisted until the young African American graduated with honors. In 1933 Arthur G. Falls, a black physician and president of the Chicago branch of the National Catholic Interracial Federation, observed that most blacks saw the church as a "bitter enemy" because of their exclusion from

56. Obituary of Victor Daniel, Baltimore *Afro-American*, December 30, 1967; Louise Daniel Hutchinson to the author, June 25, 1992.

57. John LaFarge, "The Negro Apostolate," *Commonweal*, 22 (July 5, 1935), 257. See also Hunton, *All of Which I Saw*, 119–20, 128.

Catholic schools.[58] As already indicated, non-Catholic blacks such as Du Bois and Woodson also played up the hypocrisy of the church on this issue.

That the Society of Jesus continued to exclude qualified blacks from most of its secondary schools and colleges not only deeply offended LaFarge, but it also threatened to undermine his standing with blacks in the New York area. Furthermore, such blatant discrimination by Jesuits inflicted moral anguish on LaFarge and caused him to indulge in some atypical thought and behavior. Sometime in 1931 or 1932, for example, he proposed that the Jesuits establish a separate black college in Harlem (a suggestion at odds with his interracial stance in the then on-going Turner episode) in order to avoid the scandal of blacks being rejected by surrounding Catholic institutions.[59] Moreover, LaFarge displayed one of his rare outbursts of anger when he discovered that the son of Hudson J. Oliver, a physician and a member of LaFarge's Laymen's Union, had been refused admission to Fordham University. LaFarge vehemently protested this discriminatory act to Provincial Phillips. He pointed out to the provincial that Hudson J. Oliver, Jr., was an excellent student and almost "entirely white in appearance." He curtly reminded his superior that providing a Catholic education for their children was the "sacred duty" of Catholic parents. Then he charged that the rector of Fordham had "objectively committed a very grave mortal sin" in rejecting Oliver on the basis of race, and he warned Phillips that a sense of injustice was growing among blacks. Finally, the last part of this remarkable letter revealed a side of LaFarge that he kept hidden from his black critics: "As for me, there is no course open to me but to denounce Fordham in public, either in word or in writing, or both. If I do not, I must quit all my colored work forever; for the Negroes will pay no further attention to anything I say or do. And this will be the end of most of my usefulness."[60]

58. Dorothy Ann Blatnica, V.S.C., *"At the Altar of God": African American Catholics in Cleveland, 1922–1961* (New York, 1995), 116–19; Arthur G. Falls, letter to the editor, *Am,* 50 (October 7, 1933), 21. See other similar letters by Anne M. Coveney, *Am,* 50 (October 28, 1933), 93, and J. Thomas Butler, *Am,* 53 (July 13, 1935), 333.

59. John LaFarge, "The Society of Jesus and the Negro Work in the U.S.—Some Consideration," n.d. [1931–32], in box 8, folder 22, JLFP 2.

60. John LaFarge to Edward Phillips, February 2, 1934, in box 12, folder 11, JLFP 1. See also John LaFarge to Edward Phillips, June 8, 1935, and Edward Phillips to John LaFarge, June 11, 1935, both in box 12, folder 11, JLFP 1.

This poignant letter went out just three months before the founding of the CICNY. On May 20, 1934, the very day that the council was born, LaFarge expressed his moral torment about Jesuit discrimination to the head of the Jesuit order, Vladimir Ledochowski. He related the troubling event at Fordham, informing his superior that young Oliver had been admitted to St. Peter's College in New Jersey in order to prevent "scandal." LaFarge added that the condition of blacks in the United States was "critical" and that the Jesuits had to act if they were to save "this immense and neglected race from destruction." He played on the well-known anticommunism of the Jesuit general, telling him that the Bolsheviks were capitalizing on the severe oppression of American blacks.[61]

LaFarge, however, had little power over Jesuit priorities. He was unable to change the order's educational policies or get the appropriate resources to implement his racial plans. Despite his passionate letters about Fordham, he was not about to buck authority, criticize Catholic institutions by name, or quit his racial work. In fact, he was eminently inclined to fight a prolonged, circumspect war of attrition with the inimitable Catholic hierarchical system in the theater of racial justice.[62]

The despair of LaFarge was always private and fleeting. In a rare reference to Du Bois in 1933, he upbraided the black leader for predicting that racism would not diminish in the foreseeable future. A dogged optimist, LaFarge declared that the church could never concede that human problems were insoluble.[63] Problems could be solved, he asserted, by prayer, thought, action, and organization. He nonetheless found that action and organization sometimes ran afoul of the Catholic bureaucracy. To escape the unyielding hierarchical system, priests often formed little groups to meet some social, political, or aesthetic purpose. Peter McDonough observes that "over and over again, groups of like-minded Jesuits formed in the nooks and crannies of the hierarchy" to

61. LaFarge to Ledochowski, May 20, 1934. See also "Memorandum on Negroes at Fordham University," May 20, 1934, which was also apparently sent to the Jesuit general, also in box 12, folder 11, JLFP 1.

62. McDonough, *Men Astutely Trained*, 128, 132, 186.

63. John LaFarge, "Doing the Truth: Shall Citizens Study Social Questions?," *IR*, 6 (November, 1933), 197, and "Catholic Negroes Take Stock," *Am*, 48 (February 4, 1933), 430. Du Bois' growing pessimism in the 1930s moved him toward the left and caused his firing by the NAACP.

pursue their own ends.[64] But because of the racial denial of the Jesuits, LaFarge had to build associations outside his religious order.

On November 19, 1933, LaFarge joined nine other priests in Newark, New Jersey, to form the Northeastern Clergy Conference on Negro Welfare. This informal group met every two or three months and eventually included twenty-five to thirty priests, some diocesan and some religious. The conference had no sanction from above and no formal machinery, not even a letterhead. It is difficult to single out the founder of the group. One of the members, Father William J. Walsh, pointed to Cornelius Ahern, the pastor of the Queen of Angels Church in Newark, New Jersey, as the founder. That the first meeting was held in an athletic club in Newark may mean something. More likely, though, a number of priests, including LaFarge, deserve credit for the conference's establishment. LaFarge served as secretary of the organization until its termination in 1942. Besides Ahern and LaFarge, other prominent members of the conference were Edward Kramer, the director of the Board of Colored Missions; Harold Purcell, a member of the Passionist Order and the editor of the magazine *Sign;* Monsignor Joseph Corrigan, an educator who in 1936 became the rector of Catholic University and reversed its segregationist policies; and James M. Gillis, a Paulist and editor of the *Catholic World.*[65] Gillis clearly was the most outspoken and mercurial of the lot. His impassioned speeches hammered Jim Crow Christianity and shocked and angered many. In 1932, radio networks in the South cut him off in midspeech on the *Catholic Hour.* Roy Wilkins of the NAACP described the controversial broadcast as "one of the plainest speeches by a white American clergyman on the race question ever pronounced." Unfortunately, Gillis was so extreme on a range of issues that his utility for racial reform was limited. In 1942, superiors removed him from the editorial helm of the

64. John LaFarge, "Shall We Raise Cain?" *Am,* 53 (June 15, 1935), 228–29; McDonough, *Men Astutely Trained,* 453–54.

65. *MIO,* 339–40; "Memorandum of First Meeting," in box 2, folder 9, JLFP 2, plus other material in this box; William J. Walsh, "The Clergy Conference Is Growing," *IR,* 11 (November, 1938), 172. See also these articles by LaFarge: "Publicizing Negro Welfare," *Am,* 56 (April 25, 1936), 59–60, and "Clergy Conference on Negro Welfare," *IR,* 14 (November, 1941), 168–69. Also informational are "Priest Group Confers upon Negro Welfare," *IR,* 9 (March, 1936), 47–48; "The Most Wanted Work," *IR,* 10 (December, 1937), 181; Hunton, *All of Which I Saw,* 146–49; and "Report on the Conference," March 20, 1934, in box 2, folder 9, JLFP 2.

Catholic World because of his sulfurous anti-Roosevelt views. In the early 1950s Gillis proclaimed that support for Senator Joseph McCarthy was "equivalently that of Christian ethics."[66]

The meetings of the Northeastern Clergy Conference on Negro Welfare resembled a modern-day consciousness-raising or support group. The discussion that took place was personal, frank, and largely confidential. At the first meeting some berated white Catholics for not appreciating their racial work. LaFarge informed the group that blacks would not support any religious program that did not campaign for social justice, higher education for black Catholics, and a black clergy. Opinions in the group varied significantly, but they all agreed that there was a need to make their fellow clergymen "colored conscious." They also agreed that public opinion was crucial for the "Negro's spiritual welfare" and that false opinions about the black minority had to be refuted. The group therefore sought to manufacture systematic and intelligent propaganda on racial matters and to disseminate it. The conference circulated a series of letters about the race problem to ten thousand to twenty thousand priests, pleading with them to make blacks feel welcome in the church and reminding them of Catholic social teaching. The group also used the radio to get out its message. Father Gillis and the Paulists offered the use of their radio station WLWL in New York City, first to the Laymen's Union and the Cardinal Gibbons Institute and then to the Clergy Conference on Negro Welfare. LaFarge initiated the *Catholic Interracial Hour* on WLWL in December, 1932, and it continued until the station was sold by the Paulists in 1937. Many members of the conference, LaFarge included, also spoke on such national hookups as the *Catholic Hour*, which started on NBC in 1930.[67]

In his autobiography LaFarge maintained that the Clergy Confer-

66. Richard Gribble, C.S.C., "The Fractured Inheritance of James Martin Gillis, CSP," *Journal of Paulist Studies*, 2 (1993), 52–58; James F. Finley, C.S.P., *James Gillis, Paulist: A Biography* (Garden City, N.Y., 1958), 118–20, 149, 183–86; Roy Wilkins, "Father Gillis' Broadcast," *IR*, 6 (January, 1933), 12–13; Vincent P. DeSantis, "American Catholics and McCarthyism," *Catholic Historical Review*, 51 (April, 1965), 17, 27; James M. Gillis, "President Truman and Senator McCarthy," (Baltimore) *Catholic Review*, February 22, 1952, clipping in Josephite Archives.

67. "Memorandum of First Meeting," in box 2, folder 9, JLFP 2; *MIO*, 340; La-Farge, "Clergy Conference on Negro Welfare," 169; John LaFarge, "With Script and Staff," *Am*, 42 (March 15, 1930), 554; LaFarge, "Publicizing Negro Welfare," 59–60; Hunton, *All of Which I Saw*, 147–48; "The Catholic Interracial Hour," *Am*, 48 (December 24, 1932), 274.

ence on Negro Welfare ended its activities because of the war and the deaths of such leading figures as Father Ahern and Monsignor Corrigan. In doing so, however, the Jesuit obscured the basic cause of the organization's demise in order to protect the church. In a 1949 letter to Albert S. Foley, a Jesuit historian of Catholic race relations, LaFarge disclosed that the opposition of Monsignor William J. McCann and Bishop James Francis McIntyre led to the disbanding of the conference. McCann was the pastor of St. Charles Borromeo in Harlem and supervisor of several surrounding churches with black parishioners. As the unofficial representative of the archdiocese to the black community, he had much influence. McCann resented LaFarge's interracial work because he thought it reflected negatively on his mission work among blacks. More important, Bishop McIntyre (appointed chancellor in 1934 and auxiliary bishop in 1940) agreed with McCann. Arbitrary and dictatorial, McIntyre proved to be a major obstacle to interracial work in New York City. When he was appointed archbishop of Los Angeles in 1948, he continued his opposition and quickly shut down the local interracial council there.[68]

The formation of the CICNY on Pentecost Sunday, May 20, 1934, was less a new beginning than the culmination of a decade of racial endeavors by LaFarge. Ironically, some of his failed efforts proved to be the catalysts for the CICNY. The Gibbons Institute had closed in 1933, but LaFarge could still rely on a number of people he had recruited to work for the institute, most notably the salaried secretary of the board, George Hunton. It had been the school that had led LaFarge into the FCC in the mid-1920s. When the FCC split, LaFarge then began to consider a new interracial organization more to his liking. Logically, he might have used the revamped federation, the National Catholic Interracial Federation, as an instrument for his purposes. For a number of reasons already discussed in the preceding chapter, however, he lost interest in the federation. Furthermore, his attempts to enlist the Society of Jesus in saving the Cardinal Gibbons Institute and in sponsoring a national program for blacks had failed. LaFarge, therefore, began to look in a different direction.

68. *MIO*, 340; John LaFarge to Albert Foley, S.J., November 28, 1949, in box 14, folder 11, JLFP 2; Hunton, *All of Which I Saw*, 119–20, 123–24; John O'Connor, *The People Versus Rome: Radical Split in the American Church* (New York, 1969), 70, 157, 172–73, 194.

In July of 1933 LaFarge tried to interest Mother Katharine Drexel in his plans, but he concluded that she did not grasp his ideas and would not cooperate.[69] Still, LaFarge had many resources and contacts to work with in New York. First, he had the Laymen's Union, the select group of black businessmen and professionals he had groomed for interracial work since 1928. As Hunton recalled, LaFarge "was proud . . . of the level of Catholic practice to which the group attained in a few years."[70] Second, he had the Northeastern Clergy Conference on Negro Welfare to lend support to any endeavors he might undertake in the racial field. Third, any LaFargian enterprise would have at its disposal the Catholic airwaves, particularly the Paulist station WLWL; the *Interracial Review,* a gift to LaFarge from the Jesuit William Markoe in St. Louis; and, of course, *America.* Finally, LaFarge's capacity for hard work and shrewd diplomacy promised that any organization he established would receive generous advertisement in the general Catholic press and a fairer hearing in the secular and black presses as well.

The congealing idea that brought all of LaFarge's resources together on a spring Sunday in 1934 emerged from the Cleveland convention of the National Catholic Interracial Federation the previous September. The delegates at the convention passed a resolution urging all the chapters of the federation to "hear Mass and receive Communion in a body in their respective cities" on Pentecost Sunday. Taking this cue, LaFarge sent out notices in late 1933 for a meeting on May 20 of what he tentatively labeled the "Pius XI Council in the Interest of the Negro."[71] Mercifully, this display of ultramontanism later gave way to a more palatable name.

Approximately eight hundred people, divided almost evenly between black and white, answered LaFarge's call and attended the interracial mass meeting at Town Hall in New York City. Held under the auspices of the Laymen's Union and augmented by several priests from the Clergy Conference on Negro Welfare and board members of the Cardinal Gibbons Institute, the meeting also attracted Wilfrid Parsons, editor of *America;* Day and Maurin of the Catholic Worker movement;

69. John LaFarge, "Memorandum of Conversation with Rev. Mother M. Katharine Drexel," July 15, 1933, in box 15, folder 12, JLFP 1. On Drexel, see Consuelo Marie Duffy, S.B.S., *Katharine Drexel: A Biography* (Cornwells Heights, Pa., 1972).

70. Hunton, *All of Which I Saw,* 62.

71. Quoted in Zielinski, "Promotion of Better Race Relations," 69; R. F. Downing to John LaFarge, December 15, 1933, in box 30, folder 1, JLFP 1.

and George Haynes, executive director of the Commission on Race Relations of the Federal Council of Churches. Representing Cardinal Patrick Hayes, archbishop of New York, was the Reverend Michael Lavelle, vicar general of the New York archdiocese. The principal speakers of the day included Elmo Anderson, president of the Laymen's Union; Ruth Logan Roberts, a member of the National Urban League and the wife of a black physician who had also been a board member of the Cardinal Gibbons Institute; Michael Williams, editor of the liberal Catholic weekly *Commonweal;* and Father Gillis.[72]

The two black speakers gave relatively reserved addresses, but Michael Williams was less restrained. Born in Canada, Williams left the Catholic church at an early age and entered the secular world of fiction writing and journalism. On returning to the religious fold, he had shed much of the religious defensiveness that animated so many Catholic activists at the time.[73] Williams admitted to the members of the interracial crowd that he was a latecomer to the racial cause, but he assured them that he now considered black-white relations the most critical social and religious problem in America. Then, as the following passage demonstrates, he proceeded to lacerate white Catholics for ignoring black needs and the demands of their faith:

> American Catholics have terribly and most lamentably neglected, and in some ways plainly violated, their duties as Catholics toward American Negroes. We have been indifferent and cold and callous, to say the least. . . . It is not only that we have not listened to the Negro's own claims, on merely natural grounds, on the grounds of their own status as human beings—an ostracized and exploited minority suffering terrible wrongs from the majority—worse than that, we have not listened to the teaching of our own Church which tells us that without any doubt the Negro is entitled to our love and our justice because he as much and as fully . . . as us is the son of God, and hence our brother.

Williams closed with a call for a "new crusade" by the laity to ensure that the laws of Catholic love and justice were applied to blacks.[74]

72. Hunton, *All of Which I Saw,* 67.
73. For Anderson's speech, see "As a Catholic Negro Layman Sees It," *IR,* 7 (May, 1934), 62, 69; Bredeck, *Imperfect Apostles,* 26.
74. For Williams' address, see "The New Crusade," *IR,* 6 (May, 1934), 63, 70–71.

Nobody, however, surpassed Father Gillis in sounding a call to arms. Gillis skewered Catholics for their past racial sins and lambasted gradualism. After explaining Christ's metaphors about slow growth (the mustard seed lesson) and zealous Christian action (the likening of Christianity to a fire), Gillis then thundered like a latter-day John Brown: "We have seized upon the symbol of slow growth because, in fact, we are slothful, lethargic, and lukewarm; we have obscured the symbol of rapid spread because the apostolic fire does not burn in our own hearts. Christianity should have swept from end to end of the world like a prairie fire. It should have burned away from the face of the earth bloodshed, cruelty, torture, injustice, slavery. Let us confess it; it is [a] scandal and a shame that it took Christianity eighteen centuries to eliminate slavery." Gillis claimed that anyone who practices or tolerates race hatred "contradicts and crucifies Christ." Racism, he declared, is a grave sin against the theology of "One God" and "One Brotherhood," a transgression on a par with the "crime of Cain."[75]

James Hoey, collector of revenue for the Second District in New York, summed up the proceedings of the meeting and proposed the establishment of a Catholic Interracial Council. Hoey, who was white, became the first president of the council. At the first organizational meeting in June, a committee was selected to draft a constitution for the organization. The finished document stated that the purpose of the CICNY was "to promote in every practicable way, relations between the races based on Christian principles, by creating a better understanding in the public as to the situation, needs and progress of the Negro group in America through the establishment of social justice and through the practice of mutual cooperation."[76]

What these high-sounding words meant in practice would largely be determined over the next three decades by LaFarge and his alter ego Hunton. Since the two men were inseparable, it is sometimes difficult to establish which one originated a certain tactic or idea. For the most part, however, LaFarge ruled in the realm of ideas and policies, and Hunton served as the able organizational and detail man. Officially, LaFarge was no more than the chaplain of the CICNY, a lay organi-

75. For Gillis' speech, see "One Father of All," *IR*, 6 (July, 1934), 88–89.

76. *MIO*, 338; quoted in Martin A. Zielinski, "Working for Interracial Justice: The Catholic Interracial Council of New York, 1934–1964," *U.S. Catholic Historian*, 7 (Spring–Summer, 1988), 236.

zation, but as the supreme exegete of Catholic interracialism, he suffused the CICNY and its official journal with every facet of his thought
and values, even though Hunton was the executive secretary of the
organization and the editor of the *Interracial Review*. Those values now
supplied the rationale for the CICNY. The organization stressed supernatural grace and love, education of the laity, patience with the hierarchy, interracial contact, racism as ignorance, Catholic Action (under
the control of the hierarchy), and the long, long view. Although La-
Farge emphasized social justice, the spiritual always came first, including the ever-present objective of black conversion. Sometimes LaFarge
simplified the aims and means of the organization for easy digestion,
such as in 1935 when he summed up the essence of the CICNY as
prayer, example, and education.[77] His thought nonetheless was complex, a labyrinth of cogitation, well modulated and voluminously articulated in various writings and communications; moreover, his
thought was evolving.

Not until 1937 did LaFarge attempt a major synthesis in his book
Interracial Justice. In 1950 he boasted that he had created a model Catholic Action agency in the CICNY, where, as he put it, "lay initiative
. . . can be fully reconciled with the authority and superior direction of
the Church." He emphasized strongly that ecclesiastical approval and
control of the councils were essential and that any achievements of lay
organizations should go to the bishop and the priest who acted as spiritual director of the local CIC.[78]

The mass interracial gathering in 1934 and the events of subsequent
months whipped up enthusiasm and hope among Catholic progressives.
Commonweal rhapsodized about the events of 1934 as a "real awakening on the part of white Catholics." As Hunton left Town Hall on
that balmy spring afternoon in 1934, his heart pounded with excitement. He felt that "a miracle had happened." Before long, though, he
returned to sobering reality. After all, more than half of Harlem was
on relief, the treasury of the CICNY was empty, and Cardinal Hayes
and powerful officials in the chancery office had been irked by the fiery

77. Frances Walsh, "The Story of the Conference," *IR,* 9 (October, 1936), 15.
78. LaFarge, *No Postponement,* 167–68.

rhetoric that resonated through Town Hall.[79] Nevertheless, Hunton rightly believed that a significant step in the long journey against racism in the American Catholic church had been taken. The Depression decade would see an elaboration of the movement that LaFarge had launched in the spring of 1934.

79. Editorial "The Negro Problem," *Commonweal,* 20 (June 1, 1934), 113–14; Hunton, *All of Which I Saw,* 66, 69–70, 117–20.

7

LaFarge and the
Interracial Movement
in the Depression Era

Under the tutelage of John LaFarge, the Catholic interracial movement grounded its actions on Catholic the-
ology, natural rights, and, in the Jesuit's words, "the truth of facts."
Since these facts included history, sociology, and science, all largely
academic products of the non-Catholic community, they sometimes
posed certain problems for the institutional church, especially in the
field of race relations. Although LaFarge utilized factual and theoretical
knowledge from secular disciplines (especially the social sciences) to an
unusual degree among Catholic clergymen, the Jesuit heavily stressed
the spiritual dimensions of the movement. "The Catholic interracial
program is primarily a *spiritual movement*," he declared in 1939, "based
upon spiritual principles and relying upon spiritual means." To show
the movement's interest in the religious goal of black conversion, for
example, the "Interesting Statistics" column regularly featured by the
Interracial Review highlighted the fact that nearly eight million blacks
in the United States were "unchurched."[1]

1. John LaFarge, "A Catholic Interracial Program," *IR*, 8 (May, 1935), 66, and "A
Catholic Interracial Program," *IR*, 12 (September, 1939), 134. On black conversion, see
LaFarge's articles "The Negro Apostolate," *Commonweal*, 22 (July 5, 1935), 257, and
"The Interracial Field: Interesting Statistics," *IR*, 9 (January, 1936), 2.

It is hardly surprising that a Jesuit priest emphasized the spiritual nature of the CICNY. Since LaFarge was a highly spiritual person and unflaggingly loyal to the church, the religious emphasis that pervaded the interracial movement came naturally enough. It is evident, though, that LaFarge stressed the spiritual side of the movement even more as the 1930s progressed. Here was LaFarge the master tactician at work. He knew what the hierarchy in New York and elsewhere wanted to hear, and he knew the idiom to which its members responded. He therefore downplayed the possibility that "the truth of facts" disseminated by the CICNY might subject the church to embarrassment or to troubling racial change. LaFarge knew that local members of the hierarchy viewed the CICNY with skepticism and not a few with downright hostility. To counter this attitude, LaFarge accentuated the spiritual goals of the movement in order to pacify his suspicious superiors. Ostensibly, then, he preached that black souls came before black rights.

At the top of the local Catholic pecking order sat the conservative cardinal Patrick Hayes, the archbishop of New York, described by a historian of the archdiocese as "a man of narrow range," unimaginative, plodding, and thin-skinned. The cardinal's only contribution to the CICNY, George Hunton recalled, was that he allowed it to form at all.[2] Francis J. Spellman, who succeeded Hayes as archbishop in 1939, was only slightly less skeptical of liberal reformers than was Hayes and far more willing to punish those he perceived as enemies. An organizational, central-banking archbishop in the Mundelein vein, Spellman's financial acumen resulted in greater central control over the local parishes and clergy. A favorite in Rome, Spellman quickly acquired the prestigious red hat, and by the end of World War II he had become the most powerful prelate in the United States. Often described as the "American pope," Spellman did not suffer criticism gladly.[3] While technically not under the jurisdiction of Spellman because he was a Jesuit, LaFarge knew that the CICNY could only function on the sufferance of the diocesan hierarchy. So the priest used all of his diplomatic skills to court, humor, and appease Spellman.

2. Florence D. Cohalan, *A Popular History of the Archdiocese of New York* (Yonkers, N.Y., 1983), 221; Hunton, *All of Which I Saw*, 117.

3. Dolan, *American Catholic Experience*, 355; O'Connor, *People Versus Rome*, 170; Cogley, *Catholic America*, 229–37; John Cooney, *The American Pope: The Life and Times of Francis Cardinal Spellman* (New York, 1984), 11, 88–89, 175, 182, 282, 199, 282–84, 288.

Far more menacing to the CICNY than Hayes or Spellman was James McIntyre, chancellor (and later auxiliary bishop) of the New York archdiocese. Until his move to Los Angeles in 1948, McIntyre constantly badgered the council. A biographer of Cardinal Spellman described McIntyre as a "mean-spirited and vindictive man" who did the archbishop's dirty work of surveillance and retribution. George Hunton recalled that the mass gathering on Pentecost Sunday in 1934 had caused "grave offense" in the chancery office. The CICNY in fact held its first annual meeting in a retreat house in suburban New Jersey because it feared interference from McIntyre. The chancellor made it clear to LaFarge and Hunton that he believed the religious welfare of blacks should alone concern the CICNY; the social and economic conditions of blacks, he argued, were beyond the ken of the church. When LaFarge requested financial aid for the CICNY from the newly consecrated archbishop Spellman, he discovered that he had to get approval from the chancellor. McIntyre therefore beckoned LaFarge and Hunton to his office and grilled them at length on the nature of their work. He opened his harangue by accusing LaFarge of advocating interracial marriage. With blunt but humble honesty, LaFarge informed the chancellor that his interracial cause did not include the advocacy of miscegenation.[4]

With the CICNY under close scrutiny by the Catholic bureaucracy, LaFarge and the movement walked a precarious tightrope in trying to avoid confrontation with authority. This, for the most part, limited the council's primary activity to polite propaganda through its official journal, the *Interracial Review*. In its first issue as the official voice of the CICNY, the *Interracial Review* described itself as a "progressive" journal dedicated to the principle that "all men are equal in the sight of God and equally entitled to the full measure of social justice." The journal proclaimed, as LaFarge often did as well, that one of its primary goals was to educate the laity about the conditions of blacks. On this point, however, LaFarge was not always consistent. In a letter of 1942, he indicated that the educational campaign of the CICNY was aimed more at the clergy than at the laity. Actually, LaFarge hoped that a well-informed laity would pressure the clergy toward a more enlightened view of race relations.[5] The more important question, in light of

---

4. Hunton, *All of Which I Saw*, 86, 119–20; Cooney, *American Pope*, 78–79, 88.
5. Zielinski, " 'Doing the Truth,' " 478; "New Editorial Board," *IR*, 7 (October,

the Turner and Daniel episodes, was how free lay people would be in an authoritarian church to learn all the pertinent facts and ideas about race and how free they would be to educate others about them.

Certainly, LaFarge exerted essential control of the CIC and commanded the basic facts and ideas that went into its mouthpiece, the *Interracial Review*. He impressed his thought and personality on the CICNY as surely as Franklin Roosevelt impressed his on the New Deal. At the same time LaFarge wanted to cushion himself against the wrath of the hierarchy if it found the council's actions offensive and held him and the Jesuits at fault. As McDonough has demonstrated, LaFarge possessed great "peripheral vision" and had an excellent feel for the limits of hierarchical tolerance. In 1936 he told the Missouri provincial Samuel Horine that the clergy should work out the principles of social work and leave the technical application to laymen. "This keeps us clergy and Jesuits out of controversial issues," he observed, "while it enables us to get across what really is essential."[6] Perhaps, as several of his colleagues would later charge, LaFarge worried too much about hierarchical displeasure and the image of the Jesuits. That the likable and diplomatic priest would incite serious censure by his superiors was not likely. In any case, LaFarge was given to patient slogging rather than to provocative movement, and he saw to it that the *Interracial Review* censored itself.[7]

Although the circulation of the *Interracial Review* began small and remained extremely modest (it ranged from 617 in 1934 to about 1,500 by the end of the decade), its influence nevertheless was substantial in the Catholic community. Free copies of the review went to bishops, rectors, Jesuit houses, and seminaries. Furthermore, Hunton established a close collaboration with Frank Hall, the director of the NCWC News Service. Hall fed much of what Hunton gave him to the Catholic press in the form of news releases. Always the supreme diplomat,

---

1934), 118; John LaFarge to George Moneius, November 3, 1942, in box 14, folder 28, JLFP 2.

6. LaFarge, quoted in McDonough, *Men Astutely Trained*, 128, 130, 186, 461. There is much evidence that LaFarge exercised veto power over the *Interracial Review* and had great influence over George Hunton (see George Hunton to John LaFarge, July 28, 1950, in letter box 29, CICNYP).

7. In a response to an inquiry by a contributor, LaFarge claimed that since the review was a lay journal, there was no censorship of it (see John LaFarge to L. L. Twomy, November 14, 1950, in box 21a, folder 5, JLFP 1).

LaFarge established excellent rapport with important men in the Social Action Department of the NCWC, particularly R. A. McGowan and his young protégé George G. Higgins. Monsignor Higgins recalled that LaFarge always "touched base" with the NCWC when he came to town. LaFarge also gave the New York *Times* news releases on all CICNY activities, no matter how trivial. Of course, as an associate editor, LaFarge promoted the council in the magazine *America*.[8] In a word, after 1934, LaFarge's New York council acted as a national clearinghouse of racial information for American Catholics.

The *Interracial Review* lavished much attention on outstanding blacks in all walks of life, especially if they were Catholic. This emphasis was intended to counter black stereotypes and undermine the impression that the Catholic church was a white man's institution. Much space was given to black Catholic athletes, entertainers, and artists such as Ralph Metcalf, the Catholic Olympian and teammate of Jesse Owens, and the sculptor Richmond Barthé. The review alluded frequently to black saints or whites who earned sainthood by serving blacks. Featured most often was St. Peter Claver. Called "the slave of the Negro," Claver was a Spaniard who ministered to blacks in South America in the seventeenth century. Almost as popular was St. Martin de Porres, a mulatto born in Peru in 1519. Then, too, the review often referred to St. Benedict the Moor of the sixteenth century. Finally, the journal glorified the simple and saintly Pierre Toussaint, a Santo Domingo slave in the late eighteenth century. Toussaint came to New York City with his refugee master and established a prosperous hairdressing business. Before his death in 1853, he supported his former master's widow and many Catholic charities and impressed everyone with his devotional piety. The black entrepreneur also attended to the grooming needs of the LaFarge, Binsse, and Schuyler women (he received as much as $1,000 a year per woman to create the foot-high coiffures that constituted the style of the time), and he was a confidant to the men in these affluent Catholic families. After World War II Warren Schuyler, a mainstay of the CICNY, helped revive interest in Toussaint and led the effort

8. Frank Hall to George Hunton, June 13, 1934, in letter box 8, CICNYP; interview of Msgr. Higgins by the author. See also Gerald M. Costello, *Without Fear or Favor: George Higgins on the Record* (Mystic, Conn., 1984). On circulation figures, see Zielinski, "Promotion of Better Race Relations," 122, George Hunton to Mrs. Edward Morrell, October 26, 1934, in letter box 1, CICNYP, and Dan Kane to the author, July 8, 1986.

for his canonization.[9] In its celebratory black history and journalism, the *Interracial Review* imitated earlier examples set by black magazines such as *Crisis* and *Opportunity*. The difference was that the *Interracial Review* mostly limited itself to lionizing those among the 2 percent of the black population who were Catholic, those the black press sometimes ignored.

The *Interracial Review* obviously tried hard to convey the message that Catholicism cared about blacks and recognized outstanding people of color. It was clear, however, that virtually all the review's black icons tended to be humble and peaceful types, those given to heroic piety and self-sacrifice, such as Pierre Toussaint. Missing were militant black protest leaders, Catholic and non-Catholic. Missing were the likes of the Catholic Thomas Turner and Du Bois. Furthermore, the review accentuated the positive racial news in the Catholic world and tended to avoid the negative. In its "Interesting Statistics," the journal proudly cited the number of American priests and nuns engaged in black mission work in the 1930s (about three hundred priests and eleven hundred nuns) and the number of blacks in Catholic schools (about thirty-five thousand). But the review tended to obscure how many blacks attended Catholic colleges and universities, and it was consistently unspecific on the number of black priests. *Crisis*, however, pointed out that the number of blacks who graduated from Catholic colleges in the 1930s was minuscule. The *Interracial Review* did not choose to reveal the number of black priests in its monthly statistics until 1958, when the number had risen to seventy-seven. When World War II broke out, the United States had but a half-dozen black priests, though Japan had over a hundred native priests and two bishops.[10] Some priests in the racial apostolate actually advocated the segregation of information for blacks and whites. The Josephite John Gillard explained in the *Ecclesiastical Re-*

9. For the history of black saints and saints in the racial apostolate, see Cyprian Davis, *History of Black Catholics*, 19, 23, 26; review of Arthur and Elizabeth Sheehan's *Pierre Toussaint*, in *IR*, 28 (July 1955), 120; Ellen Tarry, *The Other Toussaint: A Modern Biography of Pierre Toussaint, a Post-Revolutionary Black* (Boston, 1981), 204, 217, 238–39, 308, 353, 360–61; David Briggs (AP release), "Pierre Toussaint: Candidate for Sainthood or Uncle Tom?," Fulton (Mo.) *Sun*, July 4, 1992.

10. "The Interracial Field: Interesting Statistics," *IR*, 9 (August, 1936), 130, and *IR*, 31 (May, 1958), 74; "The American Negro in College," *Crisis*, 14 (August, 1937), 230–33; Ochs, *Desegregating the Altar*, 33, 398; CIC News Service, May 18, 1961, in box 5, CICNYP.

view in 1936 that negative information about race and the Catholic church should be reserved for whites so as not to prejudice blacks against Catholicism.[11] Apparently, Gillard believed that such duplicity was possible and deemed blacks gullible enough to swallow it.

LaFarge was not so naïve, but he nonetheless directed a steady flow of all the Catholic good news that was fit to print to the black press and moderate black leaders. Much of this was done daily through Hunton, though LaFarge had many direct contacts and extensive correspondence with non-Catholic black leaders.[12] Before the 1930s most Catholic activists worked in isolation from non-Catholic groups. LaFarge set out to change this situation, and he also worked arduously to change the attitude of the black press toward Catholicism, which was widely perceived by Catholic activists as having an anti-Roman bias. In Hunton's words, the black press's coverage of Catholic affairs was "usually garbled and preferably offensive." LaFarge in fact had reached out to non-Catholic black leaders before the advent of the CICNY. In the 1920s he had interacted at national interracial seminars with such black leaders as George Haynes, Kelly Miller, and Charles S. Johnson. After joining the staff of *America* in 1926, he began to relay problack statements by the pope and other Catholic officials to the publicity managers of the NAACP and the National Urban League. In 1928 LaFarge struck up a correspondence with James Weldon Johnson, executive secretary of the NAACP. In February of 1934 LaFarge congratulated the NAACP on its twenty-fifth anniversary in *America,* though his comments clearly placed him to the right of the civil rights organization. He pointed out that many viewed the NAACP as overly militant, but he argued that it did not impede the work of those "who resort to more peaceful methods."[13] The departure of Du Bois from

11. John T. Gillard, "The Catholic Clergy and the American Negro," *Ecclesiastical Review,* 94 (February, 1936), 152.

12. The correspondence between George Hunton and the NAACP and the Urban League is extensive, with much of it in letter box 1, CICNYP. Some letters to Hunton had scrawled across the top "for Father LaFarge."

13. Hunton, *All of Which I Saw,* 161; Osborne, *Segregated Covenant,* 138; Noah D. Thompson, business manager of the NAACP, to John LaFarge, December 19, 1932, in letter box 16, CICNYP; John LaFarge to James Weldon Johnson, April 14, 1928, and other letters in Group I, box C-327, Latin America—Haiti folder, NAACP Papers, Library of Congress, Washington, D.C. (copies of these documents courtesy of Robert L. Zangrando); John LaFarge, "Jubilee of N.A.A.C.P.," *Am,* 50 (February 24, 1934), 488–89.

the NAACP in late 1934, however, paved the way for closer relations between the CICNY and the civil rights agency. LaFarge resented Du Bois not only as a fierce critic of Catholicism but, even worse to his mind, as an agnostic who advocated birth control.

Both Walter White, the executive director of the NAACP in the 1930s, and Roy Wilkins, Du Bois' replacement as editor of *Crisis*, eagerly cooperated with the CICNY. Unlike Du Bois, neither took offense at LaFarge's role in the ouster of Turner from the FCC presidency in 1932. Both men had articles published in the *Interracial Review* in 1933. Although Hunton detected anti-Catholic prejudice in White, he admitted that he was biased against the executive director because of his part in the removal of James Weldon Johnson as head of the NAACP. LaFarge never voiced any suspicion about White. It may be that the head of the NAACP, well known for his conceit, seemed less friendly to Catholics than did the humbler Wilkins and that Wilkins' marrying a Catholic made him more open-minded toward Catholics and them toward him. In any case, White often expressed his respect for LaFarge and sought his support on many issues. Speaking on the *Catholic Interracial Hour* in 1933, White declared that the word *Catholic* evoked memories of "pleasant and profitable" associations with Father LaFarge.[14]

Both White and Wilkins, however, remained sharply critical of racial discrimination in the Catholic church. This meant that both LaFarge and Hunton received many letters from NAACP leaders concerning the gap between Catholic creed and Catholic practice. In 1933 Wilkins protested to LaFarge about Jim Crow Catholic schools in Chicago. Wilkins specifically referred to a school that denied admission to the son of Arthur Falls, the black chairman of the Chicago branch of the National Catholic Interracial Federation. Wilkins asked whether the Jesuit "through some of [his] connections" could do something to end the blatant discrimination in Chicago. No doubt, Wilkins did not know that LaFarge's influence in Chicago was quite limited or that Cardinal Mundelein had forbidden the Jesuit William Markoe to speak in

14. Roy Wilkins, "Father Gillis' Broadcast," *IR*, 6 (January, 1933), 12–13; Walter White, "Negro Citizenship," *IR*, 6 (March, 1933), 58–59; Hunton, *All of Which I Saw*, 175–78.

Chicago because of his strident attacks on segregation in Catholic institutions.[15]

Like White and Wilkins, Elmer Anderson Carter, editor of *Opportunity*, the mouthpiece of the National Urban League, cooperated with the CICNY while maintaining a critical stance toward Catholicism's racial practices. A Protestant and a Harvard graduate, Carter expressed his feelings about Catholicism in a 1934 article in the *Interracial Review*. After explaining the sociohistorical reasons for the dearth of black Catholics, he opined that the Catholic church had a great opportunity to make converts in the black community if it applied its "eternal principles" to the race problem. Near the end of the article, however, he chastised the church for the exclusion of blacks from Catholic colleges and for the paucity of black priests.[16]

Carter's article might have been more provocative had it not been altered before publication. In the original version Carter singled out Notre Dame, Holy Cross, and Fordham for excluding blacks. Carter's specificity worried Frank Hall of the NCWC News Service, who planned to carry the article. He appealed to Hunton to excise the names of the exclusionary colleges. Thus the article was published without the specific accusations.[17] Whether LaFarge collaborated in the revision of Carter's article is not known, but he surely would have approved the excision. LaFarge himself never criticized Catholic institutions by name, and he was always willing to compromise the unvarnished truth in the name of long-range goals.

In the 1930s Protestant blacks such as White, Wilkins, Carter, Miller, and Charles Houston (and later, Lester Granger, Channing Tobias, Thurgood Marshall, Bunche, and other legends of the civil rights movement) recognized the potential of Catholicism in the field of race relations. The Urban League even tried to place LaFarge on its national board of directors in 1939, but he declined because of his heavy workload. In 1955, however, Hunton became the second Catholic on the national board of the NAACP. Expectations of the CICNY by blacks such as White, Wilkins, and Carter derived from their somewhat faulty

15. Roy Wilkins to John LaFarge, October 11, 1933, in box 3, folder 7, JLFP 1. See Chap. 5 on Markoe.

16. Elmer A. Carter, "A Negro Protestant Looks at Catholicism," *IR*, 7 (July, 1934), 92–93.

17. Zielinski, "Promotion of Better Race Relations," 60.

perception that the American Catholic church, unlike Protestant sects, was highly centralized and authoritarian and therefore capable of efficiently implementing its color-blind principles. Elmer Carter proclaimed that "the very nature of the church" was good for blacks.[18]

LaFarge reached out to the black community most emphatically in his support for the federal Costigan-Wagner antilynching bill that was introduced in 1934. Designed to make local police liable for the protection of prisoners, the bill (and later the Wagner-Van Nuys-Gavagen bill) failed to pass because of southern filibusters in the Senate. Owing to the influence of the archconservative editor Paul Blakely, *America* had opposed antilynching legislation in the 1920s; and LaFarge did not openly challenge that stance after he joined the magazine's staff. The reason for Blakely's change of heart is not clear, but LaFarge undoubtedly had a hand in his reversal on the issue.[19] After 1934 both the *Interracial Review* and *America* vigorously supported antilynching bills, demanding that "Congress must act now!" and that "Lynching must go!" The files of the CICNY bulge with urgent letters and even a few telegrams that passed between the offices of the NAACP and LaFarge and Hunton on antilynching legislation. Having seized on the dramatic issue of lynching to revive the sagging fortunes of the NAACP during the Depression, Walter White was grateful for the strong support of the CICNY against vigilante murders.[20]

LaFarge and Hunton also involved themselves in the racial cause célèbre of the decade, the Scottsboro boys. In 1931 the State of Alabama charged nine black youths with the rape of two white women on a freight train. To put the situation briefly, the women had questionable characters, the state's case lacked solid evidence, and the judge displayed overt racism. The court, nevertheless, sentenced all nine of the young

18. Margaret Clark, "The Catholic Contribution: An Interview with Elmer Carter," *IR*, 9 (December, 1936), 185; James H. Hubert to John LaFarge, November 2, 1939, in box 8, folder 5, JLFP 1. See also "Kelly Miller," *IR*, 13 (January, 1940), 4–5.

19. Paul L. Blakely, S.J., "The Right Not to Be Lynched," *IR*, 7 (December, 1934), 134. On antilynching legislation, see Zangrando, *NAACP Crusade Against Lynching*.

20. Examples of support for antilynching bills are "Anti-Lynching Legislation," *IR*, 7 (December, 1934); "Anti-Lynching Bill," *IR*, 8 (September, 1935), 132–33; John La-Farge, "Present Status of Anti-Lynching Legislation," *Am*, 57 (July 10, 1937), 319–20; "Congress Must Act Now," *IR*, 10 (November, 1937), 163; "The Last Roundup," *IR*, 10 (December, 1937), 180. See telegram, Walter White to George Hunton, July 15, 1937, and letters in letter box 1, CICNYP.

blacks to death, including a lad of thirteen. The Communist party ex-
ploited the case through one of its appendages, the International Labor
Defense (ILD). In complicated maneuvering, the NAACP fought with
the ILD over legal representation of the black defendants. Ultimately,
legal appeals, new trials, and reversals brought freedom to all nine,
though some spent several years in jail.[21]

LaFarge and Hunton joined the American Scottsboro Committee
(ASC), which was founded in the fall of 1934 to publicize the facts of
the Alabama case and raise money for the legal costs of the defense.
George Haynes, the black Protestant leader who earlier had attended
the mass interracial meeting that led to the formation of the CICNY,
headed the ASC. The organization, however, was short-lived. By 1935
a united front that included the NAACP, the ILD, and the American
Civil Liberties Union (ACLU) had been formed to defend the Scottsboro nine. Rather than join hands with radicals, the ASC dissolved
itself. LaFarge seemed to worry more about tainting the CICNY with
radical associations than he did about the fate of the nine young black
men in Alabama, but one of the main reasons LaFarge had joined the
ASC in the first place was to undercut communist influence among
blacks. LaFarge constantly charged that American communists feigned
interest in racial justice and only wanted to dispense radical propaganda
to stir up the masses. He insisted that the defense of the Scottsboro
blacks was doomed to failure if the radical left had any involvement in
it.[22] Nothing about race relations worried LaFarge more in the 1930s
than the alleged appeal of communism to African Americans.

Although a federal antilynching bill never passed and the ASC was
short-lived, the CICNY's overtures to black leaders paid dividends. On
Christmas Eve in 1937, Roy Wilkins sent a special letter of thanks to
the *Interracial Review* for its "generosity in printing and commenting
upon news of the N.A.A.C.P." The letter revealed that the NAACP
offices now regularly scanned the Catholic press for news "regarding
the struggle for full citizenship rights for Negro Americans." LaFarge
and Hunton also had success in wooing the Associated Negro Press,

21. For a detailed account of the CICNY and Scottsboro, see Zielinski, "Working
for Interracial Justice," 237–90; for a more detailed account, see Zielinski, "Promotion of
Better Race Relations," 73–108. See generally Dan T. Carter, *Scottsboro: A Tragedy of
the American South* (Baton Rouge, 1969).
22. *MIO*, 344; Zielinski, "Working for Interracial Justice," 238–39, 241.

the oldest and largest black news service. Headed by Floyd J. Calvin, this Chicago-based news service supplied information to 130 black newspapers. Calvin struck up a friendship with LaFarge and Hunton, and kindly feelings toward them colored the material on Catholicism that he fed to the black press. In a 1939 article in the *Interracial Review,* Calvin lauded the "new spirit of the Catholic press" that, according to him, discussed "frankly and fairly the problems of Negroes." He praised the work of the *Interracial Review, America,* and *Commonweal* as being consistently problack. Like the officials of the NAACP and the Urban League, however, Calvin added a sobering note to his upbeat assessment. "The interracial program has not . . . been *generally accepted,*" he wrote, "even by Catholics themselves."[23]

Many of these friendly black leaders addressed the CICNY's biweekly forums held on Thursday evenings. After 1939 these meetings took place in the new headquarters of the CICNY at 20 Vesey Street in the lower downtown section of Manhattan near the Woolworth Building. Donated by an anonymous benefactor, these spacious accommodations included offices for the *Interracial Review,* a large meeting room for the forums, and a reading room and small library that was named the Martin de Porres Center. A sansculotte social actionist from Paris found the place scandalously plush for his taste. Spirited discussions on racial issues often took place in these pleasant, if not plush, surroundings. Through them all, one visitor recalled, LaFarge kept an air of "quiet dignity and composure in the midst of the interchange of ideas." And after such exchanges, he made sure that carefully worded news releases of the discussions went out to all the media.[24]

One positive result of the close working relationship between LaFarge, Hunton, and black liberals was that it spurred the interracial movement to take stronger stands on some issues than might otherwise have been taken. By avoiding the narcotic of isolation, LaFarge and Hunton opened themselves up to embarrassment when they were unable to fulfill the high expectations of their black friends that they would bring the resources of the Catholic church to bear on the race

23. Roy Wilkins to the editors, December 24, 1937, in letter box 1, CICNYP; Hunton, *All of Which I Saw,* 173–75; Brooks, *Negro Press Re-Examined,* 82; Floyd J. Calvin, "Catholic Interracial Promotion," *IR,* 12 (January, 1939), 9–10.

24. "Interracial Center Conferences," *IR,* 13 (April, 1940), 66; *MIO,* 341–42; Howard J. Herold to Jesuit Fathers (of *America*), November 26, 1963, in box 39, folder 6, JLFP 1.

problem. Although the CICNY's support for antilynching legislation posed no problem for the Catholic church, taking seriously the pleas from the NAACP and the Urban League for the council to combat racial discrimination within the church did entail certain risks. Still, LaFarge and Hunton mounted campaigns on issues they felt strongly about, even when those issues threatened to expose the church to charges of hypocrisy. In 1937, for example, the CICNY passed potent resolutions on discrimination in Catholic elementary and higher education. The resolutions on elementary education declared that the children of black Catholics had a "god-given right" to a Catholic education, and the CICNY vowed to do everything in its power "to open wide the doors of every Catholic institution to every Catholic child of whatsoever race or condition of life." The resolutions on higher education did not name offending institutions or individuals, but they confessed to the dismal record of Catholic colleges in regard to racial discrimination. Furthermore, the drafters of the resolutions promised to assail the ears of all the presidents of Catholic colleges and all the editors of the Catholic press until the injustice was rectified.[25]

From its inception, the Depression-born CICNY stressed the importance of economic opportunity for blacks. LaFarge had long preached that racial justice entailed more than the usual rights of property, suffrage, education, and freedom from intimidation and lynching. Catholics who took social encyclicals and John Ryan seriously also believed that the right to a living wage was the building block of morality and order in society. Shunning the concept of class that was so important to secular liberals and radicals in the 1930s, LaFarge linked the concept of social justice closely with the family unit, so central in Catholic social teaching. To support a family in dignity and health, LaFarge believed, a worker required a living wage. To deprive a black person of an equal opportunity for this necessity, he argued, constituted an egregious assault on the family and on interracial justice. Indeed, the first time LaFarge explicitly designated racism as a sin came in a 1934 article in which he denounced discrimination in employment. The Jesuit therefore heartily endorsed Roosevelt's National Recovery Act (NRA) in 1933 because of its prolabor and minimum wage clauses. He

25. Hunton, *All of Which I Saw,* 173; "Resolutions on Catholic Elementary Education," *IR,* 10 (October, 1937), 156; "Resolutions on Higher Education," *IR,* 10 (July, 1937), 107.

explained that the NRA adhered faithfully to the guidelines laid down by Pope Pius XI's *Quadragesimo Anno*. He lambasted those who sought to establish wage differentials for minority workers under the NRA, and he implored Catholics to abide by the humanitarian spirit of the law. "Look through your neighborhood, and offer employment to at least one colored person," he told Catholic businessmen. "If the head of the family, well and good," he implored, "but at least one person."[26]

The economic position of blacks in the United States had never been good, but the Depression rendered it catastrophic. Writing in the early 1940s, the Swedish economist Gunnar Myrdal described the economic condition of American blacks as "pathological." In 1938 the State of New York released a report that graphically revealed how much racial discrimination explained the dismal condition of most blacks. The state investigation showed that every sector of the New York economy, private and state, restricted three-fourths of blacks to the most menial, vulnerable, and low-paying jobs. Significantly, the chairman of the commission that undertook the investigation was Harold P. Herman, a Catholic lawyer, a New York assemblyman, and a member of the CICNY. Thus in the late 1930s, as the nation moved to military preparedness and thoughts of saving democracy abroad once again, the CICNY began an earnest campaign for fair employment practices.[27]

As the 1940s approached, the *Interracial Review* and *America* more and more related the domestic racial situation to world affairs. In the spring of 1941 as Roosevelt was launching the Lend-Lease program, the *Interracial Review* began to hit hard at racial discrimination in defense industries, harping on the lack of democracy in the "arsenal of democracy."[28] Meanwhile, LaFarge became involved in the work of the

26. John LaFarge, "Interracial Justice," *IR*, 12 (October, 1939), 121–23; John La-Farge, "The Negro and Wage Differential," *Am*, 50 (February 10, 1934), 442–43; John LaFarge, "Doing the Truth: The Recovery Act and the Negro," *IR*, 6 (August, 1933), 151; LaFarge, quoted in "Negro Labor and the NRA," *Am*, 49 (August 26, 1933), 493–94.

27. Myrdal, *An American Dilemma*, 205; Zielinski, "Promotion of Better Race Relations," 142–51; Hunton, *All of Which I Saw*, 79–86.

28. See, for example, the three-part series by Thomas A. Meehan, "The Economic Plight of the Negro," *IR*, 12 (March, 1939), 39–41, (April, 1939), 55–57, and (May, 1939), 75–77. See also "Negroes and National Defense," *IR*, 13 (September, 1940), 133–34; "What Price Prejudice?," *IR*, 13 (November, 1940), 163–64; George Streator, "The Illogic of Race Discrimination in Labor Affairs," *IR*, 13 (December, 1940), 189; "A Challenge

Committee on Negro Americans in Defense Industries. On May 1, 1941, the committee issued a statement that blasted employers who jeopardized the national defense by practicing racism in the job market. Both LaFarge and Hunton signed the statement, along with notables such as New York governor Herbert Lehman, mayor of New York City Fiorello LaGuardia, the presidents of Yale and Howard Universities, and Fathers Ryan and McGowan of the Social Action Department of the NCWC. The statement declared that racial justice was the true test of American democracy. "Our concern for democracy in Europe or elsewhere," the statement read, "lacks reality and sincerity if our plans and policies disregard the right of minorities in our own country." The *Interracial Review* followed up the release of the statement with an editorial that maintained there could be no racial peace as long as employers "wantonly and ruthlessly" denied to blacks the human right of a living wage.[29]

In the meantime, A. Philip Randolph had been preparing to launch an all-black march on Washington, D.C., to protest discrimination in defense industries. A militant labor-socialist leader, Randolph had conspicuously opposed America's entry into World War I. During the war the government barred from the mail Randolph's magazine *The Messenger,* self-advertised as "the only radical Negro magazine in America." In the 1920s Randolph vied with Du Bois and the black nationalist Marcus Garvey for the allegiance of the black community. Randolph's long dedication to unionism finally paid off in 1935 when the railroads recognized his trade union, the Brotherhood of Sleeping Car Porters. Owing to the rising militancy of blacks and President Roosevelt's desire for national unity as war drew near, Randolph's March on Washington Movement (MOWM) forced the government to act. On June 25, 1941, Roosevelt signed executive order 8802, which created the Fair Employment Practices Committee (FEPC).[30]

---

to the Press," *IR,* 14 (April, 1941), 51–52; and Frank L. Hayes, "Racial Bars to Defense Jobs," *IR,* 14 (April, 1941), 55.

29. "National Defense and the Negro," *IR,* 14 (May, 1941), 72; Zielinski, "Promotion of Better Race Relations," 151; "Justice for Negro Americans," *IR,* 14 (May, 1941), 68.

30. On the FEPC, see Herbert Garfinkel, *When Negroes March: The March on Washington Movement in the Organizational Politics of FEPC* (New York, 1959), 7–8, 37–61. See also Merl E. Reed, "FEPC and Federal Agencies in the South," *Journal of Negro History,* 65 (Winter, 1980), 446–67.

That LaFarge, the interracial gradualist who had earlier used his clout against the militant Catholic Turner, would endorse Randolph's class- and race-conscious MOWM was remarkable. Roosevelt's executive order of 1941 marked but the beginning of the drawn-out politics of the FEPC, and they drew LaFarge closer to Randolph than to any other black leader in the 1940s. At the famous mass rally of Randolph's MOWM in Madison Square Garden in 1942, the Jesuit stood out as the lone white speaker. LaFarge followed Randolph's lead when he helped create the National Catholic Committee on Negro Employment in 1942.[31]

If progress was slow for blacks in the Catholic church in the 1930s, the attitudes of the minority press and black leaders toward the Catholic church underwent dramatic change during that time—a change that meant tens of thousands of blacks would be presented with a more favorable picture of the Catholic church in regard to racial affairs. No one deserves more credit for this metamorphosis than LaFarge, though his close ally Hunton deserves a great deal of credit as well. In a series of nonflattering articles on American Catholicism in the Protestant *Christian Century* in 1944, Harold E. Fey devoted an article to "Catholicism and the Negro." Although Fey attacked the Catholic hierarchy for dragging its feet on the race question, he praised LaFarge as the priest who had educated Catholics up to a more liberal view of blacks. Fey further applauded the CICNY for its success in "transforming the attitude of the secular Negro press toward the Roman Catholic Church." Fey declared, "To change the attitude of that press, which largely dominates Negro thought, from hostility to warm appreciation of the Catholic Church in a decade represents a notable achievement." LaFarge rightly treasured this compliment from one of the separated brethren and quoted it proudly in his next book.[32]

By the end of the 1930s, examples of a friendlier black attitude toward Catholicism emerged. The black press began to balance its harsh criticism with positive references to the interracial work of the Catholic church. Like LaFarge, the black press now gleaned encyclicals for racial

31. Zielinski, "Working for Interracial Justice," 241–45. In *When Negroes March*, 38–42, Garfinkel explains how it was that many conservatives and the NAACP and Urban League came to support Randolph's radical proposal; see Chap. 8 for more on Randolph and LaFarge.

32. Harold E. Fey, "Catholicism and the Negro," *Christian Century*, 61 (December 20, 1944), 1477–78. LaFarge quoted Fey in his *No Postponement*, 157.

content and congratulated Popes Pius XI and Pius XII on their racial insights. Like LaFarge, too, the black press sometimes exaggerated the racial enlightenment of the church. In the early 1940s the *Interracial Review* drew attention to black praise of the Vatican in an editorial titled "Papal Interest in American Negroes." The review reprinted several editorials from black newspapers that lauded the racial attitudes in Rome. On the death of Pius XI in 1939, for example, the New York *Age,* with some hyperbole, editorialized: "In the field of racial relations the Pope was responsible for much of the Catholic Church's growing influence among Negroes and his liberalism has reflected itself all along the line in the Church so that today the Church enjoys the reputation of being the most liberal of the major denominations in its reception and treatment of Negroes." Shortly thereafter, the Kansas City *Call* expressed great hope in Pope Pius XII and proclaimed that the Catholic church was a "moral force so intelligent, so commanding" that it was "the ideal organization" to solve problems of human relations. The Chicago *Defender,* an influential black newspaper with a national readership, declared that Pius XII "in due time will prove to be the greatest force against international banditry, exaggerated nationalism and racial persecution that the world has ever had."[33]

Catholic interracialism also went to college in the 1930s, gaining a strategic foothold on Catholic campuses before the decade had ended. It started in the spring of 1933 when Mother Grace M. Dammann, president of Manhattanville College of the Sacred Heart, invited George Hunton to give a series of lectures. At the female college, which was situated at 130th Street on a cliff overlooking Harlem, Mother Dammann had been educating her students in Catholic social action for several years. After Hunton's hard-hitting lectures on the race problem, expanding, as he put it, on "several points Father LaFarge always insisted were basic," the politically aroused students asked Hunton what kind of action they should take. He suggested that they formulate a set of resolutions on race relations that could act as a guide for all Catholic students: hence, the "Manhattanville Resolutions" of 1933. These resolutions became a sensation in the Catholic educational community and

33. "Papal Interest in American Negroes," *IR,* 13 (January, 1940), 15–16; "The Church Loses," *IR,* 12 (March, 1939), 34; "The Call Editorial," *IR,* 12 (May, 1939), 69; "Pope Pius XII Praised," *IR,* 12 (July, 1939), 98.

soon became a model for the mushrooming student interracial movement. The Catholic press, including the Vatican *Osservatore Romano,* widely reprinted the eight resolutions. Their content, phrasing, and impact call for full quotation:

1. To maintain that the Negro as a human being and as a citizen is entitled to the rights of life, liberty, and pursuit of happiness and to the essential opportunities of life and the full measure of justice.

2. To be courteous and kind to every colored person, remembering the heavy yoke of injustice and discrimination he is bearing. To remember that no race or group in America has endured the many handicaps that are his today.

3. To say a kind word for him on every proper occasion.

4. Not to speak slightingly or use nick names [*sic*] which tend to humiliate, offend or discourage him.

5. To remember that the Catholic Church and the Catholic program of social justice have been called "The Greatest Hope of the Colored Race."

6. To recognize that the Negro shares my membership in the Mystical Body of Christ and the privileges that flow therefrom and to conduct myself in accordance therewith.

7. To give liberally on the Sundays of the year when the collections are devoted to the heroic missionaries laboring among the Negro group.

8. To become increasingly interested in the welfare of the Negro; to engage actively in some form of Catholic Action looking to the betterment of his condition, spiritually and materially.[34]

One Jesuit priest hailed the resolutions as "fearless and encouraging." Encouraging, no doubt, but they were more earnest than fearless. LaFarge confessed that the resolutions might appear "patronizing" to blacks, but he maintained that it was significant that anything was said at all. Even if some of the resolutions were awkwardly expressed, LaFarge's hand could be seen in some of the more substantial resolu-

34. Hunton, *All of Which I Saw,* 91–95; "Resolutions Adopted by the Students of the College of the Sacred Heart, Manhattanville, New York City," *IR,* 6 (July, 1933), 126; Louise Quigley, "Student Federation and Interracial Justice," *IR,* 12 (November, 1938), 168.

tions, especially numbers one, six, and eight. He heartily welcomed the initiative of the students. Moreover, he laid plans for broad student participation in the interracial movement.[35]

In 1935 LaFarge began a three-part series called "A Program for Youth" in the *Interracial Review*. At the second annual meeting of the CICNY at Fordham University in 1936, the conference agreed that "youth will be the backbone of the movement, since youth 'always looks at a question with unprejudiced eyes.' " The following year LaFarge declared that interracialism relied more on the "zeal and talents of Catholic college men and women" than on that of any other group. "They are," he said, "the banner bearers in this movement."[36] From the founding of the CICNY, the *Interracial Review* carried a column called "As Youth Sees It," written by and for students.

The column did not lack for material because there was an explosion of interracial activity on campus in the 1930s. First, the decade was a time of general activism on campus. Second, even in the 1920s the white avant-garde in places like New York had begun to recognize black literary artists of the Harlem Renaissance, and by the 1930s black entertainers, sports figures, and other talented individuals were making an even bigger mark on the American mainstream. Last, of course, there was the inspiration of LaFarge's interracial movement.

In 1937 some 250 invited students from twelve Catholic colleges attended the CICNY convention at Fordham University. At this meeting a standard interracial program was adopted for students, using the "Manhattanville Resolutions" as the basic guide. The delegates decided that each college should establish interracial clubs and hold intercollegiate conferences several times a year. Later that summer at the Fordham summer session, LaFarge and Hunton introduced a new technique of racial education that won high praise on campuses. The two men staged "hearings" on the model of congressional investigations. This process entailed witnesses, lawyers, cross-examination, summation, and, at the end, resolutions. LaFarge led off as the first witness, followed by two blacks from the Laymen's Union, then Elmer Carter of

35. Richard M. McKeon, S.J., letter to the editor, *Am*, 49 (June 3, 1933), 212; John LaFarge, "Doing the Truth," *IR*, 6 (August, 1933), 152.

36. John LaFarge, "A Program for Youth," *IR*, 8 (December, 1935), 182–83, *IR*, 9 (January, 1936), 6–7, and (February, 1936), 22–23; quotation in Frances Walsh, "The Story of the Conference," *IR*, 9 (October, 1936), 151; LaFarge, quoted in Amy MacKenzie, "The Philadelphia Conference," *IR*, 10 (December, 1937), 182.

the Urban League. An observer reported that LaFarge received "prolonged applause" at the end of his testimony. Carter, however, managed to raise "thunderous applause" by speaking on the economic condition of blacks. The members of the audience approved two resolutions at the end of the proceedings. One indicated that they would prod Catholic educators and students to work for black rights, and the other vowed that they would strive to "open their doors and admit duly qualified young Negroes" to Catholic colleges.[37]

A few months after the Fordham convention, Cardinal Dennis Dougherty of Philadelphia called an interracial conference at St. Joseph's College. LaFarge, Carter, and others from the CICNY's busy speaker's bureau captured the rapt attention of students with their hearings technique. The following year the CICNY held a large and highly successful conference at Providence, at which Charles Houston, the head of the NAACP legal defense team, joined LaFarge on the program. The result was another set of resolutions, similar to the "Manhattanville Resolutions" but more sophisticated.[38]

After 1937 students held scores of interracial symposia and intercollegiate conferences on race relations, sometimes drawing as many as 500 students. Significant pre-CICNY groups such as the Catholic Students' Mission Crusade, which included precollege youth, adopted interracial programs. A Catholic Action group claiming 800,000 members and led by Father Gillard, it advocated an "all-out Catholicism in behalf of the Negro" in the mid-1930s. In 1937 the newly founded National Federation of Catholic College Students also developed an interracial program. Its official magazine, *Forum*, devoted an unusually large amount of space to interracial matters. The federation encouraged all its chapters to begin interracial programs that stressed prayer, study, and work. The last, for instance, entailed such suggestions as writing articles on blacks for school newspapers, publicizing interracial affairs on bulletin boards, handing out flyers, and exploring "any other way possible" to improve the condition of black Americans.[39]

37. Harte, *Catholic Organizations Promoting Negro-White Relations*, 120; Harry McNeil, "A New Technique: Educators' Hearings on Interracial Justice," *IR*, 10 (September, 1937), 134–37.

38. MacKenzie, "Philadelphia Conference," 182–84; Louise Byles, "The Providence Pronouncement," *IR*, 11 (April, 1938), 59–61.

39. Harte, *Catholic Organizations Promoting Negro-White Relations*, 124–34;

Catholic alumni organizations soon jumped into the fray as well. In 1936 the National Catholic Alumni Federation, representing 300,000 graduates, sponsored a symposium on the race problem. In 1937 it initiated interracial programs to assist blacks in housing, health, jobs, and basic human rights. The Notre Dame Club of New York, consisting of 500 members, went on record in 1937 as supporting antilynching legislation and full rights for the black minority. Other groups, such as the Alumni Intercollegiate Interracial Committee, also formed in these years.[40] LaFarge, Hunton, and their black allies often spoke at alumni gatherings in the New York area.

Although LaFarge lacked the populistic appeal of fellow Jesuit Daniel Lord or the oratorical prowess of Fulton J. Sheen, he gained the deep respect of many college students. The Jesuit figured prominently in spawning the crucial second wave of interracialists, those who would come of age in the postwar period, when civil rights became the major domestic issue. Students admired LaFarge for his quiet nature, his dry wit, and his depth of feeling. They found him more impressive in discussions with small groups than in formal lectures. More important, they felt compelled to act after being exposed to LaFarge. Students at St. Joseph's established the Father LaFarge Society in 1938. Its stated purpose was "to obtain some measure of justice for the Negro, particularly in the field of Catholic education." To achieve this end, the students proposed to educate the public, establish personal contact with blacks, and conduct themselves as examples of racial enlightenment.[41]

One element that LaFarge held to be vital was absent from the mission statement of the LaFarge Society: the spiritual roots of interracialism. In the numerous addresses and hearings that he presented to students, he always emphasized the theological basis of interracialism. Pursuing social justice by itself, he preached, was inadequate, and in

---

"Resolutions Adopted by the Catholic Students," August 11, 1933, in letter box 13, CICNYP; outline for student interracial program in New York region, in box 12, folder 10, JLFP 1; Gillard, *Colored Catholics,* 246.

40. Harte, *Catholic Organizations Promoting Negro-White Relations,* 121; "Notre Dame Alumnae Urge Catholic Interest in the Negro," in letter box 13, CICNYP; Raymond W. Murray and Frank T. Flynn, *Social Problems* (New York, 1938), 148.

41. Interview of Dan Kane (student at St. Joseph in 1930s) by the author, Cincinnati, July 7, 1986; interview of Mathew Ahmann by the author, Washington, D.C., July 26, 1985; "Constitution of the Father LaFarge Society at St. Joseph's College," in possession of the author, courtesy of Dan Kane.

fact the goal could not be achieved without redemptive charity or supernatural love. Although LaFarge related black rights to natural rights and American values, he argued that basic human rights for Catholics derived first and foremost from God and could be extrapolated most strikingly from the doctrine of the Mystical Body of Christ. This weapon in the Jesuit's theological arsenal got increasing use in the 1930s.[42] The Mystical Body doctrine, Arnold Sparr points out, represented a dynamic view of the church as an "organic sacramental community." The old Pauline doctrine was an idea whose time had come again. The belief that all were one in Christ, acted out dramatically in the Eucharist, provided a way to achieve spiritual satisfaction through social unity. The doctrine therefore animated much of LaFarge's and Catholicism's social activism in the 1930s. A standard religion textbook written for Catholics in 1933, *Christian Life and Worship*, underscored the Mystical Body doctrine. Monsignor Sheen made the doctrine the subject of a book in 1935, and the pope reinvigorated it with a 1943 encyclical, *Mystici Corporis*.[43] Justice among the races, LaFarge insisted, required strong spiritual medicine.

Spiritual medicine, however, was not given in strong enough doses to bring about many concrete changes in racial practices on campus. In her 1936 book on Catholic education and blacks, Margaret Diggs concluded, "Catholic colleges, as a rule, are not willing to admit colored students."[44] A handful of Catholic colleges began to readmit black men in token numbers in the 1930s. The word *readmit* is appropriate be-

42. See MacKenzie, "Philadelphia Conference," 182; and Byles, "Providence Pronouncement," 59. LaFarge always asserted at youth gatherings that encyclicals such as *Quadragesimo Anno* were binding on all Catholics.

43. Sparr, *To Promote, Defend, and Redeem*, 105–106, 140; Charles E. Diviney, "The Mystical Body of Christ and the Negro," *IR*, 8 (June, 1935), 86–88; James Terence Fisher, *The Catholic Counterculture in America, 1933–1962* (Chapel Hill, N.C., 1989), 44, 49–50. See LaFarge's exploration of the social aspects of the doctrine in "Unity of Mankind Through Creation and Redemption, Basis of Interracial Justice," *Queen's Work* (December, 1934), copy in box 6, folder 26, JLFP 2.

44. Margaret A. Diggs, *Catholic Negro Education in the United States* (Washington, D.C., 1936), 125. See also Harold A. Buetow, *Of Singular Benefit: The Story of Catholic Education in the United States* (New York, 1970), 258–60, and Gillard, *Colored Catholics*, 212–15. Gillard shows that a survey of 120 Catholic colleges in 1940 revealed that 47 of them had blacks, but the total number of students was only around two hundred (figures are not reliable), including the enrollment of 2 all-black Catholic colleges. Fewer than a dozen blacks were in residence on campus.

cause some Catholic colleges, such as Catholic University, had accepted blacks until they closed their doors to the minority in the early twentieth century (one of the three black priests of the Healy family was the president of Georgetown University in the late nineteenth century, but this institution did not accept African American students until about the middle of the twentieth century). It was five years after the "Manhattanville Resolutions" before Mother Dammann was able to enroll the first black woman at the college overlooking Harlem. The first black woman graduate of a Catholic college apparently received her degree four years after the resolutions, in 1937. College officials and alumni, and sometimes significant numbers of students, resisted integration. Apologists for the church often suggested that few blacks could qualify for admission to Catholic colleges because of their educational deficiencies. A major history of Catholic education, however, states that before World War II "students who applied were admitted, and it hardly ever made any differences whether or not they were prepared to follow a *college* course of studies."[45] The interracial program for college students designed by the CICNY stipulated, with typical LaFargian restraint, that students should not agitate for black enrollment until the school was well prepared for acceptance. Nevertheless, the collegiate movement constituted a major step in breaking the vicious cycle whereby students blamed faculty, administrators, and alumni for the exclusionist policies, while the faculty and administrators blamed students, parents, and alumni for the same offense. Students, however, were definitely more favorably disposed toward change and paid less attention to the bugaboo of social equality than did their elders. Of the student body at Manhattanville, 80 percent voted in favor of admitting the first black student.[46] The student interracial movement of the 1930s helped prepare Catholic campuses for the historic breakthroughs of the 1940s and 1950s.

Whether on campus or off, the launching of the interracial movement raised great hopes among Catholics dedicated to racial reform. As the 1940s began, LaFarge wrote that the "Catholic interracial move-

45. Edward J. Powers, *Catholic Education in America: A History* (New York, 1972), 433. Powers says nothing about blacks.

46. Hunton, *All of Which I Saw,* 92, 98, 100–103; Zielinski, "Promotion of Better Race Relations," 112; Harte, *Catholic Organizations Promoting Negro-White Relations,* 123, 132–34.

ment has taken fire through the country." He declared that a "spiritual awakening" had occasioned a "wonderful increase in the spiritual welfare of the Negro." The *Interracial Review, America,* and other progressive Catholic journals spoke excitedly of the arousal of the Catholic conscience. In 1938 the *Catholic Herald* beamed, "Hardly a week goes by that His Holiness, Pope Pius XI, doesn't roundly condemn exaggerated nationalism and state that racism . . . is contrary to Christian teaching." Dennis Clark, a hard-nosed social actionist from Philadelphia who replaced Hunton in 1962 as executive secretary of the CICNY, maintains that the CICNY established an "ideological benchmark for Catholic aspirations" and that the "didactic seasoning" provided by the council served to summon youths who emerged as Catholic leaders after World War II. Mathew Ahmann, another young interracialist who took the helm of the newly formed National Catholic Conference on Interracial Justice in the late 1950s, vouched that the groundwork laid by LaFarge and the CICNY helped prepare the Catholic community to respond positively to the civil rights movement of his time.[47]

Whether or not the 1930s constituted a decisive decade in Catholic race relations, significant gains clearly occurred.[48] The amount of space in the Catholic press devoted to racial matters increased markedly during the decade. In 1940 the *Interracial Review* estimated an increase of 1,000 percent. The Catholic historian John J. O'Connor, a professor at Georgetown University, gauged the increase in racial coverage between 1934 and 1944 to be 1,200 percent.[49] As already illustrated in the case of the NAACP, the Urban League, and the black press, Catholic publicity began to reap benefits in the 1930s. Furthermore, growth in the black Catholic population, which had been flat since the Civil War,

47. John LaFarge, "Let the Negro Speak and Let Whites Listen," *Am,* 63 (September 21, 1940), 650; LaFarge, *No Postponement,* 142–43; "Educating Negro Leaders," *Am,* 54 (March 14, 1936), 536; *Catholic Herald,* quoted in *IR,* 11 (October, 1938), 160; interview of Dennis Clark by the author, Philadelphia, June 15, 1988; interview of Ahmann by the author.

48. Both Jay P. Dolan, "Religion and Social Change in the American Catholic Community," in *Altered Landscapes: Christianity in America, 1935–1985,* ed. David W. Lotz (Grand Rapids, Mich., 1989), 45, and Zielinski, "Working for Interracial Justice," 260, claim watershed-type gains in the 1930s.

49. "Five Years of Progress," *IR,* 13 (February, 1940), 19–20; John J. O'Connor, "An Educational Apostolate," *IR,* 32 (May, 1959), 89–92.

climbed upward in this period. By 1940, black Catholics numbered almost 300,000, up from a little over 200,000 at the beginning of the 1930s. Another sign of changing attitudes could be seen in the annual Catholic collection for Negro and Indian missions. In 1919 the collection averaged about three-fourths of a penny for each Catholic. By 1935, in the depth of the Depression, the figure had risen to six or seven cents per Catholic. Additionally, in Myrdal's influential study of American black-white relations published in 1944, the Swedish scholar ranked the *Interracial Review* as the third most important journal on race relations, trailing only the NAACP's *Crisis* and the Urban League's *Opportunity.*[50]

Nevertheless, on the race question the forces of continuity within the Catholic community proved stronger than the forces of change. Candid Catholic activists acknowledged that the movement had reached only a tiny fraction of Catholics. Hunton grieved that there was a "vacuum of unconcern" among Catholics. He lamented also that many of those who labored in the black missions suffered from advanced paternalism. A 1938 cartoon in the *Interracial Review* depicted an imaginary Catholic congress at which, adjacent to the occupied chairs of "Catholic Action," "Peace," "Labor," "Education," and "Liturgy," stood an empty chair representing "Interracial Justice."[51]

Early Catholic analysts had surprisingly few illusions about the CICNY. Several critics characterized the interracial movement as feeble and ineffectual. Particularly noteworthy in this regard was the Reverend Thomas J. Harte, a priest who wrote a doctoral dissertation on Catholic organizations promoting better race relations. Harte's dissertation, which was published in 1947, was directed by Monsignor Paul Hanly Furfey, a noted sociologist at Catholic University and one of the foremost defenders of Day's Catholic Worker movement. Harte described the CICNY as a small group of idealistic volunteers with no recognized authority over the Catholic population. A top-heavy and self-perpetuating board of directors, Harte claimed, controlled the organization completely. The board, not the general membership, selected

50. On black Catholic population, see Dolan, "Religion and Social Change," 44, 46, and Albert J. Raboteau, "The Black Church: Continuity Within Change," 79, both in *Altered Landscapes*, ed. Lotz, and "The Rising Tide of Negro Converts," *IR*, 11 (April, 1938), 50. On the mission collection, see Osborne, "The Race Problem," 78–79, and Myrdal, *An American Dilemma*, 909n.

51. Hunton, *All of Which I Saw*, 15–16; cartoon in *IR*, 11 (May, 1938), 4.

the group's officers, and it selected them, Harte argued, not on talent and zeal but on ideological correctness. CICNY officialdom thus emanated from a narrow circle of hand-picked black businessmen from the Laymen's Union and a small clique of whites who readily followed the lead of LaFarge and his faithful lieutenant Hunton. Usually no more than ten to twenty people attended the biweekly meetings, and their legacy consisted mostly of carefully worded resolutions avoiding attacks on specific targets that might provoke church officials.[52]

Harlem residents, Harte found out, thought that the council was largely irrelevant to their lives. In fact, Monsignor William McCann, the minister of St. Charles Borromeo in Harlem, was an ardent foe of LaFarge and the CICNY. A highly successful urban missionary who converted thousands of blacks between 1933 and 1949, McCann saw LaFarge's movement as a hindrance to his missionary work in Harlem because of its tendency to criticize the church. McCann stressed conversion, not black rights. Moreover, the Harlem priest was a confidant of Bishop McIntyre. In addition, it seems that many priests in New York were simply oblivious to the CICNY's existence. Of fifteen priests Harte interviewed in the New York area, five said they had never heard of the organization. The majority of the others believed that "Father LaFarge's group," as they called it, was "too theoretical" and "too idealistic" to be effective. No doubt, these priests noticed that the CICNY shunned all mass organization, boycotts, pickets, and demonstrations, which were standard fare in Harlem in the 1930s.[53]

Harte also judged that the highly acclaimed interracial contact in the CICNY produced no deep and lasting personal relationships across the color line. Writing about interracial groups in the *Interracial Review* in 1936, Elmer Carter of the Urban League added to Harte's insight. "The most fearful of dangers confronting any interracial program," Carter warned, "is the lack of frankness and honesty between racial groups, the chance that men may attempt to build a stable structure on the unstability [sic] of dishonesty."[54] Another Catholic com-

52. Harte, *Catholic Organizations Promoting Negro-White Relations*, 11, 15–18, 42, 58, 155, 158–61; Piehl, *Breaking Bread*, 126–27, 147. See also the critical view of Father Murphy, *Analysis of Attitudes of American Catholics*, 135, 144–45.

53. Hunton, *All of Which I Saw*, 119–20, 124; Dolan, *American Catholic Experience*, 367; Harte, *Catholic Organizations Promoting Negro-White Relations*, 55.

54. Harte, *Catholic Organizations Promoting Negro-White Relations*, 60; Clark, "The Catholic Contribution," 185.

plained of the inbred nature of the interracial program: "Too many 'interracial seminars' . . . are attended exclusively by little groups of serious thinkers who are already converted." One middle-class white woman, a ten-year member of the CICNY, said she took turns hosting "teas" for the council but had never voted or done anything important. Anna McGarry, a spark plug in the interracial movement in Philadelphia, lamented that the council was totally dominated by men. A thorough but anonymous study of the CICNY located in the council's archives concluded that the movement was "too small" and "too amateur to be successful." Casting a jaundiced eye on the leader of the CICNY, Monsignor Furfey recalled, "I fear I thought Father LaFarge just a bit ridiculous."[55]

Although Harte and Furfey had strong reservations about the methods of the CICNY, Harte concluded that the council had important symbolic significance. He acknowledged that the CICNY had made interracial work respectable in the 1930s. Moreover, he accurately stated that the council's primary contribution was to act as a "central propaganda agency." Even in the realm of propaganda, however, LaFarge and the council worked under the irksome restraints of economics; the council was always strapped for money. The *Interracial Review* constantly operated in the red, and in 1938 LaFarge informed the council that the financial condition of the review had reached a critical point. LaFarge had to spend an inordinate amount of time soliciting money from his New York friends to keep the *Interracial Review* afloat. Things eased somewhat in 1939 after he persuaded the affluent Louise Morrell to subsidize the review. Still, the CICNY never, not in its first or subsequent decades, raised enough revenue to do more than churn out relatively inexpensive propaganda. Money was so tight that the one serious spat between LaFarge and Hunton resulted from a disagreement over finances. Apparently, LaFarge thought that Hunton was not shepherding the council's meager resources wisely enough. When Hunton asked for an increase in his salary to $5,200 in 1941, LaFarge felt the request was so extravagant that he considered firing his old ally. But

55. Frank D. Whalen, "Educating the Educators," *IR*, 17 (August, 1944), 119; Harte, *Catholic Organizations Promoting Negro-White Relations*, 14, 17; view of Anna McGarry courtesy of a letter from Dan Kane to author, July 8, 1986; anonymous study of Catholic interracial councils, in letter box 25, CICNYP; Paul Hanly Furfey to Edward Stanton, September 10, 1981, in box 1, Stanton Papers.

the matter was resolved, and the two continued their fruitful collaboration for another twenty years.[56]

LaFarge also had to work within constraints set by a national hierarchy that had been silent on the race question since 1919. Many bishops refused to sanction interracial councils in their dioceses, and LaFarge strongly counseled against applying pressure to recalcitrant prelates. The result was that Catholic interracial councils spread at a glacial pace. By 1945 only seven councils had been established in the United States. Although LaFarge nudged gingerly at the edges of authority, he never openly agitated or sullied his record for obedience. He instead tactfully cultivated open-minded bishops with flattery and thoughtful little favors. LaFarge possessed an expansive mind, but he also had the stomach for those mundane tasks that came with social action and were necessitated by the bureaucratic church. Above all, he never rushed history. As a seminarian in Innsbruck, Austria, he had learned that it was not wise to contest an Alpine slope head on. He discovered that it was better to follow the meandering path of the cows, or the *Kuhpfad*, around and gradually up the steep incline.[57] *Kuhpfad* provides a strikingly apt metaphor for LaFarge's deliberate approach to the lofty summit of racial equity.

As a man of broad interests and many talents, LaFarge wore many hats. The preceding chapter has emphasized his relation to the CICNY and his role as an organizer. LaFarge, however, also served as an important theorist and propagandist for the interracial movement, and in these roles he significantly affected the racial orientation of American Catholicism in the 1930s.

---

56. Harte, *Catholic Organizations Promoting Negro-White Relations*, 24, 60–61; Hunton, *All of Which I Saw*, 71, 187; John LaFarge to Francis Talbot, August 1, 1938, in box 20, folder 1, JLFP 1; John LaFarge to George Hunton, April 2, 1941, in box 5, CICNYP; Zielinski, "Promotion of Better Race Relations," 118–21.

57. Osborne, "The Race Problem," 182–84; McDonough, *Men Astutely Trained*, x, 126, 128; interview of Dennis Clark by the author; *MIO*, 248.

8

Hurling Catholic Truth Against Communism, Fascism, and Racism
The Thirties

LaFarge reached his journalistic prime in the 1930s. He churned out well over three hundred signed articles, columns, and book reviews during the decade; moreover, the number of unsigned editorials in the *Interracial Review* and *America* added considerably to his literary bulk. In 1937 LaFarge distilled the essence of his writings on racial matters and put them in a slender volume called *Interracial Justice.* The book, which caught the eye of Pope Pius XI, became a standard reference for American Catholics who pondered the question of how the Catholic faith related to the race problem. LaFarge's stature in the American Catholic community and in the international Society of Jesus grew steadily in the 1930s. In 1939 the exclusive Century Club of New York City inducted the Jesuit into its organization of celebrities and power brokers.

LaFarge's prodigious writings on social issues (or on any kind of topic from Loyola to Lenin) almost always digressed into an attack on communism. He incessantly promoted the interracial movement as a foil to that system. Seen as the "most worthy form of Catholic social action," anticommunism was the safest way for a Catholic to bring up the subject of racism in the church.[1] LaFarge had already established impeccable anticommunist credentials prior to the establishment of the CICNY in 1934. A reader of *Pravda* and *Izvestia* and an analyst of the Soviet Union and Eastern Europe for *America*, LaFarge wrote over thirty signed articles on communism and the Soviet Union in the 1930s and authored two widely circulated pamphlets on the subject as well. Even these impressive figures greatly understate his preoccupation with communism. He warned endlessly that unless Catholics addressed the problem of racial injustice the communists would successfully sow their poisonous seed among African Americans. Yet he also observed (and historians have since documented it) that relatively few blacks paid any attention to communist propaganda. In fact, he often employed the well-worn stereotype that blacks were deeply religious and therefore not susceptible to straight doses of atheistic Bolshevism. He warned nonetheless that the black intelligentsia had an affinity for Marxist thought, popular-front activity, and fellow-traveling.[2]

Although LaFarge seldom criticized the white South, he charged that communists and southern lynchers were "brothers under the skin." The Jesuit also attacked the public schools, a favorite whipping boy of the clergy and hierarchy, as "communist-ridden" in the 1930s. LaFarge's anticommunist views made him a popular speaker on the high school and college circuits. Even the Methodists invited him to North Carolina in 1936 to discuss ways to combat the Red menace.[3] The editors of the

1. David O'Brien, *American Catholics and Social Reform*, 95. See also Donald F. Crosby, *God, Church, and Flag* (Chapel Hill, N.C., 1978), 20–23.

2. Examples of LaFarge's post-1934 writings on communism are "Liberal Thought and Moscow Terror," *Am*, 52 (March 2, 1935), 493–95; "Harlem Flats and Public Conscience," *Am*, 53 (April 20, 1935), 35–36; "Can We Cooperate with Communists?," *Am*, 53 (August 24, 1935), 465–67; "The Catholic Reply to Communism," *Am*, 54 (November 23, 1935), 150–52, (December 14, 1935), 225–27; "Communism and the Negro," *IR*, 9 (March, 1936), 39–41; "Christian Front to Combat Communism," *Am*, 55 (September 5, 1936), 108–10; "Lenin and Loyola, Parallels Real and Unreal," *Am*, 56 (March 6, 1937), 515. Pamphlets by LaFarge are *Communism and the Catholic Answer* (New York, 1936) and *Communism's Threat to Democracy* (New York, 1937). On the failure of communism in the black community, see Wilson Record, *Race and Radicalism: The NAACP and the Communist Party in Conflict* (Ithaca, N.Y., 1964).

3. LaFarge, quoted in Estelle Flynn, "The St. Paul Program," *IR*, 9 (December, 1936), 187; John LaFarge, "With Script and Staff," *Am*, 53 (October 5, 1935), 615; "Students to Take Stand on Communism," Baltimore *Review*, April 9, 1936, clipping in box 4, folder 29, JLFP 2; LaFarge, "Christian Front to Combat Communism," 108–10.

Interracial Review and *America* shared LaFarge's combative anticommunism. In the late 1930s *America* cheered on the newly created House Un-American Activities Committee, which was headed by Martin Dies, a racist and anti-Semitic Congressman from Texas.[4]

LaFarge did not limit his philippics to communism. He just considered it the worst of all the isms that he lumped under modernism: secularism, materialism, liberalism, and atheism. The irenic priest occasionally worked himself into a near rage in doing battle with modernism. In 1939 he exclaimed, "We can, and should, hurl the challenge of Catholic truth into the teeth of the modern unbelieving, materialistic world." Because of his strong feelings about modernism and communism, he was incapable of giving credit to the racial intentions or accomplishments of activists on the left. In 1935 Dorothy Day chided LaFarge and his movement for their steady drumbeat against the secular left. "Let us take what truth there is in what they say in regard to racial justice," she scolded, "and give them credit for what good they do."[5]

No doubt, the general of the Jesuits considered LaFarge one of his finest foot soldiers in the war against communism. Vladimir Ledochowski, a rabid anticommunist Polish count and the general of the Jesuits since the beginning of World War I, decided in 1934 to launch an all-out attack on communism. Ledochowski's powerful influence in the Vatican made him deserving of the sobriquet "the black pope." He had already managed to inject a potent dose of anticommunism in the notable 1931 social encyclical *Quadragesimo Anno*. In April of 1934, Ledochowski sent a letter to the American and Canadian provincials asking them to lead a systematic, worldwide crusade to save Christianity and civilization from the scourge of Marxism. In September the Maryland-New York provincial appointed LaFarge to a three-man regional committee designed to implement Ledochowski's crusade. LaFarge, whom McDonough has described as the "gray eminence" of the Jesuit social ministry, was placed second in command to Father

---

4. See George Hunton's "Communism and Catholic Action," *IR*, 8 (January, 1935), 11, and "Catholics, Communism, and the Negro," *IR*, 10 (June, 1937), 86. See also the editorials "Harlem Disturbance," *IR*, 10 (June, 1937), 57, and "Communism Is Seeking the Negro," *IR*, 10 (July, 1937), 99–100. On the Dies Committee, see the editorials in *Am*, 60 (October 15, 1938), 27; *Am*, 60 (November 5, 1938), 108; *Am*, 60 (December 31, 1938), 300; *Am*, 61 (January 14, 1939), 349; *Am*, 61 (October 7, 1939), 613.

5. John LaFarge, "Planning the Truth Before Inquiring Unbelievers," *Am*, 61 (May 13, 1939), 107; Dorothy Day, letter to the editor, *IR*, 8 (February, 1935), 33.

Edmund Walsh, the founder of the School of Foreign Service at Georgetown University. Often described as an inspiration for Senator McCarthy's anticommunist crusade in the early 1950s, Walsh was a rock-ribbed conservative who had slight interest in social reform. LaFarge, however, saw an opening in Ledochowski's scheme and hoped to use it to promote his interracial program.[6]

From June 22 to 26, 1935, Jesuits gathered at a meeting in West Baden, Indiana, to begin the "Establishment of a Christian Social Order." The plan, known as XO, proposed to battle communism directly by propaganda and indirectly by comprehensive social action designed to attack injustices on which communism fed. Meeting beneath the grand rotunda that rose 130 feet above the floor of the former West Baden Springs Hotel, once a plush gambling resort frequented by Al Capone, American Jesuits engaged in long discussions about the nature of the Christian social order they wanted to fashion. Throughout the West Baden meetings, LaFarge energetically promoted interracialism as war against communism by other means. Interracialism became a part of the XO plan of social action—a plan that encompassed thirteen different areas, including education and propaganda, labor, agriculture, and political reform.[7] LaFarge's long-awaited Christian front, the answer to the popular front of the left, seemed to be in the making.

The XO task force held several meetings in the next two years. As secretary of an interprovincial committee on fighting communism and atheism, LaFarge played a prominent role in the effort to construct a comprehensive social ministry for the Society of Jesus. Since Jesuit opinion differed widely within the international order and even significantly within the American branch, this projected ministry was a tall order. Neither conservative nor liberal, neither socialist nor capitalist,

6. "The Black Pope," *IR*, 15 (December, 1942), 179–80; McDonough, *Men Astutely Trained*, 65–68, 77, 119, 122–27; Vladimir Ledochowski to provincials of America and Canada, April 5, 1934, in box 12, folder 11, JLFP 1; Edward C. Phillips to John LaFarge, September 14, 1934, in box 8, folder 16, JLFP 1. Pope Pius XI also condemned atheistic communism at various times, especially in the 1937 encyclical *Divini Redemptoris* (see "A New Document on Atheistic Communism," *Am*, 57 [April 10, 1937], 4–5).

7. McDonough, *Men Astutely Trained*, 35; minutes of the Chicago-Missouri Province meeting on communism and atheism, West Baden, Indiana, June 22–26, 1935, in box 4, folder 32, JLFP 2; "Plan of Action for the Establishment of a Christian Social Order, Through Jesuit Activity," mailed with cover letter from Frederic Siedenburg, S.J., to John LaFarge, August 23, 1935, in box 4, folder 30, JLFP 2.

Jesuits were sui generis and largely irrelevant to mainstream reform. As LaFarge had discovered in the case of the Cardinal Gibbons Institute, American Jesuits had no desire to shift manpower and resources from the prestigious education apostolate to social reform. In addition, Jesuits were ill trained to conduct a social ministry. The order was not so much hostile as indifferent to the claims of Catholic social teaching, and race was virtually a nonissue for most Jesuits. Above all, American Jesuits, already suspect in the eyes of many Catholics as well as non-Catholics, wanted to avoid public controversy and intra-Catholic squabbles. LaFarge himself feared that the XO program might incite the hostility of the NCWC and the American bishops. Despite La-Farge's efforts, though, the society failed to establish a workable social program, so Jesuits continued as before. Individuals volunteered for social action and worked on a small scale, locally or regionally, in splendid isolation. In the end, the whole of the XO campaign, one historian concluded, "was less than the sum of its parts."[8]

In addition to promoting interracialism, LaFarge hoped to exploit Ledochowski's crusade for a Christian social order to lift the sagging circulation of *America,* which had been hard hit by the Depression. He lobbied hard to have the editors of *America* anointed as the think tank of the America Jesuit order. During his 1938 tour of Europe, LaFarge was deeply impressed by the social ministry of Action Populaire and its magnetic Jesuit leader Maurice Desbuquois. LaFarge wanted to re-create Action Populaire in New York and promote an enhanced Jesuit social program through the pages of *America.* LaFarge may have wondered if his faith in Desbuquois had been misplaced when the leader of Action Populaire later supported the Vichy regime. In any event, in 1940 Ledochowski selected the Jesuit John Delaney to head what would prove to be an ineffective Institute of Social Order. The Jesuit general placed the headquarters of the institute in Manhattan but not in the offices of *America.*[9] In the 1940s the center of Jesuit social action moved to St. Louis, where the socially progressive journal *Social Order* was established. On the whole, LaFarge's attempts to exploit Ledochowski's anticommunist crusade for Catholic interracialism came to very little. In fact, LaFarge's aggressive anticommunism served to cut him off from many black intellectuals who, like Dorothy Day, were willing to give

8. McDonough, *Men Astutely Trained,* 14–15, 37, 80–85, 180, 200.
9. *Ibid.,* 112, 122–32, 135.

credit to, if not cooperate with, leftists who conspicuously waved the banners of civil rights in the 1930s.

The militant anticommunism of liberal Catholics like LaFarge tended to blind them to the rising menace of fascism. Anticommunism often threw LaFarge into the same camp with reactionaries such as Congressman Dies of Texas. Tellingly, the Jesuit avoided direct criticism of the anti-Semitic Charles E. Coughlin, only chiding the rightist radio priest a single time for not taking a strong stand for racial justice. LaFarge clearly considered communism a much greater threat to Christian civilization and human rights than was fascism. In tune with Rome and the editors of *America*, he supported certain kinds of softer fascism in Italy and Portugal, countries that had close ties with the Vatican. With notable exceptions, such as John Ryan and James Gillis, Catholics generally supported Mussolini in the 1930s. *America* supported Italy's presence in Ethiopia, and LaFarge praised Mussolini's respect for religion and his "humane labor laws." LaFarge's high tolerance of Mussolini obviously did not help him win friends among blacks, who excoriated the Italian dictator for his African imperialism.[10]

In addition, LaFarge strongly backed the fascist general Francisco Franco. *America* published more partisan articles on Spain than on any other topic in the late 1930s. When Day and the editors of *Commonweal* chose to remain neutral on the atrocity-filled Spanish Civil War, LaFarge, with unusual vituperation, blasted his Catholic colleagues. In 1938 he accused the editors of *Commonweal* of "objective heartlessness" because of their neutrality on Spain. Francis X. Talbot, the conservative editor-in-chief of *America*, gloated that LaFarge's article would "collapse the Commonweal." When several congressmen, including a large number of southerners, announced their support for the Loyalists in Spain, LaFarge unleashed a flood of invective, declaring that the "race baiters" had embraced the "God haters."[11]

---

10. John LaFarge, "Fascism or Communism: Which the Greater Danger?" *Am*, 56 (October 10, 1936), 4–5. See also John LaFarge, "With Script and Staff," *Am*, 55 (August 15, 1936), 443, and unsigned review of *The Portugal of Salazar*, by Michael Derrick, *Am*, 61 (September 16, 1939), 549. On the lack of "moral vision" regarding fascism, see Diggins, *Mussolini and Fascism*, 185–90, 195, 197, 300–303, 306–12, 329, 333, and esp. 197 for LaFarge quotation.

11. "While Spain Burns, They Strum Impartially," *Am*, 59 (August 20, 1938), 462; "Race Baiters Embrace God Haters," *Am*, 58 (February 19, 1938), 460–61; Francis Talbot to John LaFarge, August 3, 1938, in box 20, folder 1, JLFP 1. On communism versus

Even so, LaFarge displayed greater balance on the question of communism versus fascism than most Catholic priests. By the mid-1930s he expressed great concern over the rise of a more profane, anti-Christian type of fascism in Germany. He thus took up his pen to condemn the idolatry of unfettered nationalism and its frequent companion, anti-Semitism. In April of 1938, his growing dread of Nazism prompted him to embellish the *Interracial Review* with the subtitle *A Journal of Christian Democracy.* In explaining the change, he defined "Christian Democracy" as a *"society in which the God-given dignity and destiny of every human person is fully recognized, in laws, government, institutions and human conduct."*[12] Did this change mean that LaFarge was now a full-fledged, root-and-branch antifascist? Not quite, for he constantly looked over his shoulder at superiors such as Ledochowski. At West Baden in 1935, LaFarge, showing how well he knew his superior and Vatican politics, told those at the XO session, "Father General will not approve a direct stand against Fascism." To get around the Roman obstacles blocking an attack on fascism, LaFarge engaged in a bit of casuistry. He argued that Christian democracy would undermine and taint all totalitarian systems. But what if Ledochowski asked specifically about fascism? Walsh interjected. "You might lecture against it," LaFarge shot back. On the one hand, LaFarge seemed to condemn all totalitarian states. On the other hand, he covered himself vis-à-vis Rome by insisting that Christian democracy could exist under a non-democratic and authoritarian government.[13]

Because of his personal makeup and the nature of ecclesiastical politics, the cosmopolitan Jesuit manipulated, equivocated, hedged, and accommodated so as not to provoke the hierarchy or disturb the cor-

---

fascism, see J. David Valaik, "American Catholic Dissenters and the Spanish Civil War," in *Modern American Catholicism,* ed. Kantowicz, 324–25, 331, and McDonough, *Men Astutely Trained,* 78–79, 82. See also Francis X. Talbot (editor-in-chief of *America*), "Further Reflections on the Spanish Situation," *Am,* 57 (May 1, 1937), 76–77. Talbot held that one could be a fascist and a Catholic but not a communist and a Catholic.

12. John LaFarge, "Nationalism and the State," *Modern Schoolman* (March, 1935), 58–60, copy in box 40, folder 10, JLFP 1; John LaFarge, "Christian Democracy," *IR,* 11 (March, 1938), 38–40; John LaFarge, "Christian Democracy Pledges Our Liberties," *Am,* 60 (December 10, 1938), 226–27.

13. LaFarge, quoted in McDonough, *Men Astutely Trained,* 79. See LaFarge, "Christian Democracy Pledges Liberties," 226, and his pamphlet *Fascism in Government and Society* (New York, 1938), 3–5.

porate harmony of the church. Given this hedging and trimming and his heavy religiosity, the Jesuit produced a brand of prose that had limited appeal for blacks and non-Catholics and even for some Catholics. This judgment was true of his most important book, *Interracial Justice: A Study of the Catholic Doctrine of Race Relations.* The response to this 1937 book in the liberal Catholic press, however, sounded like the Hallelujah Chorus. Senator David Walsh, a Catholic from Massachusetts, described the 194-page book as "monumental." A reviewer in *Commonweal* wrote, "It is impossible to be honest and disagree with him [LaFarge]." Another reviewer, in *Columbia,* asserted that the book "fearlessly" offered solutions to such issues as race prejudice, segregation, and interracial marriage. The reviewer in *America* judged that LaFarge had produced "a complete plank in the large platform of Catholic Social Action." A writer for *Sign* predicted that the book would become a "much used manual." One of the most laudatory reviews appeared in the NAACP's *Crisis.* This review came from the pen of Theophilus Lewis, a black devotee of LaFarge and a regular contributor to the *Interracial Review.* Lewis claimed the book rose above the parochial to present views that were "catholic as well as Catholic." More accurately, Father Francis J. Gilligan declared the study an "especially . . . Catholic book."[14] It was so Catholic that non-Catholics virtually ignored it.

Anyone who had followed LaFarge's writings since the early 1920s would have found little that was new in *Interracial Justice.* For the most part, LaFarge distilled and reiterated what he had written again and again in the previous fifteen years, material that has already been explicated at some length in this study. Therefore, only certain novel features, emphases, and additions, as well as some of the salient weaknesses and inconsistencies of this seminal volume, will be noted here. The importance of LaFarge's book was fairly obvious: it provided a thorough analysis of Catholic principles as they related to the American race question. As always, LaFarge stressed the necessity of viewing African Americans in a supernatural framework. This perspective en-

14. John LaFarge, *Interracial Justice;* Senator Walsh, quoted in *IR,* 10 (July, 1937), after 113. Reviews of LaFarge's *Interracial Justice* are: Francis A. Walsh, in *Commonweal,* 25 (April 23, 1937), 729–30; "By Brother Leo," in *Columbia,* 17 (November, 1937), 19; Francis X. Downey, in *Am,* 57 (April 17, 1937), 45; unsigned review, in *Sign,* 16 (May, 1937), 635; Theophilus Lewis, in *Crisis,* 44 (September, 1937), 284; Francis J. Gilligan, in *Catholic World,* 145 (June, 1937), 370–71.

tailed lengthy discussion of such doctrines as Christian charity and the Mystical Body of Christ. LaFarge theorized that human rights, not Negro rights, flowed inevitably from God's divine plan. Natural law, natural reason, and American egalitarian values also undergirded the inescapable logic of human rights. Finally, the facts of science supported the theological claims of the oneness of humankind. The race problem, LaFarge repeated, was a religious and moral problem, and no true Catholic could fail to face it. The tone of the book was self-effacing, calm, exquisitely balanced, and grandly optimistic. The Jesuit's stated aim was "not to intensify" racial feelings but to hasten the day they would be "forgotten." Condemning defeatism, he repeated a favorite refrain that had appeared in several of his earlier essays: "The Catholic Church does not admit that any moral problem is beyond solution." Looking serenely into the future, he predicted that all his conclusions about race relations would be accepted in a decade or so. In a passage that would essentially become his theme song in the coming years, he wrote, "I have not so much tried to persuade people to walk on a certain road, as to show to them the road that I am convinced they are sooner or later going to walk on."[15]

Interracial Justice consisted of five sections: "Subject Matter," "Doctrine," "Issues," "Solutions," and "Epilog." It contained sixteen short chapters and a bibliography. The first section, which took up more than fifty pages, dealt with the definition of race, racial differences, and the status of blacks. In this section LaFarge made greater use of social science than he had previously. Using the new cultural anthropology of Franz Boas and the environmental sociology of the Chicago School, LaFarge boldly proclaimed that race was a "myth." The idea that fixed racial traits determined destiny, he argued, was demonstrably false. There were no pure races, only population groups. Properly speaking, he said, the Negro race did not exist; only a Negro group did. Following from that, the Negro-white problem was not unique; it was just one of the many group problems, albeit sharper than most. LaFarge belabored the idea of race as a phantom of people's imagination to the point that he defied common sense. No matter how dubious the biological idea of race, experience (history), to say nothing of social science, should have told LaFarge that race was (and is) a glaring social fact that has to be dealt with realistically, not by defining it out of

15. LaFarge, *Interracial Justice*, vi–vii, 6.

existence. Indeed, LaFarge did not follow his own logic. Had he done so, it would not have been necessary to point out that one of the most important facts about blacks was their African ancestry and the color associated with it. Nor would he have written, "The Negro is deeply race-conscious." Had he heeded his own advice about the mythical nature of race, his chapter titles would not have read "The Study of Race Relations," "Racial Differences," "Race Prejudice," and "Interracial Justice." [16]

Nevertheless, LaFarge's use of social science represented a significant advance in Catholic writing on the race question. He made extensive references to noted American social scientists, black and white. Among them were Boas, Melville J. Herskovits, Donald Young, Edwin Embree, Charles S. Johnson, James Weldon Johnson, Carter Woodson, and Alain Locke. As always, LaFarge drew liberally upon Booker T. Washington. What was equally predictable, the book had not a single reference to Du Bois (or to other militant black intellectuals, such as Ralph Bunche). One thing that gave LaFarge's book a slightly odd twist was his use of European social scientists, many of them obscure, Catholic, and, more specifically, Jesuit. In the main, however, LaFarge skillfully used social science and history to explain the low status of blacks as a group and to counter white perceptions about black crime and immorality. "LaFarge had an instinct for the structural and circumstantial preconditions of 'sin,' " as one writer put it. A pioneer in applying social science to Catholic social thought, LaFarge set an example for Catholic scholars. In 1942 at Fordham University, the priest, with an assist from George Hunton, introduced one of the first race relations courses into the regular curriculum of a Catholic college. [17]

The weaknesses of *Interracial Justice* are similar to those of La-Farge's articles, except that they become more glaring in the longer work. His style suffers from untidy organization, thick religiosity, and the syllogistic meanderings of bastard Thomism. The reader is subjected to great doses of dense Catholic terminology and imagery with numbing repetition. Even appreciative Catholic reviewers rendered faint

16. *Ibid.,* 1–56. On race as a social fact around the world, see the anthology edited by John Hope Franklin, *Color and Race* (Boston, 1965), and Hoetink, *Slavery and Race Relations.*

17. Osborne, *Segregated Covenant,* 196; LaFarge, *Interracial Justice,* 28–37, *passim;* McDonough, *Men Astutely Trained,* 134; John J. Roach, "Interracialism Goes to College," *IR,* 15 (December, 1942), 182–83.

praise for the Jesuit's style. Father Francis X. Downey lauded the book's lack of "imprecations" and declared that the prose was "fiery with the cold incision . . . of truth." Downey and others indicated that the strength of the book was in its cold logic, not in the prose itself. The strongest statement the admiring Theophilus Lewis could offer in regard to the style of *Interracial Justice* was that "its brevity and the author's modest style may cause some readers to underrate its importance as a social document."[18] His friends recognized the importance of LaFarge's writings, but the more candid ones vouched that his prose "did not make for excitement." George Streator, a Columbia-educated black journalist and a friend of LaFarge, found it as difficult to understand the "mystic angels" of the priest's prose as it was to penetrate the Marxist exegesis of competing leftist factions. The Jesuit William Markoe confessed that he simply could not "plow" through his friend's prose. More than once in his career, LaFarge confessed to sloppy bookmaking, and he realized that his writing was "distasteful to a certain type of modern mind."[19]

Apparently, "monochrome" prose was endemic to the religious order. In any event, LaFarge's prose cut him off from all but the most Catholic of readers. If his ambition had been limited to only this audience, he could hardly be faulted on his style. LaFarge, however, always sought a larger audience. Moreover, he and his admirers complained bitterly about the neglect of his writings by non-Catholic scholars and activists.[20]

It was not that LaFarge was incapable of writing interesting prose. His droll humor and cosmopolitan bearing made some of his shorter, nonracial compositions sparkle, like parts of his autobiography. But he did not, or could not, apply these attributes to the issue of race relations.

18. Reviews of *Interracial Justice* by Downey, 45, and Lewis, 284.

19. See John J. O'Connor, review of *No Postponement,* by John LaFarge, in *IR,* 23 (June, 1950), 88–89; George Streator, letter to the editor, *IR,* 12 (May, 1939), 77; Markoe, "Interracial Role," 447; LaFarge, *No Postponement,* 80; and John LaFarge, *An American Amen: A Statement of Hope* (New York, 1958), 4.

20. On Jesuit style, see Aveling, *The Jesuits,* 26, 32, and McDonough, *Men Astutely Trained,* xiii, 126. In his review of Myrdal's *An American Dilemma,* in "Interracial Bookshelf," *Am,* 70 (February 5, 1944), 496, not only did LaFarge complain that the Swedish economist advocated birth control, but he also upbraided Myrdal for not recognizing the contributions of Catholic activists and scholars. See also Charles Keenan, S.J., review of *An American Dilemma,* by Gunnar Myrdal, in *IR,* 17 (October, 1944), 177.

Rather, by exploiting the inherent complexity of the race problem, by piling nuance upon nuance, by pitting tradition against change, by casting nervous glances toward the hierarchy and conservatives in general, by continually appealing to the other-worldly, and by always taking the long, long view of things, LaFarge whipped up batch after batch of historical and intellectual blandness. No wonder secular liberals, and even a few mercurial Jesuits, had trouble distinguishing LaFarge from a conservative.[21]

LaFarge's handling of certain controversial issues in *Interracial Justice* further exemplifies his tendency to compromise and even retreat. By the mid-1930s LaFarge had concluded that racism was a grave sin (years after Fathers Markoe and Gilligan). This idea was still novel to the overwhelming majority of white Catholics, clergy and laity, but it was something that black Catholics like Daniel Rudd and Thomas Turner knew instinctively. Race prejudice, LaFarge argued in 1935, was a serious moral transgression, "not a mere weakness or disease—because it is *voluntary*" (my emphasis). To the faithful he preached that "for the Catholic it [an act of racism] means that when he goes to confession he would confess as a sin any violation of interracial justice and charity."[22]

Hunton recalled that during the first annual conference of the CICNY a heated debate broke out as to whether racism was a disease or a transgression; the former view won the day. But if racism were a disease, could an individual be held responsible for it any more than a person could be blamed for contracting polio? As we have seen, LaFarge constantly held that ignorance alone caused racism. By doing so, he blurred the issue of individual culpability in regard to the sin of racism. He left a loophole for the racist when he began to speak of "involuntary" racism. He used a bewildering analogy in his book about an innocent man who, owing to false publicity, was perceived by his

21. McDonough, *Men Astutely Trained*, xiii–xv, 121, 126, 128; LaFarge, *Interracial Justice*, 5. Allitt, *Catholic Intellectuals and Conservative Politics*, 6–7, 32–33, 37–38, 97, 101, *passim*, emphasizes the similarity between Catholic liberals and conservatives on many issues such as anticommunism, abortion, separation of church and state, and lay empowerment.

22. John LaFarge, "Interracial Justice," *IR*, 12 (October, 1939), 122, "A Catholic Interracial Program," *IR*, 8 (February, 1935), 23, and "Can Prejudice Be Cured?," *IR*, 8 (August, 1935), 120–21. On social sin, see Paul Hanly Furfey, *The Respectable Murderers: Social Evil and Christian Conscience* (New York, 1966), 150–51.

neighbors as an embezzler. LaFarge asked, Were the neighbors immoral for thinking ill of the man? The inference of his question seemed to be: Were white people guilty of racism when they acted on the false publicity about blacks with which they were constantly bombarded? Thus, on the sin of racism, LaFarge retreated from his bold stand of 1935. Even Edward Stanton, LaFarge's young Jesuit colleague, believed that the priest backed off his original interpretation that racism was an unmitigated sin and fell back on the metaphor that depicted racism as a disease.[23]

LaFarge's treatment of segregation provides another example of his congenital hedging. Becoming a pressing issue by the late 1930s, the issue of segregation grew even more volatile during World War II. Not only did legal segregation rob blacks of education and economic security; it robbed them of their dignity as well. LaFarge acknowledged the importance of segregation by devoting a full chapter to the issue. He confirmed the deep resentment of blacks over legal segregation and illustrated the dire handicaps it imposed on the minority. He held that Jim Crow amounted to an "objective injustice," a crashing indictment coming from LaFarge. Yet he smothered the inherent emotional energy in the topic with subtle equivocation. He blurred the moral sharpness of the issue by making superfine distinctions between compulsory and voluntary segregation and between collective and individual segregation, and he threw in "compensatory segregation" for good measure. The last he described as segregation that was accepted by blacks to gain certain privileges they would otherwise be denied. He cited as examples of compensatory segregation black YMCAs and YWCAs and black colleges. He also argued that segregation served the moral aim of encouraging "mutual adjustment of human beings in their daily contacts of life." Furthermore, he denied the cruciality of segregation, calling it a "mere mechanical device" whose disappearance would only slightly affect the race problem. LaFarge penned no searing description of the collective misery, the personal humiliation, or the sheer absurdity of Jim Crow as practiced in the American South. Like Booker T. Washington, he counseled acquiescence where state law and folk mores necessitated Jim Crow. He gave no hint that the entire southern caste system might be unconstitutional, as some jurists, legal scholars, and

23. Hunton, *All of Which I Saw*, 87; LaFarge, *Interracial Justice*, 75, 127–28, 135; Stanton, "John LaFarge," 91.

even Catholics were suggesting. Rather, LaFarge proclaimed, "Theoretically segregation need not be unjust."[24]

LaFarge took a similar tack on the burning issue of interracial marriage. As always, he explained that marriage was a sacrament in the Catholic faith and that the church placed no impediments in the way of interracial unions. LaFarge, however, assured whites that the achievement of human rights for blacks would not lead to more, but less, miscegenation. In his review of *Interracial Justice,* Father Downey applauded LaFarge's insight into the subject when he wrote, "If we have been thinking that marriage with whites is the absorbing ambition of the Negro, we have been foolishly flattering ourselves." Based on his admittedly limited experience about the topic, LaFarge suggested that intermarriage was not an important concern for blacks. Unlike his discussion of race, he adduced no social science to shore up his argument on intermarriage. He did, however, warn his readers that there were "*grave reasons* against any general practice of intermarriage between members of different racial groups." He then detailed the dangerous family tensions that racial, cultural, and class differences brought to marriage.[25] Race ceased to be mythical for LaFarge when it came to miscegenation.

Dr. Benjamin E. Mays's review of *Interracial Justice* in the *Journal of Negro Education* provides a corrective to the laudatory one-note response of Catholic reviewers. Born in 1894 in South Carolina to former slaves, Mays received a Ph.D. from the University of Chicago in 1935. A courageous opponent of racial discrimination, Mays became president of Morehouse College in 1940 and was selected by the family of Martin Luther King, Jr., to give the eulogy for the martyred civil rights leader in 1968. King called Mays his "spiritual mentor" and "one of the great influences of his life." Mays, a Baptist minister who in 1937 was the dean of the School of Religion at Howard University, praised LaFarge for explaining the Catholic doctrine on race, but he also faulted the priest on a number of issues, most notably on interracial marriage. Mays contended that the chapter on social equality and intermarriage

24. LaFarge, *Interracial Justice,* 107–24; Marshall Smelser, "Race Conflicts Glare Through Legal Loopholes," *Am,* 63 (September 7, 1940), 596–97. C. Vann Woodward, a white southern historian, made a best-seller out of the inherent drama and absurdity of segregation in *The Strange Career of Jim Crow.*

25. Downey, review of *Interracial Justice,* 45; LaFarge, *Interracial Justice,* 137–48.

was the most flawed part of the book. He complained that LaFarge phrased the issue in such a way that he seemed to suggest it would not be prudent to pursue racial equality at all if it increased miscegenation. Mays charged LaFarge with refusing to state the obvious: that the fear of interracial marriage reflected the lurid depths of white racism and that the well-known question about the marriage of one's daughter was an evasion and a gross insult to blacks.[26]

Mays also accused LaFarge of exaggerating what the Catholic church had done for blacks. The Baptist charged that LaFarge gave the false impression that the Catholic church had outstripped other denominations in racial work. He also reproached LaFarge for not considering what blacks could do for Catholicism. Mays echoed Turner's criticism of Father Gillard's book when he wrote, "The Negro seems to be treated as a thing apart, an object for whom something is done." Mays likewise knocked down the Jesuit's argument that the tragedy of slavery was mitigated by the Christianizing of African Americans. He maintained that LaFarge ignored the fact that white masters inculcated blacks with a "subservient religion," not a "prophetic religion." Nor was Mays much impressed with the gradualistic Catholic interracial program that LaFarge extolled so enthusiastically.[27]

Like Turner, Mays readily detected LaFarge's paternalism and elitism. LaFarge, for instance, still insisted that racial work was "best promoted by small groups of conscientious, educated, and intelligent Catholics . . . under competent spiritual guidance." He observed that whites who proceeded "blissfully ignorant of what ails them" suffered more under the southern caste system than blacks did. LaFarge also disclosed his aristocratic judgment on black culture, if only by the sin of omission. He cited many outstanding blacks in various fields as an illustration of minority accomplishment in the face of great odds. He praised black classical singers of European music, such as Roland Hayes and Marian Anderson, but accorded no space to black-originated blues or jazz or its gifted practitioners, such as Bessie Smith, Louis Armstrong, and Duke Ellington. In a radio talk LaFarge offered uncritical praise of

26. Benjamin E. Mays, "A Catholic View of Race Relations," *Journal of Negro Education*, 6 (October, 1937), 631–34; Benjamin E. Mays, *Born to Rebel: An Autobiography of Benjamin E. Mays* (New York, 1971), 1–3, 57–64, 97, 266, 357; Martin Luther King, Jr., *Stride Toward Freedom: The Montgomery Story* (New York, 1958), 145.
27. Mays, "A Catholic View of Race Relations," 631–34.

Green Pastures, a grossly stereotypical play about black religion that even Father Gillard called a "pathetic travesty" upon black culture.[28]

LaFarge was so flabbergasted by Mays's criticism that he wrote a long letter to the black educator. In it, he conceded that Mays had raised cogent questions about his handling of interracial marriage (he never, however, modified his views), but he conceded nothing else and tried, in fact, to contest several of the charges made by Mays. LaFarge was especially defensive about the Catholic interracial program. He explained that the liturgical drone of Catholic doctrine might sound "flat and lifeless" to non-Catholic ears but could appear "extremely challenging to Catholics."[29] But, Mays suggested, after repeated references to the sublimity of Catholic doctrine and the recounting of the great works of the Catholic church for blacks, most Catholics might swell with pride instead of being inspired to attack racism in their church. Moreover, LaFarge's criticisms of the Catholic church were so untargeted that they lacked the power to arouse a sense of indignation and the kind of urgency that launches and propels powerful social movements.

For all its faults, *Interracial Justice* ranks as a milestone in the history of American Catholic race relations. Catholics excerpted, condensed, pamphletized, and studied the book.[30] In the second edition of a standard Catholic textbook on sociology, Raymond W. Murray, a professor at the University of Notre Dame, added twenty pages of material on the race problem after the publication of LaFarge's book. Murray's many textbooks had substantial influence on Catholic campuses. The sociologist told LaFarge of his influence in a 1952 letter: "My books have been accepted by Catholic teachers . . . largely because they reflected a viewpoint which you shaped. You do know how to shape a Catholic sense in things sociological."[31] Numerous Catholic

28. LaFarge, *Interracial Justice,* 5–6, 52, 182; script of radio talk by LaFarge, December 15, 1939, in box 41, folder 5, JLFP 1; John T. Gillard, "Catholic Green Pastures," *Commonweal,* 21 (December 21, 1934), 220.

29. John LaFarge to Benjamin Mays, October 21, 1937, in box 9, folder 28, JLFP 2.

30. A thirty-one-page pamphlet based on LaFarge's book is titled *A Catholic Interracial Program* (New York, 1939). A typical condensation appeared in *Catholic Digest,* 1 (June, 1937), 74–82.

31. Raymond W. Murray, *Introductory Sociology* (New York, 1946), 105–57 (compare with the 1935 edition); Raymond Murray to John LaFarge, February 11, 1952, in box 6, folder 7, JLFP 1. See also Murray and Flynn, *Social Problems,* and Murray's *Sociology for a Democratic Society* (New York, 1950).

interracial clubs pored over the book in search of answers to the racial dilemma. A Milwaukee group reported that it spent many evenings discussing it. A student reported in the *Interracial Review* that he won an essay contest on the "Negro Problem" after the perusal of *Interracial Justice.* The famous convert Clare Boothe Luce disclosed in a letter to LaFarge that his book had been the source of many of her talks on the "Negro question."[32] *Interracial Justice* was the Catholic equivalent of Myrdal's *An American Dilemma.*

LaFarge sent several autographed copies of his book to members of the American hierarchy and other prominent Catholics. One of these volumes went to Pope Pius XI. LaFarge followed his book to Rome in the spring of 1938 when the chief editor of *America* sent him to Budapest to cover the International Eucharistic Congress. LaFarge took advantage of this assignment to study the operation of Jesuit magazines in Europe and to observe firsthand the totalitarianism that had engulfed Italy and Germany. From April to June, LaFarge traveled extensively in Europe. After landing in England, which he described as "pagan and becoming more so," he made his way across the continent to the threatened countries of Eastern Europe. In addition to talking with prominent Catholics, he discussed the "gathering storm" on the horizon with embattled leaders such as Jan Marsaryk of Czechoslovakia. After the Eucharistic Congress ended in early June, he headed for Rome.[33]

LaFarge had hoped to attend a general audience with the pope, but on June 22, Pope Pius XI summoned the priest to his summer residence for a private meeting. At first the pope conversed with LaFarge in a combination of German and French before settling on the latter. Neither language presented a problem for the multilingual Jesuit, but he preferred one at a time. The pope indicated immediately that he had read LaFarge's *Interracial Justice* intently and liked it immensely ("C'est bon!"). The pontiff seemed delighted to see the American, and LaFarge soon discovered why. Pius XI declared that he felt as if God had sent LaFarge, for he was seeking a learned man to write an encyclical on fascism and racism. Then and there, it seems, the pope decided that his man was LaFarge. Losing little time, the pontiff instructed him on how

32. "As Youth Sees It," *IR,* 11 (August, 1938), 126, and *IR,* 12 (March, 1939), 46; Clare Boothe Luce to John LaFarge, June 15, 1950, in letter box 29, CICNYP.

33. *MIO,* 253–84; John LaFarge to Francis Talbot, May 15, 1938, in box 20, folder 1, JLFP 1; "Notes on European Trip," in box 37, folder 3, JLFP 1.

to approach the assignment: "Simply say what you would say if you yourself were the pope." Because of the explosive situation in Europe, the pope insisted on strict secrecy. After a brief discussion of the crucial task he had laid before LaFarge, Pius XI hesitated for a moment and said, "I should have taken this up with Fr. Ledochowski before speaking to you." Following another slight pause, the pope threw up his hands and exclaimed, "I imagine it will be all right." LaFarge, somewhat surprised at the pope's deference to Ledochowski, later commented, "After all, a Pope is a Pope." Certainly the pope had stunned LaFarge. In a report to the editor-in-chief of *America*, he said that he felt as if the "Rock of Peter had fallen on [him]." A month later he was still feeling "rather sacred" from his encounter in Rome.[34]

LaFarge's rapport with Pius XI was easy and immediate. Perhaps it was because the two men had much in common. The pope, formerly Achille Ratti, was, like LaFarge, a quiet and scholarly man who had earlier been the prefect of the Vatican Library. LaFarge greatly admired this pontiff who had initiated Catholic Action, encouraged native clergies, and updated the Catholic doctrine of social justice. He revered the pope who had sent in 1936, through the Sacred Consistorial Congregation, a circular letter to the American hierarchy that called for more black missions in the South. His esteem for the pope continued to rise as the Vatican began to take a stronger stand against Nazism in Germany. Pius XI had released within a week in March of 1937 an encyclical that condemned communism, *Divini Redemptoris,* and a letter to the German hierarchy, *Mit brennender Sorge,* that excoriated the Nazi "myth of blood." Moreover, the pope's tolerance of Benito Mussolini appeared to be waning rapidly by the late 1930s. Still, Pius XI had not issued a condemnation of Nazism that matched his indictment of Soviet communism.[35]

34. *MIO,* 273–74; John LaFarge, memorandum to Maryland-New York Provincial Office, July 3, 1938, and John LaFarge to Francis Talbot, July 18, 1938, both in box 20, folder 1, JLFP 1. LaFarge quoted the pope as saying, "Dites tout simplement ce que vous diriez a tout le monde si vous etiez Pape, vous meme."

35. Bokenkotter, *Concise History,* 321–23, 339–40, 367–71; Cardinal R. C. Rossi to American bishops, September 9, 1936, in Edmundite Archives, Burlington, Vermont, courtesy of the Edmundite congregation; Desmond O'Grady, "Pius XI—Complex and Imperious," *National Catholic Reporter,* December 15, 1972, p. 15; Gordon Zahn, "The Unpublished Encyclical—An Opportunity Missed," *National Catholic Reporter,* December 15, 1972, p. 9; "Comment," *Am,* 59 (August 13, 1938), 434.

Ledochowski's influence on the pope was probably one of the major reasons the Holy See had been more lenient toward Hitler's brand of tyranny than Stalin's. Pope Pius XI and Eugenio Pacelli, the Vatican secretary of state and the future pope, were both "Ignatian" in their Catholicism and were two of the most "Jesuited" popes in modern times. They shared with Ledochowski and the society a revulsion against communism and liberal capitalism. Since its restoration the Society of Jesus had been impeccably ultramontane. The Jesuits helped draft and support the *Syllabus of Errors,* and after Ledochowski became the general of the order in 1915, a number of German and Austrian Jesuits, mainly from the Gregorian University in Rome, had substantial influence in shaping a strong antimodernist Catholicism. The Jesuit Oswald Nell-Breuning had been the primary author of *Quadragesimo Anno,* and another Jesuit, Tacchi Venturi, conducted the negotiations with Mussolini that resulted in the Lateran Accords of 1929. No doubt, LaFarge's membership in the Society of Jesus influenced the pope's decision to have the New York interracialist write an encyclical for him. The pope immediately sent LaFarge to Ledochowski to iron out the details of his assignment. The Jesuit general, however, expressed strong skepticism about the pope's plan. When he heard about it, he exclaimed, "The Pope is mad!"[36]

Ledochowski feared that a confrontation with Germany might play into the hands of Stalin. The Jesuit general expressed even more concern about the secrecy of LaFarge's mission than had the pope. Without much enthusiasm, Ledochowski arranged for LaFarge to work in Paris and approved his request for two Jesuits to assist him with the encyclical. One of them was Gustave Gunlach, a German priest from the Gregorian University in Rome who had written extensively on economics. The other Jesuit was Maurice Desbuquois of Action Populaire. Before leaving Rome, LaFarge spoke for twenty minutes on the powerful Vatican radio station about the Catholic interracial movement in the United States. On June 27, he set out for Paris.[37]

36. Aveling, *The Jesuits,* 319, 324–25, 327, 332, 347–48, 351; McDonough, *Men Astutely Trained,* 56–68, esp. 135 for Ledochowski quotation; Alan Cassels, *Fascist Italy* (2nd ed.; Arlington Heights, Ill., 1985), 62–66, 68.

37. LaFarge, memorandum to Maryland-New York Provincial Office, July 3, 1938; *MIO,* 275; "The Holy Father Blesses Interracial Justice," *IR,* 11 (September, 1938), 134–36.

For the next three months, LaFarge and Gunlach worked on the encyclical at the residence of the staff of the Jesuit magazine *Études* at rue Monsieur, a quiet little street on the Left Bank. Desbuquois, it seems, was too busy to assist with the document. Sticking to his instructions from the pope and Ledochowski, LaFarge used code words in his correspondence to disguise his mission. *America* covered for LaFarge by reporting that he was undertaking "editorial investigations" and ascertaining European opinion. On the one hand, LaFarge was enthralled by the Paris episode. On the other hand, he worked himself into a state of near collapse by the end of the summer. "I know that I exhausted the very limit of my mind and body," he later wrote to a Vatican translator on the project. He found it difficult to relax in the French capital. One summer afternoon, however, he found himself sandwiched between the archbishop of Rouen and a nuncio at a Paris café, where, following their lead, he ate pig knuckles. Although he had resisted such fare while in rural Maryland, he confessed he found these porcine parts rather appetizing in such exalted company in the center of Gallic culture. "Such is life," he sighed.[38]

After finishing the encyclical, LaFarge personally took it to Rome on September 20. He delivered it not to the pope but to Ledochowski. Before boarding a ship for America, LaFarge joined with the fathers at the Jesuit Curia to hear a broadcast of a Hitler speech, an address that turned out to be a fanatical tirade aimed at a betrayed Czechoslovakia. LaFarge shivered with trepidation at Hitler's guttural barrage, but Ledochowski remained impassive throughout the speech. As the superior general prepared to leave the concerned gathering, he said, "Don't worry, there will be no war."[39]

By giving the secret document to Ledochowski, LaFarge may have aborted the encyclical. *Humani Generis Unitas* (*The Unity of Mankind*), as LaFarge and Gunlach titled the document, was never released. Many of the details of the ill-fated encyclical may be lost to history forever, but the outline of what happened is fairly clear. Although the

38. Stanton, "John LaFarge's Understanding," 170–71; "Who's Who," *Am*, 59 (August 20, 1938), 457; John LaFarge to Heinrich Bacht, S.J., October 22, 1948, in box 1, Stanton Papers; John LaFarge to Francis Talbot, August 5, 1938, in box 20, folder 1, JLFP 1.

39. *MIO*, 276–77; John LaFarge to Francis Talbot, September 18, 1938, in box 1, folder 9, Stanton Papers.

New York *Times* and the New York *World Telegram* anticipated an encyclical on world problems in late November, Ledochowski sat on the document for months. The ruling Jesuit had no desire to place Nazism on a par with Soviet communism in the pantheon of evil. Heinrich Bacht, a Jesuit who translated the encyclical into Latin, testified that Ledochowski found it "too strong and provoking." Gunlach was convinced that Ledochowski was "sabotaging" the document. Several letters passed between Gunlach and LaFarge in the fall of 1938 as they anxiously awaited the release of *Humani Generis Unitas.* On October 16, Gunlach encouraged LaFarge to write to the pope about it. On October 28, LaFarge complied. He first reviewed the brief history of the encyclical and informed the pope that he and Gunlach had produced a document that analyzed in some depth the topics of "Nationalism, Racism, and the Jewish question." He told the pope that he felt strongly that events subsequent to the completion of the encyclical confirmed the momentous truth of the document. In the conclusion of the letter, LaFarge told the pope of his "strong desire to hand over the document personally to [His] Holiness." However, he explained that physical exhaustion and "grave personal reasons" blocked this aspiration. LaFarge then informed the pope of Ledochowski's promise to turn the encyclical over to the Holy See as soon as he could. Finally, he declared that he took comfort in knowing that the document was safely in the pontiff's hands. LaFarge, of course, was subtly probing to ascertain the actual state of the document. Meanwhile, the pope had two serious heart attacks in late November and died on February 10, 1939. It is not certain that the encyclical ever reached Pius XI. Evidence suggests that it may not have reached the stricken pope until just days before his death.[40]

LaFarge took the secret of the aborted encyclical to his grave. Its existence was known to only a few insiders until an archivist began to catalog the LaFarge papers in the late 1960s. At the same time the Jesuit Edward Stanton began to piece the story together as a part of his 1972 doctoral dissertation on LaFarge. The *National Catholic Reporter*

40. Jim Castelli, "Unpublished Encyclical Attacked Anti-Semitism," *National Catholic Reporter,* December 15, 1972, pp. 1, 8, 13–14; Bacht, quoted in "Jesuit Says Pius XI Asked for Draft," *ibid.,* December 22, 1972, pp. 3–4; John LaFarge to Pope Pius XI, October 28, 1938, and John Killens, S.J. (Rome), to John LaFarge, October 27, 1938, both in box 1, Stanton Papers.

broke the story to the public in December of 1972. It carried several articles on the encyclical based on documents in the LaFarge papers. In addition to letters and memoranda on the encyclical, the LaFarge Papers included drafts of *Humani Generis Unitas* in French and in English, each over a hundred pages in length.[41]

Did LaFarge miss a golden opportunity to galvanize the Catholic church for a crusade against American racism? Much of the material in the unpublished encyclical was familiar and had appeared in earlier encyclicals, especially that in the first part on the unity of humankind, written by Gunlach (about seventy-five pages). But LaFarge's contribution on totalitarian statism, racism, and anti-Semitism (less than fifty pages) was stronger and more direct than the usual wordy and vague encyclical the Vatican dispensed. The LaFarge draft condemned Nazism as contradictory to natural law. It also asserted that "not a few decisive doctrines of Catholic faith and morals are ignored by racists." The encyclical indicted lynch law and called on people of good will "to eradicate from public life all distinctions based on race; for such distinctions can only be felt as defamatory and discriminatory." This section could be taken as a condemnation of legal segregation in America or of the Nuremburg laws in Germany. Nevertheless, as he did in *Interracial Justice*, LaFarge drew back from a total condemnation of Jim Crow, dampening the moral crackle of the issue. Although he held that racial segregation almost always caused harm, LaFarge counseled that "such differences and such social separations as brotherly love and prudence may counsel to the advantage of all different races in view of their actual circumstances no one will reasonably consider as discriminatory."[42] This kind of thought and phrasing afforded large enough loopholes for American bishops and southern segregationists to drive trucks through. Had *Humani Generis Unitas* been issued in 1938, it probably would have made no more impact on the racial situation in the United States than previous encyclicals had.

41. Curiously, the drafts of the encyclical are not now in the LaFarge Papers at Georgetown University, but copies are in the Stanton Papers. Apparently, they were removed from the Georgetown collection for the story by the *National Catholic Reporter* and were not returned. See Edward Stanton to Burkhart Schneider, February 13, 1972, in box 1, folder 4, Stanton Papers.

42. Stanton, "John LaFarge's Understanding," 182–93; LaFarge, quoted in Castelli, "Unpublished Encyclical," 14.

Would LaFarge's arraignment of Nazism and anti-Semitism have made a difference? LaFarge made it clear in the encyclical that totalitarianism was a sin and a heresy. The section on anti-Semitism also had power. Anti-Semitism, LaFarge wrote, was "totally at variance with the true spirit of the Catholic Church." It was a doctrine of hatred, a root attack on Christianity, and a recipe for violence and disorder. Unfortunately, the section on anti-Semitism also contained passages that had the potential for offending Jews. In discussing them, the encyclical spoke of "misguided souls" who "promote revolution" and deny "reverence and love of God," revealing LaFarge's inclination to link Bolshevism and Jews. He had earlier warned of the "fatal attraction" of Jews for communism, and his solution for ending tensions between Christians and Jews was Jewish conversion. In 1939 he wrote that the "only adequate solution will be when Israel finds its own soul through . . . Jesus Christ." [43]

Scholars and historians have not speculated on what impact the encyclical might have made on American race relations, but some analysts such as Gordon Zahn have conjectured that the lost encyclical might have prevented Hitler's "final solution" and at least would have made Catholics less cooperative with Germany in the occupied countries. Even some who are skeptical of this claim suggest that if the encyclical had been released in 1938, Cardinal Pacelli would not have become Pope Pius XII. With views similar to Ledochowski's, Pius XII did not share the growing intensity of opposition to fascism that had developed in his predecessor. Thus, the argument goes, if Pius XI had set a stern anti-Nazi course in 1938, Pacelli, with his more tolerant view of Germany, would not have been acceptable as pope. Then the course of history, they argue, might have been somewhat different. [44]

What is certain is that LaFarge blundered when he gave the encyclical to the reactionary Ledochowski instead of to the pope. True, LaFarge could honestly plead exhaustion and grave personal circumstances, but the basic reason for his behavior was his instinctual obe-

43. LaFarge, quoted in Castelli, "Unpublished Encyclical," 8, 14–15; Zahn, "Unpublished Encyclical," 9; LaFarge, "Christian Front to Combat Communism," 110; John LaFarge, "The Jewish Question," *Thought*, 14 (December, 1939), 534–35.

44. Zahn, "Unpublished Encyclical," 9; "A Lingering Question," *National Catholic Reporter*, December 15, 1972, p. 10; Conor Cruise O'Brien, "A Last Chance to Save the Jews?," *New York Review of Books*, April 27, 1989, pp. 27–28, 35; "Jesuit Says Pius XI Asked for Draft," 4; Zahn, "Unpublished Encyclical," 9.

dience to the head of the Jesuit order. Ironically, by putting himself in the hands of Ledochowski, the ultramontane American did the papacy and Catholicism a disservice. Gunlach told LaFarge as much, and even Father Stanton concurred in his study of the American Jesuit.[45]

Nevertheless, all was not lost with the death of Pius XI. LaFarge and Gunlach still hoped that the new pope would release the encyclical on which they had labored so feverishly. In the first months of 1939, correspondence flew back and forth between New York and Rome. LaFarge wrote to Ledochowski, Gunlach, Zacheus Maher (the American Jesuit assistant in Rome), and other contacts in the Vatican. On Easter in 1939, however, Maher fairly dashed all hopes for the document. He informed LaFarge that the priest was free to draw on the work he had completed in Paris, but Maher added that Ledochowski had ordered no allusions should ever be made to the encyclical commissioned by Pius XI.[46]

On October 20, 1939, Pope Pius XII issued an encyclical called *Summi Pontificatus (The Unity of Human Society).* Pius XII did incorporate some of the unpublished encyclical into *The Unity of Human Society,* which was drafted by Gunlach, but the pope used only the first part of the secret encyclical—the part that dealt with human unity. It cut out the heart of the earlier document, the sections on statism, racism, and anti-Semitism that were written by LaFarge.[47] In a letter to LaFarge about *Summi Pontificatus,* Maher wrote, "You have read it and have recognized some parts of it, no doubt." A decade later LaFarge wrote Bacht that some of his work had been "salvaged" by the 1939 encyclical.[48] LaFarge and Catholics in the interracial movement, of course, characterized Pius XII's encyclical as a courageous attack on racism. LaFarge labored in vain, however, to find a quotable passage in the document that hit directly at racism. He could only quote the pope as celebrating the "law of human solidarity and charity" as represented in the person of Jesus Christ. It was almost as if LaFarge read *Summi*

45. Stanton, "John LaFarge's Understanding," 194–95.

46. *Ibid.,* 175–86; Zacheus Maher to John LaFarge, Easter Monday, 1939, in box 1, folder 9, Stanton Papers.

47. Zahn, "Unpublished Encyclical," 9; Castelli, "Unpublished Encyclical," 13. For a meticulous comparison of the two encyclicals, see Stanton, "John LaFarge's Understanding," 175, 178–99.

48. Maher, quoted in Stanton, "John LaFarge's Understanding," 198; John LaFarge to Heinrich Bacht, October 22, 1948, in box 1, Stanton Papers.

Pontificatus but saw *Humani Generis Unitas.* Or perhaps he heard the echoes of what might have been had Pius XI lived but a few more weeks.[49]

LaFarge also took heart when, just a few days after the encyclical was released, the pope issued *Sertum Laetitiae,* a letter to the American bishops. The letter specifically referred to blacks but not with much originality or probity. One passage of the papal letter read as follows: "We confess that We feel a special paternal affection, which is certainly inspired by heaven, for the Negro people dwelling among you; for in the field of religion and education We know they need special care and comfort and are very deserving of it. We therefore invoke an abundance of heavenly blessings and We pray fruitful success for those whose generous zeal is devoted to their welfare." If the pope borrowed anything from the aborted encyclical on racism, he weakened it beyond recognition. Yet the *Interracial Review* called the papal letter the "most important and far-reaching pronouncement affecting the American Negro since the Emancipation Proclamation."[50]

The story of the lost encyclical raises more Hochhuthian questions about the Vatican during World War II. (Rolf Hochhuth's controversial play *The Deputy* skewered Pius XII for his failure to speak out adequately against Jewish persecution and Nazism and stimulated similar literature.) After the discovery of the aborted encyclical in the LaFarge Papers, critics had more reason to accuse Pius XII of failure to act resolutely against Nazism and its "final solution" during World War II. To be sure, the LaFarge Papers reveal that Pius XII failed to follow the promising lead of his predecessor, as instructed by LaFarge and Gunlach.[51]

When LaFarge arrived at the New York docks in October of 1938, he was exhausted and ill. He had lost thirty pounds, for the eating habits of the continent had played havoc with his defective digestion. On top

---

49. On LaFarge's use of *Summi Pontificatus,* see John LaFarge, "Mankind Is Called to Unity in Christ," *Am,* 62 (November 11, 1939), 120–21; John LaFarge, *The Race Question and the Negro: A Study of the Catholic Doctrine on Interracial Justice* (New York, 1943), 112; and LaFarge, *No Postponement,* 111.

50. Encyclical, quoted in "Pope Pius XII and the Negro," *IR,* 12 (December, 1939), 179–80.

51. "Lingering Question," 10; Zahn, "Unpublished Encyclical," 9; Rolf Hochhuth, *The Deputy* (New York, 1964). On other literature written on Pius XII and Nazism, see Gordon A. Craig, *The Germans* (New York, 1982), 98, 227–29.

of that, his favorite brother Bancel had died while he was in Paris. Shortly after his arrival in America, his oldest brother Grant passed away. Nevertheless, the CICNY was so revenue-starved that it staged a homecoming banquet for LaFarge at Town Hall in order to raise money. A still shaky LaFarge delivered a major address to an audience of three hundred on November 29. After expenses the dinner raised just $2.56.[52]

LaFarge's speech at Town Hall, however, marked a significant change in the tone of his message. Prior to his speech, he had made a neat academic division between the religious discrimination against Jews and the racist attitudes toward blacks. Now he concentrated on the relation of American racism to anti-Semitism in Europe. He warned his Town Hall loyalists, "Nazi Racism [*sic*] is coming here, for the elements are all at hand." The highly developed racism of Germany, he said, had much in common with "its pale but venomous elder cousin" in America. In effect, LaFarge warned the audience that it could happen here.[53] This speech was the first sign of a more acute resistance he had developed to all forms of racism as a result of his European trip. His diagnosis of the causes of racism, at least momentarily, seemed to deepen. Going beyond the simplistic notion that racism was generated by ignorance alone, he now preached that the source was "ingrained in our social structure, our education, even our religious practice."[54]

LaFarge's improved diagnosis still lacked completeness, however. He had not grasped the psychological dimensions of racism and how they related to its awful tenacity. He remained oblivious to the fact that white culture sustained an uplifting sense of superiority from the degradation of blacks. Whites generally defined themselves over and against blacks, whom they deemed inferior "others." LaFarge was blind to the insight that many whites hated blacks because the majority projected its evil impulses upon the minority. Some whites perhaps

52. *MIO*, 281, 283–84; Frances S. Childs (LaFarge's niece) to Edward Stanton, December 3, 1973, in box 1, folder 3, Stanton Papers; Zielinski, "Promotion of Better Race Relations," 119.

53. LaFarge's speech, "Racism and Social Unity," is in letter box 14, CICNYP, and is reprinted in part in *IR*, 11 (December, 1938), 182–84. See also New York *Times*, November 30, 1938, for its coverage.

54. LaFarge, "Mankind Is Called to Unity," 120–21. See also his "Racist Truth and Racist Error," *Thought*, 14 (March, 1939), 19–35, and "Laying the Foundations of Good Will," *IR*, 13 (February, 1940), 23–24.

sensed that the dark tendencies they saw in blacks really lay within themselves. Instead of cleansing themselves, however, they chose to devalue blacks.[55]

Nor was LaFarge ready to move beyond an elitist Catholic strategy. As a triumphalist Catholic, he was cool to overtures by liberal Protestants and Jews in the National Conference of Christians and Jews and in the Federal Council of Churches to build a united front against the increasing menace of racism. Except for his efforts to improve the image of the church among moderate blacks, LaFarge acted on the premise that Catholicism could do it alone. He, like the rest of the Catholic clergy, was largely content to cast his light in "magnificent isolation."[56]

LaFarge nonetheless grieved that *America* had grown more conservative in social thought in the late 1930s, a condition owing much to Francis X. Talbot's elevation to editor-in-chief in 1936. Despite his discontent with regression at *America*, he continued to pummel those Catholics to the left of him. He increasingly shied away from Day and her Catholic Workers, even though they set up a Harlem office and adopted interracial justice as a major theme. Although LaFarge praised the charitable instincts of the Catholic Workers, he told them frankly that they were ill suited to the task of formulating Catholic social theory. He scolded them for trying to force their radical ideas on the church, and he pointed an accusing finger at the group's lack of clerical guidance.[57]

LaFarge also snubbed Baroness Catherine de Hueck, Day's counterpart in the racial field. In the late 1930s Baroness de Hueck, a refugee from the Russian Revolution, set up Friendship Houses in Harlem and Chicago. This passionate aristocrat and her helpers not only clothed and fed blacks, but they lived in slum areas with the down-and-out. "I cannot describe the compassion, the fire of love that burned in my heart

---

55. See, for example, Kovel, *White Racism*, ix–xi, 4; Frantz Fanon, "The Fact of Blackness," in *Anatomy of Racism*, ed. David Theo Goldberg (Minneapolis, 1990), 108–26; Winthrop D. Jordan, *White over Black*, 575–82; and Ronald T. Takaki, *Iron Cages: Race and Culture in Nineteenth-Century America* (New York, 1979).

56. Michael Gannon, "Before and After Modernism: The Intellectual Isolation of the American Priest," in *Catholic Priest*, ed. John Ellis, 294–95.

57. John LaFarge, "Memorandum to the Very Reverend Fathers Provincial at the Annual Meeting," May 7, 1940, in Jesuit Missouri Province Archives, St. Louis; John LaFarge, "With Script and Staff: Some Reflections on the Catholic Workers," *Am*, 57 (June 26, 1937), 275; Piehl, *Breaking Bread*, 123.

for these people," the baroness said of poor blacks.[58] Although Hunton informed LaFarge that de Hueck was approaching racial work in a practical way, LaFarge remained wary of the impetuous Russian aristocrat. Later in his historical account of the interracial movement, he spoke of de Hueck's "genius" and praised her "remarkable and original work." However, in 1940 he asked the baroness not to consider him as an adviser to her movement, and he told her not to say anything that might convey the impression that he was associated with Friendship House. LaFarge joined a legion of priests in suspecting that de Hueck's uninhibited attacks on racism in the Catholic church constituted a sign of anticlericalism.[59]

Neither did LaFarge join hands with those Americans who wanted to defend European democracy against fascism. His rejection of pacifism and his affiliation with the CAIP suggested that he might be prone to support the collective security policy of Franklin Roosevelt in the late 1930s. But if he disagreed with *America*'s staunch isolationism, he kept it secret. Most likely, LaFarge obediently bit his tongue and went along with editor-in-chief Talbot and his conservative ally Paul Blakely. To put things in perspective, the foreign policy views of most religious leaders at the time were isolationist.[60] *America* denounced the Lend-Lease bill of 1941 as a usurpation by a power-hungry president. Even after the invasion of the Soviet Union, LaFarge continued to worry more about a communist-dominated Europe than about German aggression. However, his acquiescence in the isolationism of *America* did not keep him from presenting postwar plans for a Catholic-dominated Europe.[61]

When war came to America, it brought a disturbing increase of racial tensions and violence. Outside the South, much of the violence

58. Catherine de Hueck, *Fragments of My Life* (Notre Dame, Ind., 1979), 148; see also her *Friendship House* (New York, 1947).

59. George Hunton to John LaFarge, May 19, 1938, in letter box 16, CICNYP; John LaFarge to Catherine de Hueck, April 15, 1940, in box 16, folder 4, JLFP 1; LaFarge, *No Postponement*, 150–51. In *Catholic Organizations Promoting Negro-White Relations*, 113, Father Harte found that the majority of the priests he interviewed in the New York area believed de Hueck to be anticlerical.

60. McNeal, *Harder than War*, 12; Marty, *The Noise of Conflict*, 387–90.

61. Editorial "As We War," *Am*, 64 (March 22, 1941), 658–59; John LaFarge, "In Any United Europe Religion Must Find a Place," *Am*, 62 (February 24, 1940), 542–43, and "What Think You of Peace Even Though War Rages," *Am*, 64 (November 23, 1940), 178–79. On Catholics and foreign policy, see Flynn, *Roosevelt and Romanism*.

occurred in Catholic neighborhoods as a second wave of black migrants made their way up from the South to northern cities. The black migration presented enormous and immediate challenges to the Catholic interracial movement and to the church. The war also fastened new responsibilities on LaFarge, who rose first to executive editor and then editor-in-chief of *America*.

9

The American Race Question Through Hot and Cold Wars
Liberal Catholicism in the Forties

The winds of war spread the seeds of racial change and racial conflict across America. In 1942 the Swedish economist Gunnar Myrdal proclaimed: "This War is crucial for the future of the Negro, and the Negro problem is crucial in the War. There is bound to be a redefinition of the Negro's status in America as a result of this War." Several astute observers, including Myrdal, pointed out the global implications of American race relations. They maintained that America's quest for military victory and influence in the world depended significantly on its handling of the race problem. When a black man was lynched in Missouri shortly after the bombing of Pearl Harbor, the Jesuit editors of *America* wrote, "In perfect form, served on a platter, the town of Sikeston, Missouri, offers Hitler and Goebbels the first lynching of the new year." In 1944 the Republican standard bearer Wendell Willkie declared, "Every time some race baiter ill-treats some man in America he lessens the ability of America to lead the world to freedom."[1]

1. Myrdal, *An American Dilemma*, 997; "Comment," *Am*, 66 (February 7, 1942), 479; Willkie, quoted in Oliver C. Cox, *Caste, Class, and Race* (Garden City, N.Y., 1948), xxxvii.

The paradox and hypocrisy of a nation fighting a war against the master racist Adolf Hitler with segregated troops gave African Americans a window of opportunity to exploit the gap between the American creed and the American reality. Unlike during World War I, no W. E. B. Du Bois now told black Americans to close ranks and put away their special grievances until the rest of the world was safe for democracy. The war actually stimulated black protest. Although the overwhelming majority of blacks supported the war, their support was not unconditional. Rather, the racial manifesto trumpeted by the black press was the "Double V," victory against fascism abroad and against racism at home. Prior to Pearl Harbor, A. Philip Randolph threatened an all-black march on Washington, D.C., to protest discrimination in defense industries. Seeking unity and maximum use of black manpower for the war effort, President Franklin Roosevelt responded with an executive order that led to the establishment of the FEPC in the summer of 1941. In 1942 the Congress of Racial Equality, a direct-action, integrationist group, was formed in Chicago. In the same year a hitherto cautious group of southern black leaders issued a statement in Durham, North Carolina, that condemned "compulsory segregation." Attesting to the increased activism, the membership of the NAACP increased almost 1,000 percent during the war.[2]

The war experience marked a turning point in the lives of many young blacks. The humiliation that blacks in uniform suffered in the segregated armed forces while simultaneously being bombarded with the democratic rhetoric of the war made them angry and generally more determined to challenge the caste system. Once in uniform, and especially after combat, blacks tended to be less deferential to whites. Robert L. Carter, a lawyer who assisted Thurgood Marshall in many of the legal breakthroughs of the 1940s and 1950s, testified to the importance of his military service. "I thought I was pretty well balanced regarding the race problem," Carter recalled, "but once I got in the army, the thing was ground in my face everywhere I turned: blacks acting as lackeys to whites, and whites acting oppressively toward blacks."

2. Richard M. Dalfiume, "The 'Forgotten Years' of the Negro Revolution," *Journal of American History*, 55 (June, 1968), 97–100, 106; Neil A. Wynn, *The Afro-American and the Second World War* (New York, 1976), 102; Garfinkel, *When Negroes March*, 7–8; Harvard Sitkoff, *The Struggle for Black Equality, 1954–1980* (New York, 1981), 11–12; John Morton Blum, *V Was for Victory: Politics and American Culture During World War II* (New York, 1976), 215–18.

Carter, like many black veterans, came home from the military in a fighting mood.[3]

The rising militancy of blacks provoked strong reaction and created a racial crisis in America. In his 1943 book, *Race and Rumors of Race*, Howard Odum, a noted sociologist at Chapel Hill, North Carolina, reported on the rampaging wartime gossip. Rumors about "Eleanor [Roosevelt] Clubs," "ice-pick conspiracies," and kitchen strikes by blacks circulated wildly in the South. In 1943 Virginius Dabney, a southern liberal who was editor of the Richmond *Times-Dispatch*, wrote in an *Atlantic* article that "a small group of Negro agitators and another small group of white rabble-rousers are pushing this country closer and closer to an inter-racial explosion which may make the race riots of the First World War seem mild by comparison."[4]

These racial fears were not confined to the South. The migration of hundreds of thousands of African Americans out of the South into distant cities set off racial conflagrations in Detroit, New York, and Los Angeles. In 1943 thirty-four people died in a race riot in Detroit, twenty-five of them black. In 1944 six thousand whites struck the Philadelphia transit system when eight blacks were elevated to the position of streetcar conductor. Federal troops had to be diverted from the war effort to calm Detroit and run the war-vital transportation system in Philadelphia.[5]

The racial violence of World War II shook American liberals. When brutal assaults on blacks continued after the war, civil rights became a prominent and permanent part of the urban liberal agenda. Moreover, the executive branch assumed a major role in racial affairs for the first time since Reconstruction when President Harry S Truman in 1946 appointed a distinguished biracial civil rights committee, which the following year released a revolutionary report entitled *To Secure These*

3. Richard M. Dalfiume, *Desegregation of the U.S. Armed Forces: Fighting on Two Fronts, 1939–1953* (Columbia, Mo., 1969), 73, 89; Dalfiume, " 'Forgotten Years' of the Negro Revolution," 92–93, 96, 100; Carter, quoted in Richard Kluger, *Simple Justice: The History of Brown v. Board of Education and Black America's Struggle for Equality* (New York, 1976), 398.

4. Howard W. Odum, *Race and Rumors of Race* (Chapel Hill, N.C., 1943), 74, 97, *passim*; Virginius Dabney, "Nearer and Nearer the Precipice," *Atlantic*, 171 (January, 1943), 94.

5. Franklin and Moss, *From Slavery to Freedom*, 403–404; Philadelphia *Inquirer*, August 6, 1944, Sec. B, p. 6.

Rights. In addition to calling for a number of specific government actions to safeguard black rights, the committee recommended the elim-
ination of all forced segregation in American society. A willful band of
southern senators prevented Truman from enacting civil rights legislation, but he moved the armed forces toward desegregation with an
executive order in 1948. By courting the increasingly important black
vote in the northern states in 1948, Truman further legitimized the civil
rights issue.[6]

The Cold War also provided an incentive for racial reform. State
Department officials estimated that half of Soviet propaganda dealt with
the racial situation in America. Since the United States sought nonwhite
allies in the Third World to support its foreign policy, the fight against
white racism was considered a corollary of combating Soviet expan-
sionism. In 1947, blacks, led by Du Bois, discovered another way to
relate the American race problem to the world scene when they laid
the issue of African American rights before the newly established
United Nations.[7]

During the war the Supreme Court also began to reclaim the original intent of the Fourteenth and Fifteenth Amendments. Between 1944
and 1950, the court struck down several of the legal obstacles to black
freedom, starting with the white primary. The outlawing of state enforcement of restrictive covenants, of segregation in interstate travel,
and of separate and unequal facilities in higher education followed.
By 1950 Thurgood Marshall and the NAACP's legal defense team decided that it was time to go for broke and challenge school segregation
head on.[8]

The 1940s thus marked a watershed in American race relations. In
1945 the Julius Rosenwald Fund listed three hundred organizations that

6. On continuing atrocities, see John Hope Franklin, "Civil Rights and the Truman
Administration," in *Conference of Scholars on the Truman Administration and Civil
Rights,* ed. Donald R. McCoy, Richard T. Ruetten, and J. R. Fuchs (Independence, Mo.,
1968), 134; Harvard Sitkoff, "Harry Truman and the Election of 1948: The Coming of
Age of Civil Rights in American Politics," *Journal of Southern History,* 37 (November,
1971), 615–16; "Lynch Law Again," *Am,* 75 (August 10, 1946), 443.
7. The best and most comprehensive coverage of civil rights in the Truman era is
Donald R. McCoy and Richard T. Ruetten, *Quest and Response: Minority Rights and
the Truman Administration* (Lawrence, Kans., 1973).
8. On the civil rights cases, see Kluger, *Simple Justice,* 214–84, *passim,* and Southern,
Gunnar Myrdal and Black-White Relations, 127–50.

dealt with interracial problems. Three years later, over a thousand such groups existed. After the war a host of councils of democracy, councils for unity, and councils against intolerance were founded. The "war against bigotry" moved forward on myriad fronts.[9] No group was more engaged in this battle of the 1940s than the liberal clergy. According to the noted church historian Sidney Ahlstrom, "The most provocative new concern of religious thinkers was the place of the Negro in American society." In 1946 the Federal Council of Churches declared that segregation violated the "Gospel of love and human brotherhood." Most of the Protestant denominations condemned Jim Crow before the decade was finished.[10] By whatever index one uses, the idea of integration came of age in the 1940s.

The American Catholic church, however, lagged behind other denominations on racial matters. Unlike the Federal Council of Churches, Catholic bishops took no stand on segregation in the 1940s, and the NCWC recruited no blacks for its staff.[11] This is not to say that the Catholic church made no racial gains in the 1940s, for many advances occurred, but they were engineered by a few isolated bishops or clergymen or by small decentralized and poorly financed lay groups such as the Catholic interracial councils, organizations that had no recognized authority over Catholics in general. The lack of an adequately financed and well-coordinated Catholic program in this period meant that many opportunities for racial change were forfeited by the church.

Despite turning sixty in 1940 and suffering a number of serious health problems during the decade, Father LaFarge's activities increased and broadened, and his prestige rose. Theophilus Lewis, the black drama critic for the *Interracial Review*, wrote in 1942 that the Jesuit's influence on the Catholic interracial movement was "ubiquitous" but added that his impact on race relations was sometimes obscured by his

9. Brewton Berry, *Race Relations* (Boston, 1951), 122; Dalfiume, " 'Forgotten Years' of the Negro Revolution," 99–100. See generally Goodwin Watson, *Action for Unity* (New York, 1947).

10. Sidney E. Ahlstrom, *A Religious History of the American People* (New Haven, 1972), 962; Frank S. Loescher, "The Protestant Church and the Negro: Recent Pronouncements," *Social Forces,* 26 (December, 1947), 197–201; David M. Reimers, *White Protestantism and the Negro* (New York, 1965), 109–33.

11. Gillard, *Colored Catholics,* 261–62. Dr. George Haynes, an African American, headed the Department of Race Relations of the Federal Council of Churches from 1922 to 1947 (see Chap. 4).

many outside activities. The most important of these was his enlarged role with the magazine *America*. In July of 1942 he became the executive editor of the Jesuit journal, a new position created to give LaFarge more authority. Two years later he assumed the position of editor-in-chief, which he held through 1948. He continued as chaplain of the Laymen's Union, the CICNY, the St. Ansgar League, and the Liturgical Arts Society. In 1948 the executive board of the National Catholic Rural Life Conference gave LaFarge an award for his outstanding contributions to its organization.[12] During the war the Jesuit became the chairman of the African Committee of CAIP, a group that observed the United Nations trusteeships in Africa. He also served on various non-denominational committees to assist African students who wanted to study in the United States.[13] In addition, he joined numerous committees, such as the Committee Against Jim Crow in Military Service and Training, and he was an inveterate campaigner for the fair employment of blacks.[14]

Because of his interest in employment, LaFarge strongly supported the activities of A. Philip Randolph.[15] After the FEPC was established in 1941, Randolph broadened the agenda of the MOWM beyond jobs to include the termination of segregation in education, housing, transportation, and the armed forces. He planned a gigantic mass rally for the MOWM in Madison Square Garden in the summer of 1942. As the date of the rally approached, Randolph looked for a white speaker to deflect charges that his movement was separatist and communist-ridden.[16]

One might have thought that Randolph's leftist past would have made the black leader anathema to LaFarge. During the postwar upheavals of 1919, President Wilson had branded Randolph the "most

---

12. Theophilus Lewis, "Plays and a Point of View," *IR*, 15 (December, 1942), 187–88; *MIO*, 294–95; "Catholic Rural Life Award," *IR*, 21 (November, 1948), 165.

13. "Cardinal Spellman to Aid Fund for African Academy," *IR*, 20 (March, 1947), 48; John LaFarge to George Shuster, May 15, 1944, in box 33, folder 14, JLFP 1; John LaFarge to P. J. Holloran, S.J., September 8, 1947, in box 2, folder 4, JLFP 2. See also letters from Africans in box 49, folder 1, JLFP 1.

14. Grant Reynolds to John LaFarge, April 30, 1948, in box 10, folder 9, JLFP 1.

15. Zielinski, "Working for Interracial Justice," 242–45. See also Zielinski, " 'Doing the Truth,' " 338–84.

16. "8 Point Program, March-on-Washington Movement," copy in box 5, folder 9, JLFP 1.

dangerous Negro in America." Moreover, in 1941 Randolph defended his threatened all-black march on Washington, D.C., with the argument that "the Negro needs an all-Negro movement to fight to solve specific problems." Although LaFarge had earlier rejected the same argument by the black Catholic leader Thomas Turner, he now agreed to speak to the MOWM rally; and, what is more surprising, Bishop McIntyre let him. Even so, it was a somewhat risky venture for the priest, for southern white supremacists made grave accusations against the FEPC. Mississippi congressman John Rankin called the FEPC the opening wedge for a "communist dictatorship," and Senator Theodore Bilbo said it meant "social equality and intermarriage between whites and blacks." Not a few conservatives outside the South thought Randolph and his proposals were outright radical.[17]

LaFarge, however, had confidence in Randolph because he considered him the greatest anticommunist force among American blacks. He knew that Randolph had kept the MOWM restricted to blacks because he feared infiltration by white communists. LaFarge also favored Randolph because he believed that the black leader, though a Protestant, had great respect for organized religion. Finally, Randolph was light-skinned, handsome, well dressed, and polite. Once an aspiring actor, Randolph had cultivated an aristocratic accent as a member of Ye Friends of Shakespeare.[18] Most likely, it was these personal traits that made LaFarge such a Randolph loyalist.

In any event, LaFarge brought his impeccable anticommunist credentials and served as the token white at Randolph's massive rally of twenty thousand. On the stage at Madison Square Garden, he joined the black speakers Mary McLeod Bethune, the Reverend Adam Clayton Powell, Jr. (who announced his plans to run for Congress), and

17. A. Philip Randolph, "Government Sets Pattern of Jim-Crow," *IR*, 15 (July, 1942), 102; Wilson, quoted in Manning Marable, *Race, Reform, and Rebellion: The Second Reconstruction in Black America* (Jackson, Miss., 1984), 21; Record, *Race and Radicalism*, 124–25; Rankin and Bilbo, quoted in David R. Goldfield, *Black, White, and Southern: Race Relations and Southern Culture, 1940 to the Present* (Baton Rouge, 1990), 34.

18. John LaFarge to Merwin K. Hart, May 10, 1948, in box 3, folder 15, JLFP 1; John LaFarge to Francis J. Murphy, January 16, 1948, in box 2, folder 2, JLFP 1; "Proof of the Pudding," *Am*, 78 (March 6, 1948), 619; Benjamin Quarles, *Black Mosaic: Essays in Afro-American History and Historiography* (Amherst, Mass., 1988), 154; Paula F. Pfeffer, *A. Philip Randolph: Pioneer of the Civil Rights Movement* (Baton Rouge, 1990), 23, 30, 196, 198.

Channing Tobias. Subsequently, LaFarge decried the weakening of the
FEPC by Roosevelt under pressure from southern congressmen, and
he became an avid booster of the National Council for a Permanent
Fair Employment Practices Committee (NCPFEPC), which Randolph
established in late 1943. LaFarge served on the executive board of the
New York council founded to promote Randolph's organization. Furthermore, George Hunton became a member of the board of directors
of the NCPFEPC.[19]

Both Hunton and LaFarge testified before the House Labor Committee in favor of a permanent FEPC bill. LaFarge stressed three major
points about the proposed bill in his testimony: that employment discrimination was a national problem, that the bill was necessary for social stability and the health of the black family, and that if it failed, the
country would "be laid wide open for the worst type of revolutionary
agitation."[20] LaFarge had taken some uncharacteristic risks in his all-
out support of Randolph. He had joined hands with the most liberal
elements in the country on the FEPC issue. The actions of LaFarge and
Hunton regarding the FEPC probably gained the CICNY more respect
in the eyes of black and white liberals than any other single activity of
the council in the 1940s.

If LaFarge proved resolute on employment, he was much more
circumspect on the question of housing during the war. The changing
ethnic neighborhoods in northern cities, in tandem with the critical
housing shortage during the war, created a racially explosive situation.
Between the world wars, for example, the number of blacks in Detroit
increased from 1.2 percent to 9.2 percent of the population. Another
60,000 African Americans arrived in the Motor City during World War
II. Cleveland saw a similar increase in its black minority, and by 1940
African Americans made up 9.6 percent of the city's population. In
Chicago in the 1940s, the black population soared from 278,000 to
almost 500,000. Incoming blacks sent thousands of whites fleeing to
the suburbs. To accommodate demographic changes, one-fourth of
Chicago's parishes, serving half of the city's Catholics, were formed

19. "A Permanent FEPC," *IR*, 17 (February, 1944), 19–20; "FEPC Debate in the
House," *Am*, 73 (May 12, 1945), 112–13; "Are Negroes Citizens?," *Am*, 68 (February
13, 1943), 519; Zielinski, "Working for Interracial Justice," 244–45; Hunton, *All of Which
I Saw*, 205–207. All the speeches at the MOWM rally were carried in *IR*, 15 (July, 1942).

20. LaFarge's testimony was reprinted in "Discrimination in Employment," *Catholic Mind*, 42 (August, 1944), 487–91.

between 1940 and 1965. As southern black Protestants crowded into northern cities, they came in contact, more often than not, with working-class, immigrant Catholics.[21]

Before World War II urban Catholics had often practiced segregation by nationality, and nationality was often used interchangeably with race. Each ethnic group demanded its own priest and worship in its own language. But segregation by nationality created more ethnic or "racialist" hostility. Lithuanian and Polish students in Pennsylvania complained that they were disliked by fellow Catholics because of their "race." In Boston, immigrants from southeastern Europe were dubbed the "newer Catholic races." Although the hierarchy was discouraging the formation of national parishes by the 1940s, many of these cohesive ethnic enclaves still thrived and continued to serve the religious, social, and psychological needs of their parishioners well into the second half of this century. Since the lives of white ethnic Catholics revolved around the parish, they, if they could not flee to the suburbs, stoutly resisted the influx of African Americans. Inner-city parishes had invested substantially in real estate and had incurred hefty mortgages. Even working-class Catholics had a high rate of home ownership and the debt that accompanied it. Catholics were thus inclined to resist black newcomers from the South. They believed that blacks would depress property values and increase crime. They resisted not only incoming Protestant blacks but black Catholics as well. In fact, archbishops were still forming black parishes in the 1940s to avoid integration of Catholic institutions.[22]

To LaFarge's great embarrassment, Catholic priests often led the resistance to black urban immigrants, and the hierarchy often failed to stand up for Catholic principles. Father Thomas Love of the predom-

---

21. Dominic J. Capeci, Jr., *Race Relations in Wartime Detroit: The Sojourner Truth Housing Controversy of 1942* (Philadelphia, 1984), 4, 7; Blatnica, *"At the Altar of God,"* 15; Steven M. Avella, *This Confident Church: Catholic Leadership and Life in Chicago, 1940–1965* (Notre Dame, Ind., 1992), 76–77, 79, 250–51, 253.

22. McGreevy, " 'Race' and Twentieth Century American Catholic Culture," 7–9, 14–17; James M. O'Toole, *Militant and Triumphant: William Henry O'Connell and the Catholic Church in Boston, 1859–1944* (Notre Dame, Ind., 1992), 145. An informative case study of a changing neighborhood is in Eileen M. McMahon, "What Parish Are You From? A Study of the Chicago Irish Parish Community and Race Relations, 1916–1970" (Ph.D. dissertation, Loyola University, Chicago, 1989). See also Blatnica, *"At the Altar of God,"* 88, 220, and Joe William Trotter, Jr., *Black Milwaukee: The Making of an Industrial Proletariat, 1915–1945* (Urbana, Ill., 1988), 31, 128.

inantly Irish Gesu Parish in Philadelphia claimed that he had nothing against blacks, but he vowed to keep them out of his parish in order to save the property values of his parishioners. In a series of articles in the Philadelphia *Tribune* in 1941, black journalists reported on Father Love and other like-minded priests. The articles spoke of "Hitler's fascism in Philadelphia." Similar events occurred in other cities. On the south side of Chicago in 1946, Father Francis Quinn of St. Ambrose Parish preached a sermon that was taken down verbatim by a black parishioner. A portion of it went as follows: "The Niggers have taken over Corpus Christi church, Holy Angels and St. Anne's and now they are trying to take over this church; but if it's left to me, they will not. . . . Our forefathers from Ireland came over here and prepared the way for us . . . and the Niggers are not going to run us out." Cardinal Samuel Stritch, a southerner who liberally sprinkled his private speech with the word *nigger*, never once during the decade spoke out forcefully against Catholic-led violence against blacks in his archdiocese of Chicago.[23]

LaFarge grew deeply concerned about the racial friction in Catholic neighborhoods as the war approached. Robert Taylor of the Defense Housing Authority, a wartime branch of the Federal Housing Authority, met with the directors of the CICNY just prior to Pearl Harbor and explained to them that there was heavy, priest-led, Catholic opposition to black housing projects in "Buffalo, Detroit, and other places." Even Bishop McIntyre worried that the antiblack actions of priests in Philadelphia might make convert work in Harlem more difficult.[24]

LaFarge took his concern to the American bishops and the NCWC. On December 4, 1941, he informed Monsignor Michael J. Ready, secretary of the NCWC, of the CICNY's meeting with the defense housing director. LaFarge told Ready that laymen of the CICNY could hardly lecture priests outside New York on their racist behavior. He therefore suggested that the bishops collectively draft

23. McGreevy, " 'Race' and Twentieth Century American Catholic Culture," 23–24; Avella, *This Confident Church*, 254, 258–59, 263, 268, esp. 261–62 for Quinn quotation; Leslie Woodcock Tentler, *Seasons of Grace: A History of the Catholic Archdiocese of Detroit* (Detroit, 1990), 507.

24. Housing folders, in letter box 31, CICNYP; "Summary of Panel Discussion on Clergy Conference on Negro Welfare," June 15, 1942, in box 4, folder 4, JLFP 2; John LaFarge to Msgr. Michael J. Ready, December 4, 1941, in letter box 31, CICNYP; J. Francis McIntyre to John LaFarge, February 26, 1941, in box 29, folder 20, JLFP 1.

guidelines on housing that could be enforced in each parish. He recommended a statement that was "non-controversial" and "implied admonition directed to the laity, not the clergy, in the form of a wish that the Catholic laity should set a good example." Apparently, LaFarge held the laity to a higher standard than he did the clergy. The letter also indicated that the church's image was uppermost in LaFarge's mind. As the following passage shows, LaFarge worried considerably about the Catholic image in the black press:

> The real danger . . . seemed to be that the news of Catholic opposition, organized and unorganized, would pass from one city to another and establish a general pattern of Catholic hostility which would be extremely dangerous, not to say extremely unjust. This, then, would incur the very serious risk, or rather certainty, of a violent flare-up on the part of the Negro press as soon as this matter became known. As it is now, the lid is being kept on with considerable difficulty. The story of what has happened would, if it were made public, be front-page news for the Negro papers.[25]

Despite LaFarge's pleas, the bishops produced nothing of consequence concerning the racial crisis. In late 1943 the bishops issued the pastoral letter called "Essentials of a Good Peace," which called for political equality, better housing, and educational and economic opportunities for African Americans. However, the episcopal document relied almost entirely on soothing platitudes and proposed no specific or realistic programs to achieve its stated goals.[26]

LaFarge, however, wrote several sensible articles and editorials on the housing crisis and the race riots during the war and after. In these essays he explained at length how racism and economic and cultural problems plagued black southern migrants. Always cognizant of the sociological basis of sin, LaFarge resisted the temptation to blame the victim. Describing life in the crowded and expanding black urban enclaves, LaFarge announced that the surprising thing was, not "that so much wickedness exists, but that there is not a vastly greater amount of it."[27]

25. LaFarge to Ready, December 4, 1941; Michael Ready to John LaFarge, December 11, 1941, in box 1, folder 23, JLFP 2.

26. "The Bishop's Statement," *IR*, 16 (November, 1943), 163–64.

27. John LaFarge, "Justice Traces Patterns for Peaceful Neighborhoods," *Am*, 66

Ironically, the growing urban crisis caused the Jesuit to cling all the more to the romantic vision of the Catholic rural life program. He grieved that blacks were becoming the "Number One Proletariat" of America because of their abandonment of the land. He spoke darkly of the wrecking of rural economies and "reckless industrialization." He lamented the termination of the New Deal's Farm Security Administration, which he hoped would help keep blacks on the land.[28] Although LaFarge offered no new approaches to the urban situation, the crisis provided a magnificent opportunity for LaFarge to promote his interracial movement and proclaim anew that the Catholic church alone had the answer to the race problem. He even claimed that the Harlem riot of 1943 had been limited in scope and intensity by the work of the Catholic interracial movement.[29]

In his writing about the wartime domestic crisis, LaFarge tended to shift blame for racial strife away from Catholics. In private he accused Catholic priests and lay leaders of acting dishonorably in the bloody Detroit riot of 1943. He actually discouraged John K. Ryan of Catholic University from rebutting a report that criticized Catholic leadership in the Motor City. "Unfortunately," LaFarge told Ryan, "there is very painful evidence about the Polish clergy." But the closest LaFarge came to indicting Catholics publicly was to ask where Catholic trade unionists were during Detroit's violence. He did not hesitate, however, to villify the "hill-billy type," the "prejudiced, trouble-loving whites" who had migrated to Detroit from the South.[30]

LaFarge, of course, did not divulge to his readers that many blacks in Detroit believed a "Catholic conspiracy" had tried to deny them access to federal housing or that the black Catholic Louis Martin charged in the *Michigan Chronicle* that three Polish priests were "Nazi-

(January 17, 1942), 403–405. See also his "The Nation Can Cure Causes of Race Riots," *Am*, 69 (July 17, 1943), 397–99, and the editorials "The Detroit Race Riots," *Am*, 69 (July 3, 1943), 350, and "Blitz in Harlem," *Am*, 69 (August 14, 1943), 518.

28. LaFarge, "Justice Traces Patterns," 404, "Nation Can Cure Causes of Race Riots," 398, and "The Negro Worker and the Land," *IR*, 15 (November, 1942), 170–72. See also his "Rural Racial Problems," *Land and Home*, 7 (September, 1944), 66–67, and "Fewer Farmers Mean More Rationing," *Am*, 68 (March 6, 1943), 598–99.

29. LaFarge, "Nation Can Cure Causes of Race Riots," 398, "Justice Traces Patterns," 404–405, and "Blitz in Harlem," 518.

30. John LaFarge to John K. Ryan, November 16, 1945, and John N. May to George Hunton, October 3, 1943, both in box 1, folder 23, JLFP 2; "Detroit Race Riots," 350.

minded" and that "Catholics have abused their religion and resorted to measures which become only the Nazi heathen." Nor did LaFarge disclose that Archbishop Edward Mooney of Detroit thought in terms of a segregated church or that in 1941 priests of the Blessed Sacrament Cathedral (at the archbishop's behest) had formed a neighborhood "improvement association" to prevent black encroachment or that Mooney remained silent on the Detroit riot because he feared he might incite the numerous Polish Catholics in the archdiocese. Informing LaFarge that the Poles "by temperament [were] never phlegmatic," the archbishop added, "I must in conscience consider that any declaration of mine which might have a general apologetic value for the Church among Negroes would most certainly have a disastrously disturbing effect on the more than two-hundred thousand Polish Catholics who are part of my direct responsibility." In any case, Mooney believed that "subversive" blacks caused the riot.[31]

As LaFarge's frustrations with the continuing racial strife in Catholic neighborhoods mounted in the postwar period, he began to take a more aggressive stance on the issue of housing. He strongly supported the Supreme Court's 1948 ruling against state enforcement of restrictive covenants, and he energetically promoted integrated federal, state, and private housing projects, so much so that the new assistant to American Jesuits, Vincent A. McCormick, reprimanded LaFarge for allowing *America* to criticize the hierarchy in a 1951 article concerning housing in Cicero, Illinois. Four serious racial outbreaks had occurred in Chicago in the late 1940s, but it was the Cicero race riot of 1951 that gained worldwide attention. Cicero, a Chicago suburb, was heavily populated with Catholics whose ancestors migrated from Eastern Europe. The offending article about the riot, which was written by a lay member of the Catholic Interracial Council of Chicago (CICC), declared that "Catholic leaders, clerical and lay" must "cleanse themselves of either bigoted attitudes or timidity in the face of the challenge to our most cherished principles." The article described how a white mob of 6,000 stormed and virtually destroyed a building into which a black World

31. Martin, quoted in McGreevy, " 'Race' and Twentieth Century American Catholic Culture," 28; Tentler, *Seasons of Grace*, 508, 513; Capeci, *Race Relations in Wartime Detroit*, 85, 89–90, 129, 148, 155; Edward Mooney to John LaFarge, June 15, 1943, in box 1, folder 21, JLFP 1; John LaFarge to John May, August 4, 1943, in box 1, folder 23, JLFP 2.

War II veteran and his family had moved. Highly visible in the enraged mob were people wearing scapulars, Catholic high school sweaters, Knights of Columbus pins, and other such symbols. National guardsmen had to quell the riot, and police arrested 28 people.[32]

LaFarge told McCormick that *America,* above all, did not want to get the reputation of criticizing the hierarchy, and he added that his record as an editor was "unblemished" in this regard. Still, he apologized because the article in *America* did not make it clear that "His Eminence in Chicago" (Cardinal Stritch) was not guilty of bigotry or complacency. Having done his obeisance, however, LaFarge made a passionate defense of the article. He explained to McCormick that Cicero constituted "a national danger" in a "grave cold war." He reminded McCormick that people of color around the world were watching Cicero in anger. "A couple of more Cicero's," he declared, "will set the non-white world in blaze." He also informed his Roman superior that the "hardest accusation that Catholics must face in this country is that Catholics are muzzled" when it comes to abuses in their own church. He argued that all Catholic efforts "to uphold the teaching of the Church would fall like a house of cards if we overlooked the responsibility of Catholics for the scandalous violation of human rights in Cicero." Quoting Cardinal Spellman's condemnation of the riot as "un-American," LaFarge then asserted that Cicero was so crucial an event that it warranted the kind of article that *America* would only dare to print once in a generation.[33]

LaFarge, however, was more tentative on the increasingly pressing issue of segregation. In a 1943 update of *Interracial Justice,* LaFarge added three chapters, "The Negro Migrant in War Time," "Racism, A World Issue," and "Economic Opportunity," and gave his book a new

32. See the editorials "Restrictive Covenants," *Am,* 78 (December 20, 1947), 312, "Restrictive Covenants," *IR,* 21 (June, 1948), 85, and John LaFarge, "Manhasset Valley Houses Itself," *Am,* 80 (February 12, 1949), 514–15, as well as John LaFarge to Vincent A. McCormick, September 25, 1951, in box 20, folder 5, JLFP 1. The contested article was William Gremley, "The Scandal of Cicero," *Am,* 85 (August 25, 1951), 495–97. For an indictment of Cardinal Stritch, several of the clergy, and much of the Chicago laity, see Avella, *This Confident Church,* 249–322; on housing problems and race in one city, see Arnold Hirsch, *The Making of the Second Ghetto: Race and Housing in Chicago, 1940–1960* (New York, 1983), 4–31, 40–42, 106–107, 213–19, 229, 241–45, 253.

33. LaFarge to McCormick, September 25, 1951.

title: *The Race Question and the Negro.* He did not drop his earlier equivocation on segregation, though he acknowledged that the war had made the evil of segregation more visible. As usual, he announced that Jim Crow was "bound to disappear," but he did not insist that the issue be decided soon.[34]

Although LaFarge denounced prudence when used as a cloak for inaction, he constantly warned that there could be no reform before its time. He claimed that God himself set the example by sending his Son in the "fullness of time."[35] Time and again, LaFarge admonished impatient activists that "undue haste" caused more harm than did timidity. Anticipating William Faulkner in the aftermath of *Brown,* LaFarge responded to black militants during the war by writing, "If I were a Negro, I should sit tight, refrain from throwing brass weights at Philadelphia's Liberty Bell, keep a cool brain along with a warm heart, and thank God for the privilege of living at a time when every individual, no matter how high is the wall of prejudice, can do something for the betterment of his race and nation."[36]

Yet, more and more, LaFarge suggested that the end of segregation must come sooner rather than later. The CICNY and the Northeastern Clergy Conference on Negro Welfare condemned segregation in the armed forces early in the war. He admitted to a South Carolinian in 1942 that he had been expedient and wrong in accepting separate churches for blacks while he was in Maryland. "There is little use postponing the issue," he advised. "It must be faced in the end." Continuing exclusion of blacks from most Catholic high schools, colleges, and seminaries, especially those run by Jesuits, increasingly troubled him. Jesuits educated almost half of all Catholic students at the college level, but in 1947 Jesuit schools had only 436 blacks in attendance. Moreover, a mere handful of schools accounted for most of these black students. This number contrasted extremely poorly with the approximately 600

34. LaFarge, *Race Question and the Negro,* 157, 170, 172.

35. John LaFarge, "The Time Is Not Ripe," *IR,* 13 (January, 1940), 9, and "Evolution or Revolution?," *IR,* 18 (December, 1945), 182–85. On LaFarge's lack of focus, see McDonough, *Men Astutely Trained,* 133.

36. John LaFarge, "If I Were a Negro," *Negro Digest,* 2 (October, 1944), 45. One difference between *Interracial Justice* and *The Race Question and the Negro* is that the latter (see p. 254) expressed greater concern about black nationalism. See William Faulkner, "A Letter to the North," *Life,* March 5, 1956, pp. 51–52.

black Catholics who attended the nondenominational Howard University alone. Georgetown University did not accept its first black student, a law student, until 1948.[37]

Nevertheless, a 1948 report written by a priest happily announced that most Catholic colleges were now open to qualified blacks. Although LaFarge found the report "definitely encouraging," the author actually revealed that fewer than half of the Catholic colleges had any black students at all. This kind of interpretation of data exemplifies the tendency of LaFarge and *America* to celebrate tokenism. The outspoken Jesuit Claude H. Heithaus, however, was more demanding. Analyzing an article in *America* trumpeting the news that 17 diocesan seminaries, 52 religious seminaries, and 25 congregations of nuns accepted blacks, Heithaus pointedly noted that the American Catholic church had 47 diocesan seminaries, 285 religious seminaries, and 209 congregations of nuns. What about the majority of Catholic institutions that apparently excluded blacks? he asked.[38]

In 1944 Zacheus Maher, who in effect became the acting general of the American Jesuits on the death of Vladimir Ledochowski in 1942, gave LaFarge the opportunity to discuss the exclusion of blacks from Jesuit institutions when Maher solicited his advice on the question of fighting communism. The exchange with the acting general wonderfully illustrates LaFarge's cautious approach to reform and how he used the anticommunist club to try to move the hierarchy in a liberal direction. In his courtly and calculated fashion, LaFarge began to work on Maher with references to "Our Lady of Fatima." The miracle of Fatima instructed Catholics that the Blessed Virgin Mary appeared before a group of Portuguese children in 1917 and, among other things, warned

37. "The American Scene," *IR*, 13 (June, 1940), 85; "Clergy Conference Resolution," *IR*, 16 (June, 1943); John LaFarge to Francesca MacMurrough, March 12, 1942, in box 7, folder 8, JLFP 2; John LaFarge to William J. Bauer, S.J., in box 6, folder 24, JLFP 2; McDonough, *Men Astutely Trained*, 181; John LaFarge to James H. Dolan, Provincial of Massachusetts, June 7, 1940, in box 12, folder 11, JLFP 1; "Negro Students in Jesuit Schools and Colleges," *IR*, 22 (February, 1949), 24; Reynolds, *Jesuits for the Negro*, 201–204; Dolan, *American Catholic Experience*, 400; John O'Connor, "Washington Reporter," *IR*, 21 (August, 1948), 125; "Underscorings," *Am*, 78 (February 14, 1948), 537.

38. "Father Roche's Thesis," *IR*, 21 (October, 1948), 155–56; John LaFarge, "Race Relations—Their Tensions and Solutions," *Am*, 80 (November 13, 1948), xxix; Claude H. Heithaus, "Does Christ Want This Barrier?," *Am*, 82 (February 11, 1950), 546–47. See also Sanders, *Education of an Urban Minority*, 205–24. Sanders found segregation in Catholic schools in Chicago rampant through World War II, even in elementary schools.

against the Bolshevik Revolution. Utilizing what to many Catholics passed as the first supernatural event of the Cold War, LaFarge advised Maher, "It seems to me that by audacity, not by timidity, our Lady's favor can be won." From this lofty conversation, LaFarge then switched to a more earthly concern, suggesting to his superior that Jesuits in the New York-Maryland province should take a "qualified Negro alumnus" into one of their seminaries. In making his case, LaFarge took great pains to encase his racial advice in an elaborate ethical and supernatural framework (no sociology or history), essentially encouraging Maher to be bold for Mary.[39]

LaFarge assured Maher that by establishing the principle of not refusing a qualified African American "solely upon racial grounds," the Society would make a "tangible" gain with only "a slightly sacrificial example." Maher's inclination, however, was to do little or nothing. He acknowledged the "Catholicity" of the color-blind principle LaFarge espoused, but he argued that the suitability of the candidate depended on what was good for the order, not for the candidate. He reminded LaFarge that a prohibition against Jewish converts in the Jesuits still obtained for the good of the order. He also informed LaFarge that the church did not demand "indiscriminate admission of negroes [*sic*] to the Society in the U.S., for here we are not building up a native colored clergy." Maher said that in the end the admission of an African American depended on whether the teachers, seminarians, and the laity were ready to accept the change and whether it would be *"useful* to the Province."[40]

LaFarge hastily retreated in the face of Maher's legalistic and expedient approach. He said that he had not meant to suggest that Maher make a general rule for the admission of blacks in all American provinces; he was referring only to New York. He conceded that Jesuit principles did not require integration and that the good of a race was of secondary importance to the good of the order. Despite these concessions, LaFarge suggested that "the adoption of a Negro into the Province . . . might be something extremely useful in the battle against

39. McDonough, *Men Astutely Trained,* 161–69, 185–86, 193, esp. 186 for LaFarge quotation. On "Our Lady of Fatima," see Allitt, *Catholic Intellectuals and Conservative Politics,* 28–29.

40. John LaFarge to Zacheus Maher, August 24, 1944, and Zacheus Maher to John LaFarge, August 26, 1944, both in box 1, folder 5, JLFP 1.

Communism." In closing, LaFarge advised that if the Jesuits were to battle communism successfully, they had to be "bold" but "not [so] wildly bold . . . as to send Negroes into the Society in the South, but fairly bold, right here in N.Y."[41]

LaFarge and Maher continued their correspondence through 1944 and 1945. Finally, on May 3, 1945, Maher circulated to the provincials, in dense, scholastic prose, a supercautious statement on the integration of Jesuit schools. LaFarge reviewed the statement, assessing all the advantages—the supernatural, ethical, sociological, and political advantages—that Maher's approach would have for the Jesuits. "The presence of an occasional Negro in our ranks," he told Maher, "is an answer to a very frequent and harmful type of propaganda." With cool calculation, LaFarge weighed the cost of doing nothing (this, too, had costs) against the cost of pressing ahead in a fairly bold manner, taking acceptable risks that were only slightly sacrificial. LaFarge's subtly complex mind thus mapped out a tactically precise and minimal plan of integration that put no great strain on the Jesuits or the church.[42]

When is a Catholic leader expected to engage in truly bold acts of conscience or principle? In the past popes had issued statements that demanded such action. Pope Leo XIII declared in 1890 that "if the laws of the state are manifestly at variance with divine law . . . then truly, to resist becomes a positive duty, to obey, a crime." But what if the church itself perpetuates grave injustices? The same Leo XIII who sanctioned civil disobedience in the name of a higher law also held that the church could tolerate a situation at variance with truth and justice for the sake of the greater church good. In truth, the conflicting doctrines of Catholicism constantly pitted authority against conscience.[43] Given LaFarge's preoccupation with the unifying mission of the church (the very motivation for his interracialism) and his proclivity for faithful obedience, he was not prone to travel down "indelicate trails" that threatened upheaval in the church, even if they had the possibility of dramatic racial breakthroughs.[44]

41. John LaFarge to Zacheus Maher, August 28, 1944, in box 1, folder 5, JLFP 1.

42. Zacheus Maher to American Provincials, May 3, 1945, and John LaFarge to Zacheus Maher, June 3, 1945, both in box 16, folder 23, JLFP 1; McDonough, *Men Astutely Trained*, 189–91, 456.

43. Pope Leo XIII, quoted in Hudson, *Understanding Roman Catholicism*, 98, 102, 104.

44. McDonough, *Men Astutely Trained*, 128. LaFarge's writings are suffused with

However, three young Jesuits, Claude Heithaus, George H. Dunne, and John Markoe, who fervently believed that segregation was discriminatory and therefore sinful, sought decisive change and feared not the corporate or personal consequences. For them the "moral ethos of Catholicism" took precedence over the calculus of prudence and the fuzzy intricacies of doctrinal application to concrete racial situations. They knowingly took the risk of rebellion. In the eyes of Heithaus, Dunne, and Markoe, LaFarge appeared as an overly prudent, "safety first man." [45]

The explosion came at St. Louis University on February 11, 1944, when Heithaus, a professor of archaeology, gave a sermon at a student mass. Heithaus had painfully learned about color prejudice on digs in Syria, where Arabs stoned him because of his pale complexion. Now this imposing six-foot-two-inch priest asked the gathered students why black Christians, even if Catholic, could not attend the university whereas Moslems and Hindus could. After explaining such Catholic teaching as the Mystical Body of Christ, Heithaus asked the students to rise and pledge that they would strive to prevent further injustice to blacks. The entire congregation took the pledge. [46]

Actually, Peter Brooks, the provincial of Missouri, had considered the idea of integrating the university in 1942. Patrick J. Holloran, who became president of the university in 1943, had explored Brooks's suggestion further, but he backed down when he ran up against strong opposition from trustees, staff, and alumni. Archbishop John J. Glennon was also an obstacle, though he had no canonical power over the Jesuits; racist in attitude, Glennon had long opposed integration in his archdiocese. When Holloran retreated before the opposition, Heithaus delivered his powerful sermon, and the media feasted on it. Heithaus received accolades from far and wide, including from LaFarge. Holloran, however, reacted negatively to the sermon and the ensuing pub-

---

the theme of the unifying mission of the church; see his *Interracial Justice*, 82, and *Race Question and the Negro*, 209. See also Stanton, "John LaFarge's Understanding."

45. McDonough, *Men Astutely Trained*, 184; Markoe, "Interracial Role," 140; interview of Heithaus by Nickels; George H. Dunne, S.J., *King's Pawn: The Memoirs of George H. Dunne, S.J.* (Chicago, 1990), 97–98, 130–31.

46. William Barnaby Faherty, S.J., "Breaking the Color Barrier," *Universitas*, 13 (Autumn, 1987), 19. See also Donald J. Kemper, "Catholic Integration of St. Louis, 1935–1947," *Missouri Historical Review*, 73 (October, 1978), 1–22. Heithaus' speech can be found in "A Challenge to Catholic Colleges," *IR*, 17 (March, 1944), 40–42.

licity, silencing Heithaus on the topic of race. Along with John Markoe, Heithaus took his case to the new Missouri provincial, Joseph P. Zuercher. The provincial, though upset with Markoe and Heithaus, encouraged Holloran to integrate the school. In the summer session of 1944, the university admitted five black students.[47]

St. Louis University had taken a historic step. In a city and state bound by legal segregation, a Jesuit university had desegregated a full decade before the *Brown* decision. With the appearance of a few blacks on the campus, however, many people connected with the university warned the president about the threat of social equality and intermarriage. Holloran therefore decided to limit integration strictly to the classroom. Black students would not be allowed to attend the spring prom in 1945. At this point Heithaus broke a full year of church-imposed silence on race relations and wrote a devastatingly sarcastic article in the *University News* called "Why Not Christian Cannibalism?" Heithaus indirectly but unmistakably skewered the university's policy of accommodating racism. The professor's article was reprinted in the *Catholic Digest* and elsewhere. Heithaus further told Holloran that his conscience would not permit him to acquiesce in social segregation of blacks at the university. The Jesuit hierarchy then exiled Heithaus to Fort Riley in Kansas. Before he departed, though, he was subjected to a humiliating public penance, *decitur culpa*, before an audience of university Jesuits. Heithaus stood among the seated Jesuits while a member of the religious community solemnly read the charges of insubordination against him.[48]

Arriving in St. Louis in the middle of the controversy, George Dunne, who had just received his Ph.D. in international relations from the University of Chicago, instinctively supported Heithaus. Dunne had been a missionary in China in the 1930s, and one of his heroes was Matteo Ricci, a brilliant sixteenth-century Jesuit missionary who had greatly influenced the ruling dynasty of China but had been called home and punished by his order for his independence of mind. Although Dunne had a deep and abiding faith, the result, he claimed, of a supernatural experience, his faith did not include automatic obedience to arbitrary superiors. From the beginning of his priesthood, some of

47. Faherty, "Breaking the Color Barrier," 19–20; "St. Louis U. Admits Five Negroes," St. Louis *Globe Democrat*, June 26, 1944; Dunne, *King's Pawn*, 80–82, 87.
48. Faherty, "Breaking the Color Barrier," 20; Dunne, *King's Pawn*, 91–92.

Dunne's superiors saw him as a potential Martin Luther. Dunne clearly held truth and justice above the virtue of prudence, believing that the church was "far more damaged by the suppression of truth than by its frank admission." He even questioned the exclusion of Jewish converts from the Society of Jesus. Dunne also had an inclination toward ecumenism, a tendency furthered by graduate study at the University of Chicago. Because of Dunne's participation in the activities of the National Conference of Christians and Jews and his other ecumenical ventures while in Chicago, Cardinal Mundelein banned him from interfaith discussions. Experiences such as this convinced Dunne that the hierarchy all too readily obstructed the pursuit of truth in the name of expediency.[49]

Like Heithaus, Dunne reacted strongly against the social segregation imposed at the university. He gave speeches and penned several sharp letters of protest to Jesuit officials. The result was that Holloran presented Dunne with a train ticket back to his home province in California. Dunne, however, first traveled to Chicago, where he was scheduled to give a speech. Meanwhile, Wilfrid Parsons, the former editor of *America,* called LaFarge and suggested that he put Dunne on the editorial staff of the Jesuit weekly. LaFarge made a special trip to Chicago to discuss the matter with Dunne (so he told Dunne), but he explained to the exiled priest that it would not be "prudent" to hire him immediately, for such an action would seem to be a slap in the face of authority. "So we will wait until the heat is off," LaFarge promised, "and then bring you to *America.*" Dunne eventually received the call from the magazine but not until 1967, when Thurston Davis was editor and LaFarge was four years dead. As Dunne wryly wrote in his memoirs, after twenty-two years "the heat is off." In truth, the heat was never off a Jesuit such as Dunne. In California he took on a young actor named Ronald Reagan in the labor union wars, and his superiors "sacked" him two more times for his liberal activism. Even the Federal Bureau of Investigation compiled a five-hundred-page file on the outspoken Jesuit.[50]

49. Dunne, *King's Pawn,* 2, 18, 22, 62, 78–79, 250; Joseph Stocker, "Father Dunne: A Study in Faith," *Nation,* September 22, 1951, pp. 236–37; McDonough, *Men Astutely Trained,* 192, 487; Aveling, *The Jesuits,* 180–81.

50. Dunne, *King's Pawn,* 94–95, 97, 161, 166, 215, 233, *passim.* See Garry Wills, *Reagan's America: Innocents at Home* (Garden City, N.Y., 1987), 231, 239–40.

Although LaFarge hailed the desegregation of St. Louis University as another great victory for the Catholic interracial movement, he offered no support for the three exiled Jesuits who made it happen. He never mentioned their silencing or banishment, for he was not disposed to admit that such things occurred in the Catholic church. In hurling "Catholic truth" at Protestant critics, he had earlier written that "there is not, nor ever has been, a gag law in the Catholic Church." LaFarge agreed with Zuercher and Maher that Heithaus' behavior toward institutional authority in St. Louis was "indefensible." He opined that there was a "recognized way of going about these matters" and concluded that the St. Louis rebels lacked "a clear idea of the methods of racial reform." For LaFarge, the politically and religiously correct way for change came in 1945 when Maher gently instructed Jesuit colleges and seminaries to speed up integration, a move the editor described as another "blow to the serious heresy of Racism" and another sharp jab against communism.[51]

Interestingly, both the Missouri provincial and the American assistant of the Jesuits scolded the president of St. Louis University for not acting on Catholic principles, but they also approved the exile of Heithaus and Dunne and later John Markoe. LaFarge plainly showed more sympathy for the authorities than for the embattled priests. The St. Louis affair both disclosed how problematical it was to reconcile the warring imperatives of obedience and conscience and proved to be a harbinger of the coming crisis of the Society of Jesus and Catholicism. Since LaFarge placed paramount importance on institutional order and unity, he tended to see "true and perfect" obedience as the test of character. Heithaus, Dunne, and the Markoe brothers, however, emphasized individual conscience as the real test of their faith, and they downplayed corporate concerns.[52]

After Dunne returned to California, he wrote an incisive article on segregation that was widely circulated in the religious and secular

51. John LaFarge, "With Script and Staff," *Am*, 56 (April 3, 1937), 611; John LaFarge to Zacheus Maher, June 3 and 7, 1945, in box 16, folder 23, JLFP 1.

52. McDonough, *Men Astutely Trained*, 252–53, 256, 400–403, 456, 461; John Deedy, *American Catholicism—And Now Where?* (New York, 1987), 259–60; Jaroslav Pelikan, *The Riddle of Roman Catholicism* (New York, 1959), 86–87. John Markoe was exiled to Omaha, Nebraska. For the impact of Vatican II on the Jesuit Order, see Joseph M. Becker, S.J., *The Re-Formed Jesuits: A History of Changes in Jesuit Formation During the Decade 1965–1975* (San Francisco, 1992).

presses. Called "The Sin of Segregation," it was published in *Commonweal* in September, 1945. Not only did Dunne denounce segregation as a heresy; he also implicated anyone who cooperated with the Jim Crow system. Although LaFarge reprinted a version of the controversial article in *America,* he added a disclaimer cautioning that the essay did not apply in the South, where segregation was law. John Markoe noticed this LaFargian hedge and fired off a letter to the editor, in which he argued that Dunne's article proved Catholics should oppose immoral state laws. He pointed out that many states with segregation laws (Missouri was a case in point) did not constitutionally forbid private schools from desegregating. Markoe maintained that Catholics could no longer hide behind un-Christian laws that demeaned and oppressed blacks.[53]

Interestingly enough, critics of the Catholic church sometimes attributed more boldness to LaFarge than his record warranted. In 1944 Harold Fey, the Protestant editor of *Christian Century,* judged not only that LaFarge was "probably the most influential [person] in shaping the attitudes of the Catholic leadership on the race issue" but also that the Jesuit faced "fearlessly such controversial issues as segregation, intermarriage and equality of economic and educational opportunity."[54]

It is accurate to say, however, that LaFarge engaged in some rather bold and skillful maneuvering that led to his increased editorial influence at *America.* In a temporary reorganization of the weekly in 1940, aimed at increasing declining circulation caused by the Depression, LaFarge assumed more editorial control. He brimmed with ideas about how to make the magazine more attractive—ideas that he relayed to the provincials on the editorial board in detailed memoranda. He argued that *America* should include more material on science, art, literature, and education. He advised the provincials that the staff needed *"two or three men of wide social outlook,* men who [could] see things from the social . . . point of view" and who were free of an exaggerated anti-Roosevelt slant. He complained that *America* did not have a consistent line of thought on the social order. He even suggested that the

53. George H. Dunne, "The Sin of Segregation," *Commonweal,* 42 (September 21, 1945), 542–45, and "Racial Segregation Violates Justice," *Am,* 74 (October 20, 1945), 63–65; John P. Markoe, letter to the editor, *Am,* 74 (November 3, 1945), 139; Dunne, *King's Pawn,* 131. On John Markoe, see Smith, *From Corps to CORE.*

54. Harold E. Fey, "Catholicism and the Negro," *Christian Century,* December 20, 1944, p. 1476. This article was the fourth in a series about American Catholicism.

interprovince organization, whereby one editor was selected from each North American province, needed to be eliminated for the sake of editorial coherency. In short, LaFarge wanted a staff of Jesuits with expertise in social science and an understanding of social problems, young men whom LaFarge could initiate into the social magisterium of the church.[55]

In 1942 the provincial board gave LaFarge editorial primacy over Francis Talbot, the editor-in-chief, and his close associate Paul Blakely. Blakely had been with the magazine for almost three decades and had largely dictated editorial policy under Talbot. A Jeffersonian states' righter from the South, he considered the New Deal a tragic capitulation to statism. On becoming executive editor on July 12, LaFarge promptly began to recruit a staff of liberal, younger Jesuits. Among them were Benjamin L. Masse, Robert A. Graham, Joseph A. Carroll, and Robert C. Hartnett, a Ph.D. in political science who would succeed LaFarge as editor-in-chief. Harold Gardiner and Charles Keenan, already on the staff, quickly fell under the spell of the kindly and easygoing "Uncle John." The recruits remembered LaFarge fondly as a quiet, plain and simple man who democratized the editorial process and gave his staff considerable leeway, restricting them with but one rule: "Avoid mentioning names when writing critically of any kind of problem."[56]

Despite LaFarge's desire to avoid conflict, tension mounted at *America* through 1942 and 1943. The provincials had executed a "self-contradictory act of maladministration" by putting LaFarge in charge but retaining Talbot as editor-in-chief. Although Blakely died in February, 1943, Talbot still refused to bow to LaFarge. LaFarge routed detailed complaints to the provincials and the Jesuit American Assistant Maher about the indecisive chain of command. He argued that the ideo-

55. "Temporary Reorganization of *America*, July till December 1940," in box 7, folder 37, JLFP 2; minutes of the advisory board, March 7, 1940, in box 7, folder 39, JLFP 2; John LaFarge, "*America* Notes," February, 1940, in box 7, folder 48, JLFP 2; "Breakdown of *America* According to States," in box 7, folder 38, JLFP 2; "Memorandum on the Condition of *America*, for the Rev. Fathers Provincial at their Annual Meeting, 1941," in box 6, folder 5, JLFP 1; Halsey, *Survival of American Innocence*, 37; David O'Brien, *Public Catholicism*, 199.

56. "Who's Who," *Am*, 67 (July 11, 1942), 365; interview of Hartnett, by Stanton, December 1, 1980, and March 18, 1981; Robert A. Graham, S.J., to Edward Stanton, October 13, 1981, in box 1, folder 1, Stanton Papers.

logical cleavage on the staff had to be ended. He informed his Jesuit superiors that six of the staff supported him and that Talbot stood alone, growing "more fixed and more militant." The problem came to a head at an editorial meeting in January of 1944 when Talbot refused to run a liberal article by Father Masse. In one of his few outright rebellions, LaFarge brusquely withdrew from the meeting. In his annual report on May 3, 1944, Talbot described the conflict and confusion at *America* and offered to resign. Within two months LaFarge became editor-in-chief. In his autobiography LaFarge revealed nothing of the conflict at *America.* He simply wrote that Talbot "wished to devote himself to promotional work for the magazine." Conciliatory as always, LaFarge made glowing comments in *America* about both Blakely and Talbot on their departures.[57]

From 1944 to 1949 LaFarge put his stamp on the Jesuit magazine. He steered *America,* in his words, toward "a reasoned approach to issues of the day on a soundly liberal platform, in the light of reason enlightened by faith." LaFarge attempted to reach out beyond the Catholic audience and mold American leadership, on which, he argued, the fate of the entire world depended. But progressive Catholics, LaFarge discovered, were often branded as secular-minded radicals by ordinary Catholics and as conservatives by secular liberals. LaFarge bristled when Freda Kirchwey, editor of the *Nation,* described *America* as "highly conservative." He pointed out to her that "conservative" was not the "epithet" that most Catholics applied to the magazine. To those who saw only the option of socialistic statism or laissez-faire capitalism, the hybrid, organic social order advocated by LaFarge was puzzling. Pure capitalists became upset, LaFarge observed, "when they found that God had something to say about the marketplace."[58]

57. Interview of Hartnett by Stanton, December 1, 1980; John LaFarge, "Paul Lendrum Blakely," *Am,* 68 (March 13, 1943), 621–23; John LaFarge, "Notes on *America's* Policy," in box 1, folder 3, JLFP 1; John LaFarge to Zacheus Maher, July 30, 1943, in box 1, folder 5, JLFP 1; minutes of board meeting, January 25, 1944, in box 1, folder 6, JLFP 1; Francis Talbot, "*America,* Annual Report For the Year 1943," May 3, 1944, in box 1, folder 6, JLFP 1; *MIO,* 294–95; LaFarge, "Paul Lendrum Blakely," 621–23; LaFarge, editorial on Talbot, *Am,* 71 (July 22, 1944), 405.

58. Minutes, editorial-business meeting, October 25, 1946, in box 1, folder 6, JLFP 1; "What We Aim at in *America,*" *Am,* 79 (September 11, 1948), 508; David O'Brien, *Public Catholicism,* 223; John LaFarge to Freda Kirchwey, April 25, 1945, in box 1, folder 7, JLFP 1; *MIO,* 307.

Both *Time* and *Newsweek* noted LaFarge's ascent at *America* and spoke of the growing influence of the Jesuit magazine, but LaFarge's hope of gaining significant influence outside the Catholic community was a chimera. The *Ordinatio* under which *America* operated forbade the journal's being politically partisan. Consistent support of New Deal liberalism or globalistic foreign policy opened the magazine to the charge of favoring the Democratic party and its leaders Roosevelt and Truman. Although the death of Roosevelt, who was roundly disliked by much of the Catholic hierarchy, helped smooth *America*'s path to the left, the magazine's support of most of Truman's domestic and foreign policies soon raised the same old questions about partisanship. The strenuous balancing act dictated to *America*, along with the editors' self-confessed propensity to introduce religion "too readily to furnish an easy and universal solution to the problem under discussion," gave the editorials and articles in *America* an abstract and didactic flavor that rendered the magazine, like much of the intellectual world of American Catholicism, too "dull, drab, and defensive" to attract a significant non-Catholic following.[59]

Nevertheless, LaFarge could report to the Jesuit curia in 1947 that "*America* has become a sort of braintrust for Church policy on so many matters." Only a few months prior to this boast, Pope Pius XII sent a personal letter of commendation to LaFarge blessing his "noble apostolic mission" and citing the priest for his fruitful struggle against "State Absolutism," "racial injustices," and "economic selfishness." At the end of LaFarge's tenure as chief editor, President Truman congratulated *America* for setting an "example of fearlessness in defending the basic rights of American citizens, without distinction of race, color, or creed."[60]

Age and poor health, however, forced LaFarge to give up his position as editor-in-chief in December of 1948 in favor of Father Hart-

59. "Religion," *Time*, July 27, 1942, pp. 47–48; "LaFarge of America," *Newsweek*, July 24, 1944, pp. 87–88; John LaFarge to James P. Sweeney, provincial of Maryland-New York, May 6, 1945, in box 1, folder 5, JLFP 1; interview of Hartnett by Stanton, March 18, 1981; John LaFarge, "Century of Jesuit Journalism," *Am*, 81 (April 16, 1949), 67; "Report on 'Comments' Submitted by Mears and Masse," n.d., in box 7, folder 40, JLFP 2.

60. John LaFarge to Vincent A. McCormick, February 2, 1947, in box 1, folder 8, JLFP 1; Pope Pius XII to John LaFarge, May 13, 1946, in box 1, folder 7, JLFP 1. President Truman's letter of congratulation is reprinted in *Am*, 81 (April 16, 1949), 31.

nett. Between 1945 and 1948 LaFarge underwent surgery three times and spent at least ten months in convalescence. The exact nature of his medical problem is unclear, though he may have had complications from a botched hernia repair. In his final operation at St. Luke's Hospital, his new doctor, William MacFee, in LaFarge's words, "put in order whatever needed to be tightened up and screwed together from previous operations." On his retirement as editor-in-chief, his editorial associates made this announcement: "There was a day, they say, when '*America* meant [Richard Henry] Tierney—and Blakely.' Today and to us it means 'LaFarge.' "[61]

LaFarge's position at *America* during the 1940s gave more resonance to the Catholic interracial movement. Under LaFarge the Jesuit weekly steadily increased its coverage of race relations. In 1943 the thirty-three articles on race surpassed those on labor, the traditional focus of Catholic social action. The momentum was such that after LaFarge stepped down, the number of editorials and articles on black-white relations actually increased for a time.[62] Moreover, the new column called "Washington Front," written by former editor-in-chief Wilfrid Parsons, had more bite than anything LaFarge ever penned. John J. O'Connor's "Washington Reporter" column also added an astringent and self-critical voice. When Charles Keenan penned something about race, people took notice. His war-related article called "Jim Crow Kills White Men" drew attention from many quarters. The essay, which dealt with the refusal of the army blood bank to administer "black blood" to whites, caused the opinionated Jesuit John Markoe to comment that it was the first time he had read anything in *America* about blacks that had not been "toned down" to near sterility.[63]

LaFarge, however, continued to equivocate on the issue of segregation well into the 1950s. Father Dunne conceded that LaFarge's "quiet collaboration" and "discreet conversation" created a certain

61. *MIO*, 310; John LaFarge to Erich C. Stein, December 19, 1948, in box 14, folder 41, JLFP 2; Kittler, "The Manner Is Extraordinary," in *Wings of Eagles*, 183; "Father LaFarge," *Am*, 81 (April 16, 1949), 50. Tierney was the first editor-in-chief of *America* and served in that post from 1909 to 1925.

62. John LaFarge, "Report of Executive for the Year 1943," in box 1, folder 6, JLFP 1. See the index heading "Race Prejudice," *Am*, 82 (1949–1950), xii–xiii, which listed thirty-seven references.

63. Charles Keenan, "Jim Crow Kills White Men," *Am*, 72 (January 27, 1945), 327–28; John P. Markoe, S.J., letter to the editor, *Am*, 72 (February 10, 1945), 379.

amount of racial good will, but he doubted that LaFarge's movement
threatened American apartheid. At times LaFarge seemed on the verge
of a blanket indictment of segregation, but he always qualified his
stance. In *Survey Graphic*'s special edition on segregation in 1947,
LaFarge indulged his penchant for Ockham-like argument when discussing the types of segregation and their varying legitimacy, as he had
a decade earlier in *Interracial Justice* (see Chapter 8). He admitted that
segregation "as a Church policy . . . had had a vigorous life in the past,"
and he further noted it was preordained that the Catholic Church
"move slowly." As late as 1953 he argued that it was "practically impossible to isolate the moral aspect of segregation."[64] LaFarge's equivocation on segregation was analogous to the church's earlier position
on slavery. That so many Catholic institutions remained segregated in
both the North and the South undoubtedly influenced his cautious
stand. All-out opposition to segregation might stir up internal Catholic
strife and damage the image of the church.

LaFarge therefore picked his targets carefully and largely worked
behind the scenes.[65] For example, he publicly supported the integration
of the armed forces, the National Theater in Washington, D.C., and the
American Medical Association.[66] For the most part, however, he reported on desegregation of Catholic institutions after the fact, as in the
case of St. Louis University. LaFarge applauded when Catholic segregation ended, but he shunned forceful demands that state and federal
governments prohibit Jim Crow. As Martin Marty put it, some religious
leaders were more interested in "making unjust acts unthinkable than
in merely making them illegal."[67]

64. Dunne, *King's Pawn*, 98; "Racial Injustice Weakens Influence of U.S.," *IR*, 18
(March, 1945), 47; "The Roman Catholic Experience," *Survey Graphic*, 36 (January,
1947), 61–62, 106; John LaFarge to John Ziegler, October 29, 1953, in box 8, folder 2,
JLFP 1.

65. See, for example, John LaFarge to David Nugent, Maryland provincial, July 11,
1947, in box 12, folder 11, JLFP 1; John LaFarge to Lawrence Williams, NAACP Legal
Defense and Education Fund, September 21, 1948, in box 6, folder 30, JLFP 2; John
LaFarge to Vi Eleanor Butler, April 7, 1949, in box 23, folder 1, JLFP 1.

66. See the editorials "Segregation and Equality," *Am*, 75 (June 15, 1946), 208, "Equity and Justice," *Am*, 77 (August 23, 1947), 568, and "Doctors and the Color Line," *Am*,
79 (July 10, 1948), 323; John LaFarge to Julius Rosenwald Fund, September 17, 1946, in
box 14, folder 10, JLFP 2.

67. "Color and Catholics," *Am*, 78 (October 4, 1947), 6–7; "1947—Progress and

LaFarge's certainty that segregation was doomed deprived him of any sense of urgency about the issue. Confident about the outcome of the American dilemma, he focused on the race issue as a unique opportunity for the Catholic church to lead America down the road of social unity. As I noted previously, his optimism about race relations rested in large part on his analysis that racism was primarily a product of ignorance. In 1947, however, Joseph H. Fichter, a Jesuit sociologist and founder of the Committee on Human Relations in New Orleans, challenged this view. Fichter, who earned a Ph.D. at Harvard (where he eventually returned to teach), had several books banned by his religious superiors in the 1950s. His vast research on the South led him to argue that southern prejudice was based not "so much on ignorance as on a deep, conscious and deliberate dogma that all Negroes are inferior." He maintained that most white southerners willfully disregarded all objective evidence to the contrary. Thus, Fichter counseled, some prejudice took more than education to eliminate. He did not give the specifics of what was needed beyond education, but the next decade would prove that only massive federal force could overcome southern resistance to legal equality for blacks.[68]

LaFarge, however, clung to his complacent optimism about the demise of segregation and racism. Because of this attitude, he displayed considerable naïveté about the white South. As editor of *America* and watchdog of the *Interracial Review,* he rejected articles that sharply criticized the region below the Potomac. His writings were replete with sympathy for the plight of white southerners (in their ignorance, he claimed, they somehow suffered more than blacks).[69] LaFarge ran countless editorials and articles that hailed the "New South" and trumpeted the "crumbling walls in Dixie." *America's* reporting emphasized the failures of the reactionary obstructionists and the victories of south-

---

the Task Ahead," *IR*, 21 (January, 1948), 3; Dolan, *American Catholic Experience,* 368; Marty, *Invitation to American Catholic History,* 149.

68. "Opportunity and a Catholic Opportunity," *Am*, 77 (July 5, 1947), 367; Stanton, "John LaFarge's Understanding," 233; LaFarge, *Race Question and the Negro,* 290; Joseph H. Fichter, S.J., *One-Man Research: Reminiscences of a Catholic Sociologist* (New York, 1973), 1–3, 7, 23, 29, *passim,* and "The Meaning of Prejudice," *IR*, 20 (January, 1947), 6–7.

69. John LaFarge to Sidey J. Gilly, March 28, 1950, in box 16, folder 5, JLFP 1; John LaFarge to George Hunton, July 27, 1950, in letter box 29, CICNYP.

ern liberals, though there were many of the former and few of the latter. He frequently predicted that the South would take the lead in racial reform, if only to combat communism. *America* blasted the third-party, integrationist candidate Henry Wallace, whose candidacy LaFarge felt was engineered by the American Communist party, for "intrusive meddling" into southern racial affairs. The Jesuit magazine maintained that opposition to the Truman committee's civil rights report was "more a political stunt" than a true representation of southern white feelings. All told, LaFarge had too much faith that the South could cure itself of racism. He placed his hope for racial reform on Jim Crow liberals (or southern moderates), who trusted in what Morton Sosna has dubbed the "Silent South." This concept entailed a belief that a silent majority of good-willed white southerners existed and that it would eventually act and secure justice for black southerners, provided it was not badgered by outsiders. LaFarge thus pleaded for patience and co-operation with the South, lest the Silent South be undermined.[70] Since LaFarge had experienced the ineffectiveness of sweet reason on Catholics in Detroit, Buffalo, and Cicero, one must ask why he thought that moral or rational talk would sway the white South.[71]

To be sure, LaFarge's proclivity for compromise proved embarrassing on the issue of interracial marriage. The dictatorial Bishop McIntyre had once falsely accused LaFarge of promoting interracial marriage. Bishops and priests frequently refused to sanction interracial councils because they feared they would be charged with fostering social equality. LaFarge received more crank letters on this issue than on any other.[72] Not surprisingly, therefore, LaFarge hedged on the delicate topic of interracial marriage. Although he taught that church law put

70. Some examples are: LaFarge, *Race Question and the Negro*, 5–6; "Comment on the Week," *Am*, 70 (March 11, 1944), 617–18; John LaFarge to Lillian Smith, December 6, 1949, in box 14, folder 40, JLFP 2; "New South Emerging," *Am*, 76 (October 5, 1946), 8; "Dixie Not Looking Away," *Am*, 79 (April 24, 1948), 41–42; "Gentleman's Agreement," *Am*, 79 (May 1, 1948), 72; "States Rights," *Am*, 79 (August 14, 1948), 424; "Crumbling Walls in Dixie," *Am*, 85 (July 28, 1951), 411; "Catholic Negro Sculptor and the N.C.W.C. Honored," *IR*, 18 (November, 1945), 176. On Smith and Waring, see Southern, *Gunnar Myrdal and Black-White Relations*, 84, 139–40, 161–63, and Sosna, *In Search of the Silent South*.

71. Czuchlewski, "Liberal Catholicism and American Racism," 151.

72. See, for example, Alan T. Nolan to George Hunton, May 29, 1952, in box 5, CICNYP, and Albert F. Holder to John LaFarge, November 23, 1958, in box 4, folder 22, JLFP 1.

no impediments in the way of interracial marriage, he nevertheless discovered several prominent reasons for discouraging it, such as class and culture. He constantly tried to sell racial reform as something that would lead to fewer rather than more interracial unions, and he often couched his opposition to miscegenation in elaborate expressions of concern for the children of interracial unions. Some blacks scoffed at this concern, asking why antimiscegenationists seemed so distressed by the suffering of mixed-race children when they worried so little about the problematical fate of full-blooded African-American children.[73]

LaFarge was not the first or last influential liberal, black or white, who tried to dance around the issue of interracial marriage. The Jesuit William Markoe, however, refused to dodge the issue. Exiled by his superiors from St. Louis in 1939, Markoe ended up in Denver, where he soon exasperated a new set of superiors. After a 1946 meeting in St. Louis on race relations, held under the auspices of the Jesuit Institute of Social Order, Markoe decried the ignorance and evasiveness of his fellow priests (including LaFarge) on the issue of interracial marriage. He voiced his feelings in an essay published (though in greatly edited form) in the *I.S.O. Bulletin* in early 1947. In his indomitable style, he implored Jesuits to "get rid of our childish, emotional, and irrational thinking and feeling on the subject" and repair to the "solid ground of scientific fact and faith," on which he proceeded to expatiate at length. He ended his article by saying that nothing would please him more than to discover that he had some "Negro blood" in his veins.[74]

Markoe's article drew a venomous reply from Eugene T. Bannin, a Jesuit high school teacher in New Orleans. Bannin charged Markoe, among other things, with encouraging miscegenation. He opined that "misguided zealots" like Markoe would cause "Negro blood to run in the streets of our cities." Markoe's reply was equally caustic, but the

---

73. LaFarge, *Interracial Justice*, 146–48; "Doing the Truth," *Chronicle*, 5 (April, 1932), 72–73; John LaFarge to students, *Pascal Lamp*, April 28, 1960, copy in box 2, folder 6, JLFP 1; Mac Giolla Patrick, "My Sister's Boy Friend," *Am*, 84 (February 3, 1951), 522.

74. For the influence of LaFarge's views, see the popular textbook of Murray and Flynn, *Social Problems*, 145–47; William M. Markoe, "Miscegenation and Jesuit Thinking," *I.S.O. Bulletin*, January, 1947, pp. 2–3, copy in Jesuit Missouri Province Archives, St. Louis. At a conference of the NCWC on social and economic issues in 1946, LaFarge opposed Frederick McTerman, a New Jersey priest who wanted to condemn antimiscegenation laws.

editor refused to print his rejoinder. Markoe then began to circulate privately a set of letters about interracial marriage to other Jesuits, calling them "Enlightening Documents and Correspondence for Those of Ours." Several Jesuits, such as Heithaus, Dunne, Parsons, and William's brother John, indicated support for Markoe's views. The letters essentially held that the question of miscegenation was at the heart of the race problem. Markoe maintained that until Catholics ended their opposition to interracial marriage on the grounds of "tainted blood," no resolution to the race problem was possible. He argued that the widespread white belief in inferior black genes negatively affected all aspects of black-white relations. "It is time to explode the bomb of Catholic truth," Markoe exclaimed, "and let the chips fall where they may."[75]

George Dunne, exiled back to his home province of California, took up the topic of mixed marriage with his college friend Dan Marshall. A young Catholic lawyer who started an interracial council in Los Angeles during World War II, Marshall had liberal views that coincided with those of Dunne and Markoe. Marshall therefore decided to contest the California law against interracial marriage. He argued the case of *Perez* v. *Sharpe* in 1948—a case that involved a Catholic couple, a Hispanic woman and a black man, who wanted to marry. Marshall won the case before the California Supreme Court and struck a strategic blow against similar laws in twenty-eight other states. By a four-to-three vote, the court invalidated California's antimiscegenation law on the basis of the constitutional right to freedom of religion (that is, a Catholic marriage is a sacrament). Marshall, a devotee of Father LaFarge, was aghast to find that the minority opinion quoted five paragraphs from LaFarge's *The Race Question and the Negro.* The opinion listed several of the "grave reasons" LaFarge had given for discouraging interracial unions. This case, Dunne charged, showed how LaFarge's equivocation could cause Catholic embarrassment and provide "grist for the racists' mill!" In *The Catholic Viewpoint on Race Relations,* published in 1956, LaFarge included an appendix on "Interracial Marriage" that lauded the *Perez* case, but he never acknowledged the use of his work by the antimiscegenationists.[76]

75. Eugene T. Bannin, S.J., "In Defense of Bald Heads," *I.S.O. Bulletin,* March, 1947, p. 28, copy in Jesuit Missouri Province Archives, St. Louis; Markoe, "Interracial Role," 458–60, 464; "Interracial Papers," in box 3, Markoe Papers; George H. Dunne to the author, October 31, 1986.

76. *Perez* v. *Sharpe,* 32 C 2nd, 711, 759; Dunne, *King's Pawn,* 98; Dunne to the

If one looks for evidence of liberal enlightenment in LaFarge outside the racial question, there is scant evidence of it. The Jesuit, for example, faithfully voiced the precepts on women found in the great social encyclicals of Leo XIII and Pius XI. According to LaFarge, Catholic teaching meant that "mothers will above all devote their work to the home and the things connected with it." As editor of *America*, he worried noticeably about adhering to the rule that forbade women to speak on moral issues. He was particularly unhappy with the work of a female movie critic who worked as a substitute writer because of the wartime manpower shortage. As "Rosie the Riveter" and her kind went into forced retirement at the end of the war, LaFarge rejoiced that *America* once again had "all masculine features." Under LaFarge's editorship, *America* ridiculed the proposed Equal Rights Amendment for women.[77]

Sensitivity to the rights of Japanese-Americans at *America* was keener than that for American women. Even here, *America* at first defended the "relocation" of Japanese-Americans as a military necessity and published defenses of it during the first half of the war. To its credit, by early 1944 *America* began to talk about the "dogma of love of enemy." In 1944 the magazine called the *Korematsu* opinion, the Supreme Court's validation of the camps, another *Dred Scott* decision. By war's end the Jesuit magazine was damning the relocation of American citizens as a shameful disgrace.[78]

LaFarge had little regard, however, for the rights of native communists and fellow-travelers. As the Cold War developed in the late 1940s, he wielded the anticommunist club more than ever. He also con-

author, October 31, 1986; LaFarge, *The Catholic Viewpoint*, 125, 175–80. For critical commentary on LaFarge's view of interracial marriage by a Catholic priest, see Joseph F. Doherty, *Moral Problems of Interracial Marriage* (Washington, D.C., 1949), 35–37, 46–49, 60–155.

77. Gordon Zahn, "Social Movements and Catholic Social Thought," in *One Hundred Years of Catholic Social Thought*, ed. Coleman, 45, 57–48; LaFarge, *No Postponement*, 105; board meeting minutes of *America*, January 18, 1944, and monthly notes on *America*, January, 1946, both in box 1, folder 6, JLFP 1; "Equal Rights Again," *Am*, 72 (March 3, 1945), 431.

78. "The West Coast Japanese," *Am*, 67 (October 3, 1942), 715; Yoichi Matsuda, "Nesei and Issei Find That This Is America," 232–34, and "Return of the Nesei," 240, both in *Am*, 69 (June 5, 1943); "Beyond Atrocities," *Am*, 70 (February 12, 1944), 519–20; Charles Keenan, "Korematsu Vs. the United States," *Am*, 72 (February 3, 1945), 348–49; "The Nesei Decision," *Am*, 74 (October 20, 1945), 70.

tinued his belligerent defense of the Franco regime in Spain.[79] During the early Cold War years, American Catholics found fewer obstacles to their entry into mainstream culture. The conspicuous role of Catholics in the postwar anticommunist crusade greatly facilitated their full acceptance into American society. But now, in a kind of "inverted nativism," assimilated Catholics branded leftists as alien enemies and called them "un-American."[80] After the war LaFarge supported witch-hunting congressional committees and notorious anticommunist legislation. Under LaFarge's leadership, neither *America* nor the *Interracial Review* had any qualms about denying free speech and assembly to the dwindling number of American communists.[81] Although LaFarge never supported Senator Joseph McCarthy in the 1950s, neither did he take a public stand against him. Nor did he hesitate to announce his stand in favor of atmospheric nuclear testing as a Cold War necessity.[82]

LaFarge also continued to express his sullen distaste for secular blacks on the left. He kept files on the activities of such African Americans as Du Bois, Richard Wright, Langston Hughes, and Paul Robeson. He blamed Robeson and the communists for the famous Peekskill riot of 1949, angrily indicting them for deliberately capitalizing on the "inability of American democracy to guarantee free speech and free assembly, especially where Negroes are involved."[83]

79. "Communism and Interracial Justice," *IR*, 18 (June, 1945), 83–84; "Showdown on Civil Rights," *Am*, 78 (December 20, 1947), 315. On Spain, see *MIO*, 305; LaFarge, letter to New York *Times*, April 5, 1946; "The Powers and Spain," *Am*, 74 (March 16, 1946), 615; John LaFarge to James J. Sullivan, March 1, 1946, in box 12, folder 1, JLFP 1; John LaFarge to Carleton J. H. Hayes, March 16, 1946, in box 16, folder 2, JLFP 1.

80. David O'Brien, *Public Catholicism*, 197; Dolan, *American Catholic Experience*, 385–86; Wills, *Bare Ruined Choirs*, 233–34. On inverted nativism, see David H. Bennett, *The Party of Fear: From Nativist Movements to the New Right in American History* (Chapel Hill, N.C., 1988), 259, 288.

81. "Mundt Bill Against Communists," *Am*, 79 (May 15, 1948), 128; "Communists and Free Speech," *Am*, 82 (November 5, 1949), 120; "The Unity of All People," *IR*, 20 (July, 1947), 99–100; "The Battle for the Streets," *Am*, 81 (September 17, 1949), 630. The Jesuits savaged Henry Wallace in "Mr. Wallace's Speech," *Am*, 75 (September 28, 1946), 630; see also "The Negroes and Henry Wallace," *Am*, 79 (July 17, 1948), 338, and "Quill on Wallace Candidacy," *Am*, 79 (September 25, 1948), 555.

82. "30 Citizens Support U.S. Nuclear Tests," New York *Times*, June 12, 1958.

83. John LaFarge to Vincent P. Haas, bishop of Grand Rapids, Michigan, March 1,

On the whole, LaFarge advanced slowly along the road to ecumenism, as he continued to display "streaks of intolerance" toward
Protestants and Jews. It seems that he took literally the teaching of the
Vatican, which still defined ecumenism as submission to Christ's vicar
in Rome. Thus the editor of *America* cast sour sidelong glances at Protestants who set up a provisional World Council of Churches in Europe
in 1946. LaFarge continually worried about Catholics "being exposed
to heresy" and about the threat of "religious indifference" and "scandal." Because the wartime Springfield (Massachusetts) Plan included
interfaith church visits for the purpose of breaking down religious and
cultural differences among students in elementary and secondary
schools, LaFarge condemned it as heretical. He advised the black sociologist Charles S. Johnson that it would be "intrinsically wrong" for
a Catholic to sing in the Fisk University Choir.[84] He glibly blamed
world discord and racism on Protestantism and regularly fired broad-
sides at the public school system. He depicted converts from Catholicism to Protestantism or Judaism as rebels against God, but those who
converted in the other direction were noble souls with sublime motivation.[85] He automatically dismissed all probing critiques of Catholicism, whether by Harold Fey, Paul Blanshard, or others, and lumped

---

1948, in box 6, folder 30, JLFP 2. See clippings in box 5, folder 25, and box 6, folder 25,
JLFP 2, and "The Battle for the Streets," 630. See also "Robeson's Role at Peekskill,"
Am, 81 (September 17, 1949), 625, and "Reflections on Peekskill," *Am*, 81 (September
24, 1949), 654.

84. Cross, *Emergence of Liberal Catholicism*, 221; Samuel McCrea Cavert, *The
American Churches in the Ecumenical Movement, 1900–1968* (New York, 1968), 235,
271; Deedy, *American Catholicism*, 49; Marty, *The Noise of Conflict*, 150–51; Benny
Kraut, "A Wary Collaboration," in *Between the Times*, ed. William Hutchinson, 219–21;
"World Protestantism," *Am*, 74 (March, 9, 1946), 595; *MIO*, 322; "Speech at Madison
Square Garden," June 16, 1942, in box 42, folder 2, JLFP 1; "Some Questions as to
Interdenominational Co-operation," *Theological Studies*," 3 (September, 1942), 315–32;
John LaFarge to Mrs. W. L. Duffy, National Conference of Christians and Jews, May
20, 1941, in box 6, folder 8, JLFP 2; John LaFarge to Charles S. Johnson, November 17,
1948, in box 16, folder 7, JLFP 1.

85. LaFarge, *Race Question and the Negro*, 228; John LaFarge, letter to New York
Times, February 10, 1947. LaFarge's attitude on Jews softened in the 1940s; see his "Anti-
Semitism," *Catholic Mind*, 42 (June, 1944), 356–59. He was, however, defensive on the
meaning of "perfidious Jews" in Catholic prayer; see his letter to New York *Times*,
September 30, 1948. On public schools, see "Public School System," *Am*, 74 (March 16,
1946), 614, and " 'Public Schools' Only," *Am*, 75 (June 1, 1946), 175.

them together as part and parcel of the "new bigotry" against the Roman church. By the postwar period, however, he had upgraded Protestant America from a "pagan" to a "semi-pagan" country.[86]

LaFarge, then, was not exactly the fearless pioneer of ecumenism that some hagiographers have made him. That honor goes to such Catholic lay persons as John J. O'Connor and Anna McGarry and to such Jesuits as John Cooper, Gustave Weigel, and John Courtney Murray, all of whom denounced Protestant bashing and conceded the legitimacy of some of the questions posed by Catholic critics. LaFarge simply followed the letter of canon law too faithfully to break out in front ecumenically. He admitted to Jacques Maritain in 1945 that Catholic defensiveness had allowed the ecumenical movement to pass into Protestant hands.[87]

As concern about racial matters grew in the 1940s, LaFarge hoped to increase the number of Catholic interracial councils substantially; but despite the addition of a few important councils during the war, growth was slow. As the decade drew to a close, LaFarge bemoaned the fact that only eight new organizations had been founded. He speculated that the number should be closer to a hundred. The new councils were located in Brooklyn, Washington, D.C., Baltimore, Philadelphia, Detroit, Chicago, Kansas City, and New Orleans. Often there was a struggle before the local bishop approved an interracial council, and when he did, he seldom gave the council any real support. In Philadelphia the interracial council came about mainly because of the persistence of Anna McGarry, who had been instrumental in the formation of the Catholic Intercollegiate Interracial Council in 1937. She and a handful of black and white activists had not been able to get approval for an off-campus council from Cardinal Dennis Dougherty until 1945.

---

86. Harold E. Fey, "Can Catholicism Win America?," *Christian Century,* 61 (November 29, 1944), 1378–80, "Catholicism Comes to Middletown," *ibid.* (December 6, 1944), 1409–11, "Catholicism and the Press," *ibid.* (December 13, 1944), 1442–44, and "The Center of Catholic Power," *ibid.* (January 17, 1945), 74–76; Paul Blanshard, *American Freedom and Catholic Power* (Boston, 1950), 290–93. A series of articles published in the *Nation* in 1948 was the basis for Blanshard's book. For more tolerant, post–Vatican II references to Blanshard, see David O'Brien, *Public Catholicism,* 205–206; Reher, *Catholic Intellectual Life,* 126–27; and Cogley, *Catholic America,* 186, 188.

87. Fogarty, *Vatican and the American Hierarchy,* 347, 349–50, 368, 377, 380–82; McDonough, *Men Astutely Trained,* 400–403; Reher, *Catholic Intellectual Life,* 126–27; Reynolds, *Jesuits for the Negro,* 188–90; John LaFarge to Jacques Maritain, March 15, 1945, in box 6, folder 9, JLFP 2; Zielinski, " 'Doing the Truth,' " 262.

From the formation of the council until his death in 1951, Dougherty had no contact with the organization. The ecumenically minded McGarry found she accomplished more working on the staff of the FEPC or as an official of the Philadelphia Commission on Human Rights than by struggling with the Catholic hierarchy. Archbishop John O'Hara, who succeeded Dougherty, was highly hostile to the idea of an interracial council, and the Philadelphia council ceased to exist in 1960. The experience of the Philadelphia council exemplified the problems that the local interracial movement had. When asked for his advice on the Philadelphia situation, LaFarge gave his standard reply: nothing could be done about race relations in any diocese without hierarchical approval.[88]

LaFarge, however, carefully courted those few in the hierarchy who showed signs of racial liberalism. He went out of his way to flatter newly appointed bishops and inform them about the interracial movement. When Patrick A. O'Boyle was appointed to the See of Washington, D.C., in 1947, LaFarge wrote the new archbishop and discussed his special interest and expertise on the counties in southern Maryland, which had recently come under the jurisdiction of the archdiocese of Washington, D.C. He developed a close relationship with O'Boyle, who would soon be numbered among the most racially liberal of the American bishops. LaFarge, with a keen eye to the future of the interracial apostolate, always "touched base" with Catholics who tended toward liberal views.[89]

LaFarge had no choice but to pay close attention to Francis Spellman, the archbishop who headed the See of New York from 1939 to 1967. This powerful prelate had close ties to Pope Pius XII, who made Spellman a cardinal in 1946. In his lust for power Spellman played an adroit game of self-aggrandizement, using people as they often used him and even trying to discredit competing Catholic icons such as Bishop Sheen. During the Cold War he insisted on war "to the hilt" with the Soviets, and he worked closely with the Central Intelligence

88. John LaFarge, "A Call for Catholic Interracial Councils," *IR*, 21 (December, 1948), 183; Raymond H. Schmandt, "The Catholic Interracial Council of Philadelphia" (paper presented at the annual meeting of the American Catholic Association, Villanova University, April 13–15, 1984); Zielinski, " 'Doing the Truth,' " 126–35.

89. John LaFarge to Archbishop Patrick O'Boyle, December 12, 1947, and see also LaFarge to Francis J. Haas, Bishop-elect of Grand Rapids, Michigan, October 22, 1943, both in box 2, folder 15, JLFP 1; interview of Msgr. Higgins by the author.

Agency (CIA) and the FBI to fight communist subversion. He provided refuge in one of his seminaries for the Catholic Ngo Dinh Diem,
who was being groomed for power in South Vietnam. The cardinal's
power lust, Garry Wills lamented, worked "vast corruptions" on the
church.[90]

Nor was Spellman a racial liberal. He once declared a $500 life
membership in the NAACP to be a waste of money. LaFarge found,
however, that his diplomatic finesse was not wasted on the archbishop.
Spellman was fairly cooperative, LaFarge discovered, if he kept the
archbishop closely informed of all his activities in the archdiocese,
played on the prelate's anticommunism, and stroked his ego. Like
LaFarge, Spellman was intensely concerned about the image of the
church, and he was willing to take certain actions in the area of race
relations when shown the benefits for Catholicism and for himself.
Because of his careful handling of the ambitious cardinal, LaFarge managed to become a kind of race relations adviser and ghostwriter for
Spellman. He suggested to Spellman, for instance, that the Catholic
leader of New York should send a letter of congratulations to the
NAACP on its fortieth anniversary. LaFarge then wrote the letter for
the archbishop and read it at the NAACP celebration. Cardinal Spellman regularly routed letters containing questions on race, communism,
and related matters to LaFarge, who then supplied the answers in the
archbishop's name. LaFarge enhanced Spellman's reputation among
blacks more than the cardinal realized: Spellman was once rendered
perplexed and speechless when he was loudly applauded at an NAACP
meeting he chanced to attend.[91]

LaFarge shrewdly coaxed Spellman into contributions for the
money-starved CICNY. Whether or not LaFarge still detested fundraising, he no longer complained about the chore. Throughout the
1940s and 1950s the Jesuit bombarded Spellman with solicitations for
money. In 1943 he wrote the archbishop that the CICNY intended to

90. Cooney, *American Pope*, 11, 88–89, 253–56, 284–94; Garry Wills, "Cardinal
Sins," *New Republic*, December 10, 1984, pp. 82–85.

91. Zielinski, " 'Doing the Truth,' " 184, 188–89, 220; Cogley, *Catholic America*,
235–37; interview of Parris by the author; John LaFarge to Cardinal Spellman, January
30, 1948, in box 18, folder 4, JLFP 1; Cooney, *American Pope*, 283–84; John LaFarge to
Cardinal Spellman, September 21, 1949, John LaFarge to Msgr. Francis J. Murphy, Secretary to Spellman, November 21, 1949, Francis J. Murphy to John LaFarge, November
18, 1949, all in box 18, folder 4, JLFP 1.

expand and was "eminently deserving of substantial support" by the archdiocese. How skillfully he sometimes played on Spellman's inclinations is illustrated in this letter. "I hesitate to think what would happen if its [CICNY's] program were to be seriously curtailed and this fact were known to groups unfriendly to the Church," LaFarge warned. "Some of these groups are more active now than ever," he continued, "and I believe some of their agitation is due to their awareness of Catholic concern in these affairs." The priest managed to get a $1,000 donation from the archbishop in 1944. Thereafter, he wrote the archbishop every year to remind him of his obligation to interracialism. Longtime members of the CICNY such as Guichard Parris insisted that Spellman barely tolerated the council and gave money to LaFarge personally rather than to the organization. In any case, LaFarge persuaded Thomas E. Molloy, the archbishop of Brooklyn, to contribute $2,500 annually to the CICNY. He then informed Spellman how much Molloy was contributing and suggested that the cardinal could surely do no less. Spellman matched Molloy.[92]

The cardinal's potential for mischief, however, caused LaFarge to proceed cautiously. The imperious Spellman, who did not hesitate to put suspect subordinates under surveillance, was sometimes a hindrance to LaFarge's work. The archbishop, for instance, forbade LaFarge's serving as cochairman of Brotherhood Week, which was sponsored by the National Conference of Christians and Jews, and he periodically chastised the priest for making attacks on racism in the church, demanding that such criticism "be made with greater prudence."[93]

Worse still, LaFarge had to contend with Auxiliary Bishop McIntyre, the chancellor of the archdiocese who was designated to do Spellman's dirty work, a job McIntyre seemed to relish. The reactionary bishop hounded LaFarge with cruel pettiness. He once lashed out at LaFarge for saying prayers at a funeral in a non-Catholic cemetery. McIntyre abhorred social Catholicism and inquired incessantly about the religious content of the CICNY's programs. In a 1946 letter he cast a typical query at LaFarge: "Is not the promotion of religion amongst

92. John LaFarge to Cardinal Spellman, September 13, 1945, March 14, 1944, March 25, 1944, December 13, 1950, and June 7, 1950, all in box 18, folders 4 and 5, JLFP 1; John LaFarge to Thomas E. Molloy, October 13, 1943, September 6, and November 14, 1944, all in box 16, folder 24, JLFP 1. See also letters in box 6, folder 23, JLFP 2.

93. Zielinski, " 'Doing the Truth,' " 188–89; Cooney, *American Pope*, 78–79.

the negroes [*sic*] the most fundamental issue of the Catholic Interracial Council, or is it just interracial relations?" Later in a letter to another Jesuit, LaFarge recalled that McIntyre suspected everything he did and kept him and the CICNY on the defensive for almost fifteen years. People in the chancery, LaFarge remembered, "called me up any time, day or night, on the phone asking explanations of this or that, and so on." Of McIntyre's departure from New York in 1948, LaFarge said acidly, "Our gain is Los Angeles' loss."[94]

Yet LaFarge never once hinted in his massive publications that there was any friction between his superiors and himself. Only his heightened sense of Catholic mission, the adrenaline of antimodernism, and the sacred pledge of obedience enabled LaFarge to function and produce a respectable Catholic journal and direct an interracial movement under such ecclesiastical impediments. The distinguished and aging Jesuit had to ask permission for every foray outside Campion House, and he had to run the McIntyre gauntlet before he engaged in any sort of racial activity in New York. In addition, under Jesuit rules the superior of Campion House had authority over both spiritual and operational matters. As LaFarge was not the superior, he complained to the American assistant Zacheus Maher that he needed a free hand to run a weekly magazine. He got no satisfaction from Maher, who maintained that Jesuit discipline required that all Jesuits, including the editor-in-chief of *America*, recognize the power of the superior in each Jesuit house. By studying LaFarge, one can see the traditions of the Jesuit order creaking and groaning under the demands of modern competency and relevance.[95]

In the 1940s the CICNY attempted no changes in strategy or tactics. Under LaFarge's guidance, the council moved to the tune of a small inner circle whose main function was education. The CICNY, like the small, uncoordinated Catholic councils around the country, had little direct contact with parish life. In the nation's capital, John O'Connor, president of the Catholic Interracial Council in Washington, D.C., grieved that his council had no full-time employees, not even a secre-

94. J. Francis McIntyre to John LaFarge, February 5, 1946, in box 4, folder 40, JLFP 2; John LaFarge to J. Francis McIntyre, February 8, 1946, in box 2, folder 15, JLFP 1; J. Francis McIntyre to John LaFarge, October 16, 1946, in box 16, folder 21, JLFP 1; John LaFarge to John P. Markoe, February 27, 1951, in box 6, folder 7, JLFP 1; interview of Kane by the author.
95. McDonough, *Men Astutely Trained*, 254, 256.

tary. Unlike the Federal Council of Churches and many other religious and civic groups, the CICNY lacked the resources or the will to file *amici curiae* (friend-of-the-court briefs) in the landmark civil rights cases. The council, however, performed well in spreading its message through the Catholic press, which in 1947 had a circulation of more than thirteen million. A survey revealed that by 1947 the amount of space devoted to race relations in Catholic publications had increased 1,500 percent over that of the previous decade.[96]

During the war and after, LaFarge took on the heavy burden of public speaking. He made short-wave broadcasts to Europe for the Office of War Information, directing speeches at "Christian Working-men in Germany." He issued statements on race for the *Voice of America* and for CBS's *Church of the Air.* He lectured at a conference on "Tomorrow's Children" at Harvard Summer School, which was carried in *Vital Speeches* in September of 1947, and in the same year gave the prestigious Dudleian Lecture at Harvard, an oratorical tradition that dates back to 1740. He presented numerous talks on campuses, black and white, secular and religious. In 1946 he opened an exhibition of African American art at the Phillips Gallery in Washington, D.C.[97]

As editor-in-chief of *America,* LaFarge took a six-week journey through war-torn Europe in the spring and summer of 1947. Like the itinerary for his 1938 trip, he again spoke to important religious and political leaders throughout Europe, except that he now was restricted from parts of the continent by the Iron Curtain. He had a private, forty-five-minute audience with Pope Pius XII, and he spoke at length with Jean-Baptiste Janssens, the general of the Jesuits. In Paris, as the Big

96. John O'Connor, "Washington Reporter," *IR,* 19 (October, 1946), 158; Cavert, *American Churches,* 191; John LaFarge, memorandum on CICNY, January 8, 1946, in letter box 22, CICNYP; John LaFarge to Louis T. Achille, May 4, 1942, in box 14, folder 1, JLFP 2; "The Catholic Press and Interracial Justice," *IR,* 21 (April, 1948), 51. Catholic fiction writers also began to take up the theme of race relations: see the novel by Sylvester, *Dearly Beloved.* Hunton got involved in New York's urban programs in the 1940s; see his *All of Which I Saw,* 261–69, and Zielinski, " 'Doing the Truth,' " 303–14.

97. "Broadcast to Germany," Office of War Information, July 29, 1944, in box 42, folder 4, JLFP 1; statements for *Voice of America,* n.d., in box 8, folder 2, JLFP 1; "Religion and Education as Keys to Family and Community Living," July 10, 1942, in box 42, folder 2, JLFP 1; *MIO,* 319; copy of program for University of Scranton Lectures, 1943–44, in box 7, folder 35, JLFP 2; "Address to Fisk University," June 8, 1949, in box 43, folder 15, JLFP 1; John O'Connor, "Washington Reporter," *IR,* 19 (December, 1946), 189–90.

Three discussed the Marshall Plan, he discussed the desperate state of
Europe with Cardinal Emmanuel Suhard, the archbishop of Paris, and
the American ambassador to France, T. J. Caffrey, a Catholic.[98]

Throughout the decade hundreds of letters poured into Campion
House from African students seeking American schooling, African
Americans trying to cross the color barrier in Catholic institutions, and
poor, uneducated blacks under the heel of southern white supremacists.
These letters usually asked more of LaFarge than he could deliver, but
he gave each plea careful consideration. In one case a Jesuit priest from
Boston College informed LaFarge that a group of Protestant men were
financially supporting a brilliant black Catholic student who was studying medicine at Harvard. According to the Boston priest, one of the
benefactors remarked, "Protestants often help Catholics this way, but
you don't see the Catholics helping even their own in these matters."
The priest therefore asked LaFarge if he could raise some money for
the medical student's expenses and save face for the Catholic church.
Letters like these saddened LaFarge, for he could do little to alleviate
the problems. He also received stimulating letters from Jacques Maritain, Evelyn Waugh, Clare Boothe Luce, and other Catholic luminaries,
who hailed him as the courageous voice of Catholic interracialism.[99]

Catholics certainly could point to many advances in the racial field
by the end of the decade. The student interracial movement that La-
Farge and Hunton had inspired in the previous decade blossomed during the war. The National Federation of Catholic College Students initiated Interracial Justice Week in 1944. Nearly 150 colleges celebrated
the event by 1950, and twenty-one interracial councils were operating
on Catholic campuses. The race relations courses that LaFarge and
Hunton had introduced earlier at Fordham University greatly increased
their enrollment and spread to other Catholic campuses during the
1940s.[100]

98. "Father LaFarge Goes Abroad," *Am*, 77 (May 24, 1947), 200–201; *MIO*, 319–34.

99. Anthony G. Carroll, S.J., to John LaFarge, July 26, 1941, in box 28, folder 3,
JLFP 1. For an interesting letter to a famous novelist, see John LaFarge to Evelyn Waugh,
November 12, 1948, in "Miscellaneous Letters," John LaFarge Papers, New York His-
torical Society.

100. "International Week in Catholic Colleges," *IR*, 19 (April, 1946), 58–59; "In-
terracial Justice Week," *IR*, 23 (March, 1950), 37; "The Catholic Interracial Movement:
Progress and Achievements, 1951–52," in box 29, folder 1, JLFP 1; "Night Classes at
Fordham School of Social Science," *IR*, 16 (October, 1943), 159; Joseph F. Healy to John
LaFarge, August 31, 1942, in box 23, folder 1, JLFP 1.

In addition, Catholic leaders gained recognition in the civil rights movement as never before. The Reverend Francis J. Haas (later bishop of Grand Rapids, Michigan) became chairman of the FEPC in 1943. Monsignor Francis Gilligan, author of *The Morality of the Color Line*, published in 1928, was selected to head the Inter-Racial Commission of Minnesota and the labor committee of the NAACP. Charles Fahy, a judge, was picked by President Truman to chair the federal committee that determined the desegregation process for the armed forces. Paul D. Williams, the layman who founded the Catholic Committee of the South (CCS), replaced Howard Odum in 1945 as president of the Southern Regional Council.[101]

The visibility of Catholics in the racial field and the greatly increased coverage of race in the Catholic press apparently had some effect on African Americans. The church reported 8,851 black and Indian conversions in 1948. By the end of the decade, the black Catholic population had swollen to more than 350,000, up from about 200,000 in 1928. The jump in the number of black priests from 3 in 1930 to 30 in 1950 probably helped black conversions as well. Even the Josephites renewed the previous quest of John Slattery for a black clergy in the early 1940s under their new superior general Edward V. Casserly.[102]

Still, the number of black priests was so small that most Catholics never saw a black clergyman in this era. More than that, most of the black priests were products of a Jim Crow seminary in Mississippi, where white priests taught young black seminarians humility, obedience, and the sanctity of the status quo just as surely as Protestant white supremacists did throughout the Deep South. Many black seminarians clearly failed to meet Catholic expectations. By 1944 only 17 of the 340 black seminarians who entered St. Augustine's in Mississippi had received holy orders from the Society of the Divine Word. Although the

101. Editorial, *IR*, 16 (May, 1943), 79; "Priest Named Members of New Labor Committee," *IR*, 19 (December, 1946), 192; "Interracial Activity Becoming Nationwide," *IR*, 17 (January, 1944), 14; Richard M. Dalfiume, "The Fahy Committee and Desegregation of the Armed Forces," *Historian*, 31 (November, 1968), 1; "Williams Elected President of the Southern Regional Council," *IR*, 18 (November, 1945), 162.

102. "Circulation of Catholic Press," *IR*, 19 (May, 1946), 74; Joe K. Feagin, "Black Catholics in the United States: An Exploratory Analysis," in *The Black Church in America*, ed. Hart M. Nelsen, Raytha L. Yokley, and Anne K. Nelsen (New York, 1971), 246–53; "Negro Converts," *IR*, 22 (April, 1949), 62; "Directory of U.S. Negro Priests," *IR*, 30 (July, 1957), 119–21; Ochs, *Desegregating the Altar*, 364, 374–94.

Josephites began to cultivate black vocations again, the religious order looked to recruit blacks who were "balanced on the race question" and harbored no bitterness toward whites. Charles Ball, the first African American Josephite ordained since 1907, met the requirements fully. Ball was so light-skinned that he had trouble being accepted as black, and at the same time he had a terrible craving for white acceptance. His lack of self-identity led to a nervous breakdown and his death at the age of fifty-seven.[103] Despite the increase in black priests, the Catholic church nonetheless continued to lack for black leadership.

George Hunton admitted that in the 1940s the Catholic church fell further behind the rest of the country on the race question. The Prot estant critic Harold Fey discerned the potential of the Catholic church for racial gains, but he concluded that the American bishops had callously resisted the Vatican's efforts to bring more blacks into the American church. Throughout the period, the American hierarchy constantly advised Rome that "the time [was] not ripe." Statistics on almost any sector of the church showed the results. For example, only 8 of 368 Catholic nursing schools took blacks, no black doctor could practice medicine in the Georgetown University Hospital, and the Knights of Columbus remained lily-white in the 1940s. Dr. Mordecai W. Johnson, the moderate president of Howard University and a man known to be on friendly terms with Catholics, bluntly outlined the paternalistic orientation of the Catholic church when he told a theologians' committee on interracial justice in 1944: "You have only 300,000 Negro Catholics. Why? Because you have operated too much on the motive of charity and benevolence. . . . You have not encouraged the Negro to rise to your own stature. . . . You have not developed a Catholic Negro priesthood. . . . You have not more than a handful of Negroes in all your colleges. That's not an accident; it's a policy."[104]

It is clear that the Catholic interracial movement played a minor role in the overall scheme of civil rights in the first half of the twentieth century. In 1950 *America* lamented that the newly formed National

103. McEoin, *Memoirs and Memories*, 144–45; Ochs, *Desegregating the Altar*, 361–62, 419–20, 461.

104. Hunton, *All of Which I Saw*, 141, 144; Fey, "Catholicism and the Negro," 1476; Edward LaSalle to John LaFarge, July 26, 1943, in box 16, folder 13, JLFP 1; Joseph P. McMurray to John LaFarge, in box 1, folder 36, JLFP 2; Johnson, quoted in "Negroes and Catholics, *Am*, 72 (December 9, 1944), 182.

Emergency Civil Rights Mobilization, a coalition of race relations groups headed by the NAACP's Roy Wilkins, barely had a Catholic presence. No doubt, the consistent, quiet work of LaFarge and the interracial movement helped prepare the church for the civil rights revolution of the 1950s and 1960s. The major Catholic breakthroughs of the 1940s could not have come, however, without combative and defiant priests such as Heithaus, Dunne, and the Markoe brothers. Yet all the integrationist rebels were silenced and exiled by their tremulous superiors. Progress would also have been meager without such resourceful (essentially dictatorial) if isolated bishops as Robert E. Lucey in San Antonio, Joseph E. Ritter in St. Louis, and Patrick O'Boyle in Washington, D.C. John O'Connor realized better than most Catholic activists how little his kind influenced racial events. If Catholics would only take a hard look at the forward movement in race relations, he declared, they would "find Communists, fellow-travellers, and befuddled liberals already in the lead." The Georgetown history professor charged that Catholics excelled at passing "grandiose resolutions" and patting one another on the back. O'Connor summed up the results of Catholic policies in this way: "It is all very well to talk about the brotherhood of man and the fatherhood of God, to become truly eloquent about the Mystical Body of Christ. But the average Negro is scarcely able to distinguish between Catholic injustice and inhumanity and the contempt and ostracism of bigots and pagans. So far as he is concerned, the effect is the same. It is all part of the same conspiracy to reduce the Negro to second-class citizenship and keep him 'in his place.' " O'Connor claimed that the interracial apostolate could only make progress when Catholics reduced the "yawning chasm between Catholic theory and Catholic every-day practice" and when Catholics became more sincere in racial work and quit "carrying water on both shoulders."[105]

President Truman was not good at balancing water on his shoulders. Direct and earthy, the man from Independence addressed the race problem with rare bluntness and sincerity. At the 1947 NAACP convention, Truman stressed that federal action was necessary to protect civil rights. Denouncing the theory of states' rights, the president proclaimed that the nation could no longer allow the "slowest state or the

105. "Civil Rights Mobilization," *Am*, 82 (January 28, 1950), 487; John J. O'Connor, "Washington Reporter," *IR*, 19 (August, 1946), 126.

most backward community" in the country to determine the pace of racial change.[106] Nor could African Americans wait for the slowest church or the most lethargic bishop to declare that the time was ripe for integration. In the 1950s blacks began to take to the streets and to employ direct action in their quest for equality. As the second half of the twentieth century began, LaFarge, too, proclaimed that there could be "no postponement" of equal rights for African Americans.

106. Truman, quoted in Roy Wilkins, *Standing Fast: The Autobiography of Roy Wilkins* (New York, 1984), 199.

Father LaFarge on the *Catholic Hour,* August 5, 1956. Photograph courtesy of John LaFarge, S.J., Papers, Georgetown University Library, Washington, D.C.

Father LaFarge (left front) and the Catholic Laymen's Union at a Retreat in Glenmont, New York, 1955. Photograph courtesy of John LaFarge, S.J., Papers, Georgetown University Library, Washington, D.C.

George K. Hunton (no date). Photograph courtesy of Christopher Hunton, Washington, D.C.

Reverend Claude Heithaus, S.J. (no date). Photograph courtesy of Jesuit Missouri Province Archives, St. Louis, Missouri.

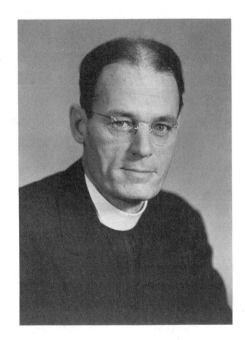

Father LaFarge with His Favorite Black Leader. LaFarge (seated second from right), A. Philip Randolph (seated in center), and some members of the Catholic Interracial Council of New York, *ca.* 1960. Photograph courtesy of John LaFarge, S.J., Papers, Georgetown University Library, Washington, D.C.

The Cardinal and the Priest, 1960. Left to right: Henry Seeger, Sr., Cardinal Francis Spellman, Lester Granger (National Urban League), and Father LaFarge. Photograph courtesy of John LaFarge, S.J., Papers, Georgetown University Library, Washington, D.C.

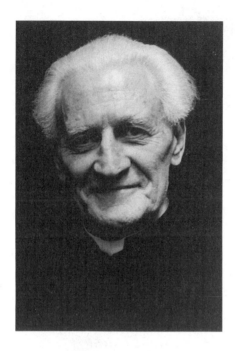

Reverend John Markoe, S.J. (no date). Photograph courtesy of Jesuit Missouri Province Archives, St. Louis, Missouri.

Reverend George H. Dunne, S.J., *ca.* 1985. Photograph courtesy of George Dunne, Los Angeles.

10

In Search of an
Orderly Revolution
1950–1958

In the 1950s civil rights became the number-one domestic issue in the United States. Moreover, between the years 1954 and 1965, from the *Brown* decision to the Voting Rights Act, African Americans essentially achieved legal equality in America.[1] The watershed events of this crucial period grew out of the circumstances that had evolved and the gains that had been won by African Americans in the previous decade and earlier. World War II and the Truman presidency lent impetus to the quest for racial equality. Black leaders such as A. Philip Randolph and the creators of the Congress of Racial Equality, Bayard Rustin and James Farmer, fought for an integrated society in the 1940s. The massive migration of blacks out of the South after 1940 gave the minority more electoral clout. Black educational and economic achievements increased significantly because of war prosperity and federal educational benefits for veterans. By 1953 twelve states and

---

1. Good starting points among the vast literature on the black revolution are Sitkoff, *Struggle for Black Equality;* Thomas R. Brooks, *Walls Came Tumbling Down: A History of the Civil Rights Movement, 1940–1970* (Englewood Cliffs, N.J., 1974); Pat Watters, *Down to Now: Reflections on the Southern Civil Rights Movement* (New York, 1971); Goldfield, *Black, White, and Southern;* and Robert Weisbrot, *Freedom Bound: A History of America's Civil Rights Movement* (New York, 1990).

thirty cities had passed fair employment practice laws. Professional sports and entertainment moved toward integration and gave blacks such as Jackie Robinson celebrity status.[2] Other factors that defy precise measurement but figured prominently in the civil rights revolution were the decline of racist ideology among well-educated people and the widespread use of equalitarian sociology in academe.[3]

The Supreme Court, prodded by the NAACP, had been steadily eroding the legal basis of American apartheid since the 1930s. Led by the talented black lawyers Charles H. Houston and Thurgood Marshall, the NAACP's legal defense team steadily chipped away at the legal fiction of "separate but equal." Meanwhile, scores of lesser-known African Americans risked life and limb in building a church-based, grassroots southern movement that would ignite the black revolt of the 1950s.[4]

Chief Justice Earl Warren provided a powerful catalyst for change when he handed down the unanimous *Brown v. Board of Education* decision on May 17, 1954. The court proclaimed in *Brown* what it had only suggested in the *Sweatt v. Painter* case four years earlier: that segregation in public education was per se unequal and therefore unconstitutional.[5] One year after *Brown*, Rosa Parks refused to give up her seat to a white man on a city bus in Montgomery, Alabama. With her arrest, blacks organized a boycott of the buses. Black Panther Eldridge Cleaver later said of Rosa Parks's defiance, "Somewhere in the universe a gear in the machinery had shifted."[6] Out of the Montgomery

---

2. Sitkoff, *Struggle for Black Equality*, 8–18.

3. Fred H. Matthews, *Quest for an American Sociology: Robert E. Park and the Chicago School* (Montreal, 1977), 163–64, 183, 189–93. See generally Southern, *Gunnar Myrdal and Black-White Relations*, and George W. Stocking, Jr., *Race, Culture, and Evolution: Essays in the History of Anthropology* (New York, 1968).

4. Sitkoff, *Struggle for Black Equality*, 11–12; Loren Miller, *The Petitioners: The Story of the Supreme Court of the United States and the Negro* (Cleveland, 1967), 340; Kluger, *Simple Justice*, Chaps. 1–21, esp. pp. 3–4, 9–25, 295, 303, 329–330, 525, 581, 667, 778. For emphasis on the grassroots, church-centered movement, see Aldon D. Morris, *The Origins of the Civil Rights Movement: Black Communities Organizing for Change* (New York, 1984), 4–16.

5. *Brown v. Board of Education of Topeka*, 347 U.S. 483. On the use of sociology in *Brown*, see Southern, *Gunnar Myrdal and Black-White Relations*, 127–50.

6. Cleaver, quoted in Sitkoff, *Struggle for Black Equality*, 42. On the boycott, see King, *Stride Toward Freedom*. King has had many biographers, but see David Garrow, *Bearing the Cross: Martin Luther King, Jr., and the Southern Christian Leadership Con-*

affair, Martin Luther King, Jr., emerged as a national black leader of high courage and captivating eloquence. Shortly after the Montgomery buses were integrated by order of the federal courts, Congress passed the first civil rights bill since Reconstruction. Three years later in 1960, college students began the sit-in movement in Greensboro, North Carolina, and formed the Student Nonviolent Coordinating Committee (SNCC). These young African Americans resented the slow pace of change. They demanded first-class citizenship without delay, and they took direct action to secure it.[7]

White supremacists, however, stoutly resisted the proposition of black equality. Segregationists in the South branded May 17, 1954, "Black Monday" and soon made massive resistance to federal law the order of the day. Whites voted for racial demagogues, and southern moderates lost office or fell silent. Significant numbers of influential whites resisted desegregation through the White Citizens' Council, through economic pressure and legal devices, and sometimes through the Ku Klux Klan and various kinds of terrorism. Most of the Deep South school districts remained segregated for more than a decade after the *Brown* decision. In 1956 the "Southern Manifesto," which was signed by 101 southern congressmen and senators, pledged to employ "all lawful means" to reverse the desegregation decision. By 1956 five southern states had defiantly enacted forty-two statutes that bolstered segregated public schools. Although President Dwight D. Eisenhower sent federal troops to Little Rock, Arkansas, in 1957 to enforce a federal court order calling for the desegregation of Central High School, the conservative president generally pursued a "go slow" policy on racial matters.[8] Many blacks grew frustrated with his sluggish pace. The separatist Black Muslims loudly voiced their distrust of all whites and

---

ference (New York, 1986), and Taylor Branch, *Parting the Waters: America in the King Years, 1954–1963* (New York, 1988).

7. Sitkoff, *Struggle for Black Equality,* 35–36, 69–96; Clayborne Carson, *In Struggle: SNCC and the Black Awakening of the 1960s* (Cambridge, Mass., 1981).

8. Sitkoff, *Struggle for Black Equality,* 25–39. Of the voluminous literature on massive resistance, start with Numan V. Bartley, *The Rise of Massive Resistance: Race and Politics in the South During the 1950's* (Baton Rouge, 1969), 3–57, *passim;* Neil R. McMillen, *The Citizens' Council: Organized Resistance to the Second Revolution* (Urbana, Ill., 1971); and Hodding Carter, III, *The South Strikes Back* (Garden City, N.Y., 1959). On Eisenhower, see Robert F. Burk, *The Eisenhower Administration and Black Civil Rights* (Knoxville, Tenn., 1984).

issued threats (the ballot or the bullet) through their magnetic young spokesman Malcolm X. In 1955 the black novelist James Baldwin sounded apocalyptic warnings of racial violence and spoke of the "naked and unanswerable hatred" that blacks harbored deep in their psyches for white society.[9] Racially speaking, the decade throbbed with both hope and disappointment.

For American Catholics, the 1950s signaled a time of arrival. In 1953 the Catholic church claimed 32,000,000 members, by far the largest unified religious group in the country. In that same year the church recorded 116,000 converts. The postwar boom propelled many working-class Catholics into the middle class and into positions of authority. The impeccable patriotism of Catholics in World War II and their leadership in the Cold War brought them new respect in Protestant America. It was a period of rich growth for American Catholicism. During the decade the number of children in parochial schools increased by 66 percent, the number of priests from 43,000 to 54,000, and the number of seminaries from 388 to 525.[10] Will Herberg, master analyst of the dominant religious groups in America, wrote the following in 1953: "Catholicism in America today stands at its highest point of prestige and spiritual power. In an age of spiritual chaos and disorientation, Catholicism stands forth as a keeper of an enduring tradition that has weathered the storms of the past and stands unshaken amidst the disasters of our time."[11]

Many white Catholics, however, were shaken when their bishops finally went against American tradition and prodded them to desegregate their churches, schools, hospitals, and social organizations. As Herberg pointed out, blacks and Hispanics remained "almost entirely unassimilated" in the Catholic community. Despite the efforts of the Catholic interracial movement, most white Catholics had not internalized the color-blind teaching of the church. Jesuit sociologist Joseph

9. Louis Lomax, *The Negro Revolt* (New York, 1962), 81, 241–47; John Henrik Clarke, ed., *Malcolm X: The Man and His Times* (New York, 1969), 177; James Baldwin, *Notes of a Native Son* (Boston, 1955), 38, 45, 97.

10. Marty, *Invitation to American Catholic History*, 175; John Tracy Ellis, "American Catholicism, 1953–1979: A Notable Change," in *Modern American Catholicism*, ed. Kantowicz, 399–402, 405–407.

11. Herberg, quoted in Ellis, "American Catholicism," in *Modern American Catholicism*, ed. Kantowicz, 399. See also Will Herberg, *Protestant-Catholic-Jew: An Essay in American Religious Sociology* (rev. ed.; Garden City, N.Y., 1960).

Fichter found that Catholics followed popular views held by white society concerning African Americans, a fact that was all too evident in the 1951 Cicero race riot. Fichter and other researchers discovered that Catholics differed little in their racial views from Protestants in the North or the South and were generally less liberal than Jews. In a poll of 68 people in a southern parish at midcentury, 47 said they would not send their children to an integrated Catholic school. In 1956 the *Catholic Digest* reported that 31 percent of white Catholics in the North and 76 percent in the South favored segregation of the races (only 45 percent of southern Jews favored segregation). Devotees of order, most white Catholics rejected nonviolent direct action as a means to black equality. In the 1950s Catholic youth looked to Southeast Asia and the anticommunist missionary Dr. Tom Dooley for inspiration rather than to Dr. Martin Luther King, Jr., and the American church showed more support for Ngo Dinh Diem, America's Catholic mandarin in South Vietnam, than for the NAACP.[12]

Nevertheless, leading Catholic interracialists such as LaFarge gained unprecedented respect in the 1950s. LaFarge, who celebrated his seventieth birthday in 1950, became a highly recognized and oft-honored figure in the last full decade of his life. The 1950s marked a series of silver and golden anniversaries for him: his twenty-fifth year at *America,* his fiftieth year as a priest, and a quarter-century as the spiritual and intellectual guide of the CICNY. Famous people from President Eisenhower on down congratulated him. *Time* magazine detailed his activities and lauded his talents on his silver anniversary at *America,* and black periodicals published flattering pieces on him. A testimonial dinner at the Waldorf-Astoria Hotel honoring his twenty-five years at *America* drew 750 people and many well-known civil rights leaders.[13]

12. Herberg, *Protestant-Catholic-Jew,* 158; Osborne, *Segregated Covenant,* 235–38; Fichter, *One-Man Research,* 44; Joseph H. Fichter, S.J., *Southern Parish: Dynamics of a Southern Church* (Chicago, 1951), 265; "Survey of Interracial Thinking," *IR,* 29 (May, 1956), 76; Wakin and Scheuer, *De-Romanization of the American Church,* 249–50. On Dooley and Diem, see Allitt, *Catholic Intellectuals and Conservative Politics,* 29–31. On discrimination against Hispanic Catholics in America, see *Puerto Rican and Cuban Catholics in the U.S., 1900–1965,* ed. Jay P. Dolan and Jaime R. Vidal (Notre Dame, Ind., 1994), and *Mexican Americans and the Catholic Church, 1900–1965,* ed. Jay P. Dolan and Gilberto M. Hinojosa (Notre Dame, Ind., 1994).

13. For the twentieth anniversary of *America,* see clippings and memorabilia in box 4, folder 55, JLFP 1, and clippings in letter box 29, CICNYP. For a list of speakers at

During the decade LaFarge garnered many prestigious honors and awards. He was elected to the American Academy of Arts and Sciences in 1950. The CAIP awarded him its Peace Prize in 1955. He won the Social Justice Award in 1957 from the Religion and Labor Foundation—an award he shared with Senator Herbert H. Lehman and Martin Luther King, Jr. In 1959 LaFarge received the American Liberties Medallion given by the American Jewish Committee. That same year the Catholic Institute of the Press awarded him a prize for furthering communication and Catholic principles. Two years later he received the Campion Award for literature given by the Catholic Book Club.[14]

Because of his recognition and his broad interests, LaFarge received countless invitations from organizations to lecture or give advice on a great diversity of topics. In 1950, for example, he was invited to participate in the Midcentury White House Conference on Children and Youth. At the request of the U.S. State Department, he took a seven-week tour of Germany to inspect religious institutions for the Division of Education and Culture of the United States Government of Occupation in Germany. He was selected to serve on the prestigious panel financed by the Rockefeller Brothers Fund to establish national goals, joining such luminaries as Christian A. Herter, Adolph Berle, Jr., Dean Rusk, Henry Kissinger, Henry Luce, David Riesman, and Walt Rostow.[15] He delivered the 1954 Phi Beta Kappa address at his alma mater

---

the dinner for LaFarge, see "Feature 'X,' " *Am*, 86 (March 8, 1952), 614–15. On his Golden Jubilee, see box 1, folders 45–46, JLFP 2 and box 37, folder, 5, JLFP 1; "A Reasoned Optimist," *Time*, March 3, 1952, pp. 76–80; "John LaFarge: Son of Famed Painter Gave Up Life of 'Gentility' to Serve Underdogs," Chicago *Defender*, April 10, 1954, clipping in letter box 29, CICNYP.

14. Memorandum, in box 1, folder 18, JLFP 1; news release, CAIP, in box 33, folder 1, JLFP 1; Clair Cook to John LaFarge, October 12, 1956, in box 21a, folder 5, JLFP 1; "Program for Social Justice Award," in box 17, CICCP; copy of program of the American Jewish Committee, in box 37, folder 10, JLFP 1; clippings, Religious News Service, February 8, 1960, in box 21, folder 2, JLFP 1; program, Catholic Book Club, October 26, 1961, in box 1, folder 6, JLFP 1. King's acceptance speech was published as "A View of the Dawn," *IR*, 30 (May, 1957), 82–85.

15. Melvin A. Glasser, Executive Director of White House Conference, to John LaFarge, July 14, 1950, in box 4, folder 43, JLFP 2; *MIO*, 355–72; John LaFarge to Nelson Rockefeller, March 1, 1957, in box 3, folder 1, JLFP 2; Gordon Tiffany to John LaFarge, February 9, 1959, in box 21a, folder 3, JLFP 1. Box 21a, JLFP 1 has seven folders of requests for LaFarge's services; see also box 3, JLFP 2.

in Cambridge. He appeared regularly on national and local television talk shows such as *Open Mind, Wisdom,* and *Night-Beat.*[16]

Ironically, at the very time LaFarge was receiving his greatest recognition, he was gradually losing his place as the foremost Catholic spokesman on race relations. In his last years LaFarge, more and more, assumed the role of "moral figurehead."[17] Had it not been for his earlier pioneering work in the racial field, he probably would have been little noticed in the decade that launched the civil rights movement. Although his ideas underwent some careful and constructive change in the 1950s, his basic message remained essentially unchanged. In the same patient tones, he restated ideas that he had espoused since the 1930s, but these ideas had grown increasingly inadequate to meet the rapidly changing racial conditions and the rising aspirations of African Americans after World War II. Younger, bolder, and more action-oriented, ecumenical Catholics would displace LaFarge as the shakers and movers of the interracial movement before the decade ended. LaFarge, like President Eisenhower, was reluctant to draw on his accumulated moral capital to try to effect a more decisive racial transformation in the church and the nation. At a pivotal point in American race relations, he seemed to experience a failure of nerve and imagination as far as making racial justice a "Catholic" issue and moving his church to the front of the civil rights movement. Instead he receded, albeit slowly and never entirely, from the center of Catholic leadership on the race issue; and the Catholic church itself, though advancing, fell further behind the faster-moving denominations and secular forces in the civil rights movement. Outside Catholic circles, where LaFarge's influence had never been great, his influence further declined.

During the 1950s LaFarge continued to publish large amounts of material. His periodical output, however, decreased during that time, and *America* published fewer editorials and articles on race than when LaFarge was editor-in-chief. During the decade LaFarge averaged only about one major article a year on blacks for the Jesuit weekly.[18] More

16. "A Conversation with Father LaFarge," *Wisdom* telecast, April 5, 1959, in box 21, folder 3, JLFP 1; Richard D. Heffner to John LaFarge, January 28, 1957, in box 21a, folder 6, JLFP 1; Zielinski, " 'Doing the Truth,' " 86; Peter P. Jacobi, NBC News, Chicago, to John LaFarge, August 29, 1958, in box 21a, folder 2, JLFP 1.

17. Interview of Clark by the author.

18. The indexes to *America* helped determine the volume of writing on race in the 1940s and 1950s.

of the writing on blacks was being done by bolder, younger writers in Campion House and by outside writers. If LaFarge's essay writing declined, his book production soared. During the decade he published five books: *No Postponement* in 1950; *The Manner Is Ordinary* in 1954; *The Catholic Viewpoint on Race Relations* in 1956; *A Report on the American Jesuits* in 1956; and *An American Amen* in 1958. In addition, two of his Campion House colleagues collected some of his essays for *A John LaFarge Reader* and brought it out in 1956.[19]

Catholic magazines eagerly cannibalized sections of LaFarge's books, and Catholic organizations compressed them into pamphlets. *The Race Question and the Negro*, originally out in 1943, had gone through five printings by 1952, and it appeared in a one-dollar paperback in 1953.[20] Yet, as earlier, no more than a fraction of LaFarge's writing in the 1950s dealt with race relations.

No Postponement was the worst and undoubtedly the least influential book LaFarge ever wrote. He confessed in a letter that the book had been "hastily slapped together," and he worried that it would be "just a lot of pastiche." As he explained to a friend during the early stages of writing the book, he first set out to explain the American race problem to Europeans. Then he decided to relate America's racial dilemma to world politics and the crusade against communism as well, entangling the quest for racial equality with Truman's Point Four program to aid the underdeveloped world. The subtitle of the book thus became *U.S. Moral Leadership and the Problem of Racial Minorities.* While pursuing these two broad objectives, LaFarge also attempted to key "to certain problems of the spiritual life."[21] Finally, he threw in a sketchy and unrevealing history of the Catholic interracial movement.

No Postponement was ill organized, highly repetitious, and saturated with religiosity.[22] LaFarge conceded that action-oriented readers

19. LaFarge, *No Postponement, MIO, Catholic Viewpoint, A Report on the American Jesuits* (New York, 1956), *An American Amen* (New York, 1958), and *A John LaFarge Reader*, ed. Thurston N. Davis, S.J., and John Small, S.J. (New York, 1956).

20. "Leadership and the Catholic Press," *IR*, 29 (June, 1956), 93. For comic books based on LaFarge's life, see Theophilus Lewis, "A Point of View: Christian Comic Books," *IR*, 27 (December, 1954), 211–12; copy of comic book, "Catholics in Action," in box 10, folder 26, JLFP 2; "The Race Question and the Negro Available in Dollar Edition," *IR*, 26 (August, 1953), 128.

21. John LaFarge to J. Minery, S.J., October 5, 1949, in box 15, folder 20, JLFP 1.

22. For LaFarge's repetition, see *No Postponement*, 154, 161. The book also con-

would not like his sermonizing or his belaboring the obvious with respect to human brotherhood. He argued, however, that a "long Baptism" or "catechumenate" was a prerequisite for change. To those who called for action, he advised more contemplation and prayer. "Prayer is action," he asserted, "the highest and most transcendent form of action." He quoted President Truman at length at least four times in trying to prove the centrality of religion in American foreign policy. Although Catholic reviewers heartily praised the book (it was almost totally ignored by others), some hinted that it contained less than felicitous prose. Writing in the *Interracial Review*, John O'Connor noted that the Jesuit's style did not "make for excitement." The book recorded only four hundred sales in the first year and a half after publication. The anemic sales bothered LaFarge, and he complained bitterly to editor Norman Cousins when the *Saturday Review* (for which LaFarge wrote book reviews) chose not to review his book.[23]

For all its faults, *No Postponement* beautifully demonstrates the continuity (as well as some significant evolution) in LaFarge's thought during an era of fast-breaking racial change. Featured prominently in this thickly didactic book was LaFarge's incorrigible optimism about the race problem. He reiterated his belief that a good Catholic could not be a pessimist.[24] But, ironically, at the same time he insisted on optimism LaFarge revealed "great anxiety" about the future. From the beginning to the end of *No Postponement*, the Jesuit inveighed against materialism and secularism. He warned that "spiritual chaos," even more than communism, threatened the world, and he stressed the need for the passionate "mysticism of Ignatius" and the "ever burning flame of spiritual holocaust."[25] One Catholic analyst refers to this strange

---

tained several factual errors, such as dating the Harlem riot in 1937 instead of 1935, on p. 167.

23. *Ibid.*, 8–9, 17, 26–37, 43–44, 55–64, 171–73, 213; John O'Connor, "No Postponement—A Review," *IR*, 23 (June, 1950), 88–90. See also Theophilus Lewis, "Point Four at Home," *IR*, 23 (October, 1950), 155; statement of royalties, in box 9, folder 19, JLFP 2; John LaFarge to Norman Cousins, August 15, 1950, in box 4, folder 5, JLFP 2.

24. The same optimistic theme found in *Interracial Justice*, ix, and quoted in Chap. 8, is repeated verbatim in LaFarge, *No Postponement*, ix; "Reasoned Optimist," 76; and LaFarge, *Race Question and the Negro*, ix.

25. LaFarge, *No Postponement*, v, 239. See also his "Secularism's Attack on World Order," CAIP pamphlet, n.d., in box 42, folder 4, JLFP 1; *MIO*, 378; *Catholic Viewpoint*, 79; and *An American Amen*, 213, *passim*. On his mysticism, see John LaFarge, "Ignatius

mixture of optimism and pessimism as the "fractured inheritance" of American Catholicism. This dualism saddled LaFarge with the tendency to blame all the ills of America on non-Catholics. In 1959 in *America* John Cogley assailed this tendency in Catholics: "We content ourselves with standing in judgment on our age as if *its* problems were not our problems, as if *its* failings were not our own, as if the challenges confronting *it* were not confronting us." [26]

LaFarge's lifelong assault on secularism, as in the past, often spilled over into anti-Protestantism. Holding fast to the idea of the "one true church," LaFarge tended to see Protestants and Jews as unbelievers or "secularists." He continued to accuse Protestants of instigating slavery and inventing racism. He still proclaimed that "the Catholic Church alone" had the answer to the race problem, though more privately and less often. As for those he perceived as unbelievers, the Jesuit could hardly conceal his contempt. He referred to Albert Einstein as a religious "vacuum," and he cast W. E. B. Du Bois' queries to him about black rights into the dead-letter file. He especially found distasteful civil rights activists who were "aggressive atheists," seldom finding a positive trait in such persons. [27]

Gordon W. Allport, a noted Harvard social psychologist and author of the influential book *The Nature of Prejudice*, published in 1954, took LaFarge to task for his assault on secularism. One of the few non-Catholic scholars to cite the Jesuit's racial work, Allport praised *No Postponement* for its "sustained warmth" and for laying out practical

---

Loyola and Our Times," *Thought*, 31 (Summer, 1956), 165–86; "The Hands of Ignatius," *Catholic Mind*, 54 (July, 1956), 382–85; "Exhortations," December 12, 1950, in box 1, folder 4, JLFP 2; Campion House Conference, "Exhortations," January 15, 1952, in box 1, folder 5, JLFP 2. See also his bitter attack on George Santayana, who died in 1952, in "Feature 'X,' " *Am*, 88 (October 11, 1952), 42–43.

26. Gribble, "Fractured Inheritance," 47, 50–51; John Cogley, "The Catholic and the Liberal Society," *Am*, 101 (July 4, 1959), 495.

27. On accusations and innuendo regarding Protestants, see *No Postponement*, 132, 143–44; LaFarge, "Christianity and the Negro," *Jubilee*, 3 (September, 1955), 52; John LaFarge to Theodore F. Cunningham, S.J., December 16, 1960, in box 21, folder 3, JLFP 1; John LaFarge, "The Catholic Intellectual and Social Movements," *Catholic Mind*, 53 (September, 1955), 556. LaFarge called Algernon Black, chairman of the National Committee Against Discrimination in Housing, an "aggressive atheist" (John LaFarge to Mathew Ahmann, May 1, 1960, in box 3, folder 42, JLFP 2). On Catholic defensiveness, see Herberg, *Protestant-Catholic-Jew*, 233–34.

steps for racial progress. However, he observed that the book was narrowly pitched to Catholics, despite general appeals for interfaith cooperation. He wondered how LaFarge and his followers could cooperate with secular reformers when the priest charged that everyone who shunned theism and embraced birth control and divorce was guilty of "ethical anarchy." He asked if LaFarge's accusations against secular reformers and scholars did not "invalidate their labor or impugn their motives" and thus undermine any chance of cooperation. Allport maintained that only by *"unrestrained cooperation and mutual respect"* among racial reformers could racial progress be achieved.[28]

Allport skillfully discerned that LaFarge's Catholic narrowness hampered his role in the growing ecumenical effort for racial equality. Ultimately, however, LaFarge had to accept the fact that America was "intrinsically pluralistic."[29] In the 1950s the Jesuit became more amenable to the concept of ecumenism. His growing fear of secularism led him to look for theistic allies with whom to war against "sophisticated materialism."[30] While never shedding all his religious intolerance or his ambivalence about ecumenism, he nevertheless encouraged more interfaith cooperation, provided Catholics did not accept the heresy that one religion was as good as another. By the end of the decade he was emphasizing that only joint action by Protestants, Jews, and Catholics could significantly advance interracial justice, and he appeared more frequently with activists from other faiths. LaFarge began to replace "Catholic" in the title of his race relations articles with "Christian." In 1957 he jointly drafted with the renowned Protestant theologian Reinhold Niebuhr a statement on tolerance that was endorsed by religious leaders from many faiths. Still, LaFarge continued to adhere closely to

---

28. Gordon W. Allport, review of *No Postponement*, by John LaFarge, in *Thought*, 26 (Autumn, 1950), 471–72. For Allport's use of LaFarge, see *The Nature of Prejudice* (Cambridge, Mass., 1954), 6, 16, and Gordon Allport to John LaFarge, October 21, 1955, and John LaFarge to Gordon Allport, November 2, 1955, both in Stanton Papers. One of the rare secular studies of significance that cited LaFarge was George Eaton Simpson and Y. Milton Yinger, *Racial and Cultural Minorities: An Analysis of Prejudice and Discrimination* (New York, 1958), 593–94.

29. Herberg, *Protestant-Catholic-Jew*, 151; Leonard I. Sweet, "The Modernization of Protestant Religion in America," in *Altered Landscapes*, ed. Lotz, 37.

30. John LaFarge, "A Catholic Statement on Tolerance," *Am*, 84 (January 6, 1951), 399–400. On the continuing conflict between faiths, see John J. Kane, *Catholic-Protestant Conflicts in America* (Chicago, 1955), and Curry, *Protestant-Catholic Relations*, 64–65.

Vatican restrictions on ecumenism, and the riskier experiments in this area were left to bolder Jesuits such as Gustave Weigel.[31]

Another change in LaFarge could be seen in his effort to place the race problem in world perspective or, perhaps more accurately, Cold War perspective. Always intensely patriotic, one of LaFarge's primary aims in *No Postponement* was to persuade Europeans that America was "fundamentally for right and justice" and ready for global leadership.[32] Putting the race problem in world perspective also heightened the Jesuit's interest in Africa and the process of decolonization. As chairman of the Committee on Africa for the CAIP, LaFarge struggled to master the intricacies of the political and social milieu of emerging Africa. He confided to a friend that Africa was "all so immense" and that it had a "thousand angles" to it. In a seven-page position paper on Africa presented to the CAIP in 1958, he lauded Africa's "sense of the family and its bonds" and proclaimed that America's goal should be to make Africa "healthy, vigorous, and democratic." Unable to see Africa apart from the East-West struggle, he warned that this goal would not be easy because the Soviets were stirring up "anti-colonialism and racism" and posing "a clear Soviet threat to penetrate the continent." He therefore grieved that America's influence in Africa was limited because of its own racist practices.[33]

In any case, LaFarge also worked hard to accommodate Africans who wanted to study in America. In 1952 LaFarge became vice-chair-

31. John LaFarge, text of speech to conference alumnae, College of the Sacred Heart, Boston, May 13, 1955, in box 21, folder 43, JLFP 1; John LaFarge, Religious News Service, February 1, 1960, in box 5, folder 40, JLFP 2; LaFarge, "Feature 'X,'" 615; LaFarge, "Christianity and the Negro," 50–55; LaFarge, "Tentative Draft of Niebuhr Proposal," January 31, 1957, and five 1957 letters from Reinhold Niebuhr to John La-Farge, all in box 17, folder 6, JLFP 1; Zielinski, "'Doing the Truth,'" 264–65; McDonough, *Men Astutely Trained*, 400–403.

32. John LaFarge, "Symbols in a Hurricane," *Am*, 91 (September 18, 1954), 590; LaFarge, *No Postponement*, vi, 5, 7–14, 239; "Catholic Interracial Program—From a European Window," *IR*, 24 (July, 1951), 107. His files contain copies of articles published in Jesuit journals such as *Month* (British), *Striven* (German), *Études* (French), *Criterio* (Spanish), *Lumen Vitae* (Belgian), and the semiofficial Vatican journal, *Osservatore Romano*. LaFarge's "Decision on Segregation," *Catholic Mind*, 52 (October, 1954), 577–78, was first printed in *Études*, July–August, 1954.

33. John LaFarge to Eleanor Waters, September 22, 1958, in box 33, folder 14, JLFP 1; "The Moral Responsibility of the U.S. with Regard to Africa," in box 33, folder 14, JLFP 1.

man of the CAIP Committee on African Students. His attempt to establish an "Africa House" in New York City was unsuccessful, but in 1960 he helped organize the African Service Institute, which assisted African students in getting housing, jobs, counseling, and emergency grants while in the United States. In addition, the African Service Center at CICNY headquarters on Vesey Street served as a meeting place for Africans and Americans to exchange ideas.[34]

If the measure of courage on human rights meant speaking out against Senator Joseph McCarthy in the 1950s, LaFarge failed the test. Although *America*'s editor-in-chief Robert Hartnett offered some fairly strong criticism of the witch-hunting senator from Wisconsin, the journal received so many angry letters from subscribers that the Jesuit provincials ordered the magazine to cease its attacks on the Catholic legislator. Ignoring McCarthy, LaFarge trained his guns on secular liberals, whom he criticized for being dangerously squeamish about denying free speech and due process to members of the American Communist party and assorted fellow-travelers.[35] Even though he admitted that the threat of communist subversion of the African American populace had vanished, his continued use of the communist bogeyman in domestic politics showed how his anticommunism could impair his strong sense of fair play and his regard for civil liberties. Scholars such as Manning Marable undoubtedly would place LaFarge in the "left wing of McCarthyism," a phenomenon that the historian claims retarded the black movement for more than a decade.[36]

34. John LaFarge to Paul C. Reinert, S.J., January 4, 1952, in box 35, folder 1, JLFP 1; Zielinski, " 'Doing the Truth,' " 65–66; Asia-Africa-Pacific News Service, "Report for 1958," in box 18, folder 6, JLFP 1; material on Africa House, in box 34, folder 3, JLFP 1; "African Service Institute of New York, Inc.," September 20, 1961, in box 34, folder 4, JLFP 1. On the African Service Institute, see *IR*, 33 (September, 1960), 210. See also letters to and from African students, in box 35, folders 2–3, JFLP 1.

35. Robert C. Hartnett, "Congress, Communists, and the Common Good," *Am*, 90 (March 21, 1954), 677–79, and the editorial "Senator McCarthy's Charges," *Am*, 82 (April 1, 1950); "Confidential Memorandum to the Editors of *America*," n.d., in box 49, folder 4, JLFP 1; Cogley, *Catholic America*, 112; John LaFarge, "Speaking of Liberals," *Am*, 94 (December 10, 1955), 299.

36. LaFarge, *No Postponement*, 113–14; Marable, *Race, Reform and Rebellion*, 33. On the use of anticommunism, see excerpts from LaFarge's speech in the Providence *Journal*, May 20, 1960, copy in box 10, folder 1, JLFP 1, and John LaFarge, "A Positive Approach to the Social Question," in *A Catholic Case Against Segregation*, ed. Joseph Eugene O'Neill, S.J. (New York, 1966), 150.

Although LaFarge's ideas slowly evolved, his caution in regard to implementing them remained monumental. Pope Pius XII, after all, had warned about "the heresy of action," reminding the faithful in 1950 that external action did not ensure salvation. LaFarge wrote as if the "long Baptism" of education had a higher priority than the accomplishment of social justice itself: "When the *moral revolution* has been accomplished, when all ambiguity and equivocation have been cleared away in every part of the country, North, South, East or West, as to the basic principles of human equality and the immorality of practices and policies that violate them—then the long and arduous process of 'evolving' the disadvantaged Negro race can make much more rapid advance."[37]

LaFarge's model of leadership was still clearly Booker Washington. If more and more blacks perceived Washington as an Uncle Tom, LaFarge's defense of the Tuskegee leader was more ardent than ever. Absent from *No Postponement*, however, were encomiums to pioneering black Catholic activists such as Daniel Rudd. There was only an innocuous reference to Thomas Turner and the FCC, and, of course, Du Bois went unmentioned. LaFarge ignored Turner altogether in the *Catholic Viewpoint*, but he indicted the FCC for its tone "of demand," which he judged as self-defeating.[38]

Although LaFarge's analysis of racism had deepened somewhat with his critique of Nazism in the 1930s, he remained staunch in his idea that ignorance, not malice, was the primary affliction of the racist mind. As in *Interracial Justice*, he attempted to downplay the importance of race in the beginning of *No Postponement* by using the trendy term "intergroup relations" instead of race relations. But, as before, he quickly lapsed into the old terminology. In 1950 he strongly denounced the much-discussed theory of certain behavioral scientists that posited an "authoritarian personality" resistant to education and interracial contact. As always, he rejected any argument that had original sin as the source of racial antipathy. He instead believed that black advances in education, along with the increasing economic cost of social and political discrimination, would cause most racism to disappear within a reasonable amount of time.[39] Stubbornly, he continued to discount

37. Pope, quoted in Herberg, *Protestant-Catholic-Jew*, 149; LaFarge, *No Postponement*, 90, 172–73.

38. LaFarge, *No Postponement*, 48, 83–90, 148, and *Catholic Viewpoint*, 64. On Washington, see Louis R. Harlan, *Booker T. Washington* (2 vols.; New York, 1972, 1983).

39. LaFarge, *No Postponement*, 20, 137; LaFarge, *Catholic Viewpoint*, 42; John

the tenacious psychological or "irrational" reasons for racism that such Catholic scholars as Joseph Fichter and Dennis Clark, along with legions of secular scholars, stressed.[40]

LaFarge and the CICNY, to their everlasting credit, persisted in stressing the need for jobs and housing and in campaigning for fair employment laws. LaFarge often alluded to Pope Pius XII's statement that "disgraceful housing conditions prove obstacles to the family tie and family life." He devoted an entire chapter in *No Postponement* to "The Changing Parish."[41] During the decade LaFarge followed the work of the young interracialist Dennis Clark, who was describing the perilous "urban frontier" and the "panic parish."[42] LaFarge's movement, however, was powerless to slow down or reverse the white flight from Catholic neighborhoods as housing-starved blacks moved in. As we have seen, the housing crisis divided Catholics and sometimes plunged them into rancorous contention. The controversy over the integration of Levittown, Pennsylvania, in 1957, for instance, helped terminate the Catholic Interracial Council of Philadelphia.[43]

Although LaFarge had long lobbied for fair employment legislation, he had not pushed hard for civil rights laws in other areas. This situation began to change in the 1950s. "The paramount issue before the country," he declared in No *Postponement,* "is the issue of national legislation regarding civil rights." He argued that legislation was "in-

LaFarge, "Probing the Authoritarian Man," *Am,* 83 (July 1, 1950), 352–54; John LaFarge to Ralph Verdos, May 2, 1952, in box 6, folder 62, JLFP 2; John LaFarge, "American Humanist Climate," *Social Order,* 3 (May–June, 1953), 268; LaFarge, *No Postponement,* 139. On the bigoted personality, see Theodore W. Adorno *et al., The Authoritarian Personality* (New York, 1950).

40. On Joseph Fichter, see Chap. 9. On Dennis Clark, see John F. Bauman, *Public Housing, Race and Renewal: Urban Planning in Philadelphia, 1920–1974* (Philadelphia, 1987), 168–69. See also LaFarge, *Catholic Viewpoint,* 42, 86–87, 89.

41. LaFarge, *No Postponement,* 109, 176, 179–93, 207; John LaFarge, "Filibuster and the FEPC," *Am,* 87 (August 30, 1952), 517–19; testimony of George K. Hunton before Subcommittee on Civil Rights of the Senate Committee on Labor and Public Welfare, 83rd Cong., 2nd Sess., transcript in box 10, folder 19, JLFP 2.

42. Dennis Clark, "Panic Parish," *IR,* 27 (October, 1954), 170–74; John McDermott and Dennis Clark, "Helping the Panic Neighborhood," *IR,* 28 (August, 1955), 131–35; Dennis Clark, *The Ghetto Game: Racial Conflict in the City* (New York, 1962), 112, 216–17. See also Dennis Clark, *Cities in Crisis: The Christian Response* (New York, 1960). Housing was a topic of a special issue of the *Interracial Review:* 32 (September, 1959).

43. Schmandt, "Catholic Interracial Council of Philadelphia." See also Hirsch, *Making of the Second Ghetto,* 4–31, 40–42, 106–107, 213–19, 229, 241–45, 253, *passim.*

304 John LaFarge and the Limits of Catholic Interracialism

dispensable" in protecting civil rights and that "able, prudent, and incorruptible administration" of such laws was needed at every level. Increasingly, LaFarge depicted the enactment of wise laws as an important part of the process of education. He pointed out that laws could not replace "social love," but he maintained that prudent legislation could be "a very great act of love." [44]

LaFarge, however, was vague on what laws he favored beyond those in employment. On housing, he seemed satisfied with the mild strictures the Supreme Court put on restrictive covenants in *Shelley* v. *Kraemer* in 1948. On voting rights, LaFarge aligned the CICNY with the NAACP in supporting the civil rights bills of 1957 and 1960, both weak and heavily compromised statutes. In 1950 he wrote that "forced racial segregation brings tangible handicaps to individuals and to families in our present complex civilization." He suggested that government should not "countenance" the separate but equal "myth" any longer. Claiming that Truman had reneged on his 1948 promise to pass a civil rights bill, a 1950 editorial in *America* asked, "How long can the Administration delay action on civil rights legislation without losing face on its election promises?" [45]

By 1952 LaFarge was convinced that the Supreme Court was going to strike down segregated public schools and that Catholics had to move on the question or be left behind in embarrassment. He told an audience at Howard University in 1952 that segregation was morally wrong and that Catholics could accept no less than "complete integration of racial groups into the total community and into each of its parts." This was the first time he publicly condemned segregation without the usual qualifications or hedging. [46]

Shortly before the historic *Brown* opinion, LaFarge published his autobiography. Unlike *No Postponement*, it was a resounding hit. The 1954 book was his most widely recognized and highly praised book. Although LaFarge was reluctant to pen his memoirs (he protested that it was not proper for a Jesuit to undertake such an immodest task), his superiors insisted that it would be good for Catholicism and for the

44. LaFarge, *No Postponement*, 61–62.
45. *Ibid.*, 183–85, 206–207, 229–30; John LaFarge, "Civil Rights Delay," *Am*, 83 (April 29, 1950), 102–103. On the CICNY's support of the civil rights bills and other activities, see the detailed account of Zielinski, " 'Doing the Truth,' " 338–427, *passim*.
46. John LaFarge, "Development of Cooperation [and] Acceptance of Racial Integration," *IR*, 25 (September, 1952), 141–43.

Society of Jesus. Thus *The Manner Is Ordinary* appeared in February, just about the time LaFarge reached the age of seventy-four. Sales of his memoirs were brisk. The book was in its fourth printing of ten thousand by 1955 and continued to sell well for several years. It seemed to appeal particularly to nuns and priests. The *Manner* was one of the selections advertised in the *Book-of-the-Month Club News* in February, 1954. A revised version was published in France in 1959 under the somewhat misleading title *Un Américain Comme Les Autres* ("An American Like Others"). In 1960 Doubleday put LaFarge's memoirs in paperback.[47]

The *Manner* was reviewed by the New York *Times,* the *New Yorker,* the *Saturday Review,* black newspapers, and virtually every Catholic publication in America that reviewed books, as well as many Catholic periodicals abroad. Catholic reviewers were ecstatic about the book, raising scarcely a quibble with it. To declare that the book (despite its title) revealed a priest whose "manner was extraordinary" became a cliché in Catholic circles. Reviewers generally commented on the aristocratic connections of the LaFarge family, the priest's humility and piety, his devotion to blacks and to social justice, his breadth of knowledge and activity, and his wit. Jacques Maritain extolled LaFarge as "a master of wisdom and witty understatement." A typical flourish appeared in the "Catholic Book Week Supplement" of *The Pilot.* Here Mary Stack McNiff advised, "For sheer pleasure, for spiritual challenge and encouragement, to quote [Gilbert K.] Chesterton, 'for God's sake,' read *The Manner Is Ordinary.*"[48]

Reviewers for secular publications articulated some criticisms of the autobiography but generally viewed it in a positive light. The *New York Times Book Review* carried its review on page one of the book review section. It included a large picture of LaFarge in one of his

47. John LaFarge to Peter S. Brown, N. S. F., February 23, 1954, in box 38, folder 13, JLFP 1; John LaFarge to J. Edward Colley, S.J., March 1, 1955, in box 15, folder 3, JLFP 1; material on French edition in box 8, folder 24, JLFP 2; John Delaney, Hanover House Division of Doubleday, to John LaFarge, August 1, 1955, in box 8, folder 34, JLFP 2. See box 4, folder 1, JLFP 1, and box 3, folder 13, JLFP 1, for royalty receipts.

48. John S. Kennedy, "The Manner Is Extraordinary," (Washington, D.C.) *Catholic Standard,* February 12, 1954, clipping in box 2, folder 11, JLFP 2; Maritain, quoted in CIC News Service, February 26, 1954, in box 9, folder 7, JLFP 2; Mary Stack McNiff, "Catholic Book Week Section," *Pilot,* February 21–27, 1954, in box 9, folder 11, JLFP 2. See also John O'Connor, "The Ordinary Way," *IR,* 27 (February, 1954), 24–26.

favorite poses, a frontal shot with his head tilted slightly upward and a studious twinkle in his eye. The noted historian and critic Jacques Barzun described LaFarge as a "saintly character" who occasionally wrote "deft and witty prose." Barzun speculated, however, that the priest was so spiritual and his thought so Catholic that he unwittingly constructed a formidable barrier between those of his world and those outside it. Still, Barzun discerned a "flexible duality" in LaFarge: the Jesuit appeared equally at home in the spiritual world and in the world of everyday affairs.[49]

Reviewing the *Manner* in the *Afro-American*, the black writer J. Saunders Redding wrote that "grace and truth and humility glow through the book like the sun through consecrated stained-glass windows." Redding continued, "The charity, the penetrating insight and the decent wisdom of the commentary warm the heart." He nevertheless concluded that the *Manner* was neither cosmopolitan nor folksy enough to rank in a class with such great autobiographies as *The Education of Henry Adams* or *Up from Slavery*. More critical was William Duffy, who charged in the New York *Post* that the book was "maddeningly sketchy," though he could have had no inkling of how much of the story about Catholic black-white relations LaFarge had omitted. Only Conrad H. Moehlman, writing in the Protestant *Christian Century*, was rude enough to chastise LaFarge for praising the reactionary pope Pius X, for paying scant attention to progressive Catholics such as Cardinal John Henry Newman, John Emerich Dalberg, and Lord Acton, and for condemning modernist critics of all stripes.[50]

LaFarge's next book on race relations, *The Catholic Viewpoint on Race Relations*, was a brief primer aimed mainly, as the title suggests, at Catholics. It contained little that LaFarge had not said repeatedly in the past. *A Report on the American Jesuits* was a piece of puffery, "a hurry-up job," LaFarge confessed. He wrote the eighty-page text, but the beauty of the book lay in the pictures by the prize-winning photographer Margaret Bourke-White. *An American Amen* was more sub-

---

49. Barzun, "Not to Count the Cost," 1.

50. J. Saunders Redding, Baltimore *Afro-American*, April 3, 1954, clipping in box 9, folder 7, JLFP 2; William Duffy, New York *Post*, February 14, 1954, clipping in box 9, folder 11, JLFP 2; Conrad Henry Moehlman, review of *MIO*, by John LaFarge, *Christian Century*, 71 (April 7, 1954), 430–31. See also the uncritical reviews by Brendan Gill, in the *New Yorker*, March 27, 1954, pp. 125–26, and Anne Fremantle, in the *Saturday Review*, March 6, 1954, pp. 40–41.

stantial and vintage LaFarge. It explored the relation between faith and the intellect and constituted a prolonged celebration of faith in God and obedience to Christ and his divine church. Here LaFarge enthusiastically proclaimed that God's goodness manifested itself most demonstrably in "the innate justice and good sense of the American people themselves."[51]

By the time the *Brown* decision was handed down on May 17, LaFarge's autobiography had been widely circulated and reviewed. In fact, a dinner party arranged by friends on May 18 to pay tribute to LaFarge and his book turned into a celebration of the Jesuit's role in preparing Catholics for the court's opinion. LaFarge had followed the school cases carefully from their inception until *Brown* was decided. In December, 1953, he predicted that the court's decision would be as momentous as the *Dred Scott* case. At the same time, he said, the court's decision would not be altogether crucial because "the simple truth is that compulsory racial segregation, as a social and educational policy in American life, is of itself doomed." Like those who argued that slavery was slated for a natural death, LaFarge contended that societal segregation would inevitably collapse under its own poisonous weight.[52] To him, justice was certain, but its swiftness was not paramount.

Anticipating the *Brown* decision, LaFarge energetically but privately encouraged bishops, his religious order, and Catholics in general to expedite the desegregation of Catholic institutions. In February, 1953, William K. Ryan, S.J., the rector and headmaster of Georgetown Preparatory School, sought LaFarge's advice on whether to enroll a well-qualified black as a day student. Ryan trotted out all the usual arguments against admission, including the southern flavor of the student body and parents' threats to withdraw their sons from the school if integration occurred. In the first sentence of his reply, LaFarge recommended straight out that the black student be accepted. Then he proceeded through four single-spaced pages to explain why. First of all,

51. John LaFarge to Schuyler Brown, June 14, 1955, in box 38, folder 13, JLFP 1; Robert Girioux to John LaFarge, November 29, 1956, in box 2, folder 1, JLFP 1; LaFarge, *An American Amen*, 11.

52. John LaFarge, "Judgment on Racial Segregation," *Am*, 90 (December 12, 1953), 289–91. See also his "Reason and the Race Question," *Social Order*, 3 (December, 1953), 452–56. On the party for LaFarge at the Parkside Hotel in New York, see New York *Herald Tribune*, May 19, 1954, clipping in letter box 29, CICNYP; see box 10, folders 6 and 9, JLFP 1 for clippings on civil rights cases.

he proclaimed: "The time is ripe. In point of fact it is over-ripe." He then informed Ryan that desegregation was proceeding all over the District of Columbia and that even Eisenhower had vowed to end Jim Crow there. He added that the archbishop of Washington, D.C., desired it and that the threats of student withdrawals from desegregated Catholic schools in St. Louis and elsewhere had not materialized. Since students would soon have to fulfill a military obligation in an integrated fighting force, he told Ryan, it would give young men the wrong message if they found out that the government was more Christian toward blacks than the church was. He also argued that the continuation of segregation at the preparatory school would be a "distinct disservice" to the cause of Catholic missions and a "serious embarrassment" in the church's war against communism. Finally, LaFarge answered a question that was not even asked but one he knew was the burning issue. Anticipating the headmaster's anxiety about social affairs, he offered certain assurances. "As for dances," he ventured, "the young people usually work things out for themselves." He also assured Ryan that the "colored have sense enough as a rule to keep out of trouble."[53]

In several of the southern and border states, bishops did not wait for the Supreme Court to rule. After the breakthrough at St. Louis University in 1944 and the desegregation of all the diocesan schools in St. Louis by Archbishop Ritter in the late 1940s, other bishops followed suit. Six southern and border states had enrolled blacks in Catholic schools by May, 1954. Archbishop O'Boyle began the process in the District of Columbia in 1949, and Bishop Vincent S. Waters in Raleigh in 1953. In San Antonio Archbishop Lucey acted a month before *Brown.* These actions elated LaFarge, but he still urged caution and kept his expectations modest. In advising Bishop Waters on desegregation in 1951, he wrote, "Undue haste can do as much harm as undue timorousness." Predictably, he advised Waters that no matter what they did, the race question would resolve itself "by the nature of our changing times." The Jesuit then announced his modest goal, "I would like to see the Catholic Church in this country a bit ahead of the times, rather than seem to be always following."[54]

53. William K. Ryan, S.J., to John LaFarge, February 2, 1953, and John LaFarge to William Ryan, February 6, 1953, both in box 4, folder 2, JLFP 1.

54. "Bishop Waters on Church Segregation," *Am,* 89 (July 4, 1953), 354; "Underscorings," *Am,* 91 (April 17, 1954), 61; Constance McLaughlin Green, *The Secret City:*

While supremely pleased with the court's 1954 decision, LaFarge warned that the desegregation opinion by the court "would not of itself make widespread sweeping and radical changes." He explained that blacks would have to initiate time-consuming suits in every school district in the South. Furthermore, he expressed disappointment that the basis for *Brown* was sociological rather than moral and religious. (Ironically, LaFarge later gave an eloquent defense of sociological jurisprudence in his intensely spiritual book *An American Amen.*) The Jesuit, however, conjectured that the spiritual basis for desegregation would emerge during the national debate on *Brown.*[55]

Just the fact that the *Brown* decision had set a clear goal fed LaFarge's congenital optimism, but the implementation, he counseled, required vigilant patience. "The pace [of desegregation] must be fast in some places, or gradual in others," LaFarge wrote, "but it must be a pace, not a crablike wiggle." Above all, LaFarge called for a quiet, "orderly revolution." He praised the Supreme Court for postponing the "when and how" of desegregation until later. He stressed, too, that the court had demanded not integration but only desegregation, a distinction that diehard segregationists would increasingly emphasize. Much of his long-range optimism stemmed from his faith in the good will and reasonableness of white southerners. He conceded that the "Ku Kluxoid agitators" would kick up their heels, but he added that "southern people had dealt with these types in the past, and will know how to deal with them in the future."[56]

LaFarge, of course, agreed with the view of the southern attorneys general in *Brown* II that school desegregation should be implemented with solemn gradualism. Although the NAACP had argued that a gradual timetable for desegregation would result in stalling by the white South, President Eisenhower, southern segregationists, and many moderates such as LaFarge applauded when the court ruled in May, 1955,

A History of Race Relations in the Nation's Capital (Princeton, 1967), 303; Joseph P. Lyford, "Race Relations Improve," *IR,* 30 (June, 1957), 100–103; John LaFarge to Bishop Vincent S. Waters, March 19, 1951, in box 19, folder 10, JLFP 1.

55. LaFarge, "Judgment on Racial Segregation," 289; John LaFarge, "Decision on Segregation," *Catholic Mind,* 52 (October, 1954), 581–85; LaFarge, *An American Amen,* 214–17; John LaFarge's address to CICNY, June 6, 1954, in letter box 16, CICNYP.

56. LaFarge, "Decision on Segregation," 585; John LaFarge, "Report on Desegregation," *Am,* 92 (October 16, 1954), 70, and "Supreme Court Voids Racial Segregation," *Am,* 91 (May 29, 1954), 238; "An Orderly Revolution," *Am,* 81 (July 28, 1949), 456.

that the schools should be desegregated "with all deliberate speed." Both *America* and the *Interracial Review* praised the "social vision" of the justices who, they claimed, acted "prudently" in leaving few loopholes for segregationists. *Brown* II, however, enabled the Deep South to "stonewall" desegregation of schools for over a decade, and it allowed a breathing spell for massive resistance to organize.[57]

The CICNY happily reported in the fall of 1954 that most of the dioceses in the Upper South and the border states had started the desegregation process in their schools. Although the *Brown* decision placed no legal demands on parochial schools, dioceses in Missouri, Arkansas, North Carolina, West Virginia, Virginia, Texas, Kentucky, Delaware, Kansas, and Tennessee began to desegregate in 1954. The ever-candid John O'Connor reported that no desegregation had occurred at all in the Deep South, to say nothing of Oklahoma or a place dear to LaFarge's heart, southern Maryland. Moreover, some of the dioceses that integrated their schools still excluded blacks from their churches. (Even O'Connor did not report that after black Catholics in Chicago were stoned at St. Kevin's, they returned to worship under police protection.) The Catholic strategy in the Deep South, O'Connor griped, was to let the Protestant majority lead (or block) the way.[58]

Archbishop O'Boyle soon discovered that, unlike the desegregating of the District of Columbia, the prospect of moving LaFarge's beloved southern Maryland toward integration was particularly daunting. In 1952 LaFarge told David Nugent, the Maryland provincial, that "nothing moves fast in the minds of Southern Maryland." He nevertheless informed the provincial that the Jesuit missions had to move on desegregation, if only at a snail's pace, and that the priests had to take the lead. Four days after the court's 1954 decision, LaFarge wrote to Nugent's successor, William F. Mahoney, and advised that no one could take refuge in the "separate but equal" fallacy any longer. He warned

57. *Brown v. Board of Education of Topeka*, 349 U.S. 294 (1955); Kluger, *Simple Justice*, 717–46; Southern, *Gunnar Myrdal and Black-White Relations*, 149; "Deliberate Speed, Majestic Instancy," *Am*, 93 (June 11, 1955), 281; "Now It's Our Job," *IR*, 28 (June, 1955), 93–94.

58. CIC News Service, September 13, 1954, in box 5, CICNYP; Charles Keenan, "Church Leaders on School Desegregation," *Am*, 91 (July 10, 1954), 378–79; "Bishop Ends Race Barrier in Richmond Schools," *IR*, 27 (July, 1954), 124; John O'Connor, "Catholic Educational Integration," *IR*, 27 (May, 1954), 81–82; Avella, *This Confident Church*, 270.

that Jesuit discrimination would now look worse than ever. LaFarge talked personally with many of the priests in southern Maryland and discovered that they all were looking to the archbishop for direction. He acknowledged the importance of the archbishop, but he suggested to Mahoney that the priests take the initiative. He even singled out the name of a certain Father Wilkinson who, in LaFarge's opinion, exhibited leadership potential on racial matters. A week later, though, he wrote Archbishop O'Boyle and informed him that the Jesuits in Maryland were waiting for his command. He advised the archbishop that the time was auspicious for Catholics in the South to show the way for interracial justice, and he suggested that Mahoney and the archbishop of Baltimore issue a joint statement on the *Brown* opinion.[59]

Soon after the *Brown* decision, someone in the Jesuit Curia inquired of LaFarge why there had been no increase in Jesuit activity among blacks. Replying to Rome on September 3, 1954, LaFarge essentially argued that rapid progress was the reason. He informed Rome that the separate black parish was fast disappearing and much of the Jesuit mission work along with it. He claimed that most of the Jesuit work was now voluntary and did not show up in the records. He predicted that all separate black parishes would be gone in five or ten years. He told Rome that the Josephites now found themselves in an "anomalous" position and were considering abandoning their exclusively racial mission. A month later, however, LaFarge informed a Jesuit in New Orleans that the church in the South was facing a long period of "storm and stress."[60]

Thus, in the main, LaFarge was realistic about the struggle ahead. He dismissed any idea that the work of the interracial councils had been completed, and in 1959 he announced that the "second phase" of the civil rights movement had begun. He maintained that desegregation was not a cure-all but only a necessary condition for the solution of the race problem. At the same time, he became more emphatic about Jim Crow. He declared that segregation was "a deadly ambiguity" for

59. Muffler, "This Far by Faith," 150; John LaFarge to David Nugent, March 31, 1952, in box 1, folder 31, JLFP 2; John LaFarge to William F. Mahoney, May 21, 1954, in box 14, folder 27, JLFP 2; John LaFarge to Patrick O'Boyle, May 27, 1954, in box 14, folder 32, JLFP 2.

60. John LaFarge to Alfonsus Smetsers, S.J., September 3, 1954, in letter box 29, CICNYP; John LaFarge to A. William Crandell, S.J., October 13, 1954, in box 6, folder 2, JLFP 2.

the church and a "grievous wrong." Almost all traces of hedging on segregation had vanished, though he continued to hold that it was impossible "to isolate the moral aspect of segregation" or pin down individual guilt. Having finally arrived at this liberal position, LaFarge brazenly asserted that neither George Dunne nor William Markoe had added anything substantial to the topic of segregation beyond the views he had offered in *Interracial Justice* nearly two decades before.[61]

One of LaFarge's greatest miscalculations was his exaggerated optimism about the white South. One could scarcely find a northern activist more sympathetic to the South than the Jesuit, who had been announcing the arrival of the "New South" and the "crumbling walls of Dixie" since World War II.[62] As racial atrocities multiplied and massive resistance accelerated in the South, *America* and the *Interracial Review* duly reported events such as the brutal murder of fourteen-year-old Emmett Till in Mississippi in 1955 (and the acquittal of his white murderers by an all-white jury). The magazines also detailed the countless subterfuges the South employed to derail desegregation: interposition, pupil assignment plans, economic pressure from the White Citizens' Council, and terror by mobs of night riders. But *America* concluded that these devices only accentuated "the incongruity of compulsory segregation in our society" and its "incompatibility" with Christian morality. LaFarge managed to find a silver lining wrapped around every southern atrocity.[63]

In fact, LaFarge refused to publish several articles by Catholics in the *Interracial Review* because he "made it a policy not to say harsh things about the South or Southerners." LaFarge preferred to direct his ire toward northern Catholic lay groups such as the Knights of Columbus, which used a "blackball" system to keep most branches of the

---

61. John LaFarge, "Interracial Justice: Second Phase," *IR*, 32 (June, 1959), 111–12; James O'Gara, "Integration—Why? An Interview with Father John LaFarge, S.J.," *IR*, 32 (December, 1959), 240; LaFarge, "Christianity and the Negro," 56; John LaFarge to John H. Ziegler, C.S.P., October 29, 1953, in box 8, folder 2, JLFP 1.

62. See Chap. 9, but also John LaFarge, "Tar Heel Catholics Show the Way," *IR*, 25 (June, 1952), 92.

63. "The Emmett Till Acquittal," *Am*, 94 (October 8, 1955), 31; "Mockery of Jury Trial," *Am*, 97 (June 15, 1957), 316; Wilfrid Parson, "Washington Front: End Runs on Civil Rights," *Am*, 96 (March 23, 1957), 694; "Civil Rights Debate," *Am*, 97 (July 27, 1957), 439.

organization lily-white. The verbal barbs he hurled at the Knights drew wounded cries from its reactionary leadership.[64] If in the past many northerners evaded their own race problem by focusing attention on southern racial atrocities, LaFarge committed the opposite error. He downplayed the southern problem by stressing northern shortcomings. Both approaches were equally flawed.

LaFarge thus minimized the true import of the 1956 "Southern Manifesto," pointing out that the 101 southern congressmen who signed it had rejected a more extreme version of the document and that the legislators had vowed to defeat the law of the land "by strictly legal methods." He incessantly praised the "brave efforts" of southern moderates, and he defined "moderate" in a way that made its practitioners appear as courageous statesmen. A moderate, LaFarge asserted, was one who had made a "hard or painful" but "definite choice." "A policy of moderation," he argued, "is a strong policy, when it is sincere." LaFarge acknowledged that some southerners gave gradualism a bad name, but if any number of white southerners made a nod in the right direction, LaFarge's hat was quickly off to them. "We cannot make too frequent and earnest a plea for moderation, patience, tolerance, and mutual good will," he taught. He frequently pointed to the example of the Jesuit founder: "Ignatius hurries no one; gives you days, months, if you wish, to deliberate. But he means action in the end." [65] Many so-called southern moderates, not to mention conservatives, did not mean action in the end. Indeed, in the late 1950s southern moderates were conspicuous by their silence. One can only speculate what LaFarge might have thought if his activities had landed him in a southern jail. It is plain, however, that he was more patient with southern moderates than was the long-suffering Martin Luther King, Jr.[66]

64. "Knights and Negroes," *Am*, 90 (March 13, 1954), 618; LaFarge attack on Knights in New York *Times*, October 29, 1955; Walter E. Walsh, Grand Knight of New York, to John LaFarge, December 14, 1955, in box 3, folder 15, JLFP 2; Christopher J. Kauffmann, *The History of the Knights of Columbus, 1882–1982* (New York, 1982), 396–400, 404.

65. John LaFarge to William J. Junkin, S.J., May 3, 1957, in box 14, folder 18, JLFP 2; John LaFarge, "Let's Accept the Challenge," *IR*, 29 (March, 1956), 41, "Southern Moderates Speak," *Am*, 98 (January 11, 1958), 410, *Catholic Viewpoint*, 165–66, and "On Moderation and Gradualism," *IR*, 29 (December, 1956), 205–207.

66. Sitkoff, *Struggle for Black Equality*, 132–33. In his famous "Letter from Bir-

LaFarge also expressed great faith in southern white Catholics. In 1951 in Charleston, South Carolina, he attended a three-day convention of the CCS, which had been formed in 1939 by Paul Williams, a layman who became president of the Southern Regional Council in 1945. LaFarge described the CCS as an agency designed to carry out the church's apostolic mission and its "undiluted social principles" in the South. He praised the small group of bishops at the convention who denounced racism in a "bold and prudent" way. Actually, the CCS hardly constituted a threat to "the southern way of life." Representing only a fraction of the 4 percent of those in the South who were Catholic, the CCS was little noticed by the white South before 1954. Besides, three-fourths of white Catholics in the South were staunch segregationists. When massive resistance began, the CCS quickly vanished from the scene altogether.[67]

As with his outlook on the South in general, LaFarge's optimism about the Catholic church in Dixie was based on low expectations. He sized up the southern situation of the church in *Catholic Viewpoint:* "In some areas of the deep South the pressure of long-standing social custom cautioned those responsible for Catholic education to withhold action until the Supreme Court had outlined its program and public opinion had become more used to the idea." In a letter to a Jesuit in New Orleans in the fall of 1954, he commented further: "It is a very big thing that the question [of desegregation] is being discussed at all. This marks a definite break from the time-honored position of hush-hush." It was no wonder some Catholics, such as Leander Perez, the notorious segregationist boss of Plaquemines Parish in Louisiana, asked the church hierarchy if segregation only became evil after the Supreme Court ruled it illegal. LaFarge told one such Catholic skeptic that segregation had been sinful all along, but the church had had no choice but to abide by local customs and laws.[68] In short, LaFarge's habit was

---

mingham Jail," King charged that when southern moderates said "wait," they almost always meant "never."

67. John LaFarge, "Southern Catholics and Applied Democracy," *Am,* 84 (February 10, 1951), 549–52; "Survey of Interracial Thinking," *IR,* 29 (May, 1956), 76; Osborne, *Segregated Covenant,* 55, 65, 68; Katherine Martensen, "Region, Religion, and Social Action: The Catholic Committee of the South, 1939–1956," *Catholic Historical Review,* 68 (April, 1982), 249–67.

68. LaFarge, *Catholic Viewpoint,* 97–98; George Hunton to John LaFarge, August 27, 1955, in letter box 29, CICNYP; John LaFarge to A. William Crandell, S.J., October

to accentuate Catholic achievements in the Upper South and border states, to muffle criticism of Catholics in the Deep South, and to exalt those few in the lower South who defied the racial mores of the region in favor of Catholic principles.

LaFarge's southern hero was Joseph Francis Rummel, archbishop of New Orleans. Rummel served in a state that had two dioceses with the largest population of black Catholics in the United States. In 1950 the New Orleans diocese had 62,000 black Catholics and Lafayette had 70,000, whereas Washington, D.C., had 29,500 and and New York had 30,302. In southern dioceses such as these, defiance of church authority on the issue of segregation matched that of general southern society toward federal law. Although Archbishop Rummel attempted no integration of schools in the fall of 1954 or 1955, he made his liberal intentions clear in the Jesuit Bend incident. Rummel had banned church segregation in his archdiocese in March, 1953. A few miles from New Orleans at the Jesuit Bend Mission, however, white Catholics refused to let a black priest celebrate Mass in October, 1955. Rummel reacted strongly and closed the mission until the parishioners showed a willingness to accept all ministers he assigned. The mission remained closed until 1958. Shortly after the Jesuit Bend controversy, Rummel issued a pastoral letter that LaFarge quoted reverently in *Catholic Viewpoint*. Rummel proclaimed that segregation was "morally wrong and sinful" on three counts: "(1) because it is a denial of the unity and solidarity of the human race as conceived by God. . . . (2) because it is a denial of the unity and universality of the Redemption. (3) because it is basically a violation of the dictates of justice and the mandate of love, which in obedience to God's will must regulate the relations between all men." [69]

Rummel's words and deeds provoked many southern Catholics to action. By the time of the Jesuit Bend incident, about 75 percent of the New Orleans White Citizens' Council was Catholic. In addition, the

---

13, 1954, in box 6, folder 24, JLFP 2; Osborne, *Segregated Covenant*, 78; Joseph L. Kimble to John LaFarge, August 26, 1957, and John LaFarge to Joseph Kimble, September 13, 1957, both in box 5, folder 10, JLFP 1.

69. "Catholic Negroes in Principal Dioceses," *IR*, 24 (March, 1951), 37; Zielinski, " 'Doing the Truth,' " 199–203; LaFarge, *Catholic Viewpoint*, 93. See also these editorials: "Word from Rome," *Am*, 94 (November 5, 1955), 144; "Rome Condemns Racial Injustice," *Am*, 95 (September 22, 1956), 581; and "Rome and New Orleans," *Am*, 97 (August 24, 1957), 518.

Association of Catholic Laymen was founded to try to stave off desegregation of the New Orleans diocese. White supremacist Catholics also founded a segregationist sheet called the *Catholic Warrior*, and Emile Wagner, Jr., organized "Roman Catholics of the Caucasian Race." Leander Perez became the name that symbolized the most strident and crudely racist type of segregationist. Rummel ultimately threatened many Catholic segregationists with excommunication, actually carrying out his threat against Perez. The Association of Catholic Laymen, however, appealed its case to Rome. Although the semiofficial organ of the Vatican, *Osservatore Romano*, supported Rummel, the pope remained silent on the issue. The parochial schools of New Orleans, which had started a very gradual plan of desegregation in 1957 (one elementary grade each year), suspended the process until 1962. Joseph Fichter, a Jesuit activist in New Orleans, lamented that Archbishop Rummel was a tired old man not up to the task of leadership.[70]

Catholic resistance in the South turned LaFarge's attention toward Rome. The assistant general of the Jesuits had earlier asked LaFarge to outline his thoughts on desegregation for the pope's use. LaFarge responded with a long letter on December 10, 1956, which urged the pope to back Rummel. He further expressed the hope that Pius XII would remove "all uncertainty" in the public's mind about where the church stood on segregation. Collectively, American bishops had avoided the subject of race since the crisis of World War II. LaFarge believed that strong statements and action by some bishops, on the one hand, and vacillation and timidity by the rest, on the other hand, had caused perplexity in the Catholic mind. Now LaFarge was asking Rome to impose racial liberalism on the American church. "Until and unless the Bishops speak on this matter with some show of unity," LaFarge declared, "the conscience of American Catholics are [*sic*] left in confusion."[71]

The Little Rock crisis in the fall of 1957 put more pressure on the bishops to act. In his initial reaction to Little Rock, LaFarge depicted

70. Zielinski, " 'Doing the Truth,' " 200–203, 205; Allitt, *Catholic Intellectuals and Conservative Politics*, 113; "Word from Rome," 144; "Rome Condemns Racial Injustice," 581; Stephen R. Ryan, "After Jesuit Bend," *IR*, 29 (February, 1956), 31; M. F. Everett to George Hunton, November 22, 1957, in box 28, folder 1, JLFP 1; Fichter, *One-Man Research*, 81–82.

71. John LaFarge to the Assistant General, December 10, 1956, in box 10, folder 3, JLFP 1.

Governor Orval Faubus as only an aberration who had temporarily derailed the benign course of southern moderates (Faubus had been a moderate, arguably a southern liberal, before the *Brown* decision). Still, with increasing urgency LaFarge lobbied several bishops, including Cardinal Spellman and Archbishop O'Boyle, for more unified and decisive action on the school question. On October 17, 1957, he wrote Bishop Thomas McDonough of Savannah that "we can no longer avoid going on record." He warned that the patience of African Americans, particularly that of black Catholics, was wearing thin. "Strains on loyalty which an older generation might endure," he commented, "can be too much for younger ones."[72]

LaFarge, however, played only a small and indirect role in the bishops' 1958 statement on segregation. The most important figure in regard to this statement was Father John F. Cronin, a Sulpician priest who was serving at this time as associate director of the Social Action Department of the NCWC. A secret speech writer and informant on the communist conspiracy for Senator and, later, Vice-President Richard Nixon, Cronin happened to be in Europe when the Little Rock crisis occurred. His strong reaction contrasted sharply with that of LaFarge. As an American abroad, Cronin was angered and humiliated by Little Rock. On returning to the United States, he urged the administrative board of the NCWC to issue a statement on segregation; he himself drafted a statement for the bishops to sign. Cronin described what followed as a "bitter" struggle. Cardinal Mooney of Detroit balked at the prospect of presenting a statement that might split the bishops. Finally, in October Pope Pius XII intervened and ordered the bishops to make a statement. Unfortunately, the pope died the day after he sent the cable, and the apostolic delegate, Amleto Cicognani (characterized by LaFarge as a prelate who exuded the "influence of timidity"), suppressed it on the pretense that the pope's message lacked the official papal seal. Cicognani's action angered Archbishop O'Boyle, who cabled several American cardinals in Rome to elect a new pope. Despite strong opposition from Cardinal McIntyre, O'Boyle persuaded Spellman to his point of view, and the O'Boyle faction prevailed. The bishops approved Cronin's statement on November 8, 1958.[73]

72. John LaFarge, "The Lesson of Little Rock," *Saturday Review*, September 12, 1959, pp. 41–42; John LaFarge to Bishop Thomas McDonough, October 17, 1957, in box 28, folder 1, JLFP 1.

73. John F. Cronin, S.S., "Religion and Race," *Am*, 150 (June 23–30, 1984), 472;

The bishops' pastoral letter was titled "Discrimination and the Christian Conscience." The letter began by quoting from the bishops' response to the racial crisis of 1943. It then reviewed the teaching of the church on human unity and the history of black-white relations since the war. It posed the problem of a nation divided "by the problem of compulsory segregation" and the "demand of racial justice." After arguing that Catholicism knew "not the distinction of race, color, or nationhood," the bishops asked, "Can enforced segregation be reconciled with the Christian view of our fellow man?" They answered in the negative, saying that segregation imposed "a stigma of inferiority upon the segregated people." In addition, the statement claimed that history showed irrefutably that segregation led to a denial of basic rights for blacks. This weighty but restrained document also emphasized Catholic "prudence." The bishops condemned "a gradualism that is merely a cloak for inaction," but they equally deplored "rash impetuosity that would sacrifice the achievements of decades in ill-timed and ill-considered ventures." But who would determine what was prudent and what was rash? Would blacks, whose constitutional rights had been denied for three centuries, have as much or more say than whites in this determination? The bishops could only suggest that the "prayerful and considered judgment of experienced counselors who have achieved success in meeting similar problems" should make the choice.[74]

LaFarge was thrilled by the bishops' letter, as were others. At least twenty-five important black leaders, including Roy Wilkins and A. Philip Randolph, and at least eight senators congratulated LaFarge and the CICNY on the statement.[75] Almost no one found fault with the bishops' letter. Only Edward Marciniak, one of the founders of the CICC, complained that the statement was not dramatic enough to move Catholics or the nation. Was it too little, too late, as Marciniak believed? According to the Josephite Joseph T. Leonard in *Theology and Race Relations,* published in 1963, only with time, experience, and

Thomas Spalding, *Premier See,* 377; Garry Wills, *Confessions of a Conservative* (Garden City, N.Y., 1979), 81; Zielinski, " 'Doing the Truth,' " 220–21.

74. "Discrimination and the Christian Conscience," in *Documents of American Catholic History,* ed. John Ellis, 642–47. The names of the assenting bishops can be found with the copy of the pastoral letter in *IR,* 31 (December, 1958), 219.

75. CIC News Service, November 23, 1958, in letter box 24, CICNYP; Zielinski, " 'Doing the Truth,' " 218–19. Senator John F. Kennedy lauded the pastoral letter in CIC News Service, February 23, 1959, in box 30, folder 2, JLFP 1.

proof could the church fathom that segregation was morally wrong.[76] Some might ask, however, why it took the Catholic hierarchy more than a decade longer than it took the Federal Council of Churches and other religious groups (some of them in the South) to make that discovery.

Because of his caution, his low-key approach, and his age, La-Farge's role as leader in the field of Catholic race relations steadily lessened. His contribution to the bishops' statement of 1958 provides a case in point. No longer fully in the ecclesiastical loop, LaFarge apparently knew nothing about the pope's directive to the American bishops. Cronin did send LaFarge an advance copy of the bishops' letter a few days before it was released. No doubt, this was a gesture of tribute to a pioneering Catholic interracialist from a man almost thirty years his junior, one who had been sternly lectured in 1949 by LaFarge because the Sulpician had ignored the race problem in his numerous books and articles on labor and economics.[77] If LaFarge supplied none of the actual words of the bishops' statement, he certainly provided the spiritual guidance for them. Monsignor Daniel Cantwell, a leader of the Chicago interracial movement, recognized this fact. In a letter to LaFarge, Cantwell said that the bishops had bestowed on the New Yorker "a great vindication, if one were necessary, of what you have been saying and teaching these many years."[78]

Despite his advancing age, LaFarge remained a master propagandist for the CICNY (and thus for himself). He was extremely effective in conveying an enhanced picture of the New York council's strength to Catholics abroad and to American civil rights leaders, both black and white. About the only thing many European church officials knew about the American church and race relations was what LaFarge had

76. Zielinski, " 'Doing the Truth,' " 219; Joseph T. Leonard, S.S.J., *Theology and Race Relations* (Milwaukee, Wisc., 1963), 282.

77. John LaFarge to Archbishop Patrick O'Boyle, November 13, 1958, in box 2, folder 16, JLFP 1; John Cronin to John LaFarge, June 14, 1949, in box 20, folder 5, JLFP 1. Compare, for example, the discussion of race in John Cronin's *Catholic Social Action* (Milwaukee, 1948) with the more ample and liberal discussions in his *Catholic Social Principles: The Social Teaching of the Catholic Church Applied to American Economic Life* (Milwaukee, 1956) and his *Social Principles and Economic Life* (Milwaukee, 1959).

78. Daniel Cantwell to John LaFarge, November 15, 1958, in box 30, folder 3, Msgr. Daniel Cantwell Papers, Chicago Historical Society, Chicago; Zielinski, " 'Doing the Truth,' " 221.

communicated by his prolific writings and extensive travels.[79] Attesting
to the effectiveness of his journalistic pleading and diplomacy was the
1959 silver anniversary of the CICNY, which was held at Town Hall
on Pentecost Sunday, the same site and same occasion of the original
meeting in 1934. The anniversary celebration was attended by five hundred people and coincided with the fifth anniversary of the *Brown* decision. Accolades flooded into the CICNY from, among others, senators, congressmen, Catholic cardinals and archbishops, the National
Council of Churches, the NAACP, the Urban League, the American
Federation of Labor, and President Eisenhower. A. Philip Randolph,
one of several distinguished speakers at the event, declared that the
CICNY had made "a constructive and creative impact upon the consciousness" of the nation, and he lauded LaFarge for his "inspired
leadership."[80]

Nevertheless, internal criticism of LaFarge and the CICNY increased in the 1950s. As I noted earlier, Catholics such as George
Dunne, Claude Heithaus, Thomas Harte, and William and John Markoe were sharply critical of LaFarge in the 1940s. Nor did the Jesuit
scholar Albert Foley spare LaFarge in his 1950 doctoral dissertation,
"The Catholic Church and the Washington Negro," a work banned
from publication by the hierarchy. Although LaFarge admired Foley's
historical work and several times pleaded the defense of the oft-cen-
sored priest vis-à-vis the hierarchy, he still lectured the young Jesuit
sternly for criticizing the interracial movement, even though it was
aimed primarily at the Washington, D.C., council. LaFarge resented
Foley's observation that the "prestigeful" CICNY was a sort of vacuous
social bandwagon onto which New York notables climbed as the civil
rights cause became more respectable. He suggested that Foley cast all
his remarks about the interracial movement in a more positive light,
citing his *No Postponement* as an example. He reminded Foley that
enemies of the Catholic movement were just waiting to seize on the
pettiest criticism. He also took strong exception to Foley's charge that
the CICNY had reached organizational old age and was stagnant.[81]

79. Zielinski, " 'Doing the Truth,' " 46, 60–61.

80. Letters to LaFarge and the CICNY can be found in letter boxes 23 and 30,
CICNYP, and boxes 30–31, JLFP 1; excerpts from Randolph's speech are in letter box
23, CICNYP.

81. Albert S. Foley, "The Catholic Church and the Washington Negro" (Ph.D.

Whether or not the CICNY was suffering from organizational old age, both LaFarge and Hunton certainly were getting well into their senior years. Celebrating his golden jubilee as a priest in 1955, LaFarge, now seventy-five, requested that the New York provincial begin to look for his replacement as chaplain of the CICNY. Although his worst medical problems were behind him, LaFarge definitely showed signs of slowing down. In an unusual bit of self-analysis, he wrote Father Gilligan in 1950: "I never feel like beginning anything at once. I always like to think it is much pleasanter to do it tomorrow, and I find that attitude is growing with the years."[82]

If he was eight years younger than LaFarge, Hunton nonetheless had several physical problems in the 1950s that affected his work, in fact, threatened his job. In the mid-1950s he developed cataracts in both eyes. Surgery improved his eyesight, but then he suffered a detached retina in his left eye in 1958 and lost sight in it. He also suffered from ulcers. In 1959 Philip Hurley, the Jesuit who was selected to replace LaFarge as chaplain of the CICNY, asked Provincial Thomas E. Neighborly to remove Hunton from his position because he was causing the CICNY "serious harm" with his inefficiency and his bad temperament. LaFarge was shocked that the assistant chaplain had gone over his head to the provincial, but he agreed with Hurley's assessment of Hunton. But LaFarge, who had nearly cashiered Hunton in the early 1940s because of excessive salary demands, said it would look bad if Hunton were removed, especially right before the silver jubilee of the CICNY. He informed the provincial that he would sort out the problems with Hunton and honorably ease him out after the anniversary dinner. As one historian of the CICNY aptly put it, the Hunton predicament had the "elements of tragedy" about it.[83]

---

dissertation, University of North Carolina, 1950); Albert Foley to John LaFarge, January 26, 1955, in box 15, folder 17, JLFP 1; Albert Foley to John LaFarge, December 1, 1958, John LaFarge to H. L. Crane, June 5, 1950, and "Report on Manuscript of Father Albert S. Foley: 'The Catholic Church and the Washington Negro,'" n.d. [1950?], all in box 8, folder 5, JLFP 2. On Foley's battles with the hierarchy, see his "Adventures in Black Catholic History: Research and Writing," *U.S. Catholic Historian,* 5 (Winter, 1986), 103–18.

82. John LaFarge to Father Provincial, July 21, 1955, in box 4, folder 31, JLFP 2; John LaFarge to F. J. Gilligan, January 10, 1950, in box 15, folder 20, JLFP 1.

83. Hunton, *All of Which I Saw,* 276; Thomas E. Henneberry, S.J., to John LaFarge, May 13, 1959, and John LaFarge to Thomas Henneberry, May 16, 1959, both in box 4, folder 31, JLFP 2; Zielinski, "'Doing the Truth,'" 82, 96–99.

LaFarge and Hunton, however, did not retire until 1962. Nor was the transition at the CICNY smooth. The much-feted leadership team left an organization that was administratively unstable and nearly bankrupt. In the crucial years of the civil rights revolution, the CICNY was in near disarray and was retrenching. As young Catholic activists were turning to King's Southern Christian Leadership Conference or SNCC for guidance, the CICNY loyally followed NAACP leadership in New York. *Time* magazine charged in 1958 that the Catholic interracial movement showed serious signs of decline. *Time* pointed to Archbishop Rummel's inability to integrate Catholic schools in New Orleans, the closing of three of five Friendship Houses, and the termination of the Race Relations Bureau at the NCWC. Even LaFarge conceded that the college interracial movement had waned in the 1950s.[84]

Time was not alone in suggesting that the Catholic interracial movement's vitality had ebbed. In 1960 LaFarge admitted in a moment of candid reflection that the racial apostolate had often been "patronizing and timid." Parish "street" priests who worked with the poor in the urban centers tended to look upon LaFarge's genteel movement as one "groping for relevance." Father Henry J. Browne, a tough, outspoken priest who worked some of the poorest sections of New York City once dropped in on a CICNY weekly forum and tartly informed LaFarge that he did not know "what the hell it's about." A Catholic journalist who had revered LaFarge and the movement as far back as the 1930s now perceived the Jesuit as an "octogenarian . . . tired from many struggles."[85]

A more energetic leadership and a better national organization of the laity were needed if the church was to play a significant role in the racial revolution that was in progress. Although a small coterie of bishops had instigated a statement condemning segregation in 1958, many bishops continued to resist or ignore the interracial movement. Cardinal McIntyre of Los Angeles was highly disturbed when he received

84. Zielinski, " 'Doing the Truth,' " 96–99, 106, 120–21, 124, 426; "Catholics and Negroes," *Time*, September 15, 1958, pp. 53–54; John LaFarge, "Short Cuts to the Kingdom," *IR*, 33 (December, 1960), 290.

85. John LaFarge to Theodore F. Cunningham, S.J., December 16, 1960, in box 21, folder 3, JLFP 1; Browne's words as recalled by Dennis Clark, interview of Clark by the author; Dolan, *American Catholic Experience*, 449; Barrett McGurn, *A Reporter Looks at American Catholicism* (New York, 1967), 191.

LaFarge's collection of sermons on interracial justice in 1958. "A sermon on interracial justice in this jurisdiction at this time could do nothing but cause what might be grave harm," McIntyre barked. "The racial groups here are happy, contented and prosperous." McIntyre, like bishops in places such as Philadelphia, Cincinnati, Mobile, and Omaha, considered the word *interracial* somewhat subversive. Yet LaFarge told John Markoe, exiled from St. Louis to Omaha by Jesuit superiors, that he should not confront his conservative bishop about the race issue. Similarly, he told Jim Shea of the *Catholic Telegraph Register* in Cincinnati to wait patiently until the attitude of the archbishop evolved. He insisted not only on hierarchical approval but also on clerical control of all councils. Not surprisingly, LaFarge's call for a hundred councils in 1949 did not eventuate in the 1950s. When the local councils met in Chicago in 1958 to consider a national organization, barely a third of that number had materialized.[86]

One of the greatest shortcomings of the Catholic interracial movement was its failure to develop black leadership. Like the white leadership of the CICNY, the original group of conservative black businessmen whom LaFarge recruited for the Laymen's Union in the 1920s had grown old and tired, and almost no young blacks had taken their places. In 1960 Hunton told the board of directors of the CICNY that a program to find and train black Catholic leadership for civil rights work was urgently needed. The councils in fact were barely able to attract enough blacks to make the term *interracial* credible. Thomas Turner, who since the early 1930s had fought the battle for black Catholics in near obscurity, closed the books on the FCC in 1952. Turner (then seventy-five) and his allies had also grown old and tired.[87]

In spite of the limitations of Catholic interracialism, the number of black Catholics increased impressively in the 1950s. Most black Cath-

86. Archbishop James Francis McIntyre to John LaFarge, January 20, 1958, in box 10, folder 13, JLFP 1; John LaFarge to John Markoe, S.J., February 27, 1951, in box 6, folder 7, JLFP 1; John LaFarge to Jim Shea, June 11, 1957, courtesy of Dan Kane, one of the founding members of the interracial council in Cincinnati. On the idea that "interracial" was subversive, see Schmandt, "Catholic Interracial Council of Philadelphia," 13. LaFarge was quoted on the number of councils in *Catholic Observer*, January 13, 1949, clipping in box 49, folder 9, JLFP 1. See box 28, folder 1, JLFP 1, for activists wanting to establish councils.

87. Minutes of board of CICNY, June 15, 1960, in box 5, CICNYP; interview of Parris by the author; "A Testimonial to Thomas W. Turner, Presented by the Federated Colored Catholics of the United States, 1952," copy in Turner Papers.

olics remained remarkably faithful to the church, and a growing number of African Americans converted to Catholicism. By 1960 the church claimed almost 600,000 black Catholics, nearly three times the number in 1928. When the *Interracial Review* first disclosed the number of black priests in its "Interesting Statistics" in 1958, the count was 77. By 1961 the number of black priests had reached 120. Ironically, in 1953 a black man from the West Indies, trained in a Jim Crow seminary at Bay St. Louis, Mississippi, was consecrated as bishop of Accra, Ghana, by Cardinal Spellman.[88] It would be more than a decade before a black man would become a Catholic bishop in the United States.

Why did black converts increase substantially in this period? Did they convert, as LaFarge claimed, because the Catholic church stood for universality and social justice? In most cases, apparently not. To be sure, the dramatic desegregationist actions of a few bold priests and bishops in the Upper South and border states impressed many blacks. Then, too, Catholics were beginning to have encouraging success in using parochial schools to recruit black students and sometimes their parents as well. Few have subjected black converts in this period to sociological analysis, but those who have suggest that many socially mobile blacks converted to Catholicism to escape the emotional worship of fundamentalist, working-class, black churches. Upwardly mobile blacks sometimes converted, it appears, to downplay their "blackness" and thereby gain social status. Certain blacks felt that membership in the Catholic church set them apart from other blacks, as indeed it did.[89]

For a black person to change his or her status to a minority within a minority could be a gut-wrenching experience. Black Catholics often found themselves cut off from the black community, which was church-

88. Dolan, *American Catholic Experience,* 370; "The Interracial Field: Interesting Statistics," *IR,* 31 (May, 1958), 74; Albert S. Foley, S.J., "U.S. Colored Priests: Hundred Year Survey," *Am,* 89 (June 13, 1953), 295–97; Ochs, *Desegregation of the Altar,* 81.

89. John LaFarge, "Christianity and the Negro," 53–54; Jon P. Alston, Letitia T. Alston, and Emory Warrick, "Black Catholics: Social and Cultural Characteristics," *Journal of Black Studies,* 2 (December, 1971), 244–45; E. Franklin Frazier, "The Negro Church and Assimilation," in *Black Church in America,* ed. Nelsen, Yokley, and Nelsen, 140; Daniel F. Collins, "Black Conversion to Catholicism: Its Implications for the Negro Church," *Journal for the Scientific Study of Religion,* 10 (Fall, 1971), 213. See also William Feigleman, Bernard S. Gorman, and Joseph A. Varacalli, "The Social Characteristics of Black Catholics," *Sociology and Social Research,* 75 (April, 1991), 133–35.

centered and overwhelmingly Protestant in most areas. Moreover, black Catholics attending predominantly white churches often felt socially isolated, and even those who attended a black parish seldom encountered a black priest. As one black Catholic put it, "And while we know that hearing Mass is the greatest privilege of all, we also know the limitation of knowledge and the frailties of human nature, and realize that being isolated from one's kind makes one a very lonesome person."[90] Whether or not the Catholic church could successfully address this isolation and loneliness would be a major question in the period ahead.

Another major question concerned the course of the Catholic interracial movement. In the 1950s many Catholic interracialists increasingly rejected the New York model of leadership. Several of the Young Turks of the movement, such as Father Cantwell, Mathew Ahmann, Lloyd Davis, and Robert Sargent Shriver, all Chicagoans, believed that events had overwhelmed the aging LaFarge and Hunton. The midwesterners also believed that their council was superior to New York's. Above all, they reasoned that a national Catholic interracial organization was needed if the church was to play an important role in addressing the American race problem, an idea that LaFarge initially resisted.[91] This intramural tug-of-war between Chicago and New York culminated as the 1950s closed and as the Catholic interracial movement intensified its search for relevance.

90. Margaret Coleman, letter to the editor, *Am,* 81 (May 28, 1949), 300. For the social price paid by black Catholics, see Blatnica, *"At the Altar of God,"* 46–47, 189–99.
91. Zielinski, " 'Doing the Truth,' " 60, 65, 427–28, 437.

11

The Final Years

*LaFarge in the Time of
Pope John XXIII, 1958–1963*

In the early years of the CICNY, Father LaFarge had enormous influence on the other Catholic interracial councils that slowly arose around the country. The new councils consulted with LaFarge and George Hunton and generally subscribed closely to the philosophy and form of the parent council, with the Jesuit attending and speaking at several of their dedication ceremonies. The New York council gained ascendancy in the interracial movement because it was the pioneering organization and because it was located in America's cultural capital. It also had the advantage of the *Interracial Review*, LaFarge's influential position at *America* and in the Jesuit order, and the free publicity afforded by the NCWC News Service and other sympathetic sectors of the Catholic press. For Catholics, the New York council acted as a de facto national forum on racial matters for twenty years or more, but with the advancing age of LaFarge and Hunton, it lost much of its vitality and influence. Leaders of the thirty Catholic interracial councils genuinely revered LaFarge as a pioneer of the movement, but by the mid-1950s several had begun to reject New York's cautious gradualism and to strike out in bolder directions.[1]

---

1. Zielinski, "Working for Interracial Justice," 249–50, 253; report, board of direc-

Most of the leaders of Catholic interracialism in the 1950s were lay persons from a generation younger than LaFarge's and Hunton's. In particular, leaders of the interracial councils in Washington, D.C., Philadelphia, and Chicago, all conceived during World War II, took a more militant stance and did more hands-on civil rights work than the council in New York. For instance, the Washington, D.C., council, led by the outspoken John O'Connor, filed an *amicus curiae* along with seventeen other organizations in the *Bolling* case, one of the school cases decided with *Brown* in 1954. Also a columnist for the *Interracial Review*, O'Connor had several clashes with LaFarge because of his harsh criticism of the Catholic church and the white South. LaFarge became enraged in 1960 when the history professor characterized the Catholic interracial movement as a "colossal failure." LaFarge accused him of dispensing "defeatism" and warned that the enemies of Catholicism would exploit such an attitude. At LaFarge's retirement celebration, O'Connor declared that as far as black rights were concerned, the clergy had "not only retired voluntarily into the sacristy but [had] retired voluntarily from the 20th century."[2] Like Father Foley, O'Connor found that strong criticism of the Catholic interracial movement was likely to be construed as an attack on LaFarge and the CICNY.

In truth, no nationally organized Catholic interracial movement really existed. LaFarge admitted as much in 1950, but he said it without a trace of regret. Rather, he praised the local autonomy and amateurism of each council and boasted that no council except New York had a full-time, paid employee. He contented himself with the perception that his movement had brought forth a "spiritual awakening" with respect to racial discrimination in the church and in the nation.[3]

In Philadelphia the activity of Dennis Clark, John McDermott, and the pioneer of the Philadelphia movement, Anna McGarry, stood out. Because of the hostility of the Philadelphia hierarchy toward interracialism, these liberal Catholics performed most of their racial work for

---

tors, CICNY, [1962], in letter box 7, CICNYP. See also Zielinski, " 'Doing the Truth,' " 105, 113, 125, 428–29.

2. John O'Connor, "Washington Reporter," *IR*, 24 (June, 1951), 93; Bob Sesner, "A View of the Catholic Interracial Councils," *IR*, 28 (January, 1955), 6–8; John LaFarge to John O'Connor, April 21, 1960, in box 3, folder 41, JLFP 1; copy of O'Connor's speech, in letter box 10, CICNYP. On *amici curiae*, see Southern, *Gunnar Myrdal and Black-White Relations*, 142.

3. LaFarge, *No Postponement*, 143.

the city and state governments. All three Philadelphians were extremely critical of the church and the hierarchy, and each engaged heavily in interfaith efforts for black rights. McDermott, for example, was the associate director of the National Conference of Christians and Jews in Philadelphia. All of these leaders were unhappy with the low profile and ineffectiveness of the Catholic interracial movement.[4]

Although LaFarge had traveled to Chicago in 1943 to launch the interracial council there, the CICC was not inclined to work in the shadow of New York. The largest archdiocese in the country, Chicago had a tradition of social activism and bold, confident leadership that went back to the 1930s and Cardinal Mundelein, Bishop Bernard J. Sheil, and Monsignor Reynold Hillenbrand. Sheil, who stated in 1942 that "Jim Crowism in the Mystical Body of Christ is a disgraceful anomaly," ran what historian Edward Kantowicz has called a "veritable social-work empire." The CICC contained a mix of hardened labor activists such as Edward Marciniak and a cohort of young, tough, and well-educated men such as Mathew Ahmann, Lloyd Davis, Robert Sargent Shriver, Gordon Zahn, and the spiritual director of the organization, Monsignor Daniel Cantwell. Both Ahmann and Cantwell had degrees in sociology, the latter having earned an M.A. at Catholic University with his thesis "Facts in Negro Segregation." Cantwell, like Marciniak, had experience in the Catholic Labor Alliance and had been the chaplain of Baroness de Hueck's Friendship House before he became the spiritual leader of the CICC.[5] "Sarge" Shriver, barely in his forties in 1958, was the president of the Chicago council. The brother-in-law of Senator John F. Kennedy, Shriver held the position of general manager of the cavernous, Kennedy-controlled Merchandise Mart in Chicago. As president of the CICC, Shriver, assisted by the black executive director Lloyd Davis, increased the council's membership from three hundred to one thousand in the late 1950s (the membership of the CICNY hovered around three hundred at that time). Although Cardinal Samuel Stritch was no equalitarian, he was interested in black converts and in stabilizing the changing Catholic neighborhoods of the

---

4. Interview of Clark by the author.
5. Avella, *This Confident Church*, 4, 23, 27, 36, 42, 45, 124, 149, 174–80, 294–97, esp. 124 for Sheil quotation; Kantowicz, *Corporation Sole*, 173. See Daniel Cantwell's astute "Race Relations as Seen by a Catholic," *American Catholic Sociological Review*, 7 (December, 1946), 242–58.

city. He even hired the radical organizer Saul Alinsky for $150,000 in an attempt to restore order to one racially troubled Chicago diocese. In the mid-1950s Stritch gave $5,000 a year to the CICC, twice as much as LaFarge was able to pry out of the deep-pocketed Spellman in New York.[6] Overall, the CICC was broader, deeper, and younger in talent than the CICNY.

The Young Turks in Chicago believed that the CICNY represented the overly mature and cautious East. In 1957 Shriver told Davis, "I have read with interest the report from New York and am happy to say that, as usual, Chicago is already doing what New York is talking about." The following year Davis commented that "Chicago and New York have been in a political war for many years." Davis continued, "New York has tended to follow the Spellman outlook on Catholic lay groups (we regard this as the old guard narrow approach) and Chicago has tended to follow a more liberal course—opening its membership to all etc., involving Protestants and Jews in its work." John McDermott, who moved from Philadelphia to become the executive director of the CICC in 1960, believed that under New York's hegemony, the Catholic interracial movement "was in the closet." McDermott favored direct action, and Gordon Zahn wanted interracial planning that involved "risk-taking and boat-rocking action."[7]

By the mid-1950s the Chicago leaders strongly favored the formation of a national interracial council. The Chicago group soon discovered that LaFarge had at least two major reservations about a national council. First, the priest feared that a national organization would fall under the jurisdiction of the NCWC. LaFarge believed that if it did, certain bishops might undermine the movement. Second, LaFarge had long worried that some junior council might steer the interracial movement in a radical direction. It was obvious, too, that the New York

6. Zielinski, " 'Doing the Truth,' " 138–39; interview of Ahmann by the author; "Fact Sheet—First National Conference for Interracial Justice," news release of the CICC [August, 1958(?)], in box 24, CICCP; "Interracial Report," *Am,* 94 (February 18, 1956), 547; Nicholas Lemann, *The Promised Land: The Great Black Migration and How It Changed America* (New York, 1991), 97–98; receipt box, in box 15, CICCP.

7. Dennis Clark, "Evaluation," in letter box 25, CICNYP; interview of Clark by the author; interview of Ahmann by the author; Robert Sargent Shriver to Lloyd Davis, June 12, 1957, in box 17, CICCP; Lloyd Davis to Vernon [no last name], in box 24, CICCP; McDermott, quoted in Zielinski, " 'Doing the Truth,' " 139; Avella, *This Confident Church,* 296, 309–310, esp. 296 for Zahn quotation.

council preferred to continue as the unofficial leader of the Catholic interracial movement. In addition, regional pride and personality conflicts also figured in the competition between the New York and Chicago factions. So preoccupied was the New York leadership with the Chicago initiative for a national organization that one historian of the CICNY suggests that it may explain the *Interracial Review*'s curious inattention to the civil rights bill of 1957.[8]

In any event, the Chicagoans believed that they had to take the lead in putting the Catholic church on the civil rights map. Cantwell assured his superior that it was "to the Chicago Council that all other Councils in the country look for leadership." Still, the leaders of the Chicago council appreciated LaFarge's many contributions to the movement, and they knew that the formation of a national organization would be difficult unless the New Yorker cooperated. As Ahmann put it, the movement needed "both the energy of Chicago and the prestige of LaFarge." Thus the CICC resorted to gentle diplomacy in regard to LaFarge.[9]

After some preliminary discussions in 1956, LaFarge and Cantwell decided to hold a meeting in New York in early January of 1957 to discuss the national conference. Cantwell presented his ideas to representatives of the councils of New York, Brooklyn, Philadelphia, and Washington, D.C. Essentially, the issue in the first meeting boiled down to Cantwell's ambitious proposal for a strong national interracial council versus New York's more limited view of a conference that would be used for intramural discussions aimed at self-improvement of the individual councils. Cantwell wanted much more consolidation and much broader scope in the national organization than what New York desired. The Chicago priest warned that the danger of "in-breeding" was great in the present councils and that experts from many fields outside the church needed to be brought into the Catholic movement. LaFarge later recalled the "cluster of troublesome questions that seemed to block the way" to a national organization.[10]

8. Zielinski, " 'Doing the Truth,' " 139, 141, 426, 478; Avella, *This Confident Church,* 296.

9. Zielinski, " 'Doing the Truth,' " 142; Daniel Cantwell to Msgr. Edward M. Burke, June 28, 1960, in box 37, CICCP; interview of Ahmann by the author.

10. John LaFarge to Daniel Cantwell, January 1, 1957, and summary of the discussion at the January 12, 1957, meeting, both in box 30, folder 1, Cantwell Papers; John LaFarge, "Preparing for the St. Louis Convention," *IR,* 33 (July, 1960), 174.

Back in Chicago, Cantwell expressed his disappointment to Hunton about the meager results of the meeting and asked the New York director to keep him informed about LaFarge's reactions to the New York meeting. Hunton had spoken for the New York council at the previous meeting because LaFarge could not attend. After the meeting, Cantwell sensed that New York was not enthusiastic about having a national conference anytime soon. Lloyd Davis told the NCWC to ignore a premature story about the proposed conference. There would be no conference in 1957.[11]

The CICC, however, continued to work for a conference, and Hunton traveled to Chicago in May, 1957, to discuss the matter further. In addition to the theoretical differences between New York and Chicago, the problem of funding the conference held up the event. The year ended as it began, with a meeting, this one on December 30 in New York, to discuss the conference. Besides LaFarge and Cantwell, Father Hurley, assistant chaplain of the CICNY, Mary Riley and Lawrence Pierce of the Brooklyn council, and O'Connor attended the meeting. Cantwell informed the group that Cardinal Stritch wanted to hold the conference in Chicago and that Sargent Shriver had gotten a promise of funding from the Kennedy Foundation. Again, Cantwell emphasized the consolidationist approach to the conference. He argued that a paper union of the councils would not allow the movement to attract foundation funding. Riley strongly agreed with Cantwell's argument, and O'Connor seemed to concur. After discussing details of costs and location for the conference, the representatives discussed a possible theme for the gathering. As one who wanted to define the organization, LaFarge was quick with the following suggestion: "This convention should create a definite sense that we have a positive contribution to make to the Church and nation. That contribution is based on natural law and fundamental virtues of justice and charity. It is extremely important that the CIC movement be stressed as a program of *strengthening* for the local as well as the national community and in a very special way *strengthening* the Church universal. We must sell the Hierarchy the truth that we are literally 'coming to the rescue' of the Church." Monsignor Cantwell then suggested that a noted scholar, "preferably a theologian," be invited to speak and tie together all the

11. Daniel Cantwell to George Hunton, January 18, 1957, and Lloyd Davis to NCWC News Service, January 23, 1957, both in box 30, folder 1, Cantwell Papers.

"ringing" pronouncements that the conference might generate. Committee members suggested the names of Gustave Weigel, John Courtney Murray, and John Tracy Ellis.[12]

In early February, 1958, the council representatives scheduled the conference for August 29–31. The CICC dutifully consulted LaFarge on many of the details of the affair. The New Yorker urged that the opening Thursday night session of the conference be a social event rather than a working session. Thursday evening's session thus officially became the "Delegates' Reception Honoring Father LaFarge." Showing his perennial worry about bishops, especially Cardinal Spellman, LaFarge axed a Chicago proposal to send out early letters on the conference to all the American bishops. In fact, LaFarge asked, "Why write them at all?" He argued further, "We can be positive they won't make any contribution to it [the conference], and there is the danger that some of them who are not very friendly to the cause will take the occasion to make a certain amount of trouble."[13]

Cantwell wanted John Courtney Murray to address the conference, and he was tentatively slated to give a speech entitled "The Philosophical and Theological Roots of the Catholic Interracial Movement." But the Chicago camp worried that LaFarge might expect to deliver the keynote address. Cantwell subtly quizzed Father Hurley in New York about LaFarge's intentions concerning the main address, and in late February LaFarge let Cantwell know that he wished to be the keynote speaker.[14]

Catholic interracialists hailed the conference as a grand success. As Ed Marciniak put it, more than four hundred men and women met and "confidently planned the peaceful overthrow of racial segregation." More than fifty Jewish and Protestant delegates participated, mostly as racial consultants. The delegates constituted a Who's Who of Catholic interracialism. Attending were George Hunton, Monsignor Daniel Cantwell, Mathew Ahmann, Lloyd Davis, Edward Marciniak, John

12. Zielinski, " 'Doing the Truth,' " 143; notes on conference held at office of *America*, December 30, 1957, in box 29, folder 7, Cantwell Papers.

13. Minutes, board of directors of CICC, February 11, 1958, in box 24, CICCP; John LaFarge to Daniel Cantwell, April 21, 1958, in box 30, folder 2, Cantwell Papers.

14. "Tentative Agenda for a National Conference of the Catholic Interracial Council Movement," n.d., and Daniel Cantwell to Philip S. Hurley, S.J., January 4, 1958, both in box 30, folder 2, CICCP; John LaFarge to Daniel Cantwell, February 24, 1958, in box 30, folder 1, Cantwell Papers.

McDermott, Dennis Clark, Anna McGarry, Judge Harold Stevens, Thomas Harte, Joseph Fichter, Monsignor George Higgins, and Monsignor Francis Gilligan.[15]

LaFarge opened the first working session of the conference on Friday morning with a seventeen-page speech. The keynote address had a familiar ring to anyone who had followed the work of the New York priest. After laudatory remarks about the Chicago hierarchy, the CICC, and his ally Hunton, LaFarge proclaimed that the thirty-five interracial councils gathered at Chicago affirmed "the great principles of God-given justice and charity." More than that, they provided the "direct answer to Marxist theory and world-Communist propaganda." La-Farge added, however, that racism would exist even if communism did not, pointing out that ignorance, poverty, "blighting secularism," and "crude materialism" were entirely sufficient to make for dangerous divisions among humankind. He further maintained that the race problem constituted an especially pressing problem that could not be left to the general agencies of social justice. Racism, he argued, was unique and could not be treated as a "mere side issue" of broader reform. LaFarge called for "reasonably prompt action" so that disorder and strife could be prevented. Despite the gathering momentum of massive resistance, he sounded his usual warning against intervention in the affairs of the South, lest southern moderates be undermined. Looking ahead, LaFarge set a goal of fifty new interracial councils. In closing, he reminded the lay delegates that the interracial movement was, first and foremost, Catholic Action under the guidance of chaplains and bishops.[16]

After the keynote address, the conference dissolved into various "commissions" and panels on specialized topics. Commissions delved into the areas of housing, employment, schools, and parochial and institutional life. Delegates from New York, Chicago, Washington, D.C., Philadelphia, and Detroit tended to dominate the panels and commissions. John O'Connor chaired the commission on schools, Dennis Clark headed the one on housing, Paul Mundy of Loyola University

15. Ed Marciniak, "Interracial Councils in Chicago," *Am*, 99 (September 20, 1958), 640–42; "Interracial Councils at Chicago," *Am*, 99 (September 13, 1958), 619; "Fact Sheet," 2–8.

16. Keynote address by John LaFarge, "Catholic Interracial Movement Looks to the Future," in box 24, CICCP. Black delegates had trouble with discrimination by Chicago hotels; see minutes, board of directors, CICC, August 12, 1958, in box 24, CICCP.

presided over employment, and Emanuel Romero, the black vice-president of the CICNY, headed the planning group on parochial and institutional life. With a minimum of drama, each commission and panel produced recommendations that essentially called for a halt to all racial discrimination in Catholic institutions and life.[17]

The delegates also passed a series of ten resolutions. The ninth resolution stood out in proclaiming that "desegregation of the nation's schools is not merely a legal question but is also a deep moral issue." Two resolutions suggested that an interim committee be established to expound on "basic Christian conduct in the area of interracial relations" and to "form a closer association of the Catholic Interracial Councils." Twenty-two people would serve on the Interim Committee. Only the New York and Chicago councils had more than one member on it. New York had Hunton, Guichard Parris, and LaFarge, the Jesuit being named the "honorary chairman." Chicagoans on the committee were Cantwell, Shriver, Davis, and Ahmann, the last chosen as secretary. Also on the committee were O'Connor of Washington, D.C., and Clark of Philadelphia. In addition to the ten resolutions, the delegates drafted a "Pledge of Allegiance to the Hierarchy" at the close of the conference. The pledge acknowledged the conferees' "indebtedness" to the American hierarchy "on all questions of human dignity and human rights" and their loyalty to the "teaching authority and spiritual guidance" of the same.[18]

The salute to the hierarchy was more a political tactic than a genuine tribute. After all, LaFarge had exclaimed that the conference would have to "rescue" the church hierarchy on the race question. LaFarge hoped that unified action by the councils would prod the bishops to make a statement on the escalating racial tension in the South. When the bishops issued a pastoral letter condemning racism and segregation in November, 1958, LaFarge wrote the following to Cantwell: "Certainly it [the 1958 pastoral letter] would not, I think, have got across if we had not had the great demonstration of Catholic solidarity on this point at the Chicago Conference. The Conference came at a critical time and it showed the bishops as a whole how deeply the laity around

17. "Fact Sheet," 2–8; "Resolutions Adopted at First National Catholic Conference on Interracial Justice," *IR,* 31 (September, 1958), 158–60. For details, see Zielinski, " 'Doing the Truth,' " 151–58.

18. "Resolutions Adopted," 158–60.

the country felt on the subject. I feel that the Conference was the spark that really helped to ignite the final explosion."[19]

However, not even the impact of the conference on the bishops had convinced LaFarge about the wisdom of a national interracial council. The *Interracial Review* and *America* simply reported the results of the Chicago conference without sounding an appeal for a new organization. In the meantime, New York and Chicago jockeyed over the time and place of the first Interim Committee meeting. Ahmann and Cantwell suggested an early January meeting in St. Louis and a later one in Chicago or New York. The first meeting, however, took place in New York on January 17 and 18, 1959. Although some progress seemed to have been made at the meeting, Cantwell still felt that New York was not cooperative. After the meeting, Cantwell confided to a colleague, "There was considerable dragging of feet on the part of the New York Council who [*sic*] would have preferred, I think, that we hadn't even had the meeting." Yet the committee moved forward and scheduled the next meeting for June 13 and 14, 1959, in St. Louis.[20]

One source of friction between New York and Chicago apparently was Hunton's dislike of the Chicago secretary Ahmann. It seems that Hunton, who was under siege in New York for alleged ineffectiveness, was envious of the young, energetic Ahmann, who was destined to become the executive director of the National Catholic Conference for Interracial Justice (NCCIJ). Probably a more serious obstacle was LaFarge's fear that the national council would be eviscerated by the bishops. LaFarge was certainly correct in thinking that the NCWC would claim jurisdiction over a national interracial conference. Back in 1932 Father John Burke, the general secretary of the administrative board of the NCWC, had informed Thomas Turner that a national interracial organization required the approval of the NCWC. In 1959 when Archbishop O'Boyle was asked about the issue, he gave the same answer as Burke.[21]

19. John LaFarge to Daniel Cantwell, November 19, 1958, in box 30, folder 4, Cantwell Papers.

20. "Resolutions Adopted," 158–60; "Interracial Councils at Chicago," 619; Daniel Cantwell to Ed [Edward Burke(?)], January 20, 1959, in box 4, folder 1, Cantwell Papers.

21. Interview of unidentified person by Edward S. Stanton, S.J., transcript in box 1, folder 4, Stanton Papers; Zielinski, " 'Doing the Truth,' " 162; John Burke to Thomas Turner, August 20, 1932, in Turner Papers; memorandum of John O'Connor on O'Boyle meeting, February 28, 1959, in box 30, folder 5, Cantwell Papers.

Even after the Interim Committee officially established the NCCIJ in June in St. Louis, the debate about the correct approach to the bishops continued. LaFarge wanted to be sure that the bishops on the administrative board were in the right frame of mind before he informed them about the formation of the national interracial council. He therefore began to feel out Cardinal Spellman on the subject in August, 1959. He assured the powerful cardinal that the NCCIJ would not intervene in local interracial council affairs and would in no way try to undercut his authority in New York. He also told Spellman that Archbishops O'Boyle, Richard Cushing of Boston, and Albert G. Meyer of Chicago approved of the new national organization. LaFarge continued, however, to advise Cantwell not to seek the consent of the bishops at the fall meeting of the administrative board: "I think it would be a mistake to announce it [the NCCIJ] at the annual meeting of the Bishops. If it were to come before them as a *fait accompli*, it might incur the displeasure of some of our unfriendly elements, and even embarrass our episcopal friends. I would rather let Cardinal Spellman take his own time and way to mention it to them, and wait until that particular coast is clear." LaFarge argued that the bishops should be allowed to come around without being pushed too much. "If we take our time and map out the ground carefully," he counseled, "we shall not be receiving shocks and countershocks later on."[22]

LaFarge had been deferential to bishops his entire career, and he was not going to change at this point, no matter how impatient the leaders of the Chicago council were. In any case, the bishops took up the NCCIJ issue at their November meeting in 1959, and the board approved of the organization's affiliation with the Social Action Department of the NCWC. The relationship of the NCCIJ and the NCWC was nominal, which meant that the interracial conference was responsible for its own budget and got practically no funds from the bishops' treasury, but this did not quiet LaFarge's fear that the NCWC might in the future try to hamstring the new organization. In June of 1960 LaFarge was once again imploring Ahmann not to contact "non-CIC bishops" about the NCCIJ, for they might take up their cudgels against the infant organization. Lay leaders such as Ahmann, Clark,

22. John LaFarge to Cardinal Spellman, August 14, 1959, in box 8, folder 6, JLFP 1; Daniel Cantwell to John LaFarge, July 27, 1959, and John LaFarge to Daniel Cantwell, September 17 and 19, 1959, all in box 30, folder 5, Cantwell Papers.

and O'Connor believed LaFarge's caution about the hierarchy to be excessive. The new generation of laypersons tended to be less deferential to clerics, and in this case they believed that LaFarge had preached once too often that the time was not yet ripe.[23]

At the St. Louis meeting in the summer of 1959, the Interim Committee decided that the NCCIJ would represent the cause of interracial justice at national and international meetings, and it would strive to enunciate the philosophy of the Catholic interracial movement. It would also encourage and nurture new local Catholic interracial councils and hold annual or biennial national conventions. Local councils would also be required to pay national dues. Yet the NCCIJ did not limit the autonomy of the local councils, a fact explained by the strength of LaFarge's lobby. In October, 1960, Ahmann became a full-time employee of the NCCIJ, with his $9,000 salary being paid by the national office. LaFarge was named honorary chaplain of the organization.[24]

The contention between the New York and Chicago councils was never bitter or petty because of the respect the Chicago leadership had for LaFarge and because the Jesuit was peaceful by nature and dedicated to serving the cause of interracial justice. But the competition between the two councils, albeit friendly, was real and prolonged. In the summer of 1961, LaFarge was still trying to headquarter the NCCIJ in New York; at this point the letterhead of the council listed both Chicago and New York as coheadquarters. In a letter to LaFarge on July 27, 1961, Ahmann insisted that the central location of Chicago was best suited for the headquarters of the NCCIJ. He also made it clear that he wanted the new organization entirely divorced from the senior council that had once acted as the national office of the interracial movement. He added that there would be a "strong negative reaction" from some of the best councils if the headquarters were moved to New York. Before long, NCCIJ stationery cited as its headquarters only one city, Chicago.[25]

23. Minutes, board of interim committee, November 28, 1959, in box 30, folder 6, Cantwell Papers; John LaFarge to Mathew Ahmann, June 7, 1960, in box 3, folder 41, JLFP 2; interview of Clark by the author.

24. LaFarge, "Preparing for the St. Louis Convention," 174–75; "Evaluation," in letter box 25, CICNYP; copy of by-laws of NCCIJ, in box 3, folder 40, JLFP 2; minutes, board of directors, NCCIJ, October 19, 1960, in box 5, CICNYP; letter to board members of NCCIJ, October 13, 1960, in box 3, folder 46, JLFP 2.

25. Minutes, board of directors, CICNY, December 14, 1959, in box 29, folder 8, JLFP 1; Mathew Ahmann to John LaFarge, July 27, 1961, in box 3, folder 42, JLFP 2.

Unlike LaFarge, the Chicagoans had little faith that white southerners would dismantle white supremacy. Ahmann informed LaFarge
in 1961 that the NCCIJ had received a grant of $30,000 from the Ta-
conic Foundation to set up a Southern Field Service. Many of the numerous statements and resolutions of the new organization, such as the
announcement of the field service, must have appeared to LaFarge as a
slap in the face. At the first NCCIJ convention in St. Louis in 1960,
Ahmann vehemently denounced southern Catholics for resisting desegregation, and he strongly praised the civil disobedience of the sit-
ins. He implored the councils to "move faster than we have been moving on all fronts," and he stressed that "lay Catholics" were guided by
their individual consciences and did not concern themselves with "the
traditionally 'apologetic.' " Ahmann declared that they were "not trying to make the Church attractive to Negroes," nor did they "want to
exist just to be able to have a few Catholic friends around to co-operate
with other organizations."[26]

Indeed, the young lay leaders of the NCCIJ sneered at exploiting
the racial situation for purposes of black conversion, and they vowed
that they would never accept "token integration" or "routine performance and mediocre achievement." Unlike LaFarge, seldom did they exploit the communist threat as a reason for pursuing racial justice. One
wonders what LaFarge, who had always danced around the issue of
miscegenation, thought of the following statement issued by the
NCCIJ in 1962: "To oppose interracial marriage because of an expressed concern for children of mixed unions was to disclose a lack of
understanding about the problems that children of all-black marriages
faced." Such opposition, the statement charged, betrayed a "white pattern of thought."[27]

LaFarge never let such statements affect his gentle temperament,
for he had no time to sulk in his tent. His last three years of life still
brimmed with activity. On February 13, 1960, he turned eighty, an
occasion for celebration by his friends, some three thousand of whom
filled the nave of St. Patrick's Cathedral to hear Archbishop O'Boyle

26. Ahmann to LaFarge, July 27, 1961; Zielinski, " 'Doing the Truth,' " 172–73;
Mathew Ahmann's address, "Our National Convention and the Social Order," *IR*, 33
(November, 1960), 272–74.
27. "Resolutions and Reports," *IR*, 33 (November, 1960), 280; statements of
NCCIJ, in box 3, folder 49, JLFP 2; statement by board of NCCIJ, February 26, 1962,
in box 3, folder 39, JLFP 2.

deliver a sermon on the racial apostolate and praise LaFarge and his work. Later at the Waldorf Hotel, an interracial, interfaith crowd of nearly a thousand attended a dinner party for LaFarge, including Roy Wilkins and Lester Granger. The Catholic and black presses sang praises to his name. Congratulations for LaFarge poured in from all over the nation and the world.[28]

In his fifty-fifth year as a priest and his forty-ninth year in the racial apostolate, LaFarge had shown a remarkable consistency of thought throughout his long career. He fervently believed in 1960, as he always had, that the universal and unifying mission of Catholicism could not be denied. "The Church of Christ," he proclaimed, "has never given up the hope of . . . a reign of justice, love and peace in the social, political, and international world." He deluged depressed Catholics with torrents of hope, and he counseled against getting back at one's enemies: "Make no accusations. Say very little, as little as possible." He preached to them to "take the opposition as a sign that the good Lord is with you." LaFarge believed his hope was built "not just on feeling, but on certainty: the certainty of God's promises."[29] His core beliefs explained not only why he acted, but why he sometimes refused to act at all.

Dualism and paradox pervaded LaFarge's life and writings. Although he voiced a robust hope about ultimate justice, his immediate apprehensions about communism, secularism, materialism, permissivism, black separatism, and black racism only increased in his last years.[30] He cheered when John XXIII, pope from 1958 to 1963, took charge of the Holy See, but he constantly bewailed the deepening divisions within Catholicism and the nation and castigated the "dead shoals of mere humanist liberalism."[31] Although LaFarge clearly favored John F. Ken-

---

28. "Father LaFarge at 80," *IR*, 33 (April, 1960), 88; "To Father LaFarge at Eighty," *Am*, 102 (February 13, 1960), 575; Cardinal Patrick A. O'Boyle, "The Racial Apostolate," *IR*, 33 (April, 1960), 92–94.

29. John LaFarge, "The Story of a Roman Catholic," *Am*, 102 (February 13, 1960), 577–80, and "Short Cuts to the Kingdom," *IR*, 33 (December, 1960), 290; John LaFarge to Mrs. [?] Kovacovsky, November 1, 1960, in box 5, folder 3, JLFP 1.

30. See also the curious mix of long-range optimism and short-range alarm in his "Our People Have Courage—And Extraordinary Spirit," *U.S. News & World Report*, February 22, 1960, pp. 77–79, and "Violence in the Streets," *Catholic Digest*, 26 (June, 1962), 28.

31. John LaFarge to Shirley Burden, February 28, 1962, in box 30, folder 4, JLFP 1.

nedy over Richard M. Nixon in the 1960 election, he wondered whether the young, jet-set Bostonian was sufficiently religious (Catholic) to supply the moral leadership the country needed or whether he was just another power-hungry relativist. Strangely enough, Cardinal Spellman and much of the hierarchy perceived Kennedy as too liberal and too soft on communism. More worrisome to LaFarge was the fact that the opportunistic Kennedy solemnly assured Protestants, Jews, and secularists that the constitution came before his religion and that he would support a sharp separation of church and state. In times past the priest would have accused such a Catholic of committing the sin of religious indifference.[32]

LaFarge held his criticism and advice for the young president until after the election. In February, 1961, just after LaFarge's eighty-first birthday, he wrote Kennedy an open letter that was published in *America*. In this rather maudlin piece, LaFarge used his old age and his Harvard-Newport ties to Kennedy (Catholicism was only implied) to justify his unsolicited advice. In essence, the letter said that it took real, "divinely inspired" religion to combat communism and that mere "liberal humanism" was incapable of combatting "the subtle, driving force of totalitarian ideology." He also reminded the new president that the race problem, a topic that went unmentioned in Kennedy's inaugural address, was a moral issue. LaFarge was surely disappointed when he later discovered that the president did not read *America*.[33]

As the civil rights movement gained momentum in the Kennedy years, young activists at the NCCIJ pressured LaFarge to speak out more boldly on such questions as direct action. For years it had been LaFarge's habit to encourage racial engagement in timid or indifferent white Catholics while lecturing militant, angry blacks and impatient white Catholics on the virtues of patience and prudence. Every instinct in the gradualist Jesuit rebelled against direct action and civil disobedience. On the NBC television talk show *Open Mind* in 1960, just days after sit-ins occurred in Greensboro, North Carolina, LaFarge argued

32. Herbert S. Parmet, *JFK: The Presidency of John F. Kennedy* (New York, 1984), 37–43; Cooney, *American Pope*, 266, 270, 272; David O'Brien, *Public Catholicism*, 229. LaFarge expressed joy over Kennedy's election; see John LaFarge to Yvonne du Halgouet, December 11, 1960, in box 38, folder 14, JLFP 1.
33. John LaFarge, "Dear Mr. President," *Am*, 104 (February 18, 1961), 670–71; "Inside *America*, Newsletter for Associates," May 21, 1961, in box 1, folder 7, JLFP 1; Cooney, *American Pope*, 273.

against the use of indignation as a social weapon. Herbert Ehrmann, the president of the American Jewish Committee, replied that people suffering severe injustice had every right to be indignant. Ehrmann declared that indignant people were usually the "bellwethers of progress." Retreating a bit, LaFarge conceded that people might usefully "flare up" but only if they did so intelligently. Ehrmann rejoined that people who flared up were hardly ever seen as intelligent or responsible in their time.[34]

To his credit, LaFarge gradually and reluctantly warmed to the idea of nonviolent direct action as a legitimate civil rights tactic. In a letter dated May 17, 1960, LaFarge told a fellow priest that the "Negro is forming a new image of himself; with indeed startlingly [sic] rapidity, as seen from the sit-down protests in the South." Although the 1960 NCCIJ convention endorsed the sit-ins as one of the "morally legitimate forms of Catholic Action," the globally publicized freedom rides of 1961 disclosed divisions within the Catholic interracial movement.[35] The *Interracial Review* endorsed the freedom rides without reservation. *America*, however, gave but grudging support to the rides and warned of the potential harm in them.[36] Since LaFarge wrote no signed articles on the freedom rides, his opinion remained unknown to the public. However, when Father Patrick J. Molloy, the chaplain of the Catholic Interracial Council in St. Louis, vehemently attacked the freedom rides as harmful to race relations and suggested communist complicity in them, LaFarge issued statements supporting the tactic.[37]

As always, a new pope stirred hope in social actionist hearts. Would Pope John XXIII, interracialists wondered, speak directly to the issue of segregation and racism in the United States? In January, 1959, the pope announced that he would call an "Ecumenical Council" (Second Vatican Council) in 1962 to update the church (*aggiornamento*). In 1961 the pope issued an encyclical entitled *Mater et Magistra* (*Mother and*

34. Transcript of program of the *Open Mind*, February 21, 1960, in box 8, folder 15, JLFP 2.

35. John LaFarge to Father [?] Mangan, May 17, 1960, in box 15, folder 2, JLFP 1; "Resolutions and Reports," 280.

36. "The Freedom Rides," *IR*, 34 (July, 1961), on front cover; "Freedom Riders," *Am*, 105 (May 27, 1961), 358; "Violence in Alabama," *Am*, 105 (June 3, 1961), 388. On freedom rides, see Sitkoff, *Struggle for Black Equality*, 97—115.

37. Zielinski, " 'Doing the Truth,' " 137; Ellsworth J. Evans to John LaFarge, June 9, 1961, in box 3, folder 42, JLFP 2.

Teacher). Like other notable social encyclicals, *Mater et Magistra* was long (25,000 words) and abstract. It dealt with magisterial European social principles, some with a medieval flavor that lent themselves to bafflement and misinterpretation in the modern age. The encyclical urged industrial cooperation between managers and workers, advocated better distribution of wealth between rich and poor nations, and praised the work of the United Nations Food and Agriculture Organization. In contrast to the earlier social encyclicals, it did not blast communism with typical Vatican fervor.[38]

Although there was much to please Catholic liberals in *Mater et Magistra*, LaFarge and *America* admitted that the encyclical offered no explicit guidance on race relations. About all LaFarge could usefully glean from the document was the pope's statement that those who placed spiritual progress first had a "surer instinct for grasping the fundamental demands of justice in different areas of human endeavor, even in those which are further complicated by the existence of widespread individual or group racial selfishness." Behind the scene, LaFarge tried to use his Roman connections to get a stronger statement from the pope on the American race problem.[39]

But, as LaFarge later conceded, neither did Pope John's controversial 1963 encyclical, *Pacem in Terris*, say anything directly about the American racial situation. Since this second encyclical spoke primarily to the issue of world order and peace, LaFarge could only infer from the papal document that racism was a "fundamental denial of order."[40]

Meanwhile, *Mater et Magistra* set off an angry exchange between liberal and conservative Catholics in the United States and offered a foretaste of the postconciliar church.[41] Alarmed at the pope's relatively tolerant attitude toward communism, William F. Buckley, Jr.'s conserv-

38. Bokenkotter, *Concise History*, 323, 376; Allitt, *Catholic Intellectuals and Conservative Politics*, 93–96; Benjamin L. Masse, S.J., "Pope John's 'Mater et Magistra,' " *Am*, 105 (July 29, 1961), 565–68.

39. Memorandum of conference between John LaFarge and George Hunton, n.d. [1960(?)], in box 16, folder 10, JLFP 2; resolution adopted by NDSAC, August 25, 1961, in box 4, folder 1, JLFP 2; "Peter Speaks Again," *Am*, 105 (July 29, 1961), 563; Mathew Ahmann to John LaFarge, April 18, 1962, in box 3, folder 43, JLFP 2; John LaFarge, "Translating into Action," *IR*, 35 (April, 1962), 93–95. In earlier times LaFarge would have discussed *Mater*, but now one of his protégés, Benjamin Masse, did; see n. 38.

40. Mathew Ahmann to John LaFarge, April 26, 1963, in box 3, folder 44, JLFP 2; John LaFarge, "Pope John on Racism," *IR*, 36 (June, 1963), 110–11, 123.

41. Allitt, *Catholic Intellectuals and Conservative Politics*, 93–101.

ative *National Review* characterized the encyclical "as a venture in triviality." The magazine further disclosed that conservatives were privately joking, "Mater si, Magistra no!" (a takeoff on Fidel Castro's statement "Cuba si, Yanqui no!").[42]

For decades LaFarge had grasped at encyclical straws in his battle against the racist flood in America, but Buckley and his allies at the *National Review* artfully demonstrated how frail a reed encyclicals were with respect to social and political questions, even ones that had moral and religious overtones. *America,* of course, responded vigorously to Buckley's irreverence, calling his editorial on the 1961 encyclical "slanderous."[43] Thereafter, the controversy between Catholic liberals and conservatives grew more belligerent. To summarize briefly, Buckley and his conservative allies argued that there was no "Catholic party line" on political issues such as civil rights and foreign policy. To substantiate this point of view, Buckley enticed one of his young protégés named Garry Wills to look into the nature of encyclicals. Wills, who had spent six years in a Jesuit seminary before earning his Ph.D. in classics at Yale, thus produced the theologically rigorous and densely argued *Politics and Catholic Freedom.* It concluded that encyclicals were largely hortative rather than dogmatic. Relying heavily on the thought of Cardinal John Henry Newman, the brilliant young syllogist argued for a developmental doctrine of the church. Wills used the concepts of historicism, contingency, and "private judgment" to attenuate the thrust of social encyclicals. Wills championed freedom for an educated laity to interpret papal letters in the light of science and reason, local conditions, and changing times. Ironically, the then-archconservative Wills made a case in his book that anticipated Vatican II. Wills later commented that Vatican II rendered his book an "instant anachronism."[44]

Even LaFarge conceded in 1960 that encyclicals were "so broadly pitched to a world audience, so traditional in style [written in abstract

---

42. Editorial, *National Review,* July 29, 1961, p. 38. A full account of the liberal-conservative dispute can be found in Wills, *Politics and Catholic Freedom,* 3–20, *passim,* and Allitt, *Catholic Intellectuals and Conservative Politics,* 93–101.

43. "Affront to Conservatives," *Am,* 105 (August 19, 1961), 622; "William F. Buckley, Jr.," *ibid.,* 624–25; Wills, *Politics and Catholic Freedom,* 6–20.

44. Wills, *Politics and Catholic Freedom,* Introduction, 61–62, 79, 82–84, 138–53, 208–11, 224, 231–38, *passim.* See also his autobiography, *Confessions of a Conservative,* 61–64.

Vatican Latin] and so solicitous about how future generations may interpret them, that they usually are not specific and concrete enough as
we would like."[45] Interestingly, Wills chastised the editors of *America*,
who had earlier assailed Buckley for selectively embracing papal teaching, for presumptuously complaining that Pope John's encyclical was
not explicit enough on racism and for expressing the hope that a subsequent document would correct the oversight.[46]

As the fracas between *America* and the *National Review* revealed,
lay activism could cut both ways. The growing numbers and confidence
of lay activists in the Catholic community had helped energize the cause
of interracialism after World War II. In the late 1950s Chicago lay activists engineered the establishment of a national interracial organization that prodded a hesitant hierarchy to condemn segregation. By the
1960s Catholic lay intellectuals on the right also stepped up their challenge to the increasingly liberal slant of the church's magisterium.[47] Lay
activism in the Deep South, though seldom led by intellectuals, was
effective in obstructing the Catholic church in the integration of its
institutions. The church unity that LaFarge so prized was in fact threatened by an increasingly educated and assertive laity.

Amid the swirling controversy between the Catholic left and right,
LaFarge and Hunton announced their retirement from the CICNY in
February, 1962. The CICNY organized a banquet to honor the retiring
interracial team at the Commodore Hotel on June 4. The theme of the
banquet, "Tomorrow Is Now," mirrored the mood of the civil rights
movement. The affair drew a large crowd of civil rights advocates from
across religious and racial lines. Mayor Robert F. Wagner of New York
presented the awards, and Judge Harold Stevens, a black member of
the CICNY and of the New York Supreme Court, acted as toastmaster.
A host of notables gave tributes to LaFarge and Hunton. Mayor Wagner described LaFarge as an "impassioned apostle of inter-racial justice"
and one of the "authentic heroes of the eternal struggle for social justice
and human rights." Letters and telegrams streamed in from outside the

45. LaFarge, "The Story of a Roman Catholic," 580.
46. LaFarge, "Peter Speaks Again," 563; Wills, *Politics and Catholic Freedom*, 11,
19, 33. Hardline Catholics like Buckley also showed contempt for LaFarge's social reform
approach to anticommunism; see Allitt, *Catholic Intellectuals and Conservative Politics*,
98–99.
47. On increasing lay activity, see Allitt, *Catholic Intellectuals and Conservative
Politics*, 97, 113–14.

banquet hall. President Kennedy's and Governor Nelson A. Rockefeller's congratulations were among them.[48]

However, as LaFarge and Hunton basked in the glow of collective praise, the CICNY was floundering. Dennis Clark of Philadelphia, who replaced Hunton as executive director, inherited an organization that verged on bankruptcy. Foundation funds were drying up, and the deficit for 1962 was $20,000 in a budget of less than $100,000. Although the CICNY increased its membership from three hundred to seven hundred in the early 1960s, usually fewer than twenty people attended the weekly forums. Furthermore, many felt that the council's polite forums had become quaint in the day of direct action. After the formation of the NCCIJ, the New York council focused more on local programs, but it had neither the personnel nor the funds to make these ventures successful. The *Interracial Review*, which never had more than 3,500 subscribers, constantly ran in the red, and in 1963 Father Hurley, the new chaplain of the CICNY, argued for its termination. LaFarge, who remained on the board of the CICNY, fought valiantly to retain the review, but it ceased publication in 1966.[49]

Under Clark the *Interracial Review* grew more strident and sociological, focusing on housing and stabilizing neighborhoods. Clark, however, resigned after about a year on the job. His final report for the year 1962 reflected his profound disappointment, if not despair. He quipped that the job had proved he was no fundraiser, the proof being the financial crisis the council faced. He argued that the council needed several skilled, full-time people to make the local programs work, but the catch was that this required more money. He grieved to the board of directors that no respectable Catholic lay apostolates existed in the social arena. According to Clark, they all suffered from "budget crisis, haphazard planning, inefficiency and stultifying self-delusion."[50]

48. "Two Founders Honored by Interracial Council," New York *Times,* June 5, 1962, p. 21; material on banquet, in box 21, folder 5, JLFP 1, and box 49, folder 9, JLFP 1; Nelson A. Rockefeller to John LaFarge, May 24, 1962, in box 1, folder 29, JLFP 2; telegram from John F. Kennedy to CICNY, June 4, 1962, reprinted in *IR,* 35 (August, 1962), opposite title page; Apostolic Delegate Egidio Vagnozzi to John LaFarge, May 28, 1962, in box 1, folder 29, JLFP 2.

49. Zielinski, " 'Doing the Truth,' " 53, 56, 69–74, 105–106, 115, 117, 120–21, 176; John LaFarge to Cardinal Spellman, November 21, 1961, in box 18, folder 6, JLFP 1. The *Interracial Review* reappeared in 1970 but only as a thin amateurish quarterly; copies of the review from the 1970s and 1980s can be found in the Josephite Archives, Baltimore.

50. Dennis Clark, report to the board of directors of the CICNY, n.d. [late 1962

In late 1963, only four days before LaFarge's death, Arthur Wright became the first black executive director of the CICNY. Wright quickly fell into heated squabbles with chaplain Hurley and other veteran staff members, and an ugly power struggle ensued. Hurley and at least one other staff member were forced to resign in 1964.[51] In the 1960s the course of Catholic interracialism would be determined not in New York but in Chicago.

Mathew Ahmann fully understood that the convergence of forces and events in the early 1960s marked the beginning of a racial revolution. In 1960 he came up with the idea of holding an interreligious conference on race, an idea that was heartily supported by Monsignor Cantwell and John McDermott. Their efforts led to the National Conference on Religion and Race held in Chicago in January, 1963, the year of the centennial of Abraham Lincoln's Emancipation Proclamation. Taking advantage of the ecumenical climate created by Pope John XXIII and the opening of the Second Vatican Council, Ahmann eventually hooked up with the National Council of Churches and the Synagogue Council of America to stage the event. The historic conference constituted a major breakthrough in recognition for the Catholic interracial movement.[52]

The national conference met at Chicago's Edgewater Beach Hotel from January 14 to 17, 1963. Sixty-seven national religious groups represented by 657 delegates attended the convention. The conference contained a mix of scholars, preachers, and racial activists, both black and white, including Benjamin Mays, president of Morehouse College, Whitney Young, Jr., executive director of the National Urban League, Dr. Abraham Heschel of the Jewish Theological Seminary, and the Reverends Fred Shuttelsworth, Ralph Abernathy, and Martin Luther King, Jr., of the Southern Christian Leadership Conference. Dennis Clark and George Hunton represented the CICNY. Too ill to attend the conference, LaFarge was limited to supplying material for some opening remarks delivered by Chicago's Archbishop Meyer.[53]

---

or early 1963], in box 30, folder 5, JLFP 1. For a sketch of this "egghead activist," see Clark's obituary in the Philadelphia *Inquirer*, September 18, 1993, and in the New York *Times*, September 19, 1993, Sec. Y, p. 22.

51. Zielinski, " 'Doing the Truth,' " 107–109, 111.

52. *Ibid.*, 256, 271–87; Avella, *This Confident Church*, 312–13.

53. LaFarge, minutes, board of directors, CICNY, January 23, 1963, in box 30, folder 5, JLFP 1; Avella, *This Confident Church*, 313–14.

Never had such a broad-based religious conference taken on such an implacable American problem, but the Chicago conferees did so enthusiastically. The gathering took place at an emotional juncture in the civil rights movement, and a feeling of optimism and solidarity pervaded the religious assemblage. Many of the delegates illustrated this heady mood in the numerous addresses given during the four-day convention. Speakers eagerly but often abstractly embraced the challenge that race presented to organized religion. Rabbi Heschel proclaimed that *"the Negro problem is God's gift to America,* the test of integrity, a magnificent spiritual opportunity."[54]

Opportunity or not, the mellifluous, cadenced voice of Martin Luther King, Jr., was the oratorial gift to the convention. King's Chicago speech marked for him the beginning of an incredible year in which he made unforgettable history at Birmingham and Washington, D.C.[55] Meanwhile, King hurled a monumental challenge at the church in Chicago. He supplied the "prophetic" voice that many young Catholics found missing in their religious tradition.[56] Although King called for healing and unity, he also charged that the churches and synagogues had forsaken "their prophetic mission on the question of racial justice." King railed against the "pious irrelevancies," the "sanctimonious trivialities," and the "pathetic irrelevancy of the Church" on the race question. He characterized the church as "an echo rather than a voice, a tail light behind the Supreme Court and other secular agencies, rather than a headlight guiding men progressively and decisively to higher levels of understanding." He quoted St. Augustine on courage and excoriated the "paralysis of analysis." The "thin veneer of religiosity" and the well-known excuses for the delay of human equality, he declared, created a "stench in the nostrils of God." In this, and subsequently in his more famous speeches and writings, King could, like few Catholics, conjure up Augustine and Aquinas to convey the "fierce urgency of now," a feeling that white interracialists like LaFarge were loath to appreciate.[57]

54. Abraham Heschel, "The Religious Basis of Equality of Opportunity—The Segregation of God," in *Race: Challenge to Religion,* ed. Mathew Ahmann (Chicago, 1963), 68. The major speeches of the conference were published in Ahmann's anthology.

55. Goldfield, *Black, White, and Southern,* 130–32.

56. John C. Bennett, "The Church as Prophetic Critic," *Christian Century,* January 6, 1954, pp. 9–11; Allitt, *Catholic Intellectuals and Conservative Politics,* 255.

57. Martin Luther King, Jr., "A Challenge to the Churches and Synagogues," in *Race,* ed. Ahmann, 155–69. See also his "Letter from Birmingham Jail," in King, *Why*

At the end of the convention, the delegates approved a resolution titled "An Appeal to the Conscience of the American People." Monsignor Cantwell of the CICC headed a committee charged with grinding out a statement that all faiths could endorse. The resolution emanating from the conference was exceedingly short and general, but it contained a substantial dose of contrition: "We repent our failures and ask the forgiveness of God. We also ask the forgiveness of our brothers, whose rights we have ignored and whose dignity we have offended." Father Cronin of the Social Action Department of the NCWC thought the "confession of guilt was too sweeping" and the view of the church too negative. A few years earlier LaFarge, rather than Cantwell, would have been involved in writing the resolution, and it no doubt would have been more to Cronin's liking.[58]

As it was, several analysts found much to criticize in the Chicago resolution. In a scorching review of the conference in the *Christian Century,* William Stringfellow, an Episcopal minister who attended the gathering, characterized most of the speeches as long on platitudes and short on realism. The meeting, he maintained, was "too little, too late, and too lily white." *Time* charged that the churches, which it characterized as mired in "awful fatalism," had always lacked resolution and originality in dealing with race, and it judged that the conference had offered little that was new or useful. LaFarge took strong offense at *Time*'s mocking review of the conference. In a letter to the editor, he assailed the magazine's view that the religious establishment had nothing to offer on the race question.[59]

LaFarge's fiery letter demonstrated his limited tolerance for criticism of the church. He preferred to put a different spin on the jarringly negative remarks made about religion at the conference. On the back cover of the collected Chicago speeches, a volume edited by Mathew

---

We Can't Wait (New York, 1964), Chap. 11, and his 1963 Washington, D.C., speech, "I Have A Dream," in *Black Protest Thought in the Twentieth Century,* ed. August Meier, Elliott Rudwick, and Francis L. Broderick (Indianapolis, Ind., 1971), 346–51.

58. "An Appeal to the Conscience of the American People," in *Race,* ed. Ahmann, 171–73; Zielinski, " 'Doing the Truth,' " 282–86.

59. William Stringfellow, review of *Race: Challenge to Religion,* edited by Mathew Ahmann, in *Christian Century,* 80 (September 18, 1963), 1135–36; John LaFarge, "Religion and Race Meeting," *Am,* 108 (February 8, 1963), 506; "That Awful Fatalism," *Time,* January 25, 1963, p. 66; John LaFarge, letter to the editor, *Time,* February 15, 1963, p. 14.

Ahmann, he assured readers that the Chicago conference recommended "calm reason combined with practical wisdom and intense concern."[60]

By the time of the Chicago conference, however, many young white Catholics had been stirred by the prophetic vision of Martin Luther King, Jr. No longer content just to tolerate direct action, they wanted to make demonstrations interracial and give them a Catholic touch. Some members of the CICC in fact went to Albany, Georgia, in 1962 and were arrested for their part in the demonstrations. Dennis Clark told the Executive Committee of the CICNY in 1962 that it was shameful that Catholics were not represented in the pitched desegregation struggle going on in Mississippi, a statement to which Chaplain Hurley took strong exception. In 1962, soon after Clark became editor of the *Interracial Review,* he penned a fire-eating editorial called "The Peril of Pussyfooting." Clark lamented that forty million Catholics had hardly made a mark on the civil rights movement. Catholics, he griped, were leery of all innovation and given to the "principle of tokenism" in racial matters. He charged that the Catholic movement was "content with rhetoric and resolutions, second guessing and mopping up." He concluded by asking if Catholics were ready to "risk jail and jeopardy in the South and stigma in the North" to reach the goal of human unity.[61]

If most Catholics hesitated to enter the racial fray, LaFarge continued to move forward in his eighties. He had come to support the sit-ins and the freedom rides, albeit reluctantly. Moreover, by the 1960s he had begun to doubt, if only slightly, the ability of southern moderates to bring peace and justice to Dixie. In late 1961 the *Interracial Review* abandoned the Supreme Court's formula "with all deliberate speed" and called for complete desegregation of schools within six months.[62]

Still, LaFarge increasingly worried about black nationalism and its image of whites. He wondered anxiously where changing black attitudes would take the aggrieved minority. The black credo, he speculated, "may become distorted, chauvinistic, anti-Christian, or it may become profoundly Catholic." LaFarge expressed fear that ghetto

60. Remarks by LaFarge on back cover of the paperback *Race,* ed. Ahmann.
61. Zielinski, " 'Doing the Truth,' " 438; minutes, executive meeting, August 29, 1962, in box 5, CICNYP; "The Peril of Pussyfooting," *IR,* 35 (June, 1962), 136.
62. "The Old Campaign Promises," *IR,* 34 (December, 1961), 304.

blacks might spurn religion and "exploit the poisonous fires of nation-alism and anti-white prejudice, with the Communists stoking the fires." He also showed heightened concern about "the lack of sound political and moral leadership in the local black community." After reviewing a book by James Baldwin and reading about Malcolm X, LaFarge decried the "voices out of the wilderness of hate." Too weak to attend the NCCIJ meeting in Chicago in early 1963, he sent advice warning Cath-olics to take the Black Muslims and Baldwin for "real—no joke."[63]

The brutal actions of police chief Eugene T. "Bull" Connor in Bir-mingham, Alabama, also had to be taken for real. Connor's police meth-ods in the civil rights demonstrations in Birmingham in the spring of 1963 proved so shocking that it prodded President Kennedy to place a far-reaching civil rights bill before Congress. In doing so, Kennedy stressed that the race problem was a moral issue, one "as old as the scriptures and . . . as clear as the American Constitution." After issuing the bill, Kennedy held a series of meetings at the White House in the summer of 1963 with religious and civil rights leaders, including La-Farge, Hunton, Ahmann, and Cronin.[64]

By the summer of 1963 another event loomed large on the horizon. Since late 1962, A. Philip Randolph and Bayard Rustin had been plan-ning a march on the nation's capital to stress the need for jobs. In 1963 other civil rights organizations joined in the planning, and Mathew Ahmann, representing the NCCIJ, was selected as one of the ten chair-men to oversee the march. In preparation for the march, Ahmann called a special meeting of the NCCIJ in Chicago on July 27. Again, LaFarge did not feel well enough to attend the meeting. By 1963 he was turning down more and more requests for his services. A medical checkup in 1960 revealed that LaFarge was suffering a "mild hardening of the ar-

63. John LaFarge to Theodore F. Cunningham, S.J., December 16, 1960, in box 21, folder 3, JLFP 1; John LaFarge, "The Incredible Daddy Grace," *Am,* 103 (April 2, 1960), 5; John LaFarge, "Voices Out of the Wilderness of Hate," *Saturday Review,* December 14, 1963, pp. 42–43; John LaFarge to George Hunton, February 20, 1963, in box 3, folder 44, JLFP 2. See also LaFarge's review of *The Fire Next Time,* by James Baldwin, in box 42, folder 5, JLFP 1.

64. Sitkoff, *Struggle for Black Equality,* 127–46, esp. 138 for Kennedy quotation; Carl M. Brauer, *John F. Kennedy and the Second Reconstruction* (New York, 1977), 240, 260–61, 266–67; telegram, President John F. Kennedy to John LaFarge, June 12, 1963, in box 49, folder 9, JLFP 1; John H. Bresnahan, O.S.A., to John LaFarge, June 27, 1963, in box 2, folder 3, JLFP 1; Zielinski, " 'Doing the Truth,' " 446–47.

teries." Although he was not especially handicapped considering his age, a creeping frailness, especially in the limbs, was spreading over a body that had never been very robust.[65]

In any case, LaFarge forwarded a long letter to Chicago detailing his view about the upcoming march. Executive director Ahmann circulated copies of the priest's comments at the meeting. LaFarge visibly struggled with his conscience and his intellect over the march, recoiling at the possibility that it might end in calamitous violence. He acknowledged that he had always stressed the slow accumulation of knowledge and interracial good will. "But today a special question confronts us," the letter proclaimed. "The hour demands dramatic action. We cannot escape a sharp confrontation on the issue." LaFarge asked if the Catholics were prepared to suffer "scorn" and "physical hardships" as had the early Christians in Rome. He declared that all hesitation must end, for there was "no honorable way of evading it [the march]." The priest's internal conflict clearly emerged in the following passage: "It is not pleasant to say these things. There may be good people who enjoy excitement and demonstration, but for most of us it is an unwilling task, one which we embark on not from any enthusiastic or revolutionary spirit, but simply because plain logic and honest faith drove us to this conclusion, as it drove the peaceful inhabitants of our original Thirteen Colonies in the summer of 1776."[66]

The NCCIJ strongly endorsed the March on Washington and Kennedy's civil rights bill. It also challenged Catholics to participate in the march. Cardinal Spellman opposed the march at first but gradually relented. In mid-July he surprised and gratified LaFarge by having a letter that supported interracial justice read in 402 parish churches. Two weeks later Bishop John Maguire, the vicar general of the New York archdiocese, approved Catholic participation in the march and urged passage of the civil rights bill. In mid-August the American bishops issued a short statement on "racial harmony" that was timed to appear before the march. The statement basically reiterated the sentiments of the 1958 pastoral letter, but it did not explicitly endorse the march on

65. Zielinski, " 'Doing the Truth,' " 447–48; William S. Norton, M.D., to John LaFarge, November 3, 1960, in box 14, folder 31, JLFP 2.

66. John LaFarge to Mathew Ahmann, July 24, 1963, in box 8, folder 19, JLFP 2; portions of the letter appeared in *IR*, 36 (September, 1963), 159–60. LaFarge also approved the direct action of two Catholic nuns in Chicago; see John LaFarge to Mother M. Clemens, July 8, 1963, in box 3, folder 44, JLFP 2.

the capital. On the eve of the march, LaFarge issued several statements pointing out how large the march loomed for Catholics as a way to eliminate "a host of ambiguities concerning the racial attitudes of religious bodies."[67]

The March on Washington was a scintillating and historic event, the emotional high point of civil rights coalition politics. On August 28, a quarter of a million people marched peacefully through the nation's capital, seventy-five thousand of them white. Thanks to the organizing efforts of Ahmann and Archbishop O'Boyle of Washington, D.C., a significant Catholic presence was evident at the affair. Besides the priests and nuns, two archbishops and five bishops attended. Archbishop O'Boyle delivered the invocation, and Ahmann, as one of the ten chairmen of the march, gave one of the many speeches that afternoon. As the earnest but often platitudinous speeches wore on during that hot day, the crowd grew rather listless. But the audience came to life with King's "I Have a Dream" speech, one of the greatest orations in the history of civil rights.[68]

Taking in the happy event were the two pioneers of the Catholic interracial movement, LaFarge and Hunton. Too incapacitated to march, LaFarge had friends reserve him a seat on the steps of the Lincoln Memorial. The story goes that A. Philip Randolph had several young black men lift the aged Jesuit above the crush of the crowd and put him in position to observe the speakers' platform. Several Catholic newspapers featured pictures of LaFarge, frocked and straw-hatted, talking intently with a black bishop of the African Methodist Episcopal church.[69] Despite the attention lavished on LaFarge by the Catholic

67. John LaFarge to Cardinal Spellman, July 15, 1963, in box 7, folder 26, JLFP 2; Zielinski, " 'Doing the Truth,' " 449–51; "U.S. Bishops on Racial Harmony," *Long Island Catholic*, August, 1963, copy in box 2, folder 17, JLFP 1; New York *Herald Tribune*, August 18, 1963, copy in box 28, folder 5, JLFP 1. For LaFarge's statements, see New York *Times*, August 25, 1963, Sec. E, p. 12, and news release from Manhattanville College of the Sacred Heart, August [13], 1963, in box 6, folder 11, JLFP 1.

68. Washington, D.C., *Catholic Review*, August 23, 1963; "Four Eyes on the Washington March," *Am*, 109 (September 14, 1963), 252; Sitkoff, *Struggle for Black Equality*, 159.

69. "Time Out for a Friendly Chat," Nashville *Tennessee Register*, September 6, 1963; "Buoyant Gaiety Sets Tone of Washington Civil Rights March," Kansas City *Catholic Reporter*, September 6, 1963; Edward S. Stanton to Daniel J. Sullivan, March 15, 1982, in box 1, folder 2, Stanton Papers.

press, the march demonstrated plainly that the torch had been passed to a new generation of Catholic leaders, represented by Mathew Ahmann and his circle.[70]

In his own mind, however, events in the last months of his life gave him a splendid sense of accomplishment. On November 7, for example, Father John McGinty, the Jesuit provincial of New York, issued a circular letter that commanded Jesuits not to follow but to lead in the fight for racial justice. Not only did McGinty call for the integration of all Jesuit schools and seminaries; he also proposed a program of affirmative action that sought out worthy blacks and awarded them scholarships. The editors at *America* correctly discerned the influential hand of LaFarge in this development. On November 16, the American bishops released the "Bonds of Union," another strong statement on black equality. By the end of 1963, the diocesan clergy had replaced the Jesuit missions in southern Maryland. The Catholic church no longer looked upon African Americans as Third World people in need of white missionaries. In the letter announcing the changeover, the Reverend John M. Daly, the Maryland provincial, referred to LaFarge, "whose faithful footprints are worn deep into the walks and the ways of southern Maryland."[71]

After the March on Washington, LaFarge returned to his normal work at *America.* He continued to attend weekly forums and board meetings of the CICNY through November 20. On November 9, the priest extended greetings to Martin Luther King, Jr., when he accepted the St. Francis Medal from the Third Order of St. Francis in New York City. Two years earlier the 106,000 lay Catholics in the Franciscan Third Order decided to devote themselves exclusively to the service of

70. An earlier indication of the declining prestige of LaFarge could be seen in the anthology *Primer on Interracial Justice* (Baltimore, 1962), edited by Robert Senser, a Catholic activist from Chicago. That Senser's *Primer* contained essays by George Dunne, Claude Heithaus, Theodore Hesburgh, and Bishop Vincent Waters but none by LaFarge speaks volumes.

71. Letter from Jesuit Provincial to "Reverend Fathers and dear Brothers in Christ," November 7, 1963, in box 1, folder 24, JLFP 2; "No Postponement," *Am,* 109 (December 14, 1963), 763; "Text of U.S. Catholic Bishops' Statement Urging Full Recognition of Negro Rights," New York *Times,* November 17, 1963; John M. Daly to Jesuit Fathers of Ridge, Maryland, May 16, 1963, in box 21, folder 6, JLFP 1; Beitzell, *Jesuit Missions,* viii.

black Americans, another sign of changing attitudes in the church. In mid-November LaFarge made his final trip to Washington, D.C., to attend a NCCIJ convention.[72]

The 1963 weekend of November 22 to 24 marked the passing of two esteemed American leaders, one tragically by violence and one peacefully in his sleep. On Friday, November 22, President Kennedy met his death at the hands of an assassin in Dallas. Two days later, on Sunday, Father LaFarge died at Campion House at the age of eighty-three. LaFarge had corrected his quota of galleys that Sunday morning, and then he took in some of the extensive television coverage of Kennedy's assassination. Watching television was rare for "Uncle John," one of his companions at Campion House recalled, but on this day the priest seemed transfixed by the electronic device. Apparently in shock over Kennedy's death, LaFarge sat before the television and whispered repeatedly, "How terrible, how terrible." Becoming weary after a while, he retired to his room. Later that afternoon, a colleague glanced in LaFarge's room to find the priest in what appeared to be a state of deep sleep. On closer examination, however, he found that the Jesuit had died, clutching tightly in his hands the Sunday New York *Times*.[73]

The voluminous coverage of the president's death diverted attention from the passing of LaFarge. Amid its coverage of the assassination, *Commonweal* stuck in a little box essay expressing its regret at the passing of the prominent Jesuit.[74] Even so, notice of LaFarge's death, and life, was extensive in both religious and secular presses. *Time* referred to him as the "longtime guiding light of the Jesuit weekly *America*" and the "staunch Roman Catholic fighter against racial injustice." The New York *Times* published a lengthy obituary. *America* and the *Interracial Review*, of course, gave extensive coverage to his death. The

72. Minutes, board of directors, CICNY, September 18, 1963, box 1, folder 24, JLFP 2; minutes, board of directors, November 20, 1963, in box 5, CICNYP; program for the St. Francis Medal, in box 7, folder 22, JLFP 2; Roy M. Gasnick, "Franciscans Pledge to Interracial Justice," *Social Order*, 12 (April, 1962), 173–77; "Interracial Council Probes Relation Between Causes of Poverty, Prejudice," Boston *Pilot*, November 23, 1963.

73. [C. P. McNapsy(?)] to Edward Stanton, October 19, [1981], in box 1, folder 1, Stanton Papers.

74. "Father LaFarge," *Commonweal*, 79 (December 13, 1963), 336. For example, see the dual coverage in Philadelphia *Catholic Standard and Times*, November 29, 1963, Washington, D.C., *Catholic Review*, November 29, 1963, and Boston *Pilot*, November 30, 1963.

priest's picture appeared on the cover of the latter in the December, 1963, issue.[75]

Since Cardinal Spellman was in Rome, Cardinal Cushing of Boston traveled to New York on November 27, only two days after offering mass for John F. Kennedy in Washington, D.C., to say a requiem mass for LaFarge in St. Ignatius' Church. Cardinal Cushing called his tribute to LaFarge "Three Great Men by the Name of John." The names of the other two Johns, of course, were Pope John XXIII and John Kennedy, all of whom, Cushing told the mourners, had "recently returned to eternity." In his sermon Cushing recalled his first meeting with LaFarge forty years earlier, and he related how he had often consulted the Jesuit on problems concerning the poor. Cushing reviewed LaFarge's multiple apostolates, depicting him as a "crusader for truth" who took up the unpopular cause of black rights and eventually goaded a reluctant church into action. The archbishop worried that his praise of LaFarge might violate the "no eulogy" rule of the Jesuit order, but it did not keep him from saying, "If I were to epitomize the personal appeal of the life and work of the beloved John LaFarge, I would say: 'Like God Himself, he was always active, yet always calm.'" Cardinal Cushing might have added that LaFarge was calm because he truly believed, as he told Constance Daniel in 1925, that the Catholic church "infallibly renders justice in the end."[76]

LaFarge's funeral attracted a large interracial crowd. People from many walks of life came to honor the priest. Letters, cards, and telegrams from around the country and the world flooded Campion House. Special masses were offered across the land by Catholic interracialists. Father John Egan, who would play a vital role in the racial apostolate after LaFarge's death, recalled that he never got to know LaFarge well because he stood "too much in awe of him." Egan made a special effort to get from Chicago to New York to attend LaFarge's

75. "Milestones," *Time*, December 6, 1963, p. 116; "Rev. John LaFarge, 83, Dead; Ex-Editor in Chief of *America*," New York *Times*, November 25, 1963; "John LaFarge, S.J. (1880–1963)," *Am*, 109 (December 7, 1963), 725; "Father LaFarge, 1880–1963," *IR*, 36 (December, 1963), 230–31. See also "No Postponement," *Am*, 109 (December 14, 1963), 762–63, and "Father LaFarge, Champion of Social Justice," New York *Herald Tribune*, November 25, 1963.

76. "John LaFarge, S.J.," 725; copy of Cushing's eulogy in box 37, folder 8, JLFP 1, also in New York *Catholic News*, December 5, 1963; John LaFarge to Constance Daniel, February 3, 1925, in box 20, folder 1, JLFP 1.

funeral, just as he later got out of bed from open-heart surgery to bid
Dorothy Day farewell. "We just owed some people too much," Egan
wrote, "and they should never be forgotten by us."[77]

The Society of Jesus worked hard to ensure that its "gray emi-
nence" was not forgotten. It rendered periodic tributes to LaFarge in
America and elsewhere.[78] Jesuits established the John LaFarge House
at Harvard University in 1964 for the use of their graduate students at
Cambridge.[79] Six months after LaFarge died, *America* founded the John
LaFarge Institute and set it up in its new headquarters at 106 West 56th
Street. Ostensibly an ecumenical endeavor to study human problems
such as race, poverty, and peace, the institute hired a full-time executive
director in 1966.[80] The new organization also established the John
LaFarge Memorial Award for outstanding interracial work. Alas, the
first award went to Cardinal Spellman.[81]

77. "Correspondence Concerning the Death of Frances, Margaret, John," in box
39, JLFP 1; Msgr. John Egan to Edward Stanton, January 25, 1982, in box 1, folder 4,
Stanton Papers.

78. See, for example, "John LaFarge: The First Anniversary," *Am,* 111 (November
28, 1964), 695–96; Thurston N. Davis, S.J., "Only the Manner Was Ordinary," *Catholic
Mind,* 63 (January, 1965), 30–34; "The LaFarge Legacy," *Am,* 113 (November 27, 1965),
663. The November 24, 1973, issue was devoted to John F. Kennedy and LaFarge on the
tenth anniversaries of their deaths; see Edward S. Stanton, S.J., "The Manner Was Extraordinary," *Am,* 129 (November 24, 1973), 397–99.

79. *New England Province News,* September–October, 1964, clipping in box 4,
folder 1, JLFP 1.

80. "The John LaFarge Institute in the New America House," *Am,* 110 (June 6,
1964), 791–93. See also memorandum, James J. Gallagher, executive director of the John
LaFarge Institute, to John Courtney Murray, February 21, 1967, John Courtney Murray
to the board of trustees of the John LaFarge Institute, May 9, 1967, James Gallagher to
John Courtney Murray, May 16, 1967, minutes of editorial board of *America,* May 27,
[1967(?)], all in box 36, folder 19, JLFP 1. From the beginning there was much controversy over the institute. James Gallagher, the first executive director, claimed that the
LaFarge Institute was being used as a money-making venture to help finance *America's*
new quarters and was being falsely advertised as an independent, ecumenical organization. Gallagher wanted to make the institute truly independent and "open." Murray argued that the institute should drop its charade of being an open, ecumenical body and
become (or remain) an organic appendage of the Jesuits. Apparently, Murray's idea prevailed. Gallagher resigned after about a year as executive director.

81. "Notes," *IR,* 38 (June, 1965), 122–26.

12

LaFarge, Race, and American Catholicism

A Summation

More than any other individual in the first half of the twentieth century, Father John LaFarge awakened the American Catholic church to the moral implications of the race problem. To the extent that a Myrdalian dilemma existed in the Catholic mind before 1963, LaFarge figured prominently in its creation. He labored for fifty years to make the crucial point that African Americans were God's creatures and should be fully accorded their God-given human rights in the church and in American society. As the spiritual and intellectual leader of the Catholic interracial movement for thirty years, the Jesuit priest made explicit what had only been vaguely implicit in American Catholic teaching: that racism was a sin and that Christian charity and justice required racial equality in the Catholic community. He was not the first Catholic to label racism and segregation a sin or the first to start an interracial organization, but he spread the message better than any other Catholic before midcentury. LaFarge understood that racial changes were in the making, with or without the church's involvement. Thus he aimed to put the church slightly out in front of the general society and to direct racial change in accordance with Catholic principles as he understood them. Cyprian Davis summed up LaFarge's notable contribution in this way: "In a sense, LaFarge saved the honor of Roman Catholicism in America by being the persistent voice of reason and justice in a time of apathy and racism."[1]

In his prolific writings and speeches, LaFarge formulated a Catholic orthodoxy for those Catholic activists interested in black rights, most notably in his 1937 book, *Interracial Justice,* and its subsequent updates. Long before the *Brown* case, his interracial movement applied pressure on the church in the North to integrate Catholic institutions, such as schools, seminaries, and hospitals. In his stint as editor-in-chief of *America* in the 1940s, he also served to make the influential Jesuit weekly a consistent voice of Catholic liberalism for the first time. Despite his lifelong emphasis on precisely stating correct principles and methods, he was not an ivory-tower idealist but, as his associates never tired of pointing out, a man who established working organizations and immersed himself in the mundane tasks that rendered palpable the social forms necessary to advance civil rights.[2]

Although LaFarge primarily bored from within the church, he broke out of the usual Catholic isolation of the 1930s and 1940s and forged strong ties with the NAACP, the National Urban League, and A. Philip Randolph's MOWM. Largely through LaFarge's efforts, the Catholic church received a fairer hearing in the influential black press, which prior to LaFarge's overtures had displayed a decidedly anti-Catholic attitude. Roy Wilkins recalled that he and other NAACP officials often went to lecture whites at the CICNY forums, but ultimately, he said, "we stayed to learn at the feet of this selfless man [LaFarge]." Still, the hard truth is that the talented Jesuit publicist was more successful at improving the church's image than in changing the church's behavior.[3]

LaFarge inspired two generations of Catholic activists to work for racial justice. Among the priests who viewed him as a mentor were such clergymen as Francis Gilligan, Albert Foley, Horace McKenna, Joseph Fichter, John Cronin, Theodore Hesburgh, and John Egan. Important lay Catholics such as George Hunton, Clare Boothe Luce, Mathew Ahmann, and Dennis Clark also acknowledged their debt to

1. Cyprian Davis, *History of Black Catholics,* 228.
2. "The President and the Priest," *IR,* 36 (December, 1963), 231; "Father LaFarge at Eighty," *Am,* 102 (February 13, 1960), 575.
3. Wilkins, quoted in Stanton, "John LaFarge," 92; Wakin and Scheuer, *De-Romanization of the American Church,* 237.

LaFarge. Just three weeks before LaFarge's death, Theodore Hesburgh, for many years a leading member of the United States Commission on Civil Rights, wrote these words to him: "You have been a great inspiration to all of us . . . since you carried the torch during the years when this [the passage of a federal civil rights bill] seemed to be a lost cause." In addition to such well-known Catholic figures, the Jesuit persuaded legions of students on Catholic campuses to take up the cause of minority rights in the 1930s and 1940s. Dan Kane, a student at St. Joseph's in Philadelphia in the late 1930s and a pioneer interracialist in Cincinnati, testified that LaFarge "gave us [students] a vision" to follow.[4]

LaFarge's success as a leader in interracialism derived from many sources, but his heroic patience and tenacity of purpose explained many of his achievements. Few have struggled for so long in the cause of racial justice. LaFarge let it be known, Kane recalled, that he was in the cause for the "long haul."[5] And because of his longevity, he simply wore down or outlived many of his opponents.

The taproot of his persistence was not difficult to discern: his deep religious faith sustained him for the long haul. "He interpreted the passing state of affairs," wrote *America*, "in the light of his Christian faith and his God—of whom, he never forgot, he was an anointed priest." His broad vision derived from his belief in the unifying mission of the Catholic church. In a pitifully discordant world, LaFarge discerned that nothing divided humankind more bitterly than race. For the glory of God and Catholicism, he resolved to do what he could to remove this obstacle to human unity.[6]

LaFarge also had a strong ambition to define the basis of black-white relations for the Catholic church. If not exactly a saint in pursuit of this ambition, he was seldom petty or vindictive. He hardly lusted for power in the usual sense. His ambition, more like a calling to him, grew naturally out of his confidence that he was the person best prepared by experience and training to address the gritty and controversial question of race in a way that, in the long run, was beneficial both to

4. Theodore Hesburgh to John LaFarge, November 6, 1963, in box 2, folder 13, JLFP 1; interview of Kane by the author.

5. Interview of Kane by the author. See also McDonough, *Men Astutely Trained*, 132, who titles his chapter on LaFarge " 'Une Longue Patience,' " a title derived from a French maxim admired by LaFarge's father: "Le genie est une longue patience."

6. "John LaFarge, S.J. (1880–1963)," *Am*, 109 (December 7, 1963), 725; Stanton, "John LaFarge's Understanding."

the institutional church and to African Americans. He did not hesitate, when necessary, to assert himself as leader of the movement. Before the revolt of Chicago interracialists in the 1950s, few Catholics questioned LaFarge's role as the self-proclaimed Catholic spokesman on the American dilemma.

An aristocrat with a sense of noblesse oblige, LaFarge had many leadership weapons in his personal arsenal.[7] His patrician background, his personality, and his linguistic talent smoothed the way for dealing with the church bureaucracy. Gentle, obedient, and diplomatically savvy, "Uncle John" worked in the sensitive area of race relations for half a century and made few enemies. His conciliatory nature was real. "He was a genuine person," vouched Monsignor Gilligan. Cardinal Spellman, LaFarge's ever-present sword of Damocles, may have thought, as he did in the case of Dorothy Day, that the Jesuit might be a saint, perhaps explaining why the prelate allowed the priest more slack than he did most liberals in the New York archdiocese. Robert Hartnett, who succeeded LaFarge as editor-in-chief of *America,* believed that LaFarge's impressive social background and his personal demeanor afforded his views a fair hearing from church officials, including those in the Vatican—the kind of hearing that other social activists did not always receive.[8] His knowledge of a dozen languages and his personal contacts also allowed LaFarge to move fluidly in influential circles abroad.

Another factor in the Jesuit's institutional endurance was his power of growth. According to his niece Frances S. Childs, he "grew by degrees," and he grew in a liberal direction until virtually his last breath. Observing LaFarge in his eighties, Mathew Ahmann said that the priest still had a "live mind."[9]

Unfortunately, as is often the case with important historical figures, many of the Jesuit's strengths also proved to be his weaknesses. His noblesse oblige gave him a taste for "uplifting" endeavors, but the business of uplift had him looking down at those below. It is instructive

7. Joseph Fichter, S.J., expressed the opinion that LaFarge had "a great social conscience" (Fichter to the author, May 29, 1992).

8. Msgr. Francis J. Gilligan to the author, June 19, 1991; Cooney, *American Pope,* 78–79, 88–90; Robert C. Hartnett, S.J., to Edward Stanton, May 18, 1981, in box 1, folder 10, Stanton Papers.

9. Frances S. Childs to Edward Stanton, October 7, 1980, in box 1, folder 8, Stanton Papers; interview of Ahmann by the author.

that the LaFarge family deeply admired Pierre Toussaint, the former Haitian slave who chose to remain a servant to the emigré family that once owned him. The saintly black man not only served as the coveted hairdresser for the LaFarge and Binsse women but also as a confidant of the patriarchs in the two prominent families.[10]

LaFarge's paternalism flowed naturally from his background and was enhanced by his fifteen years in southern Maryland. As Cyprian Davis maintains, LaFarge related better to uneducated black sharecroppers and fishermen in St. Mary's County than to the educated black elite.[11] He was particularly wary of blacks who were openly secular-minded and nondeferential. LaFarge therefore had difficulty in relating to Constance Daniel, a person not only educated, militant, and critical of Catholicism but female as well. He also had trouble dealing with Thomas Turner, simply because Turner, a Ph.D. and a layman, wanted to lead blacks in his own right. To W. E. B. Du Bois, the versatile black leader who was highly critical of the Catholic church, LaFarge could not relate at all. He related famously, however, to the Catholic Laymen's Union, the conservative group of black Catholics that he formed in the 1920s. His paternalism was particularly apparent in his timid stand on interracial marriage—a stand that cannot be explained as simply a tactical ploy. It in fact reveals LaFarge's ambivalence about blacks and their culture and recalls Father William Markoe's stinging remark that the New York priest was not quite black enough for his chosen mission.

Instead of raising a cadre of black leaders, the Catholic interracial movement actually helped create a vacuum of black leadership in the church. Historian Harvard Sitkoff has put this phenomenon in a larger context. He maintains that the interracial movement that arose during World War II in response to racial violence stunted and diluted an embryonic black movement. Liberal interracialists, Sitkoff argues, "too easily accepted the appearance of racial peace for the reality of racial justice."[12] In any event, the rise of LaFarge and Catholic interracialism in the 1930s left in its wake the precipitate decline and ultimate demise of Thomas Turner's FCC, which had the best potential for effecting

10. McDonough, *Men Astutely Trained*, 120; Tarry, *The Other Toussaint*, 204, 239, 360–61.

11. Cyprian Davis, *History of Black Catholics*, 228–29.

12. Harvard Sitkoff, "Racial Militancy and Interracial Violence in the Second World War," *Journal of American History*, 58 (December, 1971), 679. See also Marable, *Race, Reform and Rebellion*, vi, 18, 25.

change within the church. LaFarge simply disliked protest with an African American accent.

In the end, the racial mountain in America shifted because of constant and coercive pounding by African Americans.[13] Black Catholics, however, were largely absent from leadership roles in the civil rights movement. As the black Catholic priest Edward Braxton wrote, "When Jesse Jackson, Harold Washington or Alex Haley speak of the 'black church,' its power and its impact, they do not mean us." Braxton might have added that historians who consider the black church as a major source of the civil rights movement have assigned no role to black Catholics. Aldon D. Morris' highly regarded book *The Origins of the Civil Rights Movement,* which stresses the black grassroots and the black church, has no entries in its index for the Catholic church or black Catholics.[14] Black Catholics thus stood in the shadow of the larger black community, and many of them took their social action cues from Protestants such as Martin Luther King, Jr., and the young blacks of SNCC, as did many white Catholics.[15] The church of St. Sabina's in a black Chicago parish, for example, unilaterally raised Martin Luther King, Jr., to sainthood. At the same time, some black Catholics began to reject Pierre Toussaint, a candidate for beatification, as an Uncle Tom.[16]

If paternalism hampered LaFarge, excessive optimism also led the Jesuit down many false trails. His robust optimism, an outlook that

13. Czuchlewski, "Liberal Catholicism and American Racism," 159–60. See La-Farge's remarks on black Catholic leadership in his *Catholic Viewpoint,* 61–64, 73–74.

14. Edward Braxton, S.T.D., "The Key Role of the Black Laity," *Origins: NC Documentary Service,* 14 (May 31, 1984), 36; Morris, *The Origins of the Civil Rights Movement.*

15. Cyprian Davis, *History of Black Catholics,* 256; Braxton, "Key Role of Black Catholic Laity," 36. Any number of black priests and bishops invoked the names of Martin Luther King, Jr., and some referred to A. Philip Randolph, Marcus Garvey, and Malcolm X; see, for example, Roxanne Brown, "Double Dose of Divinity," *Ebony,* 44 (January, 1989), 52.

16. David Briggs (AP release), "Pierre Toussaint: Candidate for Sainthood or Uncle Tom?," Fulton (Mo.) *Sun,* July 4, 1992. Of three prominent black Catholics—Albert J. Raboteau, Beverly Carroll, and Jamie T. Phelps—asked about Toussaint by Thomas H. Stahel in *Am,* 166 (April 25, 1992), 340, 342, 354, two seemed to oppose canonization while one favored it. Ellen Tarry, a black Catholic, did much soul-searching and made a trip to Haiti before she could complete her book on Toussaint. Ultimately, she decided that Toussaint transcended racism and indignity with his piety and service (see n. 10).

seemed more utopian than Catholic, emanated from his belief that he had irrefutable possession of God's truth; and from that divine truth he claimed to have extracted unassailable social principles that ultimately assured peace and justice. Rejecting the burden of original sin, he eschewed all traces of Niebuhrian ambiguity and denied altogether a tragic sense of human relations. He seldom tempered his optimism with what Catholic philosopher Michael Novak terms "biblical realism." [17] LaFarge's "Christian anthropology" celebrated "the natural good that is man." He taught that "the goal of the best spiritual literature is—confidence." He seemed to mistake for reality the lofty aspirations of social harmony enshrined in social encyclicals, proving that arrogance of faith can be as corrupting as power when it comes to social analysis.[18]

More specifically, the Jesuit's sunshine theology inclined him toward a shallow view of racism, and it saddled him with false optimism about the white South. As Garry Wills has suggested, and many social scientists have documented, racism has a psychological dimension that seems impervious to liberal good will.[19] Had LaFarge recognized the manifold sources of white racism and the myriad factors that sustained it, he would have had to reconsider his gradualistic approach to the race problem for something stronger. If his understanding of racism had been more profound, he might have grasped the value of mass organization, black power, and coercive governmental measures to uphold the law. He even might have applauded a Notre Dame theologian who wrote, "Freedom is always taken before it is given." In the words of a

17. See Michael Novak, *Confessions of a Catholic* (New York, 1983), 132–43, and also his *Choosing Our King: Powerful Symbols in Presidential Politics* (New York, 1974), 293. On the idea of "Sin's pathetic vicious circle," see Reinhold Niebuhr, *The Nature and Destiny of Man* (2 vols.; New York, 1949), I, 250, and Robert Tabscott, "The 20th Century's Theologian: Reinhold Niebuhr's Influence Permeates Contemporary Politics and Ethics," St. Louis *Post-Dispatch*, June 19, 1992.

18. *MIO*, 311, 314. On the idea that Catholic social teaching assumed social harmony and ignored the "sociology of conflict," see Hollenbeck, *Claims in Conflict*, 162; John A. Coleman, S.J., "Neither Liberal nor Socialist: The Originality of Catholic Social Teaching," in *One Hundred Years of Catholic Social Thought*, ed. Coleman, 39–40; and Hobgood, *Catholic Social Teaching*, 254.

19. On Garry Wills, see Allitt, *Catholic Intellectuals and Conservative Politics*, 261–63. On racism, see also Van den Berghe, *Race and Racism*, 8; Schuman, Steeh, and Bobo, *Racial Attitudes in America*, 5–6, 84, 176, 179, 194–95, 201; and Kovel, *White Racism*, 4.

black Catholic historian, LaFarge erred in thinking "that racism could be combatted with good manners and reasonableness."[20]

Had LaFarge not sounded the triumphalist horn so often, he might have dissipated less of his energy on Catholic apologetics. To render plausible the idea that the Catholic church alone held the key to the race question, he had to doctor history and exaggerate the reform prowess of the church. Catholic activists who had deeper insight into the race question (one thinks of O'Connor, Ahmann, Clark, Cantwell, and the Markoe brothers) took no solace in denial.[21]

Ironically, the very breadth of LaFarge's vision detracted from the single-mindedness that often drives dynamic leaders. An infinitely complex man, he nimbly balanced the interests of competing segments of the church against the grave needs of black Americans. He constantly wrestled with the problem of conflictual pairings, such as virtue and knowledge, obedience and conscience, order and change, boldness and prudence, thought and action, humility and pride, image and substance, and the international Society of Jesus and the American church. O'Connor insightfully described him as a "paradox of obedience and personal initiative."[22] Like a centipede contemplating the movement of each foot, he found it difficult to move decisively in any one direction. His turgid prose reflected the finely crafted compromises and the conciliatory maneuvering with which he busied himself. LaFarge's highly nuanced thought revealed a facile mind, but one person's complexity of thinking is another's temporizing. A scholar who described the pre–Vatican II Jesuits as an international order "driven by contradictions straining toward integration" could have been portraying LaFarge.[23]

Then, too, his far-flung, protracted battle against modernism blurred his racial focus. LaFarge seemed to attach a real sense of ur-

---

20. James Tunstead Burtschaell, C.S.S., "Religious Freedom (Dignitatis Humanae)," in *Modern Catholicism: Vatican II and After,* ed. Adrian Hastings (New York, 1991), 124–25; Cyprian Davis, *History of Black Catholics,* 229.

21. For harsh criticisms of the Catholic interracial movement, see Robert C. Hartnett, S.J., to John LaFarge, August 12, 1961, in box 21, folder 4, JLFP 1, and Mathew Ahmann, "Strategies for the Future," in *The Church and the Urban Crisis,* ed. Mathew Ahmann (Techny, Ill., 1967), 226–30.

22. John O'Connor, "The Ordinary Way," *IR,* 27 (February, 1954), 25; Stanton, "John LaFarge's Understanding," 244. On the problem of obedience, see Pelikan, *Riddle of Roman Catholicism,* 86–89. Pelikan charges that Catholics often "lose the distinction between the church and the voice of God."

23. McDonough, *Men Astutely Trained,* xvi.

gency to only such issues as communism and birth control. Unlike his writings about race relations, his verbal assaults on communism had the lift of passion. LaFarge became equally exercised about the issue of birth control. When he heard a false rumor that the National Association of Colored Graduate Nurses planned to open birth control clinics, he addressed a letter to the secretary, instructing her to sever at once his connection with the association and "to make known this disassociation in any way possible." In addition, he berated the organization for taking a step that was sure to be "fatal to the Association's purposes," and in a final salvo he declared that birth control was "aimed directly at the freedom, progress and prosperity of the Negro race."[24]

On matters of race, however, LaFarge's tone was almost always one of detached assessment. Cardinal Cushing praised the priest's Godlike calm, but to some it signified an attitude of disengagement. Unlike Daniel Lord or Fulton Sheen, LaFarge recoiled from showmanship as a way of arousing common people. As was said of John Kennedy early in his presidency, LaFarge seemed to lack moral passion on the race question. His commitment was primarily doctrinal and intellectual.[25] Perhaps American Catholicism needed a racially advanced Lord or Sheen or even a Charles Coughlin.

In any case, LaFarge found it difficult to articulate black feelings of anguish, indignation, and humiliation. Unlike African American activists, he was in no hurry to usher in the racial justice he deemed inevitable. To him, haste and elevated emotions somehow seemed profane. One of the secrets of his unflagging optimism was that he never expected too much, too soon. As Alton Paton commented in 1954, the urge for whites to go slowly in securing the rights of others was ingrained and powerful, but the feeling, he stressed, was hardly "noble, courageous or generous."[26]

24. John LaFarge to Mabel Keaton Staupers, R.N., May 20, 1941, and Mabel Keaton Staupers to John LaFarge, June 5, 1941, both in box 3, folder 35, JLFP 2; John LaFarge, "Birth Control and Race Relations," *IR,* 33 (February, 1960), 40–41. See also Cogley, *Catholic America,* 288.

25. McDonough, *Men Astutely Trained,* xii, 125–26, 132–33. On Kennedy, see Nicholas Lemann, *Promised Land,* 115–16, and Carl M. Brauer, *John F. Kennedy and the Second Reconstruction* (New York, 1977), 11, 35–36.

26. Alan Paton, "The Church Amid Racial Tensions," *Christian Century,* 71 (March 31, 1954), 393.

The noted scholar Gordon Allport rightly scolded LaFarge for denigrating all secular liberals as purveyors of "ethical anarchy." Allport advised LaFarge that his movement should learn to work with honest and idealistic secular humanists, even if they favored birth control and divorce.[27] To his credit, late in life LaFarge took significant strides toward a position of enlightened tolerance, but he never quite banished his bigotry vis-à-vis secularists, even those fired by a love of justice.

Undoubtedly, LaFarge's historical significance will rest on his race relations work. Catholic analysts in an earlier time often ranked the interracialist high as an intellectual (non-Catholics largely ignored him). In 1960 Jacques Maritain proclaimed that LaFarge was "a priest of rare intellectual genius." Such appraisals are infrequent today.[28] Recent works on Catholic intellectuals often fail to mention LaFarge. If they do, he is seldom ranked with that small group of outspoken priests, most of them censored at one time or another, who forced Catholic thought into new and more liberal channels, men such as John Cooper, George Dunne, John Courtney Murray, and Gustave Weigel. Lacking in originality, LaFarge found it difficult to think beyond papal encyclicals.[29] A cosmopolitan generalist, LaFarge let his facile mind range widely but usually stopped at the edge of uncharted territory. Nor did he concern himself much about the intellectual shortcomings of the Catholic community as did fellow Catholics George Shuster, John Cooper, and John Tracy Ellis.[30] Preoccupied with fighting modernism, LaFarge never protested, privately or publicly, the silencing of priests such as Dunne, Heithaus, or Murray. The clash between authority and

27. Gordon W. Allport, review of *No Postponement*, 471–72.

28. Jacques Maritain, "Father LaFarge," *IR*, 33 (February, 1960), 31–32. See also Michael V. Gannon, "The Intellectual Isolation of the American Priest," in *Catholic Priest*, ed. John Ellis, 295. Gannon ranks LaFarge as one of the ten priests who achieved intellectual distinction. Cyprian Davis also ranks him high intellectually in *History of Black Catholics*, 225.

29. McDonough, *Men Astutely Trained*, 132–33. Two recent works—Reher, *Catholic Intellectual Life*, and Marty, *Invitation to American Catholic History*—do not mention LaFarge.

30. See John Ellis, *American Catholics and the Intellectual Life;* Thomas F. O'Dea, *American Catholic Dilemma: An Inquiry into the Intellectual Life* (New York, 1958); Frank L. Christ and Gerald E. Sherry, eds., *American Catholicism and the Intellectual Ideal* (New York, 1961). Thurston Davis, editor-in-chief of *America*, criticized the intellectual shortcomings of Catholicism far more than LaFarge; see his "Five Live Problems for Catholics," *Am*, 95 (May 12, 1956), 158–61.

conscience that bedeviled so many noted Catholic thinkers and activists seemed to cause LaFarge little anguish.[31]

To be fair, any appraisal of LaFarge must take into account the restraints imposed on him by the pre–Vatican II church and the racist American culture. The very nature of hierarchical, bureaucratic Catholicism stifled the kind of charismatic and prophetic leadership required of the civil rights crusade. Only in the context of American Catholicism would the mild-mannered LaFarge be pegged, as he once was, a "zealot riding a hobby [horse]" that he picked up in southern Maryland. Many non-Catholic black leaders viewed the Catholic church as a highly disciplined institution that had great potential for effecting racial change. But when it came to African Americans, the church acted more like a "ponderous anarchy than a monolith." In 1963 Sargent Shriver described the church's racial policy as "religious laissez-faire." Although the church stood firm on issues such as birth control and divorce (at the risk of scorn and mockery from non-Catholics and apostasy by Catholics), it often conformed readily to the racist American culture. Its white hierarchy simply judged doctrinal integrity on race second in importance to broader institutional interest. Before Vatican II, American bishops almost always took more interest in black conversion than in black rights or black equality, often treating black parishes as "missions" in which African American cultural styles were allowed to have no significant influence on the European-styled worship.[32]

Even when individual prelates fought determinedly against racism in the Catholic community, they often had little success. For example, in 1963 the liberal archbishop Lawrence J. Shehan of Baltimore issued an eloquent pastoral against racism and organized an impressive Catholic contingent that participated in the March on Washington. In 1966, though, only one of thirteen Catholics on the Baltimore City Council listened to Shehan's plea to vote for an open-housing ordinance. More-

---

31. McDonough, *Men Astutely Trained*, 541–42; Dolan, *American Catholic Experience*, 443; Wills, *Politics and Catholic Freedom*, p. 5 of unnumbered introduction; Novak, *Confessions of a Catholic*, 110.

32. Osborne, *Segregated Covenant*, 233–47; "No Postponement," *Am*, 109 (December 14, 1963), 762; McDonough, *Men Astutely Trained*, xii; R. Sargent Shriver, "America, Race and the World," in *Race*, ed. Ahmann, 146; Labbe, *Jim Crow Comes to Church*, 69; Hobgood, *Catholic Social Teaching*, 104; Thomas Spalding, *Premier See*, 434–36; Blatnica, "At the Altar of God," 45, 220–21, 215.

over, the church hierarchy had to contend with a determined white-supremacist Catholic flank in the South.[33]

Near the end of LaFarge's career, the Catholic church had habituated itself to rendering eloquent lip service to racial equality. Encyclicals, pastoral letters from the American bishops, and endless proclamations from the Catholic interracial councils stated the doctrinal basis for racial equality. But defining Christian ideals was one thing, implementing them, another. G. K. Chesterton encapsulated this idea: "The Christian idea has not been tried and found wanting. It has been found difficult; and left untried." Church leaders called for racial change at every level, but the institution supplied relatively meager resources toward that end. In the mid-1960s the Social Action Department of the United States Catholic Conference (formerly the NCWC) had an annual budget of just $40,000. At the same time, the social action arm of the Protestant Episcopal church, one-tenth as large as the American Catholic church, spent $3,000,000 yearly. In 1965 only one-tenth of 1 percent of American Jesuits were involved in social work. In 1967 Pedro Arrupe, the general of the Jesuits, confessed that the order had not committed its "corporate effort" to the racial apostolate "in any degree commensurate with the need of the Negro."[34]

Like church resources, the spirit of racial liberalism was too often lacking as well. Enlightenment did not easily filter down to lower levels of the church, and in fact it sometimes dissipated at very high levels. Despite the church's verbal support for racial equality, nine of fourteen Catholic bishops in California remained mute when that state repealed its open-housing law by referendum in 1964. Archbishop Thomas J. Toolen of Mobile-Birmingham tried to keep priests and nuns from participating in the Selma voting rights march in 1965, preaching that priests and nuns should stay at home and do God's work. In a tribute to LaFarge in 1965, Thurston Davis, the chief editor of *America*, sadly cited a study that showed only 26 percent of Catholics remembered a

33. Osborne, *Segregated Covenant*, 233–47; Herbert J. Gans, "Symbolic Ethnicity: The Future of Ethnic Groups and Cultures in America," in *On the Making of Americans: Essays in Honor of David Riesman*, ed. Herbert J. Gans et al. (Philadelphia, 1979), 196.

34. Chesterton, quoted in *The Oxford Dictionary of Quotations* (3rd ed.; New York, 1979), 148; Richard A. Lamanna and Jay J. Coakley, "The Catholic Church and the Negro," in *Contemporary Catholicism*, ed. Gleason, 164–65, 167–68, Arrupe quotation on 168; McDonough, *Men Astutely Trained*, 493.

priest delivering a sermon on race relations.[35] Clearly, racism continued to infect much of the church throughout the 1960s.

Black slavery and caste, of course, "deformed" all New World churches in myriad ways.[36] The eleven o'clock hour on Sunday morning probably constitutes the most segregated hour of American life. Historians have shown that white Protestants, on the whole, did no better than Catholics in living up to the true meaning of their Christian creed with respect to blacks. All sinned and fell woefully short.[37] Nevertheless, owing to their greater resources, the Protestant churches (and secular institutions) supplied most of the crucial prerequisite for successful black insurgency: educational opportunity. The contribution of Protestant institutions in this area, to say nothing of secular ones, dwarfed that of the Catholic church. Protestants poured millions of dollars into black schools, seminaries, and colleges. Consequently, most black leaders, including Du Bois and King, learned equalitarian principles in institutions financed by white Protestants. Furthermore, Protestant churches in the North committed themselves to equality and integration before the Catholic church did. By the end of the 1940s the small Episcopal church had several black bishops, many of them in the South, and its seminaries featured blacks in faculty positions. Other northern denominations soon followed. Even the General Assembly of southern Presbyterians condemned segregation in 1954, four years prior to the American Catholic bishops; and the Southern Baptist Convention endorsed the *Brown* decision in the same year it was handed down. The United Church of Christ, with only 2,000,000 members, provided 20,000 marchers for the historic March on Washington in 1963, at least double that of the Catholic church. In Washington, D.C., the "church lobby" for the Civil Rights Act of 1964 was led by the National Council of Churches. The Protestant lobby was intense and

35. Lamanna and Coakley, "Catholic Church and the Negro," in *Contemporary Catholicism*, ed. Gleason, 165; Osborne, *Segregated Covenant*, 227–30; Wakin and Scheuer, *De-Romanization of the American Church*, 247; Thurston N. Davis, S.J., "Only the Manner Was Ordinary," *Catholic Mind*, 63 (January, 1965), 33.

36. Albert J. Raboteau, "Preaching the Word and Doing It," *Commonweal*, 116 (November 17, 1989), 632; Alan Davies, *Infected Christianity: A Study of Modern Racism* (Montreal, 1988), ix–xii, 73–88.

37. See, for example, Reimers, *White Protestantism and the Negro;* Frank Loescher, *The Protestant Church and the Negro* (New York, 1948); and Wood, *Arrogance of Faith.*

conspicuous on Capitol Hill, but Catholics still worked mainly through their local interracial councils.[38]

Even so, the Catholic church began to play a greater role in the civil rights movement in the 1960s. Although liberal Protestants and Jews dominated the lobbying for the 1964 Civil Rights Act, Catholic efforts were visible. Approximately 15 percent of the mail that Congress received came from Catholics, much of it from nuns. Father John Cronin, now a familiar face in the capital, proved instrumental in getting Senate Minority Leader Everett Dirksen of Illinois to vote for cloture, a crucial step that ended the southern filibuster against the bill. For his efforts, Cronin received a pen from President Lyndon B. Johnson at the ceremonial signing of the 1964 bill. Such southern filibusterers as Senator Richard Russell of Georgia declared that civil rights was not a moral but a legal and political question. Religious leaders, however, incessantly injected morality into the issue, causing an irritated Senator Herman Talmadge of Georgia to shriek that the "godammed [*sic*] preachers beat us." Roy Wilkins analyzed the decisive role performed by Protestants and Jews in the passage of the bill, but he also allowed that the "new and very persuasive ingredient [in the bill's passage] was the committed Catholic Church."[39]

By the mid-1960s the Catholic church was beginning to devote significantly more of its resources to improvement of race relations. Father John Egan boosted the racial work of the church through the Catholic Committee on Urban Ministry, which was created in 1967. Three years later, Egan was instrumental in establishing the Campaign for Human Development, which spent some $75 million in the 1980s in the Catholic war on poverty.[40]

Other changes were evident. A 1966 survey found that almost 80 percent of Catholic priests approved of the civil rights movement, and

38. Reimers, *White Protestantism and the Negro,* 112–13, 115–17, 120–21, 132–33, 188–89; Loescher, *Protestant Church and the Negro,* 21–22, 41–45, 62–65; James L. Adams, *The Growing Church Lobby in Washington* (Grand Rapids, Mich., 1970), 12–13, 16–18, 31–32.

39. Adams, *Growing Church Lobby,* 34, 37, 42; James F. Findlay, "Religion and Politics in the Sixties: The Churches and the Civil Rights Acts of 1964," *Journal of American History,* 77 (June, 1990), 83; Adams, *Growing Church Lobby,* 6, 26, 31–32, 39; Talmadge, quoted in John F. Cronin, S.S., "Religion and Race," *Am,* 150 (June 23–30, 1984), 472; Roy Wilkins, Introduction to Hunton, *All of Which I Saw,* 9.

40. P. E. Hogan and J. B. Tennelly, "Negroes in the U.S.," *New Catholic Encyclopedia* (1967), x, 313; Dolan, *American Catholic Experience,* 447–48.

over half believed the pace of the movement was too slow. In the late 1960s Father James Groppi became a regular feature on the national news as he led open-housing marches in Milwaukee.[41]

Vatican II also opened new doors for aggrieved minorities. Many of the sixteen major documents the council produced contained the kind of statements on race that LaFarge had lobbied for throughout his long career. Two of them, *Lumen Gentium* and *Gaudium et Spes*, specifically condemned racism and demanded action to eliminate it. *Gaudium et Spes* declared that "every type of discrimination, whether social or cultural, whether based on sex, race, color, social condition, language or religion, is to be overcome and eradicated as contrary to God's interest."[42]

Ironically, just as the Catholic hierarchy was coming around to an enlightened, even prophetic, position on the race question, Vatican II actually undermined the chance for a liberal party line on the issue. In a great transformation of Catholicism, Vatican II located the heart of the church in the "people of God," not in the hierarchy, and it encouraged the laity to think for itself (that is, private judgment). White American Catholics, however, seeking to preserve their hard-won gains, were becoming increasingly conservative and antiblack. They became less and less distinguishable from other whites in the economically strapped, strife-ridden cities. Thus in the post–World War II era, sociology and human nature, more than religion, determined the behavior of the Catholic masses toward African Americans.[43]

41. Joseph H. Fichter, S.J., *America's Forgotten Priests: What Are They Saying?* (New York, 1968), 234–35.

42. Raymond A. Tucker, bishop of New Ulm, Minn., "Justice in the Church: The Church as Example," in *One Hundred Years of Catholic Social Thought*, ed. Coleman, 93.

43. Adrian Hastings, "The Key Texts," in *Modern Catholicism*, ed. Hastings, 58–62; Charles E. Curran, "Catholic Social Teaching and Human Morality," in *One Hundred Years of Catholic Social Thought*, ed. Coleman, 73; Edward Duff, S.J., "The Church and American Public Life," in *Contemporary Catholicism*, ed. Gleason, 111–12. For an article that explores the combined effect of Vatican II and the black revolution, see John T. McGreevy, "Racial Justice and the People of God: The Second Vatican Council, the Civil Rights Movement, and American Catholics," *Religion and American Culture: A Journal of Interpretation*, 4 (Summer, 1994), 221–54. Several concluded that the Second Vatican Council either sold out to secularism or conceded that Martin Luther was right after all; see, for example, McEoin, *Memoirs and Memories*, 167, and James Hitchcock, *Catholicism and Modernity: Confrontation or Capitulation?* (New York, 1979).

Had LaFarge enjoyed the longevity of Thomas Turner (the black Catholic leader died in 1978 at the age of 101), one wonders how the Jesuit would have reacted to the revolutionary period after 1963. We can be positive that he would have been gratified by the end of formal segregation and of racial exclusion in Catholic institutions, and he would have been delighted by the rising tide of color among nuns, priests, and bishops. To be sure, he would have liked the seventh National Black Catholic Congress' emphasis on strengthening the black family. He almost certainly would have applauded the new social activism of the American hierarchy, and, no doubt, he would have embraced the age's new emphasis on ecumenism and pluralism.[44]

But the "shattered fixity" of Catholicism and the "currents of anger, frustration, and bitterness" that ensued from Vatican II and the simultaneous transfer of the civil rights movement northward in the late 1960s would have set off sirens in LaFarge's head. In reaction to the 1966 demonstrations led by Martin Luther King, Jr., in Chicago, crowds of hostile white Catholics screamed "nigger" and made special targets of marching nuns and priests ("You're not a real priest"). If priests led resistance to integrated housing during World War II and in Cicero in 1951, after the Selma march liberalized nuns and priests demonstrated boldly in favor of open-housing laws. Laypersons, however, now accorded recognition as the "people of God," showed no more respect for church authority on civil rights than they would on birth control. Indeed, when a nun was felled by a rock in a July, 1966, civil rights demonstration in Chicago, Catholics in the crowd cheered loudly. It is hard even to imagine the Jesuit's anguish at such assaults on church authority.[45]

An equally intriguing speculation is how LaFarge would have reacted to the decline of the "re-formed" Jesuit order after Vatican II. Although the Jesuit general Jean-Baptiste Janssens resisted the *aggiornamento* of Pope John XXIII, one of the least "Jesuited" popes in many decades, the Second Vatican Council forced basic changes on the most powerful Catholic order. After 1965 the values of the order shifted

44. On the hierarchy, see Dolan, *American Catholic Experience,* 445–49, 452–53.
45. John Tracy Ellis, "American Catholicism, 1953–1979: A Notable Change," 401, 411, and Philip Gleason, "Catholicism and Cultural Change in the 1960s," 392, both in *Modern American Catholicism, 1900–1965,* ed. Kantowicz; Novak, *Confessions of a Catholic,* 113; McGreevy, "Racial Justice and the People of God," 235.

away from the objective toward the subjective, from the absolute toward the relative, from the sacral toward the secular, and from the institutional toward the individual. The drastically changed meanings of authority and obedience within the order, which led to a loss of "role clarity" and "religious virtuosity," would have greatly disturbed LaFarge.[46]

And how would LaFarge have reacted to the decline in the number of American Jesuits from a peak of more than 8,000 in 1965 to fewer than 5,000 in 1990? How would LaFarge have received the news that between 1966 and 1980 approximately 10,000 priests left the church and 241 seminaries closed? No doubt, the Jesuit would have been highly uncomfortable in a time when almost 80 percent of Catholics flouted the church's ban on birth control, when lukewarm "cultural Catholics" displaced "creedal Catholics," when the clergy and laity routinely raked bishops over the coals, and when underground, law-breaking priests such as the Jesuit Daniel Berrigan landed in jail and became heroes. The Jesuit Robert Graham, one of the young LaFargians of the 1940s, wondered how LaFarge would have reacted as black power swept aside his old friends at the NAACP and the Urban League. He might have wondered as well how his mentor would have responded to "black theology" and the attempt of the black militant James Forman to extract $500 million in reparations from the white churches (or, in Forman's words, "15 dollars per nigger").[47]

And what would LaFarge have made of the ultramilitant mood of the first group of black American Jesuits appearing in the 1960s? Some of these black priests predicted that the Society of Jesus was more apt to die than to change in any meaningful way. Not only did this breed of "new Jesuits" excoriate racism as endemic among the sons of Igna-

46. Aveling, *The Jesuits*, 362; Becker, *Re-Formed Jesuits*, 354–55, *passim;* Patricia Wittberg, S.C., *The Rise and Decline of Catholic Religious Orders: A Social Movement Perspective* (Albany, N.Y., 1994), 209, 211, 233, 236, 239, 243–44, 251; McDonough, *Men Astutely Trained*, 9.

47. "Many Catholics in Poll Split with Church," St. Louis *Post-Dispatch*, June 15, 1992; Deedy, *American Catholicism*, 18–21, 23, 158, 165, 213–24; Wills, *Confessions of a Conservative*, 67; Reimer, *New Jesuits*, 37–38; Novak, *Confessions of a Catholic*, 139; Dolan, *American Catholic Experience*, 437; McDonough, *Men Astutely Trained*, 5; Robert A. Graham, S.J., to Edward Stanton, S.J., October 13, 1981, in box 1, folder 1, Stanton Papers; Forman, quoted in Peter Goldman, *Report from Black America* (New York, 1971), 93–94.

tius, but they lambasted integration and equal opportunity as white devices designed to keep blacks down. When the black Jesuit Theodore Cunningham was asked in 1971 what he would do if he had to choose between the Jesuits and his race, he (reminiscent of Constance Daniel) did not hesitate to cast his lot with his race.[48]

The truth is that LaFarge thrived best in an earlier time when pluralism was absent and paternalism was rife in the American Catholic church. He operated most effectively when Catholics were a persecuted minority (making Catholic identity less problematical), when church authority asserted that Catholicism alone was the repository of Christian truth, and when the Catholic hierarchy wielded all the power and a deferential laity revered priests. He best represented the church when liberal Catholics such as himself still seriously anticipated the day when Catholics would become the American majority.

In his long career LaFarge stood on that unique ground inhabited by the Catholic liberal, an enigmatic position that fell somewhere between secular, pragmatic liberalism and Burkean conservatism.[49] Forever preaching the "Catholic ethic," the Jesuit had a limited understanding of the role of constructive radicalism in the process of historical change. As Garry Wills has eloquently argued, we depend on the radical impatience of Christians like Dorothy Day and Martin Luther King, Jr. We need the justice-driven "fanatics" in the streets, secular and religious, to nudge apathetic society along moral paths. For, in Wills's words, "Change is initiated by the principled few, not the compromising many; by the 'crazies' in the streets, not by politicians on the hustings."[50]

Society often finds the harbingers of revolutionary change frightening to behold, but by contrast they make liberal alternatives look downright appealing. Although prudent people like LaFarge might save us from the "crazies," it is the maladjusted rebels who often make society worth saving.[51] "Religion must always be, in some measure," Da-

48. Reimer, *New Jesuits*, 42, 50–51, 54, 239, 249, 250, 267. Wills, *Confessions of a Conservative*, 77, reported that Cunningham felt resentment because his entry into the Society of Jesus was delayed because of his color.

49. See Allitt, *Catholic Intellectuals and Conservative Politics*, 38, and generally Chap. 3.

50. Wills, *Confessions of a Conservative*, 162, 169.

51. *Ibid.*, 157, 162–63, 167–69. For an engaging study of the "positive radical flank

vid O'Brien has written, "an underground affair." The modern priest has to be on the "cutting edge of sacred and secular" change. He has to be prepared for a "permanent crisis, feeling always 'ambiguity and uncertainty.' "[52] As one who religiously avoided controversy, confrontation, and uncertainty and who followed instead the path of faith, obedience, and prudence, LaFarge was not well suited for the role prescribed by O'Brien. Still, for roughly three decades LaFarge was the primary spokesman for the American Catholic church on black-white relations. This fact alone speaks volumes about the church's past record in facing up to the American dilemma.

---

effect" on liberal change, see Herbert H. Haines, *Black Radicals and the Civil Rights Mainstream, 1954–1970* (Knoxville, Tenn., 1988), 1–11.

52. David O'Brien, "The American Priest and Social Action," in *Catholic Priest*, ed. John Ellis, 465.

Postscript
The Strange Career of Black Catholicism

*A*ggiornamento coincided with phase one of the civil rights movement, which culminated in the passage of the Civil Rights Act of 1964 and the Voting Rights Act of 1965. But in 1965, in the wake of the Watts riot, the movement entered phase two. Then the black movement, venturing beyond mere legal equality, set its sights on equality of condition. This change of goals was accompanied by the cry of black power and a new emphasis on black pride. The seductive mood of the movement also energized many black Catholics. These newly active black Catholics, however, seldom considered the Catholic interracial councils an adequate vehicle for change.[1] Instead they rejuvenated the 1920s vision of Thomas Turner and the FCC. In early 1968 more than fifty black priests formed the Black Catholic Clergy Caucus in Detroit, a city that had just suffered the worst race riot of the twentieth century. The black caucus proclaimed that the Catholic church was "primarily a white racist institution" and demanded a "share in the power of the church." The caucus issued a series of demands, including the appointment of an episcopal vicar for all African American Cath-

1. Sitkoff, *Struggle for Black Equality,* 213–15; Cyprian Rowe, F.M.S., "Nearly a Century in the Making," *National Office of Black Catholics,* 10 (April–July, 1980), clipping in the Josephite Archives, Baltimore.

olics, more strenuous efforts to increase the number of black priests, the incorporation of black culture and styles into the liturgies of black churches, the inclusion of black history in Catholic education and training, and provisions for more black deacons.[2]

The Black Clergy Caucus spawned a host of similar organizations, such as the National Black Sisters' Conference, the National Black Catholic Lay Caucus, and the National Black Catholic Seminarians' Caucus. In 1970 an umbrella agency called the National Office of Black Catholics was founded.[3] Although the caucuses spoke the language of black power and black consciousness and immersed themselves in African trappings, they, like Turner's earlier black federation, disavowed any intent toward separatism. The rise of black Catholic consciousness nonetheless brought an outpouring of anger and bitterness that bewildered white Catholics. The black Catholic community eventually produced counterparts to James Baldwin, Stokely Carmichael, and Malcolm X. The black Harlem priest Lawrence Lucas lent a provocative voice to alienated black Catholics in his 1970 book *Black Priest / White Church.* The Protestant minister James H. Cone also stirred black Catholic militants in 1969 with his manifesto *Theology and Black Power.*[4]

With the decline of segregation in Catholic institutions, the number of black Catholics rose markedly. In 1940 there were fewer than 300,000 black Catholics in the United States, but in 1970 the figure reached nearly 1,000,000, or an increase of 208 percent. From 1975 to 1984 the number of black Catholics increased by 41 percent while the general black population rose only a little over 17 percent. In 1985 black Catholics numbered 1,200,000, and the total reached about 2,000,000 by 1990. The percentage of black Catholics in the minority population rose from about 2 percent at the time of the founding of the CICNY to 5 percent in 1992.[5]

2. Quoted in Joseph M. Davis, "The Development of the National Office of Black Catholics," *U.S. Catholic Historian,* 7 (Spring–Summer, 1988), 269. See also Ochs, *Desegregating the Altar,* 447.

3. Ochs, *Desegregating the Altar,* 447–48; Jay P. Dolan, "Religion and Social Change in the American Catholic Community," in *Altered Landscapes,* ed. Lotz, 48.

4. Lawrence Lucas, *Black Priest / White Church: Catholics and Racism* (New York, 1970). On Cone's book, see Albert J. Raboteau, "The Black Church: Continuity Within Change," in *Altered Landscapes,* ed. Lotz, 88–89.

5. Raboteau, "Black Church," 79, and Dolan, "Religion and Social Change," 48,

Over the past quarter-century, black pressure on the Catholic church has paid impressive dividends. The increase in the number of black priests and the installation of black bishops illustrates this point. The number of black priests increased from 120 in 1961 to 165 in 1966. From there the total jumped to 300 in 1985 and climbed to around 350 by 1992.[6] In 1965 Harold R. Perry, a Divine Word priest, was appointed auxiliary bishop of New Orleans, the first black bishop selected in this century. By 1985 ten black bishops had been installed, but only one, Joseph L. Howze of Biloxi, Mississippi, headed a diocese. In 1988 in Atlanta, Eugene Marino, a Josephite, became the first black archbishop in the United States. The number of black bishops then stood at thirteen.[7] On his trip to the United States in 1987, Pope John Paul II conspicuously met with African American bishops in New Orleans.[8]

Since the establishment of the National Office of Black Catholics in 1970, the American hierarchy has issued three pastoral letters on racism. The 1979 letter, "Brothers and Sisters to Us," admitted the "subtly racist" structures in the church and society that oppressed blacks, and it vowed to eliminate discrimination and help make it possible for blacks to contribute their singular talents to Catholicism. In 1987 the United States Catholic Conference also established a Secretariat for Black Catholics as part of the bishops' administrative arm. The hierarchy also gave support to the sixth National Black Catholic Congress,

both in *Altered Landscapes,* ed. Lotz; John Harfmann, S.S.J., *1984 Statistical Profile of Black Catholics* (Washington, D.C., 1985), iii. Statistics on black Catholics are notoriously slippery and vary from source to source. The "official sources" of the church, surprisingly enough, seem to be understated when compared with the Gallup Poll and other sources. Much depends upon the definition of a Catholic: is it someone who is simply baptized, someone who attends Mass frequently or occasionally, or something other?

6. Wakin and Scheuer, *De-Romanization of the American Church,* 233–35; Dolan, "Religion and Social Change," in *Altered Landscapes,* ed. Lotz, 48; Ochs, *Desegregating the Altar,* 451.

7. Dolan, "Religion and Social Change," in *Altered Landscapes,* ed. Lotz, 48; Ochs, *Desegregating the Altar,* 451–52. In 1990, Marino resigned from his post because of alleged sexual misconduct. When Bishop Perry died in 1991, the number of black bishops fell to eleven. In 1992, however, the black auxiliary bishop James P. Lyke, O.F.M., was appointed archbishop of Atlanta.

8. In 1989, the Vatican released the document "The Church and Racism: Toward a More Fraternal Society." See Thomas H. Stahel, "The Case of Father Stallings: Bishop Emerson J. Moore," *Am,* 162 (March 3, 1990), 187–88, and Ochs, *Desegregating the Altar,* 451–52.

which met on the campus of Catholic University in Washington, D.C., in 1987 and attracted 1,500 delegates and more than fifty bishops. It was the first black national congress since Daniel Rudd and associates last met in 1894. Rudd quickly became a celebrated name among those who participated in the new black organizations. Even more prominent was the name of Thomas Turner, who lived long enough to hear his praises profusely sung. Catholic University awarded Turner an honorary degree in 1976, when he was ninety-nine. Black Catholic organizations heaped awards and honors upon the aged blind man. The black secretariat of the Washington, D.C., archdiocese named its highest achievement award after him, and the new natural science building at Hampton University became the Turner Building. Turner had long outlived his critics.[9]

Is this to say that all doubts have at last been removed as to whether a black Catholic can participate fully, and in a fulfilling way, in the predominantly white American Catholic church? Hardly. In 1990, at age forty-two, the Reverend George Stallings, Jr., formed the African American Catholic Congregation and declared his independence from the Catholic church. For this act he was excommunicated. The flamboyant minister, a prize product of the North American College in Rome and the former president of the Black Catholic Clergy Caucus, accused the church of Eurocentrism and a failure to fulfill the spiritual and cultural needs of black Catholics. Stallings regularly drew 2,000 to his services at the Imani Temple (*imani* means faith in Swahili), and millions saw the magnetic priest on *60 Minutes, Donahue,* and similar television shows. Those who attended masses at the Imani Temple, situated on the outskirts of the District of Columbia, feasted on jazz, gospel choirs, and readings from non-Catholic black writers. The black priest purports to combine "Baptist practices with the beauty and tradition of the Catholic faith." He has proclaimed Martin Luther King, Jr., a saint. In 1991 Stallings also ordained a former Catholic nun, Rose

9. Paul Elie, "Hangin' with the Romeboys," *New Republic,* May 11, 1992, p. 23; Cyprian Davis, "Brothers and Sisters to Us: The Never-Ending Story," *Am,* 162 (March 31, 1990), 320–21; Edward K. Braxton, S.T.D., "Authentically Black, Truly Catholic," *Commonweal,* 112 (February 8, 1985), 73; Marilyn W. Nickels, "A Tribute to Thomas Turner," *Impact,* 6 (April/May, 1976), 1–2, "Pioneer Honored in His 100th Year," *Impact,* 6 (April/May, 1976), 1, 4, "Black Secretariat Honors Mitchell, O'Boyle, Others," Washington *Star,* November 13, 1976, and Jean R. Hailey, "T. W. Turner, 101, Dies; Rights Activist, Educator," Washington *Post,* April 23, 1978, all clippings in Turner Papers.

Marie Vernell, into the priesthood of his church. The separatist movement then claimed some 3,800 members and had six temples around the country. Although it is too early to say with any certainty, it appears the movement may be declining.[10]

Stallings, however, struck a responsive chord in the black Catholic community. He tapped the resentments and frustrations that have plagued generations of black Catholics. Virtually all black leaders have condemned the black minister's break with the church, but most have been reluctant to criticize Stallings himself, even though some clearly think he is an ambitious grandstander. Emerson J. Moore, a black auxiliary bishop in the New York archdiocese, observes that blacks feel neither anger nor a sense of betrayal in regard to Stallings; only whites have responded that way, Moore claims.[11] The black Catholic intelligentsia in fact have broadcast their contention that Stallings has raised significant issues, and they stress the same flaws in the church that Stallings has articulated so dramatically. First, blacks believe, in varying degrees, that racism still seriously compromises the Catholic church. A 1986 study revealed that 89 percent of black Catholics expressed the opinion that racism existed at all levels of the church. Gone are the overtly scandalous types of racism that once angered and humiliated blacks, but a more elusive and insidious type of racism, blacks maintain, sullies the church today. From bishops to lay leaders, a chorus of black Catholics accuses the church of "unconscious racism" or the "racism of indifference." Albert J. Raboteau, the black Catholic chairman of Princeton's Department of Religion, stresses the "more subtle institutional forms" of racism in the church as the main obstacle to blacks.[12]

10. Laura Randolph, "What's Behind the Black Rebellion in the Catholic Church?," *Ebony,* 45 (November, 1989), 160–64; David Pitts, "Is a Separate Black Church the Answer to Black Prayers?," *Black Enterprise,* 20 (October, *1989), 28;* Cyprian Davis, "Brothers and Sisters to Us," 320; Bill Dedman, "Black Priest Severs Ties, Forms Church," St. Louis *Post-Dispatch,* February 3, 1990; "Black Catholics vs. the Church," *Time,* July 10, 1989, p. 57.

11. Stahel, "The Case of Father Stallings," 187–88. See also Stahel's interviews of two black bishops: "Carl A. Fisher, S.S.J., Auxiliary Bishop of Los Angeles," 418, and "Joseph A. Francis, S.V.D., Auxiliary Bishop of Newark," 403–404, both in *Am,* 164 (April 13, 1991).

12. Pamela Schaeffer, "Black Catholics Report Racism," St. Louis *Post-Dispatch,* November 17, 1986; Cyprian Davis, "Brothers and Sisters to Us," 320; John Deedy, *The*

These black critics protest, for instance, that 350 black priests (out of a total of 57,000) are not enough. There are so few black priests that 1,040 of the black parishes in the United States are pastored by white priests, and there is but one black priest for each 5,000 black Catholics. As evidence of racism, others point to the closing of black churches and schools in the inner cities. Beverly Carroll, the director of the Secretariat for Black Catholics, speaks accusingly of a "glass ceiling" in explaining the dearth of blacks in the front offices of the archdioceses. Father Cyprian Davis charges that the "lost harvest" of blacks is being lost once again because not nearly enough is being done to evangelize African Americans.[13]

Black critics do not deny that the church has made much progress, but they often interpret black gains differently from the way whites do. Some tend to see the rapid increase of black bishops as transparent tokenism. The militant Father Lucas of Harlem scorns American black bishops as "silent and useless." Father Raymond Kemp, a white priest who is pastor of a mostly black church in Washington, D.C., depicts the black prelates as "symbols—spooks who sit by the door." Many black Catholics demand less talk and more action by the church. More precisely, they demand "affirmative action." Blacks have little patience with trickle-down equity, which, they smirk, works no better than trickle-down economics. The buzzword of the times is "empowerment." Black leaders generally dismiss talk of integration and color-blindness as cynical ploys that deter real power sharing and stifle the spiritual vitality of blacks. Professor Raboteau discounts any kind of "spurious colorless universalism, which usually means the hegemony of the ethnic group in power at the time." Alston Fitts, III, the director of the Edmundite missions in Alabama, was mystified when a priest and a nun from the North told him that Selma's well-integrated parish was contaminating the "native spirituality" of the black parishioners.[14]

Catholic Fact Book (Chicago, 1986), 237; "The Black Catholics," *Newsweek*, January 27, 1969 p. 55; Raboteau, "Preaching the Word," 632.

13. Elie, "Hangin' with the Romeboys," 22; Ochs, *Desegregating the Altar*, 452; "30 Catholic Schools in Detroit to be Closed," St. Louis *Post-Dispatch*, January 10, 1989; "Black Catholics vs. the Church," 57; Preston N. Williams, "A More Perfect Union: The Silence of the Church," *Am*, 162 (May 31, 1990), 315–18; Thomas H. Stahel, "Beverly Carroll," *Am*, 166 (April 25, 1992), 343; Cyprian Davis, "Brothers and Sisters to Us," 320–21, 334.

14. Lucas and Kemp, quoted in Elie, "Hangin' with the Romeboys," 22; Stahel,

Black Catholics seem to keep a "prophetic distance" from the idea of assimilation. As the documents emanating from the National Office of Black Catholics and the black bishops indicate, the overarching goal is rather to fashion a church on the margins where African Americans can be "authentically black and truly Catholic." They seek "self determination" and an opportunity to express the unique "black gifts" that Du Bois championed in 1903 in his classic *The Souls of Black Folk:* the gifts of "song," "story," and "Spirit." Many phrase the challenge of the church in this manner: Ask not what the church can do for blacks; ask what blacks can do for the church. They envision a colorized Catholicism that invites a talented African American such as the late Sister Thea Bowman, a mesmerizing teacher, poet, and singer, to enthrall parishioners with her theatricality. Sister Bowman, it is reported, once "sashayed her way into a Presbyterian church in North Jackson [Mississippi] and gave a performance that had the congregation holding hands and singing 'We Shall Overcome.' "[15]

To feel at home in the Catholic church, many blacks favor, like the maverick Stallings, a separate African American rite. There are several precedents for this, the Eastern and Zaire rites, for example. In 1989 millions of Afro-Brazilians petitioned Rome for a separate rite. The 1992 seventh National Black Catholic Congress in New Orleans in fact passed a resolution calling for a feasibility study of an African American rite. Larding the liturgy with Africanisms and African American folklore and idioms has actually been going on for years in parishes such as St. Augustine's in Washington, D.C., but a separate rite could mean more than a transformation of the liturgy. It could mean a separate canonical jurisdiction that would allow blacks, for example, to appoint

"The Case of Father Stallings," 187; Thomas H. Stahel, "Norman C. Frances," *Am,* 166 (April 25, 1992), 362–63; Rhonda Reynolds, "Blacks Seek church Reform," *Black Enterprise,* 22 (November, 1991), 18; Harfmann, *1984 Statistical Profile of Black Catholics,* 9; Raboteau, "Preaching the Word," 634; Preston Williams, "A More Perfect Union," 316; Thomas H. Stahel, "Albert J. Raboteau," *Am,* 166 (April 25, 1992), 340; Alston Fitts, III, "Patching up the Peace in Alabama: Racial Conflicts Still Smolder," *Commonweal,* 117 (September 14, 1990), 515.

15. Elie, "Hangin' with the Romeboys," 26; Edward K. Braxton, S.T.D., "The National Black Catholic Congress of 1987," *Josephite Harvest,* 89 (Summer, 1987), 8–17; Preston Williams, "A More Perfect Union," 316–17; Thomas H. Stahel, "Of Many Things," front page, "James P. Lyke, O.F.M., Apostolic Administrator, *sede vacante,* Atlanta," 397, and "Jamie T. Phelps, O.P.," 367–68, all in *Am,* 166 (April 25, 1992); Mary Queen Donnelly, "Sister Thea Bowman (1937–1990)," *Am,* 162 (April 28, 1990), 421.

their own hierarchy. This is not a new idea. The first suggestion of a separate jurisdiction for black Americans was vehemently rejected by the American bishops at the Second Plenary Council of Baltimore in 1866. It might be well into the next century before an African American rite could be put in place, but it is a distinct possibility.[16]

Meanwhile, ferment permeates the church—ferment that discloses a certain ambivalence among black Catholics. A sizable number of black Catholics today seriously ponder the alternatives of integration, separation, or some yet undetermined form of liberation. Most, however, debate the narrower question of whether things are getting better or worse. A significant number of respected black Catholics believe that race relations in the church and the nation are worsening, but most think the situation is improving, if all too slowly. Some offer the paradoxical view that things are getting both better and worse. The seventh National Black Catholic Congress that met in New Orleans from July 9 to 12, 1992, suggests this ambivalence. That 2,700 delegates and ninety bishops participated in the congress denoted progress. Despite an inspirational mass filled with the richness of African American culture, the congress did not long focus on "black gifts" or what blacks could do for the church; rather, the gathering concentrated on the more somber issue of the endangered black family. After hearing hours of grim statistics on the subject, the congress approved eight public policy statements and eleven pastoral announcements designed to strengthen the African American family. The public policy statements sounded as if they had been drafted by a committee made up of representatives from the NAACP, the Urban League, the Southern Christian Leadership Conference, and the Democratic party. The congress called for universal health care, welfare reform, increased job opportunities and basic skills training programs, improved Medicaid, a multicultural curriculum for students from kindergarten through high school, and minority scholarships in higher education.[17]

Blacks are exceptional among the ethnic Catholics who have remained faithful to the Democratic party. Many analysts have also mar-

16. Cyprian Davis, "Brothers and Sisters to Us," 320–21; Kathryn Rogers, "Black Catholics Seek Culturally Meaningful Liturgy," St. Louis *Post-Dispatch*, July 25, 1992.

17. Elie, "Hangin' with the Romeboys," 18; Stahel, "Beverly Carroll," 334; Al Levine, "Troubles They've Seen," *Commonweal*, 116 (October 20, 1989), 550–51; Julie Asher, "Congress Delegates Approve Pastoral Statements," (Cincinnati) *Catholic Telegram*, July 17, 1992, clipping courtesy of Dan Kane.

veled at the loyalty of black Catholics to the American church in view of the suffering and insult inflicted on them by the institution. They are not unaware that untold thousands of blacks have left the church since the Civil War because of racism and neglect. For instance, of the seven surviving Daniel children who were raised as Catholics by Victor and Constance Daniel at the Cardinal Gibbons Institute, only two remained in the church. On the whole, however, black Catholics have been extremely loyal to Catholicism. Of the fidelity of Catholics like Daniel Rudd, Victor Daniel, and Thomas Turner, one can only say, "The manner was extraordinary." As a delegate to the National Black Catholic Congress of 1987 expressed it, "I'm Catholic born and bred, and when I die, I'll be Black Catholic dead."[18] Some stress that blacks hold to the church because they admire its catholicity, that it has incorporated millions of people of color around the globe. To be driven from the church by racism, they argue, would be to surrender to an un-Catholic aspect of the church, a view that LaFarge always preached.[19]

Unfortunately, black Catholics have been little studied by social scientists. The few empirical studies that have been done suggest that black Catholics today are younger, better educated, and more middle class than their Protestant counterparts. The sociologists Larry L. Hunt and Janet J. Hunt hypothesize that the religion of black Catholics may be consequential for "status maintenance and moderate mobility." Although studies show that the political views of black Catholics are almost identical to those of non-Catholic blacks (and far removed from the views of white Catholics), black Romanists tend to be more mainstream and conservative than other blacks. Evidence also suggests that racial identity may be less salient for black Catholics than for Protestants and that Catholics may have more integrated experiences. Whether blacks embrace Catholicism because of class and status, schools, ritual, or its universalism, they do not seem to be candidates for schism in the near future.[20]

18. Quotation in Edward K. Braxton, "The National Black Catholic Congress," *Am,* 158 (July 18–25, 1987), 30. Information on the Daniel family is courtesy of Louise Daniel Hutchinson. On the loyalty of African American Catholics, see also Blatnica, *"At the Altar of God,"* 199–203.

19. Stahel, "Albert J. Raboteau," 338; Stahel, "Jamie T. Phelps," 367; Elie, "Hangin' with the Romeboys," 20.

20. Larry L. Hunt and Janet J. Hunt, "A Religious Factor in Secular Achievement

Nevertheless, the Stallings affair signals a future of aggressive protest by the black Catholic community, accompanied most likely by a
continuation of severely strained race relations within the American
church, not unlike the strain within American society in general. The
oncoming multiculturalists and Afrocentrists have influenced black
theologians, and many, Catholic and non-Catholic alike, advocate the
"need to *trouble the waters*" of the Eurocentric church with new theological and cultural perspectives.[21] The minority problem, of course,
is not confined to African Americans. Given the differing birth rates of
ethnic groups and classes and the continuing pace of immigration by
Hispanics, Asians, and others, the minority problem will endure and
possibly worsen. Whatever the case, the church faces new and unpre-
dictable challenges. Not far into the twenty-first century, a majority of
the Catholic population in America will be nonwhite.[22] When that time
comes, one wonders if white Catholics will be as faithful to the church
as the Jim-Crowed black minority was in the past.

---

among Blacks: The Case for Catholicism," *Social Forces,* 53 (June, 1975), 597–605, quotation on p. 595. See also Feigelman, Gorman, and Varacalli, "The Social Characteristics
of Black Catholics," 133–43; Hart M. Nelsen and L. Dickson, "Attitudes of Black Catholics and Protestants: Evidence for Religious Identity," *Sociological Analysis,* 33 (Fall,
1972), 152–65; and Collins, "Black Conversion to Catholicism," 208–18. Collins rejected
the class analysis of E. Franklin Frazier and emphasized theology, world view, and ritual
as reasons for conversion. Black converts in Durham, N.C., Collins reported, wanted a
religion that was less emotional and communal, with a more trustworthy and dignified
clergy.

   21. Pitts, "Is a Separate Black Church the Answer to Black Prayers?," 28; Cain
Hope Felder, *Troubling Biblical Waters: Race, Class, and Family* (Maryknoll, N.Y., 1989),
xi–xiv, xvii–xviii, 176–77, *passim.* Felder stresses the mission ideology of the "Black
Church," holding that the black church, because of the suffering of its people, is uniquely
prophetic and suited to redeem humankind. For a historical view of this idea, see S. P.
Fullinwider, *The Mind and Mood of Black America* (Homewood, Ill., 1969).

   22. M. Reginald Gerdes, O.S.P., "To Educate and Evangelize: Black Catholic
Schools of the Oblate Sisters of Providence (1828–1880)," *U.S. Catholic Historian,* 7
(Spring–Summer, 1988), 1984. On Hispanic Catholics, see Dolan and Hinojosa, eds.,
Mexican Americans and the Catholic Church, 1900–1965, and Dolan and Vidal, eds.,
Puerto Rican and Cuban Catholics.

Selected Bibliography

It would be impractical to try to construct a bibliography
that encompasses all the sources that have shaped this study,
particularly from the rich field of black-white relations in which I have
worked for thirty years. Thus, no attempt has been made to give a
complete listing of all the works that influenced this book. Instead, this
bibliography stresses the primary sources on John LaFarge and the
secondary material that helped me most in gaining some perspective on
American Catholicism, especially as it relates to social thought and social action and, more specifically, the race problem. Only a small portion of the vast literature that pertains to black-white relations (but does
not touch on American Catholicism) is included. For those who are
interested, the footnotes provide a more complete accounting of the
sources used in this study.

With respect to primary material, the John LaFarge Papers at
Georgetown University constituted the main source for this book. The
two accessions of his papers, fifty-one and eighteen large boxes respectively, are extensive and well cataloged. During my research in the late
1980s, the library was still receiving material for the second accession,
which was opened to researchers in 1986. Unfortunately, the highly
useful Thomas W. Turner Papers were unprocessed when I used them.
The collection of CICNY Papers at Catholic University (thirty-seven
linear feet) was in a semiraw state. Moreover, the archivist allowed me
only partial access to these papers. Similarly, I was allowed only limited
use of the John LaFarge Papers contained in a larger collection of family

papers that are housed at the New York Historical Society. Immensely helpful were the Josephite Archives in Baltimore. Peter E. Hogan, S.S.J., the chief archivist for the Josephites, has collected material on virtually every aspect of the church and black-white relations, including extensive newspaper clippings. The papers of the CICC gave me crucial insight into that organization's relation to the CICNY. A summer spent in the Theodore Hesburgh Library at the University of Notre Dame gave me an opportunity to read samples of various Catholic journals and newspapers. Most important, the university had a full run of the *Chronicle / Interracial Review*.

MANUSCRIPT COLLECTIONS

Catholic Interracial Council of Chicago Papers. Chicago Historical Society, Chicago.

Catholic Interracial Council of New York Papers. Catholic University of America, Washington, D.C.

Cantwell, Msgr. Daniel. Papers. Chicago Historical Society, Chicago.

Gillard, John T., S.S.J. Papers. Josephite Archives, Baltimore.

Heithaus, Claude H., S.J. Papers. Jesuit Missouri Province Archives, St. Louis.

LaFarge, John, S.J. Papers. New York Historical Society, New York.

LaFarge, John, S.J. Papers. Georgetown University Library, Washington, D.C.

Markoe, William M., S.J. Papers. Marquette University Library, Milwaukee, Wisc.

Maryland Ridge Papers. Josephite Archives, Baltimore.

Stanton, Edward S., S.J. Papers. Boston College, Boston.

Turner, Thomas W. Papers. Moorland-Spingarn Research Center, Howard University, Washington, D.C.

BOOKS, ARTICLES, AND PAMPHLETS

Abell, Aaron I. *American Catholicism and Social Action: A Search for Social Justice*. Notre Dame, Ind., 1963.

Adams, Henry. *The Education of Henry Adams: An Autobiography*. Boston, 1918.

Adams, James L. *The Growing Church Lobby in Washington*. Grand Rapids, Mich., 1970.

Ahlstrom, Sidney E. *A Religious History of the American People*. New Haven, 1972.

Ahmann, Mathew, ed. *Race: Challenge to Religion*. Chicago, 1963.

Allitt, Patrick. *Catholic Intellectuals and Conservative Politics in America, 1950–1985*. Ithaca, N.Y., 1993.

Allport, Gordon W. *The Nature of Prejudice.* Cambridge, Mass., 1954.

———. Review of *No Postponement,* by John LaFarge. *Thought,* 26 (Autumn, 1950), 471–72.

Alston, Jon P., Letitia T. Alston, and Emory Warrick. "Black Catholics: Social and Cultural Characteristics." *Journal of Black Studies,* 2 (December, 1971), 244–55.

Anbinder, Tyler. *Nativism and Slavery: The Northern Know Nothings and the Politics of the 1850s.* New York, 1992.

Appleby, Scott R. *"Church and Age Unite!": The Modernist Impulse in American Catholicism.* Notre Dame, Ind., 1992.

Aveling, J. C. H. *The Jesuits.* New York, 1981.

Avella, Steven M. *This Confident Church: Catholic Leadership and Life in Chicago, 1940–1965.* Notre Dame, Ind., 1992.

Bartley, Numan V. *The Rise of Massive Resistance: Race and Politics in the South During the 1950's.* Baton Rouge, 1969.

Barzun, Jacques. "Not to Count the Cost." *New York Times Book Review,* February 14, 1954, p. 1.

Bauman, John F. *Public Housing, Race and Renewal: Urban Planning in Philadelphia, 1920–1974.* Philadelphia, 1987.

Becker, Joseph M., S.J. *The Re-Formed Jesuits: A History of Changes in Jesuit Formation During the Decade 1965–1975.* San Francisco, 1992.

Beitzel, Edwin Warfield. *The Jesuit Missions of St. Mary's County, Maryland.* 2nd ed. Abell, Md., 1976.

Bennett, David H. *The Party of Fear: From Nativist Movements to the New Right in American History.* Chapel Hill, N.C., 1988.

Betten, Neil. *Catholic Activism and the Industrial Worker.* Gainesville, Fla., 1976.

"Black Catholics vs. the Church." *Time,* July 10, 1989, p. 57.

Blansart, Paul. *American Freedom and Catholic Power.* Boston, 1950.

Blantz, Thomas E., C.S.C. *A Priest in Public Service: Francis J. Haas and the New Deal.* Notre Dame, Ind., 1982.

Blatnica, Dorothy Ann, V.S.C. *"At the Altar of God": African American Catholics in Cleveland, 1922–1961.* New York, 1995.

Bodnar, John, Roger Simon, and Michael P. Weber. *Lives of Their Own: Blacks, Italians and Poles in Pittsburgh, 1900–1960.* Urbana, Ill., 1982.

Bokenkotter, Thomas. *A Concise History of the Catholic Church.* Garden City, N.Y., 1977.

Boles, John B., ed. *Masters and Slaves in the House of the Lord: Race and Religion in the American South, 1740–1870.* Lexington, Ky., 1988.

Bonder, Saul. *Social Justice and Church Authority: The Public Life of Robert E. Lucey.* Philadelphia, 1982.

Branch, Taylor. *Parting the Waters: America in the King Years, 1954–1963.* New York, 1988.

Braxton, Edward K., S.T.D. "Authentically Black, Truly Catholic." *Commonweal,* 112 (February 8, 1985), 73–77.

Bredeck, Martin J. *Imperfect Apostles: The Commonweal and the American Catholic Laity, 1924–1976.* New York, 1988.

Broderick, Francis L. *Right Reverend New Dealer: John A. Ryan.* New York, 1963.

Brooks, Maxwell. *The Negro Press Re-Examined.* Boston, 1959.

Brugger, Robert J. *Maryland: A Middle Temperament, 1634–1980.* Baltimore, 1988.

Buetow, Harold A. *Of Singular Benefit: The Story of Catholic Education in the United States.* New York, 1970.

Burk, Robert F. *The Eisenhower Administration and Black Civil Rights.* Knoxville, Tenn., 1984.

Burkett, Randall K., and Richard Newman. *Black Apostles: Afro-American Clergy Confront the Twentieth Century.* Boston, 1978.

Callcott, George H. *Maryland and America, 1940 to 1980.* Baltimore, 1985.

Capeci, Dominic J., Jr. *Race Relations in Wartime Detroit: The Sojourner Truth Housing Controversy of 1942.* Philadelphia, 1984.

Caravaglios, Maria Genoino. *The American Catholic Church and the Negro Problem in the XVIII–XIX Centuries.* Rome, 1974.

Carson, Clayborne. *In Struggle: SNCC and the Black Awakening of the 1960s.* Cambridge, Mass., 1981.

Castelli, Jim. "Unpublished Encyclical Attacked Anti-Semitism." *National Catholic Reporter,* December 15, 1972, p. 1.

Cavert, Samuel McCrea. *The American Churches in the Ecumenical Movement, 1900–1968.* New York, 1968.

Christ, Frank L., and Gerald E. Sherry, eds. *American Catholicism and the Intellectual Ideal.* New York, 1961.

Christensen, Lawrence O. "Race Relations in St. Louis, 1865–1966." *Missouri Historical Review,* 73 (October, 1984), 123–36.

Clark, Dennis. *Cities in Crisis: The Christian Response.* New York, 1960.
———. *The Ghetto Game: Racial Conflict in the City.* New York, 1962.

Cockrane, Eric. "What Is Catholic Historiography?" *Catholic Historical Review,* 61 (April, 1975), 169–90.

Cogley, John. *Catholic America.* New York, 1973.

Cohalan, Florence D. *A Popular History of the Archdiocese of New York.* Yonkers, N.Y., 1983.

Coleman, John A., ed. *One Hundred Years of Catholic Social Thought: Celebration and Challenge.* Maryknoll, N.Y., 1991.

Collins, Daniel F. "Black Conversion to Catholicism: Its Implications for the Negro Church." *Journal for the Scientific Study of Religion,* 10 (Fall, 1971), 208–18.

Cooney, John. *The American Pope: The Life and Times of Francis Cardinal Spellman.* New York, 1984.

Cortissoz, Royal. *John LaFarge: A Memoir and a Study.* 1911; rpr. New York, 1971.

Costello, Gerald M. *Without Fear or Favor: George Higgins on the Record.* Mystic, Conn., 1984.

Crosby, Donald F. *God, Church, and Flag.* Chapel Hill, N.C., 1978.

Cross, Robert D. *The Emergence of Liberal Catholicism in America.* Cambridge, Mass., 1958.

Cubitt, Geoffrey. *The Jesuit Myth: Conspiracy Theory and Politics in Nineteenth-Century France.* New York, 1993.

Curran, Robert Emmett, S.J. *American Jesuit Spirituality: The Maryland Tradition, 1634–1900.* New York, 1988.

Curry, Lerond. *Protestant-Catholic Relations in America.* Lexington, Ky., 1972.

Czuchlewski, Paul E. "Liberal Catholicism and American Racism, 1924–1960." *Records of the American Catholic Historical Society of Philadelphia,* 85 (March–June, 1974), 144–62.

Dalfiume, Richard M. "The 'Forgotten Years' of the Negro Revolution." *Journal of American History,* 55 (June, 1968), 90–106.

Davies, Alan. *Infected Christianity: A Study of Modern Racism.* Montreal, 1988.

Davis, Cyprian, O.S.B. "Black Catholics in Nineteenth Century America." *U.S. Catholic Historian,* 5 (Winter, 1986), 1–17.

―――. *The History of Black Catholics in the United States.* New York, 1990.

―――. "The Holy See and American Black Catholics: A Forgotten Chapter in the History of the American Church." *U.S. Catholic Historian,* 7 (Spring–Summer, 1988), 157–79.

Davis, Harry, and Robert C. Goods. *Reinhold Niebuhr on Politics.* New York, 1960.

Davis, Thurston N., S.J., Donald R. Campion, S.J., and L. C. McHugh, S.J., eds. *Between Two Cities: God and Man in America.* Chicago, 1962.

Davis, Thurston N., S.J., and Joseph Small, S.J., eds. *A John LaFarge Reader.* New York, 1956.

Deedy, John. *American Catholicism—And Now Where?* New York, 1987.

de Hueck, Catherine. *Friendship House.* New York, 1947.

―――. *Fragments of My Life.* Notre Dame, Ind., 1979.

DeSantis, Vincent P. "American Catholics and McCarthyism." *Catholic Historical Review,* 51 (April, 1965), 1–30.

DeSaulniers, Lawrence B. *The Response in American Catholic Periodicals to the Crises of the Great Depression, 1930–1935.* New York, 1984.

Diggins, John P. *Mussolini and Fascism: The View from America.* Princeton, 1972.

Diggs, Margaret A. *Catholic Negro Education in the United States.* Washington, D.C., 1936.

Dohen, Dorothy. *Nationalism and American Catholicism.* New York, 1967.

Doherty, Joseph F. *Moral Problems of Interracial Marriage.* Washington, D.C., 1949.

Dolan, Jay P. *The American Catholic Experience: A History from Colonial Times to the Present.* Garden City, N.Y., 1985.

———. *Three Catholic Afro-American Congresses.* New York, 1978.

Dolan, Jay P., and Gilberto M. Hinojosa, eds. *Mexican Americans and the Catholic Church, 1900–1965.* Notre Dame, Ind., 1994.

Dolan, Jay P., and Jaime R. Vidal, eds. *Puerto Rican and Cuban Catholics in the U.S., 1900–1965.* Notre Dame, Ind., 1994.

Du Bois, W. E. B. *The Souls of Black Folk.* 1903; rpr. New York, 1961.

Dunne, George H., S.J. *Generation of Giants: The Story of the Jesuits in China in the Last Decades of the Ming Dynasty.* Notre Dame, Ind., 1962.

———. *King's Pawn: The Memoirs of George H. Dunne, S.J.* Chicago, 1990.

Edsall, Thomas, with Mary D. Edsall. *Chain Reaction: The Impact of Race, Rights, and Taxes on American Politics.* New York, 1991.

Elie, Paul. "Hangin' with the Romeboys." *New Republic,* May 11, 1992, pp. 18–26.

Ellis, John Tracy. *American Catholicism.* Chicago, 1968.

———. *American Catholics and the Intellectual Life.* Chicago, 1956.

———. *The Life of Cardinal Gibbons: Archbishop of Baltimore, 1834–1921.* Milwaukee, Wisc., 1952.

———, ed. *The Catholic Priest in the United States: Historical Investigations.* Collegeville, Minn., 1971.

———, ed. *Documents of American Catholic History.* 2nd ed. Milwaukee, Wisc., 1962.

Ellis, William E. *Patrick Henry Callahan, 1866–1940: Progressive Catholic Layman in the American South.* Lewiston, N.Y., 1989.

Evans, John Whitney. "John LaFarge, *America,* and the Newman Movement." *Catholic Historical Review,* 64 (October, 1978), 614–43.

Faherty, William Barnaby, S.J. "Breaking the Color Barrier." *Universitas,* 13 (Autumn, 1987), 19–21.

———. *The Catholic Ancestry of Saint Louis.* St. Louis, 1965.

———. *Dream by the River: Two Centuries of Saint Louis Catholicism, 1766–1980.* Rev. ed. St. Louis, 1981.

———. *Rebels or Reformers? Dissenting Priests in American Life.* Chicago, 1988.

———. *The Religious Roots of Black Catholics in Saint Louis.* St. Louis, 1977.

Feigelman, William, Bernard S. Gorman, and Joseph A. Varacalli. "The Social Characteristics of Black Catholics." *Sociology and Social Research,* 75 (April, 1991), 133–43.

Felder, Cain Hope. *Troubling Biblical Waters: Race, Class, and Family.* Maryknoll, N.Y., 1989.

Fey, Harold E. "Can Catholicism Win America?" *Christian Century*, 61 (November 29, 1944), 1378–80.

————. "Catholicism and the Negro." *Christian Century*, 61 (December 20, 1944), 1477–78.

Fichter, Joseph H., S.J. *One-Man Research: Reminiscences of a Catholic Sociologist*. New York, 1973.

————. *Southern Parish: Dynamics of a Southern Church*. Chicago, 1951.

Findlay, James F. *Church People in Struggle: The National Council of Churches and the Black Freedom Movement, 1950–1970*. New York, 1992.

————. "Religion and Politics in the Sixties: The Churches and the Civil Rights Act of 1964." *Journal of American History*, 77 (June, 1990), 66–92.

Finley, James F., C.S.P. *James Gillis, Paulist: A Biography*. Garden City, N.Y., 1958.

Fisher, James Terence. *The Catholic Counterculture in America, 1933–1962*. Chapel Hill, N.C., 1989.

Flynn, George Q. *American Catholics and the Roosevelt Presidency, 1932–1936*. Lexington, Ky., 1968.

————. *Roosevelt and Romanism: Catholics and American Diplomacy, 1937–1945*. Westport, Conn., 1976.

Fogarty, Gerald P. *The Vatican and the American Hierarchy from 1870 to 1965*. Stuttgart, 1982.

Foley, Albert S., S.J. "Adventures in Black Catholic History: Research and Writing." *U.S. Catholic Historian*, 5 (Winter, 1986), 103–18.

————. *Bishop Healy: Beloved Outcaste*. New York, 1954.

————. *God's Men of Color: The Colored Catholic Priests of the United States, 1854–1954*. New York, 1955.

Franklin, John Hope. *The Color Line: Legacy for the Twenty-First Century*. Columbia, Mo., 1993.

Franklin, John Hope, and Alfred A. Moss, Jr. *From Slavery to Freedom: A History of Negro Americans*. 6th ed. New York, 1988.

Fredrickson, George M. *The Arrogance of Race: Historical Perspectives on Slavery, Racism, and Social Equality*. Middletown, Conn., 1988.

Fulöp-Miller, Rene. *The Power and Secret of the Jesuits*. Translated by F. S. Flint and D. F. Tait. New York, 1930.

Furfey, Paul Hanly. *The Respectable Murderers: Social Evil and Christian Conscience*. New York, 1966.

Garfinkel, Herbert. *When Negroes March: The March on Washington Movement in the Organizational Politics of FEPC*. New York, 1959.

Garrow, David. *Bearing the Cross: Martin Luther King, Jr., and the Southern Christian Leadership Conference*. New York, 1986.

Gatewood, Willard B. *Aristocrats of Color: The Black Elite, 1880–1920*. Bloomington, Ind., 1990.

Gillard, John T., S.S.J. *The Catholic Church and the American Negro.* Baltimore, 1929.

———. *Colored Catholics in the United States.* Baltimore, 1941.

———. "The Negro Looks to Rome." *Commonweal,* 21 (December 14, 1924), 193–95.

Gilligan, Francis J. *The Morality of the Color Line: An Examination of the Right and Wrong of the Discrimination Against the Negro in the United States.* Washington, D.C., 1928.

Gleason, Philip. "In Search of Unity: American Catholic Thought, 1920–1960." *Catholic Historical Review,* 65 (April, 1979), 185–205.

———, ed. *Contemporary Catholicism in the United States.* Notre Dame, Ind., 1969.

Glenn, Norval D., and Ruth Hyland. "Religious Preference and Worldly Success: Some Evidence from National Surveys." *American Sociological Review,* 32 (February, 1967), 73–85.

Goldfield, David R. *Black, White, and Southern: Race Relations and Southern Culture, 1940 to the Present.* Baton Rouge, 1990.

Gontard, Friedrich. *The Chair of Peter: A History of the Papacy.* Translated by A. J. Peeler and E. F. Peeler. New York, 1964.

Greely, Andrew M. *The Communal Catholic: A Personal Manifesto.* New York, 1976.

———. *The Denominational Society: A Sociological Approach to Religion in America.* Glenview, Ill., 1972.

Gribble, Richard, C.S.C. "The Fractured Inheritance of James Martin Gillis, CSP." *Journal of Paulist Studies,* 2 (1993), 47–58.

Guilday, Peter. *A History of the Councils of Baltimore.* New York, 1932.

———, ed. *The National Pastorals of the American Hierarchy, 1792–1919.* Washington, D.C., 1923.

Hacker, Andrew. *Two Nations: Black and White, Separate, Hostile, Unequal.* New York, 1992.

Halecki, Oscar. *Eugenio Pacelli: Pope of Peace.* New York, 1951.

Halsey, William M. *The Survival of American Innocence: Catholicism in the Era of Disillusionment, 1920–1940.* Notre Dame, Ind., 1980.

Hammer, Andrea. *But Now When I Look Back: Remembering St. Mary's County Through Farm Security Administration Photographs.* Westminster, Md., 1988.

Harfmann, John, S.S.J. *1984 Statistical Profile of Black Catholics.* Washington, D.C., 1985.

Harrington, Michael. *Fragments of the Century.* New York, 1973.

Harte, Thomas J., C.Ss.R. *Catholic Organizations Promoting Negro-White Relations in the United States.* Washington, D.C., 1947.

Hastings, Adrian, ed. *Modern Catholicism: Vatican II and After.* New York, 1991.

Haynes, George Edmund. *The Trend of the Races.* New York, 1922.

Hebblethwaite, Peter. "The Popes and Politics: Shifting Patterns in Catholic Social Doctrine." *Daedalus,* 111 (Winter, 1982), 85–98.

Hennesey, James, S.J. *American Catholics: A History of the Roman Catholic Community in the United States.* New York, 1981.

―――. "Church History and the Theologians." *U.S. Catholic Historian,* 6 (Winter, 1987), 1–12.

Herberg, Will. *Protestant-Catholic-Jew: An Essay in American Religious Sociology.* Rev. ed. Garden City, N.Y., 1960.

Hirsch, Arnold. *The Making of the Second Ghetto: Race and Housing in Chicago, 1940–1960.* New York, 1983.

Hitchcock, James. *Catholicism and Modernity: Confrontation or Capitulation?* New York, 1979.

Hobgood, Mary E. *Catholic Social Teaching and Economic Theory: Paradigms in Conflict.* Philadelphia, 1991.

Hoetink, Harmannus. *Slavery and Race Relations in the Americas: Comparative Notes on Their Nature and Nexus.* New York, 1973.

Hollenbach, David, S.J. *Claims in Conflict: Retrieving and Renewing the Catholic Human Rights Tradition.* New York, 1979.

Hudson, Winthrop S. *Understanding Roman Catholicism: A Guide to Papal Teachings for Protestants.* Philadelphia, 1959.

Hunt, Larry L., and Janet J. Hunt. "A Religious Factor in Secular Achievement among Blacks: The Case for Catholicism." *Social Forces,* 53 (June, 1975), 595–605.

Hunton, George K., as told to Gary McEoin. *All of Which I Saw, A Part of Which I Was: The Autobiography of George K. Hunton.* Garden City, N.Y., 1967.

Hutchinson, Louise Daniel. *Anna J. Cooper: A Voice from the South.* Washington, D.C., 1981.

Hutchinson, William R., ed. *Between the Times: The Travail of the Protestant Establishment in America, 1900–1960.* New York, 1989.

Jackson, Elton F., William S. Fox, and Harry J. Crockett, Jr. "Religion and Occupational Achievement." *American Sociological Review,* 35 (February, 1970), 48–63.

Jencks, Christopher. *Rethinking Social Policy: Race, Poverty, and the Underclass.* Cambridge, Mass., 1992.

"Jesuit Says Pius XI Asked for Draft—Adds to Encyclical Story." *National Catholic Reporter,* December 22, 1972, pp. 3–4.

Jordan, Winthrop D. *White over Black: American Attitudes Toward the Negro, 1550–1812.* Chapel Hill, N.C., 1968.

Judis, John B. *William F. Buckley, Jr.: Patron Saint of the Conservatives.* New York, 1988.

Kane, John J. *Catholic-Protestant Conflicts in America.* Chicago, 1955.

Kantowicz, Edward R. *Corporation Sole: Cardinal Mundelein and Chicago Catholicism.* Notre Dame, Ind., 1983.

————, ed. *Modern American Catholicism, 1900–1965.* New York, 1988.

Kauffmann, Christopher J. *The History of the Knights of Columbus, 1882–1982.* New York, 1982.

Kennelly, Karen, ed. *American Catholic Women: A Historical Exploration.* New York, 1989.

King, Martin Luther, Jr. *Stride Toward Freedom: The Montgomery Story.* New York, 1958.

————. *Why We Can't Wait.* New York, 1964.

Kirby, John B. *Black Americans in the Roosevelt Era: Liberalism and Race.* Knoxville, Tenn., 1980.

Kittler, Glenn D. *The Wings of Eagles.* Garden City, N.Y., 1966.

Kluger, Richard. *Simple Justice: The History of Brown v. Board of Education and Black America's Struggle for Equality.* New York, 1976.

Kovel, Joel. *White Racism: A Psychohistory.* New York, 1970.

Kusmer, Kenneth L. *A Ghetto Takes Shape: Black Cleveland, 1870–1930.* Chicago, 1976.

Labbe, Dolores Egger. *Jim Crow Comes to Church: The Establishment of Segregated Catholic Parishes in South Louisiana.* 2nd ed. Lafayette, La., 1971.

LaFarge, John [1835–1910]. *Reminiscences of the South Seas.* Garden City, N.Y., 1912.

LaFarge, John [1880–1963]. *An American Amen: A Statement of Hope.* New York, 1958.

————. *A Catholic Interracial Program.* New York, 1939.

————. *The Catholic Viewpoint on Race Relations.* Garden City, N.Y., 1956.

————. *Communism and the Catholic Answer.* New York, 1936.

————. *Communism's Threat to Democracy.* New York, 1937.

————. "How the Churches Suffer." In *Discrimination and the National Welfare,* edited by R. M. MacIver. New York, 1947.

————. "If I Were A Negro." *Negro Digest,* 2 (October, 1944), 45.

————. *Interracial Justice: A Study of the Catholic Doctrine of Race Relations.* 1937; rpr. New York, 1978.

————. *The Jesuits in Modern Times.* New York, 1928.

————. *The Manner Is Ordinary.* New York, 1954.

————. *No Postponement: U.S. Moral Leadership and the Problem of Racial Minorities.* New York, 1950.

————. *The Race Question and the Negro: A Study of the Catholic Doctrine on Interracial Justice.* New York, 1943.

————. *A Report on the American Jesuits.* New York, 1956.

Lemann, Nicholas. *The Promised Land: The Great Black Migration and How It Changed America.* New York, 1991.

Leonard, Joseph T., S.S.J. *Theology and Race Relations.* Milwaukee, Wisc., 1963.

Ligutti, Msgr. Luigi, and John C. Rawe, S.J. *Rural Roads to Security: America's Third Struggle for Freedom.* Milwaukee, Wisc., 1940.

Lord, Daniel A., S.J. *Played By Ear.* Chicago, 1956.

Lotz, David W., ed. *Altered Landscapes: Christianity in America, 1935–1985.* Grand Rapids, Mich., 1989.

Lucas, Lawrence. *Black Priest / White Church: Catholics and Racism.* New York, 1970.

Luker, Ralph E. *The Social Gospel in Black and White: American Racial Reform, 1885–1912.* Chapel Hill, N.C., 1991.

Marable, Manning. *Race, Reform, and Rebellion: The Second Reconstruction in Black America.* Jackson, Miss., 1984.

Maritain, Jacques. *Reflections on America.* New York, 1958.

Marks, Bayly E. "Skilled Blacks in Antebellum St. Mary's County, Maryland." *Journal of Southern History,* 53 (November, 1987), 537–64.

Martensen, Katherine. "Region, Religion, and Social Action: The Catholic Committee of the South, 1939–1956." *Catholic Historical Review,* 68 (April, 1982), 249–67.

Marty, Martin E. "A Dialogue of Histories." In *American Catholics: A Protestant-Jewish View,* edited by Philip Scharper. New York, 1959.

———. *An Invitation to American Catholic History.* Chicago, 1986.

———. "Is There a Mentalité in the American Catholic House?" *U.S. Catholic History,* 6 (Winter, 1987), 13–23.

———. *The Noise of Conflict, 1919–1941.* Chicago, 1991. Vol. II of Marty, *Modern American Religion.*

Masse, Benjamin L., S.J. *Justice for All: An Introduction to the Social Teaching of the Catholic Church.* Milwaukee, Wisc., 1964.

Massey, Douglas S., and Nancy A. Denton. *American Apartheid: Segregation and the Making of the Underclass.* Cambridge, Mass., 1993.

Mayer, Albert J., and Harry Sharp. "Religious Preference and Worldly Success." *American Sociological Review,* 27 (April, 1962), 218–27.

Mays, Benjamin E. *Born to Rebel: An Autobiography of Benjamin E. Mays.* New York, 1971.

McCoy, Donald R., and Richard T. Ruetten. *Quest and Response: Minority Rights and the Truman Administration.* Lawrence, Kans., 1973.

McDonough, Peter. *Men Astutely Trained: A History of the Jesuits in the American Century.* New York, 1992.

McEoin, Gary. *Memoirs and Memories.* Mystic, Conn., 1986.

McGloin, Joseph T. *Backstage Missionary: Father Dan Lord, S.J.* New York, 1958.

McGreevy, John T. " 'Race' and Twentieth Century American Catholic Culture." *Cushwa Working Papers,* University of Notre Dame, Series 24, No. 4 (Spring, 1993), 1–38.

———. "Racial Justice and the People of God: The Second Vatican Council, the Civil Rights Movement, and American Catholics." *Religion and American Culture: A Journal of Interpretation,* 4 (Summer, 1994), 221–54.

McGurn, Barrett. *A Reporter Looks at American Catholicism.* New York, 1967.

McKeown, Elizabeth. *War and Welfare: American Catholics and World War I.* New York, 1988.

McMahon, Eileen M. *Which Parish Are You From? A Chicago Irish Community and Race Relations.* Lexington, Ky., 1995.

McNeal, Patricia. *Harder than War: Catholic Peacemaking in Twentieth-Century America.* New Brunswick, N.J., 1992.

McShane, Joseph M. *"Sufficiently Radical": Catholicism, Progressivism, and the Bishops' Program of 1919.* Washington, D.C., 1986.

Meier, August. *Negro Thought in America, 1880–1915: Racial Ideologies in the Age of Booker T. Washington.* Ann Arbor, Mich., 1963.

Miller, Randall M., and Jon L. Wakelyn, eds. *Catholics in the Old South: Essays on Church and Culture.* Macon, Ga., 1983.

Miller, William D. *Dorothy Day: A Biography.* New York, 1982.

Miscamble, Wilson D., C.S.C. "The Limits of American Catholic Antifascism: The Case of John A. Ryan." *Catholic Historical Review,* 76 (December, 1990), 523–38.

Moehlman, Conrad Henry. Review of *The Manner Is Ordinary,* by John LaFarge. *Christian Century,* 71 (April 7, 1954), 430–31.

Morris, Aldon D. *The Origins of the Civil Rights Movement: Black Communities Organizing for Change.* New York, 1984.

Murphy, John C. *An Analysis of the Attitudes of American Catholics Toward the Immigrant and the Negro, 1825–1925.* Washington, D.C., 1940.

Murray, Raymond W. *Introductory Sociology.* New York, 1946.

Murray, Raymond W., and Frank T. Flynn. *Social Problems.* New York, 1938.

Myrdal, Gunnar. *An American Dilemma: The Negro Problem and Modern Democracy.* New York, 1944.

Nelsen, Hart M., and L. Dickson. "Attitudes of Black Catholics and Protestants: Evidence for Religious Identity." *Sociological Analysis,* 33 (Fall, 1972), 152–65.

Nelsen, Hart M., Raytha L. Yokley, and Anne K. Nelsen, eds. *The Black Church in America.* New York, 1971.

Newby, I. A. *Jim Crow's Defense: Anti-Negro Thought in America, 1900–1930.* Baton Rouge, 1965.

Nickels, Marilyn Wenzke. *Black Catholic Protest and the Federated Colored Catholics, 1917–1933: Three Perspectives on Racial Justice.* New York, 1988.

———. "Thomas Wyatt Turner and the Federated Colored Catholics." *U.S. Catholic Historian,* 7 (Spring–Summer, 1988), 215–32.

Nolan, Hugh J., ed. *Pastoral Letters of the American Hierarchy, 1792–1970.* Huntington, Long Island, N.Y., 1971.

Novak, Michael. *Choosing Our King: Powerful Symbols in Presidential Politics.* New York, 1974.

———. *Confessions of a Catholic.* New York, 1983.

O'Brien, Conor Cruise. "A Last Chance to Save the Jews?" *New York Review of Books,* April 27, 1989, pp. 27–28, 35.

O'Brien, David J. "American Catholic Historiography: A Post-Conciliar Evaluation." *Church History,* 37 (March, 1968), 80–94.

———. *American Catholics and Social Reform: The New Deal Years.* New York, 1968.

———. *Public Catholicism.* New York, 1989.

O'Brien, David J., and Thomas A. Shannon. *Catholic Social Thought: The Documentary Heritage.* Maryknoll, N.Y., 1992.

Ochs, Stephen J. *Desegregating the Altar: The Josephites and the Struggle for Black Priests, 1871–1960.* Baton Rouge, 1990.

———. "The Ordeal of a Black Priest." *U.S. Catholic Historian,* 5 (Winter, 1986), 45–66.

O'Connell, Marvin R. *John Ireland and the American Catholic Church.* St. Paul, Minn., 1988.

O'Connor, John. *The People Versus Rome: Radical Split in the American Church.* New York, 1969.

O'Dea, Thomas F. *American Catholic Dilemma: An Inquiry into the Intellectual Life.* New York, 1958.

O'Grady, Desmond. "Pius XI—Complex and Imperious." *National Catholic Reporter,* December 15, 1972, p. 15.

O'Malley, John W. *The First Jesuits.* Cambridge, Mass., 1993.

O'Neill, Joseph Eugene, S.J., ed. *A Catholic Case Against Segregation.* New York, 1966.

Osborne, William A. *The Segregated Covenant: Race Relations and American Catholics.* New York, 1967.

Osofsky, Gilbert. *Harlem: The Making of a Ghetto, 1890–1930.* New York, 1968.

O'Toole, James M. *Militant and Triumphant: William Henry O'Connell and the Catholic Church in Boston, 1859–1944.* Notre Dame, Ind., 1992.

Paton, Alan. "Church Amid Racial Tensions." *Christian Century,* 71 (March 31, 1954), 393–94.

———. "The Negro in America Today." Part 1: *Collier's,* 19 (October 15, 1954), 52–66. Part 2: *Collier's,* 19 (October 29, 1954), 70–80.

Pelikan, Jaroslav. *The Riddle of Roman Catholicism.* New York, 1959.

Pfeffer, Paula F. *A. Philip Randolph: Pioneer of the Civil Rights Movement.* Baton Rouge, 1990.

Phelps, Jamie T., O.P. "John R. Slattery's Missionary Strategies." *U.S. Catholic Historian,* 7 (Spring–Summer, 1988), 201–14.

Piehl, Mel. *Breaking Bread: The Catholic Worker and the Origins of Catholic Radicalism in America.* Philadelphia, 1982.

Pitts, David. "Is a Separate Black Church the Answer to Black Prayers?" *Black Enterprise,* 20 (October, 1989), 28.

Porter, E. F. "Jesuits: Innovators in Education." St. Louis *Post-Dispatch,* September 16, 1991, Sec. G, p. 1.

———. "The Strike Force of God." St. Louis *Post-Dispatch,* September 15, 1991, Sec. G, pp. 1, 6.

Portier, William L. "John R. Slattery's Vision for the Evangelization of American Blacks." *U.S. Catholic Historian,* 5 (Winter, 1986), 19–44.

———, ed. *The Inculturation of American Catholicism, 1820–1900.* New York, 1988.

Powers, Edward J. *Catholic Education in America: A History.* New York, 1972.

Raboteau, Albert J. "Preaching the Word and Doing It." *Commonweal,* 116 (November 17, 1989), 631–34.

———. *Slave Religion: The "Invisible" Institution in the Antebellum South.* New York, 1978.

Randolph, Laura. "What's Behind the Black Rebellion in the Catholic Church?" *Ebony,* 45 (November, 1989), 160–64.

Ranke-Heinemann, Uta. *Eunuchs for the Kingdom of Heaven: Women, Sexuality, and the Catholic Church.* Trans. Peter Heinegg. New York, 1990.

"Reasoned Optimist." *Time,* March 3, 1952, pp. 76–80.

Record, Wilson. *Race and Radicalism: The NAACP and the Communist Party in Conflict.* Ithaca, N.Y., 1964.

Redding, J. Saunders. Review of *The Manner Is Ordinary,* by John LaFarge. Baltimore *Afro-American,* April 3, 1954.

Reher, Margaret Mary. *Catholic Intellectual Life in America: A Historical Study of Persons and Movements.* New York, 1989.

Reimer, George. *The New Jesuits.* Boston, 1971.

Reimers, David M. *White Protestantism and the Negro.* New York, 1965.

Reynolds, Edward D., S.J. *Jesuits for the Negro.* New York, 1949.

Rice, Madeleine Hooke. *American Catholic Opinion in the Slavery Controversy.* 1944; rpr. Gloucester, Mass., 1964.

Ruchames, Louis. "The Sources of Racial Thought in Colonial America." *Journal of Negro History,* 52 (October, 1967), 251–72.

Safranski, Scott R. *Managing God's Organization: The Catholic Church in Society.* Ann Arbor, Mich., 1985.

Sanders, James. *The Education of an Urban Minority: Catholics in Chicago.* New York, 1977.

Schlesinger, Arthur, Jr. *Orestes A. Brownson: A Pilgrim's Progress.* Boston, 1939.

Schuman, Howard, Charlotte Steeh, and Lawrence Bobo. *Racial Attitudes in America: Trends and Interpretations.* Cambridge, Mass., 1985.

Seaton, Douglas P. *Catholics and Radicals: The Association of Catholic Trade Unionists and the American Labor Movement, from Depression to Cold War.* Lewisburg, Pa., 1981.

Seidler, John, and Katherine Meyer. *Conflict and Change in the Catholic Church.* New Brunswick, N.J., 1989.

Senser, Robert, ed. *Primer on Interracial Justice.* Baltimore, 1962.

Shaw, Stephen J. *The Catholic Church as a Way-Station of Ethnicity and Americanization: Chicago's Germans and Italians, 1903–1939.* Brooklyn, N.Y., 1991.

Sheerin, John B., C.S.P. *Never Look Back: The Career and Concerns of John J. Burke.* New York, 1975.

Shields, Currin. *Democracy and Catholicism in America.* New York, 1958.

Shuster, George N. *The Catholic Spirit in America.* 1928; rpr. New York, 1978.

Sitkoff, Harvard. "Racial Militancy and Interracial Violence in the Second World War." *Journal of American History,* 58 (December, 1971), 661–81.

———. *The Struggle for Black Equality, 1954–1980.* New York, 1981.

Slattery, John R. "How My Priesthood Dropped from Me." *Independence,* 61 (September 6, 1906), 565–71.

Smith, Jeffrey H. *From Corps to CORE: The Life of John P. Markoe, Soldier, Priest, and Pioneer Activist.* St. Louis, 1977.

Sosna, Morton. *In Search of the Silent South: Southern Liberals and the Race Issue.* New York, 1977.

Southern, David W. *Gunnar Myrdal and Black-White Relations: The Use and Abuse of "An American Dilemma," 1944–1969.* Baton Rouge, 1987.

———. *The Malignant Heritage: Yankee Progressives and the Negro Question, 1901–1914.* Chicago, 1968.

Spalding, David. "The Negro Catholic Congresses, 1889–1894." *Catholic Historical Review,* 55 (October, 1969), 337–57.

Spalding, Thomas W. *The Premier See: A History of the Archdiocese of Baltimore, 1789–1989.* Baltimore, 1989.

Sparr, Arnold. *To Promote, Defend, and Redeem: The Catholic Literary Revival and the Cultural Transformation of American Catholicism, 1920–1960.* Westport, Conn., 1990.

Spear, Allan H. *Black Chicago: The Making of a Negro Ghetto, 1890–1920.* Chicago, 1967.

Stanton, Edward S., S.J. "John LaFarge." In *Saints Are Now: Eight Portraits of Modern Sanctity,* edited by John J. Delaney. New York, 1983.

Stocker, Joseph. "Father Dunne: A Study in Faith." *Nation,* September 22, 1951, pp. 236–39.

Sweeney, David Francis, O.F.M. *The Life of John Lancaster Spalding: First Bishop of Peoria, 1840–1916.* New York, 1965.

Sylvester, Harry. *Dearly Beloved.* New York, 1942.

Tarry, Ellen. *The Other Toussaint: A Modern Biography of Pierre Toussaint, a Post-Revolutionary Black.* Boston, 1981.

Tentler, Leslie Woodcock. "On the Margins: The State of American Catholic History." *American Quarterly,* 45 (March, 1993), 104–27.

———. *Seasons of Grace: A History of the Catholic Archdiocese of Detroit.* Detroit, 1990.

Thomas, J. Douglas. "A Century of American Catholic History." *U.S. Catholic Historian,* 6 (Winter, 1987), 25–49.

Trotter, Joe William, Jr. *Black Milwaukee: The Making of an Industrial Proletariat, 1915–1945.* Urbana, Ill., 1988.

Tull, Charles J. *Father Coughlin and the New Deal.* Syracuse, N.Y., 1965.

Van den Berghe, Pierre. *The Ethnic Phenomenon.* New York, 1987.

———. *Race and Racism: A Comparative Approach.* New York, 1967.

Wakin, Edward, and Joseph F. Scheuer. *The De-Romanization of the American Catholic Church.* New York, 1966.

Walch, Timothy. *Catholicism in America: A Social History.* Melabar, Fla., 1989.

Watters, Pat. *Down to Now: Reflections on the Southern Civil Rights Movement.* New York, 1971.

Weisbrot, Robert. *Freedom Bound: A History of America's Civil Rights Movement.* New York, 1990.

Weiss, Nancy J. *Farewell to the Party of Lincoln: Black Politics in the Age of FDR.* Princeton, 1983.

West, Cornel. *Race Matters.* New York, 1993.

White, Ronald C., Jr. *Liberty and Justice for All: Racial Reform and the Social Gospel.* New York, 1990.

Wilkins, Roy. *Standing Fast: The Autobiography of Roy Wilkins.* New York, 1984.

Williams, Michael. *The Catholic Church in Action.* New York, 1935.

Willingham, Saundra. "Why I Quit the Convent." *Ebony,* 24 (December, 1968), 64–72.

Wills, Garry. *Bare Ruined Choirs: Doubt, Prophecy, and Radical Religion.* Garden City, N.Y., 1972.

———. *Confessions of a Conservative.* Garden City, N.Y., 1979.

———. *Politics and Catholic Freedom.* Chicago, 1964.

———. *Reagan's America: Innocents at Home.* Garden City, N.Y., 1987.

————. *Under God: Religion and American Politics.* New York, 1990.

Wilson, William Julius. *The Declining Significance of Race: Blacks and Changing American Institutions.* Chicago, 1978.

————. *The Truly Disadvantaged: The Inner City, the Underclass, and Public Policy.* Chicago, 1987.

Wittberg, Patricia, S.C. *The Rise and Decline of Catholic Religious Orders: A Social Movement Perspective.* Albany, N.Y., 1994.

Wood, Forrest G. *The Arrogance of Faith: Christianity and Race in America from the Colonial Era to the Twentieth Century.* Boston, 1991.

Woodson, Carter G. *The History of the Negro Church.* 2nd ed. Washington, D.C., 1921.

————. Review of *The Catholic Church and the American Negro,* by John T. Gillard. *Journal of Negro History,* 15 (July, 1930), 106–107.

Woodward, C. Vann. *The Strange Career of Jim Crow.* 3rd rev. ed. New York, 1974.

Yuhaus, Cassian, C.P., ed. *The Catholic Church and American Culture: Reciprocity and Challenge.* Mahwah, N.J., 1990.

Zahn, Gordon. "The Unpublished Encyclical—An Opportunity Missed." *National Catholic Reporter,* December 15, 1972, p. 9.

Zangrando, Robert L. *The NAACP Crusade Against Lynching, 1909–1950.* Philadelphia, 1980.

Zielinski, Martin A. "Working for Interracial Justice: The Catholic Interracial Council of New York, 1934–1964." *U.S. Catholic Historian,* 7 (Spring–Summer, 1988), 233–60.

PERIODICALS AND NEWSPAPERS
Researched Extensively

America, 1909–93.
Chronicle, 1929–34.
Interracial Review, 1934–64.
New York *Times,* 1926–63.
St. Elizabeth's Chronicle, 1928–29.

Researched Selectively

Baltimore *Afro-American*
Brooklyn *Tablet*
Catholic Worker
Catholic World
Commonweal
Jubilee
Kansas City (Mo.) *Catholic Reporter*

Nashville *Tennessee Register*
National Catholic Reporter
Philadelphia *Catholic Standard and Times*
St. Louis *Register*
St. Louis *Review*

THESES, DISSERTATIONS, AND OTHER UNPUBLISHED MATERIALS

Fields, Kathleen Riley. "Bishop Fulton J. Sheen: An American Response to the Twentieth Century." Ph.D. dissertation, University of Notre Dame, 1988.

Foley, Albert S., S.J. "The Catholic Church and the Washington Negro." Ph.D. dissertation, University of North Carolina, 1950.

Markoe, William M. "An Interracial Role: Memoirs of Rev. William M. Markoe, S.J., 1900–1966." Typescript, copy in the Jesuit Missouri Province Archives, St. Louis.

McMahon, Eileen M. "What Parish Are You From? A Study of the Chicago Irish Parish Community and Race Relations, 1916–1970." Ph.D. dissertation, Loyola University, Chicago, 1989.

Muffler, John Paul. "This Far by Faith: A History of St. Augustine's, the Mother Church for Black Catholics in the Nation's Capital." Ph.D. dissertation, Columbia University, 1989.

Nickels, Marilyn Wenzke. "The Federated Colored Catholics: A Study of Three Variant Perspectives on Racial Justice as Represented by John LaFarge, William Markoe, and Thomas Turner." Ph.D. dissertation, Catholic University of America, 1975.

Osborne, William A. "The Race Problem in the Catholic Church in the United States: Between the Time of the Second Plenary Council (1866) and the Founding of the Catholic Interracial Council of New York (1934)." Ph.D. dissertation, Columbia University, 1953.

Pastor-Zelaya, Anthony Sean. "The Development of Roman Catholic Social Liberalism in the United States, 1887–1935." Ph.D. dissertation, University of California, Santa Barbara, 1988.

Roberts, Samuel Kelton. "Crucible for a Vision: George Edmund Haynes and the Commission on Race Relations, 1922–1947." Ph.D. dissertation, Columbia University, 1974.

Schmandt, Raymond H. "The Catholic Interracial Council of Philadelphia." Paper presented at the annual meeting of the American Catholic Association, Villanova University, April 13–15, 1984.

Stanton, Edward S., S.J. "John LaFarge's Understanding of the Unifying Mission of the Church, Especially in the Area of Race Relations." Ph.D. dissertation, St. Paul University, Ottawa, 1972.

Zielinski, Martin A. " 'Doing the Truth': The Catholic Interracial Council of New York, 1945–1965." Ph.D. dissertation, Catholic University of America, 1989.

———. "The Promotion of Better Race Relations: The Catholic Interracial Council of New York, 1933–1945." M.A. thesis, Catholic University of America, 1985.

INTERVIEWS

By the author

Ahmann, Mathew. Washington, D.C., July 26, 1985.
Clark, Dennis. Philadelphia, June 15, 1988.
Faherty, William Barnaby, S.J. St. Louis, September 2, 1986.
Higgins, Msgr. George. Washington, D.C., July 1, 1986.
Hutchinson, Louise Daniel. Washington, D.C., June 26, 1992.
Johnson, Marguerite Daniel. Washington, D.C., August 3, 1992.
Kane, Dan. Cincinnati, July 7, 1986.
Parris, Guichard. New York, July 22, 1985.

By Edward S. Stanton, S.J., in Stanton Papers, Boston College

Emerick, [?]. N.d.
Hartnett, Robert C., S.J. December 1, 1980; March 18, 1981.
LaFarge, Wer. N.d.
Lloyd, Margaret. N.d.
McCoy, Beth. N.d.

By Marilyn W. Nickels, in Josephite Archives, Baltimore

Heithaus, Claude H., S.J. June 5, 1973.
McKenna, Horace B., S.J. March 24, 1973; November [?], 1974.
Turner, Thomas W. March 24, 1973.

MISCELLANEOUS

Brown v. *Board of Education of Topeka,* 347 U.S. 483.
Brown v. *Board of Education of Topeka,* 349 U.S. 294.
Perez v. *Sharpe,* 32 C 2nd, 711.

Index

Abell, Aaron, xvii
Abernathy, Ralph, 346
Abolitionists. *See* Antislavery
Acton, Lord (John Emerich Dalberg), 306
Adams, Henry, 3, 4
African American Catholics: and history, xx; in St. Mary's County, 28; and slavery, 31; faithfulness, 31, 74, 383; and Catholic social teaching, 48; decline of after Civil War, 66–67, 68; and need for black clergy, 72, 74; and lay congresses, 74–76, 79, 372, 378–79, 383, 384; and Josephites, 78–79; and Vatican, 80–82; double-consciousness of, 129, 383–84; and education, 154, 257–58; increase of, 209–10, 377; great migration of, 242, 250–51; growth of, 323–24; sociology of, 324–25, 384; and civil rights movement, 362; and Catholic interracial councils, 376; group consciousness of, 376–77; and increase in priests and bishops, 378; and black gifts, 382
African Americans: racism toward, 29; as Protestants, 67, 74, 82, 194, 251, 362; and New Deal, 150–51; and their press, 192–95, 201–202; and World War II, 243–45; and rising militancy, 244, 245, 379–83; and segregation, 244; and Catholic church, 288; and civil rights movement, 289–92. *See also* Catholic church

African Methodist Episcopal church, 68, 352
African Methodist Episcopal Zion church, 68
Afrocentrists, 385
Aggiornamento, 341, 372, 376
Agricultural Adjustment Act, 151
Ahern, Cornelius, 178, 180
Ahlstrom, Sidney, 247
Ahmann, Mathew, xix, 209, 328, 332, 334, 335, 336, 337, 338, 346, 349, 350, 351, 353, 358, 360, 364
Allport, Gordon W., 298, 299, 366
America: and Protestant churches, 69; founding of, 84; early editorial stance, 84–86; origins and purpose of, 84–86; as most-quoted Catholic journal, 85; as official voice of American Catholicism, 86; and African Americans, 89–90, 295–96, 312; anticommunism of, 89, 216; and antilynching, 93, 195; and Franklin Roosevelt, 148; and black press, 197; circulation of, 218; isolation of, 241; and Cicero riot, 255–56; as Catholic braintrust, 268; style of, 268; political neutrality of, 268; and La-Farge, 293, 353–56; and *Brown* II, 310; and national interracial conference, 335
American Academy of Arts and Sciences, 294
American Civil Liberties Union (ACLU), 196

Cardinal Gibbons Institute: founding of,
xiv; and FCC controversy, xix; as seedbed of Catholic interracialism, 33;
opening of, 38; closing of, 39, 42, 146,
164–73; and white board, 43; as FCC
project, 79; and LaFarge, 83, 108, 152,
154–55, 157–58, 169–70, 172–73; decay
of, 159–60; mentioned, 180, 182, 218
Carmichael, Stokely, 377
Carroll, Beverly, 381
Carroll, John, 65
Carroll, Joseph A., 266
Carter, Elmo Anderson, 194, 195, 205–
206, 211
Carter, Robert L., 244
Carver, George Washington, 36, 38, 172
Casserly, Edward V., 285
Catholic Action, 88, 114, 116, 123, 124,
125, 127, 129, 141, 144, 149, 184, 210,
231, 333, 341, 336
Catholic Association for International
Peace (CAIP), 89, 241, 294, 300, 301
Catholic Board for Mission Work among
the Colored People, 81, 128, 178
Catholic church: racism and paternalism
in, xiv, 49, 66, 67, 68, 71, 77, 82, 149–
50, 207–208, 210, 251–52, 254–56, 292–
93, 314–16, 367, 369, 371, 372, 376,
380; and historical scholarship, xvii,
61–63; books on, xviii; doctrines and
nature of, xviii, 49–51, 367; on slavery
and race, xix, 62–66; and social doctrine, 32, 51–54; laity, 51, 344; immigrant nature of, 51–52; and siege mentality, 52; and labor movement, 53–55;
and unregulated capitalism, 54; and socialism, 54; intellectuality of, 57, 96–97;
and Progressive Era, 57; liberalism of,
58, 100, 370–71; and ecumenism, 59–
60; and dualism of Catholic mind, 59;
and triumphalism, 59; on public
schools, 60; demographics of, 66, 68;
and southern bishops, 66, 68, 73, 121;
and evangelization of blacks, 67; and
southern blacks, 69; and black vocations, 70–71; and racial parishes, 72;
and lay congresses, 75–76; and Vatican
policies on race, 80–82; encyclicals,
100–101; ethnic organizations in, 144;
and social activism, 147–48; and nationality, 251; and black clergy, 285–86;

and civil rights movement, 286, 353;
and race problem in 1940s, 286; and
Cold War, 292; membership of, 292;
and parochial schools, 292; and World
War II, 292; desegregation of its
schools, 310; and Little Rock, 317; and
Eurocentrism of, 367, 385; and birth
control, 373; and pastoral letter on ra-
cism, 378. *See also* African American
Catholics
*Catholic Church and the American Ne-
gro, The* (Gillard), 118–20
"Catholic Church and the Washington
Negro, The" (Foley), 320
Catholic Committee of the South (CCS),
314
Catholic Committee on Urban Ministry,
370
Catholic Digest, 262, 293
Catholic Encyclopedia, 22
Catholic Herald, 209
Catholic Historical Review, 61
Catholic Intercollegiate Interracial Council, 278
Catholic Interracial Council of Chicago
(CICC), 255, 325, 328–30, 331, 332,
334, 338, 349
Catholic Interracial Council of New
York (CICNY): founding of, xiii, 146,
180–85; as clearinghouse on race, xiv;
and Catholic Action, 184; purpose of,
184, 198–200; spiritual nature of, 186–
87; and students, 204–205; and Catholic alumni, 206; influence of, 209–10;
weakness of, 210–13; symbolic significance of, 212; on segregation, 257; slow
growth of, 278–79; and education, 282;
and African Service Center, 301; and
1957 civil rights bill, 304; decline of,
322, 326, 346; and black leadership,
323; ascendancy of, 326; and CICC,
329–30
Catholic Interracial Council of Philadelphia, 303
Catholic Interracial Council of St. Louis,
341
Catholic Interracial Council of Washington, D.C., 282, 327
Catholic Interracial Hour, 179, 193
Catholic Knights of America, 114